SWITZERLAND AND THE ALPINE REGION 1994

1994 Fielding Titles

Fielding's Australia 1994

Fielding's Belgium 1994

Fielding's Bermuda/Bahamas 1994

Fielding's Brazil 1994

Fielding's Britain 1994

Fielding's Budget Europe 1994

Fielding's Caribbean 1994

Fielding's Europe 1994

Fielding's Far East 1994/95

Fielding's France 1994

Fielding's The Great Sights of Europe 1994

Fielding's Hawaii 1994

Fielding's Holland 1994

Fielding's Italy 1994

Fielding's Mexico 1994

Fielding's New Zealand 1994

Fielding's Scandinavia 1994

Fielding's Spain & Portugal 1994

Fielding's Switzerland and the Alpine Region 1994

Fielding's Worldwide Cruises 1994

Fielding's Shopping Guide to Europe 1994

SWITZERLAND AND THE ALPINE REGION 1994

The Most In-depth Guide to the Beauty and Majesty of Switzerland and the Alpine Region

Margaret Zellers

Fielding Worldwide, Inc.

308 South Catalina Avenue

Redondo Beach, California 90277 U.S.A.

FIELDING WORLDWIDE INC.

PUBLISHER AND CEO	Robert Young Pelton
DIRECTOR OF PUBLISHING	Paul T. Snapp
CO-DIR. OF ELECTRONIC PUBLISHING	Larry E. Hart
CO-DIR. OF ELECTRONIC PUBLISHING	Tony E. Hulette
PRODUCTION SUPERVISOR	Michael Rowley
PRODUCTION MANAGEMENT	Beverly Riess
EDITORIAL MANAGER	Wink Dulles
OFFICE MANAGER	Christy Donaldson
CUSTOMER SERVICE MANAGER	Kim Martindale

EDITORS

Linda Charlton	Kathy Knoles
Tina Gentile	Evelyn Lager
Loretta Rooney Hess	Jane M. Martin

PRODUCTION

Norm Imberman	Kip Riggins
Bryan Kring	Chris Snyder
Lyne Lawrence	Lillian Tse

COVER DESIGNED BY	Pelton & Associates, Inc.
COVER PHOTOGRAPHERS — Front Cover	Van Lun Jean Yves/The Image Bank
Background Photo, Front Cover	Robert Everts/Tony Stone Images
Back Cover	Tony Stone Images
INSIDE PHOTOS	Austrian National Tourist Office, French Government Tourist Office, GeoMedia, German National Tourist Office, Italian Government Tourist Board, Slovenia Tourist Office, Swiss National Tourist Office, Robert Young Pelton/Westlight

Inquiries should be addressed to: Fielding Worldwide, Inc., 308 South Catalina Ave., Redondo Beach, California 90277 U.S.A., Telephone (310) 372-4474, Facsimile (310) 376-8064, 8:30 a.m.–5:30 p.m. Pacific Standard Time.

ISBN 1-56952-001-1
Printed in the United States of America

Dedication

This book is dedicated to Lucy, Peter and Gordon Wallace with the hope that the joy and comfort I and my generation have found in the Alpine area will await them and their contemporaries on their travels several years from now.

"Journeys, like artists, are born and not made. A thousand differing circumstances contribute to them, few of them willed or determined by the will—whatever we may think. They flower spontaneously out of the demands of our natures—and the best of them lead us not only outwards in space, but inwards as well. Travel can be one of the most rewarding forms of introspection."

"Bitter Lemons" Lawrence Durrell

QUICK REFERENCE

Tourist Offices for the Alpine Region Countries

A complete listing of central tourist offices and many regional tourist offices is included in each chapter under "Information Sources" and end-of-chapter listings. What follows is the central tourist office in the United States for each Alpine country:

Austria: Austrian National Tourist Office, Post Office Box 1142, New York, NY 10108-1142. ☎ 212+944-6880; FAX 212+730-4568.

France: French Government Tourist Office, 610 Fifth Avenue, New York, NY 10020. ☎ 212+757-1125 or 900+990-0040 (50 cents per minute); FAX 212+247-6468.

Germany: German National Tourist Office, 122 East 42nd Street, New York, NY 10168. ☎ 212+661-7200; FAX 212+661-7174.

Italy: Italian Government Tourist Office, 630 Fifth Avenue, New York, NY 10111. ☎ 212+245-4822; FAX 212+586-9249.

Liechtenstein: c/o Swiss National Tourist Office, 608 Fifth Avenue, New York, NY 10020. ☎ 212+757-5944; FAX 212+262-6116.

Monaco: Monaco Tourist Office, 845 Third Avenue, New York, NY 10022. ☎ 212+759-5227; FAX 212+754-9320.

Slovenia: Slovenia Tourist Office, 122 East 42nd Street, New York, NY 10168-0072. ☎ 212+682-5896; FAX 212+661-2469.

Switzerland: Swiss National Tourist Office, 608 Fifth Avenue, New York, NY 10020. ☎ 212+757-5944; FAX 212+262-6116.

Austria, Germany, Italy, Slovenia, and Switzerland are members of the **Alpine Tourist Commission**. For details about contacts for ATC, write to GeoMedia, #316, 1771 Post Road East, Westport, CT 06880.

Letter from the Publisher

In 1946, Temple Fielding began the first of what would be a remarkable new series of well-written, highly personalized guide books for independent travelers. Temple's opinionated, witty, and oft-imitated books have now guided travelers for almost a half-century. More important to some was Fielding's humorous and direct method of steering travelers away from the dull and the insipid. Today, Fielding Travel Guides are still written by experienced travelers for experienced travelers. Our authors carry on Fielding's reputation for creating travel experiences that deliver insight with a sense of discovery and style.

Many of us dream of hiking along Alpine mountain paths—the gentle ringing of cowbells in the distance—and waking in the early morning sunshine to the snowcapped majesty of the Alps outside the bedroom window. Travel along with Margaret Zellers as she whisks you past the crowds and tourist traps to her own special Alpine Europe. I highly recommend this guide to anyone who yearns for romantic hideaways, crisp, clean air and the hospitality of the Alps.

In 1994, the concept of independent travel has never been bigger. Our policy of *brutal honesty* and a highly personal point of view has never changed; it just seems the travel world has caught up with us.

Enjoy your Switzerland and Alpine adventure with Margaret Zellers and Fielding.

Robert Young Pelton
Publisher and C.E.O.
Fielding Worldwide, Inc.

From the Author

The Alpine region is a "country" unto itself with people drawn together by heritage as well as by geography. Mountains and their valleys have conspired to confound the architects of national borders by clipping off a tidbit of Austria, making it most accessible from Germany, or putting two segments of Switzerland together most efficiently by driving (or taking a train) through Italy, as is the case, also, in another part of Italy, with portions of southeastern Austria.

The Celts moved into this region from somewhere in the east. The Romans worked their way north, through the Alps; the Christian pilgrims traveled south, from northern Europe to Rome and places in the Holy land. The Habsburgs pushed their Empire west (as well as east, north and south) from an eventual hub in Austria, and the Burgundians stretched south and east, to swallow portions of what we know as Switzerland and Italy as their appetites expanded.

All this by way of saying that the borders many believe to be finite these days are only of recent making. Most were established in 1918, after World War I; some were modified in the 1950s, after World War II; and the most recent—those of Slovenia—were defined in 1991, early in the disintegration of what had been Yugoslavia.

It's no surprise, once these facts are acknowledged, to find that Alpine customs cross borders. What you may have thought of as "Austrian" may, in fact, be found in Switzerland, as is the case with some of the customs of Austria's Tirol and Switzerland's Valais, regions settled by the same tribes. Cheese fondue, generally considered to be Swiss, is also popular (and part of the heritage) of the neighboring Haute Savoie region of France. And many other customs and costumes cross borders, although they may not be found in distant parts of the same country.

The Bodensee, known to English-speaking folks as Lake Constance, is shared by Germany, Switzerland and Austria. Lago Maggiore, in the southern part of the Alpine region, is shared by Switzerland and Italy. And Lac Léman, better known in English as the Lake of Geneva, is shared by France and Switzerland.

It's easy, therefore, and perfectly natural, to cross national borders when you're walking, hiking, skiing, or otherwise traveling in the Alps. Be ready for the currency differences and have your passport handy to show if border "guards" are present. But most of all, be relaxed and have fun. That's what this part of the world is all about.

In the pages that follow, I share my personal thoughts about a region I have enjoyed at all times of the year for more than three decades. I have walked, hiked, skied and bicycled over countless miles of Alpine paths, trails and roads. I have enjoyed hundreds of boat rides and train rides. Although I have driven occasionally, I much prefer the remarkable public transportation, not only because it is incredibly efficient, but because it offers a chance to slide unobtrusively into the local way of life, which is a situation I enjoy.

I have often said that when I am unable to travel easily I will plant myself in the Alpine area—and rely, as those who live there do, on the security of the landscape and a way of life that nurtures independence. The region is a perfect one to travel alone, with friends and with family; I have done it all ways and will do so always. I wish the same for you.

Margaret Zellers

Introducing the Author...

Margaret Zellers

Margaret Zellers has been traveling in the Alpine countries since she was a student, when her travel was guided by limitless curiosity and a limited budget. Since those first journeys, the author has returned to the region countless times, heading for Switzerland and other Alpine countries whenever she is in Europe because, for one reason, "this is a region where everything works."

Always drawn to rural areas and sensitive to local customs, the author has enjoyed the life of the country the way the people who live there know it. Since 1977, when her first book about the region—*Switzerland—The Inn Way*—appeared, Margaret Zellers has shared her discoveries and her tips with readers of her books, newspaper and magazine articles as well as through radio, television and personal appearances.

Respected for her unique perspective, which comes from traveling on her own, unannounced, paying for her travel as her readers must, Ms. Zellers shares her experiences with enlightening and enjoyable style.

The author has served on the board of RARE Center, a not-for-profit organization involved with conservation education, and is an active member of the American Society of Journalists and Authors, the Overseas Press Club, the Society of American Travel Writers and the New York Travel Writers' Association.

As the author of the first comprehensive quide to the inns of Switzerland, a title she followed with *Austria—The Inn Way* and a series of GeoMedia Pocket Guides to the Alpine region, Ms. Zellers is also author of *Caribbean—The Inn Way,* also published by GeoMedia, and of the annual *Fielding's Caribbean* travel guide, published by Fielding Worldwide.

TABLE OF CONTENTS

LIST OF MAPS

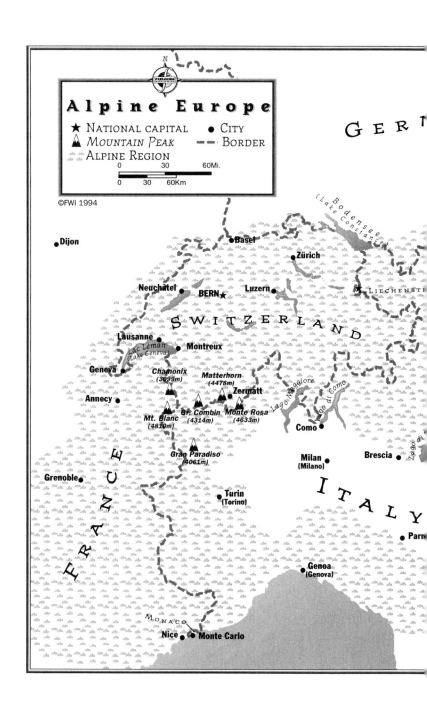

INTRODUCING THE ALPS

An inviting scenic view of the Alpine region

In September 1991, high in the Alps, in the Similaun glacier in what is now Austria's Tirol, the well-preserved remains of a man were found. That fact might not be so remarkable, if the remains had not been dated to 3000 years before the birth of Christ. The Iceman, as he came to be called, was originally thought to have lived 2000 years B.C., but carbon dating indicates that he was making his way, with his wooden backpack, in weatherproof clothing made from leather with fur and lined with hay, a thousand years earlier.

Among the possessions of the mummified body was a copper ax and a leather quiver with 14 arrows.

For at least 5000 years, then, these mountains have challenged man. Life has sprung from peaks and valleys; people have gathered together for protection—from the elements as well as from invaders. Only in the last few decades, however, has man challenged the viability of the mountains, as ski lifts stretch to the highest peaks, buildings plaster mountainsides and highways pave the valleys.

In the past few years, as development has increased at a frightening pace, conservationists and others are gathering together to protect an environment that now seems to be threatened by man. Scholars are studying the effect of acid rain on the forests, the depletion of forests on the landscape and the paving and unbridled development in some areas. Local groups are taking action; communes and villages are imposing regulations to preserve what's left of an environment that has been taken for granted.

Many things have changed in the Alpine area, but the mountain peaks—the astounding Alps—are a constant. They still provide the focal point for the villages in their orbit. They still provide the challenges, even in sport, for those who want to get over them, around them, or through their valleys.

As our work-a-day world becomes more cluttered, mountains bring magic, mystery and many moods. The stillness of remote Alpine valleys has increasing appeal. At the end of a hectic day, an hour's walk away from it all, perhaps in the green-belt that wraps around most Alpine cities, helps make the next day easier—and the evening a pleasure.

The Alps issue a perpetual invitation, but their dress (and ours) changes from season to season. The *Alpine Newsletter*, mentioned at the back of the book, will have the most current details on special excursions, currency exchange rates, accommodations, transportation, special events and more.

SWITZERLAND—A COUNTRY WITH EVERYTHING

As the consummate Alpine country, Switzerland has something of everything that makes this region special. Within its borders, you'll find each of the major Alpine languages: German, French and Italian. You'll also find astounding peaks, glorious lakes, vast meadows, varied architecture that allows both weathered farms and elaborate Baroque interiors to be neighbors. Mealtimes are memorable, not only because of fine service and setting, but also because the range of offerings allows for hearty farm fare and refined cuisine that has earned the respect of the world's gourmets. In addition, there's fine wine from vineyards that blanket strategic hillsides and a heritage of integrity that is unequalled elsewhere in the world.

The temptation to spend days wandering the Alpine region has existed since the first settlements by the Helvetian tribes prior to the birth of Christ. Goethe wandered through Switzerland's Alpine area and wrote about it. Friedrich Nietzche spent time in the Engadine, in eastern Switzerland, and Carl Jung and many others studied and practiced in Zürich. The Bernoullis taught in Basel in the 15th century; Erasmus and Holbein spent time there in the 16th.

Henri Dunant founded the Red Cross in Genève, and English poet Lord Byron spent time at Ouchy, on the lake below Lausanne. He composed portions of his "Prisoner of Chillon," a poem about the imprisonment of François Bonivard, in the 1530s. You can visit the Château de Chillon, a 13th century castle thrust into the lake from the shore east of Montreux, that lends its name to the poem's title.

Mark Twain wrote, in *Innocents Abroad* (1869) and *A Tramp Abroad* (1879), about his travels in Switzerland. You can take his route up the Rigi mountain, or stay at "his" hotel in Interlaken. And actor Charlie Chaplin took refuge near Montreux, when he left the United States in the 1950s. Richard Burton is buried in a village in the outskirts of Genève, where he lived the last years of his life.

When you travel in Switzerland, you'll be in good company, whether you choose to travel alone, with family, with friends, or with memories. I have traveled all these ways; each has its rewards. The one constant is the hospitality of the Swiss. They are innkeepers par excellence. They practice just the right amount of welcome and formality, even in the coziest small inn. They are never intrusive, but always present to be helpful wherever you wander in the country.

A CIRCLE ROUTE THROUGH SWITZERLAND

Zürich, far more than banking, business and the Bahnhofstrasse shops, shares its soul with its Zunfthaüser, as the guildhalls are known. Established by tradesmen of the Middle Ages, who gathered with their peers for mutual support and camaraderie, the most traditional guildhalls are richly embellished and open to the public for meals in historic surroundings. (Check the daily offerings on the card posted by the entrance if you want to know what's being served—and how much it costs.)

While lakeboats can take you from Zürich's Schifflände (as the boats' dock is known) to the farm country that has now become the prized place for suburban living, the trains and roads can lead to rural areas where art and architecture speak of the landscape. Within minutes of the city, there are farms where homegrown produce is served in the restaurants and lodgings offer the hospitality of the countryside.

Heading north toward the river Rhein (the Rhine), or northeast, toward the Bodensee (Lake Constance, in English), the landscape may be draped with vineyards or blanketed by farms, but it is rarely overbuilt. The architecture is distinctive from town to town. Beam-and-stucco is the style for many prominent homes; others have intricately painted facades, as is the case at Stein-am-Rhein and Schaffhausen, which are situated along the Rhein river and linked by delightful river cruises.

Villages thrive on the shores of the Bodensee, shared by Germany (on the northeast), Austria (at Bregenz, noted for its summer music festival, at the east), and Switzerland (on the southwest). Most are dotted with a lakeboat dock, punctuated with at least one traditional inn and ribboned by railroad tracks traversed by multi-stop regional trains. All the larger towns have several places to stay (and dine); some are quite special.

Austria's Bregenz, with a historic core of medieval buildings on the hillside, and Germany's Lindau, where the 12th century historic center occupies a tiny peninsula into the lake, are larger than most visitors expect, but both towns offer easy access to all entertainments of the lake and the nearby mountains, with opportunities for bicycling to places near the lake.

Similar styles of folk art can be seen when you travel south of the Bodensee (and east of Zürich), into an area that gives the Alpine region some of its trademark *naif* art. This part of eastern Switzerland, as well as southwestern Germany and western Austria, maintains most of the traditions of Alpine mountain life, with oft-repeated patterns for family celebrations and carefully planned folk festivals.

East of Zürich, the town of St. Gallen fills the bottom of a bowl of mountains. Established by Gallus, an Irish monk who wandered here in 612, the community has grown—with its tradition of embroidery and lace-making—to become a modern center with a soul.

The embellished Baroque cathedral and the amazing library, with its collection of over 130,000 volumes and illustrated manuscripts dating to the 1600s, are reason enough to pause here. But plan for time to take one of the local tram-trains, perhaps up to Trogen or certainly to Appenzell, Herisau or Gais, to walk through the countryside reflected in the paintings of farm life that you can see in museums and purchase, in copies, on postcards.

This is a region of *Bauernmalerai,* or farm crafts, common throughout the Alps, where local folks spent long winters painting, carving and otherwise working with the implements and raw materials that they know best. For anyone interested in handcrafts, this part of the Alpine area is a treasure trove.

Around Appenzell, appreciated for its painted buildings as well as for its shops and inns; there are nearby villages such as Urnäsch, where a regional museum displays many farm traditions, and other villages, where walking paths lead into the countryside. From many villages, cablecars stretch to highest peaks, where well-posted paths lead past mountain inns that prove ideal for refreshment.

Farther south, perhaps through the Principality of Liechtenstein, and the spa town of Bad Ragaz, Chur is a modern city with a historic core that dates from earliest settlements in the region. The wide Rhein valley made the area a perfect pausing place, amid travels through surrounding mountain passes. An hour's train ride from Zürich, Chur is a jump off point for the mountain resorts of Flims, Arosa, and even for St. Moritz, the fashionable resort that lies southeast of Chur and needs little introduction.

Many villages of this canton of Graubünden (known to the English as "Grisons") are little known to outsiders. Most retain traditions from their past, in the stridently independent manner of the Engadine Valley that gave Switzerland its fourth language, known as Romansch.

Several farm villages have opened their charming inns for visitors interested in walks, hikes and cross-country skiing when snow coats the ground.

South and west of this area and reached by a wonderful train ride through Italy's Tirano, the Swiss canton of Ticino, on the sunny side of the Alps, claims Locarno and Lugano as pivot points on their respective Italian-shared lakes. Locarno's vast Lago Maggiore is mostly in Italy, and is the westernmost of a trio of Italian lakes that includes large Lago di Como to the east and smaller Lago di Lugano in the middle.

Although now dedicated to banking and to tourism, both Locarno and Lugano display Italian artisans' skills with stately mansions facing central squares that prickle with café tables as soon as the weather warms. (Not only do the architecture and the artistic details speak Italian, but the voice is heard in restaurants as well.)

From Lugano through Locarno, via the cantonal capital of Bellinzona, a remarkable train ride passes through the Centovalli, shared with Italy, to change at Italy's Domodossola, for travel to Switzerland's Brig, on the Rhône valley floor.

From Brig, trains and highways stretch through the wide east-west Rhône valley or north over a remarkable scenic route toward Meirigen and Luzern or Zürich. But it is the yellow postal buses or the Brig-Visp-Zermatt cog railway that unlock the Alpine treasures high in the mountain pockets. From Brig, Sion or Sierre (valley towns worth some time on their own merits) postal buses stretch to the end of side valleys that reach out, like secondary fishbones, from the backbone route.

From Martigny, at the western end of the Rhône valley, it's almost a straight shot north to the eastern end of Lac Léman, the French-shared half-moon-shaped lake that has Genève at its western end. (From Martigny, a cog-train climbs into the mountains to the French border, to head down the mountains into France, through Chamonix.) The town is a pivot point for hikers and skiers (depending on the season) and a pausing place for people lured by the exceptional exhibits in Martigny's remarkable art gallery.

Continuing northwest along the shore of Lac Léman, a glorious span bordered on the north by Switzerland and the south by France, there are many charming towns and villages. The north coast is marked by Montreux, Vevey, Lausanne-Ouchy and, closer to Genève, by castle-studded Morges, Rolle, Nyon and the mansion at Coppet.

The lake of Geneva region, so called by English-speaking folks, reaches inland and upland from the shores of Lac Léman, as the lake is officially known in French. One noteworthy train ride climbs up through Château d'Oex and Gstaad to Zweisimmen, to head down to Spiez, on the Thunersee, a lake that takes its name from the castle-studded town of Thun, a few miles away.

Wise travelers schedule several days to enjoy the area around Lac Léman. Walking paths lead from lakeside docks through vineyards that produce some of the best Swiss wines and to villages punctuated by small chapels and stately mansions that show the continuing influence of the Italian Renaissance artists, who migrated north from Italy, plying their crafts to earn their keep.

Genève, home for international organizations of world renown, gains its soul from its neighborhoods. Make time to stroll the cobbled streets of the *vieille ville* (as the oldest hilltop of town is known in the French that's spoken here), ride a tram to Carouge, an appended village that lies across the river Arve, visit the surrounding vineyards or take a meal at an inn in Hermance, on the border with France. Shopping is superb on the streets of Genève, as well as at the bastion of shops at the rail- and bus-linked international airport.

Although the cozy restaurants, the boutiques, other shops and the eclectic museums can occupy many hours, no visit to Genève is complete without a pause at the wall of the Reformation, in the Parc des Bastions, where John Calvin stands with Beze, Farel, John Knox, Roger Williams and other great minds of the 17th century, who convened to discuss (and eventually dictate) the morals of their world.

Just overhead, strolling up the cobbled ramp where chestnut trees provide some shelter, you can stand at the wall that commemorates the defeat of the Duke of Savoy, Charles-Emmanuel, on December 11, 1602, in a battle that began with a surprise attack by an "army" of local women who dumped hot soup on the heads of the mostly-Catholic forces supporting the Duke.

Since Genève is the westernmost city of the country, a route through Switzerland now heads east, in the northern sector, where the modest hills of the Jura brush the border and share their configuration with France.

Northeast of Lac Léman (and north of Lausanne), at the western point of Lac de Neuchâtel, Yverdon-les-Bains, with its 13th century castle much restored, is the birthplace of Johann Heinrich Pestalozzi, known among educators for his unique-and-supportive homes for children. (There is a Pestolozzi village in the hills above St. Gallen, in the eastern part of Switzerland.)

Nearby, at Grandson, a castle's 11th century core was expanded in the 13th and 15th centuries to stand as testimony to the battles between Burgundians and Swiss, and the perseverence of the Swiss (Bernese) who occupied it for three centuries. Today it is a museum in a photogenic town.

Following the lake shore northeast, the town of Neuchâtel is prominent, not only for its university (which occupies several noteworthy buildings), but also for its collection of 17th and 18th century mansions, put to modern use. Although the lakefront now bristles with yachts, with a portion of the shore claimed by the recently established Papiliorama gardens, the surrounding area is the source for a popular Swiss wine (and a wine museum in a château at nearby Valangin helps to explain what's what.)

South of the southern shore of the Lac de Neuchâtel, Lac de Morat/Murtensee is a small patch of water that seems far from the mainstream. Laced with boat service, the lake's largest town is Murten/Morat (switching the double naming system, in deference to the region's language preference, to lead with the German name). And some town it is! Following the pattern established by the Dukes of Zähringen in the 12th century, the hilltop walled town bespeaks another era, especially when you stay overnight, to enjoy its quieter moments. Roman relics are highlights of the Musée Historique in the former mill (with water wheels), next to the trademark castle.

Avenches, a few miles southwest of Murten/Morat, was known as Aventicum by the Romans who built it into a significant city of 40,000 people. An important site for the Helvetian tribes prior to that time, Avenches was destroyed by the Alemanni tribes in the 3rd century. Roman ruins can be visited and the artifacts in the museum are testimony to a thriving community in the earliest centuries.

Bern, with its arcaded streets from the Middle Ages, its annual *Zwiebelemärit* (onion market) in November, and its several museums, is the federal capital of Switzerland. (Lausanne is the legislative capital; Zürich is widely considered the banking capital.) But, for visitors, it has many aspects of a small town. Buttoned onto a hilltop nub of land, set in a sharp bend of the river Aare, the city has pockets filled with charming restaurants where regional specialties are served, shops that feature handcrafts, and some of the best hotels in Switzerland, as well as several charming inns in the surrounding countryside.

Ideal as a touring hub, with its railroad station serving both international and local trains, Bern is also a source for details about the Bernese Oberland, the Alpine region to the south. (Visit the tourist office in the railroad station for travel assistance.)

South of Bern, the landscape invites wandering. In towns such as Fribourg, buildings that date from the Middle Ages line the roads from the hilltop to the valley lake that is a river bulge.

Not far away, Gruyères, a castle-capped statement in surrounding meadows, lures visitors with a history of Counts from the 11th through 16th centuries and a link with cheese that is worldwide. (The cheese comes from cows contentedly munching in the surrounding meadows; a recently-built cheese factory explains the process, at the base of the hill-climbing road that leads to the single cobbled street of the village of Gruyères.)

Interlaken—"between the lakes"—lured Mark Twain and thousands of others, not only for the awe-inspiring railway journey up and out, eventually to the Jungfrau, for many travelers, and only as far as Grindelwald or countless other mountain resorts, for others. The town that has grown on the land-link between the Brienzersee/Lac de Brienz and the Thunersee/Lac de Thoun gives visitors an astounding view of the usually snow-capped peaks of the Mönch, the Eiger and the Jungfrau.

Ideal as a base for mountain and lakeside touring, Interlaken is also rail-linked for many of Switzerland's most scenic train rides. (Not far from Brienz, at the eastern end of the Brienzersee, lies Ballenberg, where a village of historic houses and other buildings has been reconstructed from original sites so today's visitors can walk through the past.)

Lively Luzern (as Lucerne is known in German) has lured visitors through the centuries, from the time when it was a resting place for 12th century travelers before they crossed the Alps on a major route between northern Europe and Italy. These days—with its dozens of shops, comfortable inns and luxurious hotels, countless restaurants and lakeboat and train stations—the town, in a protected bay of the large-and-convoluted lake, still wins accolades.

From the shores of the Vierwaldstättersee, known to English-speaking folks as the Lake of Lucerne, visitors can walk through Swiss history. The Swiss Path, created in 1991, by the Swiss people through their cantonal governments, is a sign-posted walking path that commemorates the 700th anniversary of the founding of Switzerland. History is explained at strategic places along the route, which can be walked in easy segments, starting or ending at a lakeboat dock for the return to your choice of a "home."

The short distance between Luzern and Zürich (less than an hour by train or highway) can take days and is well worth a leisurely pace. Not only is the up-and-over mountain-and-lake route scenic, with memorable rural vignettes, but also the arrival into Zürich along the Zürichsee hints at the dozens of country inns, small villages and occasional vineyards that are within that city's reach.

Along the route, many places will surprise you with their riches: Vitznau, along the shore of the Vierwaldstättersee, with the Rigibahn cog railway to take you to the highest peaks; Brunnen, linked to nearby Schwyz, with its museum for the articles of the

Swiss Confederation, formed in 1291 and commemorated by a meadow monument across the lake; and Einsiedeln, with special events focused on its vast embellished Benedictine abbey.

Even Zürich, often wedged into the staid image of the banking fraternity that gives it its headlines, is a playground of lakeboat excursions, funicular rides (to bosky places for walks or inns for a meal), tram trips (to the hilltop zoo, for example) and regional train journeys (along the lake shore to Rapperswil or, on the other side, to Au, to walk up through the vineyard to a hilltop inn).

Zürich is also a city of charming restaurants, the best of which hide inside mellow wooden doors in the Altstadt, as the old city is known in the German spoken here. Among the lodging choices are some of the most elegant Swiss hotels and many small-and-comfortable lodgings. Zürich is an ideal gateway for the Alps, with its Hauptbahnhof, as the main railway station is called, and its international airport.

DIVERSIONS AND DALLIANCES

- The Bernina Express train climbs, sashays and descends, passing farmlands, villages with etched stucco buildings, lakes and forests on its route between Switzerland's St. Moritz and Italy's Tirano.

- A lakeboat ride between Switzerland's Locarno and Italy's Luino on Lago Maggiore is an international dalliance.

- From Switzerland's Brig, take the yellow postal coach up to Saas Fee, following the valley route that breaks at Stalden to follow the eastern branch of the inverted Y. The other prong leads out and up to Zermatt, reached by the BVZ cog-railway out of Brig or Visp.

- Between Montreux and Spiez, take the MOB train that climbs past Gstaad and other mountain resorts to Zweisimmen to descend to Spiez, for Interlaken or Thun, with their lakes.

- From Genève, take the lakeboat or the local train to Coppet or Nyon, for a luncheon or dinner at a lakeside inn, with time to walk through the home of Mme. de Staël or a historic fortress-castle.

- Plan for a boat ride on Lac de Neuchâtel, continuing through the canal to the Lac de Bienne/Bielersee, at what is obviously a Swiss language "border" between French and German. (You can return by train, or continue onward.)

- Pause long enough in one of the many castles to imagine what it must have been like to live there and then head for the nearest cozy inn for a lovely, leisurely meal—and, perhaps, a night or two.

- When you've wandered through the medieval town of Murten/ Morat, plan to pause at one of the historic hotels within the ancient walls or head down to the lakeside for a meal at a memorable inn.

- Ride the lakeboat on the Thunersee, making time to pause at Thun for a walk to the castle and at Spiez for a meal at one of the many lakeview inns and restaurants. You can take a train back to your starting point if you don't have a car.

- Settle into an inn in the countryside to enjoy the special recipes and the local wine with the area's traditional style.

WHY GO TO THE ALPS?

For one reason, there's more variety in this one area—a crescent-shaped piece of landscape that occupies approximately 765 miles east to west and from 90 to 150 miles north to south—than any area of comparable size. You can find castles and country inns, classic hotels and homes where bed-and-breakfast is offered, colorful customs and cosmopolitan cultural events including world-renowned names in music and the arts, centuries-old costumes and sophisticated couture, and, of course, locally grown produce prepared by some of the world's greatest chefs as well as by farmers who share their regional and family recipes. Meals are best enjoyed with wines that do not travel outside their region, not only because sediment may affect the quality of the wine when it is jostled in transport but also because local folks enjoy consuming their region's production.

There are festivals. Some Alpine events are brightened by regional costumes and heightened by the taste of traditional foods and by the lively sounds of mountain music. Others are world class, such as the annual ski events, including Switzerland's Engadine marathon, and other sports events. There are hundreds of museums. Some excel with collections of priceless paintings, including frescoes that have survived centuries; others are devoted to crafts, including porcelain, watches and clocks, wood carving, weaving and other time-honored skills. There are museums that focus on transportation, or Alpine mountaineers, or the Alps themselves, including their rock formations and their ice-age glaciers.

And there are the people, those you will meet on the roads and paths, and those who will be your hosts in luxury hotels, atmospheric inns and farmhouses in the country where they offer the best Alpine/European hospitality. They are the ones who help make lasting memories.

THE ALPINE COUNTRIES

AUSTRIA

Austria, the easternmost member of the group, puts its capital of Wien (Vienna, pronounced "Veen" in German) just outside the Alps on their eastern fringe. The Länder (states) of Vorarlberg, Salzburg, and Tirol, in the western part of the country, however, are marked by impressive mountains, many of which are snow-capped in summer as well as winter. Colorful folklore is woven into daily life.

FRANCE

France claims the western portion of the Alps in its southeastern sector, where the history, language and transportation routes mingle with southwestern Switzerland and northwestern Italy. Planting some of the most modern winter resorts in the Alpine region high on the flanks of impressive peaks, the French Alps played host to the 1992 Winter Olympics. From a base in the valley at Albertville participants and followers headed out to the highest peaks at Courcheval, Méribel, Val d'Isère and other areas.

GERMANY

Germany shares the Alps through Bavaria, its southernmost state, where the capital of München (Munich) combines the cosmopolitan lifestyle and the charming folklore of the Alps, not only in its museums but also on its streets, shops, restaurants and at festival times. The Zugspitze, a towering peak easily reached by cog railway from Garmisch-Partenkirchen, is "cut" by the imaginary line that is the German-Austrian border, separating Bavaria and Austria's Tirol region, and the area around Berchtesgaden is rich in history.

ITALY

Italy claims many of the most impressive southern peaks and flanks of the Alps, where the north of the country nudges against France, Switzerland and Austria, and shares a portion of its rugged Dolomites. The Valle d'Aosta, Piemonte, portions of Lombardia, the Alto Adige and the Trentino region are the stars of Italy's Alpine area, with their lovely lakes, craggy mountains and exceptional places to stay.

LIECHTENSTEIN

Liechtenstein, cupped at the Rhein valley, with Austria to the east and guardian Switzerland at the west, is a small principality with an active royal family, a thriving banking business and a standard of living that is the envy of many much larger countries.

MONACO

Monaco, a second tiny principality, grows in a niche of France on the southern flank of the Alps and faces the Mediterranean. Vacation life may focus on the pleasures of its casino and classy boutiques —and on the vast sea that is its "front lawn"—but the principality is easily accessible to Alpine areas for walks, hikes and other pursuits.

SLOVENIA

Slovenia, which became an independent country on June 25, 1991, is linking its future to the ways of its northern and western neighbors. Sharing its northern border with Austria, Slovenia also shares a Habsburg history and has always had more in common with its northern neighbors than with the former Yugoslavia, of which it was a part. The Alpine crossing at Kranjska Gora, near Austria's town of Villach, leads south to foothills of fertile farmland. The western region slides to the sea at the Jadransko Morje, also known as the Gulf of Trieste.

SWITZERLAND

Switzerland, in the heart of the Alpine countries, shares mountains with each of its neighbors—France to the west, Austria, with the tidbit of Liechtenstein, to the east, Italy on the southern border, and Germany to the north. It also shares its lakes and borrows from the languages and lifestyles of its neighbors to create a uniquely Swiss melange with dependable Swiss efficiency, security and cleanliness.

CASH, CURRENCY AND CREDIT CARDS

Although there's talk of a common European currency, at presstime the Alpine region uses six different currencies, each the king in its own realm. In Austria, the currency is österreiches (Austrian) Schillings, currently about öS 12 to US$1. The French franc is approximately FF 6 to US$1. Germany uses Deutsches (German) Marks, at DM 1.68 to US$1), while Italian lire figure at about L 1650 to US$1. Slovenia uses tolars, at a floating rate that has yet to stabilize. Switzerland and Liechtenstein deal in Swiss Francs, at about SFr 1.50 to US$1 at presstime.

> **AUTHOR'S OBSERVATION**
>
> *Plan ahead. If you're intending to head into the countryside, anticipate weekends and holidays and other times when banks and other exchange places may be closed. Visit a bank in some city or large town before you begin your travels in the countryside to cash enough travelers cheques to give you plenty of cash-in-hand.*

It may not always be easy to cash travelers cheques or to use credit cards. Some of the places mentioned in this book are local businesses where the daily routines are far removed from the international currency market. Chances are the people you're doing business with may not know (or care) about the value of the U.S. dollar.

I've found it easiest to travel with travelers cheques, readily available through your local banks, often without additional charge if you're a steady customer. For travel in the Alpine countries, buying Swiss francs travelers cheques is always efficient. Travelers cheques also come in French francs and German Marks, so give some thought as to how much time you're spending in one country if you decide to buy foreign currency cheques. One source for information about foreign currency, and for purchasing cheques, is **Ruesch International** *(1350 Eye Street, W., Washington, DC 20005;* ☎ *202+ 408-1200 or 800+424-2923; FAX 202+408-1211).*

Although credit cards are accepted at most of the places that are frequented by foreign travelers, don't assume that every place will accept your plastic card. If you're short of cash and must use a credit card for payment, shop for a place that shows the familiar decals near its doorway and always ask before you're settled in your room or at the table in a restaurant. Then, at least, if they don't accept the credit card you want to use, you can go elsewhere.

AUTHOR'S OBSERVATION

Spend some time at a café, on a train, or in your room, learning the look and feel of the local bills and coins. And then figure out some system that works for you, insofar as dividing or multiplying is concerned, to learn equivalents for easy use. Spending with the confidence of the local folk helps to break down the barriers between tourist and host.

If you'd rather not be concerned about money exchange, ask your travel agent to give you details about the *Swiss Travel Invention* and *The European Travel Invention*, travel programs organized with Swissair to sell you prepaid coupons (in dollars) that can be used at designated hotels in all categories. Germany's *Wundercheque* and *Danubecheque* programs operate in a similar way, and some hotel groups (Best Western, for one) have prepaid voucher travel plans. The individual tourist offices can give you information about special voucher programs.

CLIMATE

When you look at a map and at the parallels, it seems logical to assume that weather in the Alpine cities and countryside might be about the same as that of the similar latitude—New York, perhaps—in North America. It might be, but not always. The mountain air currents do different things to the Alpine climate. The southern side of the Alps, most of which is claimed by Italy, southeastern France, Slovenia and Switzerland's Ticino region, welcomes spring long before the northern slopes. And the sun-warmed valleys know a more temperate climate than those where mountains block the sun.

Be prepared for "everything." While it may be warm and springlike on a sun-washed lake, the afternoon cablecar ride to a mountainside perch may bring a temperature that feels more like winter. Europeans have invented the most compact fold-up umbrellas for good reason. Buy one and always carry it with you. Rain showers come without much (or any) warning. And even in mid-summer, you may find it snowing in high Alpine areas.

AUTHOR'S OBSERVATION

When you make your reservations, be sure to ask a hotel or local tourist office about the climate in specific places if it matters for your comfort. Resorts know the peculiarities of their weather patterns better than anyone else.

In summer, the weather is often warm and beautiful, but well-known resorts and cities can be crowded with Americans, Europeans, Japanese and other visitors at that time of year. Spring is one of the most beautiful times of the year; it's also when the temperature is the most variable. Winter in the cities may be chilly, or downright cold, but cozy restaurants are even more appealing when the streets are bone-chilling. Fall is known for rain, for early snows and for extremely erratic weather, but it's also the time when cool nights gild the vineyards and the air is astoundingly clear (and great for photography).

CLOTHES

Europeans who "live" in the Alps are seldom fettered with lots of luggage and they always look appropriate. Taking a cue from them, pack enough, but not too much. In fact, you'll carry your own luggage most of the time unless you're traveling with an organized group where a guide takes care of it for you. Even when you're willing to pay the premium for someone to help, it's often difficult to find anyone. Try to avoid bringing anything you cannot comfortably carry yourself.

Key items for comfort depend a lot on what you plan to do. If you are going to be in cities and want to go to gala evenings at the opera or elsewhere, women can't go wrong with black, perhaps with some dazzling costume jewelry, which you'll find in many department and other stores as you travel. For men, a dark suit is appropriate for all but the most formal occasions, when you'll need dress clothes.

AUTHOR'S OBSERVATION

Even the most compact carry-on bag takes on a life of its own if you travel from place to place. Plan to have all clothes do double duty and remember that dark and muted colors absorb the vagaries of travel better than light colors and perishable fabrics. It's possible to ship heavy sports equipment (ski boots, etc.) on rail check-in services, which are secure and convenient. It's also relatively easy to ship them home from a local post office when you no longer need them. (See "Communications" below and in the individual country chapters.)

Important items for comfortable sportswear are layers of light-weight clothing to take off or put on while you cope with the climate changes that inevitably occur at different levels and locations in the mountains. Be sure to leave some space in your luggage for on-the-spot purchases.

Comfortable (and appropriate) footwear is the most essential item. If you plan to walk or hike, bring at least one pair of "sturdy" shoes that protect your ankles and will grip the ground, with sole-padding that can absorb the impact of foot-on-rock. Many sport shoes that are appropriate for most walks and hikes and fit easily in a suitcase niche can do double duty as daily wear for walking in the countryside and hiking along a well-marked mountain route.

Most Alpine towns and cities have excellent sporting stores, often tagged "Sports" despite the language they speak. It's possible to buy everything you need when you arrive, if you allow a few extra days to shop and have the bank account to cope with the purchases.

AUTHOR'S OBSERVATION

At some of the best resorts in Switzerland, Germany and Austria, it's possible to rent boots and skis. To avoid disappointment, ask about such services before you leave home so you'll know prices and have contact names.

COMMUNICATIONS

From the U.S., telephoning most of the Alpine countries is easy, effective and inexpensive, especially in the early morning hours, when it is midmorning in Europe and U.S. rates are lowest. From the U.S., AT&T customers can dial *011* plus the country code plus the city code and the telephone number. MCI and Sprint have other international access codes. Throughout this book, telephone numbers are designated by the ☎ sign. All numbers are given for use from outside the specific country. For use in the country, add a "0" before dialing the given number.

From most of the Alpine countries, with the exception of Slovenia as this book goes to press, AT&T's *USA Direct* service allows for easy, relatively inexpensive, communication from the country to the U.S. MCI and Sprint have similar services. The system is explained as it pertains to each country in the following chapters. From Slovenia, using telephones in post offices is the least expensive way to telephone to North America.

AUTHOR'S OBSERVATION

Note that most hotels levy substantial surcharges on telephone calls made in the comfort of your room. The additional sum can double the cost of your call. Always ask, before you dial, if being forewarned is important. When you use the USA Direct service, the contact charge is a local call. The overseas charge will appear on your telephone bill.

Telephone cards are issued in most of the Alpine countries. They are slightly larger than a credit card and can be bought in specific denominations from the post office or designated shops. Your hotel or the local tourist office can point you in the right direction for card purchase. Once you have bought your card, insert it in the slot of the telephone machine, dial the number and talk. The card will eject, minus the cost of your call, when you hang up. Some phones still use coins, or, in the case of Italy, *gettones*, and some telephones gobble coins as you talk, making it necessary to anticipate the cost and have the coins handy to insert when the signal requests more money.

Facsimile systems are widely used by hotels and many other tourism interests. Although fax numbers are not always included in this text, they can be learned through the tourist offices and directly from the properties/businesses in question.

AUTHOR'S OBSERVATION

If you have a telephone answering machine that uses a coded connection, be sure to bring along the battery-operated unit that will "talk" to your tone. Because European touch-tone phones are on a different frequency, you'll need the extra apparatus to communicate with your home-tone. Most electronic stores carry the item, which is about the size of a deck of cards.

Computer links are sometimes difficult. If you plan to communicate with a computer in the U.S., be sure to work out the linkage before you leave the U.S. The fact that most of the Alpine countries operate on a different voltage can create problems with your computer when you plug it into an outlet to gain power. Modem transmission is often difficult, due to erratic pulsing signals. You may find it works better to mail a disk. If so, bring mailing envelopes. There are express international mailing services in most major cities and often through the airlines at the airports.

CONCIERGE

The person at your hotel who is in charge of daily assistance is the concierge; he's your friend-in-court (and he is still a "he" in the Alpine countries, although some North American hotels have given that job to women). His desk is usually at or near the main hotel entrance. The concierge is your source for information about shoemakers, tailors, theater tickets, taxis, public transportation routes and tickets, how to get back to your hotel from some excursion outpost, and everything else. He is also a good source for tour arrangements, dinner reservations and other daily "extras." When you use the services of the concierge, a tip is appropriate. At smaller, family-owned properties, the front desk personnel and/or the owner/manager assist with all arrangements.

DOCUMENTS

Passports are obtained through the Passport Office of the Department of Treasury in most major cities, or by mail through your local post office. A passport and an **International Driver's Permit** if you're planning to rent a car, are the key documents. The cost for a passport, valid for ten years, is $65. To obtain your passport, you must have two photographs, face-forward head shots, in specified size, plus proof of your U.S. citizenship, which can be a validated copy of your birth certificate or a copy of your naturalization papers.

If you intend to drive, visit your nearest American Automobile Association (AAA) office, listed in the telephone book, for an International Driver's Permit. The cost is $10; you'll need two passport-size photos and your valid U.S. driver's license. The permit is valid for one year from the date you designate when you make your purchase. When you rent a car in Europe, be sure to ask for the "green card," which is usually presented with your papers. It is your proof of paid insurance and is essential to show at country borders and other times.

EMERGENCIES

Major cities and many towns in Austria, Germany, Liechtenstein and Switzerland have efficient and effective methods of handling emergencies, as do many places in France and Monaco, and some in major tourism centers of Slovenia. American Express offices and representatives are good sources, especially for card holders but also for all English-speaking travelers. The local tourist office is also a good source for more complicated problems, since they have local members who usually can assist. Of course, the first place to head for help is your hotel, especially if you are staying at a deluxe resort or hotel. Even if you are staying at a small spot, the concierge at one of the major hotels is usually a good source for aid. For medical emergencies, see "Medical Facts" below.

FOOD, WINE AND OTHER BEVERAGES

Travelers who enjoy sampling local specialties will find "eating" becomes "dining" when traveling around the Alpine area, where there are many regional recipes and dining styles. The experience includes pleasant surroundings, new and different food, and cheese and cured meats, which can be enjoyed at the farms where they are made. There are many places to sample regional wines, liqueurs, beers and juices. Domestic recipes seem to ignore borders and borrow spices and other seasonings from neighbors.

Mealtimes in local inns and other restaurants can be memorable even if you're not fluent in the village language. Costs are relatively modest when you visit places known to the local folk, away from the well-trod tourist routes.

Other caveats for enjoying meals in Alpine inns include preparing for the fact that German, Italian, French and Slovene are the languages of the Alps. When you know some basic words, you'll be rewarded by knowing what you've ordered. (If you don't know some words, you can still eat. Just point and take your chances, as I have often done.)

AUTHOR'S OBSERVATION

A sum as "thanks" for service is usually included in the cost of your meal, especially in small places around the countryside and in places enjoyed mostly by local folks. Somewhere on the food listing you'll see service compris, *which is French for "service included," or* service inbegriffen *(German), or* servizio inclusivo *(Italian), and sometimes all three. "Net" also implies that a charge for service is included in the amounts. When in doubt, ask—to avoid overtipping and/or looking like a "rich American."*

Unlike the U.S. system, where many restaurants are eager to have you pay and leave, restaurants in the Alpine area expect their patrons to linger. The bill for your meal will not be presented until you ask for it. It's considered impolite to rush you. In German-speaking areas, "Die Rechnung" brings the bill. A more casual phrase, "Zahlen, bitte," means "check, please," and usually works as well. In Italy, say "Il conto, por favore" and in France, the phrase is "l'addition, s'il vous plait." Learning these phrases, how to pronounce them and be understood is worthwhile.

Die Speisekarte is the formal name for what we know as the menu, but "Karte" will usually bring the food listing. In French, the word is *la carte*, which means menu as Americans use the word. In Italian, you'll ask for "il menù," and, although any of these words will work in Slovenia, the word in Slovene is *Jedilni list.* In most of the Alpine area, the word menu is used for the meal of the day, which is the chef's choice. It's not the list of offerings. If you ask for the "menu" (pronouncing it "men-ou"), you'll have ordered the meal of the day, which is usually wonderful and may be the best way to cope with mealtime if you're timid.

Frühstuck is breakfast in German, *le petit déjeuner* in French, and *prima colazione* in Italian. In Slovene, it's *Zajtrk* that starts the day. These days, most lodgings offer a buffet of fresh breads, cheese, jam and butter, with coffee, tea, or hot chocolate. In German, *Mittagessen* is the midday meal, the main meal of the day, and *Abendessen* is the evening meal; in French, the words are *le déjeuner* and *le diner*; in Italian, *seconda colazione* and *cena*, pronounced "chay-nah;" in Slovene, the words are *Kosilo* and *Večerja.*

Walking through food shops can yield picnic fare as well as a language lesson from the names posted on the produce. Salamis and cheeses are easy to find, as is good fresh bread. Bottled water can be an elixir during long days of travel. Packages of local crackers and cookies are fun to try, as well as filling when you tire of playing restaurant games.

AUTHOR'S OBSERVATION

Don't count on having English translations on the list, especially at some of the most charming village inns. Choices for coping with the linguistic "roadblock" include carrying a pocket phrasebook, looking at what someone else is eating and pointing to it when the waitress or waiter comes to you, or pointing to something on Die Speisekarte and taking your chances.

Wine is always available. In German, *Offene Weine* is the "open wine," usually the owner's choice and often served by carafe; in

French, the phrase is *vin ouvert*; in Italian, *vino operto*. You need only say *rot, rouge*, or *rose* for red wine in German, French or Italian; white is *weiss, blanc*, or *blanco*. Amounts for the open wine are usually shown as portions of a liter.

Bavaria, the German state that covers most of that country's Alps, is famous for its beer, but all Alpine countries offer excellent brews and *Bier* sounds the same no matter how it's spelled. The same is true with *Kafe, le café*, and *caffé*, which is coffee—and usually powerful as well as costly. *Mineralwasser*, with the "w" pronounced as a "v," is bottled water in German-speaking countries, and you'll have the choice of bubbles (*mit gasse* or not which is *ohne gasse*). *Saft* is juice and can be *Apfelsaft* or *Orangesaft*, both easily translated, or *Traubensaft*, which is delicious grape juice.

Pastries are the punctuation mark on any meal and often a meal in themselves. Since the names are usually local ones, the best way to get what you want is to point—and pay.

LANGUAGE

If you want to practice just one other language, German is the one to know. It is spoken in some form and dialect by most of the Alpine region's people, and mealtime listings in the region are written in German in most places. There are some idiosyncrasies through this text, such as the use of *Wien*, which is pronounced "veen," and is the name for the Austrian capital English-speaking people know as Vienna. *München*, pronounced "moonchin," is the German name for a city many know as Munich. *Luzern* is the Swiss name for the city most British and American travelers know as Lucerne—and English-speaking folks use Lake Lucerne as the tag for the lake with the tongue-twisting name of *Vierwaldstättersee* (pronounced "feer-valled-shtodt-er-zay") which translates from the German word as "lake of the four forest cantons." (A Swiss canton is similar to a state in the U.S., and three of the four cantons are those that joined, on August 1, 1291, to form the core of what we know as Switzerland.)

Lac Léman is the official name for the Swiss-French lake that British and Americans recognize as the Lake of Geneva, a city that the French know as *Genève* (phonetically "jeune-ev") and Germans call *Genf*.

Confused? You needn't be. Just remember that, in an area with as many languages as this one, people from one village often cannot converse in a common spoken language with their neighbors over the nearby mountain pass. That makes it easy for those of us from other parts of the world when we don't know the local dialect either.

It helps to familiarize yourself with a few words and certainly with place names as they are known in the places they identify. That much is essential for traveling around and following signs that lead to the towns you will want to visit. For example, it helps to know that "*Tal*" is valley and that "*See*" is lake in German, as in Kander*tal* and Zürich*see*. The words appear in many place names and are a good tip to location.

One way to enhance your Alpine travels is to learn at least one of the languages of the area. German or French are the most useful for most Alpine countries and signing on for language lessons at your local high school or arranging with a tutor for a few weeks prior to departure can be a good investment. Foreign words used throughout this book are translated in the glossary that appears at the end of the book.

LODGING

The tourism offices for Austria, France, Germany, Italy, Liechtenstein, Monaco, Slovenia and Switzerland have accommodation listings in several forms, shapes and sizes, from inches-thick compendiums to stacks of color folders and information sheets. Each office also has staff ready to help you find a place. Travel agents are a complementary source, especially if your travel agent has been to the Alps and can share his or her personal experiences. In many cases, Alpine hotels with similar standards have grouped for communications and interbooking conveniences.

Although most U.S. chains have common ownership, most members of the Alpine groups are independently owned properties that have chosen to join, in a club style, to make it easier to book a room from one to the next or to share purchasing and promoting procedures. They are not a look-alike chain, in the U.S. sense, but they are linked.

Even with these sources, many typical Alpine lodgings do not have detailed information available in the United States, Canada and other countries. Some are not members of the national or regional hotel associations and are not, therefore, listed in the booklets offered through the national tourist offices. These are some of the many places that are best discovered on your own, traveling in the country, seeking suggestions from the local tourism office, talking with someone you meet while traveling and seeing some place you like when you're ready to pause for a couple of days—or for a meal.

AUTHOR'S OBSERVATION

Choices of places included in this book are entirely at the discretion of the author. I have included places I believe to be special for one reason or another and have paid for accommodations and meals traveling unannounced and independently.

There are some hotels in the Alpine region that look and act like American hotels, but most Alpine places do not. And some that look like American hotels may not function the same way. The European tradition known in the Alpine region is different from that of North America. Hospitality is usually more personal; decor is often Alpine country style or, in more formal situations, in the style of a manor house or villa.

Where the U.S. excels with dependable room size, routine dining room facilities (including a coffee shop), front desk systems and conveniences such as telephones in your room, television, radio and a private bathroom with tub/shower and toilet, Alpine hotels excel with personality, personal service, individuality in room shape and size, atmosphere (which is often centuries old) and regional—often exceptional—culinary skills.

Procedures in the traditional hotels, be they elegant escapes or country inns, allow for dependable quality, with flourishes established by centuries of refinement. Just as is the case with people, each Alpine hotel and/or inn will look different from the others even when it may share a name, such as "Beau Rivage," which means beautiful lakeside, "Weisses Kreuz" (white cross), or "Krone" (crown).

Palaces, estate houses and hunting lodges join established turn-of-the-century hotels and historic inns with presentations of the good life for visitors. Luxury standards are fit for kings and queens and, at some hotels, have been enjoyed by them. Rooms often vary in size or shape, decor and outlook. Prized rooms are usually big ones with the best view. Often they are suites, equipped in American style, with a small refrigerator (to chill your champagne) or minibar. The most elegant hotels, however, still bring champagne (and anything else) at your bidding, chilled and served exclusively for you.

In the days when hotels and estate houses were built with elaborate flourishes, travelers always brought their maids and other servants, who usually occupied the smallest rooms, sometimes in the nether regions of the hotels. Today, those smaller rooms are available for rent, often at modest cost, in a hotel where rates would otherwise command top price. They will be the least expensive and are often rented as single rooms—with a narrow, single bed. Even in some of the best hotels, there are a few rooms without private bathroom.

Many hotels and country inns have been modernized from early 19th-century postal coach halting places, where drivers paused to rest their horses. Rooms vary as to size, shape and location, just as they do in a private home. Some have been modernized; many I have known (and enjoyed) continue in the old style, with the toilet and tub down the hall or next door. When a room has a "private bath," it may include a shower, sink and toilet, but no tub, or a tub, sink, and toilet, but no shower, or a tub or shower and no toilet, or any combination of the above. Old-style rooms always have a washbasin in the room. The more rural, rustic and charming the place, the more varied its room style. The one constant is cleanliness.

AUTHOR'S OBSERVATION

All places that cling to the Alpine tradition bury your bed in a fluffy eiderdown, known as a duvet. It's always covered in a huge "pillow case," which sometimes is the sheet and often looks like a cloud. There's no bed cover that is as magically warm, or as easy to kick off when you get too hot. It's always crisp-clean and captures the Alpine atmosphere as effectively as anything I know.

Traditionally, continental breakfast (bread, butter, jam and a hot beverage of coffee, tea, or hot chocolate) and all taxes are included in the price of your room. Breakfast is often served in a separate room, for hotel guests only. The public is welcome in the café area, known as a *Stübli* in the German-speaking part of Switzerland, or a *Stuben* in high German. The room, whatever it's called, is often at street level, but may be up one flight of stairs and may be a portion of a room also used by hotel guests or a separate room enjoyed mostly by local folks. (For specifics about meals, refer to "Food, Wines, and Other Beverages," above.)

Among the terms worth knowing as they relate to hotels are *Halb-pension* (German), *demi-pension* (French) and *compresa la mezza pensione* (Italian), meaning "half-pension" or breakfast and one main meal per day. The second meal is usually dinner, following the style Americans know as MAP *Modified American Plan*, but that is not always the case. Be sure to inquire, if you prefer breakfast and lunch.

Garni implies a hotel with room and breakfast only. No other meals are served on the premises. The property often specifies *Hotel*

Garni (German), *l'hotel sans pension*, (French), or *l'albergo senza pensione* (Italian), in addition to *garni*.

AUTHOR'S OBSERVATION

Many lodgings give reduced rates for longer stays. It's always worth asking, so you can plan to stay longer if the price-break and your travel plans seem to warrant doing do.

"All-inclusive" in the Alpine countries implies that all service charges and taxes are included. It also usually means that continental breakfast (European-style, as mentioned above) is included, but it's wise to ask exactly what is included. Even the country's nationals are not always sure.

AUTHOR'S OBSERVATION

Service, a similar word in all the Alpine languages, implies a sum to cover the expected services provided by the maid and others. It is usually covered by the bill; nothing extra is expected (or appropriate), except in some of the deluxe hotels where special services have been provided. In fact, when you ask for special service, a small extra sum is appreciated everywhere, but it's best to tip in the custom of the country, not in lavish American fashion. The concierge in bigger hotels and the innkeeper in smaller places may be able to help with hints on local tipping customs. When in doubt, ask for suggestions about an appropriate amount.

The value-added tax, known as *Mehrwertsteuer*, or MWSt, in Austria and Germany, *Imposta Valore Aggiunto*, or IVA, in Italy, and a visitor's tax in France, has recently been voted into effect for Slovenia and Switzerland, where it may be included, without notice, in the posted price. The tax is usually included in the all-inclusive rate, although there are times when it may be noted as an extra. Always ask in advance to avoid surprises when paying your bill.

Here's a synopsis of the various styles of places to stay:

ELEGANT ESCAPES AND LUXURY LODGINGS

There are castles where you can be king or queen for a day, or longer. Many of the castles, palaces, hunting lodges, estate houses and resorts built to cater to the world's wealthy are maintained as though their original owners were present, with you as their privileged guests. In some cases, the owners *are* present. At many once private villas, visitors live in the lap of luxury in elegant, exclusive accommodations with the finest embellishments of great Italian artists. European etiquette suggests fashionable attire, sometimes with jacket for men at breakfast but always for dinner (with tie). On festive occasions at a few leading hotels, dinner jacket and long dress are not an exception. Sport clothes, when worn, are designer style.

Among the sources for several such properties are **Leading Hotels of the World**, a Swiss-based company with a U.S. affiliate *(737 Third Ave., New York, NY 10017; ☎ 212+838-3110; FAX 212+758-7367)* and **Relais & Châteaux** *(#707, 11 East 44th St., New York, NY 10017; ☎ 212+856-0115 or 800+743-8033; FAX 212+856-0193)*. **CIGA**, an Italian firm that was most recently owned by the Aga Kahn and is up for sale at presstime, has stood for ultra-luxe with Italian flourishes. CIGA (pronounced "Chee-gah") has elegant properties in Venice, Milan and other European cities; officials claim that there will be few changes following purchase by one of the bidding groups.

RESORTS AND CLASSIC HOTELS

At the turn of the century, as the 1800s climbed their way into the years before World War I, huge hotels grew at the favorite resorts of Europe's royalty and aristocracy. Many have held on to time-honored traditions, continuing to maintain the elaborate interior design in spite of the fact that many of the craftsmen and their skills are slowly disappearing. Modern plumbing, lighting and heat have been added, but little has been sacrificed of traditional ambience. Although some classic hotels accept group tours, many continue to offer the elegant service for which they are famous. Dress code is similar to that for the luxury lodgings. Although blue jeans may be acceptable for sport, they'll be designer jeans and they seldom go to dinner. Elegant boutiques set the clothing style. Leading Hotels of the World, mentioned above, is a source for details about many classic European resort hotels, as is CIGA, many of whose properties are also members of the Leading group.

FIRST-CLASS HOTELS

Some of the older hotels that exhibit high standards of service, and most of the new ones whose very newness precludes a luxury status in established European terms, such as the Hiltons, Holiday Inns, and other U.S. chains, are in this category. These are the "nouveau riche" of the lodging industry. Usually located in cities, bigger towns and the popular resorts, first-class hotels built in recent years have the modern comforts found in U.S. chains plus many that have yet to appear on American shores. A private bath is a fact of life, as are a telephone, radio and other services such as television, often with CNN. **Best Western** *(6201 North 24th Pkwy, Phoenix, AZ 85016; ☎ 602+957-4200 or 800+528-1234, FAX 602+555-5555)* operates a reservations system to which many charming European hotels belong. The properties are mostly personality places, often in historic and traditional buildings, which may come as a surprise if you associate the name with a roadside image the U.S. members used to project. Since tour groups use many of the larger first class hotels, dress standards vary with the savvy and style of the group. Conservative dress is always acceptable.

THE SPA SENSATION

Bad is not bad, but pronounced "baahd" and good. The word means "bath" in German. It refers to "taking the waters," or a mineral bath, at a spa (as well as to bathroom, when linked with general hotel rates). Towns with "Bad" in the name— Baden, Badgastein, Bad Kleinkirchheim, Bad Tölz, Bad Ragaz, Bad Reichenhall and the others—are, or were, popular spas at some time in their history. Most have spa and sports facilities now. Wise Americans are learning what Europeans have known for centuries—spas are special. The word comes from Belgium, where the town of Spa has been known as a place to take the waters since 1326, but the spa procedure and the health-giving effects were known to the Romans and before.

Spas come in several varieties. There are, of course, curative spas for serious illnesses and diseases, but there are also recreational spas with focus on diets, exercise and general health. In fact, in many Alpine resorts there's a fine line, when there's any line at all, between curative spas and sport-focused resorts where the pools are filled with water from the springs. **Spa Trek** *(475 Park Ave. S., New York, NY 10016;* ☎ *212+779-3480 or 800+272-3480, FAX 212+779-3471)* is one U.S. company that arranges spa holidays. Sports clothes are the appropriate daytime dress. Since evenings are elegant at the social spas, dress is also. Ask for guidelines from each specific spa if you care about fitting into the established system.

APARTMENTS, CHALETS AND VILLAS

Many of the Alpine resort areas have clusters of apartments for rent on a self-catering arrangement that gives you basic housekeeping facilities. In some cases, bed linens are supplied, as are cooking utensils and tableware, but it is wise to inquire. Although some people bring favorite touchstones from home, I prefer to buy local when needed. There's usually some "stock-up" place nearby. Always ask exactly what is supplied, and what there is for public transportation if you're not planning to rent a car. One U.S.-based source for apartment rentals is **Interhome** *(124 Little Falls Rd., Fairfield, NJ 07004;* ☎ *201+882-6864; FAX 201+808-1742).*

Clothing depends on your lifestyle—and the location of your "home." If you're living in a luxury area, you may want to dress for the part—and that usually means conservative, dark-colored, classy clothes and certainly suits for men. When you choose a mountain resort, comfortable sports clothes are the style.

INNS AND SMALL HOTELS

Usually family operated, with a special personality, the small places are some of the region's most ingenuous. Whether you pause at a *Gasthaus*, as the inns are known in Germany, an *auberge*, as they're called in France, a *pensione* in Italy, a *Gostilna* in Slovenia—or simply a place by the side of a country road that appeals to you—the experience will be unique. Although a few cars parked nearby can indicate that the inn is open, be aware that many of the best places look like they are closed. You'll have to go to the door to try the handle, and often you'll have to open another door inside the first, to enter either the casual pub-style room or the more formal tableclothed dining room. In all cases you are welcome, even though people may stare —and not speak your language. Go slow, and smile; watch—and wait. In most cases, someone will step forward to offer help.

Many of the inns have English-speaking staff, especially if they promote their services in North America. Some of the most charming, natural inns remain in their local sphere, however, and although any visitor is welcome, if your language is limited to American-English, sign language and smiles may be your means of communication. Those inns and others in the Alps are favorite discoveries for many of us who enjoy traveling off the beaten path.

Country-style clothes fit this scene, with evening attire about the same as daytime wear. Women wear tailored skirts or trousers, with shirts and jacket or sweater; men wear tailored sports clothes, with conservative tweed jackets or dark suit jacket. Tidy, conservative clothes are perfect for the pub-style room.

German-based **Romantik Hotels und Restaurants** *(Hörsteiner Strasse 34, Postfach 1144, D-63786 Karlstein, Germany; ☎ 37+6188+5020, FAX 37+6188+6007)* is an association of family-owned, historic hotels that pledge to maintain high standards, serve regional foods and maintain local customs. **Romantik Tours and Europa Hotels** *(Box 1278; Woodinville, WA 98072; ☎ 206+486-9394 or 800+826-0015, FAX 206+481-4079)* is a U.S. company that makes reservations for many atmospheric properties in the Alpine countries (and elsewhere in Europe). Many of the properties represented in the U.S. through **Best Western** (see above) are also appealing inns and small hotels.

FARM HOLIDAYS

Wonderful in the Alpine areas and popular with Europeans, a stay on a working farm is a favorite family vacation. Hunters and other outdoor folk also enjoy the casual comforts of the rural life. Accommodations for visitors are usually the best in the house and sometimes in a separate, newer building constructed for the purpose. Style varies, as you might expect, but most information sources provide pictures and details. If you're fluent in the local language your stay will be more meaningful, but adventuresome travelers willing to travel without sharing a language with the host can have a special experience. A week is the usual minimum stay. Country clothes are all that's needed. A scrub-up for dinner with the family is appreciated. *Urlaub am Bauernhof* is what the farm holidays are called in German. Specific details are given under "Lodging" in each country's chapter.

HUTS AND MOUNTAIN HOTELS

Unique to mountain areas, Alpine huts are usually maintained by the national Alpine association and are sometimes for use by members only. Personality varies with location (and the overseeing group), but accommodations sometimes include private rooms as well as bunk-beds and mattresses. It's a good idea to arrive midafternoon at the popular huts to be sure of "the best" bed. Mountain hotels, often reached by cableway, cog-train, or other conveyances as well as by hikers and walkers, offer woodsy, spartan surroundings with hearty country-style food. Specific contacts are mentioned in the individual chapters, in the "Lodging" section. Since the Alps are "the best" outdoors country, comfort is more important than fashion for clothes.

YOUTH HOSTELS

The Alpine region has a network of bunk-style lodgings for students and others age 26 or less. In some cases older backpackers can stay at the hostels, depending on the demand. Hostels in prime tourism areas are usually heavily booked in summer and at vacation times if they are open in winter months. Details about hostels in Alpine areas and requirements for entrance through the *International Youth Hostel Federation* are available from **American Youth Hostels** *(National Office, Box 37613, Washington, DC 20013-7613;*

☎ *202+783-6161, FAX 202+783-6171)*. Backpackers and hikers know their dress code best.

LUGGAGE

Travel light, both mentally and physically. Leave yourself open for new experiences; don't spend time worrying about your clothes. Try to travel with only carry-on luggage, but include one handy fold-up bag for items you may purchase en route. As you'll quickly realize, heavy luggage is more of a burden than it's worth. Traveling light makes it easy to move from one place to another and to get on and off trains or into and out of cars. The trick is to pack comfortable and classic clothes with colorful accents.

AUTHOR'S OBSERVATION

It's reasonably easy to mail packages to yourself, surface mail, from a nearby post office. I've done so many times from Switzerland, where the PTT sells suitable boxes, with string and labels. Although mailing costs can seem expensive, the convenience is worth the investment. And from Switzerland and the other German-speaking countries, there's no need to be concerned about whether or not your parcel will arrive. It will!

When you layer outfits for warmth, you'll need only one type of clothing. And if you travel with muted-to-dark colors, outfits can do double duty. It's possible, as I have often done, to spend the day walking in the mountains and go to a reasonably formal concert or another cultural event in the evening in the same outfit. (See "Clothes" above for further tips on what to pack.)

Put everything you think you'll need on your bed. Then put half of it back in your closet. Try to put half of what's left in your closet as well. Then carefully consider how many uses you can find for each of the items left. Pack the multi-use items, the true essentials and as many other things as you have room for in a suitcase you can easily carry yourself. That and one other small carry-on pouch are all you need.

MEDICAL FACTS

Medical services in the Alpine region are good in most communities and certainly in the major cities, especially in German-speaking areas. If you have a medical history, check with your doctor and carry copies of pertinent records in medical language, as well as the generic names of medication you need.

Study your own medical plan and inquire about credit card health plans. You're in the best position to figure out the fit between what you already have in the way of insurance and what you think you might need. The German word for accident insurance is *vor Unfall-versicherung;* insurance is *Versicherung.*

There are several firms offering medical insurance and/or assistance for travelers. Here are some to contact:

Access America International, affiliate of Blue Cross/Blue Shield *(Box 6786, Providence, RI 02940;* ☎ *800+284-8300).* You'll get a recorded message; ask for "International brochure."

Carefree Travel Insurance/Hartford Accident Insurance *(Box 310, Mineola, NY 11501;* ☎ *516+294-0220 or 800+645-2424, FAX 516+294-0268).* Ask for "customer service."

Wallach & Co., Inc. Health Care Abroad *(107 W. Federal St., Box 480, Middleburg, VA 22117-0480;* ☎ *703+687-3166 or 800+237-6615, FAX 703+687-3176).*

International SOS Assistance *(Box 11568, Philadelphia, PA 19116;* ☎ *215+244-1500 or 800+523-8930, FAX 215+244-9617).*

International Association for Medical Assistance to Travellers *(417 Center St., Lewiston, NY 14092;* ☎ *716+754-4883; #725, 1287 St. Clair Ave. W., Toronto, Ontario, M6E 1B8 Canada; 40 Regal Rd., Guelph, Ontario, N1K 1B5 Canada;* ☎ *519+836-0102; 57 Voirets, CH-1212 Grand-Lancy-Geneva, Switzerland).*

TravMed/Monumental General *(Box 10623, Baltimore, MD 21285-0623;* ☎ *410+296-5225 or 800+732-5309, FAX 410+ 825-7523).*

SEASONS

There's no one answer for what is *the* season. Seasonal "ins" and "outs" are as much a matter of personal preference as a matter of style. In the 1890s, when the smart (and rich) Britons came to Switzerland, France, Italy, Germany and neighboring countries for summer travels, that was the "in" season. By 1884, the first toboggan run was opened in St. Moritz, although the village had been known as a winter vacation spot since the 1860s. Prior to that time, village people hunkered down in winter months because winter and darkness brought out sinister powers. But from the 1880s, Alpine winter sports seasons were born. And it is still the winter months that draw Europe's rich and famous, and the world's best skiers, to the Alpine areas of Gstaad, St. Moritz, Cortina, Courcheval, Courmayeur, St. Anton, Lech and the many other classy Alpine resorts.

"The best season" will be the one you choose. I've traveled in the area at all times and find that I enjoy autumn, when many places are closed and most of the tourists have gone. The weather can be wonderful—and terrible—but the residents are relaxed and the Alpine villages are true to themselves, naturally.

Generally a "season" for the lodging facilities is the result of a complex relationship between weather and people's ability to travel. "High season" for a ski resort is when the snow is supposed to be best, plus the time when many people can travel and enjoy it. That usually means February and March as well as the holiday season around Christmas and New Year. However, in January, when the snow is often excellent, lower rates prevail, presumably because the holiday travelers have gone home and others have not yet arrived.

"High season" for a lakeside place, on the other hand, is usually July and August, both because of weather and vacation time. Rates may also be at peak level when an Alpine town or village is holding a special event, as was the case with the 1992 Olympics in France, and is true for Oktoberfest in München, Germany, or any festival that has become an annual occasion with an international following. Hotel rooms are often at a premium so if you're planning to visit at those times be sure to book well in advance.

Rates are highest in season and lower at other times, of course, but there is no one "in" or "high" season for the entire region. Some places are wonderful at all times of the year. Tourist-oriented cities, towns and summer resorts usually charge the highest rates in summer; their "off" season is November through March. The "off season" for ski resorts is usually April-May and late October–mid-December. Many hotels in high Alpine villages close for October and early November. Some ski resorts have now added an active summer sports program to give two "seasons." *(For additional information, refer to "Climate," above.)*

SHOPPING AND CUSTOMS

Handcrafts are unique in the Alpine region, where long winters have traditionally been a time to stay within the home and do "homework." The work of artisans is expensive, as is warranted by the time invested in creating the work of art. Folk paintings can be found in Slovenia, the Appenzell region of Switzerland and at *Heimatwerk* (homework or handcrafts) shops that can be found in many towns and cities.

I have found some treasures at the weekly markets that are held for local consumption in many Alpine villages and towns. Check for the days and be in the market area early in the day for the best selection.

Airport in-bond or "duty free" shops have become increasingly sophisticated with their offerings, but there's a sameness to the merchandise available in the international areas, which are after you have gone through the customs and immigration formalities at major international airports such as Genève and Zürich, München, Wien, Milano and other cities. You can count on finding the most popular tourist items, as well as a wide selection of gourmet foods and optical equipment (cameras, binoculars, radios and their ilk).

Value-Added Tax: For purchases made in stores in the Alpine countries, there's a value-added tax on most items. Known as VAT in England and some other countries, the word is *Mehrwertsteuer*, noted as MWSt, in Austria and Germany, *Imposta Valore Aggiunto*, or IVA, in Italy, and recently imposed as a separate item in Slovenia and Switzerland. Check with those countries for current facts. Details are not finalized at presstime. If you are making many expensive purchases, there may be some merit in applying for the tax refund for which you are eligible when you leave the country.

The tourist office can give basic facts about the system in advance, but also ask for details in the store where you're shopping. The usual process is to ask for a "tax refund" receipt, go to the designated place in the store to have it validated, keep it with your other important papers and pack the precious item(s) in your carry-on baggage (you'll have to show it, or them, at customs when you pass through). When you leave the country, you must allow enough time to take the form, the validated purchase receipt and the item to the customs official who will validate that you took the item out of the country. The validated customs form is then mailed to the store. Eventually, you should get the refund, which is usually a check in the currency of the country. You'll then have to go to your local bank, or some exchange center, to convert it to your own currency.

Although the system is reasonably efficient at major airports, it's time consuming, especially with security and other regulations. At railway stations, it's often a bother to find anyone to process the forms, now that border formalities are truncated in anticipation of a unified Europe from 1993 forward. When you're driving and must show your "green card" insurance form, checking your "tax refund" forms is just one more thing to think about.

In recent years, firms who are happy to handle your paper work have appeared, often with booths at the airport or at some other place. Be sure you understand what they are charging for their service. On occasions when I have inquired, their service fee eats up most of what I should be receiving in refund.

Specific tips for obtaining the tax refund will be discussed when we look at "Treasures and Trifles" at the end of each country chapter.

AUTHOR'S OBSERVATION

Although I have followed the system, in the interest of learning how it works, I find it a nuisance with little value. When I can afford some item I like, I buy it and forget about the value-added tax refund. The tedious procedures seem designed to confound and, with me, they won.

MEN'S CLOTHING SIZES

SUITS/JACKETS						
U.S.	36	38	40	41	42	44
Europe	46	48	50	50	52	54
Britain	46	48	50	52	54	56
SHIRTS						
U.S.	14	14	15	15	16	16
Europe	36	37	38	39	41	42
Britain	14	14	15	15	16	16
SWEATERS						
U.S.	36	40	40	44	46	46
Europe	44	46	48	50	52	54
Britain	44	36	38	40	42	44
TROUSERS						
U.S.	30	32	33	34	36	38
Europe	46	48	50	52	54	56
Britain	46	48	50	52	54	56
SHOES						
U.S.	9	10	11	12		
Europe	40	41	42	43		
Britain	8	9	10	11		

WOMEN'S CLOTHING SIZES

DRESSES, SUITS, COATS						
U.S.	6	8	10	12	14	16
Europe	36	38	40	42	44	46
Britain	8	10	12	14	16	18
SHIRTS/BLOUSES						
U.S.	32	34	36	38	40	
Europe	40	42	44	46	48	
Britain	34	36	38	40	42	
SWEATERS						
U.S.	34	34	36	38	40	
Europe	40	42	44	46	48	
Britain	34	36	38	40	42	
PANTS AND SKIRTS						
U.S.	8	10	12	14	16	18
Europe	36	38	40	42	44	46
Britain	10	12	14	16	18	20
SHOES						
U.S.	6	7	8	9	10	
Europe	37	38	39	40	41	
Britain	5	6	7	8	9	

When you're buying clothes, nothing compares to trying them on. Sizing systems vary, not only officially but also with all the imported merchandise that many countries are bringing in from the east and elsewhere. Here's a chart of official size comparisons:

TIPPING

"To Insure Prompt Service" is what "tips" means. The *pourboire*, as it's known in French, may be welcomed when a special service is performed, but the tradition in the Alpine countries is for the proprietor to include service charges in the total of the bill. You'll see it noted as *Service compris* in French-speaking areas, or *service inbegriffen* in German-speaking areas, or *servizio inclusivo* in Italian.

AUTHOR'S OBSERVATION

Americans generally overtip, whether from insecurity or misplaced largess. European friends advise that "when you leave an American-style tip, you ruin it for us by forcing us to do the same. We expect good service without tipping; it's part of pride in one's job." The best travelers make every effort to follow the custom of the places they visit. When in doubt, ask.

TRANSPORTATION

The Alpine countries excel with comfortable, convenient public transportation, be it express or local train, bus, cablecar, cog railway or chairlift. Around many Alpine lakes, there are boats that tie shoreside villages together, within a country or between two or more countries, and that glide along some rivers. Rental cars are available in all major cities and most towns, and there are chauffeur-driven services for those who would prefer a constant, classy guide. Cyclists can enjoy pedaling along Alpine routes. In fact, your feet—strapped to skis or wrapped in hiking boots or walking shoes—can be the best "vehicle" for wandering around the Alps.

In spite of the significant natural challenges—sheer mountain faces, deep gorges, raging rivers, wide lakes—or maybe because of them, the network of public transportation in the Alpine region is far more efficient than most people expect. Fortunately, in my opinion, not all places can be easily reached; some of the best still require the effort of hiking or climbing. But the fact is, with each passing year, more highways ribbon lakesides and tunnels burrow through mountains, making it possible to get from here to there quickly and easily.

AIRLINES

It's worth remembering that airlines are in the marketing business. They've priced packages and sell them at fares that are favorable for them and sometimes beneficial for the traveler. Airline companies have become marketing experts or have hired a partner-firm to prepare and present packages for them. Therefore, we who travel have to learn how to read between the lines to find the best "deal." Don't assume the airline is doing that for you. Offerings for tour packages and special incentives change from week to week, as airlines jockey for the competitive edge.

Your travel agent and the airlines, when you have the time and patience to wait for service, should be your first sources for the latest facts.

Several dependable charter or special fare services, often relatives of the major national carriers, offer safe and comfortable flights in addition to the regularly scheduled airlines. The charter carriers often have in-air services comparable to tourist-class service on scheduled carriers. Although not well known to American travelers, the airlines are very popular with Europeans coming to North America. Among the well-established names to mention to your travel agent are Switzerland's **Balair**, Germany's **LTU** and **Condor**, and **Jet Vacations**, a firm that's related to Air France.

CAR RENTALS

Driving is popular and relatively easy, but be prepared for heavy traffic at holiday times and on weekends, especially along narrow roads around the lakes in warm weather months and to and through the major ski resorts in winter. Up-to-date information about road construction and mountain passes (which can be blocked with snow in wintertime) is available in major European newspapers such as the *International Herald Tribune* and *The European*, available at newsstands in most of the Alpine region's major cities.

AUTHOR'S OBSERVATION

If you're planning to rent a car, you'll need an international driver's permit, available through your local American Automobile Association (AAA) for $10, upon presentation of two passport photos and your valid U.S. driver's license. The permit is valid for one year from the starting date you designate.

All of the major car rental companies have representatives in the Alpine countries, always in the major cities and also at many other towns and some villages, usually with offices at or near the railroad station. In addition, there are local firms that often have lower rates than the international ones. Inquire about train-and-car passes that allow for a combination of both methods of travel. (Several are mentioned in the chapters that follow.)

When you rent a car, be sure you have the "green card" that shows that insurance has been paid. You'll need to show it at border crossings, and perhaps at other times. Styles of cars vary; it's sometimes difficult and always expensive to get cars with automatic shift. Many gas stations are self-service, especially in Germany and also sometimes in Switzerland and Italy.

Most of the well-known U.S.car rental companies have affiliates or branches in the Alpine region. One company that has been imaginative and aggressive with promotions (and values) is **Kemwel Group** *(106 Calvert House, Harrison, NY 10469;* ☎ *800+678-0678 or 914+835-5555; FAX 914+835-5449).* Most of the national railway systems, and certainly **RailEurope** and **DER** Tours (see below), have combination rail-and-car-rental programs that allow for a few days of driving in addition to train rides. Contacts for national rail systems are given in the country chapters.

TRAINS

The joys of riding the European railways are difficult to imagine for most car-oriented North Americans, but they are many. Most of the traveling for this book has been aboard some of Europe's best high-speed trains for longer distances and on the local and regional trains for shorter distances or when I was more interested in sightseeing than in speed.

The famed "Orient Express" route passes through some of the Alpine area on routes through Switzerland or Germany and Austria to reach Hungary, or through Switzerland and Austria on the Venice Simplon Orient Express to reach Venice. There are now two versions of the "Orient Express:" the luxurious made-for-Americans **Venice Simplon Orient Express** *(1520 Kensington Rd., Oak Brook, IL 60521;* ☎ *708+954-2944 or 800+524-2420, FAX 708+954-3324)* that runs between London and either Budapest or Venice, and the normal train that takes just over 24 hours to follow close to the true route of the intrigue-studded original **Orient Express**, the legendary train that ran between Paris and Bucharest. The present train along this route is a good one, but it offers none of the special flourishes available on VSOE version, which has been set up primarily with tourist excursions in mind. (Sleeping cars are available on the route, which is shown on Table 32 of Thomas Cook's *European Timetable*, available through some travel bookstores.)

Eurail is the name to know for carefree rail travel, plus boat and bus in some cases, for most of the Alpine countries. Information and tickets are available through your travel agent or through **RailEurope** *(226-230 Westchester Ave., White Plains, NY 10604;* ☎ *800+ 438-7245, FAX 800+432-1329),* or Italy's **CIT** *(594 Broadway, New York, NY 10012;* ☎ *212+ 274-0593 or 800+223-7987);* or German-linked **DER Tours** *(P.O. 1606, Des Plaines, IL 60017;* ☎ *800+ 782-2424; FAX 800+282-7474).* Switzerland's rail network is booked through **Rail Europe** in North America and through specified travel agents.

The Eurail transportation ticket is offered only to non-nationals living outside the country. It must be purchased before you begin your travels, but can be purchased in some European railway stations upon presentation of your credentials (which is your passport, in most cases). RailEurope officials encourage purchase of the pass in your home country, prior to arrival in Europe, a plan that has some advantages if you want to know the exact dollar-cost well in advance.

The ticket is valid for travel in 17 European countries, including seven of the eight Alpine countries. Slovenia is not a *Eurail* member at presstime, but its trains and buses are very inexpensive, compared with travel in western European countries, and tickets are easy to purchase from any railway station for the many efficient, and effective, rail and bus links. Although national transportation passes for Austria, Germany, Italy, France (including Monaco), Slovenia and Switzerland (including Liechtenstein) are ideal for travel within each country's borders, a *Eurail ticket* is worth the investment if you are planning extensive rail travel in more than two Alpine countries.

AUTHOR'S OBSERVATION

The Eurail *options have become so detailed that it takes careful figuring to decide which will be the best investment. It's worth noting that the passes are a business venture for the railways and the companies set up in North America for their sale.*

Do some figuring and give careful thought to your travel plans (and wishes). In some cases you may find it makes most sense to buy the national pass for *one* country and to purchase the added routes into neighboring countries from that country's borders when you are there.

TRAIN SCHEDULE: SWITZERLAND

Luzern–Brünig–Interlaken

95 Bern 460		5 28		6 29	6 48	7 31		7 48		8 31		9 24	9 48
0 Luzern		7 12		7 46	8 12	8 46		9 12		9 46		11 04	11 12
57 Zürich HB 660						8 07				9 07		10 07	
0 Luzern						8 56				9 56		10 56	
96 Basel SBB 500	4 57		6 00	6 51	7 07		7 51	8 07	9 51		10 07	10 07	10 35
57 Olten 500	5 57		6 32	7 23	7 35		8 23	8 35		9 23		10 23	11 12
0 Luzern		7 12	7 12	8 04	8 12		9 04	9 12		10 04	11 04	11 04	11 12
SBB, Luzern	6310	6314	2452	6320	2458	2462	6324	2464		6330	2468	6336	2470

km														
0 Luzern	* 6 03	6 19	† 6 19	6 59	7 24	8 09	8 24	9 05	9 09	9 24	10 09	10 24	11 09	11 24
4 Horw 472	6 09	6 25	6 25	7 05		8 15		9 15	9 15		10 15		11 15	
7 Hergiswil Matt 472	6 13	6 29	6 29	7 09		8 19		9 19	9 19		10 19		11 19	11 34
8 Hergiswil 472, 480	6 15	6 31	6 31	7 11	7 34	8 21	8 34	9 21	9 21	9 34	10 21	10 34	11 21	11 36
Hergiswil	6 17	6 32	6 32	7 13	7 36	8 22	8 36		9 22	9 36	10 22	10 36	11 22	
12 Alpnachstad 473	6 24	6 37	6 37	7 19		8 29			9 29		10 29		11 29	
14 Alpnach Dorf	6 28	6 41	6 41	7 23		8 32			9 32		10 32		11 32	
20 Sarnen	6 40	6 48	6 48	7 30	7 48	8 40	8 48	9 25	9 40	9 48	10 40	10 48	11 40	11 48
23 Sachseln	6 44	6 52	6 52	7 34	7 52	8 44	8 52	9 29	9 44	9 52	10 44	10 52	11 44	11 52
29 Giswil	* 6 18	* 6 52	* 6 52	7 41	7 58	8 51	8 58	9 35	9 51	9 58	10 51	10 58	11 51	11 58
32 Kaiserstuhl	6 26		7 00		8 00		9 07			10 07		11 00	11 07	12 00
36 Lungern	6 45		7 07		8 07		9 15	9 52		10 15		11 07	11 15	12 07
40 Brünig-Hasliberg	6 59		7 15		8 15		9 27	10 03		10 27		11 15	11 27	12 15
45 Meiringen 474	* 7 14		7 27		8 27		9 37	10 17		10 41		11 27	11 41	12 27
			7 41		8 41									12 41

	6304	6306	6308							6328			6338
Meiringen	5 47	6 42	7 21		7 46	8 46	9 46	10 22	10 46	✳10 56	11 46	12 46	12 56
50 x Unterbach	x 5 53	x 6 48	x 7 26		x 7 51		x 9 51			x 11 01	x 11 51		x 13 01
52 Brienzwiler	5 56	6 51	7 30		7 55		9 55			11 06	11 55		13 06
57 Brienz 475	6 01	6 56	7 35		8 00	8 58	10 00	10 33	10 58	11 11	12 00	12 58	13 11
Brienz	6 02	6 58	7 36		8 02	9 00	10 02	10 35	11 00	11 12	12 02	13 00	13 12
59 Brienz West	6 04	6 59	7 38		8 04		10 04			11 14	12 04		13 14
62 x Ebligen	x 6 08	x 7 04	x 7 42		x 8 08		x 10 08			x 11 18	x 12 08		x 13 18
65 Oberried am Brienzersee	6 12	7 08	7 47		8 12		10 12			11 22	12 12		13 22
68 Niederried	6 16	7 12	7 51		8 16		10 16			11 26	12 16		13 26
71 Ringgenberg	6 20	7 16	7 55		8 20		10 20			11 30	12 20		13 30
74 Interlaken Ost	6 24	7 20	7 59		8 25	9 16	10 25		11 16	✳11 34	12 25	13 16	13 34
0 Interlaken Ost 310	6 39	7 25	8 11	7 39	8 39	9 25	10 39	11 03	11 25	11 39	12 39	13 25	13 39
3 Interlaken West	6 42	7 28	8 14	7 42	8 42	9 28	10 42		11 28	11 42	12 42	13 28	13 42
26 Spiez	7 04	7 49	8 31	7 59	8 59	9 49	10 59		11 49	11 59	12 59	13 49	13 59
41 Thun	7 16		8 42	8 10	9 10		11 10			12 10	13 10		14 10
72 Bern	7 36		9 04	8 32	9 32		11 32			12 32	13 32		14 32
Interlaken Ost	6 35	7 38	8 05		8 32	9 32	10 32		11 32		12 32	13 32	
Lauterbrunnen 311	6 57	8 00	8 27		8 54	9 54	10 54		11 54		12 54	13 54	
Grindelwald 312	7 14	8 14			9 08	10 08	11 08		12 08		13 08	14 08	

Using the Alpine area train schedules can be easy if you follow a few basic rules: spend some time to become familiar with the way the schedules look and present information; know the local names for the towns you plan to visit; become familiar with the 24 hour time designations (wherein 14 32 is 2:32 p.m.); be sure you understand the interpretation for the symbols; and have a watch that is accurate to the minute as transportation schedules are closely followed, especially in the Germanic areas of the Alpine region.

In this schedule, for example, Luzern is known as "Lucerne" to many English-speaking folks, HB next to Zurich indicates that the train leaves from the main station (the "Hauptbahnhof") and not one of the subsidiary stations, the numbers to the left of the town name indicate the number of kilometers from the major starting point, the numbers to the right of the names refer to related timetables with connections to the town and the symbols, which are translated (in the local language) on the printed timetable, indicate "stop on request," "only on Sundays," and other terms.

The various passes are:

Eurailpass, which is a first-class ticket for 15- and 21-day versions, as well as one-, two-, and three-month versions, for unlimited travel on all the Eurail members, costing $672, $876, $1078, $1482 and $1888 respectively, for the 1994 passes at presstime.

Eurail Saverpass, which is valid for 15 consecutive days, for two people traveling together, from October 1 through March 31, or for three or more people traveling together at any time for $582; for 21 days, the cost is $744; for one month, the cost is $916.

Eurail Flexipass, which is valid for five travel days out of two months for $470, or 10 travel days out of two months for $756, or 15 travel days in two months for $1000. (This pass is useful if you are going to stay some place for several days and do not intend to use local boat or bus services that would be covered by the pass, but it's expensive. You may do better to buy point-to-point tickets when you are in Europe, following specials offered in the countries you're visiting.)

Eurail DrivePass, which is a first-class pass for four days of train travel and three in a rental car, with the option to buy additional days within two months. It's the most complicated to explain, since it has many variables, such as whether you prefer an economy, small, or medium car and whether you want to purchase extra days. Most rental cars are not automatic, which makes them better for Alpine roads. Within Italy, there is no drop-off charge, but watch out for the charges elsewhere. Be sure to ask to avoid a shock.

The *Europass,* new for 1994, is used for travel in Germany, Switzerland, Italy, France and Spain. Issued for 5 days of travel in any three of the countries, the first class ticket costs $280. Additional days can be added at a per day fee. When you purchase 8 days, you are entitled to add another country. The ticket is also offered in a *Youthpass* version, for second class travel.

The *Eurail YouthPass* and the *Youth Flexipass* are available for second class travel for those under 26 years of age.

The *Thomas Cook European Timetable* is the book to have if you're planning extensive train travel in Europe. Although it does not list all train schedules, it does carry the main ones. Doing your homework with this book will make it easy to read timetables when you're wandering around the region and to plan itineraries allowing enough time for the journey. Issued monthly, the inch-thick book is available from the **Thomas Cook Publishing Office** (*Box 36, Peterborough PE3 6SB, England;* ☎ *44+733+26.89.37)* or through **Forsyth Travel Li-**

brary *(9154 West 57th St. Box 2975, Shawnee Mission, KS 66201-1375;* ☎ *913+384-3440 or 800+367-7984; FAX 913+ 384-3553)* and some bookstores that specialize in travel.

Transportation timetables are thorough, accurate and the key to carefree travel, whether you're dealing with a regional schedule or the comprehensive masterbook available at most European railway stations. The comprehensive timetable is called *Amtliches Kursbuch* (German), *Indicateur officiel* (French), or *Orario ufficiale* (Italian) in the three main languages of the Alpine area.

Once you've mastered the system for deciphering the trains' arrival and departure times and the route, you can travel happily without worrying about language confrontations. All you have to do is read!

TRAVEL AGENTS
AND TOUR COMPANIES

A good travel agent is your best source for facts and rates, especially in this time of ever-changing airfares and special promotions. If you are not already working with a good travel agent, shop around to find one. Ask your friends who they use and if they are pleased with the results. Visit travel agencies in your neighborhood; talk with personnel. Finding a good travel agent is as important as having a good doctor, dentist, or lawyer. After all, you will be investing sizable sums with the person; you should be comfortable with the relationship.

Know in advance that travel agents work on a commission from the "suppliers," which are the hotels, car rental companies, airlines and other firms that operate in the travel business. Those companies pay your travel agent a commission, usually around 10 percent, sometimes more, of the rate you pay for the booking. It makes sense, therefore, that travel agents are interested in selling the most expensive "product" possible.

Good travel agents know, however, that steady business counts; they will be willing to help, even for less expensive travel. If you want to stay in bed-and-breakfast places and are traveling on a modest budget, be prepared to do more of the research and contacts yourself. If your travel agent does the work on a journey where commissions are small or nonexistent, I believe he or she is entitled to a service fee. (Most don't, however, at least for now.)

One of the best reasons for using a travel agent these easy access, through their computers, to the best air other changes in prices or routings that can affect your t One source to learn the names of reliable, well-inform agents is ASTA, the **American Society of Travel Agents** *(1*

St., Alexandria, VA 22314; ☎ *800+828-2712 or 703+739-2782; FAX 703+684-8319)*, an association that claims 20,000 members in 125 countries. ASTA states its mission as enhancing "the professionalism and profitability of travel agents through effective representation in industry and government affairs, education and training and by identifying and meeting the needs of the traveling public."

In addition to ASTA membership, ask if your agent is a CTC, which stands for *Certified Travel Counselor*. Agents who have taken courses through the **Institute of Certified Travel Agents** *(148 Linden St., Box 812059, Wellesley, MA 02181;* ☎ *617+237-0280; FAX 617+237-3860)* to earn the CTC designation have affirmed their commitment to knowing the intricate ways of the industry. You can count on CTC agents to be well informed and diligent in their pursuit of finding you "the best" for your travels.

While travel agents are retail oriented, which means they work directly with the public, tour operators are firms that negotiate "packages," which are two major elements—hotel and air, for example, or hotel and rental car, or air and rental car, or many other combinations—and offer the result through the retail travel agent to you. Tour operators negotiate commissions of 15 percent or more, and sometimes work with hotels or airlines on a set fee for a set number of rooms or airline seats; they then offer the product to the retail travel agent, who earns 10 percent of that negotiated amount, leaving the difference as profit for the tour company. In the current very competitive market, tour operators may offer an "override," which can be an additional sum or another incentive, to encourage the retail agents to sell the product.

Tour operators and a few retail travel agents who specialize in Alpine area travel are mentioned throughout the chapters. There are several that focus on special-interest travel, whether it be bicycling, hiking, wildflower walks, ballooning, or another activity; they are mentioned both in this introductory section and under the discussion of sports for each country chapter.

SPORTS

Always a way for the leisure class to occupy its time, sports have become a major reason for traveling. Walking and hiking have been part of the Alps since the first travelers wanted to get from one place to another. There was no other way.

Since the late 1880s, skiing has become popular, but some method of getting from one place to another on snowy slopes has always ʼn a fact of life for any mountain village resident.

In the chapters that follow, specific details are given for each of the many sports available in each country. What follows are general comments on the sports offered in most of the Alpine countries.

ARCHERY

Although very popular many years ago, the sport is not practiced in many places these days. It's a recognized sport in some Italian communities and is pursued in some of the more remote Swiss and French Alpine resorts.

BALLOONING

Popular in the toniest Alpine resorts, the sensation that comes with floating high above the Alps is an experience you'll never forget. The "woosh" of the gas jets as your balloon is powered and maneuvered is often the only sound; basket passengers usually keep still, although their cameras click. Chilled champagne is the traditional celebration for a safe landing. Resort areas that are known for elitist offerings sometimes have ballooning on the list; actual dates depend, of course, on weather and wind currents. In North America, **Bombard Balloon Adventures** *(6727 Curran St., McLean, VA 22101; ☎ 703+448-9407 or 800+862-8537; FAX 703+883-0985)* have excursions to several Alpine areas.

BICYCLING

Cycling in the mountainous Alps? Yes, even for Sunday-cyclers. Of course, you will see serious cyclers pedaling multispeed bikes up (and down) some of the highest mountain passes, but anyone who enjoys bike-riding can pedal around a lakeshore or through the valley villages. Most trains and some buses have facilities for carrying bikes; some make it downright easy. Always check to find out if tickets or passes must be purchased. Whatever your age, **American Youth Hostels** *(National Office, Box 37613, Washington, DC 20013-7613891 Amsterdam Ave., New York, NY 10025; ☎ 202+783-6161, FAX 202+783-6171)* and other groups have some of the most detailed information about cycling. Among the firms that organize cycling holidays from North America are **Backroads Bicycle Touring** *(1516 5th St., Berkeley, CA 94710; ☎ 800+245-3874 or 510+527-1555; FAX 510+527-1444)*, **Travent International** *(Post Office Box 711; Bristol, VT 05443; ☎ 802+453-5710 or 800+325-3009; FAX 802+453-4806)* and **Butterfield & Robinson** *(#30, 70 Bond St., Toronto, Ontario M5B 1X3, Canada; ☎ 416+864-1354 or USA 800+387-1147; FAX 416+864-0541)*.

BIRD-WATCHING

Birders will find plenty of interest, in spite of the fact that bird-watching is not a highly organized "sport." Bring your binoculars, purchase a bird book at one of the major bookstores in your host country and head out on your own with some tips from the local tourist office. (The best binoculars are made and sold in Alpine countries if you forget to pack your own.) For specifics on bird-watching, check the "Natural Surroundings" section of each country chapter.

CANOEING/KAYAKING

Many Europeans are enthusiastic about canoeing and kayaking on the often-challenging, always-beautiful rivers in the Alpine area. Firm names are given in individual country chapters. For leisure rowing, concessionaires that operate in lakeside resort areas often have boats that can be rented. (See also "River Rafting" below.)

CLIMBING

Wherever there are the highest mountains, there are also guides available for expert climbing and places where novices can learn to climb. July 24, 1760, is generally accepted as the day mountain climbing became an official sport. That was when 20-year-old Horace Benedict de Saussure, an aristocrat from Genève, Switzerland, offered a prize for the first person to conquer Mont Blanc, on the French-Italian border—at 15,771 feet, the highest peak in western Europe. Men who spent days in the highest mountains hunting chamoix or gathering crystal became the first modern Alpine guides. The sport now tempts those fleeing the pressures of commerce as well as those challenged to balance danger and hope. In response to the increased interest, Alpine areas have associations of guides, drawn together by their knowledge of (and respect for) the towering mountains they know best. The tourism office in every Alpine town and in most villages can put you in touch with highly qualified local guides. In addition, some North American firms that take small groups of qualified climbers to Alpine areas are mentioned in the country chapters. See "Hiking" and "Walking" below for other sources. Tourist office contact numbers and addresses are given throughout the "Places Worth Finding" section of each country chapter; regional tourism offices are listed at the end of each chapter.

GOLF

The sport is becoming very popular in the Alpine communities, where farmland is being sculpted and manicured to create challenging courses. A few are draped over meadows in the highest Alps; several are closer to lake level in the wide valleys. Some are the main attraction at cosmopolitan resorts. Be specific with your questions about club rental, dynamics of the course and availability of professional services. Make arrangements for club rental when you book your hotel to be sure you'll have the clubs you're counting on. Specifics are mentioned in the "Sports" section of the individual chapters that follow.

HANG GLIDING/SOARING

Known as *Deltafliegen* in German, the sport is popular among many of the most adventuresome folks. Visiting enthusiasts are encouraged to join local clubs and associations. Hang gliding on skis is the ultimate for some. Places in Slovenia and Italy are renowned for challenging sites and the sport is offered with full equipment and teachers at several Alpine resorts. Be sure to ask if participating is crucial for your holiday happiness. The local tourist offices are your best sources for details; addresses, telephones and FAX numbers are given under "Places Worth Finding" in the chapters that follow.

HIKING

A joyful fact of life for all Alpine communities, hiking is part of the day for many folks. Many towns and villages schedule excursions with a local guide. The tourist office is one source for details and dates. If their personnel do not have full facts, they'll refer you to the place that does. Treks with local guides usually set off at specific times and return to the starting village or town each evening. Some hikes are organized from hut to hut; a few make arrangements for your luggage to be transported to the final night's lodgings. Some North American firms to contact are **Ryder-Walker Alpine Trails** *(Box 947, 5 Lake Fork Junction, Telluride, CO 81435;* ☎ *303+728-6481; FAX same as phone)*, **Wanderweg Holidays** *(519 Kings Croft, Cherry Hill, NJ 08034;* ☎ *609+321-1040 or 800+270-2577; FAX 609+321-1040)*, **Mountain Travel Sobek** *(6420 Fairmount Ave., El Cerrito, CA 94530;* ☎ *510+527-8100 or 800+227-2384; FAX 510+525-7710)*, **Travent International** *(Post Office Box 711, Bristol, VT 05443;* ☎ *802+453-5710 or 800+325-3009; FAX 802+453-4806)*, **Fred Jacobson Alpine Adventures** *(c/o Chappaqua Travel, 1 South Greely Ave., Chappaqua, NY 10514;* ☎ *914+238-5151 or 800+666-5161; FAX 914+238-5533)*, and **Butterfield & Robinson** *(#30, 70 Bond St., Toronto, Ontario M5B 1X3, Canada;* ☎ *416+864-1354 or USA 800+387-1147; FAX 416+864-0541)*. Trail snacks and light lunches are easy to arrange, from the breakfast buffet at your hotel, a local bakery, or the town's grocery store. For more information, see "Walking/Trekking" below and the information in the individual country chapters that follow.

HORSEBACK RIDING

Mountain meadows and trails through the woods are made for horses! Several of the rural hotels have horseback riding facilities and when you stay on a farm, riding is a part of the day. Some resorts have their own stables; others use a nearby equestrian center. Farmers in some villages will rent their horses for visitors to ride, and the prized experience is to ride the Lipizzaner horses, as is possible in Slovenia's community of Lipica, mentioned under "Places Worth Finding" in that chapter.

HUNTING

Popular for the local folks in the fall, hunting is not offered for visitors in all cases where the locals may hunt. There are a few hunting lodges mentioned in the following chapters, notably Jadgschloss Graf Reck in Wald im Pinzgau, Austria. Chamoix, pheasants and other wildlife are fair game at some Alpine areas, but it is essential to obtain the necessary permits and licenses. In Austria, Italy and Yugoslavia, some of the respected hunting lodges welcome visitors. The only way to hunt in Switzerland or Germany is through private sources, which usually means friends who have hunting grounds.

RIVER RAFTING

In recent years, several reliable private firms arrange for river rafting expeditions. Some of the same rivers that are good for canoeing and kayaking are good for white-water rafting, albeit in different areas. But the sport is not as well organized as it is in the United States. The white water of the Rhein (Rhine) provides challenges for some, and the Inn river runs through most of the Alpine countries.

SAILING

Boats can be rented on many lakes. The best way to size up a yacht for charter is to go to the lake and look them over before making your plans. Sailing on the lakes may surprise sailors used to open ocean. Winds are fluky and, although summertime sailing is very popular with many Europeans, the lakes are not usually crowded during the week. Races are very popular, especially on weekends, and yacht clubs have regular events. It may be possible for visitors who are members of a hometown yacht club to participate in Alpine yacht club events, but most are spectator events for foreigners. Many places rent small boats such as Snipes, Lasers and others for a couple of hours, or for a day.

SKIING

This is the champion's sport in the Alps, but it's also the way to get to school for children in Alpine villages and a family sport at many resorts. The sport is offered both winter, with the prime season February through March, and summer, in the highest Alpine areas. There's a sense of electricity in the clear mountain air of villages where the clomp of ski boots joins with the tap of walking sticks in summertime, as skiers head up to the highest glaciers. They leave in the early morning to enjoy the glacier before the sun begins to melt the surface. Some head out the night before, so that they can be skiing by the first light of dawn. The supreme experience for experts is the "Haute Route," which is any one of several routes along the "top of the Alps" between Chamonix in France through Zermatt to Saas-Fee in Switzerland. The week-long endeavor requires a guide, excellent fitness and equipment that allows for walking as well as skiing. For less ambitious skiers, skis and boots can be rented in some of the areas where the sport is popular. Be sure to check in advance if skiing is crucial to your holiday happiness. Pack jeans, windshirt and goggles—the only extra equipment you'll need for the usual places. You can buy appropriate clothing, plus powerful sunscreen, at many Alpine resorts.

SWIMMING

Not usually a reason to come to the Alps, swimming is offered by many resort hotels and in most villages where there is an immaculately maintained public sports center with a large pool. (This is not as common in Slovenia at this time, but is a fact of life for most villages in the other Alpine countries.) You can also swim in many of the region's lakes and a few of the rivers. The "beach" is usually a narrow rocky coastline, however. Spas are also popular for therapeutic swimming.

TENNIS

Not only do many resorts and luxury hotels have tennis courts, but some have focused on special tennis weeks, with Pro-Am (professionals and amateurs) tournaments in summer months. Count on public courts at many resorts, but be sure to inquire about surface, the availability of professional services and whether or not it's possible to rent equipment. Clay courts are very common in the Alps, although there are some grass courts and many with the newer low-maintenance composition surfaces.

WALKING/TREKKING

The Alps are meant for walking. It's the region's most popular activity for all ages, from babes on parents' backs to elderly folks with slow gait and firm walking sticks. Walking in the Alps is as easy as your ability to be carefree. The trick is to keep walking at a steady, moderate pace on a route that's reasonable for you. Most local tourist offices and many hotels have maps for walks and hikes. Of course, for extended walks and hikes, it's a good idea to have a backpack with a bottle of water, Band-Aids (for blisters) and high-energy snacks. The pack also acts as storage place for those layers of clothing you put on (and take off), depending on the weather. Serious hikers should bring their usual equipment, but novices can walk happily with little more than what you can put in your pocket. True botanists will climb to the highest peaks in search of tiny plants that grow above the timberline, but all of us can enjoy the first buds of spring as they break through snow patches on the highest paths. Good guidebooks for Alpine wildflowers can be found in bookstores of towns in the area. Pocket-size editions are handiest for walking. Inquire at your hotel about dates and times for guided walks, which are offered in many Alpine communities. For firms offering guided walks, see names mentioned under "Hiking," above.

WATERSKIING

Boats and equipment for waterskiing are common on some lakes —and outlawed on others. Many Europeans enjoy fast sports, and waterskiing fits that category. Resorts and private businesses can arrange for high-powered speed boats and for lessons at some lakes. When you notice waterskiers on a lake, keep an eye on their finishing point. Chances are, if they rented from a firm, that's a source for you. Wet suits are used by many skiers for the cold Alpine lakes.

WINDSURFING/BOARDSAILING

Alpine lakes are favorite places for windsurfing, not only because of strange winds but also because it's a quiet sport. If you are an avid sailor, you'll want to consider purchasing (or renting) a board to lash on the top of your rental car, so you're ready when you spot an appropriate lake. There are dozens of lakes where windsurfing is popular; some even organize competitions. Wet suits are worn by most boardsailors and special nonskid "shoes" are essential.

AUSTRIA

Salzburg, Austria

The steam that curled from my coffee assured me that the brew's heat could take the chill out of the air. The morning sun announced that the day would warm, but it was cold when I had left the inn to walk in the crisp air of dawn, along paths best known to farmers, where the only sounds—and most of the sights—are entirely natural. As I sat on the inn's sun terrace, having just returned from my day's warm-up walk, I looked off to sun-capped mountains. There's nothing like that view!

By evening, at the inn where I stayed, guests would gather for an *aperitif*, to share conversations about the day's wanderings, about a remarkable path, an ibex sighting, or perhaps about the *apfelkhuchen* that was served in a high mountain cabin, where red-checked curtains bordered the tiny windows and wood tables and chairs provided the perching points for any who opened the creaking door, clopping across word floorboards in the tempo that is natural to experienced hikers.

One of the many joys of Austria is that a day can be spent in the highest mountains and you can be in a cosmopolitan city or town for an evening concert, or another diversion usually associated with city life. The transition doesn't require a car. With attention to the well-kept timetables, you can be comfortably transported from one place to another by train or public bus, either of which permits the added asset of time for conversation or a nap on the way.

Through the centuries, the people we know as Austrians have given the world a sense of quality of life, from the awesome accomplishments of the Habsburg empire that ruled the ways of Europe and affected the rest of the world of their time for more than 700 years (from 1282 until the death of Fanz Josef in 1916) to the investment in leisure today. In Vienna's sophisticated, world-wise *cafés*, where liaisons are made—and broken, to entire villages that share a saner, simpler life, Austria's doors are open.

Hospitality shown at the smallest mountain inn or the most elegant Viennese palace-hotel, or at any of the many lodgings that make up the range of styles between these two, is serene and secure today, as it has been through the ages.

As my longtime colleague and friend, Gerhard Markus, noted, in his *Variations on Austria—A Musical Guide,*

> *Austrians had to find a way of expressing themselves that transcended the limitations of language, that went beyond any regional patois.... Being, by nature and by inclination, not a people of many words or of grand gestures, not blessed with the gift of gab or with great exuberance, yet perceptive and with profound depth of feeling, Austrians needed an adequate way of communicating their emotions, and chose music rather than the word as the most suitable vehicle.*

If "music is the food of love," as many of us believe (and as Shakespeare's *Twelfth Night* Duke Orssino declares), then Austria is a place for an unforgettable banquet.

COUNTRY CAPSULE

Austria and Germany, thought to be similar in the minds of many, are as different from each other as the United States is from En-

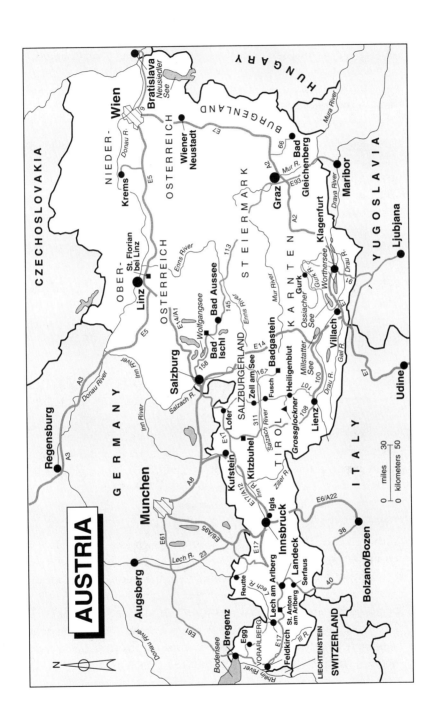

gland. To explain the difference, an Austrian friend once told me: "In Germany, a situation will be serious but not hopeless. In Austria, we say that a situation is hopeless, but not serious." Continuing this same conversation with a twinkle in his eye, he added that a German will immediately tell you his name, his job and his salary. An Austrian, on the other hand, will tell you his name, his favorite opera and the books he's read.

Austria's personality is far more cosmopolitan than the quaint villages, loden coats and dirndl dresses that come to mind and are a proud part of the country's traditions. This nation, smaller than the state of Maine, is much smaller than it was in the glory days of the Habsburg Empire, when the "sun never set" on its borders. Today's Austria is the result of decisions at the end of World War I, when the Austro-Hungarian Empire was divided into less threatening portions by the allies in that war.

The core of the country became the entire country, united and dedicated to playing a major role in east-west negotiations in the intervening years. Wien (Vienna, pronounced "veen") is the cosmopolitan, international capital, with a role far greater than its size.

LÄNDER

The nine Länder (states) of Austria represent a variety unexpected by most visitors: from the flat plains and Croatian/Hungarian traditions of Burgenland in the east to the lederhosen, dirndl, yodeling traditions of the Vorarlberg and Tirol mountain areas in the west, nuzzling the borders of Germany and Switzerland and allowing a small gap for the Principality of Liechtenstein. Throughout the country, there's a change in terrain, a change in local dialect and several completely different sets of customs.

Wien, known as Vienna to English-speaking travelers, is completely surrounded by the province of Niederösterreich (see below). It is a cosmopolitan province in its own right, and played a meaningful role throughout the "cold war" as a conduit for the cultures and currents of the eastern European countries as they met and mixed, often with tale-inspiring intrigue, with the west. Its role in the new Europe is an intriguing one of helping the west to understand the east, an area with which Austrian ties have always remained strong. The cultural heritage and present-day vibrancy of Wien is uncontested.

Niederösterreich, which translates as Lower Austria, is the land on both sides of the Donau (Danube), down-river and therefore lower than the source. The area is less mountainous and runs from just below Linz east to the Czechoslovakian border at Bratislava.

Oberösterreich, translated as Upper Austria, is the upper part of the Donau, closer to the source. It is the central part of the country, reaching to and including the Salzkammergut, the lake-speckled region bordering Salzburg. Both take the "salz" in their names from the salt mines that provided the first prosperity.

Salzburgerland, with its Mozart home-town capital, contains the traditions and picture-perfect countryside that many people assume is "Austria." The province has its borders in the valleys that surround the city, from the Austro-Bavarian border around and through the valley of the Salzach River, through Salzburg and on to Zell am See.

Steiermark, which English-speaking folk call Styria, is the timber capital of Austria. Lumbering has been second only to the province's industrial prowess since the late 18th century, when Archduke Johann, a son of Emperor Leopold II, made the city of Graz the heart of his interest in farming, industry and keeping out the invading hordes, which included Napoleon and others.

Kärnten, which is known as Carinthia in English, has been Austrian since the 900s, but in 1920 a portion was joined as part of the former Yugoslavia and since early 1992 has been recognized as the country Slovenia. (Also in the 1920s, the sliver of land that runs along the eastern boundary of the country—Burgenland—made the decision to leave Hungary and become part of Austria.) The two Länder—Kärnten and **Burgenland**—retain strong cultural influences from the countries whose early heritage they shared, and both played important roles as examples of a westernized economy and lifestyle for their neighbors to the east and south.

Vorarlberg and **Tirol** (sometimes spelled Tyrol by English-speaking folk) cup the Alpine villages in their valleys, plains and niches on their considerable slopes. These two Länder share the Alpine tradition with an outdoor lifestyle, when weather permits, and cozy inns and feather beds to warm the heart, soul and self when storms rage. While Vorarlberg is the tip of the finger of land that pokes into Switzerland between the borders of Italy and Germany, Tirol is the gnarled first and second joint.

HISTORIC HIGHLIGHTS

An international personality and a talent for looking both east and west have always been qualities of the country known as Österreich, the East Reich, or flank, a name that was first recorded in 996 and used during Carolingian times to refer to the location of the land relative to Germany. It was the Romans who settled at Vindobona, and Charlemagne (Charles the Great) who named the settlement Wien, the name Vienna carries in the German-speaking world. For more than 800 years, Wien was to be the heart of the all-encompassing dynasty that would start with Otto the Great and his Holy Roman Empire, which was not Roman and often not holy.

In 1282, the empire of the Habsburgs began with the Babenberg and Bohemian lands and stretched as far as their land claims, marriages and grasp could take it. In the 1400s Maximilian I, as Habsburg emperor of the Holy Roman Empire, married Mary of Burgundy—and acquired what we now know as Belgium, Luxembourg and the Netherlands, plus part of France. He subsequently arranged for son Philip to marry the Infanta of Spain, which brought Spain into the Holy Roman Empire. The son of Philip and the Infanta, Carlos V (Karl V or Charles V, depending on the language) ruled Spain, in his turn, and stretched the Habsburg Empire far and wide.

The Thirty Years War put a crimp in further expansion, but the Austrian Habsburgs looked east—and repelled the Turks while they took on Hungary. Thus the plays go back and forth, setting the stage for Maria Theresa, daughter of Karl VI, Habsburg by birth and hearty by nature. The considerable bulk of Austrian achievements in the arts and acquisitions seems largely due to the considerable bulk of Maria Theresa, an exceptional woman who ruled her own life from 1717 to 1780, and the life of the Habsburg Empire for the last 40 years of that period.

She came to the throne in 1740 at a troubled time, and spent her first few years making it quite clear that the empire would not be overrun by the envious and greedy potentates of Prussia, Bavaria, Saxony, Sardinia, or even France, all of whom stepped upon the Habsburg doorstep, eager to acquire the real estate. In addition to maintaining her imperial acquisitions and her elaborate palaces of Schönbrunn and the Hofburg in Wien, plus the Hofburg in Innsbruck, and other palaces around her empire, Maria Theresa bore 16 children. Among them were Marie Antoinette, who married Louis XVI of France, and her son and successor, Josef, who continued to build on his mother's good works, opening parks for the people even when it meant taking land from the wealthy—and the church. A great-granddaughter, Maria Louise, was Napoleon Bonaparte's second wife (chosen when Josephine could not produce an heir).

The Congress of Vienna (1814-15) reinstated to Austria lands that were lost during the wars with Napoleon, but it also marked the rise of Austrian Chancellor Metternich, whose dogmatic methods led to his downfall—and revolution in Wien. It was Prussia, as much as any outsider, that pushed the wedge into the Habsburg wall. The reign of Franz Josef (1848-1916), his death in Sarajevo, where he was murdered, and the Austro-Hungarian duality resulted in weak spots that destroyed the monarchy. One result was a smaller Austria.

The boundaries of today's Austria were defined at the end of World War I, when the Austro-Hungarian Empire was served at the tables of Europe. Hungary, Czechoslovakia and the former Yugoslavia were carved off, and by 1920 an empire of 14 nations became a republic of about seven million people. Hitler, who was born in the Austrian town of Braunau, annexed Austria to Germany in 1938, and soon thereafter the country became the "enemy" to the countries regarded as allies by the United States.

At the end of World War II in 1945, Austria was administratively quartered between the allied powers, at that time Britain, France, the United States, and the Soviet Union, for the purpose of restoring the area to a western-style democracy and for assistance with reconstruction. Britain, France, and the United States turned over their responsibilities when the 1955 treaty ended the allied occupation of Austria; the Soviet Union took a bit longer.

Today's Austria is the core of the matter, however, and it is solidly linked, not only within its own borders, but also to western and eastern European countries, by one of Europe's most up-to-date rail networks, good high-speed roadways, efficient telephone and postal services and regional traditions that are strong in its Alpine villages, where they survive, in contrast to the cosmopolitan lifestyle of its intriguing capital, Wien.

POLITICAL PICTURE

Dr. Thomas Klestil, former Austrian Ambassador to the United States, was elected President in early 1992. He will serve for a six year term, during which time Austria intends to play a major role as an arena for negotiations between the western democracies and the emerging democracies of what had most recently been the Soviet block of countries in eastern Europe.

The Presidential election in 1986 of former United Nations Secretary General Kurt Waldheim, took place amid revelations of "moral negligence" for his activities during World War II. His election was followed by awkward snubs from North American and European heads of state. For the government of Austria, the conservative People's Party joined in a coalition government with the Socialist Party, whose leader, Franz Vranitzky, has been chancellor since early 1991.

The far-right Freedom Party, formerly linked with aging Nazis, gained voter support as it separated itself from its past and began to concentrate on the integrity and enthusiasm of its younger leaders.

LIFESTYLE

There's a big difference between the sophistication of international Wien, the country's capital, and the rural countryside, although you will see many people dressed in traditional *Trachten* when they come to the capital. Despite their size, the towns of Salzburg, Innsbruck and Graz have more of a small-town, country style. Wien is an important crossroads between east and west. Top government officials and businessfolk dress in dark suits and conservative clothes, although immigrants from the east have set a style for more casual attire. In the mountain and countryside towns, dress is "Ralph Lauren" casual.

AUTHOR'S OBSERVATION

Music is the soul of Austria. Not only has the country lured talented composers and performers–Beethoven, Brahms, Mozart, Schubert, Haydn, Strauss, and others–throughout the centuries, but also Austria is alive with music throughout the year. For details about Austria's musical calendar, contact the tourist office.

NATURAL SURROUNDINGS

Whether you travel in the flat plains of the east or the dramatic high mountains of the west and south, there's plenty of open space in the Austrian countryside. The authorities for the *Nationalpark Hohe Tauern*, a vast tract of land south of Salzburg, publish a number of brochures about birds and other wildlife in the park areas. Most of the literature is printed only in German, but it can still be interesting if you are familiar with a few German words. Among the contact sources are the **Nationalparkverwaltung Salzburg** (*A-5741 Neukirchen am Grossvenediger Nr. 306*), the **Nationalparkverwaltung Kärnten** (*A-9844 Heiligenblut or A-9822 Mallnitz*), the **Land Kärnten Nationalparkverwaltung** (*Arnulfplatz, A-9021 Klagenfurt*), and the **Amt der Salzburger Landesregierung**, (*Abt. 16, Chiemseehof, A-5010 Salzburg*). By far the most astounding landscape is around Grossglockner, Austria's highest mountain, in this area (which is the midsection of the country). Lakes fleck the southern sectors, as well as the area around Salzburg.

The best bird-watching areas are east of the Alpine region, around Burgenland's Neusiedler See, where more than 279 species have been spotted. The area is home for storks and waterbirds. Gaissau,

Fussach, and Hard, in Vorarlberg, on the eastern shore of the Bodensee, are also good places to spot waterbirds, as are two small lakes near Judenburg in Steiermark and Friesach in Kärnten. In the Alps, seed-eating birds hover in the forest areas, leaving the higher elevations to Alpine choughs and buzzards. Birders usually focus on the Neusiedler See, sometimes also including the Alpine cliffs of Hobe Wand in hopes of spotting the rock bunting, ring ouzel and wallcreeper.

PRACTICAL FACTS ABOUT AUSTRIA

Systems within Austria are methodical, logical and easy to learn. Once mastered, the routines of living became second nature so those who don't speak fluent German can feel "at home."

INFORMATION SOURCES

Österreische Werbung is the head office at *Margaretenstrasse 1, A-1040 Wien, Austria,* ☎ *43+1+561.66.60.* In North America, contact the **Austrian National Tourist Information Office**, *Box 49138, Los Angeles, CA 90049,* ☎ *310+477-3332, FAX 310+477-5141; Box 1142, New York, NY 10108-1142,* ☎ *212+944-6880, FAX 212+730-4568; #1410, 1010 Sherbrooke St., W, Montreal, Quebec H3A 2R7,* ☎ *514+849-3708, FAX 514+849-9577; #3330, 2 Bloor St. E, Toronto, Ontario M4W 1A8 Canada,* ☎ *416+967-3381, FAX 416+967-4101.* Addresses for regional contacts are at the end of this chapter.

Throughout the chapter, local spelling is used for some words and all place names. For translation of foreign words, refer to the back-of-the-book glossary. Postal codes and telephone numbers for the tourist office are in parentheses following place names in "Places Worth Finding."

AUTHOR'S OBSERVATION

The "Vacation Kit," published by the Austrian National Tourist Office, is the most concise, fact-packed piece of information literature I know. In addition to having a detailed map of the country, the 8" x 12" foldout fact-sheet has city capsules and suggestions for day trips, walks and hikes, and other details. If there's any complaint, it's that there's too much information to absorb in one easy reading. Study the "Vacation Kit" and carry it with you for best results. It's invaluable.

CASH, CURRENCY AND CREDIT CARDS

The Austrian Schilling, österreiche Schilling (öS), is the unit of currency. At presstime, öS 11 is the equivalent of US$1, but check with your bank or the financial pages of a metropolitan city newspaper at your time of travel. As is the case everywhere, banks usually give a slightly better rate than hotels, where the rate allows for their service.

Travelers cheques seem to me to be the easiest way to carry cash, but remember to convert enough to cover costs when you are roaming in more remote Alpine areas. Many villages and inns do not have exchange facilities, partly because their lifestyle is far removed from daily international exchange rates.

Although some places accept credit cards, don't count on using plastic everywhere. Always ask at check-in at an inn or when you enter a restaurant if paying with plastic makes the difference between staying or not.

COMMUNICATION

Austria's written language is German, but the dialects spoken in many of the Alpine villages will seem strange to those familiar with high German. Spoken phrases are often local idioms. If you speak German, you can usually understand and be understood—eventually. English is widely spoken in the big resort areas. As you head into the countryside, heavy dialects mask the high German you may be prepared to speak. A phrasebook will be helpful.

To telephone Austria from North America, dial the international access code for your carrier plus 43 (country code) plus the city code and number.

AUTHOR'S OBSERVATION

Note that telephone numbers, as mentioned throughout this chapter, are given for use from outside the country. When in Austria, all telephone numbers given in this book require that you first dial "0."

Telephone calls can be made easily and efficiently from the post office. Charges are far less expensive than dialing from your hotel, where there are usually surcharges that can often multiply the cost of the call. To make a telephone call from the PTT *(Post Telefon Telegraf)*, step into the phone booth, place your call, and pay at the stamp window when your call is completed. When looking up the direct-dial code for the U.S. in the telephone book, it's helpful to know that the United States is listed as *Vereinigte Staaten von Amerika*.

For U.S. residents with an AT&T charge card, the *USADirect* system is as easy as stepping up to any phone, putting in a coin for a local call and dialing *022+903+011+* to be connected with a telephone operator in the U.S. who is part of the AT&T system. Give that operator the number in the U.S. that you wish to contact, plus your AT&T charge card number. If you do not subscribe to the AT&T system, you can still use the service to call collect, for an additional service charge. For more information in the U.S., call *800+874-4000.* For information about similar services offered through MCI and Sprint, contact the carriers.

Facsimile machines are widely used by hotels and other businesses. For tips on computer use and other communications processes, refer to "Communications" in the introduction.

DOCUMENTS AND OTHER PAPERS

You'll need to show your passport when you enter the country if Austria is your first European destination and perhaps when you enter Austria from neighboring countries, although border formalities are nonexistent or cursory in light of the plans for a united Europe beginning in 1993. When you cash travelers cheques, you'll probably be asked to show your passport. If you want to buy a foreigners-only transportation or other special ticket, you'll need your passport.

Austria has more stringent requirements than some countries for driving rental cars. You'll need to have an International Driver's permit, which you can obtain through your local American Automobile Association, listed under "AAA" in your telephone book. You'll need two passport pictures, your valid U.S. driver's license and $10, the cost of the permit for one year, which starts on the date you specify. For further details, see "Cars" under "Touring Tips," below.

MEDICAL FACILITIES

You can count on excellent medical facilities in major centers and on good emergency facilities and bone specialists in the major ski resorts. *Krankenhaus* is the German word for hospital.

TRAVEL FACTS

Public transportation systems throughout the country make it easy (and fun) to travel into the countryside from city hubs and around the cities on buses and trams. Study a map (easy to obtain through your hotel and/or the tourist office) and learn a few words of German for rural touring.

ARRIVAL

Austrian Airlines (☎ *800+843-0002 in U.S.;* ☎ *800+387-1477 in Canada*) flies between New York-JFK as well as Chicago-O'Hare and Wien as part of its network of 56 cities in 36 countries. Many of its "Friendly Austrian Holidays" tour programs include Alpine itineraries. In addition, both Germany's München and Switzerland's Zürich are convenient airports for reaching Austria's Alpine region aboard comfortable international trains that link either airport to the Alpine towns. Rental car services have offices at all major airports.

Swissair's flights to Zürich are sometimes closer to Austrian Alpine resorts than flights landing in Wien. Inquire about packages, especially those offered for ski resorts. For good-value winter ski trips, ask your travel agent about packages offered by **Icelandair** and **Lufthansa**. Check also with the airlines mentioned under "transportation" in the introductory chapter.

TOURING TIPS

Conveniently linked by an up-to-date and efficient rail network that is part of the Eurail system, Austria also has excellent, clearly posted, high-speed *Autobahnen* (highways) and many unusual transportation opportunities such as steam engines, cog railways, cablecars and other regional methods for travel. Traveling around Austria, even in the midst of winter's snow, is amazingly easy.

AUTHOR'S OBSERVATION

It helps to learn the domestic spelling of town names and some oft-used words. A few are listed in the glossary that appears at the back-of-the-book. If you're trying to find Vienna, for example, you'll have to recognize "Wien" on signs, and if you want to cruise on the Danube, you'll have to know that the word is "Donau" in German.

The public transportation system is excellent, especially with combinations of trains, buses and cablecars.

AIR TRAVEL may make sense if you are traveling the width of the country, or if you're "jet-setting" to a ski resort that happens to have an airfield, which is sometimes served by helicopter in high mountain areas. **Austrian Airlines** has a network of domestic services, linking Wien, Graz, Klagenfurt, Linz and Salzburg, and **Tyrolean Airways** operates several flights daily between Innsbruck and Wien, a distance that takes about five hours to drive or by train (when you can enjoy the scenery).

BICYCLE (*Radwanderweg*) routes are marked in many areas and local tourist offices are the best sources for information about maps, or the maps themselves. Since traveling by bicycle is very popular with many Europeans, including (of course) the Austrians, Swiss and Germans, much of the information is in German. What you want to ask for is the "Radwanderkarte," when you're looking for a map. *Rad* is bicycle in German, and bikes can be rented at many railroad stations and through some private companies. **Austria Radreisen** *(Holzingerstrasse 546, A-4780 Schärding;* ☎ *7712+55.11, FAX 7712+48.11)* is one firm that plans cycling holidays, but many of their itineraries are in Oberösterreich, north of Linz. A few are around Salzburg. Prior to arriving in Austria, the nearest bureau of the **Austrian National Tourist Office** is your best source for information and contacts in areas where you plan to (or can) visit.

BOATS operate along the Donau (Danube) as well as on many lakes around the country. Cruising along the Donau is widely promoted, especially for the segment between Linz and Krems, where tour buses and excursion boats clog the river and its banks at the height of summer. Lakeboats are a delightful way to travel from village to village, around the shores not only of the lakes in the Salzkammergut but also in the south, on the Wörthersee, Millstättersee and other lakes.

AUTHOR'S OBSERVATION

Plan ahead by visiting the village bakery and market for picnic staples when the day warrants a leisurely boat ride. Meal service is not a high point of Austrian lakeboats, if it is offered at all.

Most Austrian lakes have some scheduled boat service from earliest spring until late fall, although schedules are abbreviated and contingent on weather at the shoulder weeks. The best times for visits in the Salzkammergut and other areas that are on the well-trod tourist paths is in late spring and early fall, if you enjoy being with residents rather than tourists. Many of the lesser-known lakes can seem wonderfully undiscovered, even at the height of summer, if you avoid weekends.

BUS options include luxury touring coaches, with itineraries framed on the recognized highlights of the country, and the regional, often railway-linked, buses that stretch from many town depots into the neighboring countryside. Regional buses, both railway-linked and private, are ideal for exploring when you are looking only for some village whose appearance appeals to you as the bus approaches.

Check the timetable that is always posted at the bus stop or ask at the local tourist office when you arrive in any town, about bus trips to nearby villages. The tourist office can advise, usually in English, which villages have a sight to see, where there are pleasant walking paths, or how to find an inn that can become a worthwhile mealtime goal.

From the well-known cities—Wien, Salzburg and Innsbruck, for example—public bus service can put you in the lap of the locals and, usually, out of reach of fellow Americans. People at your hotel and at the conveniently located tourist offices are helpful about explaining the system of paying bus and tram fares, which seems to vary from place to place. They can also advise about multiride tickets that are often issued on a regional basis.

CAR is the choice for most European travelers-of-means and many Americans. The advantage, of course, is the speed and direct access between "here" and "there." The disadvantage is the problem of parking—especially in Wien, Salzburg and Innsbruck—and the isolation from the local folk and their lifestyle.

The network of roads is good to excellent insofar as surface and sign-posting are concerned. Mountain roads often allow for spectacular vistas if the weather is in your favor. Especially noteworthy and worth a day of dallying, if you're lucky enough to have clear weather, is the Grossglockner route between Winklern and Bruck, passing through Heiligenblut, an astounding ride up and around, within sight of Austria's highest mountain peak, and back again to valley level. The Austrian National Tourist Office has a folder/map, *Motoring in Austria*, that is fact-packed and full of pertinent information.

Drivers must be 21 years or older to rent a car, although only 18 to drive. Comments in English about road conditions are given daily from 6 a.m. to 10 p.m. through the head office of the **Österreichischer Automobil-Motorrad-und-Touring Club** (*ÖAMTC or Austrian Automobile Club, in Wien, ☎ 1+71.19.97*).

Train travel is comfortable and carefree. The **Österreichische Bundesbahnen** (Austrian Federal Railways) offers multiride tickets that can be purchased from railway stations in Austria. The *Bundesnetzkarte* is one multiride card, issued for either first or second class for 9 or 16 days. Senior citizen and youth fares are also available. In addition, there's a unique *Rabbit Card*, so called even in Austria, for 3 days of travel out of 10. It must be purchased outside Austria, but can be bought in neighboring European countries as well as through **RailEurope** and **DER** offices in the U.S. Although it will be discontinued at the end of 1994, some other multiride ticket is expected in its place. (The introductory chapter has further details about these and other firms, under the "Transportation" heading.)

There's more variety of service and condition of trains within Austria than in the neighboring countries of Switzerland and Germany. Trains managed by the countries of eastern Europe are older and often dowdier than those of western Europe, where excellence and speed have been top priorities in recent years. You can count on top quality on trains linking Paris and Wien, for example, or Zürich and Wien.

The Orient Express is the top of the line, but be sure you're clear about which Orient Express you want. There are two possibilities. One is the true **Orient Express** of the 1990s, which is cars on a train that follows the original route. Another is the commercial venture, the **Venice-Simplon Orient Express**, widely promoted in the United States and in some European countries, where it is often used as an incentive for company promotions.

DAILY LIVING IN AUSTRIA

Austria's Alpine area is flecked with cozy inns, many of which serve fresh farm food familiar to family life. The cities, on the other hand, often have restaurants with cosmopolitan, international style. Hospitality is a trademark, however; comfortable surroundings are assured.

FOOD, WINE AND OTHER BEVERAGES

You will dine well almost everywhere in Austria, whether you choose the elegant, cosmopolitan restaurants of Wien, or the comfortably casual, friendly *Heuriger*, as the country *bistros* that sell the first wine of the season are called, or at a wide-ranging list of places scattered in villages, towns and on farms, around the countryside.

The real spirit of Austria comes through in its cafés and small restaurants. The concept of the café is claimed as a Viennese invention, not a Parisian one, as many assume. Originally a middle-class phenomenon, the best cafés are those that have become gathering places for intellectuals, politicians, the business fraternity, the wealthy and the wanderers, but each café has its own style. In cities, cafés are the haven to which everyone heads before going home at the end of the day's work. In the country, they are the social center. A good café is a kind of living room or salon, for those who settle in to read the daily paper, offered for communal use by the café proprietor, to read a book, to write a novel, or to otherwise pass time at all hours of the day or evening. You are welcome to join the custom. It's as acceptable to linger over coffee, wine, or a soft drink as it is to do so over pastry or a full meal, but you should look for the coat rack and hang your coat on it before you settle at a table. Tables are often shared, even with total strangers, but it's polite to ask, even in sign language, if the chair you intend to sit upon is free.

AUTHOR'S NOTE

The phrase in German is Ist dieser Platz frei? *or* Ist hier frei? *If you say anything close to either one, the other person will probably understand what you mean.*

Wien claims the oft-told tale of the birth of brewed coffee, but the story comes in several versions. The basics assume that the café custom dates from 1683, when retreating Turks left bags of beans, which local residents brewed. The first batch of the elixir was served at a spot on Domgasse, and the fellow credited with its creation is Kolschitzky, a Serb who served on behalf of Wien in one of the several wars with the Turks.

There are at least three names to recognize: Beisel, Heuriger, and Konditorei. A *Beisel* is to Wien what a pub is in London, or a bistro in Paris, or an osteria in Italy. The name is supposed to have come from the Hebrew word *bayit*, which means house. Whatever you call it, be sure to go into one—for a beer and a hearty plate of food. Two suggestions in Wien are the *Weisser Rauchfangkehrer* (White Chimneysweep), with modest prices, good basic food and a cozy atmosphere in its several small, wood-walled rooms near St. Stephen's Cathedral and the *Little Café* on Franzikaner Platz.

Heuriger is a confusing word because it refers both to the "new" wine, which is actually the first pouring of last year's vintage and to the taverns where the wine is consumed. The Heuriger (Heurigen is its plural form) is an integral part of Austrian life, not only in Wien, where the hillside suburb of Grinzing has a cluster of them, but also in other wine regions such as Burgenland, the Donau valley and in the state of Niederösterreich. A Heuriger is usually, but not always, identified by a bunch of fir branches hanging at the doorway. If the branches are missing, you'll learn to recognize a good wine cellar when you see one. The custom in the countryside is to come armed with your own bread, cheese, and meats, but most of the commercially oriented Heurigen now serve meals.

Konditorei are confectionary shops unlike anything known in the United States. Some of the best also have tables where patrons can enjoy a light meal and an imperial pastry shrouded with plenty of

Schlagsahne, as it is known in high German, or *Schlagobers*, in the Austrian dialect. Both words mean whipped cream.

AUTHOR'S OBSERVATION

When you want a meal, ask for the Speisekarte, or Karte, with a pronunciation reminiscent of "cart." Karte means card and refers to the listing of food and drink offerings. If you ask for the "menu," you will have ordered the chef's special for the day, since that's what that word implies in the German-speaking world.

Jause is Austrian tea-time, with pastries and lots of *Schlagobers*. It can include any one of many delicious pastries, all of which are also available at most restaurants for dessert. *Apfelstrudel*, the Austrian's deep-dish apple pie, is best when warm and *Palatschinken* is a thin pancake dessert with a sweet sauce, sometimes chocolate.

Kaiserschmarrn is an "Emperor's omelet," a rich omelet with a sweet filling, blanketed with powdered sugar. *Germknodel*, a popular dessert in the countryside, is a snowball-size dumpling covered with mashed poppyseed. Among the more elegant offerings, *Cremeschnitter* (cut cream), known in France as *millefeuille* (thousand leaf), and in the English-speaking world as a "Napoleon," for the man in whose era they became popular, leads my list. *Sacher torte*—layers of rich chocolate cake with a raspberry filling—takes its name from the Sacher family of Wien, who claim to be its parent. But I prefer any one of the dozens of other choices that I've ordered by pointing, smiling, nodding—and paying.

Flavors from Hungarian and other cultures appear in Austrian cooking, as in the case of Hungarian paprika, for example. *Wienerschnitzel*, once you've acknowledged that Vienna is "Wien," is obviously Wien's style of *schnitzel*, which is a thin, breaded serving of veal *(Kalbsschnitzel)* or pork *(Schweinschnitzel)*. *Gulaschsuppe* is a hearty meat-based soup that is a meal in itself, with Hungarian peasant origins. *Champignons gebacken* appear as a plate of batter-fried mushrooms, served with appropriate condiments and enjoyed either as the main course or as an appetizer, depending on your appetite. *Tagessuppe* is the soup of the day and usually excellent; *Backhendl* is chicken. Omelette speaks for itself; *Schinkenbrot* is a ham sandwich of sorts.

Regardless of what you've ordered, "Guten Appetit" is the appropriate greeting to your dining companions before you start your meal.

Wine is always available—and *offene Weine* are the local vintages, either *rot* (red) or *weiss* (white), often served in a carafe, although sometimes served from a bottle as the owner's chosen vintage. Sturm is the new wine, served in early fall before the wine has matured to its full strength. *Mineralwasser* is also available, and *Saft* (juice)—*Apfelsaft, Orangensaft, Traubensaft* (grape juice), and others—is popular with adults as well as children.

LODGING

Austria excels, quite simply, with exceptional places to stay in all categories, from castles and mansions, to hunting lodges, to inns—both elegant and cozy—that are usually family-owned for several generations. There are also *Zimmer frei*, which are rooms for rent in private houses and dozens of campsites, suitable both for pitching a tent or for parking what Europeans know as "caravans," called RVs (recreational vehicles) or campers in North America.

APARTMENTS and **CHALETS** are available for rent, as wise Europeans well know. Rentals are usually for a Saturday-to-Saturday week, but other time spans may be available depending on the time of year and the level of reservations. In many cases, the units have been built recently especially for rental. Most are comfortably furnished without some of the lavish "extras," such as modern kitchens and large rooms, that some North American timeshares and condominiums usually offer. One firm with listings of chalets, villas, and condominiums for rent in Austria's Alpine areas is **Interhome** *(124 Little Falls Rd., Fairfield, NJ 07004; ☎ 201+882-6864; FAX 201+808-1742).*

CAMPING is popular at many designated campsites. There are sites near lakes in the southern part of the country, as well as in or near some of the larger Alpine resorts, such as Zell am See. Although many campsites are packed in mid-summer months when all of Europe vacations, most have adequate space in the shoulder months of May and September and at other times of the year when they are open. Detailed maps and explanation of sites are distributed through most of the local and regional tourist offices whose addresses appear at the end of this chapter. General literature about camping is also available from the Austrian National Tourist Office.

FARM VACATIONS, known as *Urlaub am Bauernhof*, are very popular with European visitors, but little known to Americans, partly due to potential language problems and also because the farm holidays have never been promoted in the North American market. Several regions print comprehensive booklets, however, with pictures and statistics about the various farms, all of which have been inspected prior to their listing. Most of the literature is printed only in German, which is your tip-off to the fact that knowledge of the language is worthwhile. *Gesundheitsurlaub am Bauernhof in der Steiermark* (**Dachstein Tauern Tours-Reisebüro**, *Bahnhofstrasse 425, A-8970 Schladming;* ☎ *3687+245.78, FAX 3687+228.73*) is a booklet with details about several farms with rooms for rent; *Urlaub am Weinbauernhof* explains details about rooms for rent with wine-growers in the Steiermark region; and *Bauernhöfe im Paradies* is the title of a thick booklet, with many pictures of properties and a German text, about farms in Salzburgerland. **Bundesverband für Urlaub am Bauernhof in Österreich** *(Hardtgasse 19, A-1190 Wien;* ☎ *222+368.01.11, FAX 222+3680.11.13)* is a nationwide association with information about farm vacations. In addition, booking offices with English-speaking staff have been established in several regions. For Salzburg area contact **Trumer Scenland Tourismus GesmbH** *(Postfach 3, A-5163 Mattsee;* ☎ *6217+6080, FAX 6217+7421)*; for Tirol, **Raiffeisen Reisebüro** *(Adamgasse 3-7, A-6020 Innsbruck;* ☎ *512+56.18.82, FAX 512+56.73.67)*; and for Vorarlberg, **Landereisebürg Vorarlberg** *(Jahnstrasse 13/15, A-6900 Bregenz;* ☎ *5574+4911, FAX 5574+473.59)*.

HUTS and **MOUNTAIN HOTELS** are important parts of the climbing/hiking network. Although the Alpine huts are primarily used by serious climbers, many of the mountain hotels welcome guests who arrive (and leave) by cablecar or another high-mountain method. There are more than 1000 huts, maintained by the **Österreichische Alpenverein**, Austria's Alpine Club, in conjunction with the **Deutscher Alpenverein** (German Alpine Club) and other Alpine mountain clubs. Hikers will find helpful information and suggested routes in Jonathan Hurdle's book, *Walking Austria's Alps—Hut to Hut.*

INNS and **SMALL HOTELS** are distinctly Austrian-style, especially in the Alpine area. There are hundreds of wonderful places; many are mentioned below, under "Places Worth Finding." German-based **Romantik Hotels und Restaurants** *(Postfach 1144, 8757 Karlstein/Main, Germany,* ☎ *49+6188+50.20, FAX 49+6188+60.07)* has a U.S. contact.

Properties considered for membership are friendly, comfortable places in historic buildings. They must be under the personal management of the owner and offer first-class regional cuisine.

LUXURY HOTELS thrive in Austria, with the elegance and time-honored hospitality, but with more personal comforts than were known in Europe to turn-of-the-last-century's travelers. **Gotha Schlossho-**

tels *(Bergstrasse 22, A-5024 Salzburg;* ☎ *662+88.16.77, FAX 622+88.16.79)* is an association of unique properties, owned by Austria's pre-war aristocracy and now open for visitors. (The name "Gotha" was used for the "blue book" of Europe's aristocracy, prior to the war and the more recent socialism.) Numbering less than 50, the group stands for the ultimate in service and style, in historic buildings that are mansions or castles. Many of the members are mentioned when they are in or near towns covered in "Places Worth Finding," below. **Leading Hotels of the World**, a registered name for a group of privately owned properties that share elegance in classic style, have a U.S. contact *(737 Third Ave., New York, NY 10017,* ☎ *212+838-1310 or 800+223-6800, FAX 212+758-7367)* for information and reservations. Among the members in Austria are Badgastein's Hotel Elisabethpark; Salzburg's Hotel Goldener Hirsch, and, at Fuschl near Salzburg, the Hotel Schloss Fuschl. In Wien (Vienna), both the Bristol and the Imperial are members.

SPAS have always offered the classiest vacation style since the times of the Romans, and certainly through the era of emperors and kings. These days they're open for anyone who can afford them, and programs are offered for weight loss, stress reduction and for more serious ailments. Villach, Badgastein and Bad Kleinkirchenheim are three of several well-known, highly respected Austrian spas.

YOUTH HOSTELS, known as *Jugendherbergen* or *Jugendgästehaus*, are located all over Austria, including in Wien, Innsbruck and Salzburg, where there are several in each city. The Austrian National Tourist Office distributes a detailed map, showing the location of dozens of hostels and other accommodations that cater to young people, with details including addresses and phone numbers on the reverse side of the map. Two additional sources for specific information are the **Österreichischer Jugendherbergsverband, Hauptverband & Travel Service** *(A-1010 Wien, Schottenring 28;* ☎ *222+533.5353, FAX 222+535.08.61)* or **Österreichsches Jugendherbergswerk** *(A-1010 Wien, Helferstorferstrasse 4;* ☎ *222+533.18.33, FAX 222+533.18.34).*

PLACES WORTH FINDING

Although there are hundreds of towns and villages worth a traveler's time, the places mentioned below are suggestions for this year's travels. Subsequent editions will highlight other places.

The letters and numbers in parenthesis following place names refer to the postal code (A-0000) and the telephone number of the local tourist

office (☎ 000+00.00.00). The difference in the number of digits in the
telephone numbers does not effect the success for phoning. When dialing
telephone numbers within Austria, begin with a "0."

BAD AUSSEE

Bad Aussee *(A-8990; ☎ 6152+2323)*, in Steiermark's Traun valley,
is a thriving spa town, long respected for its cures as well as for sports
opportunities. Not far from Bad Ischl (see below), this town was the
home of Anna Plochl, the postmaster's daughter who was wooed
and won by Archduke Johann in the late 1820s. Both the spa and
the Kurpark (where you'll find a statue of the archduke) are on a
wedge of land bordered by the Traun river, as it flows into the nearby Grundlsee and the Altausseersee. A highlight of the market town
is the **Heimatmuseum** in the Kammerhof, a palace with impressive
Salzburg-marble window frames that were put in place in the 17th
century when the town was important for the **Salzbergwerk** (salt
mines) nearby. (During World War II, artworks were stored in the
salt mines, which are open for tours from May through September.)
Chlumetzkyplatz is the center of town, where the open-air market
was held. Make time to pause at the **Spitalkirche** to look at the
15th-century Gothic panels of its altarpiece and then stroll out and
around one of several beautiful walking paths. In spring, the area is
blanketed with hundreds of narcissi and other blossoms, but the
walk is pleasant at all times of year.

The **Totes Gebirge** mountains are impressive in the distance; the
Grundlsee is active for watersports and holidays in warm weather
months; and the lovely **Altausseersee**, with its scattered village of
Altaussee at one end and the Trisselwand cliffs at the other, is a pleasant place to linger. From **Gössl**, a village at the east end of the
Grundlsee, three lakes—the Grundlsee, the Toplitzsee and the Kam-
mersee—can be toured in a leisurely combination of motorboat and
walks. Although there are dozens of walks, hikes and climbs for
every level of sportsman, the rewarding view from the peak of the
Loser is a more strenuous climb, starting from Loserhütte, easily
reached by car following a scenic road out of the town of Altaussee.

LODGING: For pleasant inns in Bad Aussee, try the gemlike **Alpenhof** *(10 rooms; ☎ 6152+2777)* or the **Villa Kristina** *(12 rooms;
☎ 6152+2017)*. The **Erzherzog Johann** *(62 rooms; ☎ 6152+2507)* is
also comfortable, although not quite as charming. In **Altaussee**
(A-8992; ☎ 6152+7643), where there are a few small hotels, the
Seevilla Maislinger Franziska *(30 rooms; ☎ 6152+713.02)* has a
lovely lakeside location.

BAD GLEICHENBERG

Bad Gleichenberg *(A-8344;* ☎ *3159+2203),* in Steiermark, was known by the Romans for its thermal springs, but lost prestige to more fashionable spas in the 18th and 19th centuries. Southeast of Graz, in a wedge of land near the Slovenian and Hungarian borders, the town has been overlooked by most western visitors. The cluster of buildings around the center of town are in Biedermeier style and although they warrant refurbishing, are impressive. But the surrounding countryside—even across the border in nearby Hungary or Slovenia—beckons wanderers and those in search of untrammeled areas.

In this area, the winding road that leads north to **Feldbach** *(A-8330;* ☎ *3152+2202)* and on to **Riegersburg** *(A-8333;* ☎ *3153+204)* is a lovely route. Charming Feldbach, with several medieval buildings gathered at its heart, has a **Heimatmuseum** that helps the unique history of this region come alive. Riegersburg is breathtaking when you come upon it as you drive along route 66. Sitting on the rocks, high above the valley, the village square and the **fortress** are enchanting. Built in the 12th and 13th centuries, the fortress was expanded in the 17th century by Elisabeth Freifrau von Gallern, a powerful woman who led a colorful life that included three husbands and planning this vast castle.

LODGING: Simple accommodations can be found in Feldbach, at the **Kulmbergerhof** *(32 rooms;* ☎ *3152+2382),* or the prominent **Gasthof** *(*☎ *3152+2741),* noted for the regional recipes served in its restaurant. In Riegersburg, Herr Fink's **Zur Riegersburg** *(33 rooms;* ☎ *3153+216)* is pinned to the hillside, near the Schloss. Although the newer part of the inn is a blight on the view as you approach the town, the rooms are comfortable when you're inside.

BAD RADKERSBURG

Bad Radkersburg *(A-8490),* about 30 minutes' drive south of Bad Gleichenberg, is a nub of Austria that pokes into Slovenia, as a result of the Mur river becoming the border in 1918. The imposing **Schloss Ober-Radkersburg** perches on a hilltop, across the Mur (and the border) in Slovenia. (The border has become a sieve in recent years, as Slovenians cross frequently for work, shopping and other errands.) The weekly market takes place in and around **Hauptplatz**, bordered by historic houses that are carefully maintained in traditional style. **Frauenplatz** and the nearby **Frauenkirche** hark back to an earlier era. If you visit either early or late in the day, or at times other than mid-summer tourist-time, this town and its squares are a step back in time. The **Gasthof Türkenloch** on Langgasse is one place to pause. Its arched doorway is large enough to allow the passage of horsedrawn carts; its several small rooms are popular with local folk, who gather around the few tables, but you are welcome. The spa is enjoyed by Austrians, whose visits are paid for by the government's health plan, as well as by other European visitors.

LODGING: Well worth finding for a sample of a pampered lifestyle little known in today's fast-paced world is **Hotel Fliederhof** *(15 rooms;* ☎ *3159+2673; open Apr.-Nov.)*, with the peace and quiet of a country estate, plus a whirlpool, sauna and noteworthy cuisine.

BADGASTEIN

Badgastein *(A-5640;* ☎ *6434+253.10)*, in Salzburg province, harks back to its 19th-century popularity as a place where European royalty and their ilk gathered to take the waters. Many of the 100-plus hotels recall that earlier era, although most have updated their facilities to include all modern creature comforts. Known as much for its sports facilities, with cablecars and ski lifts strung to high slopes, as for its health-giving hot springs, the town is lively both summer and winter. In the mid-19th century, Wilhelm I, king of Prussia, and Habsburg leader Franz Josef met and traded here, but these days the meetings are between the lesser lights on occasions that are more social than world-shattering. Located on the northern slope of the Tauern mountain, the town's best views are easily enjoyed while strolling along the Kaiser Wilhelm walk, in one direction (toward the Hotel Grüner Baum) or, in the other direction, along the Kaiserin Elisabeth walk, with pleasant but not dramatic views.

LODGING: The most elegant place to stay is the **Elisabethpark** *(115 rooms;* ☎ *64+34.25.51)*, a member of the *Leading Hotels of the World*. In addition to offering elegant dining, spacious well-appointed rooms and exceptional service, the hotel has a pool, spa facilities, and every comfort for a royal lifestyle. **Villa Solitude** *(6 suites; Kaiser Franz Josef Strasse 16;* ☎ *6434+510.10, FAX 6434+510.13)* is a manor house, built by Baron von Mesnil in the mid-1800s. Now owned by familie Blumenstein, the property is beautifully maintained, with wood paneling in public rooms as well as bedrooms, antiques throughout and an exceptional location on the outskirts of the town's bustle. The **Hotel Grüner Baum** *(91 rooms;* ☎ *64+251.60)* is another classic resort enjoyed by many for lunch or tea after a stroll and by the elitist few for extended overnight visits.

BAD ISCHL

Bad Ischl *(A-4820;* ☎ *6132+3520)*, in Oberösterreich's Salzkammergut, Austria's lake district, gains its earliest fame from its salt beds and its international élan from the curative springs that made it a famous spa, as the "Bad" (the German word for "bath") in its name suggests. In the 19th century, when the rich and famous came to take the waters, they also settled into the pastry shop opened by Johann Zauner in 1836 and noted for its consistently excellent confections. Emperor Franz Josef, who enjoyed Bad Ischl as his imperial summer palace, also enjoyed the pastries of Johann Zauner, naming him baker-confectioner to the Imperial Court. Anyone who was anyone from Wien moved with the emperor to his summer palace in Bad Ischl and into Zauner's as the gathering spot where court and other gossip was served along with the pastries. Although the mystique and courtly class that survived until the early 20th century has now been replaced by the local folk and their like-dressed visitors, the Konditorei is still in place—and the pastries alone are a worthy touring goal.

Among the mandatory stops in town, even if you're just passing through, is **Zauner's** *(Pfarrgassse 32)*, where delicious aromas from fresh pastries waft through the rooms. (There's a warm-weather restaurant on the Esplanade of the Traun river.) The Zauner name has been linked with politics and the arts for all of its history; its guest book is a veritable who's who through the ages.

BREGENZ

Bregenz *(Anton-Schneider-Strasse 4a, A-6900;* ☎ *5574+433.91, FAX 5574+43391-10)*, in Vorarlberg, claims a patch of the shore of the **Bodensee**, the Lake of Constance, which is shared with Germany and Switzerland (see map of Bodensee in "Germany"). Ideally located for mountain walks or hikes and delightful days of touring by lakeboat, the town is widely known for its lakeside summer music festival. Spreading inland and along the shore from its well-preserved **alte stadt** (old city), the town was known to Romans and Celts, and to Gallus and Columban, monks from Ireland and Scotland, who referred to the bay as the *goldene Schale* (golden bowl), for its mountain-surrounded location. In the **Oberstadt** (upper town), on a slope slightly inland from the lake, the easily recognized **Martinsturm** (St. Martin's tower) is a good pivot point for walks through the old city. Easy to spot, with its huge early Baroque onion dome, the tower has charming 14th-century paintings in its chapel. Closer to the lake, among more recent buildings, the **Rathaus** (town hall) and several museums add cultural interest to an area more easily recognized for its shops, cafés and modern commerce.

Allow some time to visit the **Vorarlberger Landesmuseum**, near the lake, walking to your left with your back to the **Bahnhof** (railroad station) and lake, where you'll find remarkable collections of early Romanesque and Gothic works from churches in the province-state. Check with the tourist office about the hours when you can visit the outstanding **Palais Thurn und Taxis**, on Gallusstrasse, to enjoy the furnishings, art collection and the palace itself. The Oberstadt, with its narrow, winding streets and medieval buildings, and the lake, with the lakeboats and their attraction, are highlights for this town.

Although the *very* modern **Bregenzer Festspiel und Kongresshaus** is a magnet when the summer festival and other important cultural events are taking place, its starkly modern bulk stands in sharp contrast to the historic buildings I prefer.

The **Bregenzer Festspiele** (music festival), which takes place on a floating stage and elsewhere in town, in late July and early August each year, has wide appeal. For programs, tickets, and other information, contact **Bregenzer Festspiele GMbH**, *Platz der Wiener Symphoniker 1, A-6900 Bregenz;* ☎ *49.20-0, FAX 49+20-228).* The **Pfänder** mountain that rises to almost 3200 feet "behind" the town is one of the town's great assets. Reached by an aerial tram from the heart of the old town in a matter of minutes, or pleasantly by foot following well-marked walking paths in a longer time, the mountain is enjoyed by skiers in winter months and by hikers and walkers when the weather warms. The views over the lake from the slope are spectacular with the Swiss mountains in view when the weather is clear.

Bregenz is an ideal base for visiting Bavaria's castles of Neuschwanstein and Hohenschwangau, nearby, in *Füssen* (see the town name, under "Places Worth Finding," in the German chapter), as well as the Principality of Liechtenstein and dozens of attractive towns and villages in Switzerland, *St. Gallen* and *Appenzell* among them. (See the Liechtenstein chapter and the town names in the Swiss chapter.)

LODGING: The two dozen-plus places to stay range from reasonably comfortable hotels to campgrounds, with several pensions in and around the Oberstadt and one exceptional Schlosshotel in the Oberstadt. One of the most highly-respected places is the **Deuring-Schlössle** *(13 rooms/apartments; Ehregutaplatz 4;* ☎ *5574+478.00, FAX 5574+478.00.80),* owned by familie Ernst Huber and restored to time-honored splendor. Its **Restaurant Zoll** is justly revered and the hotel's surroundings, in the 17th century walls of the Oberstadt, on the site of a Celtic/Roman fort, will long be remembered. This place is in a class by itself, as is each of the fellow members of the *Gotha Schlosshotels*, mentioned in the comments about "Lodging," above. Two other suggestions are the **Hotel Messmer** *(80 rooms; Kornmarktstrasse 16;* ☎ *5574+423.44, FAX 5574+42.34.46)*, with traditional offerings not far from the lake, and the **Weisses Kreuz** *(44 rooms; Römerstrasse 5;* ☎ *5574+49.880, FAX 5574+49.88.67)*, with the atmosphere of an inn.

BREGENZERWALD

Bregenzerwald (the Bregenzer forest) is a region of Vorarlberg, the western tip of Austria, where nature rules. Rolling hillsides reach to mountain heights and have sometimes been cleared for vast tracts of farmland. Rivers weave through the cleavage of deep valleys and modern intrusions are limited to a few areas. Flecked with charming farmhouses that occasionally gather into a small community, the area is similar to neighboring eastern Switzerland, with weathered-wood farmhouse architecture and the farm-oriented folk art that is the trademark of Switzerland's Appenzell region. This area is ideal for walking, hiking and winter cross-country skiing, and a popular place for farm vacations. (See the category, under "Lodging" at the start of this chapter. The local tourist offices can also help with information and reservations.)

Among the villages of note are **Egg** *(A-6863;* ☎ *5512+2426)*, on a spur road, heading slightly north, where the **Post Hotel** *(25 rooms;* ☎ *5512+2230)* can be a pleasant place to pause. Heading south through **Bezau** *(A-6870;* ☎ *5514+2295)* and **Mellau** *(A-6881;* ☎ *5518+2203)*, up into the Hochtannberg valley, the road borders the river that eventually joins the Rhein. In Bezau, the **Post Hotel** *(42 rooms;* ☎ *5514+2207; FAX 5514+22.07.22)* has on-premise sports facilities that supplement the ones nature offers, with the many walking and hiking paths (and winter ski areas) in the area. At Mellau, popular for Austrian family vacations, the **Hotel Kreuz** *(59 rooms;* ☎ *5518+2208; FAX 5518+23.33.77)* is comfortable and reasonably priced, but the small **Gasthof Bären** *(30 rooms;* ☎ *5518+2207; FAX 5518+22.36.70)* will take you back to the simple life with its farmhouse atmosphere.

Inquire, also, about **Gargellan**, an upper meadow settlement in the Montafon valley area that has grown from its original population of a few summer farmers to include a growing number of vacationers; **Vandans**, another (much larger) Montafon valley settlement, not far from **Schruns**, which is the valley's major town, just over a mile south of Bludenz; and **St. Gallenkirch**, about 3 miles southeast of Bludenz, where a cablecar and chairlifts are active in summer, for hikers/walkers, and winter, for skiing, in the Silvretta-Nova mountain area.

FELDKIRCH

Feldkirch *(A-6800; ☎ 5522+334.67)*, in Vorarlberg, at the border with Switzerland and Liechtenstein, is a fortified town with the imposing **Schloss Schattenburg**. Noted for its school of Latin in the Middle Ages, the town has preserved many of its original buildings, especially around the Marktplatz. The **Pfarrkirche** dates from the 15th century and the painting (1521) by native son Wolf Huber is noteworthy. The **Heimatmuseum** in the Schloss (palace) has some charming peasant furniture as well as samples of religious art.

LODGING: The **Alpenrose** *(24 rooms; ☎ 5522+221.75)* is one of several pleasant small hotels in town. The **Landgasthof Schäfle** *(10 rooms; ☎ 5522+222.03)* is as noteworthy for its cooking as for the attractive facade, with flags flying over second-floor windows and shutters that give warmth to stucco walls.

GRAZ

Graz *(A-8010; ☎ 316+83.52.41; FAX 316+83.79.87)*, the country's second city, is worth more time than most visitors give it. Split by the Mur river, the city was home for a branch of the Habsburg family from 1379 to 1619 and now makes the most of its many historic sights. The **Altstadt**, on the west bank of the Mur, around the Hauptplatz, is the place to start walks that can include visits to the **Rathaus** (town hall) and the **Franziskanerkirche**, marked by its 17th-century tower.

An integral part of the **Landesmuseum** is also near this square. All three sights, and many more, can be enjoyed by strolling along the cluster of streets that are the oldest part of the city, locally known as the Innere Stadt, or inner city. From the Hauptplatz, where the Rathaus is located, walk toward the river to find the Franziskanerkirche, which may seem stark inside but has beautiful stained glass windows that are truly remarkable with the benefit of sunshine. The cloister, reached through a door to the right, is a gem.

The **Landeszeughaus** *(Armory, Herrengasse, near Hauptplatz)* is a favorite part of Joanneum Landesmuseum that was set up by Archduke Johann (1782-1859), the 13th son of Emperor Leopold II, who lived in Graz and was devoted to the city and its surroundings. The armory's four floors hold more than 32,000 items, including full suits of armor (with hundreds of replacement body parts), cases of weapons and horse armor, in an intriguing display of medieval weaponry. Many of the items were made in workshops of Graz between the late 16th and late 17th centuries.

When you turn left, from the door of the Landeszeughaus toward Sackstrasse, passing the Hotel Erzherzog Johann, the Heimatwerk shop, and a huge-and-modern department store, meander to the right, on Sporgasse, to wind up the narrow shop-lined lane to Hofgasse, which spurs off to the right. Look back, when you get onto Hofgasse, for a delightful view of the **Steigenkirche** spire, before you pass (or perhaps pause at) the venerable burnished wood facade of the **Hofbakerei Edeger-Tax**, a firm that dates from 1569. (The Bakerei, the Hof Café, next to the bakery, and the Hofkeller, next to that, are all good places, for snacks and/or a full meal, depending on which place you choose.)

The **Schauspielhaus** (theater) and the **Dom** (cathedral) are in this orbit. The **Opernhaus** is not far away, on Kaiser-Josef-Platz, the site of one of the town's lively daily produce markets.

AUTHOR'S OBSERVATION

The best way to enjoy Graz is to relax and make the city your own by browsing in shops and markets, lingering in a coffeehouse and making arrangements to go to the theater, opera, or a concert.

Daily markets are held mornings on Hauptplatz and Kaiser-Josef-Platz, in the center of the old part of the city. Arrive early to enjoy the best items and then head to a coffeehouse to contemplate your morning—and your next move.

A funicular stretches up to the **Schlossberg**, where you can look at the trademark **Uhrturm** (clocktower) that dates from 1561, stroll around the park, and enjoy a wonderful view over the town.

Maria-Trost (Mary who Comforts), now a suburb of Graz, was a village in its own right when its pilgrimage church was built, from 1714 to 1725. Placed on the site of an earlier hill-capping chapel, the elaborate **Baroque basilica** holds a Gothic statue of Mary, which is credited with miracles. With a little planning, you can be in the church at the time of a concert, or, for Catholics or sympathizers, for a service, when music fills the vast space and gives added stature to the already impressive building. While visiting, allow some time for coffee or a meal (if you haven't reserved for overnight) at one of the two inns, the Mariatroster Hof or the Kirchenwirt, which are, respectively, at the bottom of the hill or up behind the church, on a site that was claimed for housing for the builders of the church. (Both inns are owned by the Pfifer family and are mentioned below).

Maria-Trost is easy to reach from the Hauptplatz, aboard tram #1, for which it is the turn-around point. (There's a Tram Museum at the terminus in Maria-Trost, but check with the tourist office about opening days and hours if you're interested in visiting it.)

The surrounding countryside is well worth exploring, by public transportation and walking or with a rental car. The fascinating wine-making areas to the south, including **Deutschlandsberg** with its castle has many pleasant inns, and the **Piber Stud Farm**, northwest of Graz, is the breeding farm for the Lipizzaner horses that perform in the Spanish Riding School at Wien.

North of Graz, at Stübing, the **Österreichisches Freilichtmuseum** is well worth a visit, if you are interested in the farm heritage of the country. Unique and traditional buildings have been reconstructed and refurbished in an open air park, as a museum of Austrian rural life. Several of the buildings house craftspeople who display their talents with traditional arts and crafts best known in the countryside.

LODGING: Insofar as places to stay in the city are concerned, the **Hotel Erzherzog Johann** *(80 rooms; Sackstrasse 3-5;* ☎ *316+81.16.16; FAX 316+81.15.15)* is on the Hauptplatz, in the oldest part of the city, convenient to the opera, the university and other focal points. A member of the prestigious *Gotha Schlosshotels*, mentioned in the "Lodging" commentary above, the one-time tavern became a Baroque mansion, and retains some of that quality today. Rooms open off the promenades that ring a 3-story atrium; the hotel is a few steps from the town-splitting river Mur. Another choice is the centrally located **Romantik Parkhotel Graz** *(65 rooms; Leonhardstrasse 8,* ☎ *316+335.11; FAX 316+335.11.05)*, restored in Biedermeier style, which has been a hotel since 1574. Its bordering park is an attraction for city lodgings and the traditions guaranteed by its membership in the Romantik hotels group add welcomed hospitality. The elegant **Schlossberghotel** *(55 rooms; Kaiser Franz Josef Kai 30;* ☎ *316+ 80.700, FAX 316+80.70.160)*, near the river, a few doors from the funicular that climbs up to the top of the hill, has a small lobby area, with discrete decor and very comfortable rooms of various shapes and sizes. All have modern furnishings and because the hotel is at the fringe of the old part of the city, the location appeals to people with private or rental cars.

On the outskirts of town, but easily reached aboard tram #1, the **Pfeifer Hotel Mariatroster Hof** *(40 rooms; Kirchbergstrasse 1;*

☎ *316+39.10.700, FAX 316+39.10.70.69)* has a historic exterior and several pleasant small rooms for dining. Bedrooms have been modernized, so that most of their historic atmosphere has disappeared, but lodgings are comfortable. Although the inn is pinned to the hillside by the road, it's convenient for people with cars and is a short walk from the tram station. Its sister-hotel, the **Pfeifer Hotel Kirchenwirt** *(45 rooms; Kirchplatz 9;* ☎ *316+39.11.120, FAX 316+ 39.11.12.49)*, has a quieter location at the hilltop, next to the large ochre-and-white, richly embellished Baroque church. With the same modern decor of its sibling, the hilltop hotel offers lovely views over the countryside from some of its bedrooms and easy access to the church. Dining rooms at both Pfeifer hotels feature traditional recipes, with farm-fresh produce and a fine wine list that highlights some rare regional vintages.

Another pleasing member of the Romantik hotel group and the Gotha Schlosshotels is **Schloss Obermayerhofen** *(20 rooms; A-8272 Sebersdorf;* ☎ *3333+25.03; FAX 3333+25.03.50)*, a country estate/ castle, a few miles east of Graz, where vacations can include country walks, bicycling and touring the historic city, an easy drive west.

Gloggnitz, north of the city and a convenient pausing point off the route to Wien. The **Burghotel Kranichberg** *(A-2640;* ☎ *2662+ 34.21.82.42)*, is a total resort that encompasses a 13th century castle. In addition to the swimming pool, the resort has tennis courts, jogging trails and nearby places for hikes and walks as well as horseback riding.

At *Heiligenkreuz*, about 45 miles (72 km) east of Graz, **Gasthof Edith Gibiser** *(A-7561;* ☎ *3325+216; FAX 3325+246.44)* offers a rare experience for your Austrian travels. Not only is the main *Gästehaus Barbara* a cozy, traditional restaurant, with a terrace café when the weather warms, but most bedrooms are in several small thatch-roofed cottages around the grounds. Many have the traditional wood walls and furniture; some have tiled stoves for warmth (and atmosphere). Located in southern Burgenland, the holiday haven is unique and popular with families and others who seek a return to the rural life, far removed from modern pressures.

GURK

Gurk *(A-9342;* ☎ *4266+8125)*, in Kärnten, less than an hour's drive north of Klagenfurt, is a tiny town with a towering Romanesque **cathedral**. Built in the late 12th and early 13th centuries, at a time when the village was a Bishop's See, the cathedral's two towers were capped with onion domes in 1682. The elaborate baroque interior can seem overwhelming, but is testimony to the considerable talents of 17th- and 18th-century artists. Allow plenty of time to look at the high altar, with "72 statues and 82 angels' heads," each with its own expression and all fascinating. (If you visit during Lent, a Lenten wrap known as a Fastentuch covers the altar, following a custom from the Middle Ages.) Spend some time wandering around the grounds, where there are several buildings from the 15th and 17th centuries.

LODGING: It's worth pausing in the small **Kronenwirt** *(12 rooms; ☎ 4266+8237)* for coffee, or to spend the night if you want to enjoy the impressive cathedral by the first light of dawn.

HEILIGENBLUT

Heiligenblut *(A-9844; ☎ 4824+2001)*, in Kärnten, hairpinned to the Grossglockner mountain road at 4200 feet, is a cluster of small hotels, gift shops and other places for the convenience of visitors. The 15th-century **church** wedged onto its mountainside holds in its tabernacle a vial of the blood of Christ (Heiligen Blut—Holy Blood), brought here in 914 from Constantinople, now Istanbul, Turkey. Several paintings are worth noting, as is the carved altar (1520). One source for information about climbing, hiking and walking in this area is **Glockner Aktiv** *(A-9844; ☎ 4824+2222; FAX 4824+20.01.43)*. The group arranges day hikes, pony trekking and ski-touring, as well as more strenuous climbing expeditions.

LODGING: The **Hotel Post** *(51 rooms; ☎ 4824+2245)*, in the middle of town, is modern in many respects, but clings to Alpine traditions with its menu and atmosphere. Rooms now include all comforts, but the Alpine wood-walled atmosphere has been maintained.

INNSBRUCK

Innsbruck *(A-6020; ☎ 512+598.50)*, the capital of Tirol, has grown where the Inn river meets the Sill, as a thriving salt-trading depot in the Middle Ages and more recently as a resort town that has twice hosted the winter Olympics (1964 and 1976) and welcomes thousands of visitors each year. (The Inn river flows through Austria, from the Swiss frontier to Kufstein, on the border with Germany.) Enchanting, with a small-town feeling in spite of its important role through history, Innsbruck's heart is its **Altstadt**, an area of intertwining streets around Maria Theresienstrasse, that can best be enjoyed by walking. The imposing **Hofburg**, built by Maria Theresa in the late 1700s, on the site of palaces built by earlier Habsburg rulers, is one popular starting point. The rooms, which can be visited with a guide at specified hours, are richly embellished with legends as well as impressive furnishings. **Dom zu St. Jakob**, nearby, is testimony to the talents of early 18th-century artists whose work covers the Baroque interior of the Tirol Catholic church. From the front door of the church, walk through the passageway to the legendary **Goldenes Dachl**, the oft-photographed and regilded golden roof-of-the-many-legends. One of my favorites among the many apocryphal stories is that a roof of gold coins was put in place by the Duke of Tirol in the early 15th century. Known as Friedrich the Penniless, he wanted to dispel the myth of his name. In fact, the roof was gilded by order of Emperor Maximilian I; the work was completed in 1500. When weather warms, the tables and chairs that sprout on the cobbles make this pedestrian area a nice place to pause, to drink in the sights (and whatever you have ordered).

Innsbruck, Austria

The **Tiroler Volkskunstmuseum**, across the street from the Hofburg, is one of my three favorite Alpine touchstones. (The others are the **Bayerisches Museum** in Germany's München and the **Alpines Museum** in Switzerland's Basel.) The exceptional collection of furniture, handcrafts and farm and household items are testimony to the Alpine people's relationship to nature and their land. Entire cozy farmhouse rooms have been rebuilt on an upper floor, having been taken piece by piece from their birthplaces in the mountains.

LODGING: There are dozens of hotels in and around Innsbruck. The **Europa-Tirol** *(125 rooms; Südtiroler Platz 2;* ☎ *512+59.31, FAX 512+58.78.00)* is considered by most to be the best in town. Located across the road from the railroad station and within easy stroll of the Altstadt, the hotel has been refurbished recently so that all modern conveniences benefit from the patina of ages on the highly-polished wood walls, not only in the public rooms on the main floor but also in the best of the bedrooms. (Rooms at the back of the house are away from street noises.) The **Hotel Sailer** *(80 rooms; Adamgasse 8;* ☎ *512+53.63, FAX 513+536.37)*, a couple of streets closer to the Altstadt, is a collection of patrician homes, gathered together at the time of total reconstruction to be a Tirolean style hotel. The several cozy dining rooms at street level give the feeling of a small hotel; the bedrooms are comfortably furnished, sometimes in true Tirolean style. The atmospheric **Goldener Adler** *(34 rooms; Herzon Friedrich Strasse 6;* ☎ *512+58.63.34; FAX 512+58.44.09)* appeals to me for its location within a few steps of the Goldenes Dachl, and for history, in spite of the fact that most rooms are small and dark. Upstairs from the tiny reception area and the informal dining area off the lobby, a more formal dining room offers Austrian specialties with elegant service. The **Gasthof zum Schwarzen Adler** *(28 rooms; Kaiserjäger-strasse 2;* ☎ *512+58.71.09; FAX 512+56.16.97)* is also pleasant, although it's at a curve of a busy road that can be noisy when you have a room facing the street.

In spite of Innsbruck's sights and shops, the appeal for many of us is the surrounding countryside. The river-split town sits in a cleavage. Mountains rise from the wide valley, to the north and south, and villages nestle in the crags and on the meadows where they are warmed by the sun. So intertwined are the mountains with this city that businessfolks and others head for the hills during lunch breaks to make a few ski runs in winter months or have a quiet walk when the snow has gone.

STUBAITAL

One delightful way to get into the hills is to take the red and white tram from the front of the Hauptbahnhof (or pick it up at another stop in town), to go up and out the Stubaital (Stubai valley), for an hour-long winding ride up to *Fulpmes*, where there are several small inns. The red-and-pale-beige tram allows for one of my favorite Innsbruck diversions: a leisurely hour's ride up to the end of the line, to wander around and perhaps walk part of the way back. The ticket costs öS55; multi-day passes are also available at a better per-ride rate. Along the route, there are many halts where walkers and hikers leave the train to stroll through the countryside. The route to walk part of the way down from Fulpmes follows well posted paths that cross the tracks from time to time and weave through meadows and woods passing inns en route. You can board a return train to Innsbruck at any one of its many halts.

RESTAURANTS AND LODGING: Even if you can't spend a few days in this area, plan to pause at one of the inns that are not too far from the paths along most of the route for a meal or a leisurely drink. **Pension Burgland** is between *Raitis* and *Kreit*; at *Telfes*, the attractive **Pension Greier** nestles near the recently restored historic church; and at Fulpmes, the **Alpenrose** *(A-6166 Fulpmes;* ☎ *522+522.10),* not far from the railway station, added a pool in summer of '93, but otherwise has a traditional Alpine style.

Another journey out of Innsbruck out the other side of the Stubaital, an excursion that can be a day trip aboard the public bus that departs from the bus depot abutting the railroad station. The route begins by passing through the wide valley entrance, where modern buildings (and the highway you'll follow) mar what had been a lovely rural area, to meet with Fulpmes near the end of the valley, and continuing on to the end, where skiers and hikers set out on challenging slopes. Near the end of the route, the village of **Neustift** has become a tourism center for hikers, climbers, and wintertime skiers. The once-small village has shops for renting sports equipment, as well as a few tourist-oriented restaurants and dozens of places to stay (often at very reasonable cost).

LODGING: The choices are many at Neustift and villages along the way. The **Hotel Bellevue** *(34 rooms,* ☎ *5226+2636; FAX 5226+26369),* where Patty and Hans Hofer welcome visitors and share their considerable knowledge, is one favorite. From here, hikers and walkers can head out on several challenging routes.

IGLS

Igls *(A-6080;* ☎ *512+598.50),* perched on a Tirolean mountainside above Innsbruck, is easy to reach by public bus from Innsbruck's Hauptbahnhof. Known as a slow-paced vacation hideaway with a few special hotels, Igls is a hub for both beautiful and challenging walks or hikes. Two pleasant goals are the **LanserSee** and the village of **Patsch**, where cozy inns serve in traditional style. Village life can be a refreshing change from busy Innsbruck, in the Inn river valley below.

LODGING: Although there are many hotels, the **Schlosshotel Igls** *(20 rooms;* ☎ *512+792.17, FAX 512+786.79)* leads my roster for its castlelike appearance and lovely rooms. Staying here is like being at a private estate. A larger relative, the **Sporthotel** *(80 rooms;* ☎ *512+ 772.41, FAX 512+333.14)* has a following for its spa facilities.

KITZBÜHEL

Kitzbühel *(A-6370; ☎ 5356+2155)*, in the Tirol, has had a skiing tradition since the late 1800s and a spectacular setting, fringed with the Kitzbühler Alps, since long before that. Copper and silver mines made the area important in the 16th and 17th centuries; sport and social tourism lure the social set these days. Although discos and other for-the-tourists pursuits tend to clutter the center of town, a few excellent restaurants, some tony shops and the spectacular surrounding scenery save the day (and nights). The town is split by a well-used main road, which can make darting from the railroad station side to the social side a bit of a challenge. Settled on the wide Kitzbühler Ache, the valley town looks out to the Grossvenediger, rising more than 12,000 feet to the south, and the Wilder Kaiser, imposing to the north. Kitzbühel is a source for skiers, with its ski club founded in 1902, the first Tirolean ski championships held in 1905, and resident Toni Sailer, champion of several Olympic and World Cup races in the 1950s, as head of the children's ski school. Although serious skiers feel throttled by the height-of-season gathering at the village-level lifts, preferring to stay near the top where the crowds disperse, Kitzbühel's popularity has not destroyed its village feeling. Whether you choose the skiers' winter, the hikers' and walkers' summer, or the border seasons when a few of the places may be closed, the Tirolean atmosphere created by beautifully painted patrician houses and tony shops and cafés is secure. In spite of the fact that portions of town have capitulated to tourism (with discos, a few yodeling and lederhosen shows and the Austrian-style casino), Kitzbühel is a classic; its appeal to the world's pace-setters is solid; its atmosphere is uniquely Austrian.

Although landscape is the prime appeal, the historic center of town recalls earlier times, with its five towers. **Katharinenkirche** has an appealing 1520s altarpiece; **Pfarrkirche St. Andreas** has 15th-century frescoes in its choir; the ceiling of the **Liebfrauenkirche** was elaborately painted in the 18th century, although the earliest part of the church was built in 1373; the **Jochberger Tor** is at a town gate from the 15th century; and the **Pfleghof** has 16th-century towers. The **Heimatmuseum**, at the south end of town, holds a charming collection of handwork from the valley and pictures of town in earlier years. The **Bauernhausmuseum**, reached by walking along the Römerweg (Roman way), is a Tirolean farmhouse fitted as it might have been in the 1800s. Above the town and the village of Aurach, the **Stang-Alm** is the town's gathering place for coffee or something stronger.

The **Kitzbühel Fair**, held early in August, features traditional handcrafts and customs. Winter's events are focused on the slopes.

LODGING: The traditional "best" place to stay is the chalet-style **Romantikhotel Herrenhaus Tennerhof** *(42 rooms; Griesenauweg 26,* ☎ *5356+3181, FAX 5356+36.36.70)*, on the site of a vast estate on the slopes of the Kitzbühel Horn. Filled with enough original antiques to give it museum status, the property thrives in response to its ambiance, impeccable service and memorable meals. Guest comforts, in addition to the natural hospitality, include a sauna and swimming pool, but you'll want/need a car to feel mobile. For convenience and country comforts, my vote goes to the small **Gasthof Eggerwirt** *(17 rooms;* ☎ *5356+2437)*, in the center of town. It's a typical Tirolean inn in the best sense of the words. Toni and Frieda Hechenberger serve excellent meals in the informal *Stübe*, in their more formal dining area throughout the year and on the pleasant terrace when weather is warm enough. Other places I've enjoyed are tiny **Bellevue** *(15 rooms;* ☎ *5356+2766)* and the **Hotel zur Tenne** *(51 rooms;* ☎ *5356+4444)*, wedged into the clutter on the main street.

KLAGENFURT

Klagenfurt *(A-9020;* ☎ *463+53.72.23)*, capital of the state of Kärnten (Carinthia), weaves its history with that of neighboring Slovenia, since wars and treaties moved the present border often through the years. The **Landesmuseum** has Roman relics and reconstructions of a Celtic fountain as well as 15th- and 16th-century religious artworks such as the altarpiece from St. Veit, a nearby village. It also has an interesting relief map that shows the region at various times in its history, when the present Austria-Slovenia border was in other places. The 16th-century **Landhaus** is occupied by government offices, but the **Grosser Wappensaal** (great coat-of-arms hall) is open, so you can see the baroque ceiling paintings of a local master in the early 18th century. The courtyard of the Landhaus was designed by an architect from Lugano, formerly part of Italy although now part of Switzerland. The most often photographed sight in town is the **Lindwurmbrunnen**, the dragon fountain that stretches in a traffic surrounded patch-park in the **Neuer Platz**, in the center of town.

LODGING: The **Hotel Palais Porcia** *(35 rooms; Neuer Platz 13,* ☎ *463+51.15.90, FAX 463+51.15.90-30)*, with a few rooms overlooking the town's central park-garden (which now has a parking lot underground), has been lavishly furnished and rebuilt in a style the building may never have known, but which harks back to the town's most prosperous years. The building's baroque facade bespeaks a palace; public rooms and bedrooms are furnished with regional antiques, many of which are in baroque style. As a member of the prosperous *Gotha Schlosshotels*, the hotel's welcome is assured. The **Romantikhotel Musil** *(15 rooms;* ☎ *463+51.16.60, FAX 463+51.67.65)*, a corner building not far from Neuer Platz, has a lovely small atrium, around which tiers of rooms are located on three levels. Best known by local folks for its pastry shop and its restaurant, the hotel has recently encouraged tour groups, which changes the atmosphere. If you're lucky enough to be here when the tours are not, try for a room for overnight.

There are dozens of pleasant places on the shores of the nearby lakes. At **Egg** *(A-9580;* ☎ *4254+2185)* on the **Faaker See**, a place I have tried and liked, both for meals and for overnight, is the **Gasthof Tschebull** *(20 rooms;* ☎ *42+54.21.91)*, wedged between the lake and the road. (For more lakeside places in this area, see "Wauorthersee," below.)

KLEINWALSERTAL

Kleinwalsertal *(A-6992;* ☎ *5517+511.40)*, in Vorarlberg, is enchantingly Alpine. Although the valley is Austrian, high mountains make an Austrian road impossible. The valley is easy to reach through Germany, by bus or car from Oberstdorf, in Bavaria's Allgäu region. Settled in the 1300s by "Walser" folk (who have a Swiss canton, known by the French as the Valais and by the Germans as Wallis), the people of this valley share many customs with their Swiss relatives.

Although **Oberstdorf**, **Hirschegg** and **Riezlern** are best known to hikers, walkers and climbers, the small church in the village of **Mittelberg** *(A-8926;* ☎ *5517+511.40)* dates from the 14th century and the **museum** of **Bodmen** gathers some of the area's traditional crafts.

LODGING: One of many pleasant inns in this quiet mountain village is the **Pension Neue Krone** *(30 rooms;* ☎ *5517+5507)*, not far from the public bus stop.

KUFSTEIN

Kufstein *(A-6330;* ☎ *5372+2207)*, about 50 miles east of Innsbruck on the German-Austrian frontier, dates from 1393, when it was established as a toll station. Capped with a remarkable hilltop castle, the town fathers have established a **Heimatmuseum**, with historic treasures, in a few rooms of the fortress. Summertime tours of the castle start at regular intervals from the **Burgwirtschaft** (castle inn). Daily organ concerts are played at the **Neuhof**, where the **Hel-**

denorgel (Hero's Organ), dedicated in 1913, occupies the top floors of the **Bürgerturm**.

LODGING: For pleasant lodgings, in the midst of the town, find the **Goldener Löwe** *(35 rooms;* ☎ *5372+621.81; FAX 5372+62.18.18)*, where familie Anton Wieser maintains the regional traditions although their inn has been completely refurbished with bedrooms furnished in modern style.

LECH AM ARLBERG

Lech am Arlberg *(A-6764;* ☎ *5583+2161; FAX 5583+3155)*, high in the mountains of Vorarlberg and best known to skiers and summer hikers, has a small **14th-century church** built by immigrants from the Valais region of Switzerland, perched on a hilltop above the main road through the sports-oriented village. Reached by bus from the railroad station in the valley, at **Landeck**, the village is also popular with Europeans who arrive by car. The once-small farming village has expanded for tourism, but its original peace-and-quiet can be found in **Oberlech**, linked by cablecar or footpath and maintained as a pedestrian area. Even the town, although its main street is lined with shops, cafés and hotels, has attractive aspects of its former village life incorporated into the now-sophisticated pace. The town-splitting river has been channeled into a carefully constructed bed and many new buildings have grown at and near its borders, but most have been constructed in chalet or compatible styles.

This is glorious sports country, for walks and hikes along 150 miles (250 km) of trails, tennis on any of 14 courts, archery, cycling or river rafting in summer and skiing (5 cable cars, 16 chair lifts, 13 T-bars) plus ski schools and sleigh rides in winter. From Oberlech, paragliding and soaring are popular.

LODGING: The tourist office operates a "room reservation" service, both on-the-spot, when you arrive and in advance, when you contact them with your request. The **Hotel-Gasthof Post** *(44 rooms;* ☎ *5583+220.60; FAX 5583+22.06.23)* is the *sine qua non* for the area, in my opinion. On the site of a building in the mid-1600s, the familie Moosbrugger have operated their hotel since they bought the property in 1937. At a point where the horse-drawn postal coaches used to stop, on their way over the Arlberg pass, the hotel is still a stop for the postal coach that continues on to the end of the village. Known to European aristocracy and to others of us who enjoy the beautifully maintained Tirolean atmosphere and the exceptional hospitality, the hotel has a devoted following of people who return year-after-year. This family-operated hotel maintains all traditions while offering full comforts and exceptional meals. Bedrooms are large and tastefully appointed in Alpine style. Service is impeccable; mealtimes are occasions on their own. The hotel is pricey, but worth it. The **Romantik-Hotel Krone** *(40 rooms;* ☎ *5583+2551; FAX 5583+25.51.511)*, with its back to the river and ski lifts nearby, also provides welcomed Alpine hospitality. Noted for the food and service in its restaurant, the hotel also takes good care of its overnight guests. The **Hotel Arlberg** *(52 rooms;* ☎ *5583+213.40; FAX 5583+21.34.25)*, regarded by many as "the best in town," has grown through the years, with several buildings in the cluster. Among the classiest places, especially at the height of winter ski season, the hotel welcomes families in summer months. On the outskirts of town, the **Silence-Hotel Angela** *(27 rooms;* ☎ *5583+2407; FAX 5583+24.07.15)* is on the flank of the Tannberg, near the Sesselbahn Schlegekopf, not far from the ski school headquarters. Across the road from the town-splitting river, the **Hotel Tannbergerhof** *(35 rooms;* ☎ *5583+2202; FAX 5583+3313)* is in the heart of the shops and other activity. Recently built in chalet style, the attractive **Hotel-Pension Haldenhof** *(28 roms;* ☎ *5583+24.44-0; FAX 5583+24.24-21)* offers warm Alpine hospitality style, with bedrooms that are comfortably furnished with all modern conveniences. It's a short walk to the main shopping street and restaurants, as well as to the ski lifts. Walking paths thread from the door. In the middle of town, the **Pension Schneider** *(12 rooms;* ☎ *5583+29.69)* has comfortable, modestly-priced rooms and a pleasant, informal restaurant where country-style food is served. Another pension, where I have lodged happily, is **Café Fritz** *(12 rooms;* ☎ *5583+26.50)*, owned by Fritz Elsenhsohn, who has a pleasant restaurant with a sun terrace in addition to small, tidy rooms with modern comforts.

In the nearby village of *Zug*, the atmospheric **Gasthof Rote Wand** *(34 rooms;* ☎ *5583+2758; FAX 5583+3625)* is neighbor to the church. Built in innovative style by a renowned architect from the region, the hotel makes the most of its Alpine location, providing bedrooms that are comfortably modern.

LIENZ

Lienz *(A-9900;* ☎ *4852+4747)*, in Osttirol, near the Dolomite mountains (and Italy), has a remarkable **Osttiroler Heimatmuseum** (East Tirol Handicraft Museum) in part of the **Schloss Bruck**, which is a pleasant walk along the river and eventually up the hillside from the center of town. While the museum focuses on regional art, the castle gallery displays the paintings of native son Albin Egger-Lienz

(1869-1926) as well as contemporary artists. There is also a display of Roman archaeology, and the Rittersaal (Knight's Hall) maintains a medieval appearance. The chapel is 15th-century style with a carved altarpiece.

LODGING: One of my favorite Austrian hotels, the **Hotel Traube** *(A-9900;* ☎ *4852+2551)*, is in Lienz. With a long family tradition and picture-perfect Tirolean Alpine style, the hotel offers exceptional food, comfortable, cozy rooms and an ideal location for walks, hikes and winter skiing. This gem would be ideal for family vacations and for the Christmas holiday, when the Wimmer family goes all out with festivities.

LINZ

Linz *(Hauptplatz 34, A-4010;* ☎ *7322+393.17.77)*, on the Donau in Oberösterreich, is a big, industrial city, not to be confused with the charming town of Lienz, above. It took me a long time to bother with stopping here. The town's first appearance is of highways, the railroad station and clunky buildings constructed after World War II, all of which can be intimidating if you've been wallowing in Austria's beautiful rural areas. Always an important commercial center, due to its location on the Donau, and a major industrial and railroad town, Linz was badly bombed during World War II, with 22 air raids in 1945 and a postwar period when the city was divided between Soviet and United States supervision. In late 1986, the city was declared a "City of Peace."

When I made some time to get to the heart of Linz, I found it well-spent in the historic center, where medieval buildings have been restored or rebuilt in the old style and some of them house museums that warrant lingering. The area is at its best, in my opinion, on Saturday mornings, when the Linz **Flohmarkt** (fleamarket) takes place on the main square. The **Donau** (Danube) that flows through the city is the lifeline for river boats and their wonderful excursions, and the **Mühlviertel**, a vast area of rolling hills, delightful farming villages and peaceful places to walk, stretches north of town (and the Alpine region). The **Salzkammergut**, with its many lakes and charming inns, lies to the south.

When you pause here, which will be when you're driving or if you're here on business, start at the tourist office for details on special art or other exhibits that may be taking place while you're in town and for a suggested walking route through the historic center. (The tourist office is also a source for the riverboat schedule.) The journey aboard the **Pöstlingbergbahn**, the railway that has been climbing "the steepest railway tracks in the world" since 1898, to reach a mountain height above Linz, might be worth some time on a very clear day, and the **Grottenbahn** that starts at the top station of the Pöstlingbernbahn, leads to an area that appeals to some children (and a few others), known locally as "fantasy land."

A short drive from Linz city, **Stift St. Florian bei Linz** *(A-4490; ☎ 7224+242.55)*, inhabited since the 11th century by Augustinians, is revered as the largest abbey in Upper Austria. It is huge and awesomely embellished. While the ceilings and illuminated manuscripts in the Bibliothek (library) are impressive, it is the elaborate Stiftskirche that holds the organ on which Anton Bruckner composed many of his masterpieces. Bruckner was born in nearby Ansfelden. He was schooled at the monastery, where he later taught, lived and composed. By his own request, he also lies buried there.

LOFER

Lofer *(A-5090; ☎ 6588+322)*, in Salzburg province, is a gem of Bavarian Alpine architecture, with many houses festooned with oriel windows and a church tower with onion domes. The **Church of Maria Kirchtal**, a place of pilgrimage, is reached by walking from Lofer.

ÖTZTAL

Ötztal, a 30-mile Tirolean valley where glaciers flow to the River Inn, stretches naturally toward the upper Adige region of Italy. It claims Austria's highest permanent settlement, at Rofen, as well as the country's highest parish, ***Obergurgl*** *(A-6456; ☎ 5256+258)*. This is the area where the Ice Man, mentioned in this book's introduction, was found. The **Gasthaus Krone** in ***Umhausen*** *(A-6441; ☎ 5255+209)*, one third of the way up the valley, maintains its 17th-century style.

ST. ANTON AM ARLBERG

St. Anton am Arlberg *(A-6580; ☎ 5446+226.90)*, the Tirolean mountain resort where Hannes Schneider first taught his Arlberg method of skiing in 1907, is as well known for summer walks and hikes as for winter skiing and discreetly chic surroundings. This is not a hustle-bustle place, except, perhaps, during the height of winter ski season, when some of the nightspots can be lively. Most lodgings, shops and other commercial ventures fringe the main road; there are a few places in the mountains at the ski lift terminals. Since it's a stop for many trains that run between Zürich (Switzerland) and Wien, and a new highway passes nearby, the town is easy to reach. The mountains are the main appeal; the **Ski und Heimat Museum**

(☎ *5446+2475)*, in town, tells the story of the Arlberg and its importance as an Alpine pass since the Romans came along the Arlberg into Switzerland in 15 B.C.

LODGING: Most hotels cluster not far from the Bahnhof; you can walk down the slight slope to many of them. The **Hotel Post** *(66 rooms;* ☎ *5446+221.30; FAX 5446+2343)* has been the traditional pacesetter, but new ownership has expanded and modernized, almost to the point of overkill. It is still a gathering point for exceptional meals served in its dining room, lively apréz ski and for the tony folks who book the best rooms in peak winter season. (At shoulder seasons, you can have the best rooms—and the place —pretty much to yourself.) My travels put me into the very pleasant **Bergheim** *(28 rooms;* ☎ *5446+2255; FAX 5446+22566)*, the Tschol family home since the 1920s, with the recent addition of modestly-priced, comfortable bedrooms. The location—just by the railroad tracks—is entertaining, but not noisy (since trains are electric); everything is within easy strolling distance. The **Schwarzer Adler** *(50 rooms;* ☎ *5446+224.40; FAX 5446+22.44.62)* is another Tirolean-style hotel, with full flourishes. And the small-and-charming **Montana Garni** *(11 rooms;* ☎ *5446+3253; FAX 5446+23029)*, on the main street pedestrian zone, is a Tirolean-style gem, with elegant atmosphere. It's open only in winter. For more remote surroundings, look at the **Hotel Montjola** *(40 rooms;* ☎ *5446+2302)*, on the hillside, above the fray, but a steep walk uphill from town. Rooms are decorated in rustic Alpine style. (Many places are closed in May and November.)

SALZBURG

Salzburg *(A-5020;* ☎ *662+88.98.70)* is greatly beloved, not only as the hometown of Wolfgang Amadeus Mozart, but also because it is an attractive town that is easy to enjoy and comfortable for visitors. The Salzach River splits the town; the hill-capping **Hohensalzburg** castle gives it style. Not far from the river, **Getreidegasse** is a narrow, shop-infested street in the heart of the old town that has become the main tourism promenade. Although it is sometimes clogged with visitors in mid-summer, it's still worth strolling along to look in shop windows, perhaps pausing in a restaurant (where tourists have set the style). At one end of the street, **Mozarts-Geburthaus**, where Wolfgang Mozart was born, has a charming small museum of his memorabilia on the third floor.

Archbishops are the ones who punctuated the town with prominent villas, castles and gardens—and gave it early class, as the dozens of guidebooks will tell you. As a crossroads during the Middle Ages, the town has historical wealth, plus the natural beauty of its three mountains—**Mönchsberg**, **Gaisberg** and **Kapuzinerberg**—and the Salzach River.

The classic walk, which I have done many times but never more enjoyably than with a nephew and his friend, is the climb from town up to the castle for a view over the Salzach River and the town. The stroll up, with views of Salzburg's spires and rooftops, is rewarded with the hill-crowning **castle** that was started in 1077 and has had several additions, many of them during the 15th century when the castle offered security for the series of archbishops who lived here. There are guided tours of the castle and its museum, with diagrams of the early city and some medieval art. The café/restaurant can be a pleasant place to pause, although there are many places that serve better food.

Before or after your climb, stroll along Festungsgasse, not far from Kapitelplatz, heading toward the castle, to the **Nonnberg Benedictine Convent**, established by St. Rupert in the 8th century. The small church dates from the 15th century. The intricate carving of the altarpiece is a marvel of craftsmanship. The crypt holds the tomb of St. Rupert's niece, St. Ehrentrude, who was the first abbess. Other more important churches are the **St. Peterskirche**, with romanesque arches and baroque embellishments inside, and the **Franziskanerkirche**, dating from 1221, but now a combination of romanesque and gothic elements.

The **Domplatz** is a wonderful place to drink in the atmosphere of the city. Not only is the **Dom** (cathedral) impressive, in mostly baroque style, but also the nearby **Residenz** and Residenzplatz, combine to give this area, just below Hohensalzburg, a strong sense of history.

Be sure to walk up, or take the elevator/lift, to the top of the **Mönchsberg**, where wise wanderers can stroll through the woods to St. Hubertus and enjoy feeling as though you're the only one(s) in town. If you're dressed for a more formal setting, call ahead for a reservation for lunch, tea, or dinner at Schloss Mönchstein, one of my favorite small-and-special hotels. (See details below.) In either setting, you're far removed from the busyness in the heart of riverside Salzburg.

The primary cultural event for many is the annual summer **Salzburg Festival** when tickets are in great demand, but if you enjoy traveling at other times (as I do), ask about the **palace concerts**.

These chamber music concerts take place from mid-April through October and during the Christmas holiday season, as well as several times weekly in other months. Performances are at either the Hall of the Knights at Residenz Palace or the Marble Hall at the Mirabell Palace. Dress warmly when you plan to attend the mid-winter events; the halls are impressive—but can be drafty.

Another event that sometimes gets short shrift from Americans, who think of puppets when they hear about marionettes, is the **Salzburg Marionette Theater**. The performances are not "puppet shows," but are impressively charming opera, with two-foot-tall marionettes performing on an elaborate small stage in a wonderfully baroque hall.

From the Salzburg railway station, several regional buses head out to the nearby lakes area of the **Salzkammergut** and the working farmland. Even without speaking German, it's easy to buy a ticket to ride with the locals to their hometown, perhaps to go to a country inn for lunch, or at least out into the countryside for a walk around the lake and a ride on one of the village-linking lakeboats. Places are clearly signposted. With map in hand, it's difficult to get lost. Adventuresome travelers will find their own towns, but you can't do better in spring through fall than to take the bus to St. Wolfgang (see below), stopping on the way as you wish. Board one of the lakeboats at St. Wolfgang and cruise to St. Gilgen, where you can pick up a bus returning to Salzburg at the end of the day.

LODGING: Salzburg has a wide variety of accommodations, both in the thick of the visitor activity, and blissfully removed, either in the mountains or in the nearby countryside. My top choices are led by **Schloss Mönchstein** *(17 rooms;* ☎ *662+84.85.55, FAX 662+84.85.59)*, in a once private, small castle-estate on the top of the Mönchsberg, where every room has its own style and each is special. Another unique choice is the **Hotel Fondachof** *(Gaisbergstrasse 46; 30 rooms;* ☎ *662+64.13.31, FAX 662+64.15.76)*, on the outskirts of town. The manor house setting gives a private home feeling with plenty of parking space if you're traveling by car. In the middle of everything, on Getreidestrasse, the **Goldener Hirsch** *(71 rooms;* ☎ *662+84.85.11, FAX 662+84.85.17.845)* claims venerable surroundings and an elegant, slightly pretentious air. A member of all the most prestigious hotel groupings, the hotel is very popular with American travelers. I've lodged quite happily in the smaller and very simple, much less expensive (and less prestigious) **Blaue Gans** *(45 rooms;* ☎ *662+84.13.17)*, a few doors down the popular street, where not all rooms have private bath, but all are clean and the price is right, even after it increased with recent refurbishing.

There are several remarkable lodgings in the area. Near **Fuschl**, two—each with its own distinct (and pleasurable) atmosphere—are the **Schloss Fuschl** at **Hof bei Salzburg** *(A-5322; 68 rooms;* ☎ *6629+225.30; FAX 6629+225.35.31)*, an imposing estate overlooking the lake, and its simpler, unpretentious hunting lodge, the **Jagdhotel am Fuschlsee** *(A-5322; 50 rooms;* ☎ *6229+237.20; FAX 6229+22.53.531)* nearby, which has recently gained a *Best Western* booking link. In **Gersberg**, a short drive from the center of Salzburg, the delightful **Die Gersberg Alm** *(35 rooms; A-5023; Gersberg 37;* ☎ *662+64.12.57; FAX 662+64.12.57.80)*, a member of the *Romantik Hotel* group, guarantees atmosphere and traditional cuisine. Die Gersberg preserved its historic charm (it claims to date from Mozart's time) when it added modern comforts in the late 1980s. With its original building in farmhouse style, the hotel sits amid a park area and offers ballooning vacations as well as special holiday weekend plans.

Although **St. Wolfgang** *(A-5360;* ☎ *6138+223.90)* is a favorite touring goal, especially in summer months, it can be charming when most of the tour buses are elsewhere. About an hour's drive east of Salzburg, it is where the Bishop of Regensburg, St. Wolfgang, sought solace by the lake—in the 11th century. One major attraction is the **Kirche von St. Wolfgang**, which dates from the 15th century. The original structure, erected by St. Wolfgang on this site in 975, burned to rubble about 1429. Although started a year later, the next church built on the site took almost 30 years to complete, to be destroyed by fire in 1480.

Although he was commissioned by Abbott Benedict of Mondsee to create an altarpiece in 1471, Michael Pacher had not yet delivered his work by the time of the 1480 fire; it was installed at a later date, in a third church built on this site. Pacher's altar, unfolded to its full splendor only on special occasions, is a Passion Play of the Middle Ages. The centerpiece portrays the life of St. Wolfgang, including his building the church and doing other good works. The neighboring mountains and other local landmarks are easy to recognize in the work. The side panels portray the life of Jesus, with the most poignant episodes portrayed on the inner panels, the last to fold open. Michael Pacher is believed to have come from an artistic family, and is known to have done the large altar for Salzburg's Franciscan Church. Most of the work on the altarpiece was done in Pacher's workshop in Brunneck. When almost completed, the altarpiece panels were carried over the Brenner Pass by mule cart and over the lakes by raft to be delivered to St. Wolfgang in 1480.

LODGING: One prized inn is the "White Horse," officially the **Romantikhotel im Weissen Rössl** *(68 rooms;* ☎ *6138+2306; FAX 6138+23.06.41)*, which is perched at lakeside in an idyllic setting and is a member of the *Romantik Hotels* group. Pleasant for luncheon, dinners and/or overnight, the inn has been immortalized in song. From spring through fall, the **Haus Appesbach** *(28 rooms;* ☎ *6138+2209)* and the tiny **Mirabell** *(6 rooms;* ☎ *6138+2276)* provide comfortable rooms with personality; the **Hotel Post** *(30 rooms;* ☎ *6138+2346; FAX 6138+234.67)* is open year-round.

A short ride south of Salzburg, **Hallein** is best known for its salt mine tours, although it is also the burial place of Franz Gruber, who composed *Stille Nacht, Heilige Nacht*, which many know as the popular Christmas carol "Silent Night, Holy Night." This area, which takes its "salz" from the salt mines, was a Celtic settlement as early as 16 B.C.; they knew salt as "Hall," a product used for trade and valued for preserving food. The small **Keltenmuseum** on Pflegerplatz displays several delightful small créches, plus the guitar on which Gruber composed the Christmas carol and his original manuscript.

LODGING: Just north of Hallein, on the route to Salzburg, the **Schloss Haunsperg** *(6 rooms; A-5411* **Oberalm bei Hallein**; ☎ *6245+26.62, FAX 6245+56.80)*, a member of the *Gotha Schlosshotels*, is a very special place. Packed with antiques and von Gernerth family heirlooms, the castle sits amid a private estate where hospitality is assured.

Near the **Altausee**, in the Salzkammergut, the **Landhaus Hubertushof** *(9 rooms; Puchen 86, A-8992 Altausee;* ☎ *6251+712.80)* welcomes its few visitors as houseguests in the 3-story country chalet, where delicious meals are served in a country-style, wood-walled room, and bedrooms have a comfortably Alpine personality. In an area enjoyed by Prince Chlodwig zu Hohenlohe-Schillingfürst and his wife in the mid-1800s, the Hubertushof was built as a wedding present for his son and his bride. Maintaining the feeling of a private home, owner Gräfin Rose-Marie Strasoldo helps guests enjoy the countryside, whether it is for skiing in winter months or at the lake or hiking when the weather warms.

SERFAUS

Serfaus *(A-6534;* ☎ *5476+6239)*, high in the Tirol mountains, was a place of pilgrimage in the Middle Ages, when two of the town's churches were built (in 1332 and 1500). These days, the mountain village is easily reached by public bus, winding up and out from Landeck, a stop on the main train route that reached between the west and east of Austria. Excellent facilities for families and others to enjoy winter and summer sports is the reason for coming to this quiet spot, where cablecars reach the Komperdellalm and the Hexenkopf mountain rises impressively to the southwest. Cars are restricted in the village; people prefer to stroll. The *Dorfbahn* tunnels under the village from a parking lot to the cablecar station, offering "subway" service for skiers as well as other passengers.

Serfaus street, with mountain view, Austria

LODGING: The most luxurious place to stay is **Das Cervosa** *(57 rooms; ☎ 5476+6211; FAX 5476+6211.141)*, owned and operated by two generations of the Westreicher family. The hotel offers all comforts, including a lovely swimming pool, a health club with saunas, dining rooms in Tirolean style with elaborate offerings, and pleasant bedrooms, many of which have exceptional views. Perched on a hillside, overlooking the children's ski slopes, the village and the far-off mountains, the hotel's sun terrace is pleasant when the weather is. My choice for in-town lodgings, which I found when I stepped off the bus from Landeck, is the **Hotel Schwarzer Adler** in chalet style with modern rooms and an excellent dining room. My cozy room overlooked a neighboring farm, with a view down the valley. The Familie Luggen (including parents and small children) provides warm multilingual hospitality to the several nationalities that are their constant guests. The **Pension Geiger** *(18 rooms; ☎ 5476+6266)*, in an old farmhouse, is wonderfully historic and cozy. For an apartment, try **Alt Serfaus** *(8 apts.; ☎ 5476+6280)*, on the main road, best known for its restaurants, which are in typical Tirolean style with plenty of *Gemütlichkeit*.

STAMS

Stams *(A-6460; ☎ 5412+2419)*, in Tirol, off the Inn valley road, east of Imst and west of Innsbruck, is known for its huge baroque **Stiftskirche** (abbey church), founded in 1273 and capped by two 17th-century towers. Originally Romanesque, elaborate changes were made in the 1730s. If the 180-room abbey seems overwhelming, find the intricately worked wrought-iron Rosengitter (rose screen) and focus on that workmanship. Many of the dukes of Tirol are buried here; some are immortalized by carved-and-gilded statues near the crypt.

STRASSBURG

Strassburg *(A-9341: ☎ 4266+2236)*, in Kärnten, north of Klagenfurt and a few miles east of Gurk, is a medieval walled town with a Gothic parish church whose baroque organ dates from the mid-18th century and the **Heilig-Geist-Spital-Kirche**, a round church with lovely frescoes. It was built from the 13th to the 16th centuries. The **Schloss**, built in 1147 and used by the Prince-Bishops of Gurk until 1780, houses a small museum with religious paintings, relics and sculpture.

LODGING: If you want to pause here to see this amazing place late in the day and/or by the light of dawn, consider the **Gasthaus Strassburg** *(17 rooms; ☎ 4266+2251)*, a simple guesthouse where most rooms do not have private bath.

WIEN

Wien (Vienna; **Wiener Tourismusverband**, *Obere Augartenstrasse 40, A-1095; ☎ 1+21.11.40, FAX 1+216.84.92*) is the capital of the country and a region unto itself. Although it is small (about 165 square miles), it is endless in offerings for a visitor's time. The city has always played a significant role in world affairs. Prior to the changes in eastern Europe, the city was a meeting place for East and West, unofficially as well as officially. These days, it is aspiring to a role as the center of the new Europe, as it was the center of the old Europe during its long Habsburg history.

AUTHOR'S OBSERVATION

Telephone numbers for Wien begin with a "1," as in this chapter, when you are dialing from outside the country. If you are dialing a number within the country, replace the "1" with "222."

The first focus for most visitors is the pedestrian mall known as **Kärntnerstrasse**, from the **Staatsoper** (Opera House) to **Stephansdom**, the city's historic and imposing cathedral. Spoking out around the cathedral, narrow cobbled streets are edged with neighborhood pubs known as *Beiseln* (see "Food, Wine, and Other Beverages," above) as well as with small shops and an occasional inn. **Graben**, another pedestrian way that spurs off near the cathedral, leads to a warren of historic streets.

AUTHOR'S OBSERVATION

Ask, when you are in the tourist office, about the Wiener Spaziergänge, the guided "Walks in Vienna" that are scheduled for specific days and times, following itineraries that are favorites for the guide. The walks provide an incomparable glimpse behind the facades of this remarkable city.

Walking along Graben is an easy and appropriate way to reach the vast complex that is the **Hofburg** (the Imperial Palace) of Wien. This "city within a city" was the heart of life for the Habsburg's Austro-Hungarian Empire, when the rulers lived in the complex and built its several noteworthy structures to accommodate the wishes of the court. Although the core of the Hofburg dates from the early 13th century, the buildings you'll enjoy today were built in three main periods, namely as a fortification until the defeat of the Turks in 1683, as a Baroque palace during the reign of Emperor Karl VI, and following Napoleon I's time in town, from 1809, when the Volksgarten, Burggarten and Heldenplatz were created on the site of the former fortifications.

The Hofburg's parks and buildings can occupy several days. Among the many sights to enjoy, in addition to the gardens and open spaces, are at least three essentials: the **Schatzkammer** (treasury), with robes, chalices, swords, jewel encrusted gold crowns and other exceedingly valuable items from the Habsburg times, all beautifully displayed with muted lighting that adds to the mystique of the gold and jewels (and protects the treasures); the **Kaiserappartements** (Imperial Apartments), where visitors walk up several banks of shallow steps to reach the many lavishly furnished rooms that exemplify the lifestyle of the Habsburg Empire; and the **Burgkapelle**, where the famous Boy's Choir performs for most Sunday services. The chapel is worth seeing as an impressive example of medieval architecture, but it comes astoundingly alive when the choir sings (even though most visitors cannot see the boys because they sing from the third tier balcony, at the back of the small chapel).

AUTHOR'S OBSERVATION

Tickets for the Sunday mass and other occasions when the Boy's Choir sings can be obtained in advance or, if you go to the ticket office early Sunday morning, before the service. The charge varies, according to the seat and the commission charged if you buy through American Express or another outlet, but ranges from öS150 to öS250.

Not far from the Hofburg, across the Burgring, two of the city's major museums reflect each other across a mall. The **Kunsthistorisches Museum** *(Fine Arts, Marie-Theresien-Platz, Burgring 5)* holds an extensive collection of sculpture and paintings that includes exhibits of Egyptian and Near East art as well as armor and ancient musical instruments, along with the expected European art. Its sister-museum, the **Naturhistorisches Museum** *(Natural History, Marie-Theresien-Platz)* is devoted to flora, fauna, anthropology and prehistory.

One touchstone for this city is its own museum, worth a visit of an hour at least. The **Historisches Museum der Stadt Wien** *(City of Vienna, Karlsplatz 4)*, not far from the Kärntnerring or the Karlsplatz underground station, is to the left, as you face the impressive **Karlskirche**, with its huge dome and gold trim. The compact collection within the museum has special appeal for anyone interested in the city's pivotal and lively history. Although rotating exhibits usually occupy several galleries to the right of the entrance, there are also some bits of 15th century and other medieval sculpture and gargoyles from historic buildings on the ground level. The two upper floors have noteworthy paintings of people and places that played important roles in the city's history. Such events as the Turkish siege of the 1680s are portrayed in paintings that give them added impact. On the second and third floors, two floor-covering models of the city, contained in the ancient walls that surrounded it, help to give a poignant frame to the city you see today. (It's easy to get your bearings, once you locate the Stephansdom.)

Wien is a city of museums, many with special focus, some that are huge repositories for grand collections and a few that are devoted to one of the many famous people who lived for a while in this city. Among the first mentioned are places such as the Museum der Stadt Wien, mentioned above, and the KunstHausWien, mentioned below, as well as the **Puppen-und Spielzeug Museum** (Doll and Toy

Museum), the **Faiker Museum** of horse-drawn carriages such as those in use around town these days and the **Gartenbaumuseum** (Museum of Horticulture).

Burgtheater, with Wien, Austria in the background

Among the second are the museums of the Hofburg and places such as the **Museum für angewandte Kunst** *(Decorative Arts, Stubenring 5)*, at one end of Stadtpark, near the Hilton hotel, which reopened after extensive restoration and new building in late '93. The MAK has several new galleries for rotating exhibitions as well as the established galleries that hold the noteworthy display of exceptional glassware, beautifully intricate lace, painted tabletops, delicate porcelain, handmade furniture, oriental carpets (some dating from the 16th and 17th centures) that were made for the Imperial household, and a complete room, reassembled within a larger room, from the Dubsky Palais in Brno. The "big MAK," as it has been called by some, is well worth a visit, not only for the style of its exhibitions, which represent the combined talents of current artists and the museum's curator, but also for the grand mansion in which the traditional items are displayed and for the gallery's shop, which is one of my favorite sources for gifts.

Another remarkable museum that has had an impact on all of Austria is the **KunstHausWien** *(Untere Weissgerberstrasse 13;* ☎ *1+ 712.04.91)*, a cultural center designed by the artist Friedensreich Hundertwasser and displaying some of his work as well as the works of other modern artists. The nearby **Hundertwasserhaus** *(Kegelgasse 36-38)* is a living space he designed for modern apartments. Both buildings are monuments to Hundertwasser's unusual "no straight lines" architecture, use of vibrant colors and environmental focus.

AUTHOR'S OBSERVATION

Gift giving takes on special emphasis in Wien, where the small shops at the Schatzkammer, the MAK, the KunstHausWien and the other museums offer exceptional items that are well worth bringing home (and cannot be found elsewhere). The major plastic charge cards are accepted for payment, as is cash, of course.

Among my favorites of the third style of museum, those that represent vignettes from the lives of famous Viennese residents, are **Figarohaus** *(Domgasse 5;* ☎ *1+513.62.94)*, a privately-owned museum on the upper floor of a historic building near the Stephansdom, where seven rooms hold memorabilia from the time when Mozart lived here; **Pasqualatihaus** *(Mölker Bastei 8;* ☎ *1+637.06.65)* for the Beethoven Memorial Rooms; and **Haydnhaus** *(Haydngasse 19;* ☎ *1+596.13.07)*, with the Brahms memorial room.

Although it may be the Staatsoper or music at one of the city's several other sources that draws some visitors, the theater is also exceptional. The **Etablissement Ronacher** *(Seilerstätte 9,* ☎ *1+514.11)* reopened, after extensive refurbishing, in early '94. With its Baroque interior restored, the small theater, with only an orchestra area and two tiers, is a gem. Any performance is worth attending, to enjoy the elegantly dressed audience and the restored theater as well as the event.

AUTHOR'S OBSERVATION

*The highlight of the season is the **Opernball** (Opera Ball), held in early February. It harks to the past and is one of a kind. Speaking German certainly adds to the evening, which is glamour at its best. Tickets should be ordered at least six months in advance by writing to Wiener Opernball-Büro (1 Goethegasse, A-1010 Wien (Vienna), Austria). Tickets are issued for entry only with an additional charge for seats at a table. Another elegant social occasion is the **Philharmonic Ball**, usually held in mid-January. For tickets, contact the **Wiener Musikverein** (Philharmonic, 12 Bösendorferstrasse, A-1010 Wien, Austria). The Staatsoper will be closed for renovations from July 1 until December 1994. Check with the Austrian National Tourist Office for details.*

Although Wien is rich with museums and music, its surroundings are well worth some time and are easily reached by tram or car. The **Wienerwald** (Vienna woods) is a goal for many who go for walks on weekends—and even for skiing when snow covers the ground. Restaurants can be found at convenient locations for a leisurely lunch or glass of wine from the region.

Grinzing, **Sievering**, **Nussdorf** and **Gumpoldskirchen** are the heart of the wine-growing region and although Grinzing is best known for its *Heurigen*, the popular "wine cafés" that have special festivities for the new wine in the fall can be found in all the surrounding areas with vineyards. Trams weave up to Grinzing from the center of Wien; the ride takes about 20 minutes.

Wien is a city with a soul. A good source for details on what's taking place while you are visiting is the tourist office on the lower level at the Opernring at Kärntnerstrasse.

LODGING: The top of my list, for elegant (and expensive) surroundings, is the **Hotel Bristol** *(141 rooms;* ☎ *1+515.16; FAX 1+51.51.65.50)*, neighbor to the Opera House and a pivot point for Viennese social circles for generations. This pacesetter is certainly the toniest hotel, from the liveried folks at its door to the chambermaids and others who attend guests. Its **Korso** restaurant is justly renowned; its **Café Sirk** is a popular place for a light meal after the opera, as well as at other times. The **Imperial** *(145 rooms;* ☎ *1+50.11.00; FAX 1+50.11.04.10)*, a neighbor a few doors away, is equally elegant in the minds of many. Both hotels offer Austrian elegance in traditional style. For special ambiance, consider the **Hotel im Palais Schwarzenberg** *(38 rooms; Rennweg 2;* ☎ *1+78.45.15; FAX 1+78.47.14)*, in a class by itself because it is in a palace by itself, with spacious gardens and impressive furnishings. It's slightly removed from the Opera House area, but convenient with taxis. (The tram also runs nearby.)

A newcomer with 1994, the **SAS Palais Hotel** *(155 rooms; Parkring 16;* ☎ *1+515.17-0, FAX 1+512.22.16)*, the tastefully-restored Palais Henckel von Donnersmarck, is ideally located across the street from the Stadtpark near the famous statue of Johann Strauss, within a few minutes' walk of Stephansdom and less than that from the recently reopened Ronacher theater, with which the hotel has a hospitality link. Definitely 5-star, the interior court of the Palais has become both reception area and the lingering area with the **Café in Palais**. Rooms include 90 bi-level suites as well as several large, well-appointed suites and regular rooms and a few tiny single rooms, one of which (#815) has been mine. (It has a memorable view of the spire of the Stephansdom framed in a circular window.) Hospitality is warm and welcoming; services have been superb. On the fringe of the Kärtnerstrasse-Opera orbit, but conveniently linked by trams, underground, buses, or a long walk, the **Hotel Biedermeier im Sünnhof** *(235 rooms; Landstrasser Hauptstrasse 28, A-1030; ☎ 1+75.55.75-0; FAX 1+75.55.75.503)* fills historic buildings on both sides of a cobbled pedestrian walkway between two streets. Often used by groups (because of its size), but comfortable and convenient under any circumstances, the hotel makes the most of its Biedermeier heritage by furnishing the rooms in period pieces or good copies.

On a smaller scale, but with plenty of atmosphere, the lovely **Römischer Kaiser** *(24 rooms; Annagasse 16; ☎ 1+512.77.51; FAX 1+512.77.51.13)*, on a side street off Kärntnerstrasse, is traditional, and the **Hotel König von Ungarn** *(31 rooms; Schulerstrasse 10; ☎ 1+51.58.40; FAX 1+51.58.48)*, not far from Stephansdom, offers modern rooms in a historic building. The **Hotel-Pension Altstadt** *(25 rooms; Kirchengasse 41, A-1070; ☎ 526+33.900; FAX 523+4901)* is a gem, occupying the upper-floor rooms of a Patrician home. All rooms have been decorated with style; management provides a gracious atmosphere. A personal favorite of long standing is the **Hotel Amadeus** *(30 rooms; Wildpretmarkt 5; ☎ 1+63.87.38; FAX 1+63.87.38.38)* where some of the tastefully modern rooms are very small, but all are very convenient to Stephansdom and other sights, as well as shops and restaurants. The **Hotel Alpha** *(70 rooms; Boltzmanngasse 8, A-1090 Wien; ☎ 1+31.16.46)*, with more reasonable rates, is in a residential area, but convenient to everything with public transportation.

Pension Nossek *(32 rooms; 17 Graben; ☎ 1+533.70.41, FAX 1+535.36.46)* is on the upper floors of a former mansion, with the lobby reached by elevator or 120-plus steps that spiral up to the cozy quarters. Once at the Pension, the hospitality is immediately obvious, with homelike surroundings in a classy style. The range of rooms carries a range of rates, with rooms on the inner side quieter but darker than those with a view over Graben. This place has been a pension for about 85 years, but its present family management (and its location) makes it ideal for visitors who want to feel "at home" on the city. Other pensions worth noting include the **Pension Domizil** *(21 rooms; Schulerstrasse 4; ☎ 1+513.30.93; FAX 1+513.31.99)*, just off Stephanplatz, in the heart of historic Wien, where all rooms, even when small, have modern comforts, including TV; and a family grouping that includes the **Pension Pertschy** *(Habsburgergasse 5; ☎ 1+534.49, FAX 1+534.49.49)*, **Pension Aviano** *(Marco d'Avianogasse 1; ☎ 1+512.83.30, FAX 1+512.81.65.65)*, **Pension Baronesse**

(Lange Gassee 61; ☎ 1+405.10.61, FAX 1+405.10.61.61) and the **Pension Christina** *(Hafnersteig 7; ☎ 1+533.29.61, FAX 1+533.29.61.11).*

Parkhotel Schönbrunn *(500 rooms; Hietzinger Hauptstrasse 10-20, A-1131 Wien; ☎ 1+878.04)* has a lovely location, across from Schönbrunn Palace, on the outskirts of town, making it pleasant if you're arriving by car. It's linked to town by bus and underground.

In the **Wienerwaldes** (the Vienna Woods), not far from Wien, **Pedro's Landhaus** *(A-3072 Dörfl, 10 rooms; ☎ 2744+7387; FAX 2744+7389)*, has an elegant indoor restaurant as well as a pleasant dining terrace and beautifully maintained gardens and grounds.

RESTAURANTS: Wien is flecked with excellent restaurants, in all sizes, shapes and prices, as you'd expect of an international city. Among my favorites of those that offer traditional food, service and style are the **Restaurant Bastei-Beisl** *(Stubenbastei 10, A-1010; ☎ 1+512.43.19)*, where *Wiener Tafelspitz* is a specialty; the **Kupferdachl** and the **Restaurant Leupold** *(Schottengasse 7, A-1010; ☎ 1+63.93.81)*, sharing the same address and owners, Harald and Susanne Leupold; and cozy **Zum Grüner Anker** *(Grängergasse 10, A-1010; ☎ 1+512.21.91)*, on a short lane not far from Stephanzplatz, in the medieval part of the city

Many visitors enjoy the **Hauswirth** *(Otto-Bauer-Gasse 20; ☎ 1+587.12.61; FAX 1+586.04.19)*, just off Maria-Hilfer-Strasse, a street known for its shops, and the **Rauchfangkehrer** ("Chimneysweep," Weibburg Gasse), not far from Stephansplatz and Kärntnerstrasse. Both places are experienced with accommodating tourists, while offering traditional Austrian and Viennese fare. My recently discovered favorite, however, is **zum Kuckuck** *(Himmelfortgasse 15; ☎ 1+512.84.70, FAX 1+523.38.18)*, which means "the cuckoo" (bird), where guests at any one of the dozen small tables can enjoy excellent meals in cozy, pleasant surroundings that are best known to local folks. (It's a short walk from both the Ronacher theater and Kärntnerstrasse, in the historic heart of the city.) Among coffeehouses I've enjoyed are **Café Prückel** (Ringstrasse), at the corner of the Stadtpark, not far from the Hilton; **Café Diglas** *(Wollseile, corner of Strobelgasse)*, a short walk from the Stephansdom; the **Café Europa** *(Kärntnerstrasse)*, convenient for pausing amid shopping; and the **Café Frauenhuber** *(Himmelfortgasse)*, which has been a restaurant since 1788 and was enjoyed by Mozart and Beethoven, according to a plaque by its door. It's also convenient to Stephansplatz and Kärntnerstrasse.

WÖRTHERSEE

Wörthersee, not far from Klagenfurt (see above), in Kärten, is not only a beautiful lake but also a favorite sports area in spring, summer, and fall. Lakeboats link many villages on their scheduled routes, and walking paths border the lake in many areas and thread up and out into the countryside.

LODGING: At the western end of the lake, near **Velden**, the **Hotel Schloss Velden** *(94 rooms; Seecorso 10, A-9220 Velden;* ☎ *4274+26.55, FAX 4272+42.26.04)* provides a memorable experience, not only for its lakeside location, but also for its castle-like surroundings, beautifully-appointed grounds and the comfortably furnished bedrooms. Speaking of another era, the oldest part of the building and grounds was built as the hunting lodge and summer retreat for Count Bartolomüs Khevenhüller, more than 350 years ago. One of many smaller and perhaps less pretentious, places to stay is the **Hotel Astoria** *(19 rooms and 6 apts.; Annastrasse 43, A-9210 Pörtschach;* ☎ *4272+3004; FAX 4272+30.04.57)*, a family-run hotel separated from the lake by lawns and a pedestrian promenade. The hotel has a small outdoor pool for warm-weather pleasure; bedrooms may seem stark, but have all comforts.

ZELL AM SEE

Zell am See *(A-5700;* ☎ *6542+2600; FAX 6542+2132)*, with its neighbor, **Kaprun** *(A-5710;* ☎ *654+8643; FAX 6547+8192)*, is one gigantic resort area that makes the most of its mountains and lake. Although there is a historic center to this massive resort, it's sometimes difficult to find and shop-infested when you get there. Reached by the same valley road and the same train route as Kitzbühel, the towns are linked thanks to a burst of building in the late '70s and through the '80s. Ski schools flourish during winter months; walking, hiking and climbing, along with sailing and swimming, are popular in summer.

LODGING: This is not a quaint village; it's big time tourism. There are hundreds of places to stay. One of my favorites has been the **Hotel Heitzmann** *(Loferer Bundesstrasse 4, A-5700;* ☎ *6542+2152; FAX 6542+21.52.33)*, built in 1900 in the chalet style of the Pinzgau region. The hotel was totally refurbished in 1991 to offer all modern comforts (TV in rooms), including a sauna and solarium. The family-owned hotel is in the center of town.

SPORTS

From the flat plains of Burgenland in the east to the mountains of western Tirol and Vorarlberg, Austria's nine Länder provide a noteworthy playground for all sports. There are all varieties of outdoor sports, from pleasant strolls to the most challenging mountain climbing, soaring and hang gliding. The Alp-surrounded state of Kärnten is speckled with lakes. Some are popular for their watersports; many are still devoted to quiet, natural pursuits. Steiermark, home for Austria's Lipizzaner horses of Wien's famous Spanish Riding School, has many places for horseback riding and almost every area—be it lakeside or mountain slope—has walking and hiking paths. Experienced mountaineers challenge sheer and craggy mountains. Grossglockner, at 12,454 feet, is Austria's highest peak, and the border between Slovenia and Austria runs through the Karnic and Karawanken Alps.

Here are tips about sports and their prime sources:

ARCHERY

Head for the Tirol, especially at specific places near Innsbruck, Kufstein, Pfunds, Reutte, St. Johann in Tirol, Serfaus and Vomp. The local tourist offices can assist with details. **Sporthotel Alpenhof Weissensee** *(Naggl 4, A-9762 Techendorf, Austria)* holds an "Archery Week Robin Hood."

BALLOONING

Inquire about plans and dates for a "Great Austrian Balloon Adventure," which has been held in the fall in Fuschl, near Salzburg. **Faszinatour Abenteuerreisen GmbH** *(Alte Bundesstrasse 27, A-6425, Haiming, Ötztal;* ☎ *5266+871.88, FAX 5266+873.11)*, a German company with offices in Austria, arranges ballooning experiences on specific dates from February through October. Itineraries are also organized through the **Bombard Society** *(6727 Curran St., McLean, VA 22101;* ☎ *800+862-8537 or 703+448-9407)*. In addition, **Die Gersberg Alm Hotel** (see "Salzburg," under "Places Worth Finding" above) holds "Balloon Basket" vacations, where several days are devoted to reenacting old customs and traditions and balloon rides are featured. About 30 miles northeast of Graz, in Schielleiten, 2 miles east of Stubenberg, ballooning championships are held.

BICYCLING

Bikes can be rented at many of Austria's railway stations. The cost is öS 90 per day; check for weekly and other rates. *Rad* is bicycle in German, so you'll want a *Radwanderkarte*, when you're looking for a map with cycling routes and facts. **Austria Radreisen** *(Holzingerstrasse 546, A-4780 Schärding;* ☎ *7712+55.11, FAX 7712+48.11)* is one firm that plans cycling holidays, but many of their itineraries are in Ober österreich, north of Linz. A few are around Salzburg. Hotels in resort areas often have information about organized itineraries. The tourist offices are always helpful with details. An itinerary that starts in the westernmost province of Vorarlberg makes it possible to cycle near and around the Bodensee (Lake Constance), perhaps to Switzerland, Liechtenstein and Germany. For planned itineraries with a guide, contact **Travent International** *(Box 711, Bristol, VT 05443;* ☎ *802+453-5710 or 800+325-3009; FAX 802+453-4806)* for their Alpine excursions and with **Butterfield & Robinson** *(70 Bond St., Toronto, Ont., Canada M5B 1X3;* ☎ *416+864-1354 or 800+678-1147; FAX 416+864-0541).* Mountain bikes can be rented in some Alpine resorts. One firm with international experience is **Austriaraft** *(Siedlungsstrasse 10, A-6425 Haiming;* ☎ *5266+8320).* They plan biking excursions with experienced guides in the Pitztal, from the Inn river.

CANOEING/KAYAKING

Tourist offices in towns along the most popular canoeing rivers provide facts about renting equipment. Among the most scenic and challenging rivers, the Drau, the Isel, and the Inn run through the Tirol. **Austriaraft** *(Siedlungsstrasse 10, A-6425 Haiming;* ☎ *5266+8320)* has guided white-water rafting expeditions along the Inn and other areas. A German company, **Faszinatour Abenteuerreisen GmbH** *(Alte Bundesstrasse 27, A-6425, Haiming, Ötztal;* ☎ *5266+871.88, FAX 5266+873.11),* organizes river rafting and other river trips in Austria, both summer and winter. In Kärnten (Carinthia), other rivers worth noting are the Gail, Gurk, Lavant, Lieser, Malta, and Moll rivers. In Salzburg Province, canoeing is popular on the Inn, Königsee Ache, Krimmler Ache, Lammer, Longa, Mur, Rauriser Ache, Saalach, Salzach, Taurach and Weisspriach, while some Tirol favorites are the Brandenberger Ache, Kossener Ache, Lech, Trisanna and Ziller. In Vorarlberg, the best rivers for canoeing are the Bregenzer Ache, Ill, Lech, and Rhein. There is even canoeing on portions of the Donau (Danube), as well as the Enns, Erlauf and Schwarza rivers in Lower Austria. **Ruefa Reisen** *(Rainerstrasse 7, A-5020 Salzburg)* is one firm that arranges canoeing vacations with lessons. **WINOGA Canoe Tours** *(Box 55, A-4560 Kirchdorf)* plans events along the Steyr, in the Pyhrn-Eisenwurzen mountains.

FISHING

Ask the **Austrian National Tourist Office** for a copy of the detailed booklet "Austria's Fishing Waters," which is also available in Austria through **Servicestelle der Fischwasser Österreichs** *(Kongresszentrum Seeburg, A-9210 Pörtschach;* ☎ *4272+36.20.30, FAX 4272+36.20.90).* Not only is the information attractively presented, but it's in English and tabulated to show areas in Kärten, Steiermark, Tirol, Salzburgerland and elsewhere that are good for fly-fishing, for catching pike, carp and other fish and for other specialties. Hotels and guesthouses mentioned in the booklet will take care of obtaining your fishing permits and will give advice and provide introductions for special fishing areas. You can have your catch prepared by the hotel kitchen when you prefer that to doing it yourself. Spring and fall are prime fishing times and you'll need an *Amtliche Fischerkarte* (official fishing license) for the province, which you'll have to obtain yourself if you're heading out on your own. Some areas issue temporary fishing permits and one-day authorizations; some also limit the number of permits. Allow a few weeks for permit processing. Kärnten claims 37 fishing areas, Salzburg

Province 29 and the Tirol 108. In Steiermark, **Raiffeisen-Reisebüro** *(Conrad von Hötzendorf-Strasse 5, A-8570 Voitsberg)* plans fishing holidays in spring and fall.

GOLF

Golf Green Austria *(Pannzaunweg 1a, A-5071 Wals/Salzburg; ☎ 662+85.08.05, FAX 662+85.81.90)* is an association of more than 90 golf courses and neighboring hotels dedicated to encouraging golfing holidays. Regulations for play include "course proficiency," which can be acquired with on-the-spot lessons, according to standards of the Austrian Golf Association and the International Golf Association. Member hotels work together to create tournaments and other activities; most have arrangements for rental of clubs and other equipment. Among the participating courses in the Salzburg area are the **Golfclub Gastein** *(☎ 6434+2775)* in Bad Gastein, the **Golfclub Goldegg** *(☎ 6415+8585; FAX 6425+8276)* in Goldegg, and the **Golfclub Europa-Sportregion** *(☎ 6542+6161; FAX 6542+6035)* at Zell am See. In Carinthia, the members are **Golfclub Bad Kleinkirchheim-Reichenau** *(☎ 4274+594; FAX 4240+82.82.18)* in Bad Kleinkirchheim, the **Golfanlage Pörtschach-Moosburg** *(☎ 4272+834.86)* in Pörtschach, the **Golfclub Klopienersee-Turnersee** *(☎ 4239+380.00-0; FAX 4239+3800-18)* at St. Kanzian and the **Golfanlage Velden-Köstenberg** *(☎ 4274+7045; FAX 4274+70.87.15)* in Velden. In Oberösterreich, members include the **Golfclub Salzkammergut** *(☎ 6132+6340, FAX 6132+6708)* in Bad Ischl. In Niederösterreich, the **Golfclub Semmering** *(☎ 2664+264)* is part of the group. In Steiermark, the members are **Golfclub Schloss Frauenthal** *(☎ 3462+5717)*, **Golfclub Gut Murstätten** *(☎ 3182+3555; FAX 3182+3688)*, the **Thermengolf Loipersdorf-Fürstenfeld** *(☎ 3382+8533; FAX 3382+82.04.87)* at Loipersdorf and the **Golf & Countryclub Dachstein-Tauern** *(☎ 3686+2630; FAX 3686+26.30.15)* in Schladming. In the Tirol, there are two member courses in Kitzbühel, the **Golfclub Kitzbühel-Schloss Kaps** *(☎ 5356+3007)* and the **Golfclub Kitzbühel-Schwarzsee** *(☎ 5356+716.45; FAX 5356+2307)*, plus the **Golfclub Innsbruck-Igls** *(☎ 512+771.65 at Lans/Innsbruck)*, the **Golfclub Innsbruck-Igls** *(☎ 5223+8177)* at Rinn-Innsbruck and two courses at Seefeld, the **Golfakademie Seefeld** *(☎ 5212+3797; FAX 5212+3355)* and the **Golfclub Seefeld-Wildmoos** *(☎ 5212+3003)*. In Burgenland, the member course is the **Golfclub Donnerskirchen** *(☎ 2683+81.71-0; FAX 2683+81.71.31)*. In addition, there are courses in and near Wien (Vienna).

HANG GLIDING/SOARING

There's a school in Zell am See, in Salzburg province and the sport is popular at many places in the Tirol, namely Axams, Galtür, Innsbruck, Inzing, Kirchberg, Kitzbühel, Kössen, Kramsach, Leutasch, Mayrhofen, Oberndorf, Tannheim, Telfs, Wildschönau and Zams, plus Sillian in Osttirol (East Tirol). Near Dornbirn, in the westernmost nub of the country, plane gliding is popular at Hohenems-Seemähder and hang gliding is the focus for the school in Andelsbuch. Instruction in parachuting is offered at a center near Graz. **Faszinatour Abenteuerreisen GmbH** *(Alte Bundesstrasse*

27, A-6425, Haiming, Ötztal; ☎ 5266+871.88, FAX 5266+873.11), a German company, arranges for hang gliding experiences with guides, on specific dates.

HIKING

Well-maintained paths are clearly marked in most of the Alpine areas, both for easy walks around the lakes and for more strenuous walks in the mountains. Most local tourist offices have good hiking maps for sale and/or as handouts. Signs are usually yellow for easy walks and red-and-white for higher elevations. One of the many joys of hiking in Austria is that the public transportation system makes it easy to reach wonderful starting points. Small trains climb deep into valleys and bus services stretch to many places not reached by the trains; cablecars and funiculars stretch to the peaks. The system of *Wandern ohne Gepäck* (walking without luggage) is popular in the Waldviertel, Altmunster and Pinzgauer Saalachtal, as well as in the Dachstein-Tauern region and around Lofer. Itineraries are arranged so that luggage is transported from one lodging to the next, leaving you free to hike without a heavy backpack. Contact **Wanderweg Holidays** *(519 Kings Croft, Cherry Hill, NJ 08034; ☎ 609+321-1040 or 800+270-2577; FAX 609+321-1040)* for details about their walks and hikes in the Tirol and in Salzburgerland. Also check with **Travent International**, and **Butterfield & Robinson**, mentioned above under "Bicycling," who offer guided hikes and walks.

HORSEBACK RIDING

Contact the **Austrian National Tourist Office** for a copy of their *Reiten in Österreich*, an attractive, informative booklet about horseback riding holidays, with information about many places, including their addresses. Among the places in Kärten, with a farm setting and exceptional horses and facilities, are the **Hotel Trattlerhof** *(50 rooms; A-9546 Bad Kleinkirchheim; ☎ 4240+81.73, FAX 4240+81.24)*, with a pool, spa and country-style comfortable rooms; the **Schloss Traubuschgen** *(15 rooms; A-9821 Obervellach; ☎ 4782+20.42)*, with an upscale manor house style that includes lessons in dressage and jumping, plus tennis, swimming and classical concerts; and the **Hotel Alte Post** *(80 rooms; A-9122 St. Kanzian am Klopeiner See; ☎ 4239+22.26, FAX 4239+22.26.78)*, which is open only in summer, with a swimming pool, sauna, tennis courts and other sports offerings. Steiermark, the state that is home for the breeding farm for the Lipizzaner horses of the Spanish Riding School (northwest of Graz, at **Piber**), has over 100 places to ride. Salzburg province-state also has several places for riding holidays, as do the states of Tirol and Vorarlberg. **Ruefa Reisen** *(Rainerstrasse 7, A-5020 Salzburg)* offers a riding program from June through November.

HUNTING

You'll need your passport, insurance, proof of your hunting ability and a passport photo to obtain a *Behordliche Jagdkarte* (hunting license) from the local authorities. That permit and a *Jagderlaubnis* (shooting permit) granted by your host/owner of the hunting preserve, is required. Many preserve owners advertise in journals such as *Osterreichs Waidwerk, Der Anblick,* or *St. Hubertus.* For addresses, contact the **Austrian National Tourist Office**.

MOUNTAINEERING OR CLIMBING

English-speaking travelers will benefit from membership in the British branch of the **Österreichischer Alpenverein** *(13 Longcroft House, Fretherne Rd., Welwyn Garden City, Herts., AL8 6PQ England;* ☎ *44+707+32-4835, FAX 44+707+33-3276)* for printed information in English and for hikes with English-speaking guides. **Faszinatour Abenteuerreisen GmbH** *(Alte Bundesstrasse 27, A-6425, Haiming, Ötztal;* ☎ *5266+871.88, FAX 5266+873.11)* arranges *Bergsport* expeditions for small groups from June through October. Heiligenblut is a starting town part way up the Grossglockner Pass. Other places, also in Kärnten, are Spittal's Klettergarten and from Faak am See up the Kanzianiberg. In Salzburg province-state, climbers set out from Abtenau, Bischofshofen, Filzmoos, Hollersbach, Leogang, Mittersill, Salzburg City, Viehofen, Wald im Pinzgau and Zell am See. In Steiermark, the most respected climbing areas are reached from Altaussee, Graz, Mürzhofen, Öblarn and Ramsau/Dachstein, while in Tirol, where there are many peaks, some of the favorites are reached from well-known Innsbruck, Kitzbühel, Mayrhofen and St. Anton as well as lesser-known Alpbach, Ehrwald, Fieberbrunn, Fulpmes, Galtür, Going, Kirchdorf, Lanersbach, Leutasch, Maurach, Neustift, Obergurgl, Reutte, Sölden, St. Leonhard and Tannheim. In Osttirol, Kartitsch and Lienz are starting points, as are Gaschurn/Partenen and Lech in Vorarlberg.

RIVER RAFTING

Near Lienz, in Osttirol, lessons and expeditions are arranged for novices along the Isel, between Ainet and Lienz. For faster currents, experts canoe along the Mittlere Isel, and on the Gail between Birnbaum and Kötschach, the Möll, and the Lieser between Trebesing and Spittal. Ask at the Austrian National Tourist Offices for facts about the **Alpine Rafting Camp** at Ainet and refer to "Canoeing and kayaking," above.

ROWING

Boats are usually available for rent through lakeside hotels and concessionaires in the resort areas.

SAILING

Almost 100 of Austria's lakes are suitable for sailing. The sport is popular in Kärnten, south of the highest Alps, on the Faaker See, Feldsee, Klopeiner See, Millstätter See, Ossiacher See, Weissensee and Wörthersee. In the Salzburg area, the best lakes for sailing are the Attersee, Fuschlsee, Mattsee, Mondsee, Obertrumer See, Wolfgangsee, Wallersee, and Zeller See. And in the Tirol, the Achensee, the Durlassboden/Gerlos artificial lake and the Plansee are popular for the sport. In Vorarlberg, you can sail from Austria to Switzerland and Germany on a day-long course on the Bodensee (Lake Constance). For sailing specifics, contact the **Österreichis-**

cher **Segel-Verband** *(Grosse Neugasse 8, A-1040 Wien, Austria)* or **Vereinigung Österreichischer Yachtsport- und Windsurfschulen** *(c/o Ing. Gaderer, Prof. Sinwel-Weg 13/13, A-6330 Kufstein, Austria).*

SKIING

Summer skiing is popular on several Austrian glaciers, some used by ski teams for their training. In the Tirol, the prime areas are Hintertux/Gefrorene Wand, Kaunertal glacier, Neustift im Stubaital, around Sölden and Rettenbachferner-Tiefenbachferner, and in the glacier area of the Pitztal. From Innsbruck, plans through the tourist office include skiing on the Stubai Glacier for öS 590. In Steiermark, head for Dachstein (Ramsau) and in the Salzburg area, the Kitzsteinhorn is the place to ski in summer.

Winter skiing focuses on the highest mountains, most of which are in the states of Vorarlberg and Tirol, the tongue of land that wedges between the borders of Switzerland and Italy to the west and south and Germany to the north. The **Austrian National Tourist Office** in New York City has a special "ski phone" *(☎ 212+944-6917)* for information about winter conditions.

Some resorts offer unlimited-use multiday lift passes at prices that range from $100 to $150 for a six-day pass, with the higher prices prevailing at the most fashionable resorts. Skis/boots/poles can be rented for about $50 to $120 for six days. Ski schools vary in price, according to style of lessons. The tourist office can provide details.

SWIMMING

Austrians enjoy their many lakes to the fullest and that includes sunbathing along and swimming from the shores of many of them as soon as the weather warms. Among the favorites, because resorts fill shoreline pockets, are those in Kärnten (the Faaker See, Millstätter See, Ossiacher See and Wörthersee), in Salzburg province-state (especially the Fuschlsee, Wolfgangsee, and Zeller See), in Steiermark at the Kumbergsee near Graz and the Sulmsee near Leibnitz as well as at the Putter See and other places. In Vorarlberg, the Bodensee (Lake Constance) is popular, but many of the smaller lakes are also lovely—and far more private. There are hundreds of municipal pools and many resort pools, especially in the areas noted for their spas.

TENNIS

Count on finding courts at resort hotels and towns such as Kitzbühel, Zell am See, Lech, St. Anton and other popular resorts, as well as near Innsbruck, Salzburg and many other resort areas. The **Austrian National Tourist Office** has a booklet called *Tennis in Österreich*, which gives complete details on facilities and contacts. Be sure to inquire about court surface, rental of tennis equipment and reservations for court time.

WALKING OR TREKKING

Everyone walks! Within minutes of the cities there are posted walking paths on hillsides and lakesides. There are even public walking paths through some vineyards as well as those linking villages up in the mountains. For planned walks, perhaps with a wildflower focus, check with the hotels and local tourist offices. See "Hiking," above, for details on more active walking/trekking.

WATERSKIING

Most of the larger lakeside resort hotels provide, or have easy access to, waterskiing. The Austria National Tourist Office can give specific suggestions, depending on your itinerary.

WINDSURFING/BOARDSAILING

Popular on many Austrian lakes, especially those mentioned under "Sailing," above, the sport has some restrictions and is prohibited entirely on some lakes. The **Austrian National Tourist Office** has information; local tourist offices have facts about places and prices for board rentals. For details about lessons and races, contact the **Vereinigung Österreichischer Yachtsport-und Windsurfschulen** *(Ing. Gaderer, Prof. Sinwel-Weg 13/13, S-6330 Kufstein, Austria).*

TREASURES AND TRIFLES

Mehrwertsteuer is what the Austrians call their value-added tax, or VAT, as it is known in England. The amount is noted on your purchase slips and if you spend more than a certain amount, you are eligible for a partial refund of the tax, providing you file the correct paper work. The item must cost more than öS 1000, including tax, and must be unused when you take it out of the country. To obtain the refund, ask the store for Form U34 and fill it out. The store must then affix the required store identification. Forms must be validated when you leave Austria, at which time the customs officer may ask to see the merchandise (so you must keep it handy).

The refund system can be a nuisance that negates the worth of the refund. Be sure to plan ahead by first asking at the local tourist office (or the store) where the nearest customs office is located and be prepared for the fact that finding customs folk at many train stations takes some time. After you've found them and your form is validated, the original must be mailed to the store where you purchased the item. Be sure to keep a copy. The store will either apply the refund to your credit card account or send you a check, in Austrian schillings (which you, then, take to your bank for an exchange). The system will be changed eventually when a United States of Europe is a reality, but for the foreseeable future it involves a lot of time and paperwork.

AUTHOR'S OBSERVATION

The **Austrian Automobile and Touring Club** *(öAMTC) has a system that, for a modest handling charge, takes care of the return. They give an immediate refund through their offices at airports and borders, as well as at the train stations at Salzburg and Kufstein, when you leave the country.*

Among the favorite items to buy are what Austrians call *Trachten*, the dirndl dresses that are modern adaptations of the traditional costumes worn in country villages. Although the entire costume is usually shown as a unit, it's possible to buy the scarf, blouse, skirt, or other elements separately. You can also expect to find superb loden coats, jackets and capes, as well as hats. Hunting and outdoor wear can be purchased in special stores or departments in larger clothing stores. Geiger sport clothes and country wear, known for style and quality, are sold in North America and elsewhere, but you'll find greater variety of merchandise in shops in Innsbruck, Salzburg and elsewhere in Austria. Other companies also offer good quality and because they may not export they may not be as well known.

AUTHOR'S NOTE

When you see something you like, buy it. Don't expect to find it in another store–or in a nearby town. The best sources for stylish clothes are the cities, namely Wien, Salzburg and Innsbruck, but make time for stores in Graz and other cities and towns where local needs are served, and in the classy resort areas.

Heimatwerk is the key to quality crafts in Austrian shops. Literally "homework," the word has come to stand for a wide range of high-quality hand-made items, from carved-wood items, to paintings, to clothes, to weaving, to glass painting and many other arts. Most major towns have at least one shop noted for Heimatwerk and several that feature *Trachten*, as the country-style costumes are called.

For those who enjoy Austrian music, tapes are sold everywhere, but ask some Austrians you meet for names of the best folk groups and be sure the tape you're buying will play on your recorder. Some of the tapes can be disappointing.

AUTHOR'S OBSERVATION

Note that VCRs in Europe operate on a different format from those in the U.S. VCR tapes are not interchangeable.

ADDITIONAL INFORMATION SOURCES

Further information about specific regions of Austria is available through the following Länder (state) tourist offices :

VORARLBERG

Vorarlberg Tourismus, *Römerstrasse 7, Postfach 302, A-6091 Bregenz.* ☎ *5574+42.52.50; FAX 5574+42.52.55.*

CITY OF BREGENZ

Fremdenverkehrsamt der Landeshauptstadt Bregenz, *Anton-Schneider-Strasse 4A, A-6900 Bregenz.* ☎ *5574+43.39.10; FAX 5574+433.91.10.*

TIROL
  Tirol Werbung, *Bozner Platz 6, A-6010 Innsbruck.* ☎ *512+53.20.170;*
  FAX 512+53.201.50.

CITY OF INNSBRUCK
  Tourismusverband Innsbruck/Igls, *Burggraben 3, A-6021 Innsbruck.*
  ☎ *512+59.850; FAX 512+59.85.07.*

SALZBURG REGION
  Salzburger Land Tourismus Ges.m.b.H., *Alpenstrasse 96, Postfach 8,*
  A-5033 Salzburg. ☎ *662+20.50.60; FAX 662+23.070.*

CITY OF SALZBURG
  Fremdenverkehrsbetriebe der Stadt Salzburg, *Auerpergstrasse 7,*
  A-5020 Salzburg. ☎ *662+88.98.70; FAX 662+889.87.32.*

UPPER AUSTRIA
  Landesverband für Tourismus in Oberösterreich, *Schillerstrasse 50,*
  A-4010 Linz. ☎ *732+66.30.21; FAX 732+60.02.20.*

CITY OF LINZ
  Fremdenverkehrszentrale Linz, *Hauptplatz 34, Postfach 310, A-4010*
  Linz. ☎ *732+239.317.77; FAX 732+27.873.*

LOWER AUSTRIA
  Niederösterreichische Fremdenverkehrswerbung, *Hoher Markt 3, 6th*
  floor, A-1010 Wien. ☎ *222+531.106.110.*

CITY OF VIENNA
  Wiener Tourismusverband, *Obere Augartenstrasse 40, A-1025 Wien.*
  ☎ *222+21.11.40; FAX 222+21.68.492.*

BURGENLAND
  Landesfremdenverkehrsamt für das Burgenland, *Schloss Esterhazy,*
  A-7000 Eisenstadt. ☎ *2682+33.84; FAX 2682+33.84.20.*

STYRIA
  Steiermärkischer Landesverband für Tourismus, *Herrengasse 16,*
  Landhaus, A-8010 Graz. ☎ *316+837.60.00; FAX 316+877.34.36.*

CITY OF GRAZ
  Grazer Tourismus Ges. m.b.H., *Herrengasse 16, Landhaus, A-8010 Graz.*
  ☎ *316+835.24.10; FAX 316+83.79.87.*

CARINTHIA
  Kärntner Tourismus Ges. m.b.H., *Halleggerstrasse 1, A-9201 Krumpen-*
  dorf. ☎ *4229+22.24; FAX 4229+20.89.*

CITY OF KLAGENFURT
  Fremdenverkehrsamt der Landeshauptstadt Klagenfurt, *Neuer Platz 1,*
  A-9010 Klagenfurt. ☎ *463+53.72.22; FAX 463+53.72.95.*

FRANCE

Annecy, France

Plump strawberries overflowed from their baskets; crusty bread (whose heart, experience had taught me, would be tongue-pleasing and tasty) filled a nearby bin; and burning-hot *café au lait* in paper cups that doubled as hand-warmers against the morning chill, was offered a few steps away. It was market day and while these three items drew me for breakfast, the narrow cobbled streets were lined with stands of country produce that offered a kaleidoscope of colors on the inevitable grey November morning.

Tabletops were covered, each in its turn, with jars of homemade honey, jams and jellies; assorted sizes, shapes and flavors of mountain cheese; tidy bundles of herbs; bursting bunches of flowers; concise piles of fruit pinched recently from its mother tree and vegetables pulled from their surrounding soil a few hours earlier.

The weekly markets of Alpine villages are integral parts of daily life, built into a lifestyle that survives in spite of the ravages of tourism. In addition to being the source of provisions for homes and restaurants, the markets offer items for a traveler's breakfast or between-meal snack.

"Perfect pictures" are framed from every angle, whether you choose to capture them with camera or memory. The mystery of village markets gives the occasions an impact far greater than the actual event. Markets bespeak a way of life that's been in place since the Middle Ages, from which many of the most charming villages' buildings date. Markets offer opportunities for a natural intercourse that transcends a spoken language, a social pact that is as strong between visitor and regular as between friends and colleagues who gather to exchange goods and gossip. Wandering along the gnarled streets of the local marketplace, you can feel the pulse of the village and its surroundings.

And then, with your personal selection of farm produce carefully stowed, it's time to board the lakeboat that leaves from the nearby dock or step onto one of the regional buses that thread out to another village, or board a train to reach some farther goal.

A day that begins with a village market is a day that sets its own pace, whether you choose to head to the hills from which some of the produce came, or to stroll through a town's museums in search of the time when life was firmly anchored to the soil.

Although today's town fathers seem to be on a rampage to cover traces of the past in many French villages and have already (tragically) plastered too much of the town's center with cement, in deference to the plague of cars that screech for places to pause, there are many places where townspeople cling to their traditions. And those are the places that are perfect for Alpine rambles and for sharing pastoral scenery, to glide, occasionally, into a country inn or a local bistro to sample the best of the Alpine life of France.

COUNTRY CAPSULE

France is a shoulder of Europe, with the Iberian peninsula reaching from its southwest border and the sea lapping at shores both north and south. Divided into 22 regions, the Alpine area of France claims portions of only four—the **Savoie**, with its division of Haute Savoie

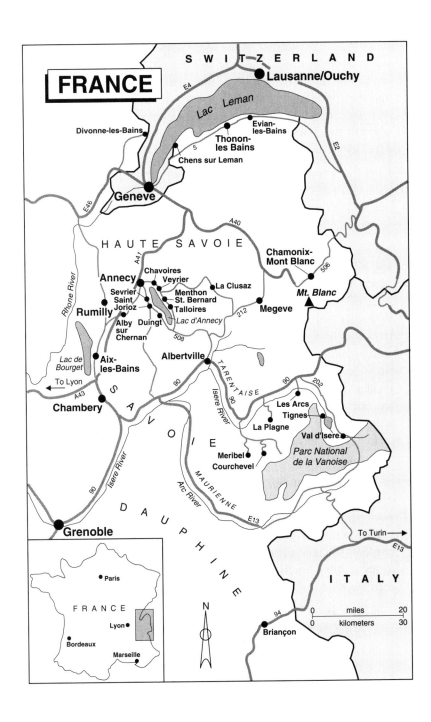

FRANCE

SWITZERLAND

Lausanne/Ouchy

Lac Leman

E4

Divonne-les-Bains

Evian-les-Bains

Thonon-les Bains

Chens sur Leman

5

E2

Geneve

E46

A40

HAUTE SAVOIE

A41

Chamonix-Mont Blanc

506

Rhone River

Annecy

Chavoires

Veyrier

La Clusaz

Mt. Blanc

Sevrier

Menthon

St. Bernard

Saint

Talloires

Jorioz

212

Megeve

Rumilly

Lac d'Annecy

Alby

sur

Chernan

Duingt

508

Lac de Bourget

Aix-les-Bains

Albertville

T A R E N T A I S E

90

To Lyon

S A V O I E

90

Isere River

90

202

Les Arcs

Tignes

Chambery

A43

La Plagne

Val d'Isere

Meribel

Courchevel

Parc National de la Vanoise

Isere River

90

M A U R I E N N E

Arc River

D A U P H I N E

E13

To Turin

Grenoble

E13

N

Paris

I T A L Y

F R A N C E

Lyon

94

miles 20

Bordeaux

kilometers 30

0

0

Marseille

Briançon

(south of Swiss-shared Lac Léman) and the Savoie region that nudges Italy to the east; the eastern portion of the **Lyonnaise-Bresse** region, mostly the district of Ain and the city of Lyon; the **Dauphiné** region, with its districts of Isère and Hautes Alpes, with some places in the western district of Drome easy to visit from the Alpine centers; and the region of **Provence-Côte d'Azur**, which wraps around minute Monaco on the Mediterranean, leaving the most mountainous regions to the Alpes Maritimes and the Alps de Haute-Provence.

What we're talking about in this chapter is an area that stretches from Lac Léman in the north to places just south of Col de Mont Cenis, Col du Galibier and Col de la Croix de Fer, to the Mediterranean sea at the south, from the Rhône river on the west to the Swiss-Italian border on the east.

While the highest peaks are along the eastern portion, where mountain passes and tunnels bring Italy and Switzerland within minutes, making them places "for lunch," the entire region is affected by the Alps, even when the highest mountain peaks may be out of sight. Where landscapes are level, they bristle with crops; where they slant to face the sun, grape vines have been trained to give maximum light to the fruit—and unique taste to the eventual wine. The produce from the land gives soul to the markets, making them one of the greatest pleasures of this region. The several-times-weekly markets are not only an integral part of the commercial system, but they are—for visitors—a time to feel what country life is all about, a time to live as the local folks, sharing their coffee, cheeses, fruits, food, wine and animated conversation.

Although tourism has stomped with a heavy foot in some portions of the French Alps (and they are mentioned as such below), there are many areas where villages survive, it seems, to be photographed and to recall a simpler, less cluttered time. There are many villages where residents still tend their crops and work their crafts, probably for sale to restaurants, hotels, and visitors these days, but still in time-honored ways.

AUTHOR'S OBSERVATION

The French seem to believe that paving the center of town is best. Many historic towns have lost every snippet of grass or lawn in an avalanche of paving for parking places and low maintenance. Rivers in many towns are constrained to ugly, utilitarian channels as they pass through the center. The result is a hot, paved area in summer months, and a loss of atmosphere.

Just outside of town, however, there are many areas, notably around lac d'Annecy, through Chambéry, high in the mountains out of Megève or in the **Parc National de la Vanoise**, where you can walk amid nature, far away from the scars of built-for-tourism development.

HISTORIC HIGHLIGHTS

As the only European country that stretches from the North Sea to the Mediterranean, France has been a pathway for most of the major strides of European history. It has been both a crossroads and a goal.

Some of the newest resort areas claim some of the oldest settlements, as is the case in the Tarentaise area of the Savoie, where relics from Bronze Age settlements have been found. They are believed to be from shepherds who roamed north from Italy. By the time of the Iron Age, around 650 B.C., tribes of Celts, who came to be known as Gauls, came from the east through an area between the Rhine and Danube rivers, settling in the area of the Isère River as it meets the Valance and into the region of Dauphiné. The Romans were next, moving north from their prosperous communities to conquer the Gauls and to bring their industry and commerce to the region. They seem to have had little difficulty with mountain passage as they carried their culture from northern Italy to the Rhône river banks.

From the 6th to the 13th centuries, feudal systems prevailed in the Dauphiné region, while, by the 11th century, the Holy Roman Empire had gathered the Savoie into its growing territory. Although daily patterns varied, as history developed in the Dauphiné region and in the Savoie, there were cross-currents that included Humbert aux Blanches from Vienne, who became the head of the new House of Savoie. The family eventually became "gatekeepers to the Alps." By the 11th and 12th centuries, monasteries developed throughout the region, and were the precursors of the many cloisters and chapels that dot the area today.

The counts of Savoie, through clever business dealings and convoluted political and economic patterns, controlled an area that stretched between Torino (Italy) and Genève (Switzerland) and included the key mountain passes through Mont Cenis and Petit St. Bernard. By 1429, Nice and Italy's Piemonte region were added to the counts' holdings.

In the area now known as Dauphiné, meanwhile, Humbert II dealt with the France of his time. Since he had no heir to continue the strategy his ancestors had set, he worked with the French to establish his region as a strong and independent dominion. (It is from this point—at the signing of the *Transport du Dauphiné*—until the French revolution, that the eldest son of the king of France was known as the dauphin.)

Both the Savoie region and the Dauphiné prospered, the former with its control of the mountain passes and the latter with an economy built on farm produce and cattle. During the years of the Reformation, religion was a catalyst for small communities, with loyalties divided between the largely Protestant Dauphiné and the Catholic-leaning Savoie. Protestant John Calvin and his followers used Genève as their base, proselytizing from there. Religious wars fragmented the region, which was also being pulled by the king of France and the Habsburg rulers in Austria.

The Savoie continued to be a powerful force in 15th-century Europe, even after the duke of Savoie moved his headquarters from Chambéry to Torino (Turin in Italy), a few steps farther from the greedy and feisty Habsburgs and farther from the reach of the kings of France. By the 17th century, however, French influence was strong in the fiercely independent Savoie, and in 1792 French forces invaded Savoie, which they renamed the départément du Mont-Blanc. By April 1868, when the Savoyards voted to join France, their independent state became two regions—Haute Savoie and Savoie —as they are today.

Although both Dauphiné and the Savoies have a farming heritage, the regions have turned to tourism since the ascent of Mont Blanc (in 1786), which started the trend of British travelers coming to the mountains on holiday. Tourism is not new to the region, although many of the facilities are. The region received an awesome investment and significant promotion from the 1992 Winter Olympics, which were held in February in the Rhône Alpes. Headquartered in the valley town of Albertville, Olympic events were held in the high mountain resorts of Méribel, Les Munières, La Plagne, Val d'Isère and other places.

POLITICAL PICTURE

President François Mitterrand's Socialist party has ruled France since the elections of May 10, 1981 and he will complete his second seven-year term in 1995. The president chooses his prime minister, usually from his own party, to head the National Assembly, which makes national and international policy. Among the many other parties, the Communists and the Conservatives have significant blocks of votes, while the small Republican party is an effective opposition. The country is divided into 22 regions, each of which is administered through its regional council. Trade union federations have a strong voice in the government. All employees are entitled to two months' paid vacation and many other benefits related to holidays, work hours, and social services.

AUTHOR'S OBSERVATION

The rampant development in resort areas, the evolution of huge vacation centers, the precise office hours, and detailed job descriptions affect tourism, not only by the appearance of places but, in my experience, by the attitude and degree of helpfulness of employees in tourism and railway offices. Be prepared to fit into the French socialist system. Although you may get exceptional service, don't expect it.

LIFESTYLE

Speaking fluent French makes life easier, as does conservative (but stylish) dress. Public offices (including tourist offices and banks) have very specific hours, which may vary from day to day, and although they may not open right on time, most close on the dot of their appointed hour. Don't expect to accomplish much business (or even shopping, in some cases) during lunch hours. Many places close from noon until 2 or 3 p.m. (which will be noted as 14:00 or 15:00, following their 24-hour time schedule).

Many years of socialism have opened up all systems for everyone. Although châteaux and other symbols of elitist life are well maintained, and several are open as hotels and/or restaurants, a lot of the construction in recent years has been block housing. Although it's most obvious in Paris and at some of the overdeveloped tourist centers, the French "attitude" that comes in for its share of brickbats can be a fact of life.

Mealtimes are events; socializing is an activity. Plan to make reservations at your favorite dining places; it's usually expected, although cafés will be happy to serve when they have space available. In contrast to their traditional style, some French folks have adopted the U.S. fast food system; they stand up as they drink and snack for a fast-paced lunchtime. The evening meal is the most important to share with friends and family.

The public transportation system is formed to provide the most comfortable methods for mass transport. Although the TGV high-speed train has been souped up for businesspeople and others who can afford "the best," most transport is strictly utilitarian. When (or if) there is someone to help with portage, expect to treat him/her like a colleague. Only the most elegant hotels will have someone to assist with your baggage. A discreetly given *pourboire* (tip) is acceptable in most cases.

The most expensive classically-elegant hotels will expect appropriately elegant attire (which may mean designer jeans), but neatly conservative clothes are appropriate everywhere. Women should leave flashy jewelry at home and wallow in quality-designed costume jewelry or no jewelry at all.

NATURAL SURROUNDINGS

Although there's plenty of spectacular scenery, some of the new resorts appear to have been built with little regard for preserving the environment. Discussions following the Olympic events, however, found some community planners talking about devoting time, energy and money to reinstate the traditional "atmosphere." In the midst of the French Alps, between the upper valleys of Maurienne and Tarentaise, the **Parc National de la Vanoise** has about 313 miles (500 km) of posted walking paths and an active summer activities program. In addition to the 19 refuges maintained by the Parc, there are a dozen maintained by the **Club Alpin Français** and about as many owned privately. The park borders the Italian park of Grand Paradiso, which means there is vast acreage that is protected from development. **L'Union Départementale des Offices de Tourisme et Syndicats d'Initiative de la Savoie**, an association of the tourism offices in areas bordering the Parc National, maintains an information center at the **Maison du Tourisme** *(24 blvd. de la Colonne;* ☎ *79+85.12.45)* in Chambéry. (See "Chambéry" under "Places Worth Finding," below.) South of Lyon, two regional parks—the **Parc du Pilat** near St. Etienne and the **Parc Vercours**, east of Valence—are marked with walking paths and educational centers.

Bird-watching is exceptional in the 50,000-acre **Parc National de la Vanoise**, as well as near the timber line, on the upper slopes of the mountains. Ptarmigan and other birds, including an occasional golden eagle, can be spotted. Near Lyon, the **Parc Ornithologique de la Dombes** *(01330 Villard-les-Dombes;* ☎ *79+98.05.54)*, created in 1970, is 50 acres with lakes and walking paths, home for more than 350 local and foreign species of waterbirds and other birds.

PRACTICAL FACTS ABOUT FRANCE

The more time you invest in learning some French, as well as French routines and currency *before* you start your travels, the happier you will be when you're traveling in France. The country's Alpine area is delightful, but helping strangers unfamiliar with the language is not a skill of most French folks (any more than it is for most people in the U.S.).

INFORMATION SOURCES

Services Officiels Français du Tourisme a l'Etranger is the head office of tourism at *17 rue de l'Ingenieur Robert Keller, 75740 Paris Cedex 15, France*. The **Maison de Savoie** is at *31 avenue de l'Opéra, 75001 Paris, France;* ☎ *country code 33 plus 1+47.03.41.05, FAX country code 33 plus 1+49.27.07.63*. In North America, information is offered through the **French Government Tourist Office**, *#303, 9454 Wilshire Blvd., Beverly Hills, CA 90212,* ☎ *310+271-6665, FAX 310+276-2835; #3360, 676 N. Michigan Ave., Chicago, IL 60611,* ☎ *312+751-5800, FAX 312+337-6339; 610 Fifth Ave., New York, NY 10020, 212+757-1125 or 900+990-0040 (50¢ per minute), FAX 212+247-6468; 1981 McGill College, Montreal, Quebec, H3A 2W9 Canada,* ☎ *514+288-4264, FAX 514+845-4868; #700, St. Patrick St., Toronto, Ontario M5T 383 Canada,* ☎ *416+593-4723, FAX 416+979-7587.*

Regional offices for specific areas are listed at the end of this chapter.

Throughout the chapter, local spelling is used for some words and all place names. For translation of foreign words, refer to the back-of-the-book glossary. Postal codes and telephone numbers for the tourist office are in parentheses following place names in "Places Worth Finding."

CASH, CURRENCY AND CREDIT CARDS

The French franc, which exchanges at about FF6 to US$1 at press-time, is the unit of currency and breaks down into 100 centimes per franc. The one-franc coin, worth about 15 U.S. cents, is the most useful unit. Travel will be easiest if you carry French francs, either buying French franc travelers cheques before you leave North America or cashing into local currency whenever you have the chance.

One source for purchase of both travelers cheques and French currency is **Ruesch International Financial Services** *(1350 Eye St., NW., Washington, DC 20005;* ☎ *202+408-1200 or 800+424-2923; FAX 202+408-1211)*. They offer full currency services for international travelers.

When you are in France, be aware that banks and other exchange centers always charge a service fee, which varies from place to place. When you have the time, shop around at several banks. Some places have a per-cheque charge (which can add up if you're exchanging several $20s rather than a few $100s). The French love and honor their holidays—and their lunch hour. You'll have to plan your check-cashing for times when banks are open, and that may take some research. In some small towns, hotels do not provide check-cashing privileges, especially if you're traveling at other than peak tourist seasons, which are generally mid-summer for lake areas and/or mid-winter for the Alpine mountain resorts.

Although many places accept credit cards, always ask before you order in a restaurant if you're planning to pay by credit card. All cards are not accepted; MasterCard (which is equivalent to Europe's Eurocard) and Visa are usually welcomed.

COMMUNICATION

Speaking French helps—a lot. Not only is it easier to communicate, but in many of the less-traveled Alpine areas there are few people who are prepared to help in English.

AUTHOR'S OBSERVATION

The clever French have devised a way for us to get information–and pay the bill for their services at the same time. The "900" number information hotline offered by the French Gorvernment Tourist Office (☎ 900-990-0048) costs 50 cents per minute for the caller, including the time they put you on hold and deliberate about your answer. To make maximum use at minimum cost, write your questions down before placing the call.

The communications system—with its use of telephone, FAX machines (which the French know as *télécopie*), television, and computers—seem far ahead of the U.S. in many ways. Most of the public telephone booths operate on a system that uses a *télécarte* and will not accept coins. The card must be inserted in the designated slot on the telephone before you can complete your call. In many towns, coin-operated phones are difficult, if not impossible, to find.

AUTHOR'S OBSERVATION

If you plan to make many local telephone calls, buy at least a 50-unit télécarte as soon as you arrive in France. You will then have a card in hand when you need it; it's not always easy to find a source for purchase at the time you choose to make a call.

Télécartes are sold at designated outlets, which are usually post offices and tabac shops. Ask for directions to the nearest source whenever you find someone with whom you can converse. During their hours of operation, the PTT usually has telephones where you can make long-distance calls with an operator's assistance, paying (in francs) for the call when it is completed. From France, use of North American companies' international dialing services can ease the language problem. For example, AT&T's *USA Direct* puts you in immediate contact with an English-speaking operator who can place your call. Simply step into the phone booth, dial *19+0011* to be connected with a telephone operator in the U.S. who is part of the AT&T system and give that operator the number in the U.S. to which you wish to be connected. If you are an AT&T card holder, you can charge the call to your card/designated phone. If you do not subscribe to the AT&T system, you can still use the service, for an additional fee, to call collect. MCI and Sprint have similar services. For information before you leave the U.S., contact your preferred long distance carrier.

AUTHOR'S OBSERVATION

Telephone numbers in this chapter are given for direct dial from the U.S., with the addition of the country code. When in France, you'll need to begin dialing out-of-town numbers with a "0."

La Poste is the post office, and it's usually near the railroad station. All communications services are offered, but not at all hours of the day. Be sure to inquire, if it matters. Many post offices have automatic purchase machines for stamps; the process may seem confusing if you're not familiar with the language and systems. When you see a post office that's open, stock up on stamps. Postcards to the U.S. cost FF3.40 for airmail.

DOCUMENTS AND OTHER PAPERS

You'll need only a passport for entry into the country. (For information on obtaining your passport, refer to "Passports" in the introduction.) For car rental, you'll need an international driver's permit, which can be obtained through your nearest *American Automobile Association* (AAA) office. Details are explained in the "transportation" coverage in the introductory chapter.

MEDICAL FACILITIES

Having your own medical insurance is a good idea for sportsfolk who expect to ski, climb, or participate in other super-active sports. Some credit card companies offer insurance programs and the medical associations mentioned under "Medical Facts" in the introduction will explain their services for France. There are good hospitals in the major cities and excellent clinics in or near some of the most popular ski resorts. Spas have specialists on call as well as doctors who are part of the spa administration. The socialist system of France means that residents are covered for medical services; charges for visitors vary. Speaking French helps, especially in smaller towns where doctors and others may not be fluent in English. In the Alpine area, there are full spa facilities for health and recuperative purposes at Aix-les-Bains, at Challes-les-Eaux near Chambéry, and some areas in the high mountains.

TRAVEL FACTS

"Club France," created by the French Government Tourist Office, is a membership organization. Members receive a Michelin *Red Guide* to France, a quarterly *France* magazine, a newsletter, discounts on some hotels and in some shops, coupons for special events and other surprises, plus an opportunity to win round-trip air tickets to Paris, a FrenchRail or rail-and-drive pass in a monthly drawing of names for special prizes. The cost for membership is $65 per year, of which $15 is earmarked as a contribution to an American Center in Paris. Ask the French National Tourist Office for details.

ARRIVAL

Air France, the national carrier, has frequent flights to Paris and, within France, to Lyon, Grenoble, and other major cities. **Air Inter** is a domestic carrier with flights to many of the smaller airports. Special prepurchased excursion tickets give good value if you are planning to make many short flights within France.

The high-speed **SNCF** TGV *(Train à Grande Vitesse)* puts Lyon within two hours of Paris and proceeds to Bourg Saint-Maurice, an Alpine train-link center, in 4-1/2 hours. There's also TGV service between Paris and Albertville, which was the pivot point for the 1992 Winter Olympics.

Lyon-Satolas is the most convenient international airport in France for reaching the French Alps. Switzerland's Genève has more convenient connecting service for the Haute Savoie, however, with bus and regional train services in addition to good roads. Grenoble may prove to be the best junction for the Dauphiné region, in the southern Alps. From Lyon, Grenoble, and Genève, inquire about bus services, especially during the ski season. For the Swiss connection, trains leave from Genève's main railroad station *(gare)* as well as from the Gare des Eaux Vives, a small station in a residential area on the south side of Lac Léman. (If you're traveling light and want to make the Genève link by public bus, ask for directions at the Genève Tourist Office in the main railroad station.)

AUTHOR'S OBSERVATION

Among the best values for touring France are the Flexi-Plan vacations offered through Jet Vacations, a tour company in the Air France family. Flexi-Meal plans allow for prepaid meals at a dollar-fixed price at specified restaurants and a Café Couette plan uses bed-and-breakfast places, at about $40 per night. Only a few plans apply for the Alpine region, but travel elsewhere in France can be linked with roaming in the Alps on your own. Ask your travel agent to give you the Jet Vacation's Flexi-Plan guide.

TOURING TIPS

France concentrates on speed, as seen with its pace-setting TGV trains, which stands for *Train à Grande Vitesse* and translates as "very fast train." The first TGV linked Paris and Marseilles in 1981; one of the newest routes linked Paris and Albertville for the 1992 Olympics. The TGV also links Paris and Lyon. High-speed highways also tie north-south destinations, as is the case with the A-6 and A-7 route, which stretches between Paris and Marseilles, following the Rhône Valley from Lyon south. (Several good roads in the A-40 series reach into the French Alpine area.) But getting from place to place within the Alpine region by public transportation, or on your own by road, is not always easy and/or efficient once the high-speed routes end. Think of it as an adventure. Many transportation schedules are seasonal, with reduced schedules in spring and fall and schedules in summer that are different from those in winter. Schedules also vary according to the days of the week.

AIR services to and within the entire country have been mentioned above. Although flying is the fastest way to get between some major city elsewhere in France or Europe to the Alps, driving is usually the most effective way to get from place to place within the area. A few resorts have small airstrips for private planes and helicopter service. Check with the local tourist offices for details.

BICYCLES are used by many, not only in the valleys and around the lakes but also high in the Alps. It's possible to rent bikes at some railroad stations, but check in advance if you want to be sure about what's available. The local tourist offices can put you in touch with private firms that rent bikes in towns you are visiting. (For further information, see "Bicycling" under "Sports," below.)

BOATS are a wonderful way to spend a day or days of leisure, not only on the lakes of the Alpine region but also on the rivers. Although not technically in the Alpine region, the Rhône River slices north-south along the western side; it was an important transportation link for travelers who headed east to the nearby Alps. River cruises can be a delightful partner for days in the Alps. The **French Cruise Lines** *(KD River Cruises, 2500 Westchester Ave., Purchase, NY 10577,* ☎ *914+696-3600 or 800+346-6525, FAX 914+696-0833; 323 Geary St., San Francisco, CA 94102,* ☎ *415+392-8817 or 800+ 858-8587, FAX 415+392-8868)* operates the 100-passenger *M.S. Arlene* between Macon, in vineyard-laden Burgundy, and through Avignon, historic city of Provence, on 7-night cruises from early April through October. Shipboard life is relaxed and comfortable, with noteworthy French cuisine, including specialties from Burgundy and Provence at mealtimes and daily excursions into surrounding countryside. (The chef is a member of the *Châine des Rotisseurs.*) The best of the spacious cabins have wide picture windows so you can enjoy the countryside from your nest.

BUSES are an easy and often convenient link between a major transportation hub and smaller places in its orbit, as well as for mountain towns from valley railroad stations. Many services are privately operated, at costs that vary depending on the time of year, length of journey, and, in some cases, whether the town is a tourist resort (higher cost) or a local village (more reasonable fares). Because it's not easy to get up-to-date local transportation schedules ahead of time, plan to spend a few minutes looking around when you arrive in a town. Many of my best "discoveries" have come as the result of hopping on some bus I saw waiting at the railroad station.

CARS may be the most effective means for travel in the French Alpine areas, especially with the highway systems put in place for the February '92 winter Olympics. However, in cities and towns, it's often difficult to find a good place to park. Rental cars are available at the airport at Lyon, from railway stations in Lyon, Grenoble and other cities or towns and at convenient locations elsewhere. One of the most effective car rental plans is the one offered by **Eurail**, where both train ticket (for longer distances) and car rental are included in one ticket. Information about the plan is available through **RailEurope** *(226-230 Westchester Ave., White Plains, NY 10607;* ☎ *914+682-2999 or 800+848-7245; FAX 914+682-8003).*

Plan your travel with careful thought to the fact that narrow roads are traffic-clogged at special holiday times, which can be winter weekends, summer vacation times (especially August) and other holidays. At such times, driving around an otherwise beautiful lake can become a nightmare. Schedule your driving in those areas for mid-week—or take public transportation.

All the internationally recognized car rental companies operate in France, in addition to many local ones that often have more reasonable rates. Speaking fluent French is almost essential if you're planning to use local firms. **Kemwel** *(106 Calvert St., Harrison, NY 10528-3199;* ☎ *800+678-0678; FAX 914+835-5449)* is one U.S.-based firm that often offers good values for rentals in the Alpine areas.

TRAINS are a wonderful way to travel in France, not only for speed, as is the case with the celebrated, pace-setting TGV modern ultraluxe trains, but also aboard some of the regional trains and a few that climb high into the mountains.

AUTHOR'S OBSERVATION

Making arrangements to ride French trains is a challenge if you want personal assistance. In the 1990s, the system in North America became, as I see it, mostly computerized, which means that when you phone you must punch a series of codes. In France, I've found some SNCF personnel to be very helpful; others seem annoyed by detailed questions. The better you know the timetables, the French system (and language) and the choices, the easier it will be to plot your travels. The alternative is to pay a premium for help through **RailEurope**, *a North American commercial venture.*

As one who enjoys riding the rails through small villages high into the mountains, I have some favorite rail excursions. Although all are pleasant at any time, obviously they're best on a clear day. The first, an easy one, is aboard the regional train that stretches between Switzerland's Genève and Annecy, in the Savoie region. The train starts (and finishes) at Genève's *Gare des Eaux Vives*, which is in a residential area across the lake from the city's main railway station. The route passes through farmlands and near lakes, offering many classic vignettes of rural life. A more dramatic journey is from St. Gervais, climbing up to Vallorcine (through Chamonix) and down to Martigny, in Switzerland, with a change of trains at the peak of the travels. A third noteworthy route is the *Chemin de Fer de la Mure*, between St. Georges-de-Commier and La Mure, through tunnels, along gorges and over bridged switch-backs along lakes and through forests, following a 20-mile (30-km) route. (This journey can easily be linked with the SNCF Grenoble-Veynes line, to St. Georges-de-Commiers to board the little red train for the climb.) Since none of the trains offers meal service, pack a picnic (or at least a sandwich and a beverage) for your travels.

DAILY LIVING

France is wonderfully, distinctively—sometimes infuriatingly—"French." Its lifestyle is its own and so are its daily patterns, even when French people seem to have adopted some of the shortcuts that started in the fast-paced U.S.A. *Joie de vivre* (joy of living) is a French phrase for good reason.

FOOD, WINE AND OTHER BEVERAGES

The region of the Rhône-Alps and the Savoie, plus the Mediterranean coast and Provence, is studded with exceptional restaurants, some of them quite simple and best known to folks who live in the area and others well known and on the cusp of becoming too commercial. Alpine areas yield some delicious cheeses, with wheels of mild and creamy *Reblochon* and slightly salty *Tomme de Savoie* two of my favorite market-day purchases. Although apples, peaches, and nuts are grown on Alpine slopes and in sun-washed valleys, the area closest to the Mediterranean yields the best crops. *Charcuterie* (sliced meats) of the Savoie are exceptional, especially as part of a picnic with some fresh-baked, crusty country bread. Count on finding a wide selection of flavorful sausages and dried meats, as well as poultry, pork, beef and lamb, served in several styles in local restaurants. Insofar as pastries are concerned, look for chardons from the Alps, especially in Annecy and Chamonix, and truffles are a specialty in Chambéry.

Lyon, and the towns and villages in its orbit, have hundreds of places to dine; most of them are exceptional. (The **Office du Tourisme**, on centrally located Pl. Bellecour, issues an annual booklet with names and addresses of many restaurants, listed according to district in the city.) Although choices are endless, some Lyonnaise specialties include *Rosette et Jesus*, the irreverent name of flavorful pork sausages; *Tablier de sapeur*, wherein tripe is cooked in white wine, with local herbs and plenty of garlic; and *Quenelles lyonnaises*, which can be made with all sorts of meat or vegetables in a baked custard consistency.

Raclette, from the French word "to scrape," is the delicious melted cheese, scraped from a half-wheel that's had its face to the fire. Served with small boiled potatoes, pungent pickles and tiny onions, the cheese dish is well known in the French Savoie region, as it is in Switzerland.

Vineyards festooned on the sunny Alpine slopes yield mostly white wines, many of them fruity, all of them crisp. "Vin de Savoie," as it is offered in many restaurants, can be white, red, or rose, sparkling or semi-sparkling and is often the choice of the patron, sometimes served from a carafe of the size you choose. It's worth noting that Evian mineral water is produced from Alpine glaciers and takes the name of the town on Lac Léman, tethered with several-times-daily boat links to Switzerland's Ouchy, the lakeside "suburb" of Lausanne.

LODGING

Among the thousands of places to stay there are some very special ones, but the extremes are far greater in France than in the German-speaking countries. In some of the recently developed ski areas all buildings are modern, with few reflections of the traditional chalet-style architecture that suggests "Alpine." Some resorts—notably Tignes and Les Arcs—are apartment-filled clusters of multi-story buildings.

APARTMENTS and **CHALETS** have become the vacation style for many Europeans, not only for the independence they offer but because they make it possible to control costs and are good choices for families and for groups of friends. Rentals are usually by the week, from Saturday to Saturday, but other time spans may be available depending on the time of year and the level of reservations. In many cases the units have been built recently and are especially for rental. Most are comfortably furnished, without some of the lavish "extras" that some North American time-shares and condos offer. **Interhome** *(124 Little Falls Rd., Fairfield, NJ 07004;* ☎ *201+882-6864; FAX 201+808-1742)* has listings of chalets, villas and condominiums for rent in Chamonix, Tignes, Val-Thorens and other communities in the French Alps, as does **Villas International** *(#510, 605 Market St., San Francisco, CA 94105;* ☎ *415+281-0910 or 800+221-2260; FAX 415+281-0919).*

CAMPING is very popular with the French and other Europeans. There are hundreds of sites throughout the Alpine area, especially the best known resort areas, where French people flock on their long, paid vacations. Among sources for information are the **Fédération de Camping for the Rhône Alpes** *(448 av. du Covet, L'Esplanade, F-73000 Chambéry),* or the **Fédération Française de Camping et de Caravaning** *(78 rue de Rivoli, F-75004 Paris;* ☎ *1+42.72.84.08, FAX 1+42.72.70.21).*

FARM VACATIONS are also popular with European families. The best sources for names and addresses are the local tourism offices and the Gîtes de France organization, which publishes a guide booklet showing pictures and giving facts about hundreds of gîtes throughout France. In the Alpine region ask about the **Gîtes Ruraux de Savoie** at the **Comite Regional du Tourisme Alpes Savoie Mont-Blanc** *(9 bd. Wilson, F-73100 Aix-les-Bains, France;* ☎ *79+88.23.41; FAX 79+35.66.14).* Although farms are not the only members, most gîtes are in rural areas. Each place is inspected in order to qualify for membership. If this kind of vacation appeals, it's a good idea to look around during one vacation to plan for your next. The printed information is not always as detailed as your own research can be.

HUTS and **MOUNTAIN HOTELS** are used mostly by hikers and climbers, but the mountain hotels that can be reached by cablecar, other public transportation or by a reasonable walk/hike offer exceptional holidays. Many of the mountain shelters are maintained by the **Club Alpin Français**. For a list of possibilities, contact the local offices or the **Gîtes Ruraux de Savoie** (See Farm Vacations, above).

INNS and **SMALL HOTELS** fleck the Alpine areas. Some can be quite exceptional, while others are more picturesque than comfortable. For lists of places at modest cost, contact the local tourism offices. Many of the most attractive (and expensive) places are members of the internationally respected **Relais & Châteaux** *(#707, 11 East 44th St. New York, NY 10017,* ☎ *212+856-0115 or 800+743-8003, FAX 212+856-0193),* an association of privately owned estate houses and other properties that are open for visitors. Properties considered for membership are well maintained in a traditional sense and often are historic buildings, with congenial multilingual management/owners and comfortable accommodations. Most members are in the luxury category, with exceptional regional cuisine.

LUXURY HOTELS, where personal comforts are tended by a well-trained staff, were staples of turn-of-the-century resorts, especially those along the Mediterranean coast, where many still thrive. These days the most luxurious accommodations are often offered at some of the inns and country hotels, especially those represented in North America by **Relais & Châteaux**, mentioned above. **Leading Hotels of the World** *(737 Third Ave., New York, NY 10017;* ☎ *212+838-3110 or 800+223-6800, FAX 212+758-7367)* is the North American arm of a Swiss-based company that represents privately owned properties with a common bond of classic style, refined service, elegance, and impressive cuisine. Among its members in Alpine France is the Royal Club Evian at Evian-les-Bains on Swiss-shared Lac Léman. French "luxury" hotels built in the past 20 years are huge, ultramodern holiday centers that attempt (and, some believe, succeed) to be all things to all guests. Thus you'll find swimming pools, bowling alleys, tennis courts, and many other activity centers, as well as big dining areas where service may not have the polish associated with traditional luxury. My favorites are mentioned below, with towns and places, under "Places Worth Finding."

AUTHOR'S OBSERVATION

Although skiers praise the no-nonsense, built-for-skiing focus of new resorts such as Les Arcs and Tignes, which have grown on prime ski slopes since 1972 (when Arc 1600 opened), these are not places noted for traditional Alpine atmosphere and "soul." The multi-story buildings hold modern apartments, often with small rooms and expensive restaurants.

SPAS appeal to the world's wealthy and, more recently, to the world's work-worn, for whom the restful days are an elixir. In addition to having specific health value, as is the case for spas devoted to work with arthritis, alcoholism or blood diseases, there are many spas that are known in Europe as "beauty farms," where weight loss, exercise and soothing-the-soul are prime features. In recent years, following a style known since the time of the Romans and enjoyed by Europe's aristocracy, many resort hotels have added spa facilities. Among the traditional spas in the Alpine area of France are Aix-les-Bains, Evian-les-Bains, and Annecy. All spas are accessible to anyone who can afford them.

YOUTH HOSTELS are known as *auberges de jeunesse*, but the **Gîtes d'Etape**, often very simple, inexpensive accommodations, can be of interest for budget travelers. Check with the tourist office for addresses and further information about both accommodations.

PLACES WORTH FINDING

There are hundreds of charming towns and villages in the Alpine area, but most are along the country roads, away from the best-known ski resorts, most of which have been built since the early 1960s. Although the new ski resorts are well-positioned for high Alpine skiing, most are huge and modern, without much traditional Alpine atmosphere. The valley villages that are away from the new highways and the Alpine communities that have not (yet) caught the eye of developers are still places worth finding, in my opinion. Many of the cities—Lyon, Annecy, Chambéry, for example—are living museums, with historic buildings alive with restaurants, museums and occasional inns.

The Tarentise area, reached from Albertville, includes Les Arcs, La Plagne, Tignes and Val d'Isère, which claims to be "the largest skiing area of such quality in the world."

The letters and numbers in parenthesis following place names refer to the postal code (F-00000) and the telephone number of the local tourist office (☎ 00+00.00.00). Telephone numbers are listed as they would be dialed from outside the country. When in France, all telephone numbers outside the local area should be preceded by a "0."

LES ARCS

Les Arcs *(F-73700; ☎ 79+07.73.73)* calls itself "the island of summits, in honor of its place among the peaks. Don't expect "quaint." This place is a forest of modern apartments and hotel rooms, planted amid the frothiest mountains, where 95 slopes have been groomed to accommodate ever increasing numbers of skiers and the *télépherique de l'Aguille Rouge* takes skiers, hikers, climbers and even sightseers to the top of the world in both winter and summer. Leaping into the spotlight for the 1992 Olympics speed-skiing events, Les Arcs is actually three "Arcs," each including its mountain height (in meters) in its name. Arc 2000, the highest (and newest) of the three, is at 2000 meters (6560 ft); Arc 1800 faces Mont Blanc valley, and family-oriented Arc 1600, the first built, is reached by funicular out of Bourg St. Maurice. For skiing and plenty of other sports, consider this; for Alpine charm, head elsewhere.

AIX-LES-BAINS

Aix-les-Bains *(Syndicat d'Initiative, Pl. Maurice-Mollard, BP 111, F-73101; ☎ 79+35.05.92)*, in Savoie, rising up the hillside from Lac du Bourget, was known to the Romans more than 2000 years ago, when they enjoyed the therapeutic springs that are still an important part of the town's appeal. Although the town is larger and busier than you may expect, relief comes with Lac du Bourget, measuring about 2 miles (31-1/4 km) by 11 miles (18 km), which claims to be the largest body of water in France. Spreading out and up from the southeast shore of Lac du Bourget, the most interesting part of town is its center, with the Roman ruins incorporated into the 20th-century commerce. The *gare* is midway up the hill, requiring a walk (or bus ride) down to the lake or up to the tourism office and the spa. Focal points are the **Thermes Nationaux**, punctuated with what's left of the Arc de Campanus (which seems to me to be overwhelmed by modern tourism); the **Hôtel de Ville** nearby, in a lovely 16th-century château that was once privately owned; the **Nouveau Casino**, in the Palais de Savoie, which was "modernized" in dreary style in 1936, although the original building dates from 1848; and the lovely parks and lake. The spa area is regarded by some as a fashionable equal to spas at Baden-Baden (Germany) and Vichy, especially at the height of season.

Allow time for the **Musée Faure** *(blvd. des Cotes)*, where the once private collection of Dr. Faure has been joined by some later acquisitions. The Impressionist collection includes works by Cezanne, Pissaro, Corot and Degas; the collection of Rodin sculptures is second only to those in the Paris collection that bears his name. Also in the museum are memorabilia of Alphonse de Lamartine, famed French poet, who took the cure in Aix when he was 26, in 1816-17, and wrote *Le Lac*, which you can buy on postcards and posterboard. Also worth some time is the **Musée d'Archeologie et de Prehistoire**, in the Temple of Diana, which holds many of the Roman artifacts found in the area.

The lakeside setting has been hemmed in by a busy highway and modern marinas, making it difficult to find places for quiet walks. Check the schedule for boat trips, which can take you away from the most heavily developed areas. Grand-Port is the departure point for boat trips. (Summer concerts are occasionally held by the lake. Check the tourism office for the program.)

Abbaye de Hautecombe, a Benedictine abbey since the Middle Ages, is one popular touring goal, even though the monks recently left the abbey for a place in the remote Durance Valley. (The area's tourism and other commerce drove them away; with them went the opportunity to hear their Gregorian chant at Sunday Mass.) The abbey's Grange Bateliere dates from the 12th century; the site holds the remains of 42 members of the House of Savoie, including Umberto II, the last king of Italy, who was buried here in 1983.

LODGING: Choices in and around Aix are many, but one special spot is **Le Manoir** *(72 rooms; 37 rue George 1er;* ☎ *79+61.44.00)*, a member of the *Relais du Silence*, with a good restaurant and cozy surroundings. It's an uphill stroll from the main square, in a quiet area. **Ruffieux**, just north of Aix, has another noteworthy member of the *Relais du Silence*, the **Château de Collognes** *(10 rooms;* ☎ *79+62.27.38)*.

Le Bourget-au-lac, across the lake, has a hideaway haven called **Ombremont** *(18 rooms;* ☎ *79+25.00.23)*, with the atmosphere of an elegant pool-punctuated private home on the hillside and a lovely view of the lake. Pleasant for walks in nearby woods and along the lake, the inn is also near a charming small restaurant, **Le Bateau Ivre** (☎ *79+25.02.66)*, nearer the lake and not far from a couple of tennis courts.

AUTHOR'S OBSERVATION

Exploring the hillsides, where there are some delightful inns and lovely views, can fill several days. The Reserve Nationale des Bauges is near enough to be a pleasant excursion for walks and hikes.

ALBERTVILLE

Albertville *(F-73200;* ☎ *79+32.04.22)*, in Savoie, at a wide place on the floor of Val d'Arly in the Rhône-Alpes, was a dreary working-class town when it was selected as the headquarters for the 1992 Olympics. Established by King Charles Albert in 1845, for its location in relation to the Alpine passes, the town had become little more than a highway crossroad in recent times. But by late 1990, the metamorphosis began, first with the opening of the Olympic Center, on a side street in the center of town, and soon thereafter with the start of the new Halle de Glace, for the Olympic '92 skating competitions. On a more meaningful level for residents and visitors, fall of '90 brought new sidewalks and the start of improved shop stock from items for the working-class residents to classier items to lure the expected influx of international visitors.

Since SNCF was a major sponsor for the Olympics, the *gare* received a total facelift, and service by the TGV. It continues to be a hub, not only for trains from Lyon and elsewhere, but also for bus services that set out from its parking lot. Buses make the 4-hour journey between Chamonix and Grenoble, stopping at Albertville and several other places (including Megève). There's also private jitney service from here to Mègeve (see below).

Conflans, the medieval fortified city on the hillside, has been Albertville's greatest asset for visitors, before Olympic fame. A chip on the mountainside when viewed from the main street of Albertville, the village is a warren of narrow winding streets, fringed with 16th-century buildings that now hold craft shops and tiny restaurants. When you look down over the Arly and Isère rivers, it's obvious why this location was selected by those interested in controlling medieval trading routes. Stroll along the Grand' Rue, allowing some time to visit the **Maison Rouge**, which holds the museum of local Savoyard history. Note especially the 17th-century pulpit in the church. Arriving by car is easiest, although there is bus service and athletic folks may enjoy the walk in spite of the fact that portions of the route are on a road shared with the traffic.

LODGING: The one exceptional inn, **Restaurant Million** *(12 rooms;* ☎ *79+32.25.15)*, is worth finding for an exceptional meal or, if you want to visit Conflans (see below) a good choice for an overnight. The public rooms on the main floor are nicely furnished with antiques. Bedrooms are comfortable; they vary in size and shape. The ones on the front have a nice view over town, but may be noisy with traffic.

ANNECY

Annecy *(F-74000, Centre Bonlieu;* ☎ *50+45.00.33; FAX 50+ 51.87.20)*, in the Haute Savoie, east of Lyon and south of Genève, is a gem with a lovely lake and a delightful medieval section that is full of good restaurants, pleasant small hotels and interesting shops. The town is at its best during the Sunday and Tuesday morning markets and at the Saturday antique market, held on the last Saturday of each month when stalls are set up in the open air, under the arches and elsewhere along the narrow streets of the medieval part of town.

Respected as the "Ville d'art et d'histoire" by the Caisse Nationale des monuments historiques et des sîtes, the dozens of buildings stretch ribbonlike along the canals, cut from the lake into the town. The **Château d'Annecy** nests on a hilltop, like a chicken over its eggs. Its Cour d'Honneur, the center courtyard, tells a story of four centuries, with the Logis Nemours dating from 1565, its Vieux Logis dating from the 13th century when the Counts of Geneva used this as their residence, to the Grand Pele, stone columns that support the first floor Grande Salle where Henry IV and Louis XIII were welcomed in 1630 and the Logis Perriere, with its tower, dating from the late 15th century. The **Musée du Château** *(*☎ *50+45.29.66)* fills the first three floors of the Logis Nemour, with displays about the natural history of the Alps and some rotating exhibits.

Two other small museums worth some time are the **Musée Sale-sian** *(*☎ *50+45.20.30)*, documenting the history of St. François de Sales and Ste. Jeanne de Chantal, and the **Musée Palais de l'Isle** *(*☎ *50+45.29.66)*, with displays pertinent to the history of Annecy.

Although modern commerce, language and other schools, and general prosperity has marked the landscape at the north end of town (and the lake), visitors who arrive by train or bus can walk from the railroad station, with the tracks at their back and be in the delightful *vieille ville* (old city) in a matter of minutes.

Annecy, France

When the weather is pleasant, lakeboats depart for excursions from the Quai du Thiou. Although some journeys are nonstop routes (for about an hour's circuit), there are also mealtime boat trips where good food is served in style as you glide around the scenic lake and trips that stop at docks around the lake. Boat service is frequent during summer and other warm-weather weekends. (See "Lac d'Annecy," below.)

LODGING: Among the many places to stay in and near the vieille ville, I have been happy at the **Hotel Carlton** *(55 rooms; 5 rue des Gliéres;* ☎ *50+45.47.75)*, not only because it is an easy walk from the railroad station and the lake, but also because I can dip into the *vieille ville* to enjoy the many restaurants and other activities. Rooms are comfortable, with private bath and traditional style. Also in the area are charming, small **Palais de l'Isle** *(23 rooms; 13 rue Perriére;* ☎ *50+45.86.87)* and the smaller, very simple **Auberge du Lyonnais** *(9 rooms; 14 quai évêche;* ☎ *50+51.26.10)*. The small **Coin Fleuri** *(3 rue Filaterie; 14 rooms;* ☎ *50+45.27.30)*, in a medieval building in the vieille ville, could be ideal, if you speak French. For standard services, try **Ibis** *(83 rooms; 12 rue de Gare;* ☎ *50+45.43.21)*, a French chain's group-oriented hotel, where the staff speaks fluent English.

RESTAURANTS: The narrow streets of Vieille Annecy are flecked with cozy restaurants, where food is often good and surroundings always are. One of my favorites is Jean Burnet's small restaurant, simply called **John** *(10 rue Perriere;* ☎ *50+51.36.15)*, where reservations are essential for the few tables, unless you want to take a chance on dining when the place opens (about 6 p.m.). **Auberge du Lyonnais**

(14 quai de l'évêche; ☎ *50+51.26.10)* is another one of the dozens of restaurants that I've tried and liked. The café tables set on the sidewalk are pleasant on warm evenings. People-watching is a favorite pastime in Annecy, where tourists flock during warm weather days.

A few miles from Annecy, **Alby sur Chernan** *(F-74540;* ☎ *50+ 68.10.10)* is worth finding for the charming **Musée de la Cordonnerie**, which you may visit by calling ahead to make an appointment for the mayor to open the doors.

Lac d'Annecy has lured devotees for centuries. In spite of the rampant expansion and modern commerce in parts of Annecy, most of the lakeside is pristine and picture-perfect. Fringed with enough inns to keep life interesting, the shore can be webbed by boats from Annecy's Quai de Thiou, by car, by public bus (departing on regular schedules from the gare) or by foot. Towns around the lake include **Sevrier**, **Saint Jorioz**, and **Duingt** on the west shore and **Chavoires**, **Veyrier** (at the point where the road starts its climb to La Clusaz), **Menthon Saint Bernard**, and **Talloires**. (See "Talloires," below.)

CHAMBÉRY

Chambéry *(F-73000;* ☎ *79+33.42.47)*, in the Savoie region, south of Aix-les-Bains and east of Lyon, is a happy surprise to those who may not know its history. As the capital of the Savoie when the region was an independent state, the town's **Place St. Léger** is remarkable not only for the Italian style of its buildings and the threadlike *trajes* (narrow lanes) that stretch from the square, but also for the restaurants and other sources for activity tucked into alcoves and on the square itself. The square is at its best on market days, but arrive early in the morning to enjoy the best produce and activity.

The **château**, on one side of Place St. Léger, serves as the prefecture, but is opened at specified times for tours with a guide. Although most of the building dates from the 18th and early 19th centuries, parts are from the 14th and 15th centuries, when it was home for the Dukes of Savoie.

La Fontaine des éléphants gets a lot of press but, frankly, it's surrounded by traffic and difficult to enjoy unless you pass by very early in the morning or late in the day, after shops have closed. Commemorating a wealthy patron, the Comte de Boigne (who gave his considerable fortunes from trade in the Indies to the building of the town), the fountain's four huge elephant heads are distinctive—and so is the fact that they have no bodies, which gave rise to the nickname "les quatre-sans-culs" that translates as "the four with no bottoms."

The nearby **Musée Savoisien** is worth visiting, as much for the Franciscan convent in which it is housed as for the relics displayed. Most have been found around Lac du Bourget and in nearby areas. It's next to the former Franciscan church, built in 15th-century Gothic style, that is now **Cathédral de St. François de Sales**.

Those who follow the travels of Jean-Jacques Rousseau will want to make a pilgrimage to the house of Madame de Warens, where he lived from 1736 to 1742. It's near the *Parc de Lémenc*, not far from the railroad station.

Worth considering for a few days to use as a touring base, Chambéry is a delightful market town with plenty of history and an active daily life. While its *vieille ville* is pleasant and cozy, in spite of some touristy places along some of the narrow lanes, the sourrounding areas offer a full range of sports, from golf and swimming to hiking, climbing, and mountain activities that are easily reached by train as well as bus or car. The spa at **Challes-les-Eaux**, between Chambéry and Aix-les-Bains, specializes in treatment of respiratory ailments.

LODGING: The **Hôtel des Princes** *(45 rooms; 4 rue de Boigne;* ☎ *79+33.45.36; FAX 79+70.31.47)* is conveniently located at the fringe of the old town, amidst the shops and commerce of the new. Maintaining a traditional style, rooms have modern comforts, even when small.

AUTHOR'S OBSERVATION

The town's a worthy halting place on its own merits, but it's also a good source for difficult-to-find facts about the region. Check for opening hours of the Maison du Tourisme *(24 blvd. de la Colonne;* ☎ *79+85.12.45), and plan to visit for information prepared by* L'Union Departémentale des Offices de Tourisme et Syndicats d'Initiative de la Savoie, *which are the tourism offices in areas bordering the Parc National.*

CHAMONIX MONT BLANC

Chamonix Mont Blanc *(F-74400;* ☎ *50+53.00.24)* is a mountain village with a long history of tourism. Recent developments, however, have paved most of the center of the former village, which is now split by both an elevated highway and the river Arve. The river flows along a huge, man-made trough that controls its path through the town when the snow melts to flood potential in the spring. Although popularity has dressed the once-small village in layers of newer buildings, the traditional Alpine architecture is often used and the atmosphere can be classy, fun, and occasionally elegant. No one has yet

destroyed the views of the mountains, including L'Aiguille Verte, le
Brévent, and les Drus. Because of its height, Chamonix often has
snow when other regions may not and is a training place for expert
climbers and skiers. The town has always had Mont Blanc and the
exhilarating **Vallée Blanche**, an 11-mile (17.71-km) ski run that
starts near the top of the impressive 12,601-foot (3842-m) Aiguille
du Midi. A cableway makes it possible even for nonskiers and non-
hikers to enjoy the scenery and sensation. The resort nestles in a valley bowl, spreading out to include newer Chamonix Les Praz and
Chamonix Les Tines, valley neighbors.

AUTHOR'S OBSERVATION

*One memorable fête is the annual Alpine Guides' Festival, held on August
15. Hosts are the mountain guides from La Bérarde and Chamonix who
entertain guides from all around Europe with the hoopla focused on traditional Alpine food, dances, games and costumes.*

Spend some time with a map to get your bearings and, summer or
winter, head out into nearby areas, preferably by car for independence, although buses do link the several parts of the town and you
can get to the Mer de Glace aboard the narrow-gauge cog-railway's
red trains that leave from the *gare superieure du Montenvers*, which is
reached by a walkway, up and over the tracks from the main railway.
Worth doing once for sightseeing and more often if you're a skier or
serious hiker, the view over the Mer de Glace (glacier) and les
Grandes Jorassess when you reach the top can be magnificent on a
day when the weather is.

AUTHOR'S OBSERVATION

*Don't count on much in the way of food from the cafeteria at the top, the
only place to eat if the nearby hotel is closed. The sun terrace off the cafeteria is a great place to pause, but bring your own snacks or a picnic.*

The Mer de Glace is the second largest glacier in the Alps, stretching from the Geant (giant) glacier for almost 10 miles (14 km). Two
Englishmen, Popock and Windham, reached this spot in 1741, a
mule track made excursions possible from 1802 and the railway
opened in 1909. The walk down from the top, following a trail that
flirts with the railway route, takes almost three hours, if you'd prefer
that to taking the return train.

In town, the **Musée Alpin** (☎ *50+53.25.93*), in the former Hôtel le Palace, has displays documenting the 17th and 18th centuries in the valley.

LODGING: There are dozens of places to stay but, with its view of Mont Blanc and Pierre Carrier's culinary expertise (which earns him many accolades), the **Albert 1er** (*32 rooms;* ☎ *50+53.05.09*) has a devoted following, in spite of the fact that a recently-built elevated highway passes near the second floor windows. Built on the northern side of the village, the inn, which has been in the Carrier family for almost 100 years, now includes discreet additions of a swimming pool, tennis court, whirlpool and solarium. Every effort has been made to fill each room with traditional Alpine furnishings, decor, and atmosphere. Among my other favorites is the elegant **Auberge du Bois Prin** (*11 rooms;* ☎ *50+53.33.51*), a member of the *Relais & Châteaux*, with traditional style set by Monique and Denis Carrier and high standards (and price). From its mountainside setting, a steep walk up from the village shops and action, it offers a superb view of Mont Blanc. One of the best-known hotels, especially as a popular cocktail-time gathering spot, is the **Hotel Mont Blanc** (*50 rooms;* ☎ *50+53.05.64*), with its heated pool. Just across the road from the railroad station, the **Gustavia** (*47 rooms;* ☎ *50+53.00.31; FAX 50+55.86.39*) has celebrated its 100th birthday and maintains a traditional atmosphere, offering comfortable lodgings at reasonable cost. Rooms on the fourth floor front side have a good mountain view. Also worth considering is the recently built **Hotel des Aiglons** (☎ *50+53.02.32*), where many rooms have a bird's-eye view of surrounding mountains. **Hotel le Labrador** (*32 rooms;* ☎ *50+55.90.09; FAX 50+53.15.85*) sits at the edge of the golf course, in grand style, attending to the comforts and wishes of discerning guests. For apartment accommodations, inquire about **Les Jardins du Mont Blanc** (*50 studios, 1-, 2- and 3-brm. apts;* ☎ *50+53.08.53; U.S. 800+366-1510*), a large complex in the heart of town.

RESTAURANTS: Among the many atmospheric places to dine, with exceptional preparation and presentation, in addition to **Pierre Carrier's Albert 1er**, is **Atmosphere** (☎ *50+55.97.97*), next to the Arve River, sharing a corner of the post office building. Specialties include raclette, fondue and other Alpine favorites, as well as tastefully prepared fish, veal and poultry dishes.

From Chamonix, it's about 20 minutes' drive, passing through the Mont Blanc tunnel (F135 for a day pass) to the lovely village of ***Entreves*** in Italy, where the granite houses lean against their neighbors along the narrow streets of the village and the pricey **Pilier d'Angle** is one place to stay. **La Maison de Filippo** *(☎ 165+899.68)* is a popular, classy place to dine, but there are several other choices along the narrow streets.

LA CHAPELLE D'ABONDANCE

La Chapelle d'Abondance *(F-74360; ☎ 50+73.51.41)*, south of Evian-les-Bains and Lac Léman, is a small village worth a pause. Check at the tourist office for entrance to **Le Museoterre**, to view the collection of arts, crafts and other tokens from the livelihood of the region. Artifacts and implements have been collected from nearby farms; people have donated skis, toys and other items from earlier, simpler times.

CHENS SUR LÉMAN

Chens sur Léman *(F-74140; ☎ 50 +26.17.22)*, another small village not far from the lake, near Thonon-les-Bains, has a **Musée de Milouti** *(☎ 50+94.01.49)*, in the Granges de Servette, which is a typical Savoyard barn, with more than 1000 tools and implements used for the traditional work of the Bas Chablais region. Lodging: For overnight in the village, try the tiny **Ecaille d'Argent** *(7 rooms; ☎ 50+94.04.16)* at Port de Tongues.

CLUSAZ

Clusaz *(F-74220; ☎ 50+02.60.92)*, a once small village that has been "buried" with an avalanche of new buildings, is mentioned primarily for its winter and summer skiing, plus walking, hiking and other mountain activities. Reached easily by public bus from Annecy, the resort is popular with families. Buildings cluster at the site of the original village, in a tumble of construction in, over and around the river that passes through the area.

LODGING: Tops, for a small spot convenient to one of the bus stops, is the newly rebuilt (on an old site) **Alp' Hotel** *(11 rooms; ☎ 50+02.40.06)*, which you can reach by walking down the steps, across the road from the bus stop. A town-operated ski bus makes regular routes past all hotels to take sportsfolk to the base station for the lifts to reach the best slopes.

If your French is top-notch, the **Pasquier family's farm**, on the outskirts of the village, offers rooms for rent on a Chambre d'Hôtes basis *(5 rooms, F-74470 Bellevaux; ☎ 50+73.71.92)*.

COURCHEVAL

Courcheval *(F-73120; ☎ 79+08.00.29; FAX 79+08.33.54)*, in Les Trois Vallées area of the Savoie Alps, is a conglomerate, with developments at five altitudes and a total of more than 50 hotels, 200 ski lifts, 450 multilingual ski instructors, 65 restaurants and 1992 Olympic fame as the site for Nordic events and ski jumping. The area boasts the fact that "250 snow canons produce fresh natural snow." The charming resort known in 1946 has been wrapped in modern trappings that have changed its traditional personality. Choices these days, starting from the top, are totally modern Courcheval 1850; Courcheval 1650, which swallowed up the hamlet of Moriond; Courcheval 1550, with a family focus; Le Praz, where some of the Savoyard traditions can be glimpsed, and Saint-Bon, where the lower altitude leads to a less frenetic pace and the one hotel mentioned by the tourism folks is the simple **Allobroges** *(9 rooms; ☎ 79+08.10.15).*

Skiing or hiking the neighboring **Vallée des Allues** (noted for Méribel and Mottaret) or the **Vallée des Belleville** (with Les Menuires and Val Thorens) is one reason for heading here and tourism is the area's reason for being. The few original buildings of the village have long been buried in new construction, most of it French-popular hotels and apartments. Comforts are assured, but don't expect much Savoyard-original atmosphere.

LODGING: As a member of *Relais & Châteaux*, **Pralong 2000** *(72 rooms; ☎ 79+08.24.82)* deserves mention. The multi-story shoebox is best enjoyed from inside, where the view from your balcony can be spectacular. Sister-member **Hôtel des Neiges** *(58 rooms; ☎ 79+08.03.77)* also has a multi-story shoebox construction, with balcony views. A conveniently located newcomer is the **Hôtel des Grandes Alpes** *(40 rooms; ☎ 79+08.03.85 or U.S. 800+366-1510)*, above the classy Galerie du Diament shopping center, but my personal vote goes to **Lana** *(76 rooms and suites; ☎ 79+08.01.10)*, with its modern-comfortable chalet style.

DIVONNE-LES-BAINS

Divonne-les-Bains *(F-01220; ☎ 50+20.01.22)*, with a view of Mont Blanc over Lac Léman, within minutes of Switzerland's Gèneve, is a classic resort with a European-style casino (a social center, not a gamblers' pit) and its attendant park. Within its orbit, at the lake, are two exceptional Swiss treasures, the town of Nyon and Mme. de Stäel's Château at Coppet (see "Places Worth Finding" in the Switzerland chapter). Worth visiting for lunch or overnight, when your plane arrives or departs from nearby Genéve or for longer if you want to enjoy the luxuries of the good life, the **Château de Divonne** *(23 rooms; ☎ 50+20.00.32)* fills an elegantly restored 19th-century estate house with the trappings of luxury living, including a good restaurant. The hotel is a member of *Relais & Chateaux.*

EVIAN-LES-BAINS

Evian-les-Bains *(F-74502; ☎ 50.75.04.26),* in Haute Savoie, on the south shore of Lac Léman, is bigger than many visitors expect. Although it is linked by boat from Switzerland's lakeside community at Ouchy below hillside Lausanne, the town climbs the hill from its pleasure-boat-fringed shore, providing easy access to the foothills of the Chablais pre-Alpine area. The maison du lac is the heart of the nautical activity, which is at full tilt as soon as the weather warms and well beyond the time of the first fall chill.

LODGING: Three prized accommodations are very different in setting and presentation, although all are luxurious and typical of the area. The **Royal Club Evian** *(158 rooms; ☎ 50+75.14.00 or U.S. 212+838-7874),* originally built in classic late 18th-century resort style, was restored and rejuvenated to offer a full roster of 21st-century amenities. **La Verniaz** *(35 rooms; ☎ 50+75.04.90)* nestles into the countryside at Neuvecelle, just off the appropriately named route d'Abondance. The swimming pool can be refreshing after walks along the shores of Lac Léman or in the mountains. For less luxurious lodgings, there are a dozen campsites around Evian, and almost 100 hotels within the town. **Hotel les Pres Fleuris sur Evian** *(12 rooms; ☎ 50+75.29.14)* is tucked into an orchard, off a spur road leading to hillside **Thollon**. Ideal for walks and hikes, the inn takes its cue from Savoyard farmhouses, but offers every comfort for its guests. Both La Verniaz and Pres Fleuris are members of *Relais & Châteaux.*

GRENOBLE

Grenoble *(F-38000; ☎ 76+54.34.36),* the capital of the Dauphiné region, is a big and busy city, cut by the Isère and the Drac rivers and surrounded by several villages that offer the contrast of a rural, quiet atmosphere. Yanked to the sport spotlight by the 1968 Winter Olympics and to international fame for its impressive science and energy research, the city's fascination for some of us is as the birthplace (in 1783) of Henri Beyle, better known as Stendahl, author of French psychological novels including *Le Rouge et Le Noir.*

For an introduction to the city, head for Place Victor Hugo and walk around between that square and Place Grenette, a residential area with some charm. Make your way toward the Isère to find the **Musée Stendahl**, in the former Hôtel de Ville, to enjoy memorabilia from Beyle's time participating in campaigns of the Napoleonic wars and his later life in Italy. Cross the Isère to spend some time at the **Musée Dauphinois**, not only for its site (in a 17th-century convent) but also for the exhibits of history and handcrafts of the Dauphiné region. Then go back across the Isère to take the Télépherique up to the Fort de la Bastille for a wonderful view over the city and its surroundings. The **Musée de l'Automobile** (old cars) may interest some; I prefer to stroll around, sample something at the restaurant and eventually walk down to town along the well-marked path. For further diversions, the **Musée de Peinture et de Sculpture** on Place de Verdun holds a noteworthy collection of French Impressionists and other artists as well as an Egyptian collection; its gallery of contemporary art and research features what's on the mind of Grenoblians today.

LODGING: South of Grenoble, at the southern end of the A-48 highway, and at the other extreme from the city for atmosphere, the **Relais l'Escale** *(F-38761 Varces; 7 chalets;* ☎ *76+72.80.19)* will be a surprise to those prepared to speed by. Noted for its restaurant, the Relais is at the foot of the Vercours mountains, which can be nice for walking.

LYON

Lyon *(Comité Regional du Tourisme, 5 pl. de la Baleine, F-69005;* ☎ *78+42.50.04),* at the confluence of the Saône and the Rhône rivers, is a big, bustling city with a big, beautiful heart and some of the best chefs in France. This second-largest city of France (after Paris) deserves as much time as you can give it, for Vieux Lyon, wedged against the hillside west of the Saône, for the restaurants and buildings around Place Bellecour on the narrow peninsula made by la Saône and le Rhône before they join, and for the dozens of unpretentious but exceptional chef-owned restaurants scattered in and around its borders. Although Lyon is a big city, the atmosphere in its various neighborhoods has a small-town quality when you carve the city into walkable portions. In addition to the two-dozen-plus museums, the parks and squares are entertaining with cafés that fleck the sidewalks with chairs and tables as soon as the weather warms. For more rural pleasures, residents (and smart visitors) head to the **Parc de la Tête-d'Or**, near the Palais des Congres Internationaux, on the east bank of le Rhône, north of the city center, for strolling or bicycling or bench-sitting.

Although walking along the streets in the oldest part of the city or taking the funicular from the station near Pont de Bonaparte up to Basilique de Fouviere can yield untold pleasures, Lyon has dozens of exceptional museums, galleries, craft centers and stores. My favorite touchstones, even when time is limited, are the **Musée Historique des Tissus et des Arts Decoratifs** *(30 rue de la Charite;* ☎ *78+37.25.05)*, for its exceptional exhibits of the silk-making that gave this city early prominence and for the early pictures and other items from historic Lyon, and the **Musée Historique de Lyon** *(Pl. du Petit-College;* ☎ *78+42.03.61)*, which shares its address with the charming **Musée de la Marionette**. Both are on a bulge of land wrapped by la Saône, just in from Quai Romain Rolland.

AUTHOR'S OBSERVATION

If you'd like a local guide to walk you through the considerable art, architecture, historic sites, crafts or something else, contact the Bureau des Guides (5 pl. Saint-Jean; ☎ *78+42.25.75) for an English-speaking person and a planned itinerary.*

The city's most important museum is the **Musée des Beaux-Arts** in the Palais Saint-Pierre *(Pl. des Terreaux;* ☎ *78+28.07.66)*, with its 19th- and 20th-century art as well as the Flemish and Dutch paintings. The cloister and the former palace are worth noting in their own right.

AUTHOR'S OBSERVATION

The Marche de la Creation and the philatelist's market on Place Belle- cour, with a stroll past the antique shops along rue Auguste-Comte to Place Carnot, make Sundays special in Lyon. The Marche is held on the Romain-Rolland quai, on the west bank of la Soane river, where stalls are filled with regional crafts and other items. People-watching can be as much fun as purchasing and pausing to enjoy the local atmosphere at cafés.

Lyon has two major railroad stations, gare de Perrache, on the pen- insula, just south of Vieux Lyon's Place Bellecour, and gare la Part-Dieu, east of le Rhône in the newer part of the city. Both trains and the new Alpine tunnel link the city easily with Paris and other cities as well as nearby villages.

LODGING: The **Hotel Royal** *(80 rooms; 20 pl. Bellecour;* ☎ *78+37.57.31, FAX 78+37.01.36)* is ideally located for exploring the city, claiming a prominant corner of the city's most important square. The small **Hotel Bayard** *(15 rooms; 23 pl. Bellecour;* ☎ *78+37.39.64, FAX 72+40.95.51)*, upstairs, with pension style, is its cozy neighbor. The **Hotel des Savoies** *(46 rooms; 80 rue de la Charité;* ☎ *78+37.66.94, FAX 72+40.27.84)*, in the Perrache district, not far from the railroad station, is more modestly priced. The recently refurbished **Hotel Pullman** *(124 rooms; 12 cours de Verdun;* ☎ *78+37.58.11, FAX 78+37.06.56)*, in an older building, to the left as you walk out of Perrache station, is comfortably modern. To the right, also in an older building, the **Hotel Bristol** *(113 rooms; 28 cours de Verdun;* ☎ *78+37.56.55)* has more modest rates. For a reasonably comfortable apartment in the Part-Dieu area, contact **Résidence Hôtelière les Citadines** *(91–95 rue Moncey;* ☎ *78+62.12.12, FAX 78+60.50.74)*.

RESTAURANTS: This city is a renowned center of gastronomy, not only for the restaurants within its borders, but also for the many highly-respected places in the surrounding countryside. Conveniently located in the center of Lyons, the rue des Marronniers, which runs parallel to Place Bellecour not far from the Hotel Royal, is bordered by wonderful restaurants. **Chabert & Fils** *(*☎ *78+37.01.94)* is one of the best. Others to consider are tiny **La Mère Jean** *(*☎ *78+37.81.27)* and **Du Côté de Chez Thom** *(*☎ *72+41.93.31)*. Although Tunisian and other styles are making inroads, this short street gains fame for lyonnaise specialties.

AUTHOR'S OBSERVATION

A bistro in Lyon is known as a bouchon, which translates literally as "cork-stopper." A leisurely meal in any one of several bouchons can go a long way toward making you feel "at home."

Among the many special spots where mealtimes are an occasion are three members of the *Relais & Châteaux*: **Nandron** *(26 quai Jean-Moulin;* ☎ *78+42.10.26)* near the Rhône river; **Pierre Orsi** *(3 pl. Kleber;* ☎ *78+89.57.68)*, with flowers cascading out of its window-boxes as soon as weather warms; and the cozy **Léon de Lyon** *(1 rue Pléneg;* ☎ *78+28.11.33)*, not far from Place des Terreaux, where special emphasis is given to Lyonnaise traditions in service.

About 21 miles (38 km) from Lyon, in *La Tour de Pin*, **Le Château** *(43 rooms;* ☎ *74+97.42.52)* offers life as it is should be lived, with an elegant castlelike manor house set in the countryside, blissfully removed from the pattern of commerce not far away. A member of the *Relais & Châteaux*, this is a lovely place to relax.

MEGÈVE

Megève *(F-74120;* ☎ *50+21.27.28)*, brought into social circles by the Baroness de Rothchild in the 1920s and still classy, is high in the mountains and blissfully atmospheric. In spite of the fact that most of the buildings are new, the village has a traditional style, with wood chalets prevailing. Jet-set chic in mid-winter, Megève can be pleasant at all times of the year, even at the traditional fall-closing-refurbishing time, when the community is best known only to its townfolk. (The social calendar, with concerts and other events, is fullest in mid-winter or mid-summer.)

Reached by car or jitney bus service up and out from Albertville or by car on a serpentine road, the town is one of my favorites and the ride is spectacular when the weather is.

Convenient, in the center of the village, the **Musée du Haut-Val d'Arly** *(173 rue St. François;* ☎ *50+21.42.10)* displays objects used in Alpine life and costumes in a small farmhouse that dates from 1809, while the **Musée de Megève** *(*☎ *50+21.21.01),* tucked into a traditional chalet-style building, shows 100 years of history of Alpine guides and life. Fashion's best names fill the many boutiques and are worn on many of the high-season visitors. The **Casino** is a central place for events and entertainment; don't expect gambling chips in the Las Vegas sense.

LODGING: Among my favorite places to stay is the cozy **Alpina** *(14 rooms;* ☎ *50+21.54.77),* convenient on the place du Casino, in the heart of town. **Le Fer à Cheval** *(Chemin du Crêt d'Arbois;* ☎ *50+21.30.39),* above the village, is a lovely, small chalet hotel, with cozy rooms, and a dazzling swimming pool for use when weather warrants. Isabelle and Marc Sibuet are hosts. **Au Coin du Feu** *(25 rooms;* ☎ *50+21.04.94),* is a Savoyard-style chalet hotel perched on the mountainside, on route du Télépherique de Rochebrune, with a sensational view of Mont-Blanc. Slightly above the village center, it's a pleasant walker's goal for dinner as well as a lovely place to stay.

For a very special holiday, plan to visit **Les Fermes de Marie** *(40 rooms, 5 suites;* ☎ *50+93.03.10; FAX 50+93.09.84; US 800+366-1510),* on Chemin de Riante Colline. Staying here is a unique, wonderfully romantic experience! Les Fermes is a collection of 10 traditional farm buildings, moved to their present location and outfitted for modern living by Jean-Louis and Jocelyn Sibuet. The reassembled "village" has a spa, with pool, exercise rooms, sauna, whirlpool, and other trappings, within a few minutes' stroll of the heart of town. Paintings around the chalets are by Mme. Sibuet. **Parc des Loges** *(53 rooms;* ☎ *50+93.05.03),* a resort relative of Lyon's Cour des Loges, is exceptionally luxurious, expensive and noteworthy.

MÉRIBEL-LES-ALLUES

Méribel-les-allues *(F-73550; ☎ 79+08.60.01)*, high in the Savoie Alps, gains international acclaim for its Olympic ski runs and the *patinoire de hockey sur glace*, as the French call an ice-hockey rink. But it has long been known to accomplished skiers as a place with challenging and long runs.

LODGING: Among the best nests is chalet-style **Le Grand Coeur** *(36 rooms plus apartments; ☎ 79+08.60.03)*, facing the slopes—and the sun, with a swimming pool and bedecked with flowerboxes in the warm-weather months. Conveniently located in town, the hotel is a *Relais & Châteaux* member.

LA PLAGNE

La Plagne *(F-73210; ☎ 79+09.79.79; FAX 79+09.70.10)* is another of the Olympic 1992 French-superlative resorts, as the site for the bobsled and toboggan events. Spread over spots between 1250 and 3250 meters (4100 and 10,758 ft), the resort touts its 107 manicured slopes, 101 skilifts, *l'ecole francaise de ski artistique* (acrobatic skiing), and *parapente*, which is parachuting from mountain cliffs with skis on your feet! While winter skiing was its raison d'etre, warmer-weather hikers and walkers enjoy the many paths, and summer skiers head for the **Gacier de Bellecote**.

The ten locales that are part of La Plagne include quiet *Champagny* (1250 m/4100 ft); *Plagne-Montalbert* (1350 m/4428 ft), with chalet-style buildings on the slopes of Tarentaise; *Montchavin* (1250 m/4100 ft), where modern developments include shops and forest walks that are popular in warm-weather months; *Les Coches* (1450 m/4756 ft), where activities and prices appeal to younger vacationers; *Aime la Plagne* (2100 m/6888 ft), where **Club Med** recently opened a massive block of rooms and apartments on a once pristine slope; *Plagne Centre* (1907 m/6255 ft), with the rectangular multi-story buildings of 25 years ago when it was built as a new town on the mountains; *Plagne Villages* (2060 m/6757 ft), with a few older buildings joined by newer ones along the road and ski lifts; *Plagne Bellecote* (1930 m/6330), a beehive of rooms and apartments in highrise buildings; *Belle Plagne* (2050 m/6724 ft), highest and newest, with a little more style than the other modern built-for-ski resorts; and *Plagne* (1800 m/5904 ft), with modern lodgings built in an out-of-scale version of the typical Savoyard farmhouses. Sports and the active life are what this massive development is all about; there's little of interest in the way of cultural attractions and the

French have scraped the countryside clear for the ski slopes, lifts and related buildings.

RUMILLY

Rumilly *(F-74150;* ☎ *50+01.09.24),* west of Annecy and north of Chambéry and Aix-les-Bains, has a charming **Musée Savoyard**, showing the history of this colorful region through its household items, costumes and documents. Housed in a 17th-century building, the collection includes elements from the neighboring Albanais region as well. Check with the mayor for entrance to the museum, which is at 11 rue Hauteville.

LODGING: For overnight or mealtime, consider the **Commerce** *(21 rooms;* ☎ *50+01.20.05),* on place d'Armes, or the **Cottage** *(15 rooms;* ☎ *50+69.53.12),* on route d'Annecy. Both are open year-round. The **Poste** *(14 rooms;* ☎ *50+01.28.61)* usually closes in October.

TALLOIRES

Talloires *(F-74290;* ☎ *50+60.70.64; FAX 50+60.76.59),* on Lac d'Annecy, is a goal for many travelers, in spite of the fact that it is a loose gathering of a few simple lakeside "houses." In fact, those who know good food genuflect at the name.

RESTAURANTS AND LODGING: This is the village of the widely acclaimed **Auberge de Père Bise** *(25 rooms;* ☎ *50+60.72.01; FAX 50+60.73.05),* which has long lured dining enthusiasts to the table of Mme. Charlyne Bise and Mme. Sophie Bise-Chevallier. Noted for presentation as well as preparation, the steady publicity may have compromised some of the quality, but overnight guests can enjoy an experience with the added dimensions of being "at home." Other inns, slightly less revered but very pleasing include **Les Prés du Lac** *(9 rooms;* ☎ *50+60.76.11),* a homelike inn with a lake view from its lawn and some rooms; **L'Hôtel Le Cottage** *(34 rooms,* ☎ *50+60.71.10),* owned by Fernand Bise; and the **Abbaye de Talloires** *(31 rooms;* ☎ *50+60.77.33),* a 17th-century Benedictine abbey perched at the side of the lake and an esteemed member of *Relais & Châteaux,* as is **Père Bise**. Preparation and serving of local produce, as well as the best items brought from elsewhere in France, are part of the mystique—and the memory—of any place in Talloires and being near Annecy puts all that town's charms in reach at times when tour buses have departed.

TIGNES

Tignes *(F-73320;* ☎ *79+06.15.55)* is neither quaint nor pretty. It's big, brassy, high-rise, and intends to be perpetually lively, summer and winter, with a sports program to appeal to all ages. Linked with

Val d'Isère for many skiers, Tignes is proud to be a "1992 Olympic resort." You're almost at eye-level with La Grande-Motte and a bowl of merangue mountains that seems surreal with a fresh snowfall. This is the Walt Disney World of skiing, with real mountains. Summer skiers head for the Glacier de la Grande Motte, for its year-round snow. There's golf, a huge lake (with speedboats!), fishing, whitewater kayaking, windsurfing, horseback riding, tennis, parasailing (which some do on skis) and many other activities. **Le Parc National de la Vanoise** awaits for summer visitors, drawn to its untrammeled aspects for hiking, walking and climbing. The options for lodgings are legion. All have been recently built; many are apartments.

LODGING: One special small spot, **le Ski d'Or** *(22 rooms; ☎ 79+06.51.60)* hangs in memory. Jeanne and Jean-Claude Brechu feature seafood in their dining room, which looks into snow-covered hillsides. Don't expect chalet style; this place is modern.

THONON-LES-BAINS

Thonon-les-Bains *(F-74200; ☎ 50+26.17.22)*, on Lac Léman, east of Evian, is a spa town that is less well known than its bottled-water-producing neighbor, but its appeal is greater for those who prefer history intact. As the historic capital of the Chablais region, the lakeside town has several buildings from the 15th to 17th centuries. The **Musée Chablais**, in the Château de Sonaz, is as interesting for its tokens from the past as for the 17th-century building. The **Plage de Ripaille** (lakeside area) offers many opportunities for sailing in warm-weather months and, although all the tourist trappings are here, the place is not usually as visitor-swamped as Evian can be at the height of summer season.

LODGING: One of the area's most charming places is near Sciez, west of the town. **Hôtellerie du Château de Coudrée** *(20 rooms; F-74140 Bonnatrait-Sciez; ☎ 50+72.62.33)*, a 13th-century château, has been painstakingly restored, including the recent addition of a swimming pool. The *Relais & Châteaux* member is on a hillside, overlooking the lake and blissfully removed from traffic and other noises.

VAL D'ISÈRE

Val d'Isère *(F-73150; ☎ 79+06.10.83)*, is often linked with Tignes in the minds of skiers—and with Jean-Claude Killy, who created Espace Killy—and was a site for the 1992 Olympics. Skiers crow over the fact that there's "every kind of skiing: Alpine, Nordic, monoski, surf, delta, etc." Although there are a few buildings left from the once charming village, most of what you'll notice—in addition to the mountains—was built before the 1992 Winter Olympics.

LODGING: One source for apartments and other rentals in the area is **Latitudes** *(Pl. de l'Eglise;* ☎ *79+06.18.88; FAX 79+06.18.87).* Individual units are small, in European style, with basic kitchen facilities and a small sunning balcony. Expect to find narrow beds. Although I usually leave the chain hotels to other guides, I've found little here of an independent nature. If you're coming to ski, consider **Hotel Mercure** *(45 rooms;* ☎ *79+06.04.41; FAX 79+06.04.41),* a link in a modern hotel chain, which offers comfort and good value, with dining choices in its *Potager* for gourmet style and the *Spatule* for regional specialties or the multi-story modern **Sofitel Val d'Isère** *(53 rooms;* ☎ *79+06.08.30; FAX 79+06.04.41),* in the same complex as the Office du Tourisme. It features a swimming pool, whirlpool, and other spa equipment, including a tanning machine.

SPORTS

French folks are your best sources for on-the-spot details about licenses and fees for sports such as fishing, golf, tennis, and skiing. While skiing is highly organized, some of the more esoteric sports will require detailed research since facts change according to the fad and the entrepreneur responsible for the concession.

ARCHERY

Popular at a few of the mountain resorts, archery is offered as an extra activity for guests. If the sport is important, be sure to ask the Office du Tourisme about specific places.

BALLOONING

Rides in hot-air balloons were popular for 19th-century travelers, and are becoming an added activity for travelers in the 1990s. In North America, **Bombard Balloon Adventures** *(6727 Curran St., McLean, VA 22101;* ☎ *703+448-9407 or 800+862-8537)* is widely respected as the first to organize ballooning vacations for Americans. Although the Loire Valley is the firm's most popular area, there are also a few places in the French Alps where ballooning is possible for visitors. Check with the FGTO for specific locations.

BICYCLING

In the country that claims headlines for its annual July *Tour de France,* a portion of which takes place on Alpine roads, you can count on cycling being a major pastime. Railroad stations are one source for bike rental. To be sure which ones have a stock of bicycles, check with **RailEurope** *(226-230 Westchester Ave., White Plains, NY 20607;* ☎ *914+682-2999 or 800+848-7245; FAX 914+682-8003).* The local **Syndicat d'Initiative** usually has lists of firms that rent bicycles and many of the larger resort hotels have bikes for use by their guests, when the terrain is suitable (as it often is around lakes and in some valley villages). Local cycling clubs often arrange excursions and are willing to include visitors. Some of the newer resorts feature mountainbikes, in keeping with the emphasis on pressure sports. For details on competitive races and other high-powered cycling events, contact the **Fédération Française de Cyclotourisme** *(8 rue Jean- Marie Jego, F-75013 Paris;* ☎ *45+80.30.21).*

CANOEING/KAYAKING

The sport is popular on many of the rivers in the French Alps. For a list of specific locations, contact the **Fédération Française de Canoe-Kayak**, *(17 route de Vienne, F-69007 Lyon;* ☎ *78+61.32.74).* One reliable firm offering guided expeditions on several rivers is **Euroraft**, which operates as **Franceraft** in at least five locations. Included in its most popular itineraries are the Durance River *(Parc d'Entraigues, F-05200 Embrun;* ☎ *92+43.44.85);* from Grenoble, along the Drac and the Severaisse rivers *(Maison de la Vallée, F-05800 St. Firmin en Vallée;* ☎ *92+55.27.89);* the Ubaye and Verdon rivers in the southern area *(F-04340 Le Lauzet Ubaye;* ☎ *92+85.55.20);* the Dranses and Giffre rivers, just south of Lac Léman and northeast of Annecy *(Route de Morzine, F-74200 Thonon les Bains;* ☎ *79+55.63.55);* and the Isère and Dora Baltee in the zone de loisirs *(F-73700 Bourg St. Maurice;* ☎ *79+07.10.59).*

CLIMBING

The Club Alpin Français *(12 rue Fort Notre-Dame, F-13007 Marseille;* ☎ *91+54.36.94)* is responsible for maintaining many of the huts and refuges in the French Alps, as well as tending trails in some areas. Many members are available as guides. Check with the local tourist offices for names of people in the areas you plan to visit. Another source for official maps and printed matter is the **Fédération Française de la Montagne** *(15 av. J.-Medecin, F-06000 Nice;* ☎ *93+87.75.41),* where you can get a list of member organizations to contact when you are in specific areas.

FISHING

There are strict regulations and seasons for freshwater fishing and, although day permits are sometimes offered, it's usually necessary to get a license and otherwise register with the district where you intend to fish. Although speaking French is not essential, it certainly makes complying with the regulations and reading the literature easier. The Haute Savoie region publishes a folder called *La Pêche.* Contact the **Fédération departé- mental de la Pêche** in Alpes Maritimes *(20 blvd. B. Hugo, F-06000 Nice;* ☎ *93+03.24.09),* in Alpes-de-Haute-Provence *(79 blvd. Gassendi, F-04000 Digne;* ☎ *92+31.57.14),* in the Hautes-Alpes *(18 rue Arene, F-05000 Gap;* ☎ *92+51.11.40),* in Isère *(1 rue Cujas, F-38000 Grenoble;* ☎ *76+44.28.39)* or at Drome *(3 pl. Dragonne, F-26000 Valence;* ☎ *75+43.17.98).* For comprehensive information about fishing in France, with addresses of local and regional information sources, contact the **Conseil Superieur de la Pêche** *(10 rue Peclet, F-75015 Paris;* ☎ *48+42.20.00).*

GOLF

Some of the biggest ski resorts have golf courses, as a response to interest in extending the "season" beyond the winter months. There are five courses in the Haute-Savoie, namely at Annecy *(year-round, 18 holes, 5216 yards, par 69)*; **Echarvines** *(F-74290;* ☎ *50+60.12.89)*; Chamonix *(end of May-Nov., 18 holes, 6625 yards, par 72)*; **Golf des Praz** *(F-74400;* ☎ *50+53 06 28)*; Evian-les-Bains *(early Feb.-mid-Dec., 18 holes, 6567 yards, par 72)*; and **Golf du Royal Club Evian** *(rive sud du lac de Genève, F-74500;* ☎ *50+75 14 00)*. There are several courses in the Savoie region, namely at Aix-les-Bains *(year-round, 18 holes, 5949 yards, par 71; av. du Golf, F-73100;* ☎ *79+61.23.35)*; Les Arcs *(end of June-Sept., 18 holes, 5307 yards, par 68)*; **Golf Arc Chantel** *(F-73700 Bourg St-Maurice;* ☎ *79+41.55.55)*; Megève *(18 holes, 6715 yards, par 72)*; **Golf du Mont d'Arbois** *(F-74120 Megève;* ☎ *50+21.31.51)*, Méribel *(18 holes, 2660 yards, par 70)*; **Association Sportive du Golf de Méribel**, *(B.P.24, F-73550 Méribel;* ☎ *79+00.52.67)*; Tignes *(late June-early Sept., 18 holes, F-73320 Tignes;* ☎ *79+06.37.42)*; and at Flaine-Les Carroz *(late June-Oct., 18 holes, 4058 yards, par 63; 74300 Flaine;* ☎ *50+90 85 44)*.

HIKING

Throughout the Alpine region, the regional members of the **Fédération Française de la Randonnee Pedestre** are excellent sources for specific facts, as are the local **Office du Tourisme** or **Syndicat d'Iniative**. The **Club Alpin Français** *(12 rue Fort Notre-Dame, F-13007 Marseille;* ☎ *91+54.36.94)* also has information about trails that are pleasant for recreational hikers. Good information is often available, also, through local bookstores. One interesting expedition starts in Modane, in the Maurienne valley, on the south side of the Massif de la Vanoise, and crosses into Italy, along portions of the Route Imperiale that was followed by both Hannibal and Napoleon. From the rivers, the *Train des Pignes* that runs between Nice and Digne, following the Val River north and then east, pauses at many mountain villages that are ideal for walking and hiking. Among them, far into the valley, are Entrevaux, Arnot, Saint-Andre les Alpes and Barreme. For U.S. firms that plan organized walks and hikes, check with **Travent International** *(Post Office Box 711, Bristol, VT 05443;* ☎ *802+453-5710 or 800+325-3009; FAX 802+453-4806)*.

HORSEBACK RIDING

The best source for details about facilities is the local **Association Regionale pour le Tourisme Equestre et l'Equation de Loisir**. There's one for the Rhône-Alpes area *(47 av. A.-Briand, F-38600 Fontaine;* ☎ *76+27.10.61)*, and for the Savoie region *(***Maison des Sports***, 6 Montee Valerieux, F 73000 Cambéry;* ☎ *79+69.69.69)*. Horseback riding is a popular activity at many of the larger resorts and often, also, at some of the high Alpine places where farmers rent their horses to visitors. Evian-les-Bains, on Lac Léman (lake of Geneva), is one place that offers riding and, at the other extreme, it's also possible high in the mountains at Tignes. For information on events being held and on special equestrian tours, contact the **Association**

Nationale pour le Tourisme Equestre *(15 rue de Bruxelles, F-75009, Paris;*
☎ *42+81.42.82).*

HUNTING

Sources for specific facts about regulations include the **Fédération dé-
partemental des chasseurs** in the Alps de Haute Provence *(79 blvd. Gas-
sendi, F-0400 Digne;* ☎ *92+31.02.43),* in Alpes Maritimes *(P.A.L. 7 M.I.N.,
St. Augustin, F-06042 Nice;* ☎ *93+83.82.39),* in the Hautes- Alpes *(quartier
Lareton, F-05000 Gap;* ☎ *92+51.16.25)* or at Isère *(6 rue St.-François,
F-38000 Grenoble;* ☎ *76+43.11.01).*

RIVER RAFTING

Several rivers are navigable for rafting, both aboard multiperson rubber
rafts and individual "flutter-board" style luges. See "Canoeing and Kayaking" above for the details about **Franceraft** *(Parc d'Entraigues, F-05200 Embrun;* ☎ *92+43.44,85),* a reliable company that operates from several
starting points in the Alpine area. Their programs are planned for international participants and, while it is best if you speak French, many of the
guides are also fluent in English. Helmets are standard equipment, as are
life-preservers.

SAILING

In the Alpine area the sailing is on lakes, but some of the lakes—such as
Lac Léman—are huge; winds are often flukey and weather can change dra-
matically within a few minutes, especially where the breezes cut through
mountain passes and are affected by many factors. Racing competition is
lively. Swiss-shared Lac Léman (lake of Geneva), the largest lake in the
area, is a challenging place for sailors. Among the places with boats for rent
are Evian-les-Bains and Thonon. Lac d'Annecy and Lac du Bourget at
Aix-les-Bains are also noted for sailing. The **Fédération Française de Voile**
(55 av. Kléber, F-75084 Paris Cedex 16; ☎ *45+53.68.00)* is a source for detailed facts and registered races.

SKIING

Famed skier Jean-Claude Killy, a favorite son, was a prime mover for the
1992 Winter Olympics, which were held in Alpine areas in, above and
around Albertville. Special preparations included the Alpine ski runs for
men at Val d'Isère and Les Menuires and for women at Méribel and the
cross-country tracks at Les Saisies. The speed ski run at Les Arcs was inaugurated in March '90. The Mont Blanc area, in the Haute Savoie region,
marks some of the best areas for skiing, with Chamonix, La Clusaz,
Megève and many places best known to French and other European families. In the Savoie region, the new and lively resorts are Les Arcs, La Plagne, Tignes/Val d'Isère, Courcheval and other Olympic areas. Although
skiers praise the no-nonsense, built-for-skiing focus of the newest resorts
such as Les Arcs and Tignes, which have grown since 1972 (when Arc 1600
opened), these are not places to come for traditional atmosphere and Alpine "soul." The multi-story buildings hold modern apartments, often

with small rooms and expensive restaurants. However, trail access is immediate, which is not always the case at long-established favorites such as Megève and Chamonix. Travelers fluent in French will find the combination of local atmosphere, good slopes, and costs refreshing at places not promoted in ski tours.

SWIMMING

Europeans enjoy swimming in their lakes, and often refer to the narrow pebbly shoreline as *la plage* (the beach). Although lake and river swimming can be fun when the weather is warm (and the sun hot), most visitors turn to the indoor pools—and some outdoor ones—that are a growing crop at the best resorts.

TENNIS

Most resort areas have public tennis courts, in addition to those at the classiest resort hotels. You can expect to find tennis courts, for example, at Tignes, which was created especially for vacationers who like sports.

WALKING/TREKKING

Randonnées Pédestres are the signs to look for and the leaflets to ask for when you stop in the local tourist office. For information and maps for some of the long-distance footpaths, contact the **Fédération Française de la Randonnée pedestre** *(64 rue de Gergovie, F-75014;* ☎ *45+45.31.02)*. Although the posted walking paths are easy to find around lakes and in most of the mountain villages and resort areas, bookstores in the various towns are good sources for specific itineraries that can take you on longer walks than you might work out for yourself. There are particularly wonderful walks in the area of Chamonix and lovely *sentiers forestiers* (footpaths in the woods) at Crêt du Maure, Sainte Catherine, Annecy and Sevrier, as well as many other areas in the French Alps.

WATERSKIING

French sportsfolk enjoy competitive waterskiing, which is offered in warm-weather months on many of the larger lakes, to the consternation of some of us who enjoy the peace and quiet of nature.

WINDSURFING/BOARDSAILING

Mistral is a well-known French name for boards and windsurfing equipment. Lakes in the resort areas, and many elsewhere in the Alpine region, are flecked with windsurfers in all weather. Wet suits are standard gear since many lakes are fed by glacial melt and winds are brisk to chilling. Check with the tourist office in areas you plan to visit if renting equipment is crucial for your holiday happiness.

TREASURES AND TRIFLES

France means fashion, and the subject is not limited to Paris. Chic boutiques may take a little longer to find in towns in the Alpine area, but they are easy to see in the center of the classiest resorts, which include Chamonix, Courcheval and Mégeve. The noted names for fashion and perfumes are well represented, but the fun of shopping for many of us is to find the *prêt-à-porter* (ready-to-wear) items that reflect the lines and style of designer clothes but don't carry the vaulted price tags.

Street markets are special times, even when the sole focus is food. (Photography can replace purchasing at those times, but rare is the person who can pass by all the stalls without buying at least some fresh fruit, homebaked bread or farm-fresh cheese.) Check with the tourist offices, if you're on a flexible itinerary, so you can be in the area on market day.

Special treats await those who make time to browse in even the most pedestrian-looking local department or grocery store. Shelves are stacked with tempting items, not only the many foodstuffs whose French labels lend an exotic note even to mustard, but also for the kitchen implements and other household items that are appreciated by the folks at home. One home furnishings store worth some time is **Castorama**, a chain that started in 1969 in the north of France and now has branches in places such as Grenoble *(rue de Champ Roman, St. Martin d'Heres;* ☎ *76+42.22.18)* or Antibes, where the huge store is in three buildings off the highway between Nice and Aix-en-Provence *(Peage d'Antibes, Route de Grasse;* ☎ *93+33.53.30).*

There are exceptional sales on ski fashions and other sports apparel, not only in the fall (if the stores remain open), before the winter stock arrives, but also in spring, before the stores turn to their summer merchandise (or close).

ADDITIONAL INFORMATION SOURCES

SAVOIE

Comité Régional du Tourisme Alpes Savoie-Mont Blanc, *9 blvd. de Wilson, F-73100 Aix-les-Bains.* ☎ *79+88.23.41; FAX 79+35.66.14.* **Office de Tourisme de Savoie**, *24 blvd. de la Colonne, F-73000 Chambéry.* ☎ *79+33.42.47.*

HAUTE SAVOIE

Association Touristique Departémentale de Haute Savoie, *56 rue Sommeiller, F-74012 Annecy.* ☎ *50+45.00. 33; FAX 50+51.87.20.*

HAUTE-ALPES

Comité régional du Tourisme Dauphine-Alps françaises, *14 rue de la Republique, F-38019 Grenoble BP 227.* ☎ *76+54.34.36; FAX 76+51.57.19.*

RHÔNE

Comité Départemental du Tourisme, *146 rue Pierre-Corneille, F-69426 Lyon Cedex 03.* ☎ *72+61.78.90; FAX 78+60.44.49.*

SAVOIE

L'Union Départementale des Offices de Tourisme et Syndicats d'Initiative de la Savoie, a group comprised of the tourism offices in areas bordering the park, maintains an information office at **Maison du Tourisme**, *24 blvd. de la Colonne, F-73000 Chambéry.* ☎ *79+85.12.45.*

VALLÉE DU RHÔNE

Comité Régional du Tourisme, *2 place des Cordeliers, F-69002 Lyon.* ☎ *78+92.90.34; FAX 72+41.95.06.*

GERMANY

St. Bartolomä, on the Königssee, Bavaria, Germany

The mid-afternoon sun gave a bronze cast to everything; the fresh spring air was welcomed, but cool enough to make me search for a seat where I could catch the last rays of sun. No matter what the date, as soon as the sun warms the pavement, tables and chairs sprout from every restaurant or *Stube* that's not on a main highway in this part of the Alpine area. So eager is everyone to see the last of winter's chill that people bundle up to sit outside, simply for the joy of feeling the sun's warmth on hands and face.

My choice for lingering in München is often in front of Augustiner, a brewery restaurant that had been established in 1328 on a site dedicated as a cloister on May 4, 1294. It's on Neuhauser Strasse, a portion of the main pedestrian mall of München, the Bavarian capital that is both sophisticated city and farmers' playground. It's appropriate to order a beer, but you'll have to know how to order the right one. So special are the brands that each is offered by its own name.

By 8 a.m., when I had started my city strolling, the fruit stands that claim a patch of pavement in this area were being set up, each variety arranged by kind, with no integration. Even at that early hour, the ice cream man was setting up his cart, in front of the Woolworth store, where young girls' dirndls were being offered for a fraction of their classy-store price.

Soon thereafter, performers would appear—both intentional artisans who mimed, played a musical instrument, or simply painted the scene before them and ordinary people who become actors on a stage when the promenade is in full swing.

Not far away, the squeal of tram wheels indicates that the city is in motion. Most people are hustling to work, while others are wandering aimlessly, window shopping and watching the city in motion. In spite of its size, München has a small town feeling that I enjoy. It is easy to nibble digestable portions: the area from the Hauptbahnhof to the Altes Rathaus on Marienplatz, including Neuhauser Strasse and Kauflingerstrasse, one long route that changes names occasionally; the area around the Sigistor, a tower marked with an arch that divides Leopoldstrasse from Ludwigstrasse and is the pivot point for the University area; Maximilianstrasse, with its shops, hotels, and the theaters around Max-Joseph Platz; and, of course, the Englisher Garten, where "everyone" goes to walk, ride bikes and linger at the Chinesischer Turm, as the Chinese tower that marks a favorite café is called.

The heart and motor for Germany's Alpine life is in this city, which is tethered by railway lines to most of the villages in mountains and by lakes to its south.

COUNTRY CAPSULE

Germany wears the North Sea for a hat, and the Alps as boots. Stretching for a north-south distance of approximately 530 miles (848 km), the countryside and lifestyles vary greatly, from what appears to be the industrialized Prussian north to the farmlands and back-to-the-earth rural atmosphere of the south. While Hanseatic links are obvious in the architecture and manners of the north, the southern region shares the Alpine tradition—where mountains,

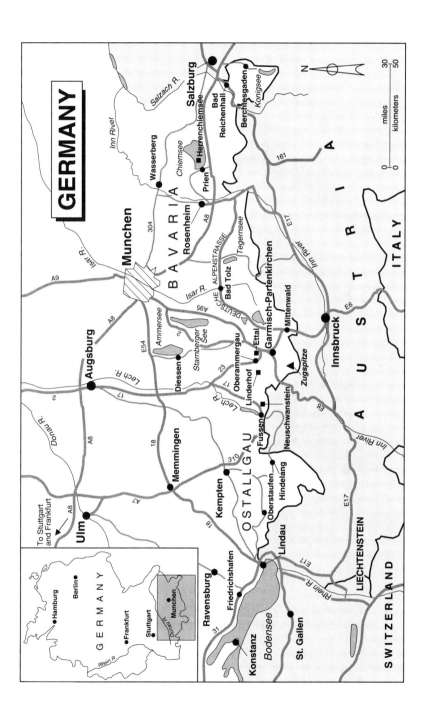

fields and lakes provide the cause for colorful festivals and harvest celebrations and the landscape inspires artisans, sportspeople, and wanderers. The rich traditions of Bavaria set the pace for Germany's Alpine area, with its Catholic heritage adapting pagan ceremonies and its farms putting plump produce on the table.

Bavaria's capital of München thrives on its folklore, but it is a cosmopolitan city with an impressive culture that is obvious with its museums, concerts, opera and symphony. Just south, sometimes in sight, are the Alps with the Zugspitze, Germany's highest peak, easily reached by cog railway from Garmisch-Partenkirchen. (The top of the Zugspitze is at the border between Bavaria and Austria's Tirol.)

HISTORIC HIGHLIGHTS

When the Romans ranged over much of western Europe, settling in many places including the now-German town of Trier (in 58 B.C.), Germanic tribes occupied the land wrapped by the Elbe, the Donau, and the Rhein rivers, and the Celts settled in southern areas as they moved from eastern Europe in the 6th and early 5th centuries B.C. But it was Charlemagne, born in Aachen in 742 and known by Germans as Karl der Grosse, who extended the Holy Roman Empire to include all of today's France, Germany and Austria, as well as vast tracts of northwestern Spain and Italy to Naples, which was a kingdom of its own at that time. Germany was to be the heart of that empire for 700 years, with Rudolf, Count of Habsburg, bringing the crown to Austria when he became emperor in 1273. In 911, during the years when Germany was the seat of the empire, Conrad I, Duke of Franconia, was elected king of Germany, after the Treaty of Verdun (843) had created a German state. Eventually Otto the Great, who ruled after his father Henry I, was crowned emperor of the Holy Roman Empire by the Pope in 962.

As the boundaries of the empire fluctuated with whims and wars, the vast tract grew on one side while it was whittled away on another. To the northeast, meanwhile, Prussia became a significant power, and a thorn or more in the side of the empire as the feisty Prussians grasped more land. But it is the south that interests for its Alpine area.

Among names worth noting is that of Frederick Barbarossa (red beard), a pre-Habsburg emperor of northern Franconia who, after he became emperor in 1152, grappled with revolts among vassals at home, with disagreements with the Pope (ultimately resolved with a ceremony in Venice), with the capture of Milan and Rome, and with the plague that almost annihilated his troops, before he was drowned while on a crusade in 1190.

"Munichen," the early spelling for München, translates as "the monks," a name that comes from the fact that Benedictine monks, related to those of the important Tegernsee Abbey, settled on the banks of the Isar river in the 9th century. Their new abbey and its works were noteworthy by 1102, mostly because Otto, Bishop of Freising, maintained a toll bridge to tax salt coming along the Isar from Bad Reichenhall, Berchtesgaden and Hallein. But it was Henry "the Lion," a Saxon duke, who began the commerce for München, after Frederick Barbarossa gave him the area in 1156. He destroyed the Bishop's bridge and built a bridge over the Isar at München. As time passed and sterner souls prevailed, he paid one third of the toll that he gathered to the bishop. On June 14, 1158, München officially became a town, with a bridge, market and mint on the signing of a document by Frederick Barbarossa and walls were built around the area.

After Henry was stripped of his titles and banished for his independent actions, the Bavarian dukedom was given to Count Otto von Wittelsbach, whose family ruled the city and Bavaria for over 700 years. Salt was still the prized "gold" when Duke Ludwig the Severe made München his residence in 1255, after he had received Upper Bavaria and the Palatinate. Town gates and new walls were built under his reign. Lavish palaces rose in and around München, as a statement of the wealth and importance of their occupants and to occupy the leisure time of the new aristocracy who aspired to equal (or surpass) the lifestyle known in the French court. Elector Ferdinand Maria built a palace for his electress, as did his son and his grandson. Ludwig I, patron of the arts, embellished his favorite spots, and Ludwig II, the king of fantasy, built his Neuschwanstein, Linderhof and Herrenchiemsee, three castles that still impress all who visit them. Bavaria built its landmarks.

After a lull from the mid-14th century to the early 16th century, partially the result of sieges of the Black Plague, München was to emerge as a center of the arts—in spite of a brief recurrence of the plague, brought to the city by Spanish soldiers during the Thirty Years' War.

Napoleon's involvement with northern Prussia in the early 1800s and his eventual victory resulted in redistricting and reform. The kingdom of Bavaria was created in 1806, in the heat of the Napoleonic wars, when the southern states declared themselves independent. (Even after the combined forces of Prussia and Russia led to the defeat of Napoleon in 1814, the southern states continued on their own course.) Bavaria's six kings—all of the Wittelsbach dynasty—ruled until 1918, the end of World War I.

It's impossible to travel in Germany today and not be aware of World War II, especially as it has been recalled with the unification of the country in late 1990. Although the villages of the Schwarzwald (Black Forest), at the northwestern fringe of the Alps, and many of the Alpine lake and mountain communities, may mask their historic role with natural attributes, portions of the cities and many towns have been rebuilt since the mid-1940s, albeit often in historic style. The economic strides are amazing, and a past has been recreated, but authentic prewar buildings are rare and almost every building that survived the war has tales of the war to tell. Most furnishings, although of the era, were brought to replace those that vanished or were destroyed during the wars.

POLITICAL PICTURE

At midnight on Tuesday, October 2, 1990, East and West Germany joined, under the name used by West Germany during the years of partition, the Federal Republic of Germany. They had been two separate countries following partition on May 23, 1949, when the Federal Republic of Germany was established, and was soon followed by the German Democratic Republic, as East Germany was known under Soviet occupation.

The Federal Republic of Germany has 16 states, after reunification of the 11 states of West Germany and the five states of what had been East Germany (known as *Deutsche Demokratische Republik* or German Democratic Republic). As is the case with western-style democracies, the federal government responds to the wishes of the states. Social services for the people are a key responsibility of the government; all programs work toward that end, as has been obvious prior to and following reunification.

The first all-German elections since 1933 took place on Monday, December 3, 1990, when parliamentary elections selected Helmut Kohl as Chancellor of a united Germany. Kohl's CDU (for *Christlich Demokratische Union* or Christian Democrat party) won 44 percent of the vote, and the *Freie Demokratische Partei*, which became his coalition partner, added another 11 percent. The leftist SPD (*Sozialdemokratische Partei Deutschlands* or Social Democrats) won 33.5 percent of the vote, but lost their standard-bearer, Oskar Lafontaine, who resigned his party post to return to his home area of Saarland.

The other major party involved in the government is the CSU, which is the *Christlich Soziale Union* (Christian Social Union).

Although villages near the states' borders share characteristics, each state has its own personality. One needs only to travel the length of Germany to notice the differences between the industrial north and the farmlands of the south.

LIFESTYLE

The atmosphere of the southern region is much livelier, colorful and rural than that of the north, not only because the Alps are in view, but also because the influence of the mountains that have spawned the need for village life, where mutual support for survival against the elements and invaders has led to a clan-like existence. The Bavarian kings—and Wittelsbach lavish living—responded to cues from the courts of France, and any other court when it established fashion for that time. They set the pace for Alpine Germany's social life. Although many of Germany's best-known castles are on its Mosel and Rhein rivers north of the Alpine area, the three castles of King Ludwig II—Herrenchiemsee, Linderhof and Neuschwanstein—punctuate the Bavarian Alps and set a regal tone. Although München is a cosmopolitan city, it has the soul of the countryside. Bavarian-style clothing—dresses with bodice and shawl, loden coats, stylish hats (often with feather decoration)—are worn in the city, even for dressiest occasions, and often are seen on the streets of towns and in the countryside. The style is elegant; it's not a "costume" affair. Since high-powered business people are frequent guests at München's best hotels, most men wear dark suits and women are elegantly dressed. Attire in the Alpine regions focuses on sports at all times of the year. Although clothing for mountain sports has become almost psychedelic insofar as colors are concerned, away from the international cities and chic resorts most local folks still wear dark colors and conservative clothing. Layered outfits work best when you are traveling from mountain peak to lakeside in one or more days.

NATURAL SURROUNDINGS

Bavaria is mostly rolling countryside that soars to Alpine peaks at the border with Austria and slopes to a lovely lake, the Bodensee, at the western "corner." Where Bavaria meets Czechoslovakia to the east, the Bavarian Forest and the Palatinate forest mingle with fir and spruce growing from a terrain that is mostly crystalline massifs. One of the highest areas, the Pfahl, is a vast area of quartz. Lovely lakes, often with forests rising directly from the edges and small villages nestled into the trees, are ideal places for walks, hikes and outdoor vacations. Testimony to the residents' appreciation of nature is the space given to parkland in München, where the Englisher Garten is a favorite place for walks, bicycling and lingering at a *biergarten* and the promenade areas along the Isar river that runs through the city.

Bird-watching is enjoyed by many. Although there are few organized walks, if you're interested in birds, bring your binoculars. When you're in the countryside or riding a cablecar high into the Alps, you can often spot unfamiliar species. There are bird sanctuaries at Lower Inn and Ortenburg, south of the Donau river.

PRACTICAL FACTS ABOUT THE GERMAN ALPS

Once you've mastered the mechanics—money exchange rates, how to read timetables, where to find them and a few words of German—the routines of daily life will seem easy.

INFORMATION SOURCES

Deutsche Zentrale für Tourismus e.V. is the head office for the German National Tourist Office, at *Beethovenstrasse 69, D-60325 Frankfurt/Main 1, Germany;* ☎ *49+697.57.20.* For Bavaria, one source for facts is **Fremdenverkehrsverband München-Oberbayern**, *Sonnenstrasse 10, Postfach 200929, D-80331 München, Germany;* ☎ *89+59.73.47.* Other offices include **German National Tourist Office**, *52nd floor, 122 East 42nd St., New York, NY 10168-0072,* ☎ *212+661-7200, FAX 212+661-7174; #750, 11766 Wilshire Blvd., Los Angeles, CA 90071,* ☎ *310+575-9799, FAX 310+575-1565;* and *#604, 175 Bloor St., E, Toronto, Ontario M4W 3R8, Canada,* ☎ *416+968-1570, FAX 416+968-1986.*

Information is also available from the regional tourism offices whose addresses are at the end of the chapter.

Throughout the chapter, local spelling is used for some words and all place names. For translation of foreign words, refer to the back-of-the-book glossary. Postal codes and telephone numbers for the tourist office are in parentheses following place names in "Places Worth Finding."

CASH, CURRENCY AND CREDIT CARDS

The Deutsche Mark (DM), the unit of currency, is one of the world's strongest. At presstime, DM 1.50 equals US$1, but check with your local bank to learn the equivalent at the time you're planning to travel.

Consider buying Deutsche Mark travelers' cheques before you leave North America. There are distinct advantages to "living" in

German marks while you are in the country. Because you know how much you have exchanged prior to your travel, you'll be able to keep track of how much you're spending. In addition, when you are in small villages and elsewhere, there'll be no confusion about exchange rates when you want to cash a cheque.

If you prefer to buy dollar denomination travelers' cheques and play the odds (which can change daily), there are convenient currency exchange booths at airports and major railway stations, making it easy to cash into Deutsche marks when you arrive in the country. If you plan to cash large amounts, checking the service charges and the exchange rate prior to doing business may prove worthwhile. Although American Express does not charge a service fee for cashing its own travelers' cheques, I have found that the exchange rate may not be as good as that offered at the banks. If the bank you choose has a large service charge, however, the result may be about the same.

When you intend to travel for extended periods away from the many towns and cities, plan to have deutsche marks, either cash or travelers' cheques, to use for purchases. Inns and other places in villages often do not know (or care) about the Deutsche mark's value in dollars.

If using your credit card is important, always ask if it is accepted before doing business with a place away from the international mainstream.

AUTHOR'S OBSERVATION

If you buy merchandise and plan to take it out of Germany, you're entitled to a refund of the Mehrwertsteuer, the value-added tax imposed within the country. Procedures to obtain the refund are tedious and may seem more trouble than they are worth, except for very expensive purchases such as an automobile. For details on the system, refer to "Treasures and Trifles" below.

COMMUNICATIONS

Although German is the national language, dialects in villages in the Alpine region may cause linguistic puzzles for visitors familiar with *Hochdeutsch*, or "high German," as the best German is known. If you're familiar with the written language, however, touring is easy. You'll be able to decipher signs, restaurant offerings and even newspapers.

From North America to Germany, telephone direct dial is easy, using your carrier's international access code, plus 49 for Germany, plus the routing code and local number.

AUTHOR'S OBSERVATION

Throughout the chapter, telephone numbers are given for direct dial from outside the country. When used within Germany, all out-of-town telephone numbers begin with a "0."

Germany's telecommunications system is efficient and simple to use, especially since every PTT (*Post Telefon Telegraf*) office in any town, city, or village has facilities for overseas telephone calls as well as for local calls. You can dial direct from the telephones in cabinets near the stamp-selling windows. In lieu of coins, many phones require a *Telefona Corte*, about the size of a credit card, which you can purchase at the PTT. AT&T's *USA Direct* system works well from any phone, anywhere in Germany. Simply step into the phone booth, dial 0130+0010 (for the cost of a local call) to be connected with a telephone operator in the U.S. who is part of the AT&T system. Give that operator the number in the U.S. that you wish to contact. If you are an AT&T card holder you can charge the call to your card/designated phone. If you do not subscribe to the AT&T system, you can still use the service for an additional fee. Inquire about similar services, available through MCI and Sprint.

Facsimile machines are "everywhere," and are used by all businesses. You can fax to or from most places, either from your hotel (where they usually slap on an amazing surcharge) or from the local PTT office, where charges are more reasonable.

DOCUMENTS AND OTHER PAPERS

You'll need to show your passport when entering Germany and sometimes for identification when cashing travelers cheques. Refer to the introduction for the procedures and costs. If you want your passport stamped, to have as a souvenir or record, you'll have to ask specifically. Not all immigration officials are willing to stamp the passport; they seem proud of the fact that it's not necessary in the "new" Europe!

If you are planning to drive a rental car, you'll need an International Driver's Permit, which you can get through your nearest AAA (American Automobile Association). The cost is $10; you'll need two passport photos and a valid U.S. driver's license. The permit is valid for one year from the starting date you select.

MEDICAL FACILITIES

You can count on top-notch bone surgeons in the ski areas, and good medical services throughout Germany. In the introductory chapters, under "Medical Facts," several companies offering international travel insurance and other medical services are listed. In Germany, the word for accident insurance is *Unfallversicherung.* You'll usually find excellent doctors at spa communities as well as at the major ski resorts. In cities and towns, large hotels usually have a doctor on call; some have doctors in residence. Helicopter services are extremely efficient at plucking injured skiers from the slopes, and Murnau, near Garmisch, is one place where the *Krankenhaus* (hospital) specializes in emergency medicine. Fees are expensive, as they are in the U.S.

TRAVEL FACTS

Most travel around Bavaria starts (or ends) in München since transportation links—both roads and trains—fan south from the capital. In less than an hour, you can be in the Alps.

ARRIVAL

Frankfurt had been the main airport for international flights, until the new international airport, München II, opened May 17, 1992, outside München (Munich). It has two runways for long-range international flights and a completely modern terminal with shops and other services. München II is linked to the center of the city by S-Bahn. By 1995, a second S-Bahn line will connect the west of München, via Neufahrn. The *Airport Express* train links Frankfurt and Stuttgart to the München airport, via Ulm and Augsburg. **Lufthansa**, Germany's national airline, uses München as an important hub, both for travel to the eastern countries and to the Far East.

In addition to Lufthansa's service, there are charter services operating from several North American cities by Frankfurt-based Lufthansa subsidiary **Condor Flugdienst GMBH** *(875 N. Michigan Ave., Chicago, IL 60611;* ☎ *312+951-0005).* Their flights operate on specified days at fares that are usually lower than the major carriers, but count on close quarters and full planes. Long popular with German and other European travelers, the service is not well known to most North American travelers. Although popular with European travelers, and known to a few wise North American travelers, **LTU** *(*☎ *800+888-9200)* operates from Los Angeles, San Francisco, Miami and New York. It's another German-based carrier with reasonable rates.

TOURING TIPS

Traveling around Bavaria is easy, pleasant and fun whether you choose to drive yourself in a rental (or purchased) car or use the excellent public transportation system aboard trains, buses, lakeboats, cablecars or trams. In München, the bus and tram system is easy to learn and inexpensive for traveling distances; most towns are walking size. When distances require bus transport, it's available, usually starting at the Bahnhof.

AUTHOR'S OBSERVATION

WunderCheck and DanubeCheck are two voucher plans offered for travelers who prefer to know lodging costs in U.S dollars. At presstime, the cost is $54 per night, per person, based on two sharing one room, for room, breakfasts, tips and taxes. Some places include additional items. The WunderCheck can be used at about 100 hotels throughout Germany; the DanubeChecks can be used at specified hotels in the Donau (Danube) river region of Germany, Austria and Hungary. Cost for an accompanying booklet of four to seven discount and free-entry coupons is an additional U.S. $11-or-so. For details explained in a leaflet, contact the German National Tourist Office.

AIR TRAVEL within Germany is possible on **Lufthansa**'s local services and on regional air services for personalized itineraries to some of the Bavarian resorts, but train or road travel allows for sightseeing en route. Garmisch-Partenkirchen and a few other resort areas have helicopter service. Check with the Bavarian tourist office in München about such services elsewhere.

BICYCLES can be rented at many sport shops and approximately 250 *Bahnhofen* (railroad stations). Although bicycle rental from the railroad stations is less expensive when you show your rail ticket or pass, it's possible to rent there when you are in a town where the service is offered and have the urge to cycle. Bicycles must be returned to the same station you've used for rental, in most cases. Many towns and villages, and even the city of München, have well-marked bicycle paths that are used by residents and available for visitors. Detailed maps are usually available at the local tourist office.

BOATS offer both excursions and point-to-point transportation, on the many Bavarian lakes and rivers. The lakeboats are popular for outings during warm-weather months, even when the weather may not be ideal. Since many boats have enclosed sections, the weather need not force travel plans to change. Schedules are skeletal during winter months, when they exist at all, but they usually operate for weekends and holidays. The village-fringed **Bodensee** (Lake Constance), shared with Switzerland and, for a tiny wedge at Bregenz, with Austria, could be a playground for an entire vacation. Lindau is a good place to begin Bodensee excursions. Among the Bavarian lakes, both the **Chiemsee** and the **Starnbergersee** have frequent services linking towns that have charming inns, pleasant walking paths, and/or provide a relaxing atmosphere. The smaller **Ammersee** is popular with yachtsmen and other watersports enthusiasts.

BUSES link train services and outlying villages, as well as provide transportation within the larger towns and cities. Routes usually begin (and end) at the *Bahnhof* (railroad station), with a schedule that is posted near the *Halte*, as the bus stop is called. In the cities, your hotel concierge and/or front desk personnel can help with advice about the system and routes. For tips about the best multiride tickets and when they are available, talk with people at the local tourist office. München has special price day touring tickets as well as multiride tickets that make transportation costs very reasonable and can help with point-to-point travel.

CARS, in the country that gave birth to the Mercedes, BMW, and Volkswagen, give maximum freedom, with the option to use the highspeed *Autobahn* when time is more important than sightseeing. Most rental companies have desks at the major airports; your hotel can also assist. International airlines (Lufthansa and others) have fly-drive plans that are worth investigating.

If you're interested in buying a German-made car, visit your local dealer to discuss available programs. The usual system is to buy in U.S. dollars through your hometown dealer and pick up the car in Germany. You must place your order at least three months before you want to pick up the car. After you have driven your car, the typical plan is to take it to the shipping port, where you will fill out the appropriate papers, sign over your car and wait until it arrives in the U.S. designated port. Anticipate some additional expenses (over and above those that are listed), such as the cost for the first inspection, which can seem staggering at German labor costs if you are transacting in U.S. dollars.

There are dozens of car rental firms. Comparing prices can be worthwhile, especially if you're armed with the knowledge that the household names (**Hertz, Avis, Dollar, Europcar, National**, and others) have waged price wars in recent years. Local firms sometimes have the best rates, but you'll do better when you can negotiate in German. Inquire about special multiday package plans, and—if you're a frequent flier—look into special offers through your chosen airline. **Kemwel** (☎ *914+835-5454* or *800+678-0678*) and **Europe by Car** (☎ *212+581-3040* or *800+223-1516*) are two of the many companies that offer good values on multiday rentals.

TRAIN services are excellent. Trains are direct, efficient, clean and comfortable, as you'd expect from the Germans. The **Deutsche Bundesbahn** (German Railways) and the **Deutsche Reichsbahn** (German Peoples' train) joined in May 1990, to create 22,000 daily trains in the east and west. Although 40 years of neglect seriously affected the bridges and rolling stock that operated through the eastern part of Germany, the new DB services are countrywide. Some of the older stock was retired; some was delightfully refurbished, when it could be. The high-speed *InterCity Express* (ICE) network links major cities along popular routes throughout the country. Some of those trains reach speeds of 165 miles per hour where roadbeds allow.

GermanRail, the name used by the North American promotional arm of the *Deutsche Bundesbahn*, sells tickets through **DER Tours** *(Box 2056, Des Plaines, IL 60017;* ☎ *800+782-2424; FAX 800+282-7474)*. But your travel agent is also able to sell all the tickets, and you may find that the personal service available in your hometown is far more helpful that the telephone system. Your travel agent can assemble the facts and details on individual passes so you can do some homework, with a map in hand, before settling on the type of ticket that will be best for your travels.

Ask about bonus coupons, discount admission fees and excursion tickets that are included in some of the tickets purchased through GermanRail. One of the most useful special passes sold outside Germany for foreign travelers is the *Flexipass*, which can be purchased in 5-, 10-, and 15-day versions, to be used within one month. Costs are as follows:

# OF DAYS	COACH	1ST CLASS
5-DAY PASS	$130	$190
10-DAY PASS	$200	$300
15-DAY PASS	$250	$275

AUTHOR'S OBSERVATION

DER's telephone is computerized, with a baffling list of alternative numbers. Have paper and pencil handy when you call and be prepared to deal with the fact that your specific questions will have to be phrased in a way that fits into the way the office has its information tabulated.

One advantage to buying your ticket in U.S. dollars before you arrive in Germany is that all the challenges of dealing in another language with another currency disappear. You can simply read the posted rail schedules and board trains as you wish, showing your prepurchased rail card to the conductor if and when you see one.

If you're comfortable with the currency and language, however, you may find that point-to-point tickets are as easily purchased after your arrival in Germany and that domestically offered excursion and other special-price tickets are less than your advance-purchase ticket.

AUTHOR'S OBSERVATION

München's railway information services are excellent, but there are often long lines for personal assistance. Pick up some of the printed regional schedules, do some homework about possible journeys, and plan your questions so that you can ask them at one time. Also, familiarize yourself with the methods for deciphering the posted railway schedules. I've found that early morning is the best time to get fast information; midday can be a nightmare!

In addition to the speed and efficiency of the **Deutsche Bundesbahn** network, some of the most scenic routes in the Alpine region are aboard regional trains, many of which head out of München toward the Austrian border.

DAILY LIVING

The Alpine atmosphere of Bavaria is obvious even in cosmopolitan München. Although people dress well for social events in the city, you'll see plenty of folks in hiking and other outdoor gear around the railroad station, as they head out to the country for walks, hikes and other sports.

FOOD, WINE AND OTHER BEVERAGES

German food is much more than the hearty *wurst* and *sauerkraut* that immediately comes to mind. In fact, many restaurants have developed a lighter German fare, using the same ingredients without the high cholesterol count and heavy gravies. However, when you're traveling to country inns, you'll find plenty of fresh farm produce. *Kartoffel* (potato) and *Würste* (sausages) can be found almost everywhere, as can fresh salads. It's worth noting that *Braten* means roast, so you'll know the preparation for *Kalb* (calf-veal) when it appears as *Kalbsbraten*. The same goes for *Rind*, which is beef, or *Schwein*, which is pork. *Schinken* is ham, *Huhn* is chicken, and the *Wurst* comes in several forms, one of my favorites being *Bratwurst*, which is a veal sausage. *Nürnberger Bratwürstl*, however, are small pork sausages, often served with *Sauerkraut*, which is—as most know—pickled cabbage.

München, in addition to being an exceptional city for the arts, is the unchallenged capital for beer! It claims at least half-a-dozen major breweries, and a calendar with several major beer-focused events. Its several beers—*Löwenbräu, Augustinerbräu, Pschorrbräu, Paulaner*, and others—are served everywhere, but beer is seldom served more effectively (or with more fun) than the Hofbräu Bier is served at the famous Hofbräuhaus, in the center of the old city. (See "München" below for details on beer-halls.) German wine, offered throughout the Alpine region, is also good. Most of the best grapes are grown north of the Alpine region, on the banks of the Rhein and Mosel rivers. The first wine of the fall, known as *Federweisser*, is a young wine enjoyed before the vintage has come of age and full alcoholic content.

LODGING

Germany's Alpine region offers a wide range of lodging styles, from inns and small hotels to hunting lodges, castles, private estates, spas, full-fledged resorts, and—of course—deluxe, elegant hotels. There's also a network of campgrounds, used by many Europeans who travel with caravans, which are known in the U.S. as campers or RVs (recreational vehicles). Although the three castles of King Ludwig II set an elegant style, there are no castle lodgings in the Alpine area. But Ludwig's confections have proved to be such tourist magnets that each has spawned several lovely inns and pleasant hotels in its area.

APARTMENTS and **CHALETS** freckle the mountain areas, especially in and around noted resorts. Always popular with Europeans, many of whom own a chalet, which they may put into a rental pool, rentals are usually for a Saturday-to-Saturday week, but other time spans may be available depending on the time of year and the level of reservations. Units are adequately furnished, without some of the lavish "extras" that some North American time-shares and condos offer.

CAMPING (*das Lagern*) is very popular, especially near lakes and at high Alpine resorts. Campgrounds are designated and often filled by midday in the most popular areas. The German Tourist Office has useful maps for campsites and a comprehensive booklet about camping, but, after you arrive in Germany, the local tourist offices can direct you to some of the most interesting places. Campers, which the

British have made popular as caravans, can be rented through many car rental firms.

FARM VACATIONS, known as *Urlaub auf dem Bauernhof*, are popular with many European visitors, but little known to Americans, partly due to potential language problems and also because the farm holidays have never been promoted in the North American market. Several regions print comprehensive booklets, however, with pictures and statistics about the various farms, all of which have been inspected prior to their listing. Most of the literature is printed only in German, which is your tip-off to the fact that knowledge of the language is worthwhile. The best sources for details on farms offering lodging are the regional tourist offices, whose names and addresses are available through the German National Tourist Office.

HUTS and **MOUNTAIN HOTELS** cling to the high Alpine slopes. Although the huts are strategically placed as shelter for hikers and climbers, many of the mountain hotels are easily reached by anyone willing to take a cablecar, funicular, or mountain railway. Some of the mountain hotels are a short walk from the transport station, but the walk is usually an easy one in anticipation of guests coming up for meals and for overnight with a rucksack. The **German Alpine Club** is known as the **Deutscher Alpenverein e.V.** *(DAV, Praterinsel 5, D-80331 München 22;* ☎ *89+23.50.90-0)* and is the group responsible for maintenance of most of the Alpine huts. In addition to providing valuable information about hikes, climbs and the huts, the DAV is a good source for printed material and for dates of Alpine treks that might include visitors.

INNS and **SMALL HOTELS** are truly Alpine-style, in Bavaria as well as in the rest of the Alps. Many places have only a few rooms; most are known for the home-cooking as well as for the cozy rooms. Prices are usually moderate; hospitality is assured.

ROMANTIK HOTELS UND RESTAURANTS *(Horsteiner Strasse 34, Postfach 11 44, D-63786 Karlstein/Main, Germany;* ☎ *6188+950.20, FAX 6188+6007)* is an association of atmospheric properties that have grouped for promotional purposes. Properties considered for membership are friendly, comfortable places, often in historic buildings. They must be managed by the owner and must offer first-class regional cuisine. Several of the members are mentioned when this book looks at "Places Worth Finding" below. **Romantik Tours** *(Box 1278, Woodinville, WA 98072;* ☎ *206+486-9394* or *800+826-0015),* formerly the U.S. representative for the German-based company, has expanded to represent other properties in similar style, as well as to assemble holidays that visit more than one inn on a planned itinerary.

A French-based organization, **Relais du Silence** *(7 Passage du Guesclin, F-75015 Paris;* ☎ *country code 33 plus 1+45+66.77.77; FAX country code 33 plus 1+40+65.90.09)* is a collection of rural properties that guarantee a quiet, nature-oriented lifestyle. Although not all members are small inns, many are—and all properties have special features and welcomed hospitality.

Many private homes that have all the qualities of a very small inn can be found by driving along the country roads and responding to a "Zimmer frei" sign, which means "room free" in a bed-and-breakfast kind of place. The German National Tourist Office distributes an annual "Bed & Breakfast in Germany" booklet with details about some places and how to spot others. The local tourist offices in Bavarian towns and villages are good sources for places in the area where you are traveling.

LUXURY HOTELS are led by the Bayerischer Hof mit Palais Montgelas and the Vier Jahreszeiten Kempinski, both in München and members of the Leading Hotels, a registered tag for a group of privately owned properties that share elegance in classic style. The U.S. contact for the group is **Leading Hotels of the World** *(737 Third Ave., New York, NY 10017;* ☎ *212+838-3110* or *800+223-6800, FAX 212+758-7367)*. Another organization of unique luxury properties is the French-based **Relais & Châteaux** *(#707, 11 East 44th St., New York, NY 10017;* ☎ *212+856-0115; FAX 212+856-0193)* where member properties usually offer exceptional atmosphere and cuisine. Both organizations publish annual directories of their member properties.

SPAS have been popular since the Romans discovered the therapeutic values of the mineral springs and harnessed them for public baths. These days, the spas offer updated programs for specific illnesses as well as for weight loss, stress reduction, or just plain relaxation. The German word *Bad* means "bath," or spa. Baden-Baden leads the list of classy German spas. Although it's west of Stuttgart, on the fringe of the Black Forest, and not in the Alpine area, it's near enough to be a possible tangent to time spent in the Alps. Bad Tölz and Bad Reichenhall are also spas, as their names indicate. Among the Bavarian lakes where you can find spas are the Tegernsee, at Rottach-Egern (Hotel Bachmair am See) and Bad Wiessee (Der Jägerwinkel); on the Starnbergersee at Ambach (Wiedemann Spa &

Health Resort); and on the Bodensee at Meersburg (also a Wiedemann Spa & Health Resort).

YOUTH HOSTELS vary from one extreme (pleasant, comfortable) to
the other (crowded, almost-too-basic) throughout the Alpine region
of Germany. All are very popular with young travelers, especially
during summer months when they are often packed by noontime.
For entry, you'll need an International Youth Hostel membership
card, available through the New York Office for the **American Youth
Hostels**, which is mentioned in the "Lodging" section of the introductory chapter, or through the **Deutsche Jugendherbergswerk**
(*Hauptverband, Bismarckstrasse 8, postfach 220, D-32756 Detmold*).
The Deutsches Jugendherbergswerk can also supply a list of hostels,
with details, if you send DM10, to cover the cost of the booklet and
postage.

PLACES WORTH FINDING

Although there are hundreds of towns and villages worth a traveler's time, the places mentioned below are suggestions for this year's
travels.

*The letters and numbers in parentheses following place names are the
postal code (D-00000) and the telephone number for the local tourist office (☎ 000+00.00.00). All German postal codes were revised for 1994,
in response to the unification of the east and west. The "D" stands for
Deutschland, which is how Germany calls itself. Information in parentheses following mention of hotels and restaurants refers to street address
when necessary and telephone number, plus the FAX number, when
there is one.*

The *Deutsche Alpenstrasse* (German Alpine Road) stretches from
the Bodensee (Lake Constance), shared with Switzerland and Austria, to the Königsee, a lovely pastoral lake near Berchtesgaden,
about 15 miles from Austria's Salzburg. The route through the Bavarian Alps passes towns and villages where chapels stand as testimony to God in this strongly Catholic region and artists do their best
work in His honor. Musical events, fairs, market days and folk festivals fill the calendar.

Travelers who visit many parts of the Alpine region will note simi-
larities between the wood chalets found throughout the Alpine region and in the elaborately painted houses with what Bavarians know
as *Lüftlmalerei* that welcomes visitors in villages such as Mittenwald,
Hindeland, Lindau and others.

While Wagner received inspiration from the area (and sponsorship from King Ludwig II), Wagnerian music is by no means all that is featured at concerts in Germany's Alpine region. München is undoubtedly the best-known source for culture, but there are noteworthy events and sights at most Bavarian towns and many villages.

Although the area south of München has been more trammeled than some of the Alpine areas in Austria and Switzerland, and certainly than areas in Slovenia, there are many towns and villages that still offer a natural Alpine experience. Here are some of my favorites:

BAD TÖLZ

Bad Tölz *(D-83646; ☎ 8041+700.71)*, halfway between the Alps and München, is a spa town rich with Bavarian folk customs. Split by the Isar river, the **Altstadt** is the traditional heart, with Marktstrasse (market street) almost too artfully maintained. Richly painted facades yield to merchandise spilling from shops at street level. Kalvarienbergweg, with the stations of the cross, has been a place of pilgrimage for the intensely Catholic Bavarians, and is a popular walk for folks who are in town to take the cure. If your travels are in the fall, plan to be here for November 6th, the saint's day, when horsecarts make a procession to the two chapels at the head of this route, where there's a lovely view over the Isar river valley.

Since 1845, when the therapeutic waters were first channeled toward promotion as a spa, many of the buildings on the "other" side of the river have been dedicated to taking the waters—and shopping.

LODGING: The **Residenz Hotel König Ludwig** *(93 rooms; ☎ 8041+8010; FAX 8041+80.11.27)*, with a Best Western reservation link, is near a lovely park at the center of town. The smaller **Posthotel Kolberbräu** *(41 rooms; ☎ 8041+9158; FAX 8041+9069)* has local atmosphere, and modest prices. **Hotel Bellaria** *(17 rooms; ☎ 8041+800.80 , FAX 8041+80.08.44)* built in Patrician style, offers pleasantly homelike surroundings in the spa district.

BAD WIESSEE

Bad Wiessee *(D-83707; ☎ 8022+820.51, FAX 8022+86.03.30)*, less than an hour's drive or trainride from München, is known within Germany as a spa resort, but most North American visitors are drawn here for the activities on the Tegernsee, the pleasure of strolling along the lakeside promenade, and the proximity to München, less than 35 miles (54 km) away.

LODGING: There are several pleasant hotels, but one of my favorites is a small spot, the **Hotel Marina** *(32 rooms; ☎ 8022+860.10, FAX 8022+86.01.40)*, in chalet style, on a hillside with a sun terrace and pleasant views from balconied rooms. The **Hotel Gasthof zur Post** *(38 rooms;* ☎ *8022+860.60, FAX 8022+860.61.55)* is also in traditional style, with an appealing dining room and comfortable, cozy bedrooms.

BERCHTESGADEN

Berchtesgaden, Germany

Berchtesgaden *(D-83471;* ☎ *8652+5011; FAX 8652+633.00)*, 16 miles (24 km) north of Salzburg, Austria, was part of Austrian Berchtesgadener Land from 1803 until 1810 when it became part of Bavaria under Napoleonic decree. Augustinian monks, heading north from Salzburg, settled in this sensational Alpine location in the 12th century, establishing a convent in 1102. Their former abbey caught the eye of Wittelsbach kings in the 1800s, when they secularized it for their home, the **Schloss Wittelsbach**, open as a museum since the death of Prince Rupprecht in 1955. In addition to exceptionally fine woodwork, the Renaissance rooms of the palace are richly furnished. The neighboring 12th-century **abbey** holds wood sculptures by Tilman Riemenschneider and Veit Stoss, two remarkable craftsmen of the Middle Ages. Both Berchtesgaden and Salzburg gained great wealth from their crop of salt, which was the "gold" of medieval times. Emperor Frederick Barbarossa gave the town its charter and the monks the right to work the saltmines they found in 1212. The **Salzbergwerk** (Saltmines) that were opened in 1571 can be visited today, after you don miner's garb, board a small train for a short ride and slide down a chute to reach the level of the salt lake where you can take a short boat ride. In the town, the **Heitmatmuseum** is well worth a visit for its extensive collection of folk art from the region, including furnishings, costumes and tokens from the farming lifestyle. In addition to toys, crafts, and household implements, antique *Spanschachteln*, hand-painted boxes, are charming and are sold in modern versions in almost every store.

The exhilarating mountain air and the presence of the 8,900-foot (2,713 m) Watzmann mountain peak have made Berchtesgaden special through many centuries. In recent times, the town's notoriety comes from der Führer, Adolph Hitler, whose hideaway, the **Adlerhorst** ("Eagle's Nest") is a major tourist attraction. The residence, **Kelsteinhaus**, now a restaurant (open May through October), has some rooms furnished as they were at Hitler's time, but it is the route to reach this aerie that is breathtaking. It's the "highest road in Europe," reaching 6,345 feet (1,934 m). Used only by special buses of the RVO (Upper Bavarian Transport Co.), the road winds from Obersalzburg, at 3,200 feet (976 m), up a 27% grade and through several tunnels for four sensational miles. The road was built in just over a year's time; the "Eagle's Nest" is reached by elevator, rising up a 407 foot (127 m) shaft, from the parking area. Given to Hitler on his 50th birthday, the aerie perch was seldom used.

Berchtesgaden can be enjoyed, however, solely for its natural Alpine surroundings. There are endless opportunities to walk, hike, climb, ski or indulge in many other sports, depending on the time of year.

The **Königssee**, a lovely 5 x 1-1/4-mile lake nestled near the border south of Salzburg, maintains its pastoral and peaceful atmosphere. Although there are boat trips along the lake, the boats are electrified, quiet, and the only way to reach tiny **St. Bartholomä chapel**, a favorite touring goal. Allow some time for the boat trip that operates year-round, except when the lake is frozen.

Refer to "Sports" at the end of this chapter for the many activities offered in Berchtesgadener Land.

LODGING: There are several choice places to stay in this area. One of the most revered is the **Hotel Geiger** (*49 rooms;* ☎ *8652+5055; FAX 8652+5058*), a member of the prestigious Relais & Châteaux group. Not only is its setting peaceful and stunning—amid a lovely park just outside the town, but the Bavarian furnishings and the soothing hospitality make this an ideal base for walks, hikes and skiing, depending on the season. Even the newer rooms have plenty of Bavarian atmosphere. All guests can enjoy the small indoor pool and the excellent meals. The **Hotel Vier Jahreszeiten** (*61 rooms;* ☎ *8652+5026; FAX 8652+5029*) is another good choice. In the countryside, not too far from the town center, the **Alpenhotel Den-ninglehen** *(24 rooms; ☎ 8652+5085; FAX 8652+647.10)* offers Bavarian-style decor, with painted furniture in its rooms and traditional recipes served from its kitchen. One special small spot, the **Gast-haus-Pension Maria Gern** *(D-83471 Maria Gern/Berchtesgaden; 12 rooms; ☎ 8652+3440)*, nestled next to a tiny pilgrimage church, offers a wonderful opportunity to enjoy country life. Regional specialties are served in the wood-walled dining room. A viewful dining terrace is used when weather warrants; all bedrooms have private bathroom, TV and balcony or terrace. For in-town lodging, try **Al-penhotel Kronprinz** *(65 rooms; ☎ 8652+610.61; FAX 8652+33.80)*.

BODENSEE

Bodensee (Lake Constance), shared with Switzerland and, at Bregenz with Austria, is fringed with charming villages, many of which are linked by lakeboats of the **Bodensee-Schiffsbetriebe der Deutschen Bundesbahn** *(Bodenseeverkehrsdienst, D-88048 Friedrichshafen, Seestrasse 22; ☎ 7541+20.13.89)* as well as boats of the Schweizerische Bundesbahnen, a Swiss lakeboat company, mentioned under "Bodensee" in the Swiss chapter.

The best way to enjoy this lake is to allow several days and to travel with minimal luggage, using one of the multiday travel passes to get on and off the lakeboats as your spirit moves. There are several lovely inns, many villages with sights worth seeing and limitless choices for walking, bicycle riding, or otherwise traveling along the lakeside from place to place.

LODGING: In addition to the towns of Lindau and Konstanz, at the eastern and western "ends" of the lake (and described below), there are many villages and small towns that provide a unique base for enjoying the lake. **Immenstaad** *(☎ 7545+20.11.10, FAX 7545+ 20.11.08)*, a shoreside village, has the **Gasthof Adler** *(40 rooms; Dr. Zimmermann Strasse 2; ☎ 7545+14.70, FAX 7545+13.11)*, noted for its chef/owner's style as well as for being in an appealing village.

Both **Stockach** and **Friederichshafen**, near Konstanz at the northwestern end of the lake, have noteworthy lingering places, namely **Zum Goldenen Ochsen** *(Zoznegger Strasse 2, D-78333 Stockach; ☎ 7771+20.31)*, and the Baur family's **Buchhorner Hof** *(65 rooms; Friedrichstrasse 33, D-88045 Friederichshafen; ☎ 7541+2050, FAX 7541+326.63)*.

Another worthy contender for lakeside lodgings and/or dining is **Insel Reichenau** *(☎ 7534+276)*, a tiny island that is popular with local folks for Sunday walks and for the rest of us at any time of the week. By road it's best reached through Switzerland, although it's part of Germany, but the isle is also touched by the lakeboats of both countries.

RESTAURANTS AND LODGING: The **Romantik-Hotel Seeschau** *(24 rooms;* ☎ *7534+257, FAX 7534+78.94),* which has been in the same family for more than 60 years, is well known for its restaurant but especially prized for its charming, lake-view bedrooms. Although there's a special atmosphere in warm weather, when you can dine on the terrace overlooking the lake, the dining rooms are especially cozy in the evenings and on cold, dreary days.

(For information about other places around the Bodensee, refer to "Konstanz, " "Insel Mainau," and "Lindau" listed alphabetically, below, and to "Bodensee" in the "Places Worth Finding" section of both the Austria and Switzerland chapters.)

CHIEMSEE

Chiemsee, a lake on the route between München and Austria's Salzburg, is worth visiting for its impressive **Schloss Herrenchiemsee**, created at the bidding of Ludwig II in the style of Versailles. It is on an island where you can walk or take a horse-drawn carriage. On the **Fraueninsel**, the Benedictine monastery was known in the 13th century, but was rebuilt in the 15th.

LODGING: When you're willing to make time for the best of Alpine life, reserve a room at the **Inselhotel zur Linde** *(14 rooms; Haus 1, D-83256 Chiemsee-Frauenchiemsee;* ☎ *8054+316),* where dining takes on special meaning. For more spacious surroundings, try the **Hotel Gut Ising** *(88 rooms; 3 Kirchberg, D-83358 Seebruck-Ising am Chiemsee;* ☎ *8667+790)* a once private estate now open for the guests to enjoy elegant lakeside living.

On the southwestern shore, at **Prien** *(D-83209;* ☎ *8051+90.50),* the **Yachthotel Chiemsee** *(Harrasserstrasse 49;* ☎ *8051+6960)* appeals to sailing folk as well as to anyone who appreciates comforts at a sports-oriented place. In addition to a lakeside location, with a lawn separating the hotel from its marina, there are tennis courts, a swimming pool, sauna and solarium.

DIESSEN

Diessen *(D-86911;* ☎ *8807+41.48),* on the Ammersee, a few miles southwest of München, is a popular summer resort. In its suburb of St. Georg, the 18th-century **Stiftskirche** that stands on the site of an earlier Augustinian monastery is the work of Johann-Michael Fischer, a famous Bavarian architect.

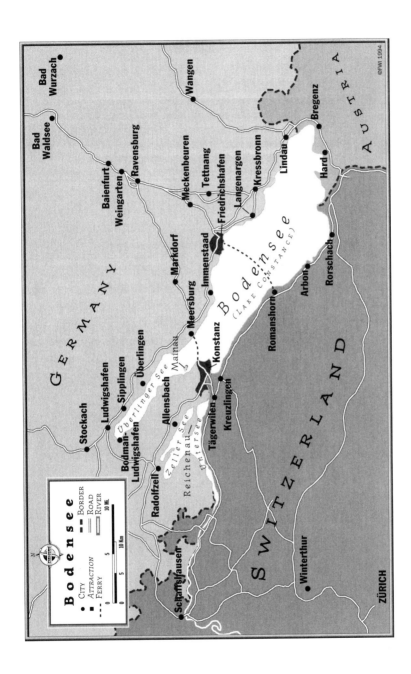

©FW 1994

Bodensee

- • CITY
- ■ ATTRACTION
- --- FERRY
- ■■ BORDER
- == ROAD
- ▭ RIVER

| 0 | 5 | 10 Km |
| 0 | 5 | 10 Mi. |

GERMANY

AUSTRIA

SWITZERLAND

Bad Wurzach

Wangen

Bad Waldsee

Bregenz

Ravensburg

Meckenbeuren

Baienfurt

Tettnang

Kressbronn

Weingarten

Friedrichshafen

Langenargen

Lindau

Hard

Markdorf

Immenstaad

Bodensee
(LAKE CONSTANCE)

Meersburg

Überlingen

Rorschach

Arbon

Sipplingen

Überlinger See

Mainau

Romanshorn

Ludwigshafen

Allensbach

Konstanz

Stockach

Bodman-Ludwigshafen

Zeller See

Kreuzlingen

Radolfzell

Reichenau

Untersee

Tägerwilen

Winterthur

Schaffhausen

ZÜRICH

BODENSEE BOAT SCHEDULE

Schaffhausen–Stein am Rhein–Reichenau–Konstanz–Kreuzlingen

4.-25. April=an Sa/†
1.-22. Mai=täglich
23. Mai–3. Oktober (Saisonschluss)

Stationen	Kurs Nr.	613 ★	521	503	618 ★	523	617 ★	619 ★	505	507	529
Von Zürich	ab		7 04	8 52		10 52			12 52	14 52	16 54
Von Winterthur			7 16	8 13		10 13			13 13	15 13	17 13
Schaffhausen	ab	9 25	7 45	9 15		11 15			13 40	15 40	17 30
Büsingen	ab	9 40	8 10	9 40		11 40			14 05	16 05	
Diessenhofen	ab	10 00	8 40	10 10		12 10			14 35	16 35	18 20
Stein am Rhein	an	10 20	9 40	11 10		13 10			15 35	17 32	19 15
Stein am Rhein	ab		9 45	11 15		13 15			15 40	17 40	
Öhningen	ab		10 02	11 32		13 32			15 57	17 57	
Mammern	ab		10 09	11 39		13 39			16 04	18 04	
Wangen	ab		10 15	11 45		13 45			16 10	18 10	
Hemmenhofen	ab		10 27	11 57		13 57			16 22	18 22	
Steckborn	ab		10 33	12 03		14 03			16 30	18 28	
Gaienhofen	ab		10 39	12 09		14 09			16 37	18 34	
Berlingen	ab		10 49	12 19		14 19			16 47	18 44	
Mannenbach	ab		10 59	12 29	13 52	14 29			16 57	18 54	
Reichenau	ab		11 07	12 37	14 00	14 37	14 37	16 35	17 05	19 02	
Ermatingen	ab		11 19	12 49		14 49	14 49	16 55	17 20	19 14	
Gottlieben	ab		11 40	13 10		15 10	15 10	17 15	17 40	19 35	
Konstanz	an		12 00	13 30		15 30	15 30	17 35	18 05	19 55	
Konstanz	ab		12 05	13 35		15 35			18 10	20 00	
Kreuzlingen-Hafen	an		12 15	13 45		15 45			18 20	20 10	
Nach Romanshorn			13 02	14 02		16 02			18 33	21 02	

	529	507	505
Von Zürich	16 54	14 52	12 52
Von Winterthur	17 13	15 13	13 13
Schaffhausen	17 30	15 40	13 40
Büsingen		16 05	14 05
Diessenhofen	18 20	16 35	14 35
Stein am Rhein an	19 15	17 32	15 35
Stein am Rhein ab		17 40	15 40
Öhningen		17 57	15 57
Mammern		18 04	16 04
Wangen		18 10	16 10
Hemmenhofen		18 22	16 22
Steckborn		18 28	16 30
Gaienhofen		18 34	16 37
Berlingen		18 44	16 47
Mannenbach		18 54	16 57
Reichenau		19 02	17 05
Ermatingen		19 14	17 20
Gottlieben		19 35	17 40
Konstanz an		19 55	18 05
Konstanz ab		20 00	18 10
Kreuzlingen-Hafen		20 10	18 20
Nach Romanshorn		21 02	18 33

Kreuzlingen–Konstanz–Reichenau–Stein am Rhein–Schaffhausen

4.–25. April=an Sa/†
1.–22. Mai=täglich
23. Mai–3. Oktober (Saisonschluss)

Stationen	Kurs Nr.	502	614 ★	504	618 ★	526	508	619 ★	528	620 ★	530
Von Romanshorn		8 55		10 55		12 55	14 55		15 55		
Kreuzlingen-Hafen	ab	9 05		11 40		13 50	15 05		16 05		
Konstanz	ab	9 15	10 25	11 55	13 00	14 00	15 15		16 15	16 15	
Gottlieben	ab	9 35	10 45	12 15	13 20	14 20	15 35		16 35	16 35	
Ermatingen	ab	9 55	11 05	12 35	13 40	14 40	15 55		16 55	16 55	
Reichenau	ab	10 07	11 15	12 47	14 00	14 52	16 07	16 35	17 10	17 10	
Mannenbach	ab	10 15		12 55			16 15	16 43			
Berlingen	ab	10 25		13 05			16 25				
Gaienhofen	ab	10 35		13 15		15 10	16 35		17 30		
Steckborn	ab	10 41		13 21		15 16	16 41		17 36		
Hemmenhofen	ab	10 47		13 27			16 47				
Wangen	ab	10 59		13 39			16 59		17 55		
Mammern	ab	11 05		13 45			17 05				
Öhningen	ab	11 12		13 52			17 12				
Stein am Rhein	an	11 25		14 05		15 50	17 25		18 15		
Stein am Rhein	ab	11 30		14 10		15 55	17 35		18 20		20 45
Diessenhofen	ab	12 05		14 45		16 30	18 10		18 55		21 20
Büsingen	ab	12 20		15 00			18 25				
Schaffhausen	an	12 45		15 25		17 05	18 50		19 30		21 55
Nach Zürich		13 08		16 08		18 08			20 08		22 46
Nach Winterthur		13 46		15 46		17 46			19 46		22 46

Zeichenerklärung

= 4. Juli – 29. August

= An Sonntagen:
4. Juli – 29. August

= Dienstag, Donnerstag, Freitag, 13. Juli – 6. August

= Täglich vom 4. Juli – 29. August
Donnerstag, Sa/† vom 23. Mai – 3. Juli + 2. Sept. – 3. Okt.

= Nicht an Sonntagen vom 4. Juli – 29. August

= Anschluss von und nach Radolfzell

† = Sonn- und allg. Feiertage

= Kurse der URh mit Restauration – Frühstück erhältlich
Für Gruppen ab 30 Pers. auf Vorbestellung Mahlzeiten erhältlich

★ = Kurse der Deutschen Bundesbahn

The Bodensee, one of the multi-national lakes of the Alpine region, allows for pleasant meandering between Austria, Germany and Switzerland by foot, train, car or lakeboat. The Swiss boat schedule between Schaffhausen and Konstanz indicates the rail links with its mention "von Zurich" and "von Winterthur" ("von" is "from"), but it does not indicate that the train station is a short walk from the boat dock at Schaffhausen. It's important to know that "an" refers to "ankunft," which means "arrive" (in German), and "ab" refers to "abfahrt," which means "depart." The "4.25. April=an Sa/†" means that from the 4th to the 25th of April, the service operates only on Saturdays and Sundays (Sunday is indicated by the cross); "täglich" means "daily." The schedule is presented on the 24 hour clock, making 2 p.m. "14 00." The schedule to the left of the place name is for the trains; the schedule to the right is for the boat service, which gives the user full details to get off at any stop and take the most convenient train to continue the journey or return to his starting point. Be sure to remember that the schedules read from top to bottom, as is shown by the schedules on pages 188 and 189, wherein travel is shown from Schaffhausen to Kreuzlingen-Hafen (harbor) and from Kreuzlingen-Hafen to Schaffhausen.

RESTAURANTS AND LODGING: The small **Hotel Gasthof Maurerhansl** *(7 rooms;* ☎ *8807+342)* is a page from the past, not only with its atmosphere, but also because the homestyle cooking brings traditions to today's table.

ETTAL

Ettal *(D-82488;* ☎ *8822+534)*, north of Garmisch (see below) and a star in its own right, is the site of a huge and impressive **abbey** founded by Emperor Ludwig in 1330. As rich for the many treasures in its interior (paintings, sculpture, architectural appointments) as for its solitary location amid beautiful scenery, the Abbey is a marvel of the Alpine area.

RESTAURANTS AND LODGING: The appropriately named **Ludwig der Bayer** *(70 rooms;* ☎ *8822+66.01, FAX 8822+744.80)* is the best hotel in town; **Zur Post** *(24 rooms;* ☎ *8822+596)*, its neighbor on Kaiser-Ludwig Platz, is cozy, atmospheric and less expensive. The **Schlosshotel Luinderhof** *(29 rooms;* ☎ *8822+790, FAX 8822+43.47)* appeals to businesspeople and to families who enjoy the elegant surroundings and international cuisine offered in the dining room.

FÜSSEN

Füssen *(D-87629;* ☎ *8362+7077)*, on the Lech river, about 70 miles (112 km) west of München, is the nearest town to Schloss Neuschwanstein, a castle confection created for Ludwig II. The Schloss stands prominently on a mountainside peak less than a mile from Füssen. Castle tours allow for seeing several rooms, some with wall and ceiling paintings depicting characters from Wagnerian operas (Richard Wagner was befriended by Ludwig II). The **September Music Week** is a pinnacle of pleasure, with formal attire preferred by most guests and champagne and candlelight part of the evenings.

In Füssen, the **Stadtpfarrkirche** (parish church) is a delightful example of the work of an 18th-century artist from this region, Johann-Jakob Herkommer, who was both artisan and architect. The vast **Klosterhof**, a baroque confection, is also the work of Herkommer. Part of the complex is the **Heimatmuseum**, with restored rooms that are richly furnished and open for viewing. The hilltop **Schloss**, rebuilt on earlier foundations in the 16th century and home for the bishops of Augsburg, has some rooms that are decorated with paintings from the 15th-century Swabian school. Its park-surrounded location makes it a favorite for leisurely walks.

LODGING: Among my choices for a place to stay is **Hotel Sonne** *(32 rooms;* ☎ *8362+60.61, FAX 8362+60,64)*, the small and reasonably comfortable hotel is conveniently located at the railroad station, but the **Kurhotel Filsur** *(33 rooms; ☎ 8362+2068)* is favored by some. The **Hotel Alpenblick** *(46 rooms; Hopfen am See; ☎ 8362+505.70, FAX 8362+50.57.73)*, a modern hotel in chalet style, about a mile (4 km) from the railroad station, has a country atmophere and easy access to pleasant walking trails.

The nearby **Forggensee**, a man-made lake formed by the Rosshaupten dam, has become a recreational area with a fringe of camp sites, hotels and inns plus dozens of sailboats and other boats on its surface.

GARMISCH-PARTENKIRCHEN

Garmisch-Partenkirchen *(D-82467; ☎ 8821+1806)*, two villages that joined together for the winter Olympics of 1936, stands as one highly respected resort community with a snow focus. It is not far from the towering Zugspitze, the highest point in Germany, with the Alpspitze and the Waxenstein in view (on clear days) from the streets of town. In summer months, there are concerts at the **Alte Kirche** in Garmisch, on the bank of the Loisach river, where 14th- and 15th-century paintings remain on the walls and the Gothic vaulting dates from the 16th century.

The Zugspitze railway has prized appeal year-round, not only for skiers and hikers who use it to reach the highest peaks, but also for sightseers who can ride the route to the top, or stop off along the way to settle into an inn and enjoy the view.

LODGING: Among the many places to stay, my favorites include a few in the thick of things, downtown and a special spot on the mountainside, offering sensational views. The majority of the hotels make the most (sometimes too much) of Bavarian folkart atmosphere. One memorable nest is the **Romantik-Hotel Clausings Posthotel** *(30 rooms; ☎ 8821+7090; FAX 8821+70.92.05)* in Garmisch, on Marienplatz in the heart of town, within a few steps of shops and other activities. The sometimes overwhelming Bavarian decor includes the bedrooms, the beer garden and the more formal dining area. The similarly named, but unrelated **Posthotel Partenkirchen** *(50 rooms; ☎ 8021+510.67, FAX 8021+785.68)*, at Ludwigstrasse 49, also has Bavarian decor and a long tradition of inn-keeping. Restaurants in both hotels serve Bavarian specialties. **Riendl's Partenkirchner Hof** *(80 rooms; ☎ 8821+580.25)*, convenient on the Bahnhofstrasse, has spectacular mountain views from some bedrooms and the traditional Bavarian folkart throughout. Its grill restaurant is one of the town's most esteemed. On the mountainside, find the quiet and lovely **Grand Hotel Sonnenbichl** *(96* *rooms; 97 Burgstrasse;* ☎ *8821+70.20; FAX 8821+70.21.31),* even if you head here only for a memorable meal while you are in the area. Another place that might appeal, built in traditional style although it's new, is the **Alpenhotel Waxenstein** *(49 rooms; Eibseestrasse 16, WD-8104 Grainau;* ☎ *8821+8001),* which has a swimming pool, sauna and fitness room, in addition to being in the orbit of the Zugspitze for walks, hikes and more adventuresome and strenuous mountain activity.

For other places in the area, see "Ettal" above and "Mittenwald" below.

KEMPTEN

Kempten *(D-87435;* ☎ *8312+52.52.37),* in the Allgäu, dates from 2000 years ago, when Cambodunum, mentioned in documents of 18 A.D., was established as a Celtic and then a Roman community. Rising from the banks of the Iller river, today's town has grown around its historic medieval heart, with several noteworthy buildings and museum collections. Wrapped in a commercial cloak that can be disarming, Kempten is a bigger city than you might expect. If you arrive by train, take a taxi to the historic center, where the knot of medieval buildings sets an atmosphere quite different from the "modern Germany" feeling in the newer part of town.

Lorenzbasilika (St. Lorenz' Basilica), dating from 1651-1652, stands as the first Baroque church to be built in southern Germany after the Thirty Year's War. It is the city's trademark today, since its twin steeples, with their modified onion domes, can be seen from far away. The **Rathausplatz**, with remarkable patrician buildings and the **Rathaus** (Town Hall), is a good starting point for strolling. Built on the site (in half-timber style) in 1368, the Rathaus was rebuilt in stone in 1474, and restyled in 1934 when the present facade was added.

The Baroque **Residenz**, which was also started in 1651, on the site of a Benedictine monastery, has several lavishly furnished rooms, in Rococo style. In addition to noting the furnishings, be sure to look at the structure of the building itself with all its embellishments.

Zumsteinhaus, built in classical style in the early 1800s, is the place to get an overview of the Roman town that lies (in ruins) across the river. Many items found on the Roman site are displayed in the museum, in addition to the displays that show the geology and other qualities of the Algäu region. Be sure to allow time for the garden, especially when the weather warrants.

On the other side of the river, **Cambodunum** is thought to have originally been built by Celts, in wood. After the time of Nero, when this town shared the fate of many by being burned, the community rebuilt in stone. Restorations of the Roman settlement have been undertaken since 1982, according to specific plan; discoveries are on-going, with the best of the artifacts on display at Zumsteinhaus.

LODGING: The **Hotel Fürstenhof** *(74 rooms;* ☎ *831+253.60, FAX 831+25.61.20)* is conveniently located on the Rathausplatz. If you're traveling by car, consider stopping at the **Goldenes Kreuz** *(Marktplatz 1, WD-8961 Wiggensbach, Germany;* ☎ *8370+8090)*, in a nearby suburb, for an interlude in a traditional half-timber building, where bedrooms have modern comforts and meals served in the restaurant are made according to regional recipes.

KONSTANZ

Konstanz *(D-78465;* ☎ *7531+28.43.76; FAX 7531+73.32.74)*, on the western end of the Bodensee, was built on the site of a former Roman fort. Today, the city, which is known as Constance in English, is a thriving, modern city with a charming medieval core. From the shore to the Romanesque-Gothic cathedral, the Niederburg (old part of town) is a warren of narrow streets and charming buildings that now hold pubs, shops and restaurants. At its best when opera performances are held in the Renaissance Rathaus, the town has several interesting museums and an ever-fascinating lake.

LODGING: Although there are many comfortable places to stay in Konstanz, led by the **Steigenberger Inselhotel** *(100 rooms;* ☎ *7531+12.50, FAX 7531+264.02)*, elegantly sited on its own island tethered to the town, give some thought to staying in **Gottlieben**, a lakeside Swiss town that's within walking distance (and easy trainride or drive). (Refer to "Gottlieben," in the chapter about Switzerland.) In Konstanz, the **Rega Parkhotel am See** *(38 rooms;* ☎ *7531+510.77, FAX 7531+501.43)* has a lovely location on the lakeside promenade. The **Hotel Halm** *(102 rooms;* ☎ *7531+12.10, FAX 7531+218.03)*, reopened in May '91 after extensive refurbishing that gave all rooms TV, minibar and telephone with a FAX outlet. Meals are served in the intricately lavish *Maurischer Saal* (Moorish room), as well as the spartanly appointed *Brasserie*. The best bedrooms offer a view of the lake. First opened in 1974, the hotel has regained its former glory. In addition to the lavish places best known to businessfolk, there are several smaller places to stay. One worth noting is the **Hotel Deutsches Haus** *(42 rooms;* ☎ *7531+270.65, FAX 7531+272.66)*, on Marktstätte, a short walk into the old city from the railroad station. Bedrooms are small and spartanly furnished, but the Grüner family offers welcomed hospitality. **Apartment Hotel Konstanz** (☎ *7531+980.60, FAX 7531+980.67.77)*, within a short walk of the historic buildings, has apartments furnished with basics only at reasonable rates.

LANDSHUT

Landshut *(D-84028; ☎ 871+92.20.50, FAX 871+892.75)*, northeast of München (about as far from the Franz-Josef Strauss airport heading northeast as München is heading southwest), is a historic city that takes on bigger-than-life proportions at the time of its famous **Landshuter Hochzeit 1475**, held every four years in the summer. The reenactment of the 15th century wedding of Georg, the Landshut duke's son, and Hedwig, the daughter of the Polish king, most recently took place early July 1993; the next event will be in 1997.

Although 1993 was a big year for Landshut, with the wedding reenactment, the celebration of the 500th anniversary of **Landshuter Brauhaus** (brewery), and the **Jahrhundertmarkt der vergessen künste** (Turn of the Century Market of Forgotten Arts), held in May '93, the historic town has enough of interest to warrant a visit whenever you are in the area. Since Landshut is about an hour's train ride from the München Hauptbahnhof, a day trip is possible.

The Wedding of 1475 is a lavish presentation, with more than 2000 townspeople and others dressed in medieval costume assuming the roles of 15th century folks. The wedding procession starts in the historic part of town, with a parade to the *Wiesmahd*, the plot of land where the bride was supposed to have first entered town to be met by her future husband prior to the wedding. In the outdoor arena, the honored couple sit at a long banquet table, with other important guests, to enjoy a performance that includes flag throwing, jousting matches and other spectacular events.

Trademark of the town is its **Schloss**, grandly placed on the peak of the hill. The several streets of beautifully-restored medieval houses lie below the hill-capping castle, providing hours of entertainment, not only with the architecture, but also with the stores, *Stuben*, as the pub-like bars are known, and several interesting museums. The **Martinskirche**, with its intricate steeple and birckwork designs, has riches displayed in its museum, as well as within the church itself. **Stadtmuseum** has an intriguing collection of relics and crafts related to the town's history as well as an impressive collection of paintings.

Moser and Göttlicher, a renowned manufacturer of the traditional *Alpentraum trachten*, is located in Landhut, although clothes from the house are sold at boutiques and specialty stores here and elsewhere.

In addition to pleasures offered by the buildings and shops within the town, the outskirts of Landshut are laced with walking paths and with pleasant places to ride bicycles.

LODGING: Although it's possible to visit Landhut in a day trip from München, there's a lot to be said for settling here, perhaps making it your base for day trips into the bigger city. The **Romantikhotel Fürstenhof** *(24 rooms; ☎ 871+820.25, FAX 871+890.42)*, in a gabled-roof art nouveau villa, within easy stroll of the enchanting buildings of the old part of town, is my first choice for lodgings, not only for the hospitality offered by Hertha Sellmair and others, but also for the traditional atmosphere made all the more pleasing with the regional specialties served in the hotel's dining room. The **Lindner Hotel Kaiserhof** *(139 rooms; ☎ 871+68.70, FAX 871+68.74.03)* has modern rooms and facilities appealing to tour groups, but I've also enjoyed the smaller **Hotel Gasthof Ochsenwirt** *(9 rooms; ☎ 871+234.39)* and the slightly larger **Hotel Goldene Sonne** *(55 rooms; ☎ 871+230.87, FAX 871+240.69)*, which seem to me to have more atmosphere (and less expensive rates).

LINDAU

Lindau *(D-88131; ☎ 8382+5022)*, at the eastern end of the Bodensee, is delightful, especially if you're here when the tour buses are not, which usually means visiting overnight or in fall, winter, or early spring. The medieval part of the town, on a small island across the Neue Seebrücke, is the heart of the matter, with cafés placed at appropriate places for lingering. **Hauptstrasse**, the main street, and the **Altes Rathaus**, the old town hall, are places to start wandering, following the narrow streets, which veer off at all angles. Although the Hafen (harbor) is always a nest of tourists, it is the departure point for boats that set out on the lake whose borders are shared by Germany, Switzerland, and at Bregenz, Austria.

LODGING: There are dozens of hotels near the lake. The **Bayerischer Hof** *(104 rooms; ☎ 8382+50.55, FAX 8382+505.52.02)* has claimed its piece of lakefront for more than 100 years. Now refurbished, with the best of the large bedrooms offering views of the Bregenzer Bucht and the Alps (on clear days), the hotel has a swimming pool and terraces that are pleasant in warm weather months. The smaller, more intimate **Insel-Hotel** *(28 rooms; ☎ 8382+50.17,*

FAX 8383+67.56) or the **Lindauer Hof** *(25 rooms;* ☎ *8382+40.64)* have cozy atmosphere in congenial surroundings. The **Hotel Reute-mann** *(37 rooms;* ☎ *8382+50.55, FAX 8382+50.54)*, near the railroad station at the lakefront, shares an ownership link with the Bayischer-hof, mentioned above, as does the **Hotel Seegarten** *(27 rooms;* ☎ *8382+50.55, FAX 8382+50.54)*. Both hotels are in traditional style with modernized bedrooms that have TV, duvets and other comforts. These hotels also have pools and are in the historic part of Lindau at the lakefront.

INSEL MAINAU

Insel Mainau (☎ *7531+30.30, FAX 7531+30.32.48)*, a 100 acre (45 hectare) island in the Bodensee, easily reached from Lindau, is unique. It's now a labor of love (and business) that is shared with all who make the time to visit. Owned by the family of Count Lennart Bernadotte and maintained as a national monument in his name, the island is an environmental and ecological preserve. Established as a charitable foundation in 1974 by Countess Sonja and Count Len-nart Bernadotte, the island was the summer residence for Grand Duke Friedrich I of Baden in 1853, when he began to create the re-markable arboretum, as a showcase for tree specimens from around the world. Its worthy goal has been sustained under supervision of Count Lennart, Grand Duke Friedrich's great grandson, and, more recently, by his family. Excavations in the 1930s yielded evidence of six houses from the New Stone Age and a Roman settlement in the first century A.D. when the Rhaetian tribes lived in the region. These days, it is the works of the German Horticultural Society, founded in 1822 and reestablished in 1955 (with Count Lennart as its president after the end of World War II), that have turned the is-land into a delightful garden. From the time of Count Lennart's marriage to Countess Sonja, in 1972, the island has become both an idyllic place for visitors to enjoy flourishing gardens, each in its sea-son, as well as a place for studies of botany and other environmental pursuits.

In additon to the joys of the gardens, the Heraldic Hall and public rooms of the castle are open at specific times, and there are concerts and other events held on a detailed schedule. The **Restaurant** (☎ *7531+30.31.56)* is open year round. Linked to the mainland with a bridge, the island is a short walk from the center of Lindau. Public transportation—buses from the central rail station as well as fer-ries—also link the island to Lindau.

MITTENWALD

Mittenwald *(D-82481;* ☎ *8823+1051),* about 12 miles from Garmisch on the trade route through the Brenner Pass between Augsburg and Verona, has been a home of stringed instruments since Matthias Klotz returned from Cremona in 1684. He brought with him an expertise in stringed instruments that has led to the violin school and to the **stringed instruments museum** that can be visited today. Still made painstakingly by hand by a few local craftsmen, the violins can be enjoyed from wood choice through creation and final polishing. Although the town has capitulated to tourism these days, it is still a pleasant place to use as a base for mountain walks and hikes —and for winter skiing for those who enjoy cross-country skiing as well as downhill.

Mittenwald, Germany

LODGING: For mealtime or lodging, my choice is the **Post** *(160 rooms;* ☎ *8823+10.94, FAX 8823+10.96),* which has a good location on the main street and a lovely Bavarian atmosphere. Among the several smaller spots, my vote goes to the **Gasthof Gries** *(10 rooms;* ☎ *8823+55.54),* which is best known as a restaurant and puts tables outside as soon as the weather warms. If you have a few days to spend in this area, consider the **Hotel-Pension Jagdhaus Drachenburg** *(27 rooms; Elmauerweg 20;* ☎ *8823+1249),* a modestly-priced hunting lodge in the nearby woods, with a small sauna and a big view.

MÜNCHEN

München (*Rindermarkt 5, D-80331;* ☎ *89+239.11),* the capital of
Bavaria, has many exceptional museums as well as a full roster of
opera, concerts and other musical events. The rollicking, frollicking
fall beer festival, the Oktoberfest, has its international following, but
München is even better, in my opinion, before or after that event
and throughout the winter, when the cultural season is in full swing
and the city takes its rightful place as a sophisticated center with a
fun-filled heart.

Sharing the other side of the München coin with the country-style,
fun-loving, foot-stomping Bavarians is a cosmopolitan city that fills
its streets with the latest models of Mercedes and BMWs, its shops
with couture fashions and punctuates its outskirts with palaces that
have provided city escapes through several generations.

München has many historical points of interest, in spite of the fact
that most buildings were destroyed by 66 bombing attacks in the
early 1940s. Rising phoenixlike in the late 1950s, as was the case
with many German cities after World War II, many of München's
most impressive monuments and buildings were reconstructed according to their prewar status. Most are in Renaissance style, which
was followed by a Baroque and Rococo period during the reign of
Elector Ferdinand Maria, when the Palace of Nymphenburg was
started and architects and sculptors built as well as beautified. Late in
the first half of the 19th century Ludwig I made München a focus
for the arts, while he oversaw the creation of Königsplatz, Ludwigstrasse, and several galleries, including the **Gyptothek**, the **Neue
Staatsgalerie**, **Alte** and **Neue Pinakothek**, and the **Allerheiligen-
Hofkirche**.

The **Kleine Stadtrundfahrt** (little city tour) is an ideal way to get
your bearings. The tour operates several times daily in summer and
at least twice a day the rest of the year; the bus departs from the Bahnhofplatz, next to Hertie Department Store. The route touches the
high points: Max-Josef-Strasse, Königsplatz, past Siegestor (Victory
Arch), Maximilianeum (Bavarian parliament), the Residenz (royal
residence of the Bavarian rulers), the Hofgarten (court garden), zig-
zagging across the midsection of the city so that you get an idea of
where things are located.

One route for wandering in the historic and shop-filled Altstadt is
to start at **Karlsplatz**, just off the big, wide, heavily trafficked Maximilianstrasse, the ring road around the Altstadt. Neuhauser Strasse,
when linked with Schützenstrasse and Kaufingerstrasse, is a pedestri-

an way, which makes it a wonderful place to window shop and people watch. München's world promenades along the long street, from early morning to late in the evening. In addition to the big stores and small shops, street musicians play for whoever will listen, and when weather warms, the seasons' crop of café chairs and tables for serving wurst and steins of beer sprout on the pavement. **St. Michaelskirche**, rebuilt after devastating bombing of this area on November 2, 1944, is along this route, as is the **Deutsches Jagd-und Fischereimuseum** *(German Museum of Hunting and Fishing, Neuhauser Strasse 53)*, on the site of the Augustiner-Klosterkirche, built in 1291. The museum has been here since 1966, and holds trophies, mounted deer heads with antlers and other hunting items, in addition to prints and documents.

A detour to the left at Kaufingerstrasse will bring you to Frauenplatz and the famed **Frauenkirche**, a München landmark. Most of the original church was built from 1468 to 1488 by Jörg von Polling, also known as Jörg von Halspach, and nicknamed Ganghofer. The parish church is in typical Bavarian style. The twin 325-foot domed towers were added later, in 1525. The fact that the building was partially destroyed during the war helps to explain the stark interior, but a number of medieval artworks have been donated to the new church.

Erasmus Grasser made the marvelous wood figures on the choir stalls in 1502, and a few of the stained-glass windows are from the 14th and 15th centuries. It's hard not to notice the wooden Christ suspended on the upper wall over the altar, but be sure to look at the monument of Kaiser Ludwig, in late Gothic style, with the pairs of laughing angels looking at the coat of arms.

Veer off to Marienplatz and, if you've timed your arrival for 11 o'clock, you'll witness the "show" of the dancing figures on the tower of the **Glockenspiel** at the Rathaus.

Among the many exceptional museums, there's one touchstone for Alpine travelers. The **Bayerisches Nationalmuseum**, founded by King Maximilian II in 1855, holds over 20,000 objects, most of them related to life in the Alps. The selection of "European Art and Handicraft of Nine Centuries" is the best of its kind, and the unique collection of 17th- to 19th-century nativity scenes, known as *Krippen* in German (or *crèches* in French, which is often mis-translated as "crib" in English), portray village life as the craftsman knew it. Christ and those around him often wear the dress and are in surroundings that the artisan knew best. Special areas are also devoted to textiles, applied arts, costumes and home furnishings, as well as porcelain and faience.

Schloss Nymphenburg, on the outskirts of München, is noteworthy not only for its impressive building, interior stuccowork, paintings and lovely gardens—a legacy of the Italian workmen who were brought in to build the place—but also for the Nymphenburg porcelain atelier that occupies one "arm" of the huge-and-impressive palace. (The atelier is to the right as you face the palace.) The estate was in full swing and elegant when Baron Charles Louis von Pollnitz wrote enthusiastically about it in 1737. It was started in 1663 and was given to the Electress Henriette Adelaide of Savoy from her husband, Elector Ferdinand Maria, who was jubilant about the birth of his heir. The original palace is the core of the palace that now stands. The approach, off the main Stuttgart-Ulm-Augsburg road, is magnificent, with wrought iron gates and an esplanade dividing a wide avenue where 18th-century carriages would have stood. The canal was built by the Turks (prisoners of war) and used to have gondolas on it. The waterway is now popular for the sport of curling, when it freezes in the winter months.

Schloss Nymphenburg can be reached by tram #12 from the center of München.

RESTAURANTS: The **Schlosswirtschaft zur Schwaige** (☎ 89+ *17.44.21, FAX 89+178.41.01)*, originally the oldest farmhouse in an area that was all farmland, was a restaurant before the palace was built. The setting is very attractive, with several small rooms, each with its own style, from country-formal to mansion-elegant. The menu features specialties from the region, often prepared in traditional style. Reservations are advised.

The gardens are popular with local folks, especially on weekends and holidays. The Pagodenburg, a Chinese-style pavilion that was the away-from-it-all place for Maximilian Emanuel, and the lovely Amalienburg Pavilion, built in 1734 by Elector Karl Albrecht, son of Maximilian Emanuel, for his wife, Electress Maria Amalia, are two of the many charming follies throughout the gardens. The pavilion, which is small enough to see in an hour or so, is reached by passing through the left arcades as you face the schloss. It was the inspiration of François de Cuvillies, the Walloon dwarf befriended by Elector Maximilian Emanuel, who hired him, at the age of eight, to be the court dwarf—an honor in those days. Cuvillies was sent to schools in France, but he returned to devote his life and his considerable talents to the family—father and son. He designed this masterpiece, plus the

202 FIELDING'S SWITZERLAND AND THE ALPINE REGION 1994

Altes Residenztheater in München and other rooms and buildings for the Wittelsbach family.

Today's München combines many traditional customs and time-honored costumes with the best of modern public transportation, restaurants, and hotels.

LODGING: My top vote for a place to stay goes to the elegantly historic **Hotel Rafael** *(D-80331; 35 rooms; Neuturmstrasse 1;* ☎ *89+29.09.80; FAX 89+22.25.39)*, in the old part of the city, sharing a block with the famous Hofbräuhaus, but quite different from that earthy atmosphere. From the rooftop swimming pool, there's a spectacular view of the city; many rooms offer nice views of and over the city's rooftops. This *Antic Haus* was restored to its 1924 design where possible and meaningful. The city's *Leading Hotel* is the **Vier Jahreszeiten** *(314 rooms; Maximilianstrasse, D-80539;* ☎ *89+ 23.03.90)*, pronounced "fear yahr-it-zeye-ten," and translating as "Four Seasons," a prestigious place within walking distance of everything that matters in this city. This hotel is a classic, beloved by businessmen and tony travelers who want to enjoy an elegant lifestyle. The **Hotel Platzl** *(170 rooms;* ☎ *89+23.70.30, FAX 89+23.70.38.00)*, in this same area, with a history that belies its present spruced up appearance has a rooftop fitness center and rooms with modern appurtenances. A cozy old-style hotel when I first stayed here, this property has been totally gutted, reappearing as a modern hotel, within a historic shell, a few steps from the famed Hofbrauhaus.

Among the many other hotels, here's my choice of a few small spots, some of them very modestly priced, and all conveniently located between Hauptbahnhof and the Altstadt. The **Andi** *(30 rooms; Landwehrstrasse 33, D-80539;* ☎ *89+59.60.67; FAX 89+55.34.27)* makes the most of its tiny lobby and small bedrooms with attractive, fresh decor; **Hotel Germania** *(99 rooms; Schwanthalerstrasse 28, D-80336;* ☎ *89+516.80; FAX 89+59.84.91)*, at the corner of Schillerstrasse, used to have a Best Western reservations link, but is now linked with a popular German hotel group; and the small **Hotel Schwiez** *(45 rooms; Goethestrasse 26, D-80336;* ☎ *89+53.95.85, FAX 89+53.98.26.63)*, a short walk from the Hauptbahnhof, charges modest rates for its small, clean rooms and serves an ample breakfast in a rooftop room. Near the Hofbräuhaus, both the **Alcron** *(21 rooms; Lederestrasse 13, D-80331;* ☎ *89+228.35.11)* and the **Hotel Adler** *(30 rooms; Lederestrasse 8, D-80331;* ☎ *89+22.39.91, FAX 89+228.94.37)* are convenient and adequate, with small-but-tidy bedrooms. Both are wedged into narrow doorways on shopping streets, within a few steps of many noteworthy sights of the old city.

The **Hotel Uhland** *(27 rooms; Uhlandstrasse 1, D-80336;*
☎ *89+53.92.77, FAX 89+53.11.14)*, in an interesting 5-story mansion, is convenient to the Oktoberfest grounds and only about 10
minutes' walk from the Hauptbahnhof.

RESTAURANTS: Don't miss the **Haxenbauer** *(at Lederestrasse and
Sparkassenstrasse)*, not far from the Glockenspiel at the end of the
shopping promenade, noted for its various recipes for pork hocks,
the best of which (in my opinion) are those that are roasted on a spit,
which you can see turning by 8 a.m. For reasonably priced meals,
with good regional specialties, try the **Augustiner Grossgaststätten**
(Neuhauser Strasse 16; ☎ *89+55.19.92.57)*, which has a typical beer
hall atmosphere. To mingle with the social set of München, stop by
for tea at **Alois Dallmayr**, an elegant specialty food shop that has
been open at the same site since 1671. (The shop has been of service
to 15 monarchies and countless numbers of the rest of us.) To enjoy
the "other" face of München, visit the **Hofbräuhaus**, always a commercial venture, as a lively, bustling beer hall, not far from the
Rathaus in the Altstadt. At Marienplatz, a window seat at the 6th
floor **Hoch Café** is as close as you'll get to eye level with the animated
clock and Glockenspiel on the tower of the Neues Rathaus (which
also has a restaurant in its basement). The dowdy entrance is near the
street level Peters Keller and a Benetton shop.

OBERAMMERGAU

Oberammergau *(D-82487;* ☎ *8822+1021)*, on the Laine river,
about 12 miles (18 km) from Garmisch, dates its Passion Play from
1634, when it was performed by grateful citizens who had been
spared the plague that had wiped out many nearby villages. The
plays have been performed, with few exceptions (a major one being
World War II), at ten-year intervals ever since. Although crowds
swell the village at the time of the **Passion Play** and tickets (and
hotel reservations) must be obtained many months in advance, the
village is worth visiting for its own Bavarian-Alpine personality at
other times as well. The shops that fleck the town's streets are filled
with woodcarvings that take inspiration from both religious and sec-
ular sources.

About 10 miles west of Oberammergau, **Schloss Linderhof** stands
as another example of the late 19th-century castle creations of Wittelsbach King Ludwig II. Its fountain-studded gardens can be as fascinating for leisurely strolls in pleasant weather as the castle itself is
for prowling through its richly embellished rooms amid the many

legends. (When in this area, "Ettal" (see above) is also worth some time.)

LODGING: Although the number of places to stay is longer and fuller for nearby Garmisch-Partenkirchen, there are some worthy lodgings in Oberammergau, which has developed as a tourist town. The once-cozy **Alois Lang** *(St.-Lukas-Strasse 15; 70 rooms;* ☎ *8822+760; FAX 8822+4723)* has grown to include a new building with rooms in modern style. The facade recalls the traditional buildings of the town; the restaurant fare is reasonably good. The **Hotel Bold** *(König-Ludwig-Strasse 10; 62 rooms;* ☎ *8822+3021; FAX 8822+7021)* has also added a block of new rooms to its traditional stucco and wood style. Another convenient choice is the **Turmwirt** *(Ettaler Strasse 2; 44 rooms;* ☎ *8822+3091; FAX 8822+1437)*; the **Parkhotel Sonnenhof** *(König-Ludwig-Strasse 12; 80 rooms;* ☎ *8822+1071; FAX 8822+3047)* is slightly grander and bigger. All hotels welcome groups at the time of the passion play, but usually have available rooms at other times.

OBERSTAUFEN

Oberstaufen *(D-87534;* ☎ *8386+2024)*, in the Allgäu, about 100 miles (155 km) southwest of München, is a major health and tourism center. Although many of the hotels in the town are devoted to health cures and such rituals, there are many others in charming villages in the surrounding farm country. One worth finding is the **Traube** *(Thalkirchdorf; 25 rooms;* ☎ *8325+451; FAX 8325+756)*, although the **Gasthof Zum Ochsen** *(Thalkirchdorf; 9 rooms;* ☎ *8325+242)* is a pleasant, small pension where 5 rooms have private bathroom.

ROSENHEIM

Rosenheim *(D-83022;* ☎ *8031+300.10; FAX 8031+30.01.64)*, a cultural center with a style reminiscent of the Mediterranean, nestles in the valley of the Inn river. Its impressive buildings, marketplace, and museums give it a special appeal.

LODGING: If you're planning to stay here and want some atmosphere, head for the small **Goldener Hirsch** *(33 rooms; Münchener Strasse 40;* ☎ *8031+120.29)*.

TEGERNSEE

Tegernsee *(D-83684;* ☎ *8022+18.01.40; FAX 8022+3758)*, south of München and east of Bad Tölz, is the name for both a popular Bavarian lake and one of the villages at its shore. Noteworthy as the abbey from which Benedictine monks founded München, the village is on the eastern side of the lake, where the original abbey, dating from 711, was incorporated in 1803 into a palace enjoyed by Maximilian I Josef. The Schloss also holds a Brauhaus where beer has been made for centuries. The Heimatmuseum in the Schlosskirche has a collection of regional crafts and pictures of rural life through the centuries.

The lake is a favorite for sailing, swimming and motorboat rides. There are several pleasant walking paths around the shore, plus more strenuous walks and hikes in the nearby mountains.

On the western shore, across the lake from Tegernsee village, the **Wiesseer Hof** *(54 rooms; Sanktjohanserstrasse 46, D-83707 Bad Wiessee;* ☎ *8022+820.61)* has an Alpine feeling, especially in its rooms with balcony and window boxes. Meals are served on a pleasant sun terrace when the weather is warm enough; otherwise, meals are served in the cozy dining rooms on the street level. Nearby, **Der Jagerwinkel** combines modern spa treatments with traditional Bavarian atmosphere in its new buildings. This area is very popular for farm holidays. (See further comment under "Lodgings" above.)

Rottach-Egern *(D-83700;* ☎ *8022+67.13.41; FAX 8022+67.13.47)*, a two-village community on the southern shore of the lake, is a popular warm-weather vacation area for Germans and other Europeans in search of a lakeside holiday.

LODGING: The luxurious **Hotel Bachmair am See** *(250 rooms; Seestrasse 47;* ☎ *8022+2720; FAX 8022+27.27.90)* is a tony spa resort with a truly Bavarian atmosphere. In addition to its spa facilities, the resort has tennis courts, indoor and outdoor pools, opportunities for sailing and windsurfing in warm weather and skiing nearby in winter. There are dozens of other hotels, many of them small pensions, in the area.

SPORTS

The southern part of the state of Bavaria claims most of Germany's Alpine region, and sports are an important part of the Bavarian lifestyle. Even in München, people can enjoy river-rafting, bike-riding and walks in the woods and along the riverside. In addition, the Alps that rise in the south are easily reached by public transportation as well as by car. People shrouded with skis, rucksacks and other trappings of the outdoor life are familiar sights in the München Bahnhof (railway station).

In the Ostallgäu, to the southwest, where there are 30 lakes, the ridge of the Allgäu High Alps is a challenging route for experienced climbers. The area around Füssen and Bad Faulenbach, with Weissensee and Hopfensee, offers both lakes and mountains. The southern end of the Romantic Road reaches Germany's Alpine area at Schwangau and Füssen. Travelers who then head east, along the Alps, will be richly rewarded with lakes, mountain peaks and many lovely villages and towns. The two-town resort of Garmisch-Partenkirchen lies in the valley of the Loisach and Partnach rivers, at the foot of the Alpspitze and near the Zugspitze, Germany's highest peak at 9731 feet. Berchtesgadener Land is a popular area for outdoor sports, both from a base at Berchtesgaden and from the many small towns in the area. The Königsee, nestled near the Austrian border (and Salzburg), is the deepest lake in Oberbayern (Upper Bavaria). In all cases the local Verkehrsverein (tourist office) is your on-the-spot source for facts as well as for walking maps and itineraries, costs and times for guided walks and hikes.

Here are tips about where to enjoy specific sports:

BALLOONING

Berchtesgaden is one place that offers hot air ballooning. In past seasons, **The Bombard Society** *(6727 Curran St., McLean, VA 22101;* ☎ *800+862-8537* or *703+448-9407)* has planned special trips in Bavaria, using Füssen as headquarters.

BICYCLING

About 100 Bavarian railroad stations have bicycles for rent, for about DM 8 per day when you show your rail ticket and about DM 10 without a rail ticket. Ask for a map-guide when you rent your bike. The local tourist offices are prime sources for information about inn-to-inn journeys, the guided bike tours that cover long distances with overnight lodging at inns along the way. Bicycles can also be rented through hotels and shops at many resort centers, especially those on lake shores. Check with the tourist offices at Füssen, for example, or at Bad Reichenhall, Berchtesgaden, towns around the Ammersee and at many places in the Chiemgäuer Alps and around the Chiemsee. Even from the most popular resort areas such as Garmisch-Partenkirchen, it's possible to get into very rural countryside within a few minutes' ride from the place where you rent a bike.

CANOEING

Popular rivers include the Isar, Vils, Rott and Inn in Lower Bavaria, south of the Donau (Danube). The local tourist offices are your best sources for names of firms who rent canoes and lead expeditions. See "River Rafting," below. *Wildwasser-Kanufahrten,* translated as "wild-water canoeing," can be arranged.

FISHING

The many Alpine lakes and rivers offer good fishing possibilities. Although some resorts have temporary permits for visitors, it's best to check with the local tourist offices well in advance of your travels to be sure you have the necessary licenses, or know where you can get them expeditiously after you arrive. In some places you can get a day permit for DM 10 from the city hall. Bring extra passport photos, which you'll need for the permit. Among the lakes noted for fishing are the Königsee, Waginger See, Chiemsee, Tegernsee, Schliersee, Starnberger See, Ammersee and Wörthsee, as well as the rivers Inn, Isar and Loisach. The Bertchesgaden area also has rivers for trout fishing. Fisherfolk should make time, while passing through München, to visit the **Deutsches Jagd-und Fischereimuseum** *(German Museum of Hunting and Fishing, Neuhauser Strasse 53, D-80331 München;* ☎ *89+22.05.22).* Although the museum has several special exhibits that seem to have little to do with its stated focus, there are some good relief maps of various parts of the German Alpine areas and some displays of interest.

GOLF

There are well-maintained courses near München and at Garmisch-Partenkirchen, as well as at Bad Wiessee, Berchtesgaden, Oberstdorf and Lindau. Be sure to ask about the course and about the equipment for rental. The tourist office and specific resort hotels are your best sources.

HANG GLIDING/SOARING

The sport is very popular, especially off the Unternberg and Hochplatte above Marquartstein, in the Chiemgau Alps. In the area around München, contact tourist offices in Dachau, Erding, Wartenberg, Ingolstadt, Moosburg, Neuburg/Donau and Pfaffenhofen an der Ilm. Not far from Berchtesgaden, Schongau am Königssee *(D-86956)* offers the sport. Contact Franz Wenig *(Richard Voss-Strasse 73;* ☎ *8652+2363).* In the valley of the Tegernsee, tourist offices in Rottach-Egern and Tegernsee have the facts. There are also places in Ander-Aufham, in the Bad Reichenhall-Saklzstrasse area and near Wendelstein (mountain) at Niederaudorf, Oberaudorf and Samerberg. Near the Schliersee, inquire at the tourist offices of Bayischzell and Fischbachau. The sport is also popular at the Tegelberg (mountains), near Schwangau, southwest of München and around Garmisch-Partenkirchen, Oberammergau and Landsberg am Lech in the Ammersee area. Contact the German National Tourist Office for names of soaring schools. Rottach-Egern on the Tegernsee is one place to note.

HIKING

Spazierwege (beginner's trails) are clearly marked, usually with brown signs and yellow script. *Wanderwege* (intermediate trails) have white signs with blue script, and the sometimes strenuous *Bergwanderwege* (mountain trails) have black signs with white script. Sport shops sell good maps with hiking routes clearly marked. The local tourist offices often double as headquarters for the mountain-guide association. Even when they don't, they are still the best sources for guide information and for daily activities that often include planned hikes and walks. The area around the two-town resort of Garmisch-Partenkirchen claims "185 miles of footpaths and promenades" and the Chiemgau, southeast of München, has 1620 miles. Berchtesgadener Land is also popular for walking and hiking; the Alpenverein maintains an office near the Kurgarten entrance *(Maximilianstrasse 1;* ☎ *8652+2207).* Footpaths thread through rural countryside and drape around Alpine heights everywhere in southern Germany. The **König-Ludwig-Fernwanderweg** *(King Ludwig Hiking Path)* stretches between Starnberg, Schwangau and Füssen. If you're familiar with German, most bookstores have good supplies of *Wanderkarten* (trail maps) and books outlining hikes and walks. One valuable source for trail details and information about mountain huts is the German Alpine Club, known as the **Deutscher Alpenverein** *(DAV, Praterinsel 5, D-80538 München 22;* ☎ *89+29.49.40).*

HORSEBACK RIDING

Most spas and resort centers offer trail rides and equestrian lessons. Known as *Pfaffenlehen*, the sport is popular in Garmisch-Partenkirchen, Berchtesgaden, Bad Reichenhall and Bad Tölz, but inquire also at smaller towns such as Prem am Lech in the Pfaffenwinkel area and Miesbach near the Schliersee for wonderfully rural riding. On the Chiemsee (see "Places Worth Finding," above), inquire at Hotel Gut Ising at Seebruck- Ising am Chiemsee about their equestrian center.

HUNTING

The sport is very restricted, and therefore not easy for outsiders' participation. Your best bet is to have a friend who owns a "Jagd," as the private hunting grounds are called. In München, the **Deutsches Jagd-und Fischereimuseum** *(German Museum of Hunting and Fishing, Neuhauser Strasse 53;* ☎ *89+22.05.22)* is worth visiting. It's convenient on the main promenade, not far from the moving clock.

MOUNTAINEERING/CLIMBING

Most of the Alpine resorts have expert guides; some arrange expeditions, but it's best to do preliminary research on the spot. The **Deutscher Alpenverein** *(German Alpine Association, Praterinsel 5, D-80538 München, Germany;* ☎ *89+29.49.40)* maintains more than 24,000 miles of trails and offers introductory climbing courses as well as guides for accomplished climbers. Contact the organization with your specific questions. Areas that are good starting points, with expert guides available, include Garmisch-Partenkirchen, Berchtesgaden, Oberstdorf and Mittenwald.

RIVER RAFTING

Facilities range from the party-style recreational raft that makes its way between Wolfratshausen to München along the Isar to challenging whitewater rafting and canoeing. Known as *River-trekking* or *Wildwasserprogramm*, the sport of riding the rapids is popular wherever rivers allow. **Meuwly & Eichhammer** *(Postfach 1321, D-83301 Traunreut, Germany)* is one contact for organized rafting trips. (See "Canoeing," above.)

ROWING

Mostly recreational, the rowboats can be rented from lakeside resorts and *Bootsverleih*, the concessionaires along the most popular lakes.

SAILING

Southeast of München and about 35 minutes' ride on the S-Bahn, the "five lakes district"—the area around the Starnberger See, Ammersee,

Wesslinger See, Pilsensee and Wörthsee—offers a full range of watersports. Within easy distance of Garmisch-Partenkirchen, there are sailing centers at Walchensee, Eibsee, Riessersee and on the shores of other lakes. Rottach-Egern on the Tegernsee is a sailing source, and the sport is also popular on the castle-punctuated Chiemsee. Southwest of München, the Forggensee and Bannwaldsee are popular for sailing. Ask for details from the local tourist offices.

SKIING

For winter skiing, the prized winter resorts are led by Garmisch-Partenkirchen. The resort is also the platform from which late-spring skiers set out for an area high on the Zugspitze, where snows usually last into May. The German National Tourist Office in New York (☎ *212+661-7200)* and Los Angeles (☎ *310+575-9799)* have constantly updated information about snow conditions during winter months.

SWIMMING

Many of the lakes are enjoyed by vacationing Germans and others. The Bannwaldsee, the Foggensee and the Schwansee, in the Ostallgäu, are popular European resorts. The lakes that lie southeast of München are also very popular, but the best resort hotels often have swimming pools, and there are usually public pools in the towns.

TENNIS

Most resort areas have tennis courts, many of which are enclosed to allow for year-round play. Both at Füssen and at neighboring Hopfen am See there are courts and many Bavarian resorts feature tennis. Look into Bad Tölz and Bad Reichenhall, for example, and count on courts at Garmisch-Partenkirchen.

WALKING/TREKKING

Paths are well marked and "everywhere," especially in the Bavarian forest, in the wide valleys around the Wendelstein and on the rolling hills between the Ammersee and the Lech river. (See "Hiking" above.) Although some of the Alpine resorts offer occasional guided wildflower walks, you'll do best on your own with a handy book you can purchase at one of the many bookstores.

WATERSKIING

Resorts on the shores of the bigger lakes are sources. Kiefersfelden, on the Hecht See, is one place that has a *Wasserskischule,* for those who want to learn the sport.

WINDSURFING/BOARDSAILING

The sport is very popular on most Bavarian lakes. Many of the sailors wear a wet suit for protection from the spring-fed or glacier-fed lake water; regulation "shoes" are essential in brisk and flukey winds.

TREASURES AND TRIFLES

The shops in Alpine towns are great sources for high-quality outdoor wear, especially during the fall and early January sales.

AUTHOR'S OBSERVATION

Mehrwertsteuer is the value-added tax for Germany. When you are making expensive purchases it may be worthwhile to apply for the tax refund, for which foreign visitors are eligible when the item(s) are taken out of the country. The complicated procedure includes asking for the refund forms at the time of purchase, having them stamped at the store, then keeping the forms and the item(s) handy to show to customs officials when you leave the country, at which time they will stamp the form. After that, you must mail the form to the store and await your refund–which will be sent to you in German marks, for you to convert through your local bank or another source of currency exchange.

München has many elegant shops where merchandise is top of the line (as are the prices). Maximilianstrasse is the long respected fashion center, but many of the boutiques nestle on side streets and elsewhere in the area. Among the shops, you'll find several that sell traditional Bavarian dress, either piecemeal (scarf, bodice, apron, skirt, petticoats and so on) or as a total outfit. **Ludwig Beck**, near Marienplatz, has sold *München Heimatwerk* since 1876 and has a wonderful collection of Bavarian-style clothes that could appear in social settings without looking like a costume. **Wallach**, on Residenz Strasse, is one of several shops to find for handcrafts.

The **Rosenthal Porzellanhaus Zollner** is the place to see Rosenthal porcelain, and **Dallmayr** is a favorite for food items. Both shops are worth visiting just to look, if not to buy. Displays are enchanting.

AUTHOR'S OBSERVATION

*December is a charmed month for München, with the annual **Christkindlmarkt**. Marienplatz is the heart of the celebration, but there are events throughout the Altstadt. Inquire about the Münchner Christkindl-Schlussel, a promotion that includes several bargains and events for visitors. The tourist office has details.*

Oberammergau, best known for the Passion Play that takes place there on a ten-year schedule, is also known for woodcarving. Shops are filled with all manner of small creatures and characters, with crèche figures a popular purchase and various farm figures also worth noting.

Landshut, easily reached by train from München, is the homebase for the *Alpentraum* name, used by the **Moser and Gottlicher** firm for some of the typical Bavarian clothing they manufacture. Planned for today's lifestyle, the Bavarian costumes can be found in elegant boutiques and special departments in the best stores in Germany.

For department stores, **Hertie** is one name that is prominent in München. Purchased by **Karstadt** department store in late 1993, the company will probably maintain its own name, which is widely respected in the southern and eastern parts of Germany. The multi-story department store on Schützenstrasse, near the Hauptbahnhof, is full of tempting items, not only clothing but also housewares and tinned foods, that are easy to pack and make good gifts.

ADDITIONAL INFORMATION SOURCES

Further information about the Alpine region of Germany can be obtained from the following addresses and telephone numbers. When telephoning or faxing from the U.S. dial the international access code followed by the country code for Germany, which is 49, and then the numbers given below. When you are telephoning from one area code to another within Germany, begin with a 0. Here's the form for addressing letters:

Fremdenverkehrsberband
Street Address
D-00000 Town name
GERMANY

BERCHTESGADENER LAND
Kurdirektion, *D-83471 Berchtesgaden.* ☎ *8652+5011; FAX 08652+633.00.*

BODENSEE AREA
Fremdenverkehrsverband Bodensee-Oberschwaben e.V., *Schutzenstrasse 8, D-78462 Konstanz.* ☎ *7531+222.32; FAX 7531+164.43.*

BAVARIA
Landesfremdenverkehrsverband Bayern e.V., *Prinzregentenstrasse 18/IV, D-80538 München.* ☎ *89+21.23.970; FAX 89+29.35.82.*

ALLGAU AREA
Fremdenverkehrsverband Allgau/Bayerische-Schwaben e.V., *Fuggerstrasse 9, D-86150 Augsburg 1.* ☎ *821+333.35; FAX 821+383.31.*

MÜNICH AND SOUTHEAST
Fremdenverkehrsverband München-Oberbayern e.V., *Sonnenstrasse 10, D-80331 München 22.* ☎ *89+59.73.47; FAX 89+59.31.87.*

EASTERN BAVARIA
Fremdenverkehrsverband Ostbayern e.V., *Landshuter Strasse 13, D-93047 Regensburg.* ☎ *941+56.02.60; FAX 941+570.41.*

ITALY

Riva di Garda, Italy

Clutching the telephone to her ear, her dark hair bouncing in the breezes, the young woman continued her energetic pace (and her animated chatter) without a pause, even when her pocketbook fell down to the crook in her right arm when she flung her left arm for emphasis. Bypassing her, at an even greater pace, a young man bellowed orders into the mouthpiece of the phone that was his link between hand and ear. A third person huddled in a doorway, punching numbers into his portable phone, as his body pushed his briefcase onto a ledge nearby. Milano is on the move.

I watched in disbelief from my pausing place at a streetside *trattoria*, partially sheltered from the buzzing noises of the street by a flank of eye-high trees-in-boxes. The city swirled around me. Milano is complicated and cosmopolitan; it moves at a peripatetic pace—and seems to take perverse pleasure in throwing its wastepaper and other rubbish into the street and letting its potentially beautiful gardens and parks thrive with weeds. Unkempt and perhaps unmanageable, Milano is a marvel.

Yes, the vast *Duomo* is awesome. (From first sighting, it has always recalled, for me, a gigantic seaside "castle," playfully made from dribbled white sand.) And its neighborhood, with *Teatro La Scala* and other cultural monuments vying with traffic-clogged streets for space, is memorable, not only for the impressive facades designed by notable architects, but more so for the talent that caused the buildings to be. It's true that today's mass tourism threatens to overwhelm this arena, but "mass" tourism has been part of the scene since the cathedral first lured the devout (and the merchants who sought to sell to them), when it was started in the 14th century and through its years of embellishments (which lasted well into the 18th century).

Even Como, growing from its lakefront, less than an hour's train ride away, seems almost suburban, but it is far more peaceful, even though it's a bigger community than most first-time visitors imagine.

The Alpine region of Italy, although tethered to the commerce, communication and convoluted politics of Milano, is a marvel of contrasts. Within an hour of the festering city (which has some of the country's best restaurants, by the way), you can stroll along mountain paths with only the local farmer for company. Although cars are the fastest way to make the link, trains allow for carefree time to contemplate the changing scenery.

And it is in these hills and valleys that the soul of the southern Alpine region survives. Art and architecture from northern Italy make an impressive mark, not only here but throughout the Alpine area. As artisans of the Middle Ages were lured onward in search of work, they paid for their travel by plying their skills—in tiny chapels of a mountain village, in the mansions of wealthy landholders, and in public buildings that seem to vie with their nearest neighbors for opulance, and take their first cue from the celebrated monuments created by the fashionable artists in the thriving cities of their time.

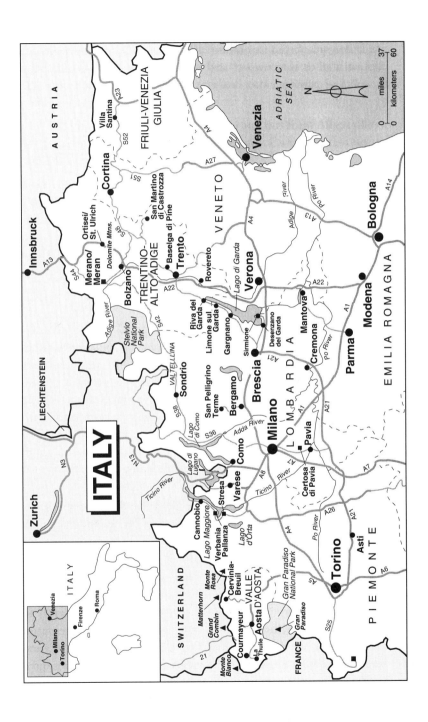

It is the farmlands and the valley villages, with the often-jagged mountains looming overhead, that speak softly of Alpine life. It is the home-grown produce that has been cajoled, by family recipes, into unforgettable sensations that keep certain *alberghi* in mind. It is the local wine, served from the vintner's private (and modest) cellar, that serves the senses. It is the open spaces, the spontaneous village festivals, the market that surprises a wandering traveler (although it has taken place on that day at that time for centuries). It is the sense of timelessness, the sense of permanence, the sense of nature—and natural people—providing hospitality, not because they have to, but because it comes from the heart, that makes the mountain villages of the Italian Alps so wonderfully appealing.

COUNTRY CAPSULE

Although Italy is some 745 miles long, only the top of the boot-shaped country is trimmed with the Alps. Claiming the "sunny side of the Alps," the southern side, the several regions that share the mountains also share a rich culture that crosses national borders and mingles languages in many communities. From the Celts and the ancient Romans to modern "invasions" of visitors, the region celebrates more than 2000 years of recorded history. Roman ruins fleck some areas while the small chapels that stand in remote villages are testimony to the talent of Italian artisans who embellished ceilings, walls and plasterwork in their inimitable way. Important cathedrals, public buildings and some of the homes fringe town piazzas and dot the countryside. Villas mark many of the region's lovely lakes, and nature's own art is intact, from the lakes and larch trees to the jagged mountain peaks.

Marked at its western border by the Gran Paradiso National Park, which joins the Parc National de la Vanoise of France and at its eastern border by parklands that abut those of Slovenia's Triglav National Park, the Alpine region of Italy is very developed in some areas and underdeveloped in others. The landscape is splintered with hundreds of narrow valleys, some of which are best visited on foot. Life is harsh in the most remote communities where accommodations for visitors are very simple when they exist at all.

Three important cities stud Italy's boot top: **Torino** in the western third, **Milano** at the middle and **Venezia** in the east, on the Gulf of Trieste. But it's the regions north of these cities that lead the Alpine life. In some cases, where ski slopes have been groomed for winter sport, burgeoning resorts call to the world's wealthy—and to the rest of us who enjoy life naturally. In others, villages remain as they have been for centuries, with their traditional customs intact and their daily life devoted to farming and to making a living from the land. Each valley weaves threads of the nearest great culture into something uniquely its own. From the western regions of Lombardia and Piemonte, with the Valle d'Aosta a nick on the northwest border, through the Alto Adige and Dolomite areas to the northeast's Friuli-Venezia Giulia region, the mountain villages often have a mild Mediterranean climate, warmed by the sun and often warm winds. While many of these villages enjoy rural simplicity, the cosmopolitan resorts are active with daytime sports and evening events.

The western **Piemonte** region, sharing the border (and some of its lifestyle) with France, claims Gran Paradiso National Park, the busy city of Torino, the resort of Sestrière, which was established by the Agnelli family, and the valley of the Po river, with its many lovely towns. A sliver of Piemonte reaches north of the Swiss town of Lugano.

The **Valle d'Aosta** region, which shares the border with France and Switzerland, is the northwestern nub, marked by Monte Rosa and several smaller valleys such as the lovely Valtounanche, Val d'Ayas and Valgrisanche. The resorts of Courmayeur and Cervinia-Breuil are better known to sportsfolk than the small town of Aosta that lends the valley its name.

Lombardia borders Switzerland, with towering Piz Bernina (13,371 feet), the lovely Alpine foothill lakes—including Lago Maggiore, Lago di Como, Lago d'Iseo and Lago di Garda—and the business that is the motor for the Italian economy. Long known for the excellence of its silk, and for the lure of its lakes, the region's economy revolves around Milano and, more recently, a thriving tourism.

The rugged, majestic Dolomite mountains, with the Trentino valley at the eastern portion of Italy's Alps, present a range of pleasures that include outdoor activities, historical sites, colorful festivals and countless inns and elegant hotels—all with a backdrop of gray-toned limestone mountains that assume awe-inspiring shapes and proportions.

The regions of **Trentino** and **Alto Adige**, sharing the border with Switzerland and Austria, claim a Ladin heritage related to that known in Switzerland's eastern Engadine valley. The Trentino, part of the Austro-Hungarian empire prior to World War I, rises from lakes to Alpine heights, tucking villages with red-tile roofs into pockets protected by natural terrain. The Alto Adige, called the Sud Tirol in German, borders Austria's provinces of Tirol and Vorarlberg. Because it runs north and south, and the sun can warm both sides, spring comes early to the Adige river valley.

Although Italian is the national language, French is also spoken as the Aosta valley stretches toward Mont Blanc and toward the Great St. Bernard Pass, which links Italy to Switzerland. And German is the common language in many villages of the bilingual Alto Adige/Sud Tirol area.

The arts and Italy are intertwined, from the time of the Etruscans through the Roman Empire, to the establishment of the Vatican as the home of Catholicism, and into the Renaissance, when the Medici and other patrons sponsored names that are now part of the world's culture. The influence of the grandest cultural capitals stretched north over the Alps, from Rome, Florence and other cities south of the Alpine region as well as from Torino, Milano and Venezia, the triumvirate on the southern side of the mountains. Reflections of styles appeared in architecture, in painting, in sculpture and in spirit. Imposing buildings still stand as testimony to affluence in lakeside towns and at staging points for Alpine crossings.

HISTORIC HIGHLIGHTS

Gateway to the Valle d'Aosta and Piemonte's Alpine resorts, Torino sits astride the Po River. Although its present fame may come from the Fiat Motor Company, its charm is the result of the many historic palazzi and piazze that set the tone. Far more than a lively city, with shops, restaurants and impressive social events, the city is the heartland of Italian unification. It was here, in 1870, that modern Italy was established.

Milano also has a venerable past, although it is best known by many as the heart of today's Italian fashion industry. Bustling with modern commerce, overwhelming and cluttered to first-time visitors, the city has been a crossroads since the time of the Celts, the ancient tribes that came from the east, through the Rhein and the Donau in the first millenium B.C. Referred to as Gauls by the ancient Romans, whose region they invaded in 390 B.C., the Celts maintained camps in the area now known as Milano. A Roman center at the time of Constantine, it was in this city—in 312—that he declared Christianity the religion of the Roman Empire.

The ubiquitous Romans marched through the Alps to settle points in the north, where their town plans and a few of their buildings can still be seen today. Barbarians swept through in subsequent years, with the Franks and Burgundians yielding to the invasions. Two names to note: Charlemagne and Napoleon. Charlemagne was king of the Lombards, following the area's invasion (in 765) by his father, Pippin, King of the Franks. Napoleon's troops stormed Milano, which Napoleon then made the capital of the Cisalpine Republic in 1797. It should come as no surprise, given its lively history, that the area—especially the Valle d'Aosta—is freckled with medieval fortresses and castles, most dating from the 10th to 15th centuries.

POLITICAL PICTURE

Italy has been referred to as the "fifth industrial power in the world," and most of the headline-making industry that drove the country into that position is in the north, where companies such as Fiat have their headquarters. Italian politics, however, is not as easily defined. The Italian Republic is administered through regions, which are made up of provinces. Each province has its capital, but is comprised of several towns, villages and communities, each of which also has its administrative official. The rampant corruption burst into headlines almost two years ago and housecleaning since that time has helped give the people a voice. In elections during 1993, candidates representing change won handily over the long- ensconced politicians.

A region may, and often does, have several different ethnic groups and more than one language. Italy has had more than 50 governments since the the mid-1940s and is undergoing a major catharsis as this book goes to press. Elections held in April '92 resulted in political convulsions, with both the Christian Democrats and the Socialists losing votes (and prestige), and political turmoil continued into 1994. By June '92, Giuliano Amato had been selected as prime minister, but he has been succeeded by others, in turn, in anticipation of parliamentary elections of March 27, 1994. Among the rival parties, major players are the Socialists and the Communists, with the Republican party and the Liberal Party joined by assorted special interest factions. The Italian Communist party has been known as the Democratic Party of the Left since early 1991, after Soviet-style Communism became the scapegoat for eastern Europe's economic paralysis. A *New York Times* reporter explained that "Italian politics is often described as Byzantine and difficult to fathom, but in fact there are a few basic rules that anyone can understand. If political language has entered the high-decibel range, it means that a government crisis is under way. If not, it means that a government crisis will be under way before long." In the meantime, daily life in Italy continues apace and visitors will experience its vagaries, which include protests and strikes as part of the mix.

LIFESTYLE

The egalitarian effects of the socialist government may seem obvious in cities and working-class neighborhoods, but Italian "aristocracy" continues to set a jet-set pace for a life of posh resorts and luxurious living. Italy's location on the sunny side of the Alps contributes to a relaxing, casual way of life that liberates the creative spirit, which is obvious in design and high style, regardless of the cost. Discos and colorful clothes are key elements for some resorts, but the earth-toned browns and stone grays sometimes set more somber notes for small villages that are away from the mainstream. Nature (and Catholicism) are woven into the daily patterns for life in villages within minutes of the cosmopolitan cities, as well as deep into the Alpine valleys. High-fashion mingles happily with tradition in some places, especially in small restaurants, where food takes its special flavor from well-orchestrated use of fresh produce with herbs and spices. Mealtimes are social events in Italy's Alpine region—tradition keeps food cooking in the kitchen most of the time and sprinkles rural roadsides with expanded homes-turned-inns where a good meal is assured. A real treat for visitors is to be present for one of the village festivals which are usually prompted by a harvest, the new wine, a religious event, or the end of winter.

NATURAL SURROUNDINGS

The Alpine areas now claimed by Italy include many of the area's most impressive peaks, namely the Matterhorn, Monte Bianco, Monte Rosa, Gran Paradiso and Gran Combin, all 4000-meter peaks in the Valle d'Aosta, plus awesome glaciers and flourishing forests. The high Alpine areas are freckled with lakes, some of them small and isolated, making them a special joy when you come upon them during walks and hikes. The slate roofs of the region's typical stone houses provide the perfect foil for the acres of meadows, dotted with wildflowers and snow-capped peaks in the distance. *Gran Paradiso*, covering 585 square kilometers between the Valle d'Aosta and Piemonte, was the first national park in Italy; it shares borders with the *Parc National de la Vanoise of France*. The five main valleys in Italy's park include the Val di Rhemes, the Val Savarenche and the Val di Cogne, which run north-south from the Valle d'Aosta, as well as the Orco and Soana valleys in the Canavese area. The narrow valleys on the south side slope down to the Orco valley.

Bird-watchers can find species such as snow finches, wall creepers, ptarmigans and choughs in the highest zones, and perhaps can spot the golden eagle, which lives in these mountains although it is not strictly an Alpine bird. Although mountain walks have special appeal, the green areas that border the Ticino river, from Sesto Calende on Lago Maggiore to Pavia, where the river joins the Po, are exceptional for wildlife. Hunting and shooting are outlawed in this area and picking the wildflowers is discouraged. Check with the tourist office in Bormio and with some of the larger hotels about guided walks in the Stelvio National Park, which borders eastern Switzerland's Engadine Valley.

PRACTICAL FACTS ABOUT ITALY

The more you know about where things are and how to find them, the happier your travels will be. It's not easy to find reliable information sources while you're traveling in Italy, especially if you don't speak Italian. Learn at least a few words and ask, in your hotel or a nearby big one as well as at the local tourist office, for leaflets that may give facts about the town you're in and its neighbors.

INFORMATION SOURCES

Ente Nazionale Italiano per il Turismo (ENIT) is the head office of tourism at *Via Marghera 2, I-00185 Roma, Italia,* ☎ *649+712.82.* Other offices include the **Italian Government Tourist Office**, *#550, 12400 Wilshire Blvd., Los Angeles, CA 90025,* ☎ *310+820-0098, FAX 310+820-6357; 630 Fifth Ave., New York, NY 10111,* ☎ *212+ 245-4822, FAX 212+586-9249; #1914, 1 Place Ville Marie, Montreal, Quebec, H3B 3M9 Canada,* ☎ *514+866-7667, FAX 514+392-1429.* Information is also available from the regional tourism offices whose addresses appear at the end of this chapter.

Throughout the chapter, local spelling is used for some words and all place names. For translation of foreign words, refer to the back-of-the-book glossary. Postal codes and telephone numbers for the tourist office are in parentheses following place names in "Places Worth Finding."

CASH, CURRENCY AND CREDIT CARDS

Italian lire are the units of currency. At press time, US$1 buys about 1650 lire, but check with your local bank, or on the financial pages of a major metropolitan newspaper or the *Wall Street Journal* to learn approximate equivalents at the time you plan to travel.

Banks, tourist offices and other possible money-changing places operate on schedules that I find difficult to anticipate, what with holidays, lunch hours, early closings and the vagaries of the Italian lifestyle. Plan ahead so you can exchange travelers cheques or bills when you're lucky enough to find a place that's ready to do so. Exchange booths and/or banks at railroad stations are usually (but not always) a safe bet, but you may have to wait in line for service.

AUTHOR'S OBSERVATION

For those who have difficulty, as I do, with the many zeros on Italian bills, make some time (while you're in your hotel room) to become familiar with the equivalents and then simply put your thumb over most zeros to deal with a smaller number.

Credit cards are widely accepted at major cities and in resort areas, but be prepared to pay cash, in lire, when you stop at a small trattoria by the side of the road in some out-of-the-way place.

COMMUNICATIONS

If you speak Italian, it helps—a lot. If not, watch for a while and practice some of the hand, eye and shoulder motions as well as the facial expressions that are as much a part of Italian conversation as the words. Adopt them as your own, if you can do so comfortably. Learning the Italian spelling and pronunciation for place names is the key to finding some of the most charming places. Although people you meet along the road or in the villages may not recognize an Anglicized pronunciation, if you print the word on a piece of paper, chances are someone can point you in the right direction. Although it's easy to decipher Milano and Roma, and recognize that Torino is Turin and Venezia, Venice, some other places may be more difficult to fathom. In northwestern Italy, some villages converse in both French and Italian. In the Alto Adige, also known as the Sud Tirol, Italian and German words are often mingled in the same sentence, and conversations are sprinkled with words in the local dialect. An added spice in this verbal stew is Ladin, related to the Swiss Engadine valley's Romansch and spoken in neighboring Italian valleys.

AUTHOR'S OBSERVATION

When dialects are strongest I find it easiest to spend some time with a good map and make my own discoveries. The most effective communication is face-to-face. Mail service can take forever; telephone service can be difficult; but standing on the spot and sprinkling conversation with genuine smiles seems to get results.

Telephone service works reasonably well when you're trying to reach Italy from outside the country, especially when Italian operators are not on strike and the phones are in working order. The country code for Italy is 39, which follows the international access code of your chosen carrier. The country code is followed by the city code and local number, which are the numbers given in the text that follows. Most businesses and many individuals have facsimile machines.

AUTHOR'S OBSERVATION

Telephone numbers in this chapter are given for direct dial from outside the country. Within Italy, you'll need to begin dialing out-of-town numbers with a "0."

While traveling in Italy, remember that telephone calls to the U.S. and other out-of-the-country places carry a large surcharge, especially when they are from the comfort of your hotel. International calling services, operated through U.S.-based companies rather than through the Italian telephone system, can result in much more reasonable costs. AT&T's *USADirect* was the first international service to put you immediately in touch with a U.S.-based operator who, obviously, speaks American English. The AT&T system is easy and effective, from any telephone anywhere in Italy. Simply step into the telephone booth, deposit your coin or card, dial *172+1011* and talk with the telephone operator in the U.S., who will then place your call over U.S. lines, charging it to your own telephone account in the U.S. or collect, as you specify. MCI and Sprint now have similar services.

In order to activate most public telephones, you'll need either a *gettone* (pronounced "gee-tone-eh"), a coin you can purchase for 200 lire from the *Tabak* shops, news stands and some coffee shops, or a plastic telephone card, the size of a charge card, that you can purchase at the post office and specific other places. Although the coin system is being phased out in favor of telephone cards, it's worthwhile having a few *gettoni* in case you can't find a card phone.

DOCUMENTS AND OTHER PAPERS

In addition to your passport, if you plan to rent a car, arrange through your nearest **American Automobile Association** (AAA) to buy an international driver's permit. (Further details are in the introductory chapters, under "Transporation.") Bring extra passport-size photos for ski passes, fishing permits and other passes you may want to purchase while in the Alpine areas.

MEDICAL FACILITIES

There are hospitals in major cities and towns and private clinics at many Alpine areas known for therapeutic springs and/or healthful weather. Hotels can locate doctors, when needed, but do not expect English to be spoken by all. The larger resort hotels that cater to North American or other English-speaking visitors will be your best route for finding English-speaking doctors. Bone specialists are available at key ski resorts; check on the availability of helicopters if the subject concerns you. In the Trentino region, more than 800 volunteers man 35 medical stations. VVFF helicopter service *(6 Caproni Airport Group;* ☎ *115.461)* is on call throughout the province and an avalanche dog rescue team operates in the high mountain areas. For information about insurance and international medical associations, see "Medical" in the introduction.

TRAVEL FACTS

Italians care less about efficiency and speed than they do about personal gratification. For that reason, trains may be late, buses may not run on the posted schedule, signposting may be hard to find and strikes can bring the entire system to a halt. Be prepared—either with plans for a rental car or for stressless travel that allows you to happily modify your itinerary when public transportation "schedules" don't meet your expectations.

ARRIVAL

Milano is the most convenient international Italian airport for the Alpine region, although Switzerland's Zürich or Genève airports are easily linked by fast train service and by winter ski buses, to Alpine areas of Italy. Arriving in the Italian Alps is also easy by road or by train from France (Lyon) through the Mont Blanc tunnel. The rail journey from Genève takes about five hours aboard a comfortable train that follows a spectacular route around lakes and through mountains.

AUTHOR'S OBSERVATION

Be aware that major railroad stations have become gathering places for assorted souls. Guard your possessions carefully and do not be flustered if someone flutters papers at you. That's a well-known tactic whereby another person takes your purse while you deal with the paper-flutterer. Chances are you'll not be bothered, but be alert.

TOURING TIPS

Italy's network is akin to those known to travelers in Switzerland, Germany, Austria and France, but it's a bit ragged on the edges; life is more laid-back in this country—and breaches of transportation systems are common. Relax. Expect to enjoy the inevitable quirks of travel in Italy by finding a comfortable *trattoria* or *albergo* to wait out the time or continue your travels by another method. "Schedules" indicate approximate times only, unless you've cut the time close. Then the train, bus, or lake boat will leave exactly on time, if my experiences are any indication.

AUTHOR'S OBSERVATION

The adventure of traveling aboard public transportation in northern Italy includes the challenge of finding the appropriate departure points and the correct train or bus. The more research you do in advance, the more alternatives you'll have when your first-choice method doesn't work out. Ask lots of questions so you can make your own decision by consensus. (I've often had wonderful travel experiences when I've gotten "lost.")

AIR SERVICE is possible to the small airports at some resorts, as well as by helicopter in the toniest areas. Check with the local tourist offices if arriving by air is important. Small charter planes can be arranged, as can helicopters in some cases, but you'll sacrifice seeing some lovely landscape from ground level and may not gain much in speed.

BICYCLES are used both for leisurely pedaling around a lake and for strenuous sport. (See "Bicycles" under "Sports.") The systems, however, are not as efficient as in Austria, Germany and Switzerland, and theft is a real problem in Italy. If you are planning to travel by bike, be sure to have a good lock and be sure to ask a lot of questions about the best way to protect your possessions. Don't plan on taking anything of real value.

BOATS offer a wonderful way to explore, not only on many of the lakes that dot the Alpine region, but also in the Gulf of Trieste, which is *Golfo di Trieste* in Italian (and *Zaljev Trieste* to the Slovenians who share its southern shore), and the larger *Golfo di Venezia*, between Venezia and Slovenia's towns. The village-linking boat service on most lakes operates at full tilt in summer months and often on weekends and holidays when the weather is warm enough to make excursions worthwhile. Two of my favorite international boat trips are on Lago Maggiore, where boats connect Italian towns with

Swiss ones such as Locarno and neighboring Ascona, and on Lago di Lugano, where boats link Italian villages with Swiss Lugano. Italy's own Lago di Garda is criss-crossed and wrapped with boat services, not only between Torri del Benaco and Moderno, but also between villages around the shores.

Athough some of the larger lake boats have dining facilties, it's always a good idea to be sure. If there's no service on board and if you haven't planned to take a boat to a lovely lakeside restaurant for your meal, plan to stop at one of the many bakeries to pick up something to make your own picnic.

BUS SERVICE is worth considering for longer distances if you don't plan to rent a car because it's a good way to sightsee, even when you are on a domestic (not a tourist) service. In fact, since traveling by bus gives you the freedom to look out the window instead of clenching the wheel, I have often found bus links to be delightfully carefree. Buses are also the most effective way to cover short distances in most cities and towns.

Many of the mountain passes—Piccolo San Bernardo between France and Italy, Gran San Bernardo between Switzerland and Italy, the Brenner pass between Austria and Italy—offer sensational journeys, especially when the weather cooperates (but often, also, when weather is dreary and you are in your comfortable bus-cocoon for the journey).

In cities and larger towns, since bus systems and routes are geared for residential use, they usually pass city highlights, are easy for visitors to decipher and will be convenient for your own travels. In often-frantic Milano (see "Places Worth Finding"), the efficient underground system is the best way to cover longer distances, once you've mastered the routes. It's the only way to avoid the traffic snarls that lock cars and buses in horn-honking, exhaust-choking knots.

AUTHOR'S OBSERVATION

For travel around towns and cities, ask at the local tourist office, or at some hotel (even if you're not an overnight guest) about route maps and suggestions for the best use of the public transportation system. Multi-ride tickets are often a very good value, but they usually have to be purchased before you board the bus. Bus tickets are often sold at newsstands and at Tabac kiosks, where you also buy magazines, newspapers, and postcards.

Avoid all public transportation at rush hours when the local folk use the system to capacity and have little time to help visitors. Plan your touring so you can use the systems when residents are ensconced at their offices, schools, or homes!

CAR is the most convenient way to cover the countryside, but driving can be perilous—or at least nerve-racking—in cities. Negotiating one-way streets and convoluted street patterns can be a challenge, and signposting is not reliable around the countryside. The *autostrada* (high-speed toll roads) are fast, direct and well marked, but it's easy to skim past some of the most charming towns. I find these roads best when time is crucial. For meandering, head for the secondary routes.

Prepare for the fact that lakeside driving on summer weekends is a stop-and-go affair, often with long chains of traffic that move at a snail's pace. Whenever possible, plan to do your scenic drives at times when the local folks are not apt to be doing the same.

The scenic Alpine border passes, mentioned for bus travel, require stamina for drivers not experienced with climbing mountain roads and their hairpin switch-backs. The several through-border tunnels may be fast, but they cut out some spectacular mountain scenery. Among them are the Mont Blanc between Italy and France (7-1/2 miles long), the Frejus Tunnel, also between France and Italy (just over 8 miles), the St. Gotthard tunnel between Switzerland and Italy (just over 10 miles), the San Bernardo tunnel, also between Switzerland and Italy, and the tunnel between Zernez in Switzerland and Italy's Livigno (3.5 miles).

AUTHOR'S OBSERVATION

Not every Italian drives an Alfa Romeo or a Maserati, but most people behind the wheel seem to act as though they own the road. Speed is a fact of life, even on wiggly roads, and so is tailgating–and car theft. When you rent a car, lock it when you are not in it, and park it overnight in a garage or some hotel-protected place whenever possible.

All the major car rental companies have affiliates in Italy and several local firms offer cars in towns and villages you may be visiting. If the recent past is any indication, you can count on the well-known U.S. firms to have the highest rates unless you can track down some promotion (or are using a frequent flyer coupon). Two recommended firms are **Kemwel**, *(106 Calvert St., Harrison, NY 10528-3199;* ☎ *914+835-5454 or 800+678-0678; FAX 914+ 835-5449)*, with a number of "SuperSaver" and other promotional rates that might fit with your travel plans, and **Europe by Car**, *(14 West 49th St., New York, NY 10020* ☎ *212+581-3040 or 800+223-1516, FAX 212+246-1458)*, with both rental and new car purchase plans.

Ask your travel agent to help with research about the car-and-rail plans offered through **RailEurope** and about car rental deals offered through **Alitalia**, **Swissair**, **Lufthansa** and other airlines.

For driving in Italy, it's best to have an international driver's permit, available in the U.S. through the American Automobile Association for $10 and valid for one year from the designated starting time. Your own license *may* be sufficient, but you'll have to have all papers translated into Italian for the local offices.

The **Automobile Club Italiano** *(Automobile Club of Italy, Via Marsala 8, Roma I-00185 Italy;* ☎ *6+499.81, FAX 6+499.82.34)*, the counterpart of Triple-A in the U.S., is very active, both with road services and with good driving maps and other information. Although most of the printed information is in Italian, the maps obviously can be deciphered by experienced travelers. ACI has offices in most cities, as well as emergency telephones every 2 km on major highways. If you use the telephones, begin by asking for an English-speaking person and speak very slowly. The **Touring Club Italiano** *(Corso Italia 10, I-20122 Milano;* ☎ *2+852.61, FAX 2+852.63.62)*, founded in 1894, is also affiliated with international organizations. It is a good source for route maps, details on special sites and manuals.

AUTHOR'S OBSERVATION

Ask the Italian Tourist Office about gas coupons and whether the system is still in place. In the recent past, a "Tourist Incentive Package" was offered with coupons to redeem for tolls and gasoline purchases at discounts. If it is still being offered, figure out how much driving you intend to do and whether or not the advance purchase is worthwhile.

TRAINS are the best way to cover distances if you want carefree sightseeing en route. The national network is **Ferrovie Italiane**. The best of the Italian State Railways' trains are the *Intercity*, some of which charge a supplement and some of which are international trains, which are also known as *Eurocity* trains. *Espresso*, which do not require a reservation or a supplementary fare, can also be international trains, but are usually made up of older (but comfortable) cars. *Diretto* trains make several stops, but are said to be fast between stops (which I've seldom found to be true) and may be commuter trains. The *Locale* are the stop-and-start local trains, which used to be called *Accelerato*, which they definitely are not. The Locale are the best for leisurely exploring, when you may want to get off at a place that appears to be attractive and take a later train to your ultimate goal. In fact, any train that goes where you want to go is a good one; it's often difficult to tell one version from another.

CIT, officially **Compania Italiana Turismo** (*#207, 342 Madison Ave., New York, NY 10173;* ☎ *800+223-7987 or, weekday mornings, 212+697-1482*) is the major outlet for ticket sales in the United States. For the U.S. West Coast, contact CIT, (*#980, 6033 W. Century Blvd., Los Angeles, CA 90045;* ☎ *310+338-8616; FAX 310+670-4269*). In addition to providing information about Italian State Railways, CIT sells the passes and charges $10 per ticket for their service (which I've found to be extremely helpful, once you get through the interminable busy signal).

AUTHOR'S OBSERVATION

Schedules and other facts are most easily obtained through your travel agent, who can access the information through the computer system and save you the aggravation of the busy signal and phone waiting.

The *Biglietto Turistico di Libera Circolazione*, called the BTLC-Italian Railpass, is the prepurchased ticket that allows for unlimited travel during the specified number of days.

COSTS FOR THE BTLC TICKETS		
Time Frame	First Class	Tourist Class
8 days	$226	$152
15 days	$284	$190
21 days	$330	$220
30 days	$396	$264
COSTS FOR THE FLEXI RAILCARD (IFR)		
4 days out of 9	$170	$116
8 days out of 21	$250	$164
12 days out of 30	$314	$210

In addition to the special tickets mentioned above, there is an *Italian Kilometric Ticket*, valid for 20 trips on the entire Italian rail system, over 1875 miles (3000 kilometers) within two months. The ticket may be used by up to five people traveling together. In Italy,

CIT offices are prominent at Italian railroad stations and elsewhere in cities and larger towns. Italy's trains are part of the Eurail network, mentioned under "Transportation," in the introduction. CIT sells Eurail tickets and you may find their office easier to deal with than the RailEurope office, also mentioned in the introductory chapter.

DAILY LIVING

The Italian lifestyle is far more relaxed and laid-back than that of the Germanic countries. However, when it comes to mealtimes and to checking in or out of hotels, visitors are expected to respect the appointed hours. For your host, in some of the most popular tourist places, you are "a job." As you travel in the countryside, however, the local *trattorias, alberghi* and other places are as pleased to help you as they are to help their neighbors.

FOOD, WINE AND OTHER BEVERAGES

Northern Italian cuisine is distinctive, especially in the Alpine areas. Generally, it is lighter and more elegantly presented than the noteworthy pastas and other dishes known throughout North America as "Italian." Specialties vary from region to region, especially in the valleys of the Alps where climates and customs vary. The northwestern Piemonte region is justly proud of its *bagna caoda*, a pungent potion of olive oil, garlic and anchovies brewed hot in a clay pot to serve as a sauce for bite-size pieces of fresh vegetables that are happily devoured by the forkful. Fall is the time for bagna caodas, which must be ordered in advance to assure the proper vegetables. The area around Nizza Monferrato, southeast of Asti, is known for its special *cardoon*, a member of the thistle family (like an artichoke) that is called *cardi gobbi* and is dipped into the bagna caoda. Sweet red peppers, artichokes, celery and other vegetables are favorites for the bagna caoda table. *Soma d'aj* is garlic-rubbed, crusty, country-style bread dipped in olive oil and eaten with fresh grapes. The country wine most often served with this peasant food is a Barbera, from nearby vineyards. The traditional finale for a bagna caoda is an egg that has been cooked in hot olive oil, after it has gathered the flavors of the seasonal vegetables that provided the main course.

In this area, veal, mountain cheeses and fresh vegetables are often cooked in time-honored ways. *Fonduta* is their rich, melted cheese fondue, with fontina cheese and egg yolks. *Tartufo bianco*, the white truffles of Alba, are a widely praised delicacy. Barolo and Barberesco wines are among the regional favorites, but there are many other good wines in the Alpine region. In the Trentino, for example, fruity Teroldego from the Campo Rotaliano, as well as dry, red Marzemino, and many sparkling wines are served with meals that make good use of the *Trentina grana* and *Vezzena* cheeses as well as fruit that grows in that area. And in the Valle d'Aosta, where many dishes pivot around Fontina and Toma (a cheese best known in the lower valleys), *Valpeileunentse* is the name of a delicious farm soup and *carbonada* is a hearty main meal that is based on polenta. *Mocetta* is the dried meat (usually chamois) from this region, but most Alpine areas have some version of the air-dried meat that is flavorful when used for seasoning and wonderful with farm bread when served, thinly sliced, as a main course.

In Lombardia, *vitello tonnato* is boiled veal, sliced paper thin and served with a white sauce made from canned tuna, anchovies, capers, white wine and a touch of homemade mayonnaise; *arrostino annegato* is a saddle of veal, flavored with white wine, salt pork and rosemary; and a *cotoletta alla milanese* is what appears in Austria as Wienerschnitzel, which is floured veal cutlet, dipped in egg and breadcrumbs before being fried in butter. *Ossobuco con gremolada* is veal bone, cooked in white wine, tomato, onion and celery, with herbs (including garlic). *Minestrone*, the hearty vegetable soup, is well-known everywhere; *panettone* is a traditional Milanese white egg-and-butter cake, flavored with raisins and candied fruit.

LODGING

The style was set by the Romans with their spacious villas and followed by the popes with theirs. The pursuit of art in the Cinquecento (16th century) added an important design to Renaissance gardens with villas in the area of Vicenza (Villas of Palladio and Scamozzi). The baroque era was next, in the 17th and 18th centuries—when lavish interiors had their counterpoint in beautiful gardens with distinctive flower beds such as those still seen at Villa Carlotta on Lake Como.

Most inns and small hotels in Italy's Alpine area offer warm and welcoming service, with some of the resorts—notably Cortina—among the region's classiest vacation areas. Many of the lakeside hotels, especially those on Lago di Como, continue time-honored traditions, with a leisurely lifestyle that allows time for walks, sitting in lakeside gardens and reading books. Of course, there are sports resorts as well. Standards of innkeeping vary considerably in Italy's Alpine area, however. Only the best *alberghi* have rooms with private bath; some in rural areas may not have hot water.

Lago di Garda, Gargnano, Italy

The local tourist offices are usually known as **Aziende Autonome di Soggiorno e Turismo**; the provincial offices are **Ente Provinciale per il Turismo**. Either can supply some listings. The *Annuario Alberghi d'Italia* is the hotel guide.

Information about some of the small but special places in and near the Dolomites, the Valle d'Aosta, Piemonte and Italy's other Alpine areas is given when towns are mentioned (in "Places Worth Finding").

AUTHOR'S OBSERVATION

Speaking some Italian will certainly add to your enjoyment, although people in the larger resorts will speak some English. Recognizing basic Italian words and knowing their meaning is essential when you stray from the well-trod tourist routes.

APARTMENTS and **CHALETS** are available for rent in many Alpine areas, as wise Europeans well know. Rentals are usually for a Saturday-to-Saturday week, but other time spans may be available depending on the time of year and the demand for reservations. In many cases, the units have been recently built with rentals anticipated. When that is the case, furnishings are often spartan and units are usually in dense blocks. Although some places are comfortably furnished, don't expect some of the lavish "extras" found in the best North American timeshares. Always ask for exact appointments. Three North American firms specializing in Italian housekeeping rentals are **Vacanze in Italia** *(Box 297, Falls Village, CT 06031;* ☎ *413+528-6610 or 800+533-5405; FAX 413+528-6222),* **Villas In-**

ternational *(#510, 605 Market St., San Francisco, CA 94105; ☎ 415+281-0910 or 800+221-2260; FAX 415+281-0919)*, and **Inter-home** *(124 Little Falls Rd., Fairfield, NJ 07004; ☎ 201+882-6864; FAX 201+808-1742)*.

CAMPING is a very popular way for most Europeans to vacation. Campsites in the Alpine region vary insofar as facilities and size are concerned. One reliable source for preliminary information is the booklet *Campeggi in Italia*, published by the **Touring Club Italiano** *(Corso Italia 10, I-20122 Milano; ☎ 2+852.61; FAX 2+852.63.62)*. Two other helpful resources for campers are the list of campsites on a map issued through the **Federazione Italiana del Campeggio e del Caravanning** and a book called *Guida Camping d'Italia*. Ask at the Italian State Tourist Offices about obtaining copies, which are sometimes available through their offices.

CONVENTS and **MONASTERIES** sometimes have rooms for overnight guests. A list of places that rent rooms can be obtained by writing to the *Arcidiocesi* (Archdiocese) in the city of interest. Sometimes, in small towns, a visit to the parish priest can yield names of places to stay and the local tourist office is another possible source.

FARM HOLIDAYS are popular with many European visitors, but little known to Americans, partly due to potential language difficulties and also because the farm holidays have never been promoted in the North American market. The plan is known as **Agriturist**, for **Associazione Nazionale per l'Agriturismo**, **l'Ambiente il Territorio** *(Corso Vittorio Emanuele 101, I-00186 Roma; ☎ 6+685.2342; FAX 6+685.24.24)*. The nationwide network makes it possible to stay with working farmers in most parts of Italy. In the areas where German is spoken, farm holidays are known as *Urlaub am Bauernhof*. Several regions print comprehensive booklets with pictures and statistics about the various farms all of which have been inspected prior to their listing. One U.S. source for information is **Italy Farm Holidays** *(547 Martling Ave., Tarrytown, NY 10591; ☎ 914+631-7880; FAX 914+631-8831)*.

HUTS and **MOUNTAIN HOTELS** fleck the high Alpine areas. A system of almost 600 Alpine huts is maintained by the **Club Alpino Italiano** *(Via Ugo Foscolo 3, I-20122 Milano; ☎ 2+7202.30.85)*. Refuges in the Gran Paradiso National Park, above the Valle d'Aosta, for example, are usually built of stone and are reasonably comfortable. There are also simpler climbers' huts that can accommodate about 6 people, year-round. The **Touring Club Italiano** *(Corso Italia 10, I-20122*

Milano; ☎ *2+852.61; FAX 2+852.63.62)* includes mountain itineraries in its book of excursions.

INNS and **SMALL HOTELS** can be found in many of the more remote valleys, where the surroundings are at their pastoral best. Roadsides in the rural areas are punctuated with buildings tagged "albergo" or "pension," which are the names to look for (and ask for) when you're searching for an inn. In the U.S., a choice selection of inns is represented through **Romantik Tours** *(14178 Woodinville-Duvall Rd., Box 1278, Wodinville, WA 98072;* ☎ *206+486-9394 or 800+826-0015; FAX 206+481-4079).* Many of the inns used in their plans are members of their former affiliate, **Romantik Hotels und Restaurants** *(Hörsteiner Strasse 34, Postfach 1144, D-63786 Karlstein/Main, Germany;* ☎ *49+6188+950.20, FAX 49+6188+ 60.07),* an association of privately-owned atmospheric properties, grouped to promote their traditional qualities. Member properties must be owner-operated, with friendly management for comfortable accommodations in historic buildings. All must also offer first-class regional cuisine. Another source for appealing inns is **Relais et Châteaux** *(#707, 11 East 44th St., New York, NY 10017;* ☎ *212+856-0115; FAX 212+856-0193).* Noteworthy inns are mentioned under "Places Worth Finding."

LUXURY LODGINGS and elegant escapes are an Italian specialty. Italian villas lend themselves to the pursuit of the good life. Properties known to royalty and their ilk in the late 1800s have been refurbished and are open as deluxe properties. Some, such as Cernobbio's Villa d'Este and Bellagio's Villa Serbelloni, both on Lago di Como, have a worldwide following. Courmayeur and Cortina, Italy's best-known Alpine resorts, have their luxury properties, as well as a wide range of resorts that are popular both in winter and in summer. Milano's Excelsior Hotel Gallia is a traditional pacesetter for that cosmopolitan city. San Vincent has its Billia Grand Hotel with the neighboring European-style casino. Cervinia-Breuil, sharing the Matterhorn with Switzerland's Zermatt, also shares the sensational skiing—with a ski-lift and ski slope link, and Stresa and even Verona have their Alpine connection. As mentioned, several exceptional small properties in northern Italy are represented in the U.S. by Relais et Châteaux. "Leading Hotels" is a registered name for a group of privately owned properties that share elegance in classic style. The U.S. contact for the group is **Leading Hotels of the World** *(737 Third Ave., New York, NY 10017;* ☎ *212+838-3110 or 800+223-6800; FAX 212+758-7367).* Among the members in Italy are the Bauer Grunwald and the Hotel Cipriani in Venezia. **CIGA**

Hotels, whose acronym stands for *Compagnia Italiano Grande Alberghi*, has long stood for the pinacle of luxury in Italian lodgings. The firm, purchased some years ago by the Aga Khan, is being courted for purchase by several noteworthy hotel groups at press time, but its prestige and status are assured. CIGA hotels in the places included in this book are the Villa Cipriani in Asolo, the Diana Majestic, Duca di Milano, Palace and Principe di Savoia in Milano, the Danieli, the Europa & Regina and the Gritti Palace in Venezia along with the Hotel Des Bains and the Excelsior on the Venezia Lido.

SPAS have offered the classiest vacation style since the times of the Romans and certainly through the era of emperors and kings. These days they're open for anyone who can afford them, and programs are offered for weight loss, stress reduction and for more serious ailments. Acqui Terme, in the Piemonte, southeast of Torino (Turin), is one of Italy's premier spas. Bormeo, above Milano, is another. Courmayeur, better known by sportsmen for its skiing, is also a popular spa and many other smaller towns are known for their curative springs. In Abano, not too far from Venezia, the Hotel Trieste & Victoria has long been known among Europeans for its spa facilities. The property can be booked through **Spa Trek Travel** *(475 Park Avenue South, New York, NY 10016;* ☎ *212+779-3480 or 800+272-3480, FAX 212+779-3471).*

YOUTH HOSTELS and other student lodgings are scattered throughout Italy, including in the cities of Torino, Milano, and Como. The provincial tourist offices can be a great help with suggestions about hostels and other inexpensive places to stay. The official organization is the **Associazione Italiana Alberghi per la Gioventù** *(AIG, the Italian Youth Hostels Association, via Cavour 44, I-00184 Roma;* ☎ *6+46.23.42; FAX 6+488.04.92).* In addition to the network of hostels, many towns provide university accommodations in places that are used by students during their study year, but are available for others at other times. Inexpensive meals are often available at universities. A *Guide for Foreign Students* and other booklets are available through the **Instituto Italiano di Cultura** *(686 Park Ave., New York, NY 10021;* ☎ *212+879-4242, FAX 212+861-4018).*

PLACES WORTH FINDING

Alpine villages are folded into the deep valleys and planted on meadows in the high mountains, as well as along the valley floor. Although buses reach some villages, times for travel are not always dependable. Rental car is the best way to assure independence if you want to visit several places. The towns around the lake shores are sometimes laced together by ferries and often touched by pleasure boats that set out from one of several marinas. Lago d'Iseo, surrounded by hills and mountains, is punctuated with Italy's largest island-in-a-lake, Montisola, enjoyed for fishing and camping. In many border valleys in northeastern Italy, German is spoken. Thus Alto Adige is also known as Sud Tirol and all places in that area bear two names. The same is true in border valleys in northwestern Italy, where French is spoken by many and places carry both a French and an Italian name. In Italy, "Turismo" is your tip-off to most local tourist offices. Although there are hundreds of towns and villages worth a traveler's time, the following places are suggestions for this year's travels.

The letter-number notation, I-000000, is the postal code. The telephone and FAX numbers that are in parentheses following each place name apply to the tourism office, which is the source for further information. Information following mention of hotels and restaurants includes street address, where necessary, and telephone numbers. To reach the Italian telephone numbers when you are in Italy, begin by dialing "0."

AOSTA

Aosta *(I-11100;* ☎ *165+333.52)*, capital of Valle d'Aosta (to which it gives its name), still has the grid plan given to it when it was a Roman military camp. Many Roman buildings remain, including the **Pretoria Gate** and the **Arch of Augustus**, dating from the first century B.C. The **Duomo** is well worth pausing to enjoy. Its chancel has a charming 13th-century mosaic floor with designs that are worthy of study; the choir stalls are 15th century; the sculptures on the facade are 16th-century pieces; and the facade itself dates from the 19th century.

ASTI

Asti *(Piazza Alfieri, I-14100;* ☎ *141+503.57)*, in the Piemonte plains, southeast of Torino (Turin), is marked by the Romanesque campanile of its **Duomo**, most of which was built in 14th-century Gothic style. The town's a pleasant excursion at all times, but is a frantic center of activity during the mid-September palio, when the townsfolk dress in traditional costume and horses race through town. Piazza Alfieri takes its name from that of a favorite son, poet Vittorio Alfieri, who was born here in 1749. Most travelers will become familiar with Asti's name through the wine made from grapes grown on surrounding hillsides.

Nearby **Barbaresco** is also noted for its wine, which is rich and red and can be tasted in the wine cellar at San Donato, a former church. The area is flecked with castle-capped villages that blanket their slopes with vineyards. One worthwhile goal is the medieval hill town of **Nieve d'Alba**, where Claudia and Tonino **Verro's restaurant** offers home-cooked regional specialties, including bagna caoda (see "Food, Wine, and Other Beverages") in its season, which is from the end of the wine harvest in the fall until cold weather leaves in the spring.

BERGAMO

Bergamo *(via Papa Giovanni 106, I-24100;* ☎ *35+23.27.30)*, in Lombardia, is, in fact, two towns: the historic **Città Alta** (upper town), wrapped in Venetian walls built in the 1600s, and the lower town, where you'll find the **Academia Carrare** (art gallery) and several 16th-century palaces scattered among more recent (and mostly uninteresting) buildings. Among the highlights in the Academy are the several portraits of people who played pivotal roles in Bermago's history and that of its region. Also worthy of note, especially if you can attend a performance, is the room devoted to the **Bergamasque**, a colorful and fun-loving folkloric dance/theater, better known in Italy as the *commedia dell'arte.*

The heart of Bergamo's upper town is the **Piazza Vecchia**, with the **Pallazo della Ragione** (from 1199) in sight while you sit at one of the cafés to drink in the activity in the square. The **Capella Colleoni**, designed by the architect of the Carthusian monastery outside of Pavia, has exceptional paintings and intricate interior work in addition to its impressive facade. The originally Romanesque, later re-modeled, **Chiesa dei Santa Maria Maggiore** is also worth some time.

LODGING: A rustic gem for overnight is the charming **Agnello d'Oro** *(24 rooms; via Gombito 22;* ☎ *35+24.98.83)*, nestled amid ancient neighbors, near the piazza Viejo. Rooms are modestly priced, tiny and furnished with only basics; the restaurant is memorable, even if you overnight elsewhere.

About 16 miles (25 km) north, through the Val Brembana, **San Pelligrino Terme** *(via B. Tasso 1, I-24016;* ☎ *345+210.20)* gives its name to the widely exported San Pelligrino sparkling water and is noted around Europe for the health-assuring springs at its spa.

In addition to the scenic drive through the chalk hills of the **Val Brembana**, it's worth driving through the **Val Seriana** to the Passo della Presolana, for memorable vistas as you make the climb.

BOLZANO/BOZEN

Bolzano/Bozen *(Piazza Walter 8, I-39100;* ☎ *471+975.656)*, capital of the Alto Adige/Sud Tirol region (hence its Italian and German names), is a big city that serves as one departure point for visits to the Dolomite mountain valleys. The **Piazza delle Erbe**, with its 15th-, 16th- and 17th-century buildings, is most colorful at the time of the fruit market, when tables are set up to be piled high with lush, ripe apples, quince and other local produce. The **Duomo** has Germanic elements in its interior; the 15th-century frescoes at the **Convento dei Domenicani** are noteworthy; and the 14th-century cloisters of the **Chiesa dei Francescano** help give quality to the commercial life of the city in the Middle Ages.

LODGING: North of Bolzano, at historic *Bressanone-Brixen*, on the road toward the **Brenner Pass** (and Austria's Innsbruck), the **Hotel Dominik** *(29 rooms;* ☎ *472+301.44; FAX 472+365.54)* is like a country home. It's a member of the *Relais et Châteaux* group, mentioned when "Lodging" is reviewed, earlier in the chapter.

BRESCIA

Brescia *(corso Zanardelli 34, I-25121;* ☎ *30+434.18, FAX 30+293.284)*, not far from **Lago di Como** in Lombardia, does not have instant appeal. It's a big industrial city, but its historic heart is secure, albeit surrounded by modern commerce. Step into the Piazza della Loggia (and try to shut out traffic and its noise) to notice the impressive buildings that surround you, especially the 15th-century palaces of **Monte Vecchio** and **Monte Nouvo**, separated in building dates by less than ten years, as well as the name-giving **Loggia** and the **Pallazzo dell'Orologio**, with Moorish figures on the top. The **Pinacoteca** holds paintings and other work by regional artists, plus a reasonable collection of Venetian-style work and many paintings that document historic events that took place in and around Brescia, a town that held out against the Austrians for ten days in 1849 and was besieged by Venetians in February 1512. One name to note: Tullia of Aragon, a revered courtesan, whose statue (and legends) appear around town.

COMO

Como *(Piazza Cavour 33, I-22100;* ☎ *31+27.25.18)*, in Lombardia, at the south end of the lake that bears its name, grows from its **Piazza Cavour** in a pattern taken from ancient Roman camps. These days, however, the city has grown to grand proportions, so take a deep breath, look at a map and get your bearings before starting out. The 12th-century **Torre di Porta Vittoria**, a landmark that's easy to spot, is part of the Roman walls. The **Duomo** that was started in Gothic style in the 14th century was finished in the Renaissance period. The intricately designed marble and the statues (and the tales they tell) are noteworthy; the tapestries and paintings in the interior tell stories from the Old Testament. Although ransacked for its success by Milanesi in the early 12th century, the town's prosperity gave rise to master builders who took their artistry throughout Italy and north through Europe, wherever sponsors could be found. The town's location, lakeside to the south of the Splugen, Bernina and St. Gotthard Alpine passes, gave rise to its prosperity.

AUTHOR'S OBSERVATION

It's worth noting that Switzerland's Lugano, a more peaceful and relaxing lakeside town, is less than an hour's train ride and an even shorter drive, from Como.

LODGING: Places to stay in Como are legion. At the top of my list is the **Villa Flori** *(44 rooms;* ☎ *31+57.31.05)*, elegantly situated on the via Provinciale per Cernobbio, but the luxurious **Hotel Barchetta Excelsion** *(80 rooms; Piazza Cavour;* ☎ *31+3221; FAX 31+30.26.22)* is more centrally located on the piazza facing the lake and preferred by some. Also worth considering, if you want a major player, is the **Metropole Suisse** *(71 rooms; Piazza Cavour;* ☎ *31+26.94.44)*. Among the smaller, but also top-of-the-line, places, look into the **Firenze** *(31 rooms; Piazza Volta;* ☎ *31+30.03.33)* or the elegant **Petit Château** *(10 rooms; Viale Innocenzo XI;* ☎ *31+26.23.36)*. The tiny **Posta** *(17 rooms; via Garibaldi;* ☎ *31+26.60.12)* is more modestly priced.

At **Cernobbio** *(I-22010)*, just outside Como, one of the world's great hotels stands at the side of the lake. The **Grand Hotel Villa d'Este** *(172 rooms;* ☎ *31+51.24.71; FAX 31+51.20.27)* celebrated its 100th birthday in 1973. Thoroughly modern insofar as comforts are concerned, ownership takes great pride in maintaining Europe's traditional "grand hotel" style with service and decor. A huge heated swimming pool has been built into the lake; a landing pad awaits helicopter arrivals and the gorgeous garden-park stretches up the hillside behind the hotel. Each room has its own style and personality, with either lake or garden view. Meals in either the *Verandah* room or the *Sporting Grill* are memorable, not only for the menu but also for the setting. The hotel is open from March through October. At Montorfano, 7 miles from the hotel, the hotel maintains its golf course and clubhouse.

In the hills just above Cernobbio, at **Erba** *(I-22036)*, two historic small hotels have a link with Villa d'Este. Both are known in the area for serving elegant meals and for their medieval architecture. **Hotel Castello di Pomerio** *(27 rooms; via Como 5;* ☎ *31+62.75.16; FAX 31+62.82.45)* is in 12th-century style, with gardens, an indoor and outdoor swimming pool, tennis courts and a spa program. The **Hotel Castello di Casiglio** *(29 rooms; via Como 5;* ☎ *31+62.72.88; FAX 31+62.96.49)* has been tastefully rebuilt from a 13th-century castle palace, complete with a square turret. Both small hotels are goals for walkers, who settle into the renowned restaurants for either lunch or dinner.

Lago di Como, the left (western) branch of a body of water vaguely shaped like an inverted Y (Lago di Lecco is the eastern branch), is one of the Alpine region's loveliest playgrounds. Not only is it fringed by picturesque villages, many of which are docking places for lakeboats, but the lakeside promenades and country walks around its shores draw many visitors, especially when the weather warms. This area has almost the perfect mix of time-honored traditions and modern comforts for an Italian lakeside resort.

LODGING: Among the many special places to stay in villages around the shore are the **Villa Serbelloni** *(82 rooms;* ☎ *31+95.02.16)* at **Bellagio**, at the crook of the Y; the **Castello di Pomerio** at **Erba** *(58 rooms;* ☎ *31+61.15.16)*; and the **Grand Hotel Victoria** *(53 rooms;* ☎ *31+320.03)* at **Menaggio**, across the lake from Bellagio, at the neck of the Y, and road-linked to tiny Lago di Piano and on west to Lago di Ceresio, which the Swiss know as Lago di Lugano and claim as their own.

COURMAYEUR

Courmayeur *(I-11025;* ☎ *165+84.20.60)*, in the northwest Valle d'Aosta, nestles at the base of Monte Bianco, near the tunnel to Chamonix, France, where the mountain peak is known as Mont Blanc. (The route southwest from Courmayeur, through Pré St. Didier, leads to Albertville, France, the hometown for the 1992 Winter Olympics.) Known to the Romans more than 2000 years ago and to pioneering mountain climbers in the 19th century, the once forgotten village is now a chic, busy resort with spectacular scenery and sports facilities, plus shops and hotels that appeal to the international sporting set. (Restaurants could be better than they are.)

Skiing in winter and walks, hikes and climbs in summer months are reasons for heading here, although there's also golf at La Palud, where the lovely Val Ferret opens out for cross-country skiing and walks along its river. **Duca degli Abruzzi**, a museum of Alpine life, is well worth some time if you can be here when its open.

LODGING: There are dozens of places to stay in the knot of roads just off the highway between Aosta and the tunnel, as well as in the neighboring areas of **Dolonne**, across the river, and **Entrêves**, **La Palud**, **La Saxe**, and **Val Ferret** at higher elevations. **Pavillon** *(50 rooms;* ☎ *165+84.24.20)*, a member of Relais et Chateaux, is tops, not only for the sensational views from the rooms, but also for the atmosphere created by the furnishings throughout. The **Palace Bron** *(27 rooms;* ☎ *165+84.25.45)* is one of the toniest places to stay, slightly removed from the hubbub, in the Plan Goret area, but near enough to walk to town. Small **Edelweiss** *(28 rooms;* ☎ *165+84.15.90)* is modestly priced, on the fringe of in-town activity. Also small, the **Hotel del Viale** *(23 rooms;* ☎ *165+84.22.27)* has Alpine atmosphere, comforts and higher prices in the heart of things. In the untrammeled Val Ferret, **Belvedere** *(9 rooms;* ☎ *165+891.19)* has rooms with private bath, while the **Plampincieux** *(12 rooms;* ☎ *165+899.48)* is quiet, pleasant and modestly priced for rooms with shared bath.

RESTAURANT: Allow time to drive to **La Maison de Filippo** *(*☎ *165+899.68)*, a noteworthy restaurant about 10-minutes' ride out of the center of town, in Entreves.

CREMONA

Cremona *(I-26100, Piazza del Comune;* ☎ *372+217.22)*, in Lombardia, is where the fiddle became the violin in 1566 at the "finishing school" of Andrea Amati and where Antonio Stradivarius studied under Nicolo Amati, Andrea's son. It's an enchanting city, about two hours by train from the bustle of Milano and a diversion southeast of the Alpine area. Dozens of **palazzi** and elegant **country villas** are as much a testimony to the fact that Cremona is a liveable city these days as to the affection that Bianca Maria Visconti felt for the city she received as a wedding gift from Milanese scion Francesco Sforza in 1441. Cremona is easy to enjoy, by strolling from the station along the via Palestro, pausing at **Museo Stradivariano** in the Palazzo dell'Arte, for its visual history of violins and their creators, and the **Museo Civico**, in the Pallazo Affaitati, for a palatable collection of fine arts (on the spur of via Dati). Then proceed along Corso Garibaldi, lingering at the garden-filled **Piazza Roma**, the heart of town life, to Piazza del Comune, the hub for cultural sights. Here's where you'll find the imposing **Duomo** from the 12th century and its

Torrazzo, a campanile from the 13th, as well as other noteworthy buildings in and around the area.

LAGO DI CALDONAZZO

Lago di Caldonazzo *(I-38056 Levico Terme;* ☎ *461+70.61.01; FAX 461+70.60.04)*, in Trentino's upper Sugana valley, was first respected for the thermal springs that gave rise to therapeutic spas on this lake and the smaller neighboring Lago di Levico. These days, opportunities for fishing, sailing and hiking lure campers and others to the area in warm weather months. Not far from Trento, the area is easily linked with Venezia on highway A22 to Verona, where you head east to Venezia on A4.

LAGO DI GARDA

Lago di Garda, shared by the provinces of Lombardia and Veneto, with a tiny northern tip in the Trentino-Alto Adige/Sud Tirol region (giving this area its Germanic atmosphere), is the quintessential lake. Not only do warm springs feed its waters, but the high Alps protect it from the harshest winds, giving it a climate far warmer than its location (on the latitude of Maine, Montreal and London) would seem to deserve. Beloved by Virgil, Pliny and Catullus, and by Goethe and Stendahl, as well as by countless others, the shores seem to thrive on the adulation of ever increasing numbers of visitors.

Although the traffic numbs the roadways at height-of-season summer, many small hotels seem to be unaware of the bustle around them. The western side of the lake is the most interesting (and elegant), especially if you're driving it when others aren't—or you've chosen to travel by boat.

Lakeboats that dart from town to town and on touring itineraries, are the best means of travel not only when the road traffic is knotted, but also for the pleasing views and pace. One plus for driving, however, is the opportunity to pause at the pretty villages between the dozens of tunnels along the Gardesana, as the route is known.

At **Gardone Riviera**, mid-lake, where the shore begins to narrow to the north, is a nest of villas, parks, gardens and vacation facilities, with the historic center mercifully declared pedestrian. Cafés line the lakefront. At **Gardone di Soto**, the **Giardino Botanico Hruska** has more than 2000 varieties of plants and flowers and a re-creation of the Dolomite landscape to make appropriate flora feel at home. Just off the square marked by the 14th-century **Chiesa di San Nicola**, find the entrance for **Il Vittoriale**, where Gabriele D'Annunzio was buried in 1938. His is a name to remember, not only for the villa and gardens, but also for his writing, military feats and lifetime escapades, which are recounted in printed matter you can find in local bookstores.

LODGING: A noteworthy place to stay is the **Grand Hotel Fasano** *(47 rooms;* ☎ *365+210.51)*, a former Habsburg hunting palace in the style of the late 1800s, when this area was a winter haven for European aristocracy. Now with modern comforts, the hotel retains its turn-of-the-century atmosphere. For more modest lodgings, check out the inexpensive **Pensione Hohl** *(14 rooms;* ☎ *365+201.600)* on the route to Il Vittoriale, blissfully removed from the street noises in the lakeside area, but don't count on private bath.

Driving is the best way to enjoy the scenery between Gardone Riviera and Gargnano, and on as far as Limone sul Garda, with detours inland to the heights of Monte Magno and Costa Mignone, where there's an ancient Franciscan monastery with a charming cloister. Not to be missed along the lakeside link are **Bogliaco** and **Villa**. From **San Faustino** to **Riva**, the views along the lake rimming road are broken by countless short tunnels.

RESTAURANTS: At Villa, south of Gargnano, the restaurant **Baia d'Oro** is a special favorite, for its lakeside setting and pleasing atmosphere, but **Gargnano's La Tortuga** *(*☎ *365+712.51)*, in the center of the town, not far from the harbor, is widely praised for the special attention the Filippinis give to their choice of menu, preparation, and guests.

Allow time to visit **Limone sul Garda** *(via Comboni, I-25010;* ☎ *365+95.40.70)*, pinned against rocky cliffs that drop to the lakeshore. Legends romantically claim that lemons, brought to Gargnano from Tuscany and Umbria by Franciscan monks in the 14th century, gave the town its name; some scholars claim otherwise. That controversy aside, the town suggests the building style of Venice with its straight walls, window balconies and aging rust-colored, tile roofs. But the village has little of the tourist-commercialism that has come to be part of the pattern for Venezia.

LODGING: For overnight, try for a room at **Le Palme** *(28 rooms;* ☎ *365+95.46.81)*, in a lovely villa not far from the lake.

Riva del Garda *(I-38066;* ☎ *464+55.40.04)*, a few miles north of Limone, but in the Trentino region, has **La Rocca**, a 13th-century castle and the **Torre Aponale**, a 13th-century tower, as two noteworthy sites. Clustered at the northern end of the lake, the town is a popular resort surrounded on three sides by modern buildings. But it's the medieval core of the lakeside town, around **Piazza 3 Novembre**, that charms with its medieval buildings, red-tile roofs and piazza life. The classic, mammoth **Hotel du Lac et du Parc** *(57 rooms; ☎ 464+ 55.02.02)* sets the tone, with gardens, pools, lakefront and sports facilities, but the smaller **Hotel Sole** *(32 rooms; ☎ 464+55.26.86)* is ideally located on the Piazza 3 Novembre, amid the medieval touchstones.

In the orbit of Lago di Garda, whether you are in the region of Trentino (the north), Lombardia (the west shore), or Veneto (the eastern shore), many villages have distinct charm, usually focused on ancient buildings, but often, also, on a restaurant or inn.

At the southern end of the lake, **Desenzano del Garda** *(I-25015; ☎ 30+914.15.10)*, west of Sirmione, is where you'll find Gian Domenico Tiepolo's *Last Supper*, in the small church (rebuilt in 1586), Roman mosaics from the 3rd century in the Villa Romana along the via Scavi Romani and at Capo la Tarrare, the upper part of town, there are remnants of a 13th-century **castle**. The **Antiquarium** holds some of the ancient treasures found in the area. Although modern lodgings are growing on its outskirts, the castle-studded center of town, as it faces the lake, is still lovely—and a special place when the Tuesday-morning market takes place in and around Piazza Malvezzi.

LODGING: The **Lido International** *(16 rooms; ☎ 30+914.10.27)* and the **Villa Rosa** *(38 rooms; ☎ 30+914.19.74)* are two of the few hotels that are open year-round in Desenzano. Both have earned four stars from the local tourism officials.

Praised by Dante, Virgil and dozens of others, **Sirmione** *(I-25019, ☎ 30+91.61.14)* is in the south, with its greatest treasure—a cluster of cheek-by-jowl houses at the base of the 13th-century **Castello di Scaligers**—saved from clutter by the fact that it's on a speck-size islet, once attached to the sliver of a peninsula that pokes into the lake. Wrapped in tourists by noontime at peak travel times, the castle and its surroundings are exceptional both early and late in the day, which is one of the best reasons to linger in this area.

RESTAURANTS: East of the castle, the **Vecchia Lugana** restaurant is a pleasant lakeside pausing place.

At the end of Sirmione's peninsula, the Roman ruins at the **Grotte di Catullo** are a major tourist attraction. They are worth seeing if you can arrive when hordes of others don't and the view from the point is sensational.

LODGING: Among the hotels worth noting in and around Sirmione are two five-star properties, the **Villa Cortine Palace** *(54 rooms; ☎ 30+91.60.21)* and **Grand Hotel Terme** *(57 rooms; ☎ 30+91.62.16)*. Others to consider are the **Continental** *(53 rooms; ☎ 30+91.61.72)*,

Olivi *(60 rooms;* ☎ *30+91.61.10)*, and the **Sirmione** *(76 rooms;* ☎ *30+91.63.31)*. If you'd prefer an apartment, **Punta Gro** is a modern complex of apartments with a pool as the focal point. It is one of several rental units available through **Europlan Reservation Service** *(Via Mirabello 15, I-37011 Bardolino, Verono;* ☎ *45+721.02.00; FAX 45+721.21.30)*.

In the hills above the lake, ***Tignale*** *(I-25080;* ☎ *365+55.20.66)*, at a mid-point on the west side, is reached via a memorable road of switchbacks. From the church of **Madonna di Monte Castello**, at tiny **Gardola**, there's a spectacular view over the lake. The town has an active tennis complex with several clay courts, lessons and tournaments.

LODGING: The family-style **Hotel Tignale** is used by **C.B. Tours** *(*☎ *365+734.85; FAX 365+734.92)* for its guests. Down the hillside at the lake, there are facilities for windsurfing and boating.

Other places to stay on and near Lago di Garda include the tiny village of ***Costermano***, known to the Romans as Castra Romanum. The village is noteworthy today for its rural pleasures and for **Residence Hotel La Filanda** *(26 apts.; via Tavernole 7/11. I-37010 Costermano VR;* ☎ *45+720.09.77)*, created around an 18th-century spinning mill, amid a vineyard. Although the bedrooms have been austerely modernized, the landscape and surrounding countryside support a rural atmosphere, about two miles (4 km) from the lake. There's a pool on premises. Nearby, the **San Carlo** *(29 apts.)* has also been created around a swimming pool. The vacation village **Poiano**, half way between Costermano and the lake, has tennis courts, sauna, a swimming pool and children's facilities. **Parco del Garda** *(80 villas and apts.)* is set in what had been a thriving olive grove. Two swimming pools and plenty of game areas are part of the complex which is popular with British travelers.

At ***Vignol/Caravelle***, there are several bungalows and apartments with swimming pools scattered among the units. At ***Bardolino/Cisano***, the **Residence Casetto** clusters apartments around its swimming pool, not far from the lake. At ***Peschiera***, **Al Cappuccini** is a modern apartment complex with swimming pools, tennis courts, and other activities on premises and **La Madonnia** is another pool-centered complex popular with British travelers.

LAGO MAGGIORE

Lago Maggiore, shared with Switzerland and known to the earliest traders and conquerers, is studded with islets such as the one called **Castelli di Cannero** for its 15th-century castle and **Isola dei Pesca-**

tori *(I-28049 Stresa;* ☎ *323+301.50),* which survives as a medieval fishing village, capitulating to tourism only in the summer months. Near Stresa, the small isle seems removed from modern times. Buildings with straight walls and gradually slanted weathered-tile roofs cluster around the square bell tower with its dunce-cap roof. For an unforgettable experience, make a reservation at **Hotel Verbano** *(via Ugo Ara 2;* ☎ *32+33.04.08),* where one of Alberto Zacchera's half-dozen rooms will allow you to enjoy the quiet peace of the Isola. The sun terrace blisters with day visitors who enjoy meals and lingering during warm weather months, but you can have the evening pretty much to yourself.

At **Verbania Pallanza**, about 25 miles (40 km) southwest of Switzerland's Locarno and 60 miles (96 km) northeast of Milano, **Villa Taranto** is easily reached by lakeboat as well as by public transportation. Its sensational gardens are open daily from April 1 through October. Started in 1931 by a Scotsman named Captain Neil McEacharn, the **Giardino Botanico** (botanical garden) is on the northern slopes of the promontory of Castagnola. The villa is not open to the public; it is used by the Italian government for official functions.

RESTAURANTS AND LODGING: Among the many noteworthy places around the lake to stay and/or dine are the **Milano** *(51 rooms;* ☎ *322+72.65)* and the tiny **Villa Treves** *(9 rooms;* ☎ *322+764.61),* which is administered through the much larger **Villa Carlotta** *(101 rooms;* ☎ *322+764.61)* in **Belgirate**; the **Pironi** *(11 rooms;* ☎ *322+706.24)* in **Cannobio**; and many places in Stresa. (See "Stresa.")

LAGO D'ORTA

Lago d'Orta, just to the west of Lago Maggiore, is a gem little known to American travelers. Suggested first stop is **Orta San Giolio** *(via Olina 9-11, I-28016;* ☎ *322+90355),* for a coffee at one of the places on the town square and a visit to the *Azienda di Promozione Turistico Lago d'Orta* for suggestions about walks, places to see and other information. Don't leave town without visiting the **Palazzotto**, dating from 1582, and looking carefully at the 20 panels showing the life of St Francis of Assisi on the walls of Sacro Monte. Dotted with the **Isola di San Giulio**, which has a charming 12th-century Roman **basilica**, the lovely lake is fringed with villages such as **Pettenasco**, **Vacciago** and **Gozzano**, with 15th-century frescoes in the tiny **church** at **Luzzara**. There are pleasant views from many villages in the surrounding hillsides.

LODGING: One quietly lovely place to stay in town is **San Rocco** *(39 rooms;* ☎ *322+903.90).* **La Bussola** *(16 rooms;* ☎ *322+901.98)* is also pleasant if you're lucky enough to secure a room.

MERANO/MERAN

Merano/Meran *(Coso Liberta 45, I-39012;* ☎ *473+352.23),* Italian with an Austrian personality and German mother tongue (hence the two names of the town), is in the Sud Tirol, a region ceded to Italy at the time of the break up of the Austro-Hungarian empire, at the end of World War I (1918). The town is 10 miles from the Austrian border. Known for its spas long before Kaiser Karl V went there in 1522, the town claims 150 years as a "modern" spa. The **Cathedral of St. Nicholas** is a town landmark, with its stained glass windows and mosaic floors.

RESTAURANTS AND LODGING: Among the several castles in the area is **Castel Labers**, dating from the 11th century and now a 32-room inn with orange-tile roof, prominent tower and medieval furnishings. Nearby **Castel Rametz**, another medieval castle, maintains a restaurant.

Not far from Merano, ***Novacella*** has an Augustinian convent maintained since the 12th century. The several buildings include a 12th-century chapel as well as Romanesque buildings and some 20th-century living quarters for the monks who make today's wine in a cellar that was built in the 1300s. (Sampling is encouraged.)

MILANO

Milano *(via Marconi 1, I-20123;* ☎ *2+80.96.62),* capital of Lombardia, is a confusing, sometimes chaotic city, with the ruins of a Roman wall worked into the traffic pattern. The Ligurians settled on the plains, south of the Alps, long before the birth of Christ, yielding to the Umbrians, who then yielded to the Etruscans, the Celts, and finally the Romans—who settled here in about 222 B.C.

But that's only the beginning. Partially because of its location (on the south side of the Alps amid fertile plains capable of providing plenty of fresh food), Milano was tossed back and forth between the big names of Europe when they were playing political volleyball. Francis I (in 1515), Charles V (in 1535), Philip II (soon after Charles V) and Maria Theresia of the Habsburgs, and even Napoleon—ceremoniously crowned King of Italy in the Duomo in 1805 only to have his representative, Eugene de Beauharnais (Josephine's son), tossed out with the emperor's fall from power in 1814. At that time the Austrian-based Habsburgs returned again.

All that seesawing of power resulted in a cosmopolitan city with a populace dedicated to the good life, no matter what. The city still has that feeling, even with the modern confusion of strikes, economic turmoil, socialism in light of aristocracy and the changes of a united Europe.

Milano, fashion capital of Italy (some say of Europe), can be an overwhelming city with its many drab gray buildings, the knotted traffic in its streets and the busyness of the Milanese, who appear to have little time for "non-belongers," but it is worth a visit.

AUTHOR'S OBSERVATION

Arrival at either airport or railway station seems chaotic, but both arrival areas can be easily navigated, if you pause, take a look around and then proceed directly to your train, the exit, or the tourist office to ask questions. Be aware of pickpockets and gypsies, especially around the train station. They've been known to flutter papers in your face or beg, with a child in arms, while a colleague steals from or walks away with your luggage.

The best way to get around the city, which is knotted with fume-spewing traffic, is a combination of walking and using the local bus, taxis, or, for longer distances, the metro. The *Uffizio Provinciale* and the *Touring Club Italiano* have speckled the city with yellow signs noting the best route to each of the major sights, but the traffic on the main routes and the gnarled streets in the more charming, older areas of town conspire to challenge walkers.

In spite of its obvious tourist appeal, the **Duomo** is the major sight in town. Grandly gaudy, the cathedral takes on a carnival atmosphere, with souvenir stall, postcard salesfolk, guides and tours. It's certainly the heart of the matter for tourists, on a piazza that's set up with kiosks selling guidebooks, postcards and other tourist items, wrapped in a ring of traffic-clogged roads. Via Dante cuts a swath from the Palazzo dei Giureconsulti, easily reached from piazza del Duomo, to the Castello Sforzesco; Teatro alla Scalla is just the "other" side of the covered Galleria.

Bus tours depart from the piazza del Duomo, on the via Marconi side, about 9 a.m. and 2:30 p.m. daily, to travel to piazza della Scala, past the Palazzo Marino to piazza dei Mercanti, the center of town in medieval days, past the church of **Santa Maria delle Grazie** (for Leonardo da Vinci's *Last Supper*) to **Castello Sforzesco** and on to **Famedio** (cemetery), to return passing piazza della Republica and via Manin. The exact route may vary, depending on traffic, but the highlights will be covered and this is a good way to get your bearings. The guide who gives information and history can be a good source for answers to any questions you may have.

LODGING: Milano is a major, cosmopolitan city. There's little in this city that has the charm and atmosphere usually associated with Alpine life, but there are several places to stay that meet expectations of worldwide travelers savvy in the style of Europe's "elite." Everyone knows the high rise luxurious **Palace** *(223 rooms; ☎ 2+63.36)* and the turn-of-the-century lavish **Principe di Savoia** *(302 rooms; ☎ 2+6230)*, fashionable neighbors facing each other across the Piazza della Repubblica, and two of the most expensive hotels in town. Millions have been spent by the CIGA group on these two hotels and their sibling, the elegant **Duca di Milano** *(100 suites; ☎ 2+6284; FAX 2+655.59.66)*, totally refurbished in 1992, next door to the Principe. (The Piazza della Repubblica on which these three face has not been the lovely park you might imagine; it was weed- and derelict-filled when I recently visited the city and a depressing sight when you step out the front door of your luxurious hotel.) For ultimate luxe, I prefer the **Excelsior Gallia** *(252 rooms; ☎ 2+6785; FAX 2+30.26.22)*, which maintains its old-world class and art deco style after extensive renovations. It's on Piazza Duca d'Aosta, a short walk from the main railroad station. The **Four Seasons Milano** *(98 rooms; via Gesù 8; ☎ 2+79.69.76 or 800+332-3442, FAX 2+7708.50.04)*, which opened in April '93, brings a new level of efficient comfort to the city. With high ceilings, soothing decor and marble bathrooms, the bedrooms seem palatial. The Palazzo-convent that has become the hotel dates from the 14th century.

One smaller place I have tried and liked is the centrally located **Pierre Milano** *(52 rooms; ☎ 2+72.00.05.81 or 800+323-7500)*, on via De Amicis, not too far from the Duomo. The **Hotel Diana Majestic** *(47 rooms; viale Piave 42; ☎ 2+2951.34.04)* can also be pleasant when you have a room at the back of the house, overlooking the garden. (Front rooms are very noisy, as is the case with most hotels that face onto busy streets). Charming and small, the **Hotel Manin** *(35 rooms; via Manin 7; ☎ 2+659.65.11)*, just off piazza Cavour, near the Giardini Pubblici (public gardens), has viewful rooms on its 7th floor. The tiny **Antica Locanda Solferino** *(12 rooms; ☎ 2+659.98.86)*, on via Castelfidardo, has a few rooms above its memorable restaurant in a now-chic nest of streets and lanes. Although rooms are small, this place puts you into a neighborhood that seems far removed from the international style of the big-and-lavish hotels, but is chic enough these days to have several good restaurants and some appealing boutiques.

RESTAURANTS: Worth seeking out for memorable meals are **Cucina delle Langhe** *(Corso Como 6;* ☎ *2+655.42.79)* and its relative, **Piccolo Teatro Fuori Porta** *(viale Pasubio 8;* ☎ *2+657.21.05),* both with interesting menus and pleasant presentation. **Bagutta** *(via Bagutta;* ☎ *2+760.027.67)* is a classic, enjoyed by four generations of Milanese and still owned by the Pepori family. It's multi-roomed, casual and busy at lunchtime as well as dinner, just off via Montenapoleone where you'll find some of the best boutiques. In the warren of short streets around Antica Locanda Solferino, mentioned above, look for **La Briciola** *(via Solferino near via Marsala;* ☎ *2+655.10.12)* and **Giollo** *(via Milazzo 6;* ☎ *2+657.15.81),* which is just off via Marsala. Both are pleasant places offering excellent food in trattoria surroundings. **Osteria del Binari**, **Osteria della Lanterna**, *(via Mercalli 3;* ☎ *2+551.31.43)* and **Osteria La Granseola** *(via Tortona 20;* ☎ *2+8940.24.45)* are three typical multi-course city restaurants that bustle at mealtimes. Among the city's best restaurants, Michelin gives 3 stars to **Gualtiero Marchesi** *(via Bonvesin de la Riva 9;* ☎ *2+942.00.34),* an oft-touted, very expensive, place to see and be seen, while enjoying the city's finest cuisine. But those in the know go to the informal, less expensive **Brunch** *(via Santa Rodegonda 3;* ☎ *2+87.71.59),* opened by the same owner, or to his **Bistro** *(via San Rafaele 2;* ☎ *2+87.71.20),* on the top floor of La Rinascente department store, where you can enjoy a bird's eye view of the Duomo in addition to good food. Other places worth finding are **Baretto** *(via Sant' Andrea 3;* ☎ *2+78.12.55),* just off via Montenapoleone and its wonderful shops, which is filled with Milano's "beautiful people" who seem to enjoy the offerings; **Giannino** *(via Amatore Sciesa 8;* ☎ *2+545.29.48),* where meals have been served since 1899; and **Antica Trattoria della Pesa** *(via Pasubio 10;* ☎ *2+655.5741),* with traditional Milanese recipes served to a devoted following of city folk and others who are lucky enough to find a table.

For an excursion, consider a reservation for a meal at **Antica Osteria del Ponte** *(*☎ *2+942.00.34),* a charming place with delicious food, south of Milano at the village of **Cassinetta di Lugagnano**. (It's possible to reach the Osteria del Ponte by train, from Milano to Abbiategrasso, but you'll have to contact the restaurant to arrange to be picked up.)

AUTHOR'S OBSERVATION

This confusing city seems somewhat easier to navigate if you've studied What's On in Milan, *a fact-filled English-language leaflet distributed in hotels, Alitalia offices, some car rental offices and the Milan information offices at the airport and the railway stations. If you'd like a copy in advance, write to* What's on *(Corso Venezia 18, I-20121 Milano, Italia).*

ORTISEI/ST. ULRICH

Ortisei/St. Ulrich *(via Rezi, I-39046; ☎ 471+796.328)*, in the Alto Adige's Val di Gardena (which runs northeast of Lago di Garda), is known for the craft of its woodcarvers. The town is deep in the Dolomite mountains, between Bolzano and Bressanone, in a little-known area that encourages exploring on foot as well as by car. Local folk converse in Ladin, a Romansch language related to that spoken in Switzerland's Engadine valley. Students at the woodcarving school work mostly in pine and chestnut, carving religious and farm figures as well as other objects.

PAVIA

Pavia *(I-27100; Via Fabio Fitzi 2; ☎ 382+272.38; FAX 382+322.21)*, a university town on the Ticino river in Lombardia, is south of Milano and the high Alps, but the town is worth a lengthy visit for its longtime links with both. The amount of history that is packed into Pavia's streets, churches and castles can seem overwhelming until you get your bearings. The Romans called it Ticinum; for the Lombard kings, it rivaled Milano; to people in the Middle Ages the city was known as Pappia, *civitas centrum turrium*, for the many towers that make the skyline look like a lively stock-market graph. Among my favorite touchstones in this town are the **Castello Visconteo**, designed by Galeazzo Il Visconti in the late 14th century, which has a lovely courtyard; the **Duomo** is gigantic, with a dome that guides will tell you is the "third largest in Italy," and **San Pietro in Cielo d'Or**, a lovely and relatively small Romanesque church. The Romanesque **San Michele church**, which was the coronation church for Charlemagne, Henri II, and Frederick Barbarossa, is also worth some time.

About 5 miles (9 km) away, at *Certosa di Pavia*, the **Gratiarum Cartusia** (Carthusian Monastery) is astounding! Founded at the end of the 14th century, the monastery benefitted from 15th- and 16th-century builders whose work makes this place what it is today. In addition to the richly embellished interior of the church, with its charming cloisters, a leisurely stroll around the grounds, enjoying the Lombard Gothic style of the exteriors, can consume pleasant hours.

Also near Pavia, **Salice Terme** *(via Marconi 8, I-27056;* ☎ *383+912.07)* is of interest for its thermal springs and spa status.

SAN MARTINO DI CASTROZZA

San Martino di Castrozza *(I-38058;* ☎ *439+681.01; FAX 439+683.52)*, deep in the Trentino region, on a wiggly mountain route that bisects the Parco Naturale Paneveggio-Pale di San Martino, has been in the tourism business since 1872, when the **Alpino Hotel** joined a monastery to welcome travelers. The town is still a worthy goal—for the amazing vistas of the Dolomites, so named for French scholar Marquis Deodat de Dolomieu, who conducted scientific studies of these mountains in 1788. (Prior to that time and still, for some, the mountains were—and are—known as the Pale mountains.) This small village is as interesting for the travel to and from as for the time spent in town.

SESTRIÈRE

Sestrière *(Piazza G. Agnelli, I-10058;* ☎ *122+762.76; FAX 122+763.17)*, in Piemonte, was Italy's first full-fledged ski resort, planned at the behest of Fiat's Giovanni Agnelli in the late 1940s, with an eye to recovery after the trauma of World War II. And it's still regarded by many as *the* fashionable spot at the height of winter or summer season. The installation of snow-making equipment assures good skiing throughout the winter, with plenty of walking and hiking opportunities when the weather cooperates the rest of the year.

LODGING: Among the dozens of places to stay, look into the **Grand Hotel Sestrière**, *(97 rooms;* ☎ *122+764.76)*, which aspires to elegance and is within walking distance of the ski lifts, and the **I Cavalieri** *(63 rooms; via Plagnol, 2 bis;* ☎ *122+768.77)*, an all-suite hotel in a style favored by Europeans who enjoy the independence offered by the kitchenette.

Less than an hour's drive from Sestriere and about 54 miles (87 km) from Torino, **Sans Sicario** *(I-10054;* ☎ *122+89.202)* grew from a small village to a popular ski resort from the mid-1950s. Brace yourself for a modern resort, with shops, restaurants and all other facilities catering to tourists. A monorail links the outlying areas. From its slopes you can ski or hike into France, depending on the weather. (A winter ski pass links the two areas.) Although you can count on hearing both French and Italian, don't count on fluent English. Do what you can in one of the other languages.

STRESA

Stresa *(via Principe Tomaso, I-28049;* ☎ *323+301.50, FAX 323+325.61)*, on the Piemontese shore of Lago Maggiore (see above), holds on to its elegance in spite of the fact that it is a bustling lakeside resort that can be crowded in mid-summer. Justly adored for its surrounding scenery, which includes the beautiful Borromean Islands—**Isola Bella**, **Isola dei Pescatori** and **Isola Madre**—as well as towering Mottarone and other mountains that allow for glorious views, Stresa is a lovely place to linger. Well known to the world's wealthy since leisure travel became fashionable in the late 19th century, the town has dozens of hotels, several excellent restaurants and many pleasant lingering places that include sun-warmed cafés as well as enclosed places that are pleasant when the weather cools. To avoid the peak-season crowds that inject a discordant note, plan to visit in early spring or late fall, when places are in full swing and it's relatively easy to get a good table in the best restaurants.

In addition to being a nice place to rest up between more strenuous travels, Stresa is an ideal home base for boat travels around Lago Maggiore. The **Navigazione Laghi Maggiore Garda Como Iseo** *(via L Ariosto 21, I-20145 Milano;* ☎ *2+481.20.86)* offers regular tours on Lago Maggiore, as well as the lakes of Garda, Como and Iseo. Some boat services start as early as March; others operate only from April through September.

LODGING: Top of the list for luxury is **Des Iles Borromees** *(120 rooms;* ☎ *323+304.31)*, part of the prestigious Italian CIGA group, but some of my other favorites are the small **La Fontana Meuble** *(19 rooms;* ☎ *323+327.07)*, where guests have the feeling of being in a home, and the larger **Astoria** *(106 rooms;* ☎ *323+30.259)*, **Bristol** *(251 rooms;* ☎ *323+326.01)* and **La Palma** *(128 rooms;* ☎ *323+302.66)*, all considered 4-star properties by the local tourist officials.

LA THUILE

La Thuile *(via Collomb 4, I-11016;* ☎ *165+884.179)*, in a wide spot of the Valle d'Aosta, on the branch that stretches southwest toward the Little San Bernardo (St. Bernard) pass, is mentioned so that you can arrange to pass through, unless you're lured by the massive resort complex that dwarfs the original, small village that was known for anthracite mining. From the town there's a grand view of the Grand Assaly and the Rutor and, when you continue along the road that crosses the San Carlo pass and goes through Morgex, there's a lovely view of Monte Bianco/Mont Blanc from Tete d'Arpy. Lago Verney sits amid the high mountain peaks, on a route that has been known since the Middle Ages and passes close to the ancient monastery of the San Bernardino monks, which has been closed since the end of World War II. The route sashays down to Bourg-Saint-Maurice, in France.

Now appreciated by Europeans as a family resort, mostly because the **Planibel** complex *(I-11016;* ☎ *165+88.45.41)* has everything from pinball machines and an ice-skating rink to an Olympic-size swimming pool and outdoor tennis courts, La Thuile concentrates on tourism. Cable cars stretch up and out from town, allowing visitors to ski or hike (depending on season) between Italy and France. The **Rutor glacier** is reached by helicopter, making it possible to ski the glacier and be in La Rosière in France for lunch, to head up again and return to La Thuile by nightfall.

TORINO

Torino *(via Roma 222, I-10121;* ☎ *10+535.181)* is first and foremost a big city; brace yourself for hustle and bustle befitting the home of Fiat. The city is also the gateway to the many rural Alpine towns and villages, easily reached by road, train (the main Porta Nuova station, plus the west side's Porta Susa, and local Torino Ceres station), trams and buses, which head into the Valle d'Aosta for Chamonix, Sestrière, and other mountain resorts. (Caselle airport, not far from the city, is linked with major European cities.)

Early Romans defined the area as Augusta Taurinorum, but the House of Savoy gave the city its French flavor, from 1574, when the headquarters were moved from Chambéry (see France chapter) to this place, which was the northern fringe of the lands then claimed by Spain. Filiberto Emanuele had reclaimed his lands after defeating the French at San Quentin in 1557. Kept under wraps for most of the next two centuries, communities in the Piemonte valley dug deeper into the earth that gave them sustenance, letting most of the influences from that time pass them by. Many of those villages still shrug at modern development, although their alberghi and trattorie welcome wanderers.

Via Roma, with Porta Nuova station as one of its goal posts, is the street to find for elegant shops and easy strolling, and Via Po, which branches off of it at Piazza Castello, is fringed with cafés that are ideal for lingering (and for people watching), when you close out the din and fumes of traffic. From Piazza Carlo Felice, at the front of the station, to Piazza Castello, with the Giardino Reale at its "back," an easy stroll will take you through lovely Piazza San Carlo, where Filiberto Emanuele sits on a prancing stallion, as he has since he was cast in bronze by Carlo Marchetti in 1838.

While the two churches (**San Carlo** and **Santa Cristina**) are pleasant to explore, study and enjoy, the **Palazzo dell'Accademia delle Scienze** holds the astounding Egyptian Museum, as well as the Galleria Sabauda (paintings) and the Galleria Gualino (collection of 15th- and 16th-century Florentine art, plus gold and silver work).

When the choices for museum-filled palazzos seems overwhelming, head for one of the many parks. **Parco del Valentino**, on the far bank of the Po, is laced with walking paths, dotted with enough buildings to keep things interesting and filled—at one portion—with the **Giardino Botanico**, where good maps define the plants and trees along your route.

Teatro Regio, highly respected among the local folks for the operas and other performances, was the location for the premier of Giacomo Puccini's *La Bohème*, on February 1, 1896, when *La Stampa* newspaper carried Carlo Bersezio's report that noted that "Just as *La Bohème* does not leave much impression in the mind of the listeners, it will not leave much impression on the history of our lyric theater."

Easily reached from Torino, towns such as **Alba** *(Piazza Medford, I-12051;* ☎ *173+358.33; FAX 173+36.38.78)*, **Nieve d'Alba**, **Asti** *(Piazza Alfieri 34, I-14100;* ☎ *0141+503.57)*, **Masio** and **Rochetta Tanaro** are all worth visiting, as are many other small spots.

LODGING: My first choice for a place to stay in Torino, if you're lucky enough to get a room, is the **Villa Sassi** *(12 rooms; via Traforo del Pino 47;* ☎ *10+89.05.56)*, a 17th-century manor house in a pleasant park, east of the Po and away from the city's bustle. Other choices in the heart of the city are the **Torino Palace** *(70 rooms; via Sacchi 8;* ☎ *10+51.55.11)*, a few steps from the Porta Nuova station, which makes it convenient for day touring to Alpine towns and villages. The **Hotel Piemontese** *(35 rooms; via Berthollet 21;* ☎ *10+669.81.01)* provides reasonable comforts at more modest prices, in the same area.

RESTAURANTS: For a dining experience, try **Vecchia Lanterna** *(Corso Re Umberto 21;* ☎ *10+53.70.47)*, which may appear to be austere but provides exceptional food. **Tre Galline** *(via Bellezia 37;* ☎ *10+546833)* may seem more memorable for its setting (in a 17th-century palazzo) than it does for its food, but it's worth a try. And then, experiment amid many choices of small places scattered along the streets in the center of the city. The antipasti are usually intriguing and tasty, regional specialties are fun to try and pasta dresses in many styles.

Outside town, but within easy driving distance, there are many exceptional places to dine. Try for a reservation at **La Contea** (☎ *173+671.26*), on *Piazza Cocita 8*, in Nieve d'Alba, or at **Ristorante Da Aldo** (☎ *141+20.60.08*), a few miles east of Asti. The **Trattoria Losanna** (☎ *131+77.95.25*), *on via San Rocco*, in Masio, a few miles east of Rochetta Tanaro, is also worth visiting. With plans made in advance and a special request to management, it's possible to enjoy a hearty *bagna caoda*, mentioned in the "Food, Wine, and other Beverages" section at the start of this chapter, at each of these restaurants.

TRENTO

Trento (*I-38100, via Alfieri 4;* ☎ *461+98.38.80*), capital of the Trentino region, in Italy's northeastern Alps, is a place D. H. Lawrence called "a pure Italian ancient city." Most of Trentino province is flecked with villages that time has forgotten.

From Milano, it takes about three hours by train to reach Trento, from which other trains and buses stretch into many of the less-traveled valleys. Although a rental car gives greatest freedom to explore the byways, some ski programs, such as those of **Italiatour** (☎ *800+237-0517*), include bus transportation from the airport at Milano to Trento and other places.

Trento is a cultural cache on the Adige river, on the way to the Brenner Pass. Marked by **Castello Buonconsiglio**, where the Council of Trent was held (1545-63), the town thrives on its history, along narrow streets as well as in places that have been modernized for today's traffic. Just to look at the town is to sink into the world of the arts at a confluence of Austrian and Italian talents. Many remarkable buildings date from 1027 through 1803, when the town was ruled by bishops of the Holy Roman Empire. The **Duomo**, in Lombard-Romanesque style, has a wonderful wheel-of-fortune window, but the rose window is also spectacular, especially when the sky is bright. Sixteenth- and 17th-century Venetian-style palaces line many streets; some have frescoes or painted walls. The **Museo Diocesano**, in the 13th-century Palazzo dei Pretorio, holds the paintings, 16th-century tapestries and other treasures of the cathedral. **Santa Maria Maggiore** is a Renaissance church, although its tower dates from Roman times.

For an overview of the town, be sure to go to Dosso Trento, where you'll also find the **Museum of the National History of the Alpine Soldier**.

South of Trento, **Rovereto** *(I-38068; ☎ 464+43.03.63)* is marked by its 14th-century Castello, standing watch over the maze of narrow streets of the medieval town that nests at its base. Although little remains from several 12th-century forts, built by the Castelbarco family to gain control of the trade route to Germany, several buildings enjoyed today are from the years when the town was controlled by Venice, from 1416 to 1509. Austria's Tirol region also played a role in town rule, when Maximilian annexed the town in the first half of the 16th century. Always at a crossroads, Rovereto was on the front line in World War I and its role affects its personality today, with the war museum in the castle and the nightly tolling of the Campana dei Caduti, one hundred times, in memory of those fallen in the wars.

In almost every direction out of Trento the valleys hide tiny villages that seem far removed from fast-paced 20th-century life. Although they have known trials and turmoil throughout their history, many are quietly asleep these days, waking only to serve good wine and home-cooked food to the occasional passer-by. The area is one of the most dramatic in the Alps, with the jagged Dolomites, small villages that hide astounding artworks in their churches, daily life focusing on markets that recall an earlier era and places with exceptional opportunities to enjoy walks, hikes, skiing, history, inns and special restaurants.

Three of dozens of worthy goals are **Aldeno**, deep in the Adige valley, south of Rovereto, where the grapes for Marzemino wine are cultivated; **Andalo** *(I 38100; ☎ 461+58.58.38)*, northwest of Trento, on the eastern fringe of the **Parco Naturale Adamello-Brenta**, with a cable car link to La Paganella; and **Baselga di Pine** *(I-38042; ☎ 461+55.70.28)*, on the shore of Lago Serraia, a popular resort area with several tiny communities within easy walking distance.

TRIESTE

Trieste *(I-34121, Castello San Giusto; ☎ 40+30.92.98; FAX 40+30.93.02)* is a busy knot of commerce between Croatia's Istrian Peninsula and Venezia. Overwhelming at first glance, the city is freckled with historic sights and rimmed with a coastal road that offers magnificent views of the Golfo di Trieste and its commerce.

If you have time for only one sight, make it **San Giusto Hill**, smack in the center of town, for the view as well as for the remnants of the 2nd-century **Roman Basilica**, the imposing **Castello** and the 15th-century **Cathedral of San Giusto**. The 6th- and 7th-century mosaics and the many 11th-, 12th- and 13th-century frescoes inside the cathedral are especially worth noting. The Castello is behind the cathedral. Started in 1470 by order of Frederick III and enlarged by a round bastion in 1508, when Trieste was under the Venetian Republic, the castle was "completed" in 1630. Its Lalio bastion was added in 1561. Now used for art exhibitions, the Castello holds a museum of antique furniture and arms as well as the main tourist office. Try to plan your visit to coincide with a performance in the *Cortile delle Milizie*, the large courtyard that is the stage for periodic events.

Check the schedule also for performances at the **Teatro Verdi**, reminiscent of Milan's Teatro della Scala and also designed by Pertsch and Selva. Conveniently located between the waterfront's Riva Tre Novembre and Piazza G. Verdi, the building was first used for performances on April 21, 1801. Inquire, also, about performances at **Teatro Rossetti**, on *viale 20 Settembre*, which was inaugurated with a performance of Giuseppe Verdi's "Un ballo in maschera" on April 17, 1878.

AUTHOR'S OBSERVATION

Trieste is a natural pausing place between Slovenia's resort area of Portoroz and Venezia. For those who are traveling on public transportation, buses leave from the Piazza della Libertà Coach Station, not far from the Central Railway Station, for the connection between trains from Venezia and the bus into Slovenia for Portoroz.

The bustle around **Piazza Unità d'Italia**, opening to the sea, is constant and confusing, as you might expect from the "largest square in Italy." Although it's difficult to get a sense of history these days, make some time to look at the **Fontana dei quattro Continenti**, (the Fountain of the Four Continents), which was the waterworks terminal during the reign of Habsburg Empress Maria Theresa. And pause to look up at the several impressive buildings around the perimeter of the square. In addition to the Duchi d'Aosta Hotel mentioned below, there's the 18th-century **Palazzo Pitteri** and the neo-16th-century **Palazzo di Lloyd Triestino**. Also on the square are the **Palazzo Modello**, the **Palazzo del Governo** (Government House), and the neoclassical **Palazzo Stratti**, best known these days for the Caffé degli Specci, a popular gathering place.

Other squares of special note are the **Piazza della Bourse**, with both the old and new stock exchange buildings on its edges, and the **Piazza S. Antonio Nuovo**, with many 19th-century buildings in a part of the city that was built during Maria Theresa's (Habsburg) reign. On a sour note, the cluster of buildings known as **Risiera di S. Sabba**, built as a rice husking depot from 1913 to 1943, was put to use as a concentration camp during the years of Nazi occupation. On the outskirts of the city, it has been a national monument with a museum since 1965.

About 10 miles outside the city, **Borgo Grotta Gigante**, the name both for a town and for the "largest cave in the world," is a popular tourist attraction, as much for the caves themselves as for the neighboring **Museum of Speleology**. It is linked to the city by the Opicina trams that depart from the station at Piazza Oberdan. Opened in September 1902, the tram links the waterfront area to the residential area of Opicina. (It's pulled on its route by a unique combination of cables that pull it to the top of the grade and then cast it loose to coast to its destination.)

A network of marinas lines the coast, with charter facilities and an active program of yacht races. West of Trieste, the nearest large facility is at Porto San Vito in **Grado** *(I-34073; Riva G. da Verazzano;* ☎ *431+846.22).*

VALLE DI FIEMME

Valle di Fiemme *(I-38033 Cacalese;* ☎ *462+302.98)* and **Val di Fassa** *(I-38032 Canazei, via Costa;* ☎ *462+624.66; FAX 462+622.78),* in the northeastern part of the Trentino region, are punctuated with a few towns that have adapted for today's visitors and many villages and hamlets that have not. The mountains set the mood, with the sun playing off their considerable bulk, warming some valleys and bringing shade early as it moves behind the peaks. Nature rules in these valleys, with thick forests in some areas and sheer rock face in others.

VALTELLINA

Valtellina stretches for 75 miles (125 km) following the Adda river, between Lago di Como and the Stelvio Pass. It links Italy with Switzerland on a route that stretches to St. Moritz. The valley made headlines in the mid-1980s when the spring thaw and torrential rains conspired to create mudslides that devasted many of the valley villages and towns. Funds were allocated for rebuilding and refurbishing, by both Italian and Swiss communities, and a complex network of dams and channels was built for the riverbed. The region has returned to normal, which is primarily as farming country with the more recent addition of tourism.

In Lombardia's lovely Valtellina, **Sondrio** *(I-23100, via C. Battisti 12;* ☎ *342+51.25.00)* is a pleasant center for walks, hikes, and history. Many of the town's historic buildings benefitted from funds available for rebuilding and refurbishing after the mid-1980s floods.

Modern comforts have been added to some buildings, but the traditional valley architecture of stone walls, decorated with balconies and window shutters, has been maintained. Although damaged at the time of serious floods in the late summer of 1980, the now restored early paintings inside the church by regional artist Pietro Ligari are worth a look.

VARESE

Varese *(viale Ippodromo, I-21100;* ☎ *332+28.46.24)*, in Lombardia, is a busy center for touring, but it's worth some time for a stroll through the **Giardini Estensi** at the **Pallazo d'Este**, which was built for Duke Francesco III from 1768 to 1780. The best thing about Varese, in my opinion, is its surrounding lake-studded, mountainous landscape and views from places such as Santa Maria and Campo dei Fiori, as you drive into the Alps. Within 6 miles (9 km) of Varese, Bisuschio's 16th-century **Villa Cicogna-Mozzoni** is worth visiting, but check for opening hours if you care about touring the villa.

VENEZIA

Venezia *(Castello 4421, I-30122;* ☎ *41+522.61.10)*, the romantic city in the Veneto region, is magic, in spite of the fact that it is (and has been always) a tourist city of the highest order. Threatened both by tourists and by frequent flooding, from the fact that it is sinking and the tides are rising, the canal-threaded city is the grande dame of tourism—and beautiful, in spite of its overwhelming tourist-commercial lifestyle. Magnificent palazzi show their most elaborate facades to the canals; charming foot-bridges link narrow lanes into a complex labyrinth; exotic art lives side by side with tourist trash, much as the worldly, cosmopolitan Venetians and others share restaurants and other public places with tourists and rip-off artists. There is no place like Venezia, in spite of the many cities that claim they are "the Venice of the north" or elsewhere.

AUTHOR'S OBSERVATION

Ask at your hotel, and/or the tourist office, for a copy of the English version of "Un Ospite di Venezia," which translates as "A Guest in Venice," and is valuable for maps, information about current events and other tips.

Walking is the best way to enjoy the city, window-shopping along the narrow lanes and pausing at sidewalk cafés and other places to watch people and feed the pigeons. There are three ways to navigate the canals: *vaparettos* that ply regular numbered routes from the

Stazione St. Lucia are the city's bus equivalent and the least expensive water route for travel; *motorscoffi* that wait at the dock across from Stazione St. Lucia and are on call as taxis; and the popular *gondolas* that have been the traditional (and most romantic) ways to glide along the canals. These days gondolas are hard to find and very expensive, having yielded to more modern methods and succumbed to traffic jams.

Rialto Bridge, a city landmark, is the place to find for the market, daily from before 8 a.m. until about 1 p.m., an event held on this spot since 1097. Start at Campo di Rialto, near San Giacomo di Rialto church, which dates from the late 11th century. Be sure to pass by the Pescheria, the fish market that resides on the Grand Canal, in a photogenic Gothic-Venetian building.

AUTHOR'S OBSERVATION

Do some homework with a detailed map before arriving, so you know what's where. Hardened hosts are not above giving you wrong directions; you're on your own to figure out what's correct—and to figure out what to pay. Spend some time learning the value of Italian lire; they go fast, especially to scalpers and others who seldom have your interests at heart when they quote prices.

Palazzo Grassi, near Piazza San Marco, on the east side of the Grand Canal, has been restored to its 18th-century splendor and is used for special exhibits and other cultural events, sponsored by the Fiat Motor Company. There's an admission charge.

AUTHOR'S OBSERVATION

Advance reservations are the only way to be sure of a room in your choice of hotels, but I've always found some reasonably pleasant place, even if it has been very simple, when I've arrived without reservations.

LODGING: Gritti Palace *(2467 Campo Santa Maria del Giglio;* ☎ *41+79.46.11)* is the most sensational hotel, in the opinion of many of us. The classy, canal-front palazzo is furnished with priceless antiques in a style that complements the 15th-century doge's mansion. The best rooms offer an unmatched view of the canals and several nearby palazzos. Expect rates that are as breathtaking as the view, at this member of the CIGA, which is also an esteemed member of *Leading Hotels of the World*, both mentioned when we look at "Lodging" in the introduction. **Romantik Hotel Metropole** *(4149 Riva degli Schiavoni;* ☎ *41+520.50.44; FAX 41+522.36.79)* is another memorable place, with less pretentious surroundings. Placed where the Grand Canal meets the lagoon, a short walk from piazza San Marco and convenient to the S. Zaccaria boat station used by lines 2 and 34, the comfortable hotel is convenient to all the touchstones of Venezia.

Other places, with more modest prices and a long list of devoted guests, include the tiny **Hotel Flora** *(calle Bergamaschi 2283a;* ☎ *41+520.58.44)*, with a courtyard garden, and its neighbor, **Do Pozzi** *(Corso do Pozzi;* ☎ *41+520.78.55)*, also between San Marco and the Grand Canal. Near Teatro la Fenice, in the heart of things, is the small **Hotel Kette** *(San Marco;* ☎ *41+7200.11.80; FAX 41+86.06.77)*. Two modestly-priced places in the "middle" of Venezia's hubbub that I've seen and liked are the **Hotel Serenissima** *(34 rooms; calle Golldoni, San Marco;* ☎ *41+520.00.11)*, just off the Piazza, with basic rooms and a great location; the **Hotel Austria e de la Ville** *(47 rooms; Lista di Spagna;* ☎ *41+71.53.00)*, a short walk from the railway station, which seems very attractive if you have much luggage. Rooms are comfortable; the terraced dining area is nice for alfresco meals.

Near, but not in, the center of things are several attractive places to stay. All offer rooms in calm surroundings within easy traveling distance from the highlights. Three places, all booked through the **Humania System** *(via Ponte Vetero 22, I-20121 Milano;* ☎ *2+7200.11.80; FAX 2+86.06.77)*, are the **Hotel Villa Mabapa** *(Riviera San Nicolò, Venezia Lido)*, with a homestyle atmosphere, and a terrace where candlelight dinners are served in summertime; the **Relais di Campagna al Leon d'Or** *(via Canonici, Mirano, Venezia)*, once a farm that was used as a retreat for churchmen at the turn of the century and was restored in 1980 as a lovely country inn; and the **Hotel le Boulevard** *(Venezia Lido)*, in a traditional hotel building, with viewful rooms and easy access to the Lido and Piazza San Marco.

RESTAURANTS: Memorable meals are legion in this city, where many places are as enticing for their atmosphere as for their food. Among my regular touchstones are **Antica Besseta** *(calle Salvio, Santa Croce 1395;* ☎ *41+72.16.87)*, for good basic Venetian food in a family-owned small spot, and **Al Graspo de Ua** *(5094/a calle dei Bombaseri;* ☎ *41+70.01.50)*, near the Rialto Bridge, where the chef makes good use of the best of the fresh produce from the Rialto market. Other places for memorable meals include **Ristorante Colombo** *(Corte del Teatro, San Marco;* ☎ *41+5222.26.27)*, serving Venetian specialties in a nest behind the Teatro Goldini, with a courtyard that is pleasant when the weather is, and the **Ristorante alla Borsa** *(calle delle Veste, San Marco;* ☎ *41+528.51.57),* near the Teatro Fenice and popular with performers and others who follow theater.

SPORTS

Italian sportsfolk take their prowess as a personal badge of courage. Fast skiing, tortuous bicycle riding and perilous rafting through rapids appeal to the super sportsfolk. You can participate or ogle, but be aware when you're on the ski slopes that others may ski past you with daredevil abandon.

AUTHOR'S OBSERVATION

The greater the amount of time you invest in tracking down sports options the better your experience will be. Contacting government agencies and tourist offices is time consuming and requires endless patience and persistence. Crucial questions, such as those about what equipment is available and how to obtain licenses, should be asked of several people. Then balance the answers and form your own opinion.

Here are suggestions about some of the places to look for specific sports:

ARCHERY

Recognized as a sophisticated sport and enjoyed by many Europeans, equipment has a place at established resorts such as Cortina d'Ampezzo, nestled in the Dolomite mountains, or Courmayeur, near Mont Blanc and France. The **Federazione Italiana Tiro con l'Arco** *(Archery, via Cassia 490, I-00189 Roma;* ☎ *6+331.24.04; FAX 6+366.38.60)* is your source.

BICYCLING

Many resort centers have bicycles for rent, but some bicyclers bring their own. If you're devoted to the sport, consider buying an Italian Bianchi bike to ship home after your travels. Some trains have a special car that has hooks for hanging the bike; inquire at railroad stations. Secondary roads are excellent for cycling, especially around the little-known lakes and in the wider valleys such as that of the Adige river and from the Piemonte plain into the Valle d'Aosta. The sport is popular in Lombardia, where there are reasonably flat areas. The local tourist offices can suggest firms that rent bikes and some of the resort hotels have a supply for their guests. More specific details and some good maps can be obtained through the **Federazione Ciclistica Italiana** *(via Leopoldo Franchetti 2, I-00194 Roma;* ☎ *6+3685.72.55).*

CANOEING

Some of the most popular rivers are the Bembo, the Oglio, the Po and the Ticino, as well as a branch of the Adda that passes through Valtellina. The supreme challenge is the route that runs near Milano to the Adriatic Sea, following the Naviglio Pavese canal and the Ticino and Po rivers. It's a sportsman's route and worth doing, but professional equipment is advised. One reliable firm that arranges white-water rafting excursions is **Euroraft**, with contacts in Austria, France and Switzerland as well as Italy, where the firm uses the name **Italiaraft** *(Parc d'Entraigues, I-05200 Embrun;* ☎ *33+9243.44.85).*

FISHING

In addition to the many rivers that carve their routes through the Alps, Lago di Endine in Lombardia is popular with fishermen who camp on its shores. In the Alto Adige (Sud Tirol), the Adige river is popular with anglers. And the area of Cortina d'Ampezzo, in the Dolomite mountains, is also noted for fishing. A fishing license must be obtained from the **Federazione Italiana Pesca Sportiva** or, in German for the bilingual Alto Adige/Sud Tirol, the **Landesamt fur Jagd und Fischerei** (Federation for Hunting and Fishing); you'll also need a day permit in many areas. Speaking Italian is very helpful. The Italian Government Tourist Office has details and specific addresses, as does the **Federazione Italiana Pesca Sportiva** *(viale Tiziano 70, I-00196 Roma;* ☎ *6+39.47.54).*

GOLF

There are many golf courses in and around Italy's Alps; Lombardia has 13 courses plus one on the outskirts of Milano; Piemonte has 15 including 36 holes at Torino, and the Veneto has 8 areas of play, including 18 holes at the Lido di Venezia. Among the best-known courses in Lombardia are the **Golf Club di Varese** *(via Vittorio Veneto 32, I-21020;* ☎ *332+22.93.02),* the **Menaggio e Cadenabbia Golf Club** *(via Golf 12, I-22010 Grandola e Uniti Como;* ☎ *344+321.03),* and the **Barlassina Country Club** *(via Privata Golf 42, I-22030 Birago di Lentate;* ☎ *362+56.06.21),* near Milano. Other good courses are at the **Golf Club I Roveri** and the **Golf Club Torino**, both near Torino; and the **Golf Club Monticello** is near Como on its famous lake. There is also a golf course at Courmayeur. Avid golfers should get specific details from the Italian Government Tourist Office and the named resorts, as well as from the **Federazione Italiana Golf** *(via Flaminia 388, I-00196 Roma;* ☎ *6+39.46.4l, FAX 6+322.02.50).*

HANG GLIDING/SOARING

One popular area is from the Mendelgebirge to the upper Adige area and around Brixen/Bressanone, Ahrntal/Valle Surina and on the Kronplatz/ Plan de Carones, using the German/Italian names for the dual-language towns. The Seiseralp/Alpe di Siusi lures many enthusiasts. The ultimate challenge is hang gliding with skis, which is popular with a few fearless sportsfolk.

HIKING

The *rete di sentieri* (route of hikes) are marked in many places, perhaps not as diligently as in the northern Alpine countries, but adequately for leisurely hikes and walks, after you've checked with the local tourist office. Cortina d'Ampezzo, respected for its winter sports, has hiking and walking paths around its mountain lakes, through its forests and along ridges in sight of the dramatic saw-toothed Dolomite mountains. The Monte Baldo, rising between Lago di Garda and the Adige river, is as wonderful for wildflowers and views as it is for the challenge of the hikes. The Gressone Valley, in Valle d'Aosta in the west, is crossed by the Lys and offers hundreds of beautiful walks and hikes, as do many of the side valleys in the Valle d'Aosta. In Alto Adige/Sud Tirol, to the west, there are also many miles of hiking and walking paths, including a section of the European Hiking Trail from Radein across Salurn to the mountains. In springtime, the Eppaner mountain path in the Adige Valley is a favorite, as are the paths through vineyards from Auer to Pinzon. One Alpine expedition is The Route Imperiale, from Modane (France) into Italy. The **Club Alpino Italiano** *(CAI, via Ugo Foscola 3, Milano;* ☎ *2+92.023.085)* is the source for maps and other specific facts.

HORSEBACK RIDING

Horse people interested in riding the Haflinger of the Sud Tirol can find them through lodgings and the local tourist offices. Varese and the Po Valley are two other places where riding is popular. Check with some of the riding clubs, such as those at Lainate, near Lodi at Ca del Ponte, Casorate, Sempione, Cremona and in the Alto Adige/Sud Tirol, places in Radein, Leifers and the Upper Adige Valley around Kaltern, as well as near Toblach/Dobbiaco. In Trentino, there are several **Centro Ippico** offices. Contact the **Federazione Centri di Equitazione Alpina** *(*☎ *465+210.36)* for a list. In addition, the Cortina Riding Club, in the Dolomites, holds special events throughout the spring, summer and fall. For information about riding schools, contact the **Associazione Nazionale per il Turismo Equestre** *(via Tiziano 70, I-00196 Roma;* ☎ *6+368.51).*

HUNTING/SHOOTING

In the Sud Tirol, the St. Joseph's competition takes place at Tramin/Tremeno in March and there are other events throughout the year. For those who can read Italian, contact the Ministry of Agriculture and Forestry for their annual booklet about regulations and seasons. Be sure to allow several weeks to get the necessary hunting permit from your nearest Italian Consultate before departure from North America. The permit is good for 30 days; the cost is about $25. The **Federazione Italiana Caccia** *(viale Tiziano 70, I-00196 Roma;* ☎ *6+3685.83.44)* is a source for additional facts.

MOUNTAINEERING/CLIMBING

Europe's highest peak, Mont Blanc (15,771 feet), often reached from Courmayeur, was conquered on August 8, 1786, by Michel Paccard and Jacques Balmat. Even before that date, mountaineers had been challenged by Alpine peaks in this area bordering France. Professional guides are available at most of Italy's Alpine resorts. The tourist office is your best source for facts about hiring an Alpine guide or accompanying an organized climb. Some resorts give classes in rock climbing. There are rock-climbing schools in Radein, Aldein and Margreid in the Alto Adige/Sud Tirol, where the walls, ridges and peaks are respected by experts and more than 100 shelters are maintained by the mountaineers. The area lists over 30 safeguarded climbs, including some in summer snow. Two contacts for mountain-climbing schools are **Scuola Alpina Alto-Adige** *(Piazza Parrocchia 4/11, Bolzano)* and the **Scuola di Roccia** in Courmayeur. For maps and information about huts and other mountain climbing facilities, contact the **Club Alpino Italiano** *(CAI, via Ugo Foscola 3, Milano;* ☎ *2+92.023.085).*

RIVER RAFTING

In the Alto Adige/Sud Tirol, programs are arranged along the Rienz, from St. Lorenzen to Muhlbach, and along the Rienz to the Eisack and the Noce on a two-day excursion. Contact the Alpine Rafting Camp. (See "River Rafting" for Austria.)

ROWING

Sometimes available at lakeside resorts, rowing can be arranged with the help of your hotel. Some places have their own boats. The sport is popular with local clubs, but it is often difficult for visitors to do more than watch the races. If you're serious about participating, speaking some Italian will help with negotiating arrangements through the local tourist office or another town organization suggested by your hotel.

SAILING

Italians are enthusiastic sailors and competitive racers. Sailing is especially popular on Lago di Garda, the largest lake in the Alps, and Lago di Caldaro/Kaltersee, which claims to be the warmest Alpine lake. Riva del Garda is one of the many places with marinas for boat charter. Other areas where sailing is popular include the small Lago di Ledro, west of Riva, and the Reschen Stausee in Alto Adige/Sud Tirol. Houseboats are available for rent on Lago di Como at Pognana Lario and on Lago di Garda at Sirmione. For details on permits and on lake sailing as well as on the Mediterranean, contact the **Federazione Italiana Vela** *(viale Brigata Bisagno 2/17, I-16129 Genova;* ☎ *10+56.57.23, FAX 10+59.28.64).* The best sources for facts about day sailing are the local tourist office or hotels near or on the many lakes.

SKIING

Skiers will find snow on the highest Alps, even in the middle of summer. If you'd like to ski when you find snow, it's a good idea to travel with jeans, a wind-shirt and suitable layers of clothing. You can buy powerful sunglasses and essential sunscreen lotions (and sometimes ski wear on sale). If summer skiing is important for your holiday happiness, be sure to line up skis and boots through the hotel when you make your reservations. (If they don't have an in-house rental system, chances are they can suggest a nearby sport shop.) Places with summer skiing include the Colle de Gigante out of Courmayeur, within sight of Monte Bianco (Mont Blanc); the Plateau Rosa, out of Breuil-Cervinia for the highest glaciers (in the Valle d'Aosta and also reached out of Zermatt, Switzerland); the Presena Glacier in Trentino; Passo Dello Stelvio near Bormio; and the Marmolada, famed Dolomite peak. One source for details is **Dolomiti Superski** *(via Meisules 183, I-39048 Selva di Val Gardena)*, near Bolzano. For information about skiing and other winter sports, contact **Federazione Italiana Sport Invernali** *(via Piranesi 44/b, I-20137 Milano;* ☎ *2+754.31, FAX 2+738.06.24).*

All these places offer exceptional facilities for winter skiing, as do many other resorts, both big and small. Daily information about winter snow conditions is offered, during winter months, through the Italian Government Tourist Office *(*☎ *212+245-4822).*

TENNIS

Most resorts have well-maintained tennis courts. Although it's often pleasant to play outside in warm weather, many resort centers also have covered courts that allow for all-weather, year-round tennis. Passo del Brallo in Pavia has been used as a training center for top tennis players. For further facts, contact the **Federazione Italiana Tennis** *(viale Tiziano 70, I-00196 Roma;* ☎ *6+3685.82.10).*

WALKING/TREKKING

One of the most interesting areas is the Stelvio National Park, best reached out of Bormio. The **Stramilano**, a non-competitive walking event, is held every spring in Milano. Italy's little-known villages in the less traveled valleys are good starting points for wildflower walks, especially in the early spring when the sun warms the southern side of the Alps. Rare daphnes and wild orchids are two species found in the Adige Valley. Around Cortina d'Ampezzo and Courmayeur, local tourist offices are good sources for guided walks—and maps, which are also sold at local bookstores. Near Trento, the Pine high plateau is ideal for walkers of all ages, with its meadows and woods, and the Fassa Valley, better known to experienced climbers for the challenges of the Dolomites, is fascinating as a stronghold of the Ladin language and customs.

WATERSKIING

Head for the busiest resort towns along the shores of Lago di Garda and Lago Maggiore, the largest and next-to-largest lakes of Italy. (The latter's northern tip pokes into Switzerland.) The waterski school at Lezzeno, on Lago di Como, teaches barefoot skiing. For facts about events, contact the **Federazione Italiana Sci Nautico** *(via Piranesi 44b, I-20137 Milano;* ☎ *2+7611.02.40).*

WINDSURFING/BOARDSAILING

Klaus Maran, two-time world champion, has a windsurfing school on the Lago di Caldaro/Kaltersee in the Alto Adige/Sud Tirol. In the same area, the Val Senales/Schnalstal, the Reschensee, Ulten Lake and Vernagt reservoirs are popular areas. On Lago Maggiore, which juts into Switzerland, the sport is also popular. You can rent boards at a few places, but traveling with your own (perhaps strapped to the top of your car) assures compatible equipment. Lago di Garda, west of the Dolomite mountains and regarded by some as having the "finest windsurfing conditions in Europe," is flecked with board-sailors.

TREASURES AND TRIFLES

Milano is the shopping center, with via Monte Napoleone and its side streets one of the prime areas for the elegant fashions that make this city world famous. The boutiques of Missioni, Giorgio Armani, Trussardi and others lure wise shoppers, and Pecks is the place to find for gourmet specialties that you might not find at home.

Torino's via Roma has elegant shops with Italian designers' specialties, and bookshops and antique stores are favorite places to browse and buy.

Silk produced in Lombardy, with Como as a center, is special—whether you choose to buy a ready-made item or yards of fabric to have fashioned at home.

Scarves and ties are ideal items for gifts, since they take up little luggage space, and other items to consider are the many leather wallets, gloves, key cases and other practical pieces that are well made according to patterns of Italian designers.

Expect to find folk art in the mountain villages, with the focus on pottery, weaving and a large selection of wooden crafts. The woodcarvers of Oritsei, in the Val Gardena, northwest of Lago di Garda, are famous for their artistry; purchases from that village can be real treasures.

Italy's Value-Added Tax, Imposta Valore Aggiunto, or IVA, is rebated to foreign visitors who intend to leave the country with the purchases. Offered only on single purchases over L 930,000, the rebate requires endless form-filling and—in my opinion—creates more headaches than it's worth. If you can afford to make a purchase of that amount, chances are that the rebate procedure will be too much bother. Here's the procedure: when you make your purchase, ask the store for the receipt, which you must have checked against the merchandise and stamped when you leave the country. The plan may not sound too difficult, but it's often time-consuming to find the proper authority at the airport or road border-crossing and is impossible, if my experiences are typical, at any train station.

If you do find the proper authority, you have to have the merchandise ready to show and the form ready to be stamped, which means keeping it separate from your checked-through luggage. The form is then mailed back to the store. It can take *weeks* (or "forever") to receive the rebate, which will be in Italian lire, if it arrives at all.

ADDITIONAL INFORMATION SOURCES

For further information on specific regions contact:

REGIONE FRIULI-VENEZIA GIULIA

Direzione Regionale del Commercio e del Turismo, *via S. Francesco d'Assisi 37, I-34133, Trieste, Italia;* ☎ *40+73.55; FAX 40+36.21.09.*

REGIONE PIEMONTE
Assessorato Regionale al Turismo, Sport, Tempo Libero, Caccia e Pesca, *via Magenta 12, I-10128 Torino, Italia* ☎ *11+432.11; FAX 11+432.24.40.*

REGIONE DOLOMITEN ITALIEN
Landesverkehrsamt Sudtirol/Ufficio Provinciale per il Turismo, *I-39100 Bozen/Bolzano, Pfarrplatz 11-12;* ☎ *471+99.38.80; FAX 471+99.36.99.*

REGIONE TRENTINO-ALTO ADIGE
Provincia Autonoma di Trento Azienda per la Promozione Turistica del Trentino, *via S. Sighele 3, I-38100 Trento, Italia.* ☎ *461+98.39.39; FAX 461+98.24.35 or 23.15.97.*

REGIONE AUTONOMA DI TRIESTE
Azienda Regionale per la Promozione Turistica, *via Rossini 6, I-34132 Trieste, Italia.* ☎ *40+36.51.52; FAX 40+36.54.96.*

REGIONE VALLE D'AOSTA
Assessorato Regionale del Turismo, Urbanistica e Beni Culturali; Ufficio Regionale per il Turismo, *piazza Narbonne 3, I-11100 Aosta, Italia.* ☎ *165+30.37.25; FAX 165+401.34.*

REGIONE LOMBARDIA
Assessorato Regionale al Commercio, Turismo, Sport, Tempo Libero, e Industria Alberghiera, *via Fabio Filzi 22, I-20124 Milano, Italia.* ☎ *2+67.651; FAX 2+67.655.428.*

Bergamo I-24100, *via Emaluele 20;* ☎ *35+21.31.85.*

Bescia I-25121, *corso Zanardelli 34;* ☎ *30+434.18; FAX 30+29.32.84.*

Como I-22100, *piazza Cavour 17;* ☎ *31+26.20.91, FAX 31+30.10.51.*

Cremona I-26100, *piazza del Comune 5;* ☎ *372+232.33; FAX 372+217.22.*

Mantova I-46100, *piazza Andrea Mantegna 6;* ☎ *376+35.06.81.*

Milano I-20123, *via Marconi 1;* ☎ *2+80.96.62; FAX 2+7202.24.32.*

Pavia I-27100, *via Fabio Filzi 2;* ☎ *382+272.38; FAX 382+322.21.*

San Martino di Castrozza e Primiero *I-38058* • ☎ *439+681.01, FAX 439+98.39.39.*

Sondrio I-23100, *via Cesare Battisti 12;* ☎ *342+51.25.00, FAX 342+21.25.90.*

Terme di Levicio, *Lago di Caldonazzo, I-38056* • *Levico Terme,* ☎ *461+70.61.01; FAX 461+70.60.04.*

Trento I-38100, *via Sighele 5;* ☎ *461+23.89.38; FAX 461+23.15.97.*

Trieste I-34121, *piazza della Cattedrale 3;* ☎ *40+30.92.42, FAX 40+30.93.02.*

Valle di Fiemme I-38033, *cavalese, via Fratelli Bronzetti 4;* ☎ *462+302.98; FAX 462+206.49.*

Valle di Fassa I-38030, *canazei, via Costa;* ☎ *462+624.66, FAX 462+622.78.*

Varese I-21100, *viale Ippodromo 9;* ☎ *332+28.46.24; FAX 332+33.17.37.*

Venezia I-30121, *Castello 4421;* ☎ *41+529.87.11, FAX 41+523.03.99.*

LIECHTENSTEIN

Liechtenstein

When the smartly-styled yellow and white postal bus arrived in Vaduz, the air was crisp, the view was in shades of grey and the countryside was trimmed with ice-diamonds that sparkled in response to sun beams. It was the cusp of winter, the temperature had frozen middle Europe's inevitable drizzle and the sun was just breaking through the clouds when I stepped off the bus. Liechtenstein, a tongue-challenging word that has always conjured up fairytale images, appeared to be a magic land.

And so it always has been for me, whether I've chosen to dip into the country for a lingering luncheon near the castle or a few stolen

271

days of walking along mountain paths or an hour or two of conversation with friends, in a small *Stübli*, as the pub-style room of an inn is known in German-speaking areas of the Alps.

Of course most people arrive in a Mercedes or some other tony European car (and I've done that), but there's an insousiance that comes with stepping off the Swiss postal coach, sliding anonymously into one of the world's most sophisticated commercial centers and strolling around with the inner confidence of a resident.

The castle that's pinned to the mountainside above the town, where aloofness is assured by the surrounding forests and the angle of the slope, is far more obvious than the banking intrigue that fills the offices (and lines of communication) of the principality. In Liechtenstein, numbered bank accounts are still a viable option and mind-boggling sums are swept along the airwaves.

Vaduz, the most important town of the principality, has lost some of its appeal in the many years I've known it. Where it was once a small town with one bustling street, it is now a warren of traffic-clogged roads. It is made ever more congested by the swarms of tour buses that pass through on their route between "here" and "there" and the prosperity that plants stores and other buildings along the roadsides. As a clutter of commerce brings ever-more affluence to the residents, I head for the hills, where the rustic, magical lifestyle that lured me here many years ago manages to survive, albeit with some commercial overtones.

The singing nuns, their black habits' swinging as they moved their wooden rakes when I watched them haying a field several summers ago, no longer work the pasture across from their church in Schaan. Only a patch of field remains to be tilled by mechanical means; the rest has been built upon. But the walking and hiking trails on the Eschnerberg and in other areas are more clearly marked, and the challenges of the upper ridge remain constant, as does the ever-changing weather at that height.

COUNTRY CAPSULE

Fürstentum Liechtenstein, the official name of the principality, is set in the border between Austria and Switzerland. The tiny country measures a mere 61.76 square miles and its highest peak is at 8525 feet. But that's enough to inspire the village of Malbun to become a ski resort in winter and acquire a walking-hiking focus in summer months. Operating as a constitutional principality on a system similar to that known in Britain, Liechtenstein is one of the world's most

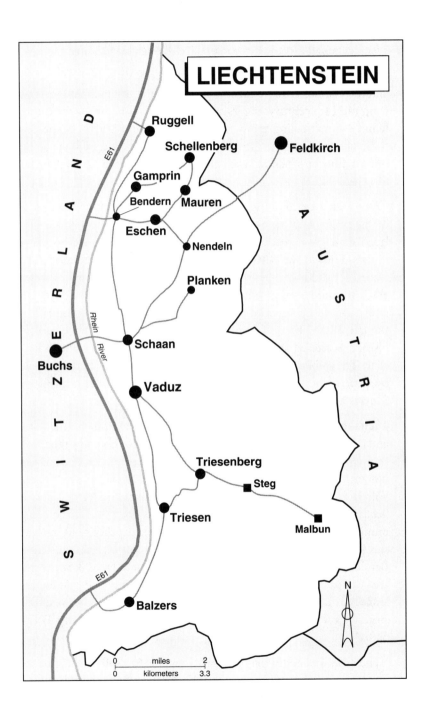

prosperous countries. Total unemployment had been tallied at 242 in August 1993, when Liechtensteiners also "felt the recession." The average annual income has been tallied at over US$25,000.

The castle that perches on the hillside overlooking the Rhein valley and the commerce of Vaduz incorporates parts of a medieval fortress from the 14th century. But its modern interior is home for the ruling family—Fürst (ruling prince) Hans Adam II and Fürstin Marie, his wife. The family of the Prince of Liechtenstein is said by some to be one of Europe's richest, even though much of the family land in Czechoslovakia was confiscated after World War II.

Although a swath of the Rhein valley is part of Liechtenstein, most of the principality blankets Alpine mountains that are occasionally laced with good roads and walking paths. There are eleven communes. **Triesen** was settled in Roman times and was mentioned in records of 1155 when it was the home of several noble families. **Balzers**, the southernmost village, is mentioned in records of royal estates that were drawn up around 850. In **Triesenberg**, founded in the late 1200s, the village museum documents some of the earliest history. Scattered around the higher areas of the principality, especially Triesenberg and **Planken**, are a few original wood chalets built by settlers who share a heritage with people who live in southwestern Switzerland, in the canton of Valais.

Schaan was mentioned in Carolingian records as Scana in the 830s and a Roman helmet unearthed several years ago dates from the first century A.D. Today most of antiquity is covered with modern development; the few historic sites are mentioned below, under "Places Worth Finding." The small chapel at Planken, a nice walk above Schaan, has some peculiar copies of Old Masters, but it is the community of **Gamprin-Bendern** that holds the principality's oldest treasures. There's evidence of a farm near the hill by the church in Bendern that is thought to have stood in about A.D. 500, when the area was part of what is now the Swiss canton of St. Gallen. At **Schellenberg**, marked by two historic castles, the ruins of the medieval structures dot what is marked as the "Historic Eschnerberg Footpath."

The other villages of the principality include **Ruggell**, the northernmost community of the principality; **Mauren/Schaanwald**, which borders Austria; and **Eschen**, incorporating the village of **Nendeln**, which has yielded Stone Age artifacts from 5000 B.C. and is now an area for small companies as well as a popular residential area.

HISTORIC HIGHLIGHTS

The royal family of Liechtenstein traces its lineage back to the 12th century when the knight Hugo lived in Liechtenstein Castle (which is not in this country, but in Austria, south of Wien). Ties with Austria have been strong, both legally through much of the principality's history and sentimentally even today. Not only did the lords of Liechtenstein, as those who lived in the Austrian castle called themselves, rally to the aid of the Austrian government, but they also bore the effects of its discipline, when John of Liechtenstein fell into disgrace and all the lands south of the Donau (Danube) were taken from Liechtenstein's domain.

When the Duke of Babenberg died in battle against the Hungarians, Henry I of Liechtenstein led the Austrians on to victory; when Rudolf of Habsburg fought against Ottokar, the king of Bohemia, Henry II of Liechtenstein was at his side; and in the Middle Ages, George III became chancellor of the University of Vienna, before he was Bishop of Trent and before he became a cardinal.

It was Charles I of Liechtenstein, however, who earned what has become the principality. He was a friend (and more) to the Habsburg dynasty, serving as a loyal lord high chamberlain and taking over as imperial governor of Bohemia after the Bohemian Rebellion (the start of the Thirty Years' War) had been crushed. He also loaned money from his then considerable coffers to the emperor for his war against the Turks. For all his services, in 1608 Charles of Liechtenstein was given the rank of prince.

Since status among princes of an empire depended on having a suitable territory, Charles' grandson had the task of finding the proper place. The impoverished head of the house of Hohenems seemed the answer to the prayers of Prince John Adam Andres. Purchase of the lordship of Schellenberg was negotiated in 1699. When that proved not quite big enough to qualify for principality status (and the money was not quite enough to cover Lord Hohenems' debts), a second purchase of the county of Vaduz was negotiated in 1712. In 1719, the emperor of Austria was willing to see the two purchases joined in the Imperial Principality of Liechtenstein, named for the land holdings in Austria.

Liechtenstein's princes continued to live in Austria until 1938, when Fürst Franz Josef II, father of the ruling prince, moved to the land holdings between the borders of Austria and Switzerland. Previous princes governed their principality through emissaries who dealt with the Landamanner, the spokesmen for the people. That system lasted through the 18th and 19th centuries during periods when the principality was to become one of the 16 member states of the Confederation of the Rhein under Napoleon in 1806. (That fact gave the principality the sovereignty it holds today.) Subsequently, after Napoleon's fall from grace, Liechtenstein became a member of the German Confederation as a result of the 1815 Congress of Vienna.

Although officially terminated with the collapse of the Austro-Hungarian Empire in 1919, Liechtenstein's links with Austria are still strong. Prince Hans Adam II received his middle schooling at the Schottengymnasium in Wien (Vienna), and his parents were both born and educated in Austria. Since 1984, Prince Hans Adam has acted as sovereign, although his 83-year-old father, Prince Franz Josef, was titular head until his death in November 1989.

POLITICAL PICTURE

The principality is a "constitutional hereditary monarchy," governed both by the prince and the people. It is built upon a "democratic and parliamentary basis," as stated in the constitution of 1921 and is the last monarchy remnant of the Holy Roman Empire. The two rival parties formed a coalition government in 1938 and have continued to agree on government positions and to respond favorably to any suggestions made by the prince since that time. The people separate themselves, in a general way, as Oberlanders and Unterlanders, according to historic traditions. The communities in the Oberland, the south, are Vaduz, Balzers, Schaan, Planken, Triesen and Triesenberg. The Unterland, the north, includes Eschen, Ruggell, Bendern-Gamprin, Mauren-Schaanwald and Schellenberg. Malbun, Steg, Silum, Gaflei, Masecha and Sucka are part of the Alpen region.

For a brief period immediately following the collapse of the Habsburg Empire (in 1918), Liechtenstein set up and patrolled its own borders. With an economy tied to and using the Austrian schilling, Liechtenstein's political and financial fortunes fell. The principality turned to neutral Switzerland and, in 1923, signed a customs treaty that was the foundation of the strong relationship that continues today. All customs and trade treaties signed by Switzerland also apply for Liechtenstein, unless the principality specifically declines to participate. Swiss neutrality during World War II included Liechtenstein, and the flourishing economy of the principality benefits from that fact—and from the keen business sense of several Liechtensteiners. In 1990 Liechtenstein became a member of the United Nations, and in 1991, a member of the EFTA, intending to have a relationship with the European Economic Community when the customs and other contracts with Switzerland (who voted against joining) are worked out.

LIFESTYLE

Although Malbun takes on a festive air at peak winter ski season, most of the principality has a country-conservative lifestyle. Business and banking guide the social circuit these days, but the hard-working life of the fields and farming is not too far in the past. Most folks hold on to those basic values. The Catholic church plays a meaningful role in daily life. Most Liechtensteiners wear business clothes for their work in banks, insurance companies, tourism-related industries and other offices. Visitors are expected to follow the reasonably formal lifestyle, with jacket and tie for men, and dark-and-classic clothes for women, especially when dining at the Parkhotel Sonnenhof, the Hotel Real and other elegant places. Country clothes are worn for walks, sightseeing and other leisure activities.

NATURAL SURROUNDINGS

The entire principality is a parkland, some of it owned by the prince and other portions owned by the several communities. Very little is owned in the name of the principality. For this reason, Liechtenstein assumes the aspect of a gigantic park, freckled with an occasional village. Rising from the Rhein valley to jagged mountains, the principality boasts, in one of its official booklets, of "6380 square yards of land per inhabitant." Relaxation in restful surroundings is appealing for visitors, as well as for residents.

Pleasant for walking and other outdoor activities, the principality has 93 miles (150 km) of walking and hiking trails in the Alpine areas and another 74 miles (120 km) in the Rhein valley area. Bird-watchers will enjoy walks in the Eschnerberg area, where the woods provide cover. Although it can only be visited by special permission, one of the best places for birding is the 247-acre Ruggeller Riet, which is protected by law as a nature conservation area. Inquire at the tourist office in Vaduz.

PRACTICAL FACTS ABOUT LIECHTENSTEIN

Liechtenstein is easy to enjoy, not only because the lifestyle is orderly, as you can expect with Swiss systems, but also because the size allows for easy touring, even by foot.

INFORMATION SOURCES

Liechtensteinische Fremdenverkehrszentrale, the Liechtenstein Tourist Office, can be reached through *Box 139, FL 9490 Vaduz, Liechtenstein;* ☎ *41+75+232.14.43 or 236.61.70, FAX 41+75+392.16.18.* In the U.S., contact the **Swiss National Tourist Office**, *608 Fifth Ave., New York, NY 10020;* ☎ *212+757-5944, FAX 212+262-6116,* and elsewhere. (Refer to "Switzerland" for additional addresses and telephone contacts.)

Throughout the chapter, local spelling is used for some words and all place names. For translation of foreign words, refer to the back-of-the-book glossary.

CASH, CURRENCY AND CREDIT CARDS

The official currency of Liechtenstein is the Swiss franc, which is approximately SFr. 1.5 to US$1 at press time. Many of the stores in Vaduz welcome credit cards, but some of the inns and small hotels accept only cash. Be sure to inquire before checking in if paying with plastic is important to your travel budget.

COMMUNICATION

German, with unique Liechtenstein dialects in the villages, is the language of the principality, but many internationally oriented people in Vaduz and elsewhere speak fluent English. Almost everything that is a fact for communications in Switzerland applies also in Liechtenstein since Swiss systems have been adopted throughout the principality. One exception is Liechtenstein's postage stamps, which are made in Austria and Switzerland. They are unique, and are prized by stamp collectors as well as tourists.

Telephoning to Liechtenstein from the U.S. is as easy as dialing the international code for your chosen carrier, plus 41 (the same code as Switzerland), plus 75, which is the "city" code for the Principality of Leichtenstein and the local 7-digit number.

AUTHOR'S OBSERVATION

Telephone numbers in this chapter are given for direct dial from the U.S., with the addition of the country code. When in Liechtenstein, or in Switzerland, you'll need to begin dialing out-of-town numbers with a "0."

From Liechtenstein, you can make international telephone calls, as well as local ones, of course, from any post office, even in the smaller villages. The procedure involves advising the personnel attending one of the sales windows (with gestures, if you don't share a common spoken language), stepping into a booth and dialing your number—including the country code. After you've finished talking, go to the stamp window to pay. The amount will be shown on a receipt. To dial into *USADirect* or another U.S. call-expediting service, the cost is the same as a local call. Deposit a coin, dial *046+05.00.11* to reach the AT&T operator in the U.S. and tell him or her the number you wish to reach in the U.S. AT&T subscribers can have calls charged to their U.S. telephone account at a minimal service charge; anyone can use the system to call collect. For more information in the U.S., call ☎ *800+874-4000*. Sprint and MCI have similar services with different access codes.

DOCUMENTS AND OTHER PAPERS

Your passport is required for entry into Switzerland, and, therefore, also for Liechtenstein, but when you've entered Switzerland you may travel without further check to Liechtenstein. Border formalities are nonexistent when entering through Sargans or Buchs in Switzerland and minimal through Feldkirch, Austria. Even if there is someone to look at your passport, as there has been occasionally when I've arrived from Feldkirch, it's difficult to get your passport stamped. For a modest fee, however, the *Verkehrsbüro Vaduz* will put an official stamp in your passport when you make the time to stop by their office.

MEDICAL FACILITIES

The *Krankenhaus* (hospital) in Vaduz is efficient and well equipped for normal problems. The most serious medical cases may be taken to St. Gallen, less than an hour's drive into Switzerland. (One of the principality's most important exports is false teeth, made at factories in the valley.)

TRAVEL FACTS

The principality is small enough, with a landmass of 61 square miles (160 square kilometers) to enjoy with a combination of postal bus and walking. The public transport system operates on a two-fare system, with rides up to 13 km costing SFr. 2 and longer rides costing SFr. 3. A ticket for unlimited rides for one month costs SFr. 15.

ARRIVAL

Liechtenstein has no airport or railroad station. Trains passing through Liechtenstein stop at the Swiss towns of Buchs and Sargans, where the Swiss postal bus service makes a link with Vaduz. Although Liechtenstein has no national trains, the Austrian Federal Railway maintains a road bed through the principality. (The border stop in Austria is at Feldkirch.) As part of the agreement, the Austrian railway is required to hire a certain number of Liechtensteiners to work on the railroad, but the standard of living and the availability of desk jobs in Liechtenstein results in few, if any, applicants. Major highways between Switzerland and Austria pass near Liechtenstein, with spur roads making access easy.

TOURING TIPS

Public **BUS** service and walking paths can take you "everywhere." Since the postal buses are part of the Swiss system, Swiss transportation passes can be used for travel on them. Schedules are posted at the PTT station in Vaduz and at appropriate stops along the routes.

CAR is the fastest and most efficient way to climb from Vaduz and the Rhein (Rhine) valley floor up the mountainside to Malbun and other villages. There are **taxis** and rental car companies in Vaduz, but most people driving in this region have rented cars in Austria or Switzerland, or even France or Germany, to pause in Liechtenstein on travels elsewhere.

On **FOOT** is the best way to wander around, although there are no quaint and pleasant strolling streets in downtown Vaduz, unless you're shopping. Every village has well-marked walking and hiking paths. You can easily walk up and out from Vaduz, past the prince's vineyards, the *Parkhotel Sonnenhof* and beyond into the hillside in the direction of the prince's palace or Schaan. When you get into any of the villages, walking from place to place is pleasant and easy. There's a well-posted Fürstenweg (prince's walk) from Vaduz to Schaan. For professional climbers who don't mind heights, the Fürstensteig threads along the peaks between the Rhein and Samina valleys from the hamlet of Gaflei. The *Historischer Hohenweg Eschnerberg* is a bosky walking path that passes near the Schellenberg castle ruins.

DAILY LIVING

FOOD, WINE AND OTHER BEVERAGES

Meal offerings include items familiar in neighboring Switzerland and Austria, with emphasis on veal, pork and fish for the main course. Some restaurants excel in homemade wurst and country-style cooking, as can be expected in an area that was essentially a farming community until recent years. *Salamibrot* is salami with farm bread and *Kasesalat* is a salad with small pieces of cheese.

Liechtenstein has several noteworthy restaurants. The two best, for European *haute cuisine*, are owned by brothers: the **Hotel Real**

(☎ *41+75+232.22.22),* in downtown Vaduz, opened by Felix Real and now managed by his son, Martin, and **Parkhotel Sonnenhof** (☎ *41+75+232.11.92),* well known for Emil Real's culinary skills and now managed with his son, Hubert. At the Sonnenhof, window-side tables give you a wonderful glimpse of the Prince's Castle, which is enchanting by day or night. The Parkhotel Sonnenhof is open only for the hotel's overnight guests, but it's worth telephoning to inquire about a possible exception for the midday meal.

Other places offering exceptional European food and service are the **Waldhof**, where the gourmet menu is legendary and the atmosphere is better than you might suspect from its location (on the road that links Austria's town of Feldkirch) and the **Landgasthof Schtazmann** (☎ *41+75+232.90.70),* in Treisen, which has gained a reputation as "one of the five best restaurants in the country."

One of the most traditional places to dine on regional specialties and enjoy Liechtenstein wine is the **Torkel** (☎ *41+75+232.44.10)* on the northern side of Vaduz. It takes its name from the 17th-century wine press that has been incorporated into the main room and is now acknowledged as one of the principality's best restaurants with local recipes as well as international specialties.

Other good country-style restaurants include the **Hotel Saroya** (☎ *41+75+233.15.84)* in a vintage building in Planken above Schaan; the **Gasthof Engel** (☎ *41+75+234.12.01)* in Balzers, where you can enjoy farm-style recipes; and the **Wirthschaft zum Löwen** (☎ *41+75+233.11.62)* in Schellenberg, in a traditional building with wood walls and wrought-iron latches. The place has been in the same family for many generations and is where I first enjoyed *Käsknöpfle*, made with *Sauerkäse*, a pungent homemade mountain cheese that is a Liechtenstein specialty. The restaurant also serves homemade *Schwartenmagen*, which is head cheese, and other traditional food.

The princely vineyards provide three noteworthy wines—*Vaduzer Süssdruck, Vaduzer Beerli* and *Vaduzer Chardonnay*—and private vintners provide the rest of the different types of wine that are produced on about 35 acres of the principality. The Torkel restaurant, mentioned above, sits amid the prince's vineyards and is a comfortably rustic setting for wine tasting. Wine tastings can also be arranged at the **Hofkellerei des regierenden Fürsten von Liechtenstein**, the wine cellars of the prince, by special reservation *(Feldstrasse 4, FL-9490 Vaduz;* ☎ *41+75+232.10.18)* and in Nendeln at **Schächle's Weinstube** *(Churer Strasse 263, FL-9485;*

☎ *41+75+373.41.44, FAX 41+75+373.43.67)*, where the cellar holds more than 350 European wines.

LODGING

A rate sheet for hotels and pensions is distributed through the tourist office. In addition, the Triesenberg area issues an annual *Unterkunfts-und Restaurantliste* (list of lodgings and restaurants), with pictures of most properties and prices on an accompanying list. Most of the accommodations are new, with modern facilities, small bathrooms, and, in some cases, noteworthy cuisine. Although many have been built in the Alpine chalet style, there are few, if any, original historic inns. Most places are small and family-operated and some have added rooms in an owner-inspired style. For names of specific places, check each community mentioned below.

PLACES WORTH FINDING

The letter-number notation, which is the postal code, and the telephone and fax numbers in parentheses following each place name apply to the tourism office, one important source for further information.

The main town, **Vaduz**, is a small, modern city that doesn't look like much, especially if you arrive in summer months when tour buses pour their passengers into the few streets of town. If you're staying a few days, head for the hills—to villages such as Schaan, Triesen, Triesenberg and Malbun, or elsewhere on the valley slopes, to Planken or Schellenberg, to enjoy a rural life and the scenery.

BALZERS

Balzers, in the Rhein valley, is marked by its picturesque **Gutenberg castle**, best enjoyed from the outside.

MALBUN

Malbun has become a tourist community in recent years. Most of the recently built hotels, restaurants and apartment clusters are tastefully constructed in a style reminiscent of traditional Alpine chalets. The **Alpenhotel** (☎ *41+75+263.11.81*), where I've stayed (and dined), is a chalet style inn that has been in the same family since 1908. (Its sister hotel, the **Galina**, has a local reputation for its pastries!) A new chairlift from Malbun takes vacationers to the highest peaks via Sareis for skiing in winter or walking in summer.

PLANKEN

Planken, the smallest parish, takes its name from *plaunca* or *planca*, a Rhaeto-Romansch word that means high pasture. Settled by peo-

ple from the Valais region of Switzerland at the end of the 13th century, the landscape is dotted with tiny weathered-wood chalets in
traditional style. The jagged rocks of the **Dreischwesternmassiv**
(massif of the three sisters) is best reached from here. Although the
Gafadura mountain inn is only open in summer, when it's enjoyed
by hikers and climbers, the **Hotel Saroja** (☎ *41+75+373.15.84)* and
the **Restaurant Hirschen** (☎ *41+75+373.13.03)* are popular walking
goals.

SCHAAN

Schaan's Sylva im Sax (☎ *41+75+232.39.42)* is a modern hotel,
built in traditional style, and the **Dux** (☎ *41+75+232.17.27)* above
the main community on the hillside, with a weathered-wood barn
across the road and fields nearby, is known for its food. A popular
newcomer with traditional atmosphere is the **Hotel Schaanerhof**
(☎ *41+75+233.18.77, FAX 41+75+233.16.27)* with a pool and a
pleasant restaurant. A jogging track and tennis courts are offered for
visitors as well as residents.

SCHELLENBERG

Schellenberg's Gasthof Krone (☎ *41+75+373.11.68)*, a small inn
when I first knew it, has modernized to provide all comforts including a swimming pool.

STEG

Steg, on the other side of the mountain-burrowing tunnel on the
road to Malbun, is a small gathering of wood chalets and a few newer
buildings that are beginning to come into focus for vacationers. The
two small hotels are the Lampert family's **Hotel-Restaurant Steg** *(10
rooms;* ☎ *41+75+263.21.46)*, where most rooms do not have private
bath, and the Beck family's **Berggasthaus Suecka** *(5 rooms;*
☎ *41+75+232.25.79)*, on a quiet hillside, a pleasant walk from the
village.

TRIESEN

Triesen, south of Vaduz in the valley, is a pleasant rural area. The
Hotel Schlosswald *(33 rooms;* ☎ *41+75+392.24.88, FAX 41+75+
392.24.36)* is a comfortable, modern hotel with nicely-appointed
rooms in two- and three-story buildings with an outdoor pool. The
Landgasthof Schatzmann *(Landstrasse 779;* ☎ *41+75+393.42.22)*,
mentioned earlier for its exceptional restaurant, has a few rooms and
a cozy atmosphere with its modern building following traditional
style. The long-popular **Hotel-Restaurant Meierhof** *(41 rooms;*
☎ *41+75+399.00.11)*, owned by the brother of the Schlosswald, has

modernized all rooms, equipping them with TV and minibar, and added a fitness room as well as a small outdoor swimming pool.

Village of Triesenberg above the Rhine Valley, Liechtenstein

TRIESENBERG

Triesenberg, about 15 minutes' drive above Vaduz, has a charming **Walser Heimatmuseum** (Folkmuseum), with an eclectic collection of art, crafts and exhibits from the land and traditions shared with the 13th-century people who migrated here from the upper Rhone valley, in the area of Switzerland known as the canton of Valais (in French, or Wallis in German). Pictures of Liechtenstein up to the 1950s are interesting as is some of the equipment used by the village craftsmen and farmers and the folk art. Rudolf Schadler, a woodcarver who was doing remarkable work well into his 80s, responded to the spirit he felt in pieces of wood he picked up during his mountain walks to bring out the people and animals he saw in them. One highlight for newcomers is the slide show that is offered, with commentary in German, French and English.

VADUZ

Vaduz has several tourist shops, an exceptional museum and plenty of places to buy stamps. The **Liechtensteinische Staatliche Kunstsammlung**, on the main street of Vaduz, is the place to see a portion of the prince's art collection and special exhibitions of the work of contemporary and other artists. What you will view of the prince's collection is a mere fraction of an awesome collection that has been gathered by the royal family since the 16th century. The entire collection constitutes one of the oldest art collections in private hands.

The treasures include baroque items and tapestries and many Viennese Biedermeier works that were purchased from the artists while they were alive.

AUTHOR'S OBSERVATION

As impressive display of "Five Centuries of Italian Art" from the collection of the Princes of Leichtenstein is being featured for 1994. The special show is scheduled to last for about three years.

Liechtensteinisches Landesmuseum, on the main street, is the national museum, founded in 1954. It is presently closed for renovation and expects to remain so for another two or three years. Housed in a former inn that became the seat of the government prior to its acquisition in 1972 as the museum, the interesting displays have included maps showing the principality, some items from the Roman period (from 15 B.C.) and folk objects. Inquire about status, or other areas where these items might be on display while you're in town.

LODGING: My top hotel choice continues to be the **Parkhotel Sonnenhof** *(29 rooms; ☎ 41+75+232.11.92)*, set amid well-tended gardens on a hillside above Vaduz, but within pleasant walking distance of the center of town. This comfortable family-owned hotel, which has long been a member of the prestigious *Relais et Châteaux* group, has been my home on several occasions. It's a restful hideaway, with a lovely swimming pool set in its gardens and walking paths nearby. In downtown Vaduz, Felix Real's **Hotel Real** *(11 rooms; ☎ 41+75+232.22.22)* is also worth noting, although it's wedged in the commerce of town. The **Hotel Löwen** *(12 rooms; ☎ 41+75+ 232.00.66)* is a special inn with historic significance. On the same site for more than 600 years, the present building dates from 1388. Its mansard roof was added during the French Revolution; the entire property was extensively renovated from 1986 to 1989, with comfortable rooms decorated in traditional style. Antiques or good copies set the tone; the surrounding vineyards provide the wines.

Some of the best dining choices are mentioned above, under "Food, Wine and Other Beverages." Other places include the attractive *Lutherstube* and other rooms at the **Hotel Gasthof Löwen** *(35 Herrengasse; ☎ 41+75+232.00.66)*. The **Adler** *(2 Herrengasse; ☎ 41+ 75+232.21.31)* is unpretentious with reasonable prices and home-style food that make it popular with Liechtensteiners.

PLACES WORTH FINDING

In addition to the places mentioned throughout the chapter, many other places worth finding are in neighboring Austria and Switzerland. Just as visiting Liechtenstein for lunch or dinner is a possibility from those countries, so it is possible to stay in Liechtenstein and go, for example, to Zürich for the day or to Feldkirch for lunch and shopping. The express train to Zürich takes about an hour from Buchs or Sargans, both easily reached by the postal bus service from Vaduz.

SPORTS

Outdoor activity on your own is a feature of life in Liechtenstein. There are not many highly organized sports, except for skiing. Archery and ballooning are not popular in Liechtenstein.

BICYCLING

It's possible to rent a bike through the Swiss system, at their railroad stations, and to arrive in Liechtenstein's Vaduz by bicycle. The flat areas around the Rhein valley are easy for bicycling; the mountain roads require more effort. Check with the tourist office about places to rent bikes when you arrive in town if you haven't made plans in advance.

FISHING

The Rhein river that makes the border between Liechtenstein and Switzerland is an area used by local folk, but permits and other formalities are difficult for visitors to obtain.

GOLF

The nearest real golf course is about 20 minutes' drive from Vaduz in Bad Ragaz, Switzerland.

HANG GLIDING/SOARING

There are launching places in the mountains above Triessenberg. Passenger flights can be arranged through **Flugcenter Schönauer** (*Gewerbeweg, Postfach 615, FL-9490 Vaduz;* ☎ *41+75+232.72.88*). Check with the Vaduz tourist office, or with Flugcenter Schönauer, about costs and details.

HIKING

The tourist office has an extensive and detailed selection of maps showing marked trails, graded by ease. Some paths are merely walks through the woods; others are more strenuous. The ski center at Malbun is a popular starting point for hikers when the weather warms. The chairlift takes you to the Sareiserjoch, at 656l feet, where there are well-marked paths. Augstenberg is a goal for hiking the highest route, which is a favorite among experienced hikers when the weather is clear and the snow has melted. The northernmost village of Ruggell is a good place to walk along the Rhein, and Balzers, in the south, is favored for the nearby woods.

HORSEBACK RIDING

Horseback riding is not offered in Liechtenstein.

HUNTING/SHOOTING

The tourist office has details on the methods for hunting, which is usually thanks to the courtesy of a resident who will take you to his private hunting grounds.

MOUNTAINEERING/CLIMBING

Several guided mountain tours are offered, with assistance and guides from the **Liechtensteiner Alpenverein**; call for dates of planned hikes (☎ *41+75+232.98.12).* Among the most popular hiking routes are from Malbun to Saas, Fürkle and the Schönberg, returning to Malbun through Guschg in about five hours, and the six-hour hike from Malbun, through Saas and Fürkle to Matta and the Galinakopf, on the border with Austria, returning via Guschgfiel through Hintervalorsch, Guschg, and Fürkle to Malbun. For details and a guide for the high ridge, which is narrow, challenging and spectacular when the weather is clear, check with the tourist office. One mountain guide, a member of the United International Alpine Association, is Michael Bargetze *(Poska 459, FL-9495 Triesen;* ☎ *41+75+ 392.42.25).*

SKATING

Skating is at the rink in Malbun in winter months.

SKIING

Skiing gets a boost from the fact that Liechtenstein's best skiers train above Malbun, and vacationers can enjoy almost 12 miles of trails and downhill runs. There are cross-country areas at Malbun and in the Valuna valley in Steg. For special rates for ski schools and equipment rental, contact either **Skischule Franz Beck** (☎ *41+75+263.26.36)* or **Skischule Malbun AG**, Engelbert Buhler (☎ *41+75+263.97.70).*

SWIMMING

Swimming is in pools, indoor for winter and outdoor in warm-weather months. Several villages have public swimming pools that are meticulously maintained for the benefit of residents—as well as for visitors.

TENNIS

Tennis courts are community facilities and not generally open for visitors. Some hotels can assist with special permissions, however, if the counts are not being used by the club members. If you're an avid player, be sure to inquire about the court surface and, if you'll need to rent a racquet, the availability of racquets and tennis balls.

WALKING/TREKKING

The tourist office has information and detailed maps for walks and hikes in the area. Ask especially for the "Radwanderwege" folder, which fits easily in your pocket and maps out two clearly marked routes. In addition to printed information, people at your hotel and at the tourist office are happy to share details about their personal favorites.

TREASURES AND TRIFLES

Postage stamps, printed in Switzerland and Austria, are prized by collectors around the world. Issued four times a year, in March, June, September and December with a regular issue and a special one each time, the stamps can be ordered through **Postwertzeichenstelle der Regierung** *(FL-9490 Vaduz;* ☎ *41+75+236.64.44, FAX 41+75+236.66.55).* As a matter of interest, stamps brought in about 13.3 million Swiss Francs in 1992, which was 3.1 percent of the principality's total revenues. Shop at the **Philatelic Service**, next to the post office, or at the **Post** itself, for new issues.

Most of the other items for sale in Vaduz are offered with tourists in mind. For an excellent selection of books, including some about the princely art collection, visit the Tourist Office in Vaduz as well as the shops in town. The **Bücherwurm**, opened in winter '92, has an impressive selection of books on all subjects.

"Duty-free" shopping, similar to that found in many airports, is the style of many shops. Many items (knives, key rings, Alpine flowers, and pot holders for example) are reminiscent of items you'll find in Switzerland. In Nendeln, the **Schaedler Keramik** *(*☎ *41+75+373.14.14; FAX 41+75+ 373.28.85)* makes **pottery**, sometimes to order if you have enough time to wait for completion. In Schaan, the **Haas Keramik** is a family pottery. The chunky, country designs have been molded into useful plates, pitchers, bowls and other crockery. Six members of the family are among the workers on the pottery.

ADDITIONAL INFORMATION SOURCES

For telephone and FAX contact with all places in Liechtenstein, the country code is 41.

MALBUN
 Verkehrsbüro, *FL-9497 Malbun.* ☎ *75+263.65.77; FAX 75+263.73.44.*

SCHAAN
 c/o **Postillion-Reisen AG**, *Landstrasse 5, FL-9494 Schaan.* ☎ *75+232.65.65; FAX 75+232.70.37.*

SCHAANWALD
 Quick Tourist Office, *Vorarlberger Strasse 59, FL-9486 Schaanwald.* ☎ *75+373.11.88.*

TRIESENBERG
 Verkehrsbüro, *FL-9497 Triesenberg.* ☎ *75+262.19.26.*

VADUZ
 Verkehrsbüro, *Städtle 37, FL-9490 Vaduz.* ☎ *75+392.11.11 or 232.14.43; FAX 75+392.16.18.*

MONACO

Monte Carlo's Belle Epoque

There's nothing to compare with a first glimpse of this nugget from the sea, unless—perhaps—it's the heady lift of arriving by helicopter. Like an elaborately frosted wedding cake, Monaco rises from the shoreline, encrusted with all manner of man-made contributions.

Of course sashaying along roads plastered to or cantilevered off the side of steep mountains has its thrills, but essential concentration on the road ahead means that the full impact of Monaco's sensational location is compromised. Traveling by train to nearby Nice or Cannes, while it may not sound romantic to North Americans inured by only-average rail service, also has its appeal, especially if you settle into a first class compartment on one of the more traditional trains and set your mind back to the times at the turn of the century, when Europe's royalty (in fact and in fiction) were aboard, en route to their winter playground.

Monaco is a place of many moods—and most of the best are sea centered. Of course there are many visitors who fold themselves into the classy casinos to stare at cards, chips, or dice in preference to the yachts, "beautiful people" and diamonds that appeal to many of the rest of us, but when you can find yourself a sunwashed table at a sea-view café, to settle in with your newspaper (preferably French), you become a "belonger."

Minute Monaco, known also by the name of its original community, Monte Carlo, is made for memories. It's impossible for most Americans to be here without invoking the images of the late Princess Grace, a Philadelphia-born woman of classical grace with a movie star aura that surrounded her naturally. Or of Cary Grant, immortalized in so many ways, but certainly for this place, in *To Catch a Thief*. And then there's the image of Jacqueline Kennedy Onassis, whose shenanigans, sometimes with her sister, Lee Radziwell, and certainly with her late husband, Aristotle Onassis, filled hours of conversation. The Onassis' yacht seemed hotel-like when it was moored to its harbor-home, but it was only one of dozens, albeit the largest one.

Although these legends are culled from a vibrant past, Monaco is magic—still. Not only does it claim an astounding piece of real estate, to which the city fathers append new plots that they have recovered from the sea, but it *is*, unto itself. Admittedly a chosen playground, the tiny principality has a social conscience that belies its attitude of seeming insouciance. Behind most of the fun and frolic on the social calendar is a serious cause to which the coffers of the rich and famous are cajoled into making a substantial contribution. Monaco works—while it plays.

COUNTRY CAPSULE

Considering its small size (about two miles long and just over half a mile wide), Monaco offers a wealth of man-made diversions. The cosmopolitan seaside life focuses on elegant cafés and bikinis on beaches with watersports offshore during daylight hours and switching to the calculated clatter of casinos and pulsating, flickering discos by nightlight. There are botanical gardens and pocket parks pinned

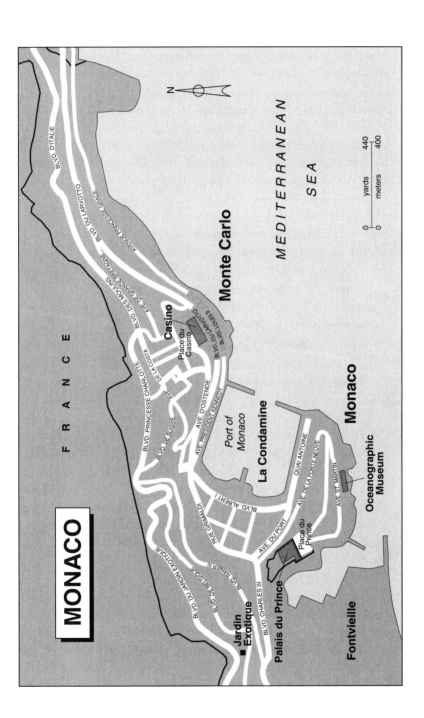

to hillsides draped with mountain-climbing roads; luxurious yachts fill the harbor of the tiny *Principauté de Monaco*. France wraps around its mountainside borders and the Italian Riviera lends its insouciance to the east. There is no place like this place!

The principality is the smallest in the world, but it is slightly larger than its famous Monte Carlo area. It includes the original town of Monaco-Ville plus La Condamine, with the port separating Monaco-Ville and Monte Carlo. Most of the pricey portions of flat land have been reclaimed from the sea, with the two newest being Fonteville, planned as an industrial area, and Lavotto, which focuses on the sea and resort activities.

Palm trees and other tropical growth fleck the shoreline, and gardens and parks are welcome oases in this bit of land that has its back against the Alpine foothills. For most visitors, however, it's not the Alps but the Mediterranean that gives Monaco a sense of space.

The land area is almost entirely covered with modern commerce. The small area of *vieille* (old) Monaco seems to have more soul, with its narrow streets and older buildings.

HISTORIC HIGHLIGHTS

The first Grimaldi of record was a Genoese who served in the court of Frederick Barbarossa, German king and Holy Roman emperor, who conquered Milan in 1152 and added Rome to his realm a few years later. With the 13th-century conflicts between the Guelphs and the Ghibellines—the rival factions who drew their "party line" in support of the pope or the emperor, respectively—the Grimaldis fled to Provence.

The present palace of the principality began life as a Genoese stronghold perched on a cliff over the Mediterranean. Traveling in the robes of a Franciscan monk, François Grimaldi and a colleague crept into the fortress, conquered the resident Genoese and declared the palace their own. They never left.

The Grimaldi dynasty claimed the fortress and its surrounding lands as home—and adopted a coat of arms that features two Franciscan monks. When the last male Grimaldi died in 1731, the French Goyon-Matignon family (who married into the Grimaldi family) adopted the Grimaldi name, which has been carried forward to this day.

During the 15th and 16th centuries, Grimaldi holdings on the Mediterranean coast proved profitable. They skillfully taxed all who wanted to travel between Genoa and Provence, which was most of the merchants of the day. Until the 19th century, the principality also included Menton and Roquebrune, both shaved off following Sardinian rule (1814-48).

In 1612, Honore II was recognized as prince of Monaco by Louis XIII of France. But it took until 1932 to work out a firm agreement ensuring the right of the principality to manage its own affairs while receiving customs and currency assistance from the French.

In the late 1800s, not long after Prince Charles of Monaco dedicated his lifestyle to emulating the successes of the Duke of Baden, the principality became a mecca for the wealthy—or for those who wanted to bask in their glow. The still elegant Hotel de Paris, built in 1887, has been the holiday home of the Dowager Empress of Russia, the Queen of Portugal, the Emperor and Empress of Austria, the King of Sweden, and countless others who came with entourage and weighty trunks to take up temporary residence with the sun and the sea.

When the vintage royalty that gave Monaco its panache died off, so did Monaco's lure as a vacation haven. The years of World War II were dreary ones for the principality. By the mid-1950s, however, Monaco captured the imagination and headlines of Americans and others. While in Cannes for the film festival for her role in *To Catch a Thief*, Philadelphia-born actress Grace Kelly met the bachelor prince of Monaco. About a year later, on April 18, 1956, when she had completed the movie *High Society*, they were married in Monaco's Cathedral of St. Nicholas. The fortunes of the principality thrived on the post-war prosperity—and the publicity. The world focused on the attractive pair, their family and the efforts of Princess Grace and Prince Rainier to revitalize their community. Prince Rainier is often called the "Prince Developer" for the many urban projects that have been successfully completed during his reign.

Endless publicity also came from the activities of the flamboyant Greek shipping magnate, Aristotle Onassis, who later courted and married Jacqueline Kennedy following the death of President John Kennedy. In 1953, Onassis acquired major control in *Société des Bains Mer*, as Monte Carlo's legendary casino is known. Conflicts between Prince Rainier's wish to move his principality into the future and Onassis's plan to keep "his" enclave for the world's wealthy brought Monaco into the public eye. The principality made headlines more for social gossip than for tourism statistics. By 1966, when Onassis released his control on the principality and devoted his energies to other areas, Monaco began to build for increasing tourism—with a plan that included the new American-style Loew's hotel and a tourism and convention thrust to appeal to more than royalty and aristocracy.

POLITICAL PICTURE

Monaco is a principality. H.S.H. Prince Rainier III succeeded to the throne in 1949. Princess Grace died following an automobile accident in September 1982. Their three children are U.S.-educated Prince Albert, successor to the throne; recently widowed Princess Caroline, whose husband, Stefano Casiraghi, died tragically in a racing boat accident during the World Offshore Championships in late 1990; and Princess Stephanie, the youngest, whose jet-set activities make her a favorite topic for tabloids and tony magazines.

LIFESTYLE

The 25,000 Monégasques occupy 468 acres, most of which is vertical. The principality "lives" on at least two levels, which have little to do with the sheer mountain terrain as it slopes to the sea. On the royal level, life is very posh, with Rolls-Royces lined up in front of the Hôtel de Paris and designer clothes de rigeur for the style-conscious winter season when the **Monte Carlo Philharmonic**, the **Ballets de Monte Carlo**, **L'Academie de Danse Classique Princess Grace**, the **Red Cross Ball**, and even the **International Circus Festival** held in the Princess Grace Rose Garden occupy the social calendar. The annual **Bal de la Rose**, held in early March at the Monte Carlo Sporting Club, is an elegant event, not only for the Italian and French designers that show their newest collections, but also for the styles worn by the names-you-know guests. (Tickets cost about FF4000, and benefit the Princess Grace Foundation for the arts.) Other colorful events are the Theatre de Fort Antoine, the Fireworks Festival and Folkloric events, all held during the summer months.

On the more pedestrian tourism level, life is strictly surface—with busloads or smaller groups arriving to "look and see," hoping to catch a glimpse of the royals and certainly to walk where they have walked, including portions of the 200-room palace, when it is open. Between these two, there's a wide swath of daily living, where hours can be happily spent lingering in sun-washed cafés, strolling the seaside promenades, or browsing through shops that hold some of the world's poshest potential purchases.

NATURAL SURROUNDINGS

The principality has covered almost all of the seafront with buildings, and pulled silt out of the sea to create the land to build some more. For natural surroundings other than people, head for the hills—to the botanic gardens or outside the principality in France or Italy. There are a few pocket-parks in the area near the Oceanographic Museum, along Avenue Princess Grace, as well as one remarkable Exotic Garden, clinging to the mountainside. The *Jardin Exotique* (Exotic Garden) is world famous, not only for its collection of cacti but also for the rock garden and the thousands of other plant specimens, many of which have been collected by the garden's director, Marcel Kroenlein, during his worldwide travels.

PRACTICAL FACTS ABOUT MONACO

INFORMATION SOURCES

Direction du Tourisme et des Congrés, *2a bd. des Moulins, Monte-Carlo MC-98030, Monaco,* is the head tourism office. Other information offices include the **Monaco Government Tourist and Convention Bureau**, *542 S. Dearborn St., #550, Chicago, IL 60605,* ☎ *312+939-7863, FAX 312+939-8727; 845 Third Ave., New York, NY 10022,* ☎ *212+759-5227, FAX 212+754-9320.* In England, the office is at *3-18 Chelsea Garden Market, Chelsea Harbour, London SW10 0XE, England,* ☎ *44+71+352-9962, FAX 44+71+352-2103.*

Throughout the chapter, local spelling is used for some words and all place names. For translation of foreign words, refer to the back-of-the-book glossary.

CASH, CURRENCY AND CREDIT CARDS

The French franc is the unit of currency, exchanging at about FF6 to US$1 at presstime. Check the equivalent prior to your time of travel and, if you want to have ready cash at hand when you arrive, consider buying some travelers cheques in French francs to avoid the bother of exchange rates and service charges. Your local bank can make arrangements, with a few days' notice. If you choose to travel with travelers cheques in U.S. dollar denominations, you can exchange some for French francs at the airport upon arrival. Credit cards are widely accepted.

COMMUNICATION

French is the spoken language (as well as the lifestyle), but Monaco is an international playground. You'll hear all languages, including English. Monaco uses the French systems, with phone cards, post services and international telephone systems as they apply for France. (See the France chapter for specifics.) Expect *La Poste* to be closed on all holidays, as well as on weekends, and know that your hotel's concierge is your "friend in court."

AUTHOR'S OBSERVATION

Telephone numbers in this chapter are given for direct dial from the U.S., with the addition of the country code, which, for Monaco, is 33. When in Monaco, you'll need to begin dialing out-of-town numbers with a "0."

To make international telephone calls to North America from Monaco, simply step into the phone booth, dial the code for your chosen international carrier, which is *19+0011* to be connected with AT&T's *USADirect* telephone operator in the U.S., and give that operator the number in the U.S. that you wish to contact. If you are an AT&T card holder, you can charge the call to your card/designated phone or place the call collect. If you use another carrier, check with them prior to leaving the U.S. for their system. For more information about AT&T in the U.S., call ☎ *800+874-4000*. Similar services are offered by MCI and Sprint.

DOCUMENTS AND OTHER PAPERS

North American visitors need a passport for entry into Monaco, as well as for identification at the casinos. In addition, if you plan to rent a car, you'll need an international driver's permit, which can be obtained—with two passport pictures, a valid U.S. driver's license, and $10—through your nearest AAA (American Automobile Association) office.

MEDICAL FACILITIES

There are good hospital facilities in Monaco, with full services offered in nearby Nice.

TRAVEL FACTS

Within the principality, cars are the preferred transport, although there is domestic bus service and limousines are the preferred transport for those who can afford them. Taxis are plentiful—and expensive.

ARRIVAL

Unless you're planning to tour the Mediterranean (perhaps on a private yacht), the usual arrival is at the international airport at Nice/Côte d'Azur in neighboring France. From there, a helicopter service makes easy links. The drive takes about 45 minutes to cover the scenic distance of some 60 miles.

AUTHOR'S OBSERVATION

The Passeport pour Monte Carlo *is issued through travel agents in several European countries, for special benefits that include free helicopter transfer from Nice to Monaco and preferential hotel rates. Inquire about getting one prior to your visit.*

TOURING TIPS

Although many visitors arrive by car, either rental or personal (preferably chauffeured), there is also convenient train service, aboard the SNCF (French Railways). Buses link areas within the principality, as well as stretching to neighboring Italy and surrounding France.

BOATING is aboard charter yachts (see "Sailing," under "Sports," below). Throughout its history, Monaco has been a port of call, most flamboyantly in recent times when the pleasure ships of Aristotle Onassis anchored off Monte Carlo. One Onassis yacht served as the honeymoon retreat for the Prince and Princess (and for opera diva Maria Callas, Jacqueline Kennedy Onassis and others). These days, the $30 million *Atlantis II* of Stavros Spyros Niarchos is a familiar and impressive harbor sight. Monte Carlo has emerged as a prized port of call for luxury ships, including a coterie of yacht cruise ships such as the *Sea Goddess*, the *Wind Star*, the *Wind Spirit*, and the *Sea Cloud*.

CYCLISTS interested in mopeds and motorcycles should check with **Motos Garage** *(7 rue de la Colle)*. If you want a moped at the height of the season, contact them in advance and secure your reservation by credit card or another deposit method.

CARS are easy to rent, if you haven't rented one elsewhere to arrive by car. You won't be expected to match the prowess of the professionals who tear through the streets of Monte Carlo in the Rallye Monte Carlo in January or the **Grand Prix** in May, but you will have the challenge of finding a parking place.

HELICOPTER touring is possible, thanks to the landfill area known as Fonteville, where the expanding heliport allows for frequent flights linking Monaco with the Nice/Côte d'Azur international airport.

TRAIN service is frequent, with international trains stretching from London or Amsterdam through Paris to Nice and via Monaco to Ventimiglia, Italy. The TGV train between Paris and Marseilles also has a link to Monaco. Since April 23, 1990, the Orient Express has included Monte Carlo in its itinerary between Paris and Venice, on a route that can start (or end) in London.

WALKING is the best way to enjoy the "real" Monaco, especially when you join others for the classic promenade along the seafront.

DAILY LIVING

The good life is the real life for Monaco, where elegance is a by-word and style is what everyone strives to acquire or display.

FOOD, WINE AND OTHER BEVERAGES

Expect French service and preparation in some of the best restaurants, where elegant dining is the accepted style, and Italian in others. Alain Ducasse has earned 3 stars for his **Restaurant Louis XV** (☎ *93+30.23.11)* in the Hôtel de Paris on Place Casino and has a devoted following for his specialties; **Rampoldi** *(3 ave. des Spelugues;* ☎ *93+30.70.65)* is top-of-the-list for people-watching in grand Italian style. Also serving Italian specialties, but with a less pretentious atmosphere, is the **Sans Souci** *(42 blvd. d'Italie;* ☎ *93+50.14.24)*. The Hôtel Mirabeau's **La Coupole** *(1-3 ave. Princess Grace;* ☎ *93+25.45.45)* exudes affluence, extols the good life and serves French favorites. Other hotel restaurants provide variety, with U.S. offerings readily available at the Loews Hotel, where you can find hamburgers, pizza and that ilk in the coffee shop equivalent and classier cuisine at their upscale restaurants. Pizza and other fast-food places are popular; some are offered café style, as at **Le Texan** *(4 rue Suffren-Reymond;* ☎ *93+30.34.54)*, a gathering place for younger folk and the slightly tonier **La Polpetta** *(2 rue Paradis;* ☎ *93+ 50.67.84)*, in a trattoria style with Italian pastas and other specialties featured. A favorite café, open only in warm-weather months, is **La Vigie**, on the rocks at the Monte Carlo Beach Hotel *(☎ 93+ 78.21.40)*. For informal dining in town, search out the **Castel Roc** *(pl. du Palais;* ☎ *93+30.36.68)* for pleasant, reverse-chic atmosphere, or the **Café de Paris** *(pl. du Casino;* ☎ *93+50.57.75)*, with a name that suggests a swankier place than this one is.

LODGING

The real flavor of traditional Monaco is best enjoyed when you wallow in turn-of-the-last-century elegance, updated to the highest 1990s standards. The style suggests romantic novels; you'll be in surroundings that have hosted the famous names that appear in magazines and social columns. Among the best are the palatial **Hérmitage** *(236 rooms; sq. Beaumarchais, Monte Carlo;* ☎ *93+50.67.31; FAX 93+50.47.12)*; the oft-touted, much-revered **Hôtel de Paris**

(229 rooms; pl. du Casino, Monte Carlo; ☎ *93+50.80.80; FAX 93+25.59.17)*; the **Metropole Palace** *(170 rooms; 4 av. de la Madone, Monte Carlo;* ☎ *93+15.15.15; FAX 93+25.24.44)*, or the small and quite special **Hôtel Balmoral** *(68 rooms; 12 av. de la Costa;* ☎ *93+50.62.37; FAX 93+15.08.69)*. A newcomer for the '91 season was the **Abela Hôtel** *(56 rooms; 23 av. des Papalins, Fontvielle;* ☎ *92+05.90.00; FAX 92+05.91.67)*, near the sea and the Princess Grace Rose Garden.

Choices for budget-minded travelers include the **Hôtel Alexandra** *(55 rooms, 35 of which are air conditioned; 35 bd. Princess Charlotte, Monte Carlo;* ☎ *93+50.63.13)*; **Hôtel du Louvre** *(34 rooms; 16 bd. des Moulins, Monte Carlo;* ☎ *93+50.65.25; FAX 93+30.23.68)*; the **Hôtel le Siècle** *(35 rooms; 10 av. Prince Pierre, Monaco;* ☎ *93+30.25.56; FAX 93+30.03.72)*; the **Miramar** *(14 rooms; 1 av. Président J.F. Kennedy, Monaco;* ☎ *93+30.86.48)*; and the tiny **Hôtel le Versailles** *(15 rooms; 4 av. Prince Pierre, Monaco;* ☎ *93+50.79.34)*, with rooms above the restaurant of the same name. The very modest **Hôtel Helvetia** *(28 rooms, 18 of which have bathtub or shower; 1 bis rue Grimaldi, Monaco;* ☎ *93+30.21.71)* is on the upper floors, over shops on a side street.

PLACES WORTH FINDING

Many of the most interesting places are in neighboring Italy or France, either one of which is only a few minutes' drive—or a boat ride—from the principality.

Wander around Monaco-Ville, the oldest part of town. You can start at the **Palais** at La Porte Neuve (new port). Known as La Rocher, this area has a maze of small streets that lead around the **parliament house**, the **Palace of Justice**, and the **Cathedral of St. Mary**, where Princess Grace and Prince Rainier were married in 1956. From this hillside spot you can overlook the rest of the principality—and then go to rue des Fours, named for the bakery ovens that used to line this street and to rue Basse, where the bakery founded by Alexandre Canis is still open for business.

For leisurely strolling, follow boulevard des Moulins (home base for the tourist office), turning off on the side lanes when the spirit moves. A dazzling view of the principality and spectacular views of the sea are your rewards when you follow the road/path along the coastline from the beach at Monte Carlo. After you've walked for about half an hour, look back at the view of the principality.

Musée Oceanographique *(Oceanographic Museum, 2 ave. St.-Martin;* ☎ *93+15.36.00)* perches at Le Rocher. It was built in 1910, and, until 1989, Jacques-Yves Cousteau was director. Although it is an obvious visitor attraction, the museum's main purpose is as a research institute. As many as 90 tanks hold whales as well as colorful tropical fish; there are also ships, shells and other sea specimens on display.

Casino de Monte Carlo is also worth some time, even if you're not a gambler. Although spruced up for the 1990s, the 19th-century casino is what gave the principality its panache during the legendary years when jewel-draped ladies and elegant tuxedoed gentlemen clustered at the quietly elegant gaming tables.

Other places worth finding are in the mountains or along the coast, outside the boundaries of the principality. One prize for mealtime dalliance is **Le Roquebrune** *(100 av. Jean Jaures, Corniche Inférieure, France;* ☎ *93+35.00.16)*, a pleasant restaurant where people-watching can be as entertaining as the view. Many other small spots as well as some well-known places are in France (Nice, Cap Ferat, and Menton) or Italy (San Remo), which are best reached by car.

SPORTS

The sea is the prized playground; sailing and windsurfing are popular. With the exception of tennis, most of the land-based sports are enjoyed in neighboring France or Italy.

AUTO RACING

Auto races are led by the 2065-mile **Monaco Grand Prix** in May or the **Rallye Monte Carlo** in January, covering a course of about 1900 miles (3145 km). If you want tickets for the Grand Prix, contact the Monaco Tourist Office several months in advance for an order form, which you then mail, with the fee in French francs, to the **Club de Voitures de Monaco** *(Automobile Club of Monaco, 23 blvd. Albert I, Monaco)*.

BICYCLING

Following the French system, it's possible to rent a bike at the railroad station, but the roads are so traffic-clogged that novices may find the experience intimidating. Serious bikers will find the hairpin turns on the corniches challenging; others can enjoy a leisurely pedal along the bike paths on or near the Mediterranean shore. Check with the tourist office about other places to rent bikes when you arrive in town if you haven't made plans in advance.

FISHING

The source for charter yachts for fishing is the **Yacht Club of Monaco** *(*☎ *93+50.58.39)*, where arrangements can be made for a day's outing. It's also worthwhile to wander along the waterfront to see what motorboats are tied up, but confirm the names with the concierge at your hotel or the tourist office to be sure of credentials.

GOLF

The nearest golf course is at Montangel, 2000 feet above sea level, with spectacular views from the 18-hole PGA course. The biggest golfing event in the Principality is the annual *Monte Carlo Golf Open*, held in early July. If renting clubs is important, confirm your dates of play well in advance of your arrival in Monaco.

HANG GLIDING/SOARING

Places along the nearby coast in France are your best sources. Check with the tourist office in Monaco for names of people who can help with your plans.

HIKING

The tourist office has good maps with marked trails, graded by ease. Some paths are easy walks through the woods or promenades along the Mediterranean shoreline; others are more strenuous. The nearby French mountains offer the most interesting areas for hikes and climbing.

HORSEBACK RIDING/HUNTING

There are no stables where visitors can go horseback riding in Monaco and hunting is not a sport for the principality. There's no suitable landscape.

MOUNTAINEERING/CLIMBING

Check with the tourist office for details about places in neighboring France.

SAILING

Best, of course, when it's aboard your private yacht, sailing can be aboard a charter through the **Yacht Club of Monaco** (☎ *93+50.58.39*). To be sure a yacht's available, make arrangements well in advance of your intended sailing date(s). When you're on the spot, a check at the Yacht Club may yield a day's charter. Charters can also be arranged through **Agence Maritime** (*1 bis av. Président J. F. Kennedy*) or through **Monaco Shipchandler** (*9 av. Président J. F. Kennedy*). The **Sailing School** (☎ *93+30.63.63*) is located at the Yacht Club. There are several yacht races held throughout the year, with the **Primo Cup** in February, the **Inter-Banques J-24 Challenge** and the **Optimist International Challenge** held in April and other events. Ask the tourist office for a schedule.

SKIING

Although there's no skiing in Monaco, some of the best Alpine resorts in France are easily reached by train or car from the principality. You can split your vacation, with a few days here and a few days skiing.

SWIMMING

The Mediterranean shoreline is a coarse-sand beach, where fashion and well-tanned skins appear to be more important than swimming-for-sport. There are also several huge swimming pools.

TENNIS

The Monte Carlo International Tennis Championships are held in April at the **Monte Carlo Country Club**, where there are 20 clay courts on land that is rented from France. It's also possible to play, at more modest cost, at the **Monaco Tennis Club**, *off bd. Belgique*, not far from the Jardin Exotique.

WALKING/TREKKING

The tourist office has information about nearby trails, festooned over the mountains that are part of France. In addition to printed information, people at your hotel and at the tourist office are happy to share details about their personal favorites.

TREASURES AND TRIFLES

Count on finding the top-of-the-line names for exceptional (and expensive) jewelry. Piaget, Cartier, Bulgari, Harry Winston and Van Cleef & Arpels are top names among the many classy shops. **Cartier**, *at place du Casino*, claims a corner by the main entrance for the Hotel de Paris and **Louis Vuitton**, down the street at *6 avenue des Beaux Arts*, fills its cabinets and cases with the easily recognized dark leather, with the trademark superimposed LV. Also on avenue des Beaux-Arts, you'll find the couturier shops of **Celine**, **Lavin**, **Yves Saint Laurent**, **Dior**, **Givenchy** and others. **Valentino** is on *avenue de Monte Carlo*, nearby. Many Italian designers have clustered on *avenue de la Costa*, in the Allees Lumieres building and **Adonis** claims a three-story building on *avenue Princess Grace*.

Be sure to visit **La Boutique de Rocher**, either at *11 rue Emile de Loth*, near the Prince's Palace, or at *1 avenue de la Madone*, for lovely handmade items, including children's clothes. The *Princess Grace Foundation* operates the shop; profits are used for the arts.

For the fun of it, stop in **Chocolatierie de Monaco**, at *7 rue Bioves*, for a small sample—and to look at the creative confections that seem to take on art-gallery appearance.

SLOVENIA

Ptuj, Slovenia

The *schnaps* smelled like gasoline, but I downed it in one gulp. It was impossible to do otherwise. Within a few feet from where I sat, the farmer/owner stood proudly with his wife and watched me. A few minutes after our arrival, he had disappeared to his cherished wine cellar, to return with the grandest bottle of his homemade elixir and share his prized possession with "visitors from the United States."

Although the conversation was fast and animated, I understood not one word of it. The smiles, voice tones and arm-waving were a language of their own. He and his wife were thrilled to have visitors from North America; they had a son who lived in the United States.

And he had a wife and four children, whose pictures were proudly passed around, from his wife to the four of us who had driven up the winding road to their hilltop farmhouse. It had grandeur greater than a castle, because it was theirs and they loved it—and shared it.

Our host had been a Partisan in the fierce and wiley battles fought in the terrain he had known since birth. He had fought in these convoluted mountains, against the Germans (but sometimes with them) —and for his independence, at the behest of Field Marshall Jozip Broz Tito, whose picture hung prominently in the cozy living room.

We sat in a small front parlour, where larch-wood walls lent a pungent smell to the surroundings. My nephew and his friend had worked their way half way around the wooden table, where the bottle of *schnaps* was the centerpiece and were watching, warily. Our thimble-sized glasses were refilled as soon as they'd been ceremoniously emptied. There was a lot to talk about and, with the help of our student interpreter, we had a lot to learn.

Life on the farm is shared these days. The farming couple continue to live in their hilltop homestead and farm the surrounding lands. An attractive recently-completed annex provides a kitchen, four bedrooms-with-sink (and running water), one modern (shared) bathroom with tub and shower and a separate room with a toilet for paying guests. Views from each of the small-and-friendly rooms were over unblemished landscape, in colors that changed with the season; the world at its pristine best.

Built for European travelers, for whom farmhouse vacations are a family staple, the tourist house is clean, tidy and comfortable. All the basics are here and the hosts—the farming couple—are nearby to help with anything you might want to accomplish.

A German guest and his son were heading out to hunt, with full (and proper) hunting attire, including reasonably benign guns. The irony of the partisans' territory becoming a sporting playground for tourists, using similar "implements" in very different ways, was not lost on the visitors from North America. And the day's game would appear on the dinner table at the farmhouse two days later, for a special meal enjoyed by all of us, speaking our own languages, or tidbits from another, haltingly, in deference to the fact that we shared no common spoken lexicon. A far greater means of communication— seeing, sharing and smiling, punctuated with appreciative noises in response to the farmwife's recipes—would lead to a far greater understanding of other ways of life and provide memories that last forever.

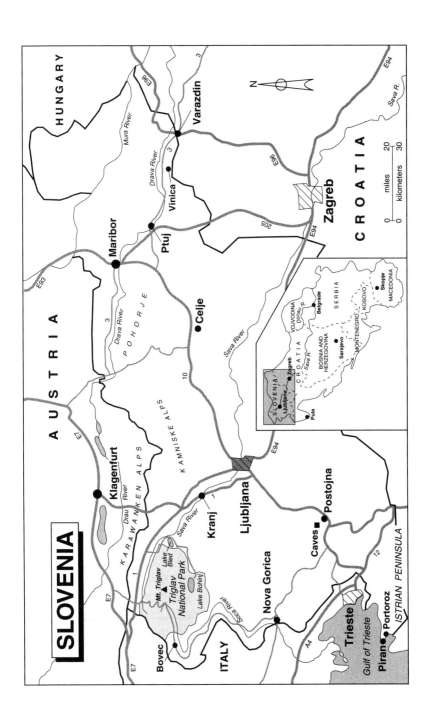

COUNTRY CAPSULE

The country of Slovenia was created in June 1991, when the citizens of the northernmost republic of what had been Yugoslavia declared their independence from the regions to their south. Recognition of the new country was officially granted in December by Germany, soon to be followed by France and the other European countries and eventually by the United States.

Slovenija, spelled Slovenia in the western world (since the "j" has the sound of an "i"), shares the Alpine heritage and, from its northern border, the Alps themselves. Rolling hills, farmland and villages are trademarks for most of Slovenia's landscape. Linked to Austria for much of its history and to Italy for some of it, Slovenia claims about 7800 square miles, about the size of Massachusetts, and is, with its neighboring republic of Croatia, the most prosperous part of the former country of Yugoslavia.

Small white churches mark many hilltops within Slovenia, testimony to the depth of the Catholic tradition. Some of the chapels have richly embellished interiors that hark back to their Bohemian and Habsburg heritage and all are in clear view of the neighboring farmers, who still work their fields in time-honored ways. The mountainous area has harbored partisans through much of its modern history.

Along the coast of the Adriatic Sea, known in Slovenia as Jadransko Morje, small fishing villages have buildings capped with red tile roofs and churches that are often rich with religious relics. Some towns and villages have awakened to the alarm clock of tourism in recent years, but most are little known to American visitors. Most offer plenty to intrigue those who seek destinations that maintain a natural personality.

Slovenia's mountain resorts give it special appeal for skiers, climbers, hikers and other adventurers; its many lakes and forests are havens for those who enjoy hunting, fishing and woodsy walks. Dramatic caves at Postojna intrigue even those not normally enthusiastic about underground exploring, while other visitors enjoy the horse farm at Lipica, the original home of the stock for the highly trained stallions that perform at Austria's Spanish Riding School. (The Austrian performers are now bred and boarded at a farm across the border, near Austria's town of Graz.)

Insofar as architecture and art are concerned, Gothic and Romanesque influences are immediately evident, while the Turks have made their mark with markets and minarets.

HISTORIC HIGHLIGHTS

Although Slovenia stands proudly on its own as an independent country since June 25, 1991, its prior history deserves some mention. Before independence, Slovenia was the most prosperous and most western-oriented republic of the former Yugoslavia, a disparate group of five nationalities living in six republics, with four religions, three languages and two alphabets.

The country that was Yugoslavia until mid-1991 had been established on November 29, 1945, as the Federal People's Republic of Yugoslavia. Socialist/communist Army Marshall Jozip Broz Tito was the leader of that new country, a position he was granted at the Yalta conference at the behest of Josef Stalin, to reward him for partisan efforts during World War II. In 1947 some areas of Italy's Venezia-Giulia region were added to Yugoslavia by treaty, the result of overlapping cultural, historic and family influences, and those lands are part of present day Slovenia.

From 1953 until his death in 1980, Marshall Tito ruled his fragmented country with a strong hand that created a measure of stability. It was on his watch in 1963 that the country's name was changed to the Socialist Federal Republic of Yugoslavia. And it was ten years after his death that the fall of the Soviet Union presaged the collapse of Yugoslavia. But the Balkan area, of which Slovenia is a part, has always had a tumultuous history.

Slovenia occupies 7816 square miles (20,251 sq km) of land from the borders with Italy and Austria in the Alpine north to the border with Croatia to the south. More than two million people live in the area, which has more in common with its northern neighbors than with its former countryfolk to the south. Its population of about two million people, 340,000 of whom live in the capital of Ljubljana, is mostly Slovenian, with relatively small numbers of Italians and Hungarians. Archeological excavations indicate that Stone Age people lived on these lands, and that Illyria included the southern border of Slovenia. Illyrians lived on the site of the present capital, Ljubljana, and vestiges of Celtic communities have also been found. Tribes of Slavs left their homeland to the east, migrating almost to the Adriatic in about A.D. 600, bringing their rich language. (*Slav* came to be synonymous with "speaking people," and the Slavs are known to have referred to foreigners as "the dumb," or those who cannot speak.)

While the Slavs contributed a language, the Romans brought a measure of civic organization when they sailed east across the Adriatic and came overland at the bend of land where we now find Trieste to do battle with the resident Illyrians and Greeks. They claimed the settlement at Ljubljana, calling their town Emona.

Slovenes of the 7th century lived in areas around Austria's Klagenfurt and Graz as well as Ljubljana. Although ruled by dukes, they joined with the Bavarians and, eventually in 788, with the Franks. Bavarian missionaries brought Christianity to Slovenia in the 9th century. In fact, each group has left its mark in buildings as well as behavior.

By the 14th century, the Turks attacked and continued to do so intermittently until the peace treaty of 1606, after which their influence declined. During most of the Habsburg era, German was the major language of the area, although Slovenian customs were allowed to thrive. When Napoleon came into Ljubljana in 1797, he decreed that the language of Slovene should be accepted as the regional tongue, to be widely spoken and taught in schools. And the French influence was strong between 1809 and 1813.

For a long time, the lands of the former Yugoslavia were divided between the Holy Roman Empire of the Habsburgs in the north and the Eastern Roman Empire in the south. Slovenia was part of the Habsburg empire from the late 1200s until 1918, when the Austro-Hungarian Habsburg influence came to an abrupt end with the collapse of the empire.

By way of background, the former country of Yugoslavia was created from the union of Serbia and portions of the Austro-Hungarian empire, particularly Croatia, Slovenia and several Slav provinces. Montenegro joined what was then a limited monarchy in 1921.

Although portions of the country that resulted from that arrangement sided with Germany at the start of World War II, Slovenia officially joined with the Serbs, Croats and the less developed Balkan states in the south only when its people felt threatened by an Italian invasion. The country later attempted neutrality, only to be occupied by the Nazis soon after March 1941.

The partisans and their underground, with Jozip Broz Tito as the leader, waged war on the Germans and Italians, to a point where the Italians retreated to an enclave in Ljubljana, surrounding it "with barbed wire and bunkers" until they were routed from the area.

Many people credited the former Yugoslavia's nonaligned status to Tito's negotiating ability and his arms-length relationship with both the former Soviet Union and with western countries. Although Yugoslavia could continue on Tito's momentum for many years after his death, it could not survive the dissolution of the Soviet Union when various factions began to assert their independence. With its western-oriented economy, Slovenia was the first and the most successful at breaking from the communist government headquartered in Zagreb.

Although Slovenia's path toward independence was long and tortuous, by the time amendments were made to the Slovenian constitution in 1989, there were many who had dreamed of independence for the northern republic for several years. At the first postwar free parliamentary elections held in 1990, more than 80 per cent of the Slovenian population voted for independence. Achieving it came later, after the "Ten Day War," in October 1991, when the last of the Yugoslav army troops withdrew from Slovenian territory. After October 25, 1991, Slovenes took control of the government and established their new autonomous country.

AUTHOR'S OBSERVATION

The relative economic strength of ethnically homogeneous Slovenia and its long affiliation with its border countries to the north and west (Austria and Italy), makes the new country an interesting and pleasant place to visit. Vacationers can expect to find comfortable facilities and a warm welcome in Slovenia.

POLITICAL PICTURE

Slovenia declared its independence from the former country of Yugoslavia on June 25, 1991 and adopted a new constitution on December 23, 1991. Slovenia's status as a new nation was recognized by Germany when that country upgraded its consulates to embassies on January 15, 1992. Soon thereafter, other western powers, including the United States, recognized the newly independent country, an act which some claim contributed to the tragic events in the former and present Yugoslavian lands to the south.

Slovenia's constitution established the country as a democratic republic and affirms "the permanent and inalienable right of the Slovenian people to self-determination."

Elections are to be held every four years for delegates to the State Chamber, which has 90 representatives, elected from the Slovenian people. Hungarian and Italian minorities each elect one representative to the State Chamber. In addition, a 40-member State Council is an advisory body, made up of four representatives from employers, employees, farmers, craftsmen and independent professions as well as six representatives from noncommercial interests and 22 members from the local communities.

The mandate for the State Council is five years. The President of Slovenia is elected in general elections every five years and chooses his Prime Minister. He also serves as Commander-in-Chief of the defense forces. The government's daily operation is the responsibility of the Prime Minister and his council of Ministers, who are selected with the approval of the Prime Minister and the State Chamber.

Judicial power is in the hands of the judges, who must abide by the constitution and are elected by the State Chamber, after recommendations from the Jurisdictional Council. The first elections to the State Chamber were held on December 23, 1992.

LIFESTYLE

Although the 40-plus years of socialist/communist government had their effect on the economy and mores, Slovenia has quickly and proudly reasserted its traditional links with its northern and western neighbors. Many of the resort areas, such as that of Portorož, which is less than 10 miles from the Italian border, and of Croatia's Istrian peninsula, which is an easy drive (or boat ride) from the Italian border, have been popular vacation centers for Europeans for several years. The rest of Slovenia, where the influence from border neighbors Italy and Austria have filtered south in recent years, is developing along patterns familiar in democratic free-market systems.

Slovenia's landscape is occasionally marred by the industrial architecture and styles of the former Communist block, but most of the landscape is rolling farmland that had been overlooked by the strident socialism that was the way of life prior to the events of the early 1990s. Although bright colors expected in resort communities lighten up daily life in some of the border communities, grays and other sober colors dominate in the rest of the countryside, not only with the rocks and the austere angular architecture that was the style of Eastern Europe's socialist countries, but also the tone and style of clothing worn in small towns and villages.

Although field workers use hand-hewn implements in many areas, tractors and other mechanized farm equipment are appearing in ever increasing numbers. Vignettes of life in the countryside of Slovenia sometimes reflect western Europe of the 1950s, but 1990's prosperity, once limited to the coastal regions and, to a lesser degree, to Ljubljana and Maribor, are beginning to filter through the entire country.

NATURAL SURROUNDINGS

The Julijske Alpe (Julien Alps), craggy and crumpled, fill the northwest sector of Slovenia. They have been hideouts for resistance forces for centuries; some areas are now havens for skiers, rock-climbers, and adventuresome hikers who challenge their peaks with less threatening pursuits. Larch forests blanket many of the lower slopes, as they sink to the sometimes verdant valleys and the welcome plains that encourage subsistance farming. Castles perch on hilltops, often marking important trade routes that gained added prominence in the years of battles with the Turks.

The Drava river, known as the Drau in German-speaking Austria, weaves through Maribor and Varazdin on its route to join the Donau (Danube). Its banks are castle-studded; its bordering towns and villages have several historic buildings that are being put to modern use. While the fertile valley of the Soca river is marked with farms, the karst country is laced with caves. Postojna and škocjan are two that have been prepared for visitors. The škocjan Caves have been acknowledged as a UNESCO World Heritage Site. The Logar river valley, rural and weaving, is flecked with villages that take their cue from the talents of their past.

Lakes nestle quietly amid tall forests. Although only a few of the lake areas have elaborate resort facilities, all are enjoyed by those who prefer natural surroundings without "enhancements." Since cultural development in the early years often followed the rivers that were the route for trade, it is along their banks that today's visitors can find the most interesting man-made sights (and, occasionally, some of the most unsightly socialist-inspired factories).

Bird-watching can occupy pleasant hours in many parts of the Slovenian countryside. One prized place is Triglav National Park, in the Julijske Alpe, near the Italian and Austrian borders. Although there are few organized walks, avid birders will enjoy the natural surroundings. Be sure to bring binoculars and a bird book of the Alpine area.

PRACTICAL FACTS ABOUT SLOVENIA

Slovenia is adapting and developing as it gains security as an independent country. While many structural changes are still to be made, many of the facilities for tourism are already firmly in place. As the economy becomes more secure, new areas are opened for visitors and facilities are being improved. At the time of this edition, Slovenia is still little known to most North American travelers, although it has been a popular holiday destination for neighboring Germans, Austrians and other Europeans for many years.

INFORMATION SOURCES

Center za turistično in ekonomsko propagando pri Gospodarski zbornici Slovenije (*Kotnikova 5, 61000 Ljubljana;* ☎ *386+ 61+171.32.95, FAX 386+61+133.12.20*) is the head office for tourists. Another office for information on Slovenia is **Turistični Informacijski Biro**, *Slovenska 35, Ljubljana, Slovenija SL-61000;* ☎ *386+ 61+22.42.22; FAX 386+61+22.21.15.* In North America, information about Slovenia is available through the **Slovenian Tourist Office**, *122 East 42nd St., New York, NY 10168-0072;* ☎ *212+ 682-5896, FAX 212+661-2469.* Additional information sources are listed at the end of this chapter.

For information on Croatian places easily visited while touring Slovenia, see the separate "Croatia" commentary at the end of the "Places Worth Finding" section.

Throughout the chapter, local spelling is used for some words and all place names. For translation of foreign words, refer to the back-of-the-book glossary. Postal codes and telephone numbers for the tourist office are in parentheses following place names in "Places Worth Finding."

CASH, CURRENCY AND CREDIT CARDS

The Tolar was created at the time of Slovenia's independence as the unit of currency; it is divided into 100 Stotins. At press time, it exchanges at about SIT$110 to US$1, but rampant inflation affects the exchange rate daily. Money can be changed at a reasonable fee through the post office. Slovenians are eager to have hard currency, which means U.S. dollars, German Marks, Swiss Francs and other stable currencies, and may offer to change money independently.

COMMUNICATIONS

Slovene is the language of Slovenia. Many people in Slovenia and Croatia also speak German or Italian, depending on which neighbor's border is the closest and a few involved with tourism also speak English. French is spoken in some places that cater to French vacationers.

To telephone Slovenia from North America, use the code for the international carrier of your choice (AT&T uses *011*), plus *386* plus the telephone numbers as they appear throughout this text, with the city/town code and the specific number.

Two pronunciation tips may help you recognize names when you hear them: "J" has a "y" sound, which leads to Slovenia's capital of Ljubljana, being pronounced "LOO-blee-anna." "Z" is sometimes pronounced "sh," when it is marked with the breve (˘) sign, as in Portorož (Porto-rosh). "Č" has a "ch" sound. When in doubt, ask a resident to pronounce the name and, if you can't get your tongue around it, write it out—or have someone else do so—with the correct accent marks. *Veselica* is a Slovene word that signifies fun and festivities; it's a word to look for, to find special festivals that take place on specific dates throughout the year.

There are pay telephones in most post offices, but it may be difficult to find a private booth. Most phones are in public places where the entire room can share your conversation. Tokens, which can be purchased in post offices and at newsstands, are required for many pay phones; plastic telephone cards, also purchased in various denominations at the post office, are required for the telephones available in the post offices and for a growing number of public telephones elsewhere.

DOCUMENTS AND OTHER PAPERS

Your valid passport is all you'll need to travel in Slovenia. If you plan on renting a car in a neighboring country to drive into Slovenia, be sure you get the green card that indicates international vehicle insurance. The International Driver's License, issued through the *American Automobile Association* (for a fee of $10, plus passport size photos), is accepted in Slovenia.

MEDICAL FACILITIES

In the well-known Slovenian spas of Bled and Portorož, there are multilingual doctors in charge of the clinics and available for consultation. Medical services are available to all people, including visitors, who will pay a small fee for treatment. Drugstores, called *drogerije*, are obvious in most towns, but it may be difficult to find someone who speaks fluent English. When you are in a major city, the U.S. consulate or other North American service organization offices are good sources for information about doctors. Otherwise, work through your hotel or the nearest international-style hotel when you need medical assistance.

TRAVEL FACTS

Trains make links between major cities within Slovenia between Ljubljana and Maribor as well as along international routes. The main roads are good and clearly signposted (with Slovenian spelling, of course), and the long established network of local and regional buses continues to provide transportation links for most of the population. Tickets seem inexpensive for North Americans and others used to dollar equivalents.

AUTHOR'S OBSERVATION

It's often possible to invite a student to be your guide for time in Ljubljana and, depending on the schedule, for a few days' traveling around the countryside. Expect to pay expenses and to give something extra. Discuss fees ahead of time, and arrange a generous tip if fees are refused.

ARRIVAL

Many Europeans drive into Slovenia for their holidays. Although it's easy to dip across the border from Austria or Italy, train service is also comfortable. Arrival by train allows for leisurely sightseeing en route and the possibility of renting a car or taking buses to link sights you want to see.

AIRPORTS at Ljubljana-Brnik, Maribor and Portorož are served by the national carrier, **Adria Airways**, as well as other European airlines. **Swissair**, **Lufthansa**, **Austrian Airlines** and other European airlines fly from their major city (or cities) to Ljubljana. **Crossair**, a small-plane relative of Swissair, also links Ljubljana with Zürich and other Swiss airports. From the U.S., air links are usually made through a neighboring European city. Your travel agent can supply the details. Ljubljana is the major airport. Private planes touch down at all three airports, especially at Portorož, near the Italian border.

TOURING TIPS

For spontaneous travel, renting a car is the best method. For adventuresome travelers, linking the public system of buses with trains can be very inexpensive, especially for the excellent service between Ljubljana and Bled, which is used by many international visitors.

BOATS web the Adriatic with several crossings between Italy and ports along the Istrian peninsula as well as with Portorož, near Trieste. Many shore towns and villages and the islands of Croatia are linked to other Mediterranean ports, as well as to Yugoslav ports, as has been the case throughout history. When political conditions permit, cruise ships stop at historic ports and small boats flit like dragonflies between seaside towns and villages. There is hydrofoil service, for example, linking Portorož and Piran to Venezia (Venice), Trieste and other Italian ports for day excursions as well as for longer journeys.

Some lakes also are threaded with small boat service. One of my favorites, Lake Bled, does not allow motor boats. You'll be rowed, in a style reminiscent of the gondoliers of Venice, in boats that are hand built, following a pattern used for the past 100 years or more.

AUTHOR'S OBSERVATION

If a boating excursion sounds like fun, ask ahead of time to find out what days and times the services operate. Schedules fluctuate; not all services operate every day–or year-round.

BUSES are the best link between cities, towns and villages in Slovenia's Alpine area unless you rent a car. They are usually comfortable and air conditioned. There is regular bus service between Trieste (Italy) and Portorož, for example, and also between Ljubljana and Bled, a popular route for visitors. If you're planning to take a bus to reach the coastal resorts of Croatia, heading southwest from Slovenian towns, note that the schedule is not frequent and the route is often wiggly. (Take Dramamine or another antidote if you tend to get motion sickness.)

CAR RENTALS can be arranged, either in another Alpine country such as Italy or Austria, or in Slovenia. In Ljubljana, **Budget** (☎ *61+21.17.81 or 61+21.14.39, FAX 61+21.39.47*), **Avis** (☎ *64+ 26.16.85*), and **Kompas Hertz** (☎ *61+57.19.87 or 61+57.20.05, FAX 61+57.20.88*) are represented, in addition to several domestic companies.

> ### AUTHOR'S OBSERVATION
>
> *Ask about insurance coverage and rates. Be prepared for what seem to be excessive charges. There's been a brisk business in stolen rental cars in many of the former communist countries and the problem occasionally hits Slovenia as well. Most roads in Slovenia are clearly marked and, in many cases, in good repair. You may notice the difference between roads in neighboring Austria and the rural areas of Slovenia as soon as you've crossed the border, but overall the roads are good and well-marked.*

Border formalities are reasonably easy. You'll be requested to show your car rental papers and your passport. Be sure that you have your "green card," which is the essential insurance document for your car. If you don't have the document, you can obtain a temporary insurance permit in Slovenia.

Driving defensively has advantages. Mountain roads are often winding and many European drivers I've encountered seem to be trying for the Grand Prix. **Auto-Moto Zveza Slovenija** (**AMZS**, *Dinajska 128, SL-61000 Ljubljana;* ☎ *61+34.13.41; FAX 61+34.23.78*) is the Slovenian Automobile Federation and the source for information about driving in Slovenia. AMZS maintains a roadside service system; you can contact them by dialing 987 from designated telephones, but be sure to begin your conversation with "Do you speak English?" unless you are fluent in Slovene. Fill up when you see a petrol station, which will be at border crossings and on the outskirts of major towns and cities. (There may be others, but these locations you can count on.)

> ### AUTHOR'S OBSERVATION
>
> *If you're planning to drive from another western European country into Yugoslavia, be sure to advise your car rental company at the time you rent. You must have papers in the car to show that you have, in fact, rented a car that will be returned to its point of origin. If you plan to drive between Slovenia and the Croatian resorts on the Istrian peninsula, be sure to inquire about border formalities well in advance of your intended crossing date.*

TRAIN service between European cities and Ljubljana is reasonably good; it's also reasonably inexpensive for the Slovenian portion since you'll be paying a tolar-priced ticket. **Slovenske Železnice** (the Slovene Railways) works closely with the international trains of its neighbors to the north and west. The *Eurocity Mimara* highs-peed train links Ljubljana and München (Munich) in about 6 hours; Ljubljana and Venezia (Venice) is a 5 hour journey; Ljubljana to Wien (Vienna) is about 6 hours by train.

Trains usually offer both first- and second-class service. North American travelers usually purchase and will be more comfortable in first class; most local folks travel second class.

Some railroad cars may seem "old-fashioned" if you've recently traveled on the French TGV, the German high-speed trains, or the high-speed trains in Switzerland, Austria, or Italy. The compartments are usually arranged for six people, sitting three facing three, with a corridor down the side. You're expected to stow your luggage on the overhead rack and, since most Europeans travel with very little luggage, North American travelers with lots of luggage will be very conspicuous.

Count on waiting in line when you buy your train tickets in Slovenia. Slovenske Železnice offers discounts on travel from 10 to 30 days, both first and second class, but at presstime tickets must be bought in Slovenia. Check with the Slovenia Tourist Office (see "Information Sources") for possible sales outlets elsewhere at the time of your visit. There are also special tickets for students (30 percent discount), families traveling together, senior citizens (over 60 years), and others. A "Tourist Ticket" for four days of traveling in Austria includes a pass for public transportation in Wien. Always inquire at the tourist office or a tourist agency in Slovenia if you must transact in English language. It's a good idea to plan ahead—even a day ahead—and make an adventure out of buying your ticket.

YACHT CHARTER is a popular way to visit shore points. **Le Boat** *(Box E, Maywood, NJ 07607;* ☎ *201+342-1838 or 800+922-0291; FAX 201+342-7498)* had operated "Flotilla Sailing Holidays" prior to traumatic times south of Slovenia, especially in Bosnia and Serbia. Although Italian charters sail along the Croatian coast at frequent intervals, the North American firms are not operating in the area at press time. Check with them about possible plans in the future. The best sailing times, for weather and winds, are from mid-April to mid-October.

DAILY LIVING IN SLOVENIA

FOOD, WINE AND OTHER BEVERAGES

Slovenian mealtimes are an adventure, especially for travelers most familiar with French-style presentation. Fine service had not been a priority when Slovenia was part of socialist Yugoslavia. Even these days, napery and other tableware may look a bit worn. The food can be delicious, a symphony of tastes drawn from many ethnic traditions and, it seems, from every transient who lingered long enough to add spice to the kitchen. Cooking styles and flavors of western Europe mingle with spices and flavors from the east and Slovenia's location—bordered by the Mediterranean, the Alps and Eastern Europe—as well as its people's farming tradition, affects its culinary heritage. Central Europe's buckwheat appears as an ingredient for *struklji* (strook-lay), the favorite dumplings that are a mealtime staple and the cornmeal polenta is a favorite with goulash, which takes its cue from Hungarian fare. *Chevapchichi* (chee-vap-chi-chi)—the spelling may vary, but the pronunciation is about the same—is well known to eastern Austria as well as to Slovenia. Because the recipe is Serbian (and Serbs are *personna non grata* in Slovenia), the item was taken off many menus after Slovenia's independence. But the spicy ground beef "fingers" are beloved by all and now are appearing once again. They could please the palates of Americans craving hamburgers, but brace yourself for coriander and other flavors. On their own, they are delicious, especially if you like spicy food. *Pleskavitzka* is ground meat in another shape, but also spicy and served with special sauce(s) on the side. *Vampi* is a tasty tripe stew, and *krapi* or *krofi* are delicious raised doughnuts. Recipes for homemade bread differ in each town; I find them all delicious.

At the seaports of Portorož and Piran and around the Istrian peninsula, the scampi are real scampi of the crawfish family, not the shrimp in garlic that most Americans know as "scampi." Italian neighbors have lent risotto to mealtimes in border areas, and other pastas also appear on restaurant offerings.

Slovenia's wines can be very good. Each of the three major wine-producing regions has its own specialty. The vineyards on the hillsides near the Adriatic produce hearty reds and dry white wines. Noteworthy regions are those around Korper, Karst, Vipava and Brda. The valley of the Sava river produces red and white wines as well as a light rosé. The four wine-producing areas of this valley are the Dolenjska region, which includes the communities of Novomesto, Mokronog, Krško and Gorjanci; the Bela Krajina district, which includes Metlika and Čmomelj; the area around Bizeljsko-Semič; and the Smarje-Virštanj district. The third major area is around the Drava valley—Maribor, Radgona-Kapela, Srednje Slovenske gorice, and Prekmurske gorice, where the grapes respond to the warm, dry climate to produce white wines. Pinot Gris, Pinot Blanc, Chardonnay, Riesling, Traminer and Yellow Muscatel are the most popular white wines; Merlot, Cabernet Sauvignon, Barbera, Rofosco and Cabernet franc are the most popular reds.

AUTHOR'S OBSERVATION

Try the dark red (and strong) wine, a Rofosco, called Teran. Exceptional in the Lipici area, the wine is best when joined by pršut, as the air-dried pork is called. (It's pronounced to sound something like "phr-shoot.")

LODGING

Although a few of the farm houses that dot Slovenia's Alpine area have rooms for rent and there are several comfortable resorts, hotels and spas throughout the country, most of the traditional resort hotels and apartments are gathered in towns at or near the shoreline of the Istrian peninsula, on the Gulf of Trieste and at the lakeside resort of Bled, as well as at the sports-oriented places at Kranjska Gora in the highest mountains. The rural area, from the peaks of the Julian Alps to the undulating foothills that reach south, has some small and basic lodgings in villages and towns as well as rooms in private homes and on farms.

Bookings and guide services can be arranged through the tourist agencies such as **Sterling Tours**, *(#105E, 1106 Cayton Lane, Austin, TX 78723;* ☎ *512+467-1707 or 800+367-2328; FAX 512+453-1153).* The **Slovenian Hotel Association** *(Slovenska 41, SL-61000 Ljubljana;* ☎ *61+135.01.22)* can provide information about its members. It's also possible to travel on your own, without advance reservations, taking your chances by either stopping at the tourist office in the main towns (but you must plan to be there when you know the place will be open) or by asking people at one lodging about possibilities in other places you plan to visit.

AUTHOR'S OBSERVATION

Some knowledge of German or Slovene–and Italian, if you travel near that country's border–is essential for spontaneous travel in Yugoslavia. Even if you can't speak fluently, it's important to know the proper words for "bedroom," "food" and other essentials. If you can't pronounce them in recognizable fashion, write them on a paper to show to someone en route.

APARTMENTS and **CHALETS** are not as omnipresent as in Italy, Austria and Switzerland, for example, but there are many in the coastal resort areas of Croatia (see the end of the "Places Worth Finding" commentary below) and more will appear now that life is settling down and tourism is acknowledged as an important industry. Self-catering accommodations can be arranged through the local tourist offices and with **Sterling Tours** *(#105E, 1106 Clayton Lane, Austin, TX 78723;* ☎ *512+467-1707 or 800+367-2328; FAX 512+453-1153)* or another tour operator specializing in Slovenia. **Villas International** *(#510, 605 Market St., San Francisco, CA 94105;* ☎ *415+ 281-0910 or 800+221-2260; FAX 415+281-0919)* lists a few rental properties in Slovenia and coastal areas of the neighboring country of Croatia.

CAMPING is very popular for nationals of the country as well as visitors. People enjoy the back-to-nature aspects and the cost factor. The coastal areas are freckled with campsites, as are some mountain areas, especially those near the three-country border with Austria and Italy. The islands have many campgrounds, all of which are very popular (and often crowded) in summer. Camping is not allowed at other than designated campsites unless special permission has been obtained in advance. Although some sites have chalets and bungalows, most are for tents, which can sometimes be rented at modest cost. If you're bringing a tent or bicycle, the items are allowed into the country duty free, but they must be declared at the border. Cafeterias and medical aid are usually available near the sites. Although tenting is popular, some camps have facilities for RVs (recreational vehicles, campers or caravans). Ask the tourist office for the booklet about camping or contact **Turistično Družtvo Lesce** *(SL-64248 Lesce;* ☎ *64+775.00 or 64+742.60, FAX 64+780.70)* for their booklet that shows pictures of many campsites and offers site maps to help pinpoint locations.

FARM VACATIONS, known as *kmecki turizem*, are possible in the Alpine foothills, where many farmers have built new rooms for visitors. Germans and British are especially fond of this vacation style, which is enjoyed by many European visitors. In most cases, the unit will have several rooms for guests who share the bathroom and kitchen, as in a home. In some cases, there are also rooms in the farmer's own living area. In all cases, the guests' comfort comes first. Food will be homecooked when it is offered at the main house and usually home grown. Hospitality is heartfelt, even when the spoken language is not the same for all. The tourist office has a comprehensive booklet, *Farmhouse Holidays: Back to Nature on the Sunny Side of the Alps*, with full details about dozens of farmhouses and pictures of many properties. **Zadružna turistična agencija VAS** *(Miklošičeva 4, SL-6100 Ljubljana;* ☎ *61+21.94.47; FAX 61+21.93.88)* is one agency that handles information about and reservations for farmhouse vacations, in addition to providing assistance with transportation and sightseeing.

HUTS and **MOUNTAIN HOTELS**, favored by hikers and climbers, can be found in Slovenia's Alpine region. The network in place throughout the Alps stretches into the Julian Alps, with maintenance undertaken by Slovenes in partnerships with neighboring Alpine Clubs.

INNS and **SMALL HOTELS** gather at places designated for tourism development. If you want a truly authentic Slovenian place, *Gostlina* is the word to look for. You'll usually find it on a building or two at a village crossroad or along the road. Although most inns are locally known for their restaurants, which is usually the village gathering place, some also offer simple rooms for rent. Do not expect fancy flourishes or a private bath. Chances are the bath will be down the hall. Some places will not have hot water, although most do have running water.

LUXURY RESORTS and **CLASSIC HOTELS** can be found, but the atmosphere found in western Europe is available only when the turn-of-the-century buildings have been saved as an official residence. Many of the former grand hotels were torn down or turned into offices or used for other purposes during the days when communism/ socialism was being firmly established. Luxury living, as it is interpreted in the western-capitalist world, is not a byword for Slovenia, but there are some top-quality resorts. Villa Bled, which was Tito's private villa from 1945 to 1980, is a luxury hotel and Hotel Toplice, also in Bled, has been a favorite of the world's wealthy through the generations. At Lipica, the Klub Hotel Lipica and the Maestoso accommodate the horsey set who stay to ride the Lipizzaner stallions. And the mountain resort of Kranjska Gora caters to skiers and summer vacationers. On the coast at Portorož, the modern luxury Hotel Metropol provides all comforts. Its casino is popular with Italians and other Europeans. The top city hotels have expected services and private bath, often in Eastern European style, but not always private telephone and other flourishes expected by most North American travelers. Among the exceptions is the Holiday Inn in Ljubljana which has many of the U.S. chain's conveniences.

SPAS operate in the traditional European style where the emphasis is on cures and relaxation. The **Skupnost Slovenskih Zdravilisc** *(Slovene Spa Community, Tomšičevtrg 7, SL-63000 Celje;* ☎ *63+ 280.17, FAX 63+280.24)* publishes an attractive, informative guide (in English) to a dozen spas in Slovenia, some of which were known to the Romans, who give the word *Rimski* to some. A few are mentioned in documents dating from 1147 and for their healing powers, in writings in the 17th century. Although popular with nationals, as part of government-financed health cures and with Germans and others who have known of these spas through history, the places are little known to North Americans. Procedures available at the various spas vary considerably. Two of the most familiar towns for spa-seeking international visitors are Bled, about an hour's drive northwest of Ljubljana and Portorož, on the Gulf of Trieste. Both communities have well-maintained spa facilities that mingle curative services with all the trappings of a full-fledged modern resort. The Hotel Palace in Portorož has "winter therapeutic" and "slimcure" packages, both of which are popular with European travelers. Bled's Hotel Toplice (which means baths) also offers spa plans.

YOUTH HOSTELS are not often designated as such, although pensions, rooms in private hotels and camping facilities are very inexpensive. They seem to have supplanted youth hostels for students and other cost-conscious travelers. University towns such as Ljubljana and Maribor can be very interesting places for young visitors (and others). The local tourist offices can advise about lodging in student rooms, available from May to October when students are not in residence and about rooms in private homes which are sometimes available.

PLACES WORTH FINDING

The mountainous region of Slovenia is dotted with villages, most of which have small churches that sometimes have lavishly trimmed interiors. Castles fleck many hilltops along the historic trading routes. Although some have been partially restored, most castles have been neglected, but all are worth visiting to turn pages of Slovenia's rich past when the land was the crossroads for travel between the Balkans and Central Europe as well as from Northern Europe to the Mediterranean. Since cultural development in the earliest years often followed the rivers that were the route for trade, many of the most interesting sights are along their banks. For example, along the Drava river (the Drau in German) that weaves through Maribor and Varazdin on its route to join the Donau (Danube), there are several castles and some villages have historic buildings that are being put to modern use.

While the fertile valley of the Soča river is marked with farms, the karst country in the northeast is laced with caves. Postojne and Skocjan are two vast cave complexes that have been prepared for visitors.

The Logar river valley, rural and weaving, is flecked with villages that take their cue from the talents of their past.

AUTHOR'S OBSERVATION

One of the pleasures of traveling in Slovenia is that it has not (yet) been overdeveloped for tourism. Although Germans, French, Swiss, Austrians, Italians and some British are frequent visitors, the natural lifestyle is still in the tradition of the region.

After each place name, the letter-number notation (SL-00000) is the postal code; ☎ *telephone and FAX numbers are for the local tourism office, known as "turizem" in Slovene, your source for further information. SL indicates Slovenia, the country that was created on June 25, 1991. As noted under "Communications," above, to telephone within Slovenia, you must first dial "0" before the numbers given. From outside the country, you will need the country code and, from the United States, dial an international access code before the country code, which is 386.*

BLED

Bled (*Tyristično Društvo, Cesta svobode 15, SL-64260;* ☎ *64+774.09, FAX 64+778.38*), nestled at lakeside and respected through history for its spa, thrives as a favored resort area for Europeans. Occupied by the Romans and the Slavs, the town was awarded by the German emperor to the Bishop of Brizen in 1004. Not only is the resort town comfortable, with good hotels and pleasant restaurants and shops, but also it is picture-perfect with a tiny isle in the middle of the lovely lake and no power boats to disturb the tranquil scene. Although Bled is busiest in midsummer months when it is a popular vacation goal for Europeans and others, it is also beautiful in spring, fall and winter. When conditions are right, it's possible to play golf and ski in the same day.

Although Bled's **Grad** (castle), which dates from 1004, was shorn of its treasures by the Germans during World War II, the charming landmark is regaining its wealth as some items are returned and new ones are added. It is a museum, with most furnishings dating from earlier times. The 17th-century frescoes in the chapel and items from the Bishops of Brixen in the castle rooms are noteworthy. Although it dates from the 11th century, the **Church of St. Maria** on **Otok**, a tiny island that rises in the lake, is in baroque style from the early 17th century and the **Church of St. Martin**, in the lakeside town, claims modern frescoes in its Turkish period walls.

In addition to shops, several hotels and restaurants and the entertainment offered by the lake, the area is host to the headquarters for the **Triglav Nacionalni Park** (Triglav National Park). From the shops and festivity of Bled, it is only a short drive to peace and quiet—and walks and hikes—at the peaceful, calm **Jezero** (lake) **Bohinj**.

LODGING: Among my top choices are the **Vila Bled** *(31 rooms;* ☎ *64+774.36, FAX 64+773.20)*, a member of the *Relais & Châteaux* group and the **Grand Hotel Toplice** *(205 beds;* ☎ *64+772.22)*, which is wedged between the lake and the main road, within easy walking distance of shops but enough removed to be peaceful and pleasant. Vila Bled, a vacation villa for Josep Tito, became an elegant hotel in the mid-1980s. Although its furnishings are tediously 1950s style, the location and history of the villa lend it style. The Grand Hotel Toplice, with large rooms and a style familiar in the grand hotels of Europe, has modernized some rooms, but maintains the traditional atmosphere that drew Europe's notables to the hotel as the 19th century turned to the 20th. Among the other choices are the **Golf Hotel** *(290 beds, 64+775.91)* and the **Park** *(400 beds,* ☎ *64+779.45)*, both of which are big hotels with resort facilities catering to touring groups.

Two smaller places, known and enjoyed by wise Europeans, are **Hotel Lovec** *(75 rooms; Ljubljanska cesta 6;* ☎ *64+776.92, FAX 64+760.21)*, a 3-story Italianate building with bedrooms furnished in spartan style and the **Pension Mlino** *(18 rooms; Cesta svobode 45;* ☎ *64+773.21, FAX 64+787.76)*, at lakeside, in a farmhouse style with sparsely-furnished rooms that are clean and neat, as well as a sun terrace for café dining when the weather is warm enough.

BOHINJ

Bohinj *(Ribčev laz 48, SL-64265;* ☎ *64+72.33.70, FAX 64+72.33.30)*, a quiet area devoted to summer and winter sports, has miles of walking paths, challenging hikes and climbs, and, in winter months, two groomed ski areas—Vogel and Kobla—as well as guides to take experienced skiers on ski touring expeditions. The lake and nature are the reasons for coming to Bohinj.

LODGING: Most of the hotels focus on Alpine atmosphere. The **Zlatorog Hotel** *(75 rooms;* ☎ *64+72.33.81, FAX 64+72.34.46)*, at Ukanc, near the lower cable station for the Vogel, has a pool, as well as TV in the rooms. The **Hotel Kompas** *(58 rooms;* ☎ *64+72.34.71, FAX 64+72.31.61)* and the **Hotel Jezero** *(55 rooms;* ☎ *64+72.33.75, FAX 64+72.33.75)* are neighbors near the lake, not far from the St. John's Church. Bedrooms at the Jezero have TV; most of the bedrooms at the Kompas have viewful balconies. Both hotels are relatively new and built in modern chalet/mountain style. The area also has many apartments, pensions and bed-and-breakfast places.

Bohinj, Slovenia

BOVEC

Bovec *(SL-65230;* ☎ *65+863.70)*, in the Soča river valley, in northwestern Slovenia, is in the midst of the Triglav National Park. The valley, incidentally, was featured in Ernest Hemingway's *Farewell to Arms*. North of Trenta, in a mountain-rimmed bowl, Bovec and the surrounding areas are popular in winter for skiers who set out from here on the funicular to Kanin where there are lifts, a restaurant and other ski facilities. The mountainous Bovsko region surrounds the village which is placed about 10 miles (17 km) from the Italian border and about 75 miles (140 km) north of Ljubljana. Little known prior to 1972 when it was designated to be developed for skiing, the town has lost some of its former appeal but now offers most expected visitor services. This area—the Kanin Alps—was bitterly contested between Austria and Italy in World War I and was caught in a "taffy pull" at the end of World War II when Trieste was also being claimed by both Italy and Yugoslavia.

Not far from Bovec at the foot of the Julian Alps, **Trenta** is in the Soča river valley. Nature is its main attraction with the Soča canyon, the Mlinarica gorge and starting points for climbs of at least four major peaks—Triglav, Prisojnik, Jalovec, and the Razor—reasonably nearby. The road that runs along the valley continues on through the Vrsic mountain pass and on to the resort area at Kranjska gora.

LODGING: For hotels in Bovec, ask about the **Kanin** *(150 rooms;* ☎ *65+860.21, FAX 65+860.81)* and the **Alp-Hotel** *(125 rooms;* ☎ *65+860.40, FAX 65+860.81).* Both have been built in recent years for skiers and others who come to the area for outdoor pursuits. Bedrooms are basic, furnished in spartan style. **Gotour** *(39 beds; Trg Golobarskihžrtev 50;* ☎ *65+861.03, FAX 65+861.03),* is a small hotel with basic facilities and an informal atmosphere. The **Scabiosa Turistična Agencija Bovec** *(*☎ *65+860.41, FAX 65+860.41)* lists private homes with rooms for rent.

CELJE

Celje *(SL-63000;* ☎ *63+294.45),* southwest of Maribor, on the route to Ljubljana, is worth a visit for its museums. Other small villages will surprise you with the richly embellished interiors of their churches and chapels.

LODGING: The handful of places to stay are reasonably small with basic furnishings. The largest is **Hotel Europa** *(120 beds; Titov Trg 4;* ☎ *63+212.33, FAX 63+241.26),* which is centrally located and used by groups. Other choices are the **Hotel Celeia** *(95 beds; Mariborska 3;* ☎ *63+291.41, FAX 63+256.46),* the **Hotel Merx** *(38 beds; Ljubljanska 39;* ☎ *63+219.18, FAX 63+219.19)* and the **Hotel Turška Mačka** *(43 beds; Gledališka 39;* ☎ *63+251.50, FAX 63+285.21),* whose name translates as "Turkish Cat" and whose restaurant has a traditional café-style atmosphere from a time when it was a popular gathering place for artisans. Known as the **Istrska Konoba**, the restaurant features regional recipes, especially those from the Istrian peninsula and good Slovenian wines. (See "Croatia," at the end of "Places Worth Finding.")

KRANJSKA GORA

Kranjska Gora *(Ticarjeva 2, SL-64280;* ☎ *64+88.17.68, FAX 64+88.11.79),* high in the mountains at the edge of Triglav National Park, has been respected as a ski resort since the 1920s when the first intrepid skiers enjoyed challenging slopes on surrounding mountains. Now, with an atmosphere akin to that found in other Alpine areas, the town focuses on skiing in winter and walking, hiking and climbing when the snow has left the lower slopes. The annual *World Cup Final Ski Jump* event is held each year on the third weekend in March, the *European Cup Downhill* is held at the end of December, and an interesting *Ski-Tour 3*, which crosses Italy, Austria and Slovenia, has its counterpart in the *Three-Country Run*, held each July. Although there's not much that's historic about this place, there's plenty for sportsfolk to enjoy. One favorite walk in warm weather months is up to the Vrsic mountain pass where there is a **Russian chapel**. In town, sights to see include the remarkable paintings inside the 14th-century **Gothic church** and the 17th-century **Liznjak house**.

Since the town is on the main road linking Ljubljana to both Villach (Austria) and Tarvisio (Italy), the resort is easy to reach by car, as well as by public bus that links the town to Bled, as well as to Ljubljana and to Jesenice.

LODGING: The resort has ten tourist hotels and dozens of smaller places in addition to rooms in private homes for a total of almost 4000 tourist beds. Among the most popular hotels are the **Hotel Kompas** *(156 rooms;* ☎ *64+88.16.61, FAX 64+88.11.76)*, a modern hotel with sauna, pool, exercise room and the feeling of an Alpine ski lodge in winter months, as well as the convenience of being in the center of town, and the **Hotel Alpina** *(106 rooms;* ☎ *64+88.17.61, FAX+88.13.41)*, with comfortable, but slightly simpler, facilities, near the ski lifts and not far from a lakeside hunting chalet, **Gostišče Jasna**, where the management arranges special parties. Guests at the Alpina can use the health club facilities at the Kompas Hotel. One pleasant smaller spot is the **Hotel Lek** *(80 rooms;* ☎ *64+88.15.20, FAX 64+88.13.43)*, on the main street and near the ski lifts, with a modified chalet-style architecture.

LJUBLJANA

Ljubljana *(Promocijski Informacijski Center, Trubarjeva 5, SL-61000;* ☎ *61+133.31.55, FAX 61+133.20.07)*, the capital of Slovenia, weaves romance, revolts and Renaissance art into its rich history. The city is a wonderful melange of baroque, Renaissance, art nouveau and tumbling buildings, with a few 1950s and more recent high-rise buildings to yank you back to modern times. Illyrians settled in the B.C. years and a Roman town received a charter here in 34 B.C., but by the time the Slovenes came in from the east, they found a deserted area that they settled and named Lubigana. The name appears in records of 1142. By 1282, the town was incorporated into the Habsburg domain, following its capture in 1270 by Ottokar of Bohemia, although some date the start of Habsburg rule to 1335. There's no doubt, however, about the fact that, except for five years under Napoleon (during which time the Slovenian language was "saved"), the city was Habsburg until the end of World War I, when the empire was dissolved. It's not surprising, therefore, that the city is reminiscent of Austria's Salzburg, with a river cutting the city and a hilltop castle that's a favorite goal for strollers.

AUTHOR'S OBSERVATION

The Turistična magistrala, *a walking tour, is clearly marked within the town. Many buildings have identifying plaques, in Slovene and other languages and a two-hour walk is also marked. Ask for a copy of "Where?" a pocket-sized booklet, in English, with good detail about the primary sights of Ljubljana.*

The town-splitting river is embroidered with Venetian-style bridges. The **Cevljarski Most** (Shoemaker's Bridge), designed by a local architect, Joze Plecnik, after the end of the Habsburg rule, is an ideal pausing place to note the medley of medieval, baroque and Renaissance buildings. The **Zmajski Most** (Dragon's Bridge), designed by Jurij Zaninovic, was built in 1901, to replace a wooden bridge that linked the "other" side of town with the market square.

The **Stolnica** (cathedral), at the market square, was founded in 1708, at the site of a medieval church dedicated to St. Nicholas, the patron saint of fishermen and boat owners. In the 15th century, when the bishopric of Ljubljana was established, a larger church was built over the early Romanesque church, and by the second half of the 17th century, when the church was tumbling down, plans were laid to build a new church on the same foundations. The impressive frescoes are by Italian painters and are mostly the work of Giulio Quaglio, an Italian from a village near the town of Como. (The first-choice artist, Andrea Pozzo, who had done the frescoes for the Jesuit church, was committed to work in Vienna.)

Legend claims that Napoleon stayed in the nearby Renaisssance style **Škofijski Dvorec** (Palace of the Archbishop) in 1797; the Catholic bishop lives there now. The early morning market that is held on the cathedral square is well worth some time, not only to see what's for sale (and perhaps to buy some handmade lace or handcrafted implements), but also to gain an impression of daily life in Ljubljana. After browsing around the marketplace, stroll up to the hilltop **Grad** (castle) for an overview of the town. Be sure to climb the tower for the best views. The hilltop was a Roman fortress and prior to that, was used by the Celts and Illyrians as their fortified lookout.

Portions of the buildings date from the 9th century, but much was added in repairs following the earthquake of 1511, and again in the late 1600s, when the castle was being readied for the provincial rulers who lived here. The chapels are very popular these days for weddings. A monument to the Slovene peasant uprising in 1974 stands near the castle.

Prešernov Square, named for Slovenia's revered intellectual and poet, France Prešern (1800-49), is marked with his statue, which faces the building that was the home of the woman he loved. Nearby the Venetian-style **Tromostovje** (three bridges), designed by Plečnik, arches over the Lubljanica river. The **Uršulinska Cerkev**, (Ursuline convent, an impressive baroque structure, reflects some elements of the Italian Palladian architecture. The Trinity at the front of the church was originally portrayed in wood, in thanks for survival from the plague in 1693; the stone rendition now in place is a copy of an original work that is in the museum.

As the capital of the country and a university town, Ljubljana is home for many cultural activities throughout the year. **Cankarjev Dom** is the cultural center and the city's great pride and joy. Built in modern Eastern European style in 1982, the building appears drab for some tastes. In order to sample Ljubljana's social life, try for tickets for any event that's held in the concert and convention hall where there are several auditoriums, meeting rooms and recording studios. In addition to being an impressive home for the performing arts, the public halls are decorated with tapestries that follow designs of well-known Yugoslavian artists.

The **University**, established in 1919, sets the city's youthful tone. The several streets are good places to stroll and to chat with students, many of whom speak good English.

For on-the-spot touring assistance, if you arrive in Ljubljana on your own and want a guide, the **Kompas Turizem D.D.** (*Pražakova 4;* ☎ *61+12.71.27, FAX 61+31.98.88*) can help with reservations, tours and car rentals. Another source is the **Slovenijaturist** (*Pivovarniška 1;* ☎ *61+31.61.89, FAX 61+32.14.86*).

For information about cultural events, contact **Slovensko narodno gledalisce Drama** (*National Theater; Erjavceval, SL-61000 Ljubljana;* ☎ *61+22.14.62*), **NNG Opera in balet** (*National Opera and Ballet, Zupanciceva 1, SL-61000 Ljubljana;* ☎ *61+33.19.45*), **Slovenska filharmoniza** (*Philharmonic, Kongresnia trg 10, SL-61000 Ljubljana;* ☎ *61+21.34.60*) or the **National Gallery** (*Cankarjeva 20, SL-61000 Ljubljana;* ☎ *61+21.97.16*).

Southeast of Ljubljana along the Krka river, **Grad Otočec** is both a castle and a hotel within easy distance of **Novo Mesto**, founded in 1365 as Rudolphswerth by Habsburg ruler, Rudolf IV. The medieval core of this delightfully photogenic town seems to thrive in the past. Not far from here, **Kostanjeviški samostan**, a monastery, is impressive, although only men are invited to visit its inner sanctum.

(Women can visit the gardens around the historic buildings.) Two other medieval clusters, **Grad Mokrice** and **Grad Brežice**, are rectangular fortress castles that should be on your itinerary if you are driving. Both are imposing for their sites as well as for turrets and thick walls.

LODGING: The **Holiday Inn** *(215 beds; Miklošičeva Cesta 3;* ☎ *61+15.50.51, FAX 61+15.03.23)* offers the expected HI accouterments, which seem strangely out of place in Ljubljana. A sprucing up has come with Slovenia's independence, making this well-located place popular with touring groups, business folks and independent travelers, but service seemed slack when I visited. Because it has more local personality, I prefer the **Grand Hotel Union** *(270 rooms; Miklošičeve Cesta 1;* ☎ *61+15.41.33, FAX 61+21.79.10)*, which may not seem grand by western European standards, but I find its eastern European style fascinating and its sparse rooms reasonably comfortable. **Austrotel** *(40 rooms; Miklošičeva 9;* ☎ *61+12.61.33, FAX 61+30.11.81)*, popular with business folks, is well located, reasonably priced and reasonably comfortable. **Hotel Lev** *(125 rooms; Vošnjakova 1;* ☎ *61+13.21.55, FAX 61+32.19.94)* is used by European and other travel groups. It's high-rise-modern, with TVs in the bedrooms.

Maribor, Slovenia

MARIBOR

Maribor *(SL-62000;* ☎ *62+212.62)*, Slovenia's second largest town, masks many of its cultural attractions with an overlay of modern building in tedious architectural style. Although Austrian for much of its history, Maribor was assigned to Yugoslavia in 1918.

Those who persevere, in light of the town's industrial appearance, will be rewarded by finding **Glavni Trg**, the main square, marked by a column that commemorates the plague of 1680. The **Town Hall**, on the square, holds the coat of arms under its prominent balcony. Inside, the council chamber is richly embellished with stucco work and painted ceilings.

Go through the wrought-iron gates to visit **Alojzijeva Kapela** (St. Aloysius's chapel), and then proceed along the pedestrian area to **Katedrala Sv. Jožefa** (St. John's cathedral), originally built in the 17th century. In the 16th-century Gothic choir area, the bishop's throne is marked by a statue of A. M. Slomsek, the first prince-bishop of Marburg.

Although Maribor's **Grad** (castle) has capitulated to modern industry, with the monument for the struggle for Liberation at its entrance, the regional museum in its interior holds many treasures. The painted ceiling in the great hall depicts a battle with the Turks in addition to other historic events. Calvary Hill, rising at the fringe of town, is capped by **Kapela Sv. Barbara** (St. Barbara's Chapel).

While in Maribor, wake early one morning to walk up to the nearby tower for a good view of Maribor and its surrounding countryside. The town's at its best at that hour. By midday, plan to select one of the chairs at the square near the Orel Hotel to people-watch, as others are doing, while you sip some wine, a cola, or a beer. Walk through the park, along the promenades, to the **Mariborsko Jezero** known as the "Park of the Three Lakes," where there are no lakes now, but there is a dining pavilion in a farmhouse style where meals are served in one of the rooms inside as well as at tables outside (which I prefer) when the weather warms.

One on-the-spot source for touring assistance is **Slovenijaturist**, a small firm, *(Grajski trg 3A; ☎ 62+289.90, FAX 62+288.51)*, but **Kompas**, and other nationwide touring companies also have their representatives here. All can arrange car rentals and hotel rooms as well as local and regional tours.

LODGING: Don't expect quaint, atmospheric hotels, but I've found the **Hotel Slavija** *(192 beds; ☎ 62+236.61)* to be convenient and reasonably comfortable. The **Orel Hotel** *(228 beds; ☎ 62+261.71)* is also popular with many foreign travelers, although most of its style reflects its eastern European links.

The **Pohorje valley**, along the Drav river, west from Maribor, is mostly an unspoiled rural area, where farming is the major occupation and tiny churches cap many hilltops. There is, however, one touristy area, with a cluster of hotels and a nearby campsite.

PIRAN

Piran *(SL-66330;* ☎ *66+733.42)*, a pre-Roman town about ten minutes' ride by public bus or by car from Portorož, is worth a visit in early morning to watch the fishermen depart. Plan to return at dinner time to enjoy their catch at one of the many good restaurants that line the harborfront. **Tartinijev Trg**, the main square, is named for Giuseppe Tartini (1692-1770), who stands prominently (in bronze), peacefully playing the violin with which he became famous. The surrounding car-clogged "square" is fringed with shops (and the post office); it's a good starting point for most meanderings along the narrow, winding streets that are lined with well-kept medieval buildings. Be sure to climb up to the **church** for a rewarding view of the sea beyond the red-tile rooftops. This venerable seaside village claims Illyrian, Celtic, and Roman roots, with each group occupying the area in turn—and squabbling with others in the meantime. I like this town for its cluster of old houses leaning against each other up the hillside, for the church that caps its hill (and gives those who reach it a lovely view out to sea), and for the harborside cafés and restaurants which take on special appeal when there's activity around the fishing boats that tie up nearby. These are lingering places, where mealtimes are an occasion to be enjoyed, with fresh fish a specialty and homecooking assured.

Punta, the "point" of the peninsula at Piran, was fortified in Roman times. Patches of the 15th-century walls still stand. Many of the old buildings are dwellings; a few around the town square and along the harbor are shops and casual seafood restaurants. A Venetian influence is obvious in the buildings and bridges, with interesting discoveries possible along almost any path.

PORTOROŽ

Portorož *(Obala 16, SL-66320;* ☎ *66+763.72, FAX 66+730.54)*, known as Porta Rosa to neighboring Italians, is a thriving summer resort that was highly regarded as a spa visited by royalty and the world's wealthy at the turn of the century. Today it's a lively tourist town on the shore of the Gulf of Trieste with a strong and welcoming personality. Most visitors are Italians or other Europeans who enjoy the cafes and shops that line the waterfront. There are concessionaires who rent boats and arrange other lake activities. The dozens of hotels include resort style and small spots; the tourist office on the waterfront is manned by English-speaking personnel who I've found to be very helpful.

LODGING: Among the many places to stay, the **Grand Hotel Metropol** (*610 beds;* ☎ *66+735.41*), a complex that incorporates several separate buildings, is modern in accepted western style. There's a casino on the premises (you'll need your passport for entrance), in addition to several shops, a large pool and full resort facilities. The smaller **Apollo** (*192 beds;* ☎ *66+735.42*), joined with others for a group of tourist hotels as is the socialist policy, is on the main waterfront boulevard. Its rooms are basic but convenient.

POSTOJNA

Postojna (*SL-66230;* ☎ *67+210.77*), widely acknowledged for its sensational caves, is a major tourist site. In spite of the fact that it is a pausing place for bus tours of the area, the caves are well worth seeing. About an hour's drive east of Portorož, and slightly less going west from Ljubljana, the caves are threaded with an electric train that follows less than a mile (5 km) of paths, broken by a short walk with a guide who speaks your choice of languages. Bring a lightweight jacket, even on a hot day, and some head covering if you're going to be bothered by an occasional drip of water from the moistened cave walls.

PTUJ

Ptuj (*SL-62250;* ☎ *62+775.69*), pronounced "pi-tooey," rises on the banks of the Drava, in a picture-perfect setting, about 30 minutes' drive east of Maribor. It is a charming historic city, wedged into the crop of a river. Capped by a 12th-century castle that now holds the **Pokrajinski Muzej**, the town is one of Slovenia's most picturesque, historic and easy to visit. The museum is filled with portraits and furniture left by the Herberstein family when, after World War II, they reportedly went to live in nearby Austria. The village is a tapestry of narrow, winding streets bordered with medieval buildings. Known to Celts in the 4th century B.C., the town was settled by Romans in 35 B.C. to protect the route from northern Italy to the east. Linked into the Habsburg realm for part of its history, the town shares the Hungarian, Bohemian, Austrian history of its neighbors across today's national border.

PLACES WORTH FINDING IN CROATIA

The independent country of Croatia was the heartbeat of tourism for the former country of Yugoslavia, when it was a Yugoslav republic, prior to its independence in 1991. Although some of the southern inland portions of the country have known the devastation of war since 1991, the Istrian peninsula, nestled between Slovenia and Italy, seems to be "a world away" from that activity. The ragged coastline that splinters into "a thousand islands," heading south, is flecked with charming villages that date from the Middle Ages, as well as with the holiday virtues of a sea-oriented location. The coastal areas are regions where tourism professionals are working tirelessly to assure a safe and hospitable climate for vacationers, leaving the horrors of the wars of independence as part of a tragic recent past. Always popular with Europeans, the region looked first to its neighbors for the reintroduction of its coastal resorts.

Most of the companies mentioned elsewhere in this chapter, for their assistance for travel in Slovenia, are active with travel to and around neighboring parts of Croatia. In addition, there are several attractive vacation programs offered through British and European tour companies. One company with comprehensive programs in Slovenia and Croatia is **Phoenix Holidays Ltd.** *(INA House, 210 Shepherds Bush Rd., Hammersmith, London W6 7NL, United Kingdom; country code 44 plus:* ☎ *71+371.66.00, FAX 71+371.11.19)*. North American travelers can join Phoenix plans upon arrival in London. Each town has its own tourism office, with contacts given in parentheses when mentioned below. One domestic tour company with facilities in several tourism centers around the coast is **Istriaturist** *(POB 54, C-51440 Poreč;* ☎ *531+364.44, FAX 531+341.18)*.

Istria, a large arrowhead of land pointing into the Adriatic sea, is easily enjoyed as part of a visit to western Slovenia or eastern Italy. The peninsula, reached from a point just south of Trieste or Portorož or even from Postojna or Ljubljana, has dozens of coastal villages with important Roman ruins and medieval buildings. The coastal fringe of one-time fishing villages is worth exploring at a leisurely pace, allowing time to pause at places that appeal. Some villages are being developed for tourism but many have been spared the ugly, boxy, gray buildings that socialism inspired and remain with their original medieval aspect intact.

AUTHOR'S OBSERVATION

Although Croatia welcomed hordes of refugees during the most difficult days of the war, most people have been settled either inland or elsewhere in Croatia; most of those that remain in the resort areas are there with jobs.

Most of the fascinating places to visit—and stay—are along the coast, in walled towns that have grown from early Roman settlements, on sites known before the time of Christ or on the offshore islands, easily reached by boat services.

BRIJUNI

Brijuni *(National Park Brijuni, C-52214 Brijuini-Hrvatska;* ☎ *52+224.55, FAX 52+447.42),* known as **Brioni** to most English-speaking folks, was famous as one of the special havens for Jozip Broz Tito, the illustrious and all-powerful ruler of Yugoslavia for much of its history since World War II. Designated as a **National Park**, the archipelago is actually 14 small islands, northwest of Pula, and reached by boat from **Fažana**, across a narrow channel. Praised for its mild climate, as well as for its 250 bird species and the close to 700 species of plant life, the area is a popular vacation area made exclusive by its island status.

LODGING: In addition to the campgrounds, there are comfortable (not lavish) hotels, some of which have been used for high-powered secret meetings during the Tito years. The **Neptun** *(85 rooms;* ☎ *52+52.51.00, FAX 52+421.10)* is one large hotel with all modern conveniences and a decor that hints of former times. The **Karmen** *(45 rooms;* ☎ *52+52.54.00, FAX 52+421.10),* its neighbor, has slightly more atmosphere, partly due to its smaller size. Both hotels are boxy, with rooms furnished with the basics, in 1950s style. Views and the natural park are the main reasons for staying overnight at either place. In addition to these two, there are some smaller hotels, called villas, with as many as 25 rooms and a few very basic lodgings.

NOVIGRAD

Novigrad *(*☎ *531+514.66)* linked to the mainland only since the 18th century, has been noted in official records since about 450. The most intriguing part of town is, not surprisingly, the oldest part, now joined by a neck of land that leads to a dreary landscape of boxy, modern, multi-story buildings. Walls of the oldest part of town date from the 1200s; the pencil-point church steeple marks a prime starting point for strolling the narrow streets. The band of rocky shoreline that passes as a beach will not thrill people familiar with Caribbean beaches, but the marina offers an expanding fleet of yachts, many of which are for charter for day sails or longer

LODGING: The **Emonia** *(45 rooms;* ☎ *531+573.22; FAX 531+ 573.14)* is one modestly-appointed place to stay.

OPATIJA

Opatija *(C-51410;* ☎ *51+27.17.10, FAX 51+27.16.99)* is a gem. Worthy of an excursion for its own merits, the town's riviera runs for some 25 km along Istria's eastern coast. Famous among the European world's pace-setting travelers in the mid-1800s, Opatija's mild climate and beguiling scenery lured A.P. Chekhov, Gustav Mahler, Isadora Duncan and various royalty to the elegant hotels and seaside promenades during the fashionable winter seasons when the mild semitropical climate was most appreciated.

Even today, the elegance enjoyed by past generations can be felt, not necessarily in the lifestyle, but in some of the surroundings. Appealing palacios line the waterfront, where restaurants, hotels and a few shops claim space. The **Bay of Kvarner** is a playground for yachts and smaller boats, many of which are available for charter excursions. Horseback riding is possible on the flanks of the **Učka mountain** or in the other inland areas and a journey to Venezia (Venice) can be easily arranged.

LODGING: Because it is a popular touring base, the town has dozens of places to stay. The **Kvarner-Amalia** *(95 rooms;* ☎ *51+27.12.33, FAX 51+27.12.02)* is modern, conveniently located and reasonably comfortable. The huge **Ambassador** *(325 rooms;* ☎ *51+27.12.11, FAX 51+27.17.22)* needs tour groups to survive (or be lively), but its rooms are standard, some are viewful and all have modern comforts.

POREČ

Poreč **(Turistička Zajednica Općine,** *Pionirska 1, C-51440 Poreč;* ☎ *531+35.11.31, FAX 531+35.13.31),* at a midpoint on the western coast of the Istrian peninsula, is the name of the town as well as of the riviera that stretches between the Mirna river and the Limfjord. Mentioned in travel guidebooks used by steamship passengers in the mid-1800s, Poreč was also noted in writings of the 16th century for its pleasant location, historic buildings and appealing climate. At the end of the 19th century, when the town was the capital of the region of Istria and a significant part of the Austro-Hungarian empire, important people of the time came to Poreč for holidays. The first modern hotel—the Riviera—was opened in 1910, and prior to the first World War, the town had a total of six hotels with less than 200 rooms. The building boom that is evident these days began in 1957, but was brought to an abrupt halt with the domestic wars that surrounded the division of Yugoslavia which began in 1991.

The nearby islet of **Sv. Nikola**, a prized resort area, is easily reached by boat. Not only is its long shoreline flecked with comfortable hotels, but the historic center of town is marked by the monumental **Basilica Euphrasiana**, where classical and other concerts are presented year round.

The harbor at Poreč is busy, not only with commercial fishing and other boats, but also for recreational boating, especially sailing to nearby islands and along the coast. Italy's Venezia (Venice) is a 2-hour hydrofoil ride from the harbor, making it an easy (and popular) day trip.

LODGING: Although the modern hotels share none of the classic style of the earlier hotels, there are hundreds of places to stay. The holiday village that is the trademark of socialist investments in tourism, wherein self-contained places offer "everything" in a style first advertised by the post-war Club Méditerranée, is popular along the Poreč riviera. Areas are set aside for camping, as well as for apartments and what's known locally as "villa," which is a small hotel that might have once been a private home.

Huge resort hotels, some of them with reasonably interesting architecture, mark the coastline. All are used by tours of German, Italian and British travelers, who flocked here prior to the break up of Yugoslavia and are returning once again. My top choice among the dozens of places to stay is the time-honored **Riviera** *(50 rooms;* ☎ *531+35.14.22)* where history speaks. Although attempts at "modernization" have masked some of its original charm, the hotel's location—near the oldest part of town, on the harbor—gives it added appeal. Other related places nearby, with shared management and the style of turn-of-the-century villas, are the **Depandanca Jadran** *(22 rooms;* ☎ *531+35.14.22)* and the **Parentino** *(10 rooms;* ☎ *531+35.14.22).* All are open from April through October, when their harbor-front cafés are favored lingering places. (The balconied rooms overlooking the harbor are the best situated.)

PULA

Pula *(C-52000;* ☎ *52+226.62)* is one of Croatia's prized historic sites. Its amazing well-preserved Roman theater gives an indication of the sophisticated culture that thrived in the earliest years in communities south of the Alps. The town's buildings were the inspiration for many buildings in Italy's Venice and other cities to its north. Illyrians settled in the neighborhood of the castle in the 5th century B.C., to be followed by the Romans. Legends of earlier times link Jason and Medea to Pula in the adventures of the Argonauts. Capable of holding 32,000 spectators and wrapped in a 102-foot wall, the theater was coveted by Venetian senators who voted (in 1583) to dismantle it for reconstruction in the Italian city. The plan was foiled by Gabriele Emo, who is honored with a plaque on one of the towers facing the sea.

Today the theater is the site of a summer festival of the arts, with events taking place through the warm-weather months.

ROVINJ

Rovinj *(C-52210)*, with its trademark baroque **Church of St. Euphemie** capping a hill in the center of a net of medieval buildings, is a favorite touring goal. Although it can be crowded with day trippers who arrive on tour buses and cars, an overnight stay gives the reward of stepping back into the 13th century as you wander through the narrow lanes at twilight or dawn. This remarkable town is a knot of medieval buildings covering a bulge of land that has recently been embroidered to the coast by well-appointed marinas. Fishing boats nestle with sleek yachts, confirming the mixture of work and play that is the lifestyle of the town. **Katarina** and **Red Island**, not far offshore, are linked by boats.

Limfjord, just south of Vsrar, is marked by the ruins of a **Benedictyine abbey** and its **Wildlife Preserve**.

SPORTS

The Alpine area of Slovenia is well known to neighboring Germans and French and some other Europeans who have been introduced to the area through battles and have come to love it for its pastoral charms and modest prices as well as for the challenges offered by the mountains. The region is little known to most North Americans, however. There are only a few areas where sports facilities are comparable to those found in neighboring Alpine countries, namely in the **Triglav National Park**, around Lake Bled and in the area north of Ljubljana, around Kranjska Gora, a respected area for winter sports.

Slovenia has long been treasured by people in search of pastoral pleasures. It claims the southeastern Alpine foothills, an area known as the Dinaric Alps, which begins as a wedge between Italy's Trieste and Ljubljana, Slovenia's capital, and stretches to the southeast. Many communities share qualities of the bordering regions of southwestern Austria and northeastern Italy. Facilities for specific sports are beginning to be organized, with special offices in charge of arranging permits and other assistance. The natural attributes of the area are especially appealing for adventuresome travelers. Wise Europeans, especially Germans, have enjoyed hunting, fishing and hiking in the area for centuries. Bohinjsko Jezero (Lake Bohinj), not far from Bled, is easily enjoyed from the small village of Bohinjska Bistrica, a pleasant base for walks to the Savica Falls as well as around lovely lakes. The rural areas of Slovenia are best traveled by car and/or foot; the bus and train service touches only the largest towns.

In the region, detailed information is available through the **Turistični In-formacijski Biro** *(Slovenska 35, Ljubljana, SL-61000 Slovenija;* ☎ *61+22.42.22, FAX 61+22.21.15).* **Albatros Tours** *(Ribenska 2, SL-64260 Bled; FAX 64+763.19)* or **Janko Humar** *(Ribcev 1a2 50, SL 64265 Bahinjsko Jezera;* ☎ *64+72.34.41, FAX 64+72.34.46).*

For specific sports, refer to the headings below.

BICYCLING

One popular resort ride is around Blejsko Jezero (Lake Bled), perhaps with a pause at an inn on the far side. Some hotels rent bikes and Bled's tourist office can give you names of other sources. Other areas where hotels have bikes for rent are Bohinjsko Jezero (Lake Bohinj) and Bovec to ride along the Soca river, high in the montains at Kranjska Gora and Lipica, better known for its Lipizzaner horse farm.

CANOEING/KAYAKING

Although it may be difficult to rent a canoe or kayak, the tourist offices in Ljubljana, Bovec, Kranj and other towns can help with information about local groups that welcome visitors on their outings. The best rivers for the sport are the Soca, in the northwest from Bovec along to Tolmis; the Kokra, northeast of Kranj; and around Bled. Enthusiasts claim that the Soca is one of the best areas in Europe for kayaking and none can deny that its milky turquoise water is spectacular. Check with Swiss-based **Eurotrek** *(Malzstrasse 17, Case Postale, CH-8036 Zürich;* ☎ *country code 41 plus 48+02.14.35)* for details on their expeditions. They arrange adventure holidays in Slovenia for small groups, reaching the area by bus from Villach, to go canoeing along the river Sava Bohinjka and the Soca, with trains for transportation between major starting points. Some of the activities on a recent 10-day holiday were in the Triglav National Park and around Bled. (Speaking French and/or German will be useful on Eurotrek journeys, since most of the participants are Europeans.)

FISHING

Still natural, with little or no pollution, the mountain rivers of Slovenia are full of fish. Officials boast about the possibility to fish in "crystal clean alpine rivers, fabulous chalk streams, deep lakes, small brooks flowing through meadows and wide rivers running through plains." Avid anglers should bring waders, rod and other equipment, at least until things improve economically and independent rental shops can thrive in the new spirit that allows private ventures. Residents tout the pleasures of areas around Bohinj, in the Sava river and in the lake, as well as along the Soca river. Ask the tourist office for a brochure about fishing.

GOLF

There's an 18-hole course near Bled, designed by David Haradine and well maintained. Clubs can be rented, but scratch golfers should be specific with their questions. Consider bringing golf clubs if you plan to stay in Bled for a while. There are also golf facilities at Lipica.

HANG GLIDING/SOARING

Slovenians seem fearless! They soar from the peaks of Triglav mountain into "the beyond." In anticipation of landing on snow fields, some experts soar with skis. One place with a soaring center is Smarna Gora, about 12 miles from Ljubljana. Contact the Ljubljana tourist office for other sources in the area. For winter sports, Slovenians enjoy the ski-flight competitions that are held each year in Planica.

HIKING

The sport is popular with most Yugoslavs, as well as with people from the neighboring Alpine areas. One lovely hike is from Bohinjsko Jezero (Lake Bohinj), near Bled, past the Savica Falls up to Crno Jezero (Black Lake). Another is what's been referred to as the "hidden valley," Logarska Dolina, which is reached from Celje or Ljubljana. North of Ljubljana, there are many areas with marked paths. The region of the Kamniske Alpe, known as the Kamnik Alp in German or the Karnack Alps in English, is popular with those who know the area well and Triglav National Park is a prized area. (See "Mountaineering/Climbing.")

HORSEBACK RIDING

The opportunity to ride one of the Lipica horses, made famous by the highly disciplined horses that perform in Wien (Vienna), Austria, is unique. Austrian Archduke Karl founded this farm for the special horses in 1530, when the territory was part of the Austro-Hungarian Empire. Reserve a room at one of the hotels on the grounds if you want several days of riding or lessons. Bring your own boots, hat, breeches and riding attire. Most people—and especially visitors—tend to wear the accepted uniform out of respect for the sport. For further information, contact the **Kobilarna Lipica** (*Sezana, SL-66210 Slovenia*).

HUNTING/SHOOTING

Inquire in Lipica about riding to hounds; fox hunts are scheduled. For nonhorsemen, hunting clubs welcome visitors, but a common spoken language may be a challenge for visitors who do not speak Slovene, Croatian or at least some German. The Slovene Tourist Association in Ljubljana can give you on-the-spot assistance, but allow several days to organize your plans. Bled is one area where shooting is popular in season, but the best-known area is one beloved by Tito, in the region around Kamnik. Another is between the Hungarian and Austrian borders. Deer, pheasant, and rabbits are the main prey, but brown bear, mouflon and wild boar are hunted in the Kiprivnica hunting grounds, where the Mercator company takes its guests. For details, contact **Mercator Turist** (*Tolstojeva 63, Ljubljana, SL-6100 Slovenia*). Check, also, with **Kompas** (*Prazakova 4;* ☎ *61+32.77.61*) and **Globtur** (*Wolfova 1;* ☎ *61+248.41*), both in Ljubljana.

MOUNTAINEERING/CLIMBING

The sport is enjoyed by experts. The Triglav, at 9394 feet, is the country's highest peak. Its sheer north face is challenging for rock-climbers, but the entire national park and its surroundings offer many demanding climbs. One noted hike is from Vrata to the top of Triglav, overnighting at mountain huts. The Slovenian mountain clubs maintain mountain huts, which have both dormitory-style and semiprivate rooms. Be sure to get the detailed maps available through the mountain clubs. Experienced climbers should contact **Planinska Zveza Slovenije** *(Mountain Association of Slovenia, Dvorzakova 9, Ljubljana, SL-61000 Slovenia;* ☎ *61+31.25.53)* and/or **Planisko Drustva Ljubljana, Matica** *(Mountain Club, Miklosiceva 17, Ljubljana, SL-61000 Slovenia).* (See also "Hiking.")

RIVER RAFTING

Major rivers in Alpine Slovenia are the Soca between Bovec and Tolmin and the Sava between Bohinj and Bled. (The Mura and the Drava, a branch of the Danube that flows near Maribor, in the eastern sector, have hydroelectric plants that mar their beauty.) *Rijeka* or *Reka* are words for "river" in Croatian and Slovene, respectively.

ROWING

There are boats for rent on the shores of Lake Bled. Here the traditional boats are a gondola style many will recognize as being similar to those of Venezia (Venice). European rowing championships are held on the lake of Bled from May through October. Near Maribor, the Drava reservoir is a watersport complex in a style widely known in Europe. The campsite has small boats for rent.

SAILING

The Adriatic Sea is a challenging sailing area, with harbors best known to European sportsfolk. Boats can be chartered for day or longer sails out of Portorož and Piran, on the Zaliv (Gulf) of Trieste. Plans are best made on the spot, with help from your hotel or the local tourism officials, or by visiting the Yacht Club at the marina. Piran is home port for commercial fishing boats, as well as for motor boats and a few sailing craft. Among the U.S. firms with yachts for charter in the region are **Le Boat** *(Box E, Maywood, NJ 07607;* ☎ *201+342-1838 or 800+922-0291; FAX 201+342-7498)* and **The Moorings** *(#402, 1305 U.S. 19 South, Clearwater, FL 33546;* ☎ *813+535-1446 or 800+535-7289; FAX 813+530-9747).* When the political situation has cooled and the climate is suitable for pleasure boating, these firms will be ready to set up cruising holidays along the coast, stretching south from the areas of Slovenia covered in this book.

SKIING

On the flanks of the Karavanke mountains and the Julian Alps in the northern part of the country, there are several ski resorts. Although they may lack the jet-set chic of some of the best known Austrian, Swiss and Italian resorts, the Slovenia resorts offer well-maintained trails and places to stay that charge a fraction of the cost of holidays at the oft-touted resorts. Kranjska Gora is the prized area for Slovenia. Not only are lifts in reasonably good condition, but trails are well maintained and there are several comfortable places to stay. In addition, there are facilities at Krvavec, northeast of Kranj; Vogel and Kobla, southwest of Bled and Bohinj; and Kanin, near the Italian border. Bled can be used as a base, for day skiing at places such as Pokljuka, Zatrnik and Straza. Summer skiing is strictly for the true athlete and nature-lover; the snow-covered slopes are reached by climbing, with the glacier of the Skuta mountain one area for the sport. Most snow slopes are pockets on the shady side of the Alps and difficult to reach. You'll have to bring your own equipment. The mountain associations (see "Mountaineering/Climbing,") can provide information, maps and sometimes companions. The **Planinska Zveza Slovenije** *(Slovene Alpine Association, Dvorzakova 9, 61000 Ljubljana;* ☎ *61+31.25.53)* is one source for details.

SPAS

The tourist office has a special booklet about spa facilities. Among the most interesting are the one at Dobrna, not far from Celje, west of Maribor and east of Ljubljana. It claims a spectacular site at the foot of Mount Paski Kozjak. Known since the 16th century, Dobrna specializes in sports-related injuries. Radenci, near the Mura river banks, in the niche that marks the border with Austria and Hungary, also specializes in sports.

SWIMMING

Resort hotels in Bled and Portorož have swimming pools, but it is the spas there and elsewhere in Slovenia that get most attention from knowledgeable European travelers. As is the custom in most European countries, topless sunbathing is acceptable on Yugoslav beaches.

TENNIS

There are well-maintained courts at the resort centers, especially at Bled and Portorož and at several of the spas, as well as in the capital, Ljubljana. If tennis is crucial for your holiday happiness, be sure to ask about the surface of the courts, the availability of rental equipment, the on-the-spot purchase of tennis balls (it's wise to bring a few cans of your own) and the facilities offered by the tennis pro.

WALKING/TREKKING

One of the joys of Slovenia is that a lot of the landscape is undeveloped. It is possible to walk almost everywhere, but it's wise (and courteous) to ask questions at the local or regional tourist office so that you do not trespass on a farmer's lands. For those comfortable speaking at least German or Italian, staying in some of the farmhouse accommodations gives entree to the world of rural living. Insofar as wildflowers are concerned, with a good flower guidebook in hand, even hobby-botanists can have a wonderful time. Don't count on highly organized walks unless you sign on with a group with leader from outside the country.

WATERSKIING

The waterfront at Portorož, on the Zaliv (Gulf of Trieste), is dotted wiith several entrepreneurs who offer waterskiing, as well as pedal boats and other waterborne activities.

WINDSURFING/BOARDSAILING

Count on finding plenty of activity in the Adriatic Sea at coastal resorts such as Portorož, as well as at some of the resort lakes. Check with the local tourist office or through your hotel if the sport is crucial to your holiday happiness.

TREASURES AND TRIFLES

When you see something you want, buy it. Don't count on finding similar items in several shops—or in another town. You can expect to find the largest selection in the resort areas, where items are made and displayed for tourists. Handcrafted items of high quality are difficult to find, but a few inquiries can sometimes lead to craftsmen who sell from their workshops.

Among frequently seen items are peppermills and pottery, smock dresses with embroidery and slippers with leather soles and knitted tops. Many women make lovely lace in traditional patterns. Some can make items to order, but be sure to bring measurements (in meters) and designs, if you want a particular pattern. For names of lacemakers, visit the tourist office and ask at your hotel. Often the name is that of the person's mother, sister, or aunt.

Slovenians are justifiably proud of their crystal, most of which is cut in elaborate patterns. There are selections of glasses, bowls, plates and other items at the resort area shops as well as in the cities.

Sport clothes that have been designed and made in Beograd (Belgrade) are fashionable and well priced. Leather jackets, skirts and other items are good quality, but prices have risen in recent years to keep pace with the expectations of affluent visitors. Bargains are hard to find.

String-knit dresses, skirts and shirts have been popular in recent seasons. Almira is one label that stands for quality. Fur-lined slippers are also popular.

In Ljubljana, the open market on the Cathedral Square is one of the best spots to find local handcrafts and housewares, as well as for photographing flower and produce stalls. There are some department stores—the art-nouveau **Centramerkur department store** is one—around town, but the merchandise is geared to local needs and of minor interest to most visitors from western countries. Look for the **Dom** shops around town. There's one facing the market square. Near the Shoemaker bridge on the cobbled way from the Town Hall, the **Salon Pletenina** has fashionable, colorful dresses. **Elmira**, underground near the market, also has fashionable dresses.

ADDITIONAL INFORMATION SOURCES

In addition to the central tourism office in Ljubljana and in New York City (see "Information Sources"), there are some firms in the United States that specialize in travel to Slovenia.

Four to contact are:

Atlas Travel, *60 East 42nd St., New York, NY 10165;* ☎ *212+697-6767, FAX 212+697-7678.*

Kollander World Travel, *971 East 185th St., Cleveland, OH 44119;* ☎ *216+692-1000 or 800+800-5981; FAX 216+692-1831.*

Kompas Travel, *2826 East Commercial Blvd., Ft. Lauderdale, FL 33308;* ☎ *305+771-9200 or 800+233-6422; FAX 305+771-9841.*

Sterling Tours, *#105E, 1106 Clayton Lane, Austin, TX 78723;* ☎ *512+467-1707 or 800+367-2328; FAX 512+467-1707.*

SWITZERLAND

Luzern, Switzerland

The meal they brought us—*salad melée* and *filet des pêrches*—was picture perfect, as was the lakeside setting. The day was sunny and warm; the bottle of white wine was crisp and cool. It was a perfect foil, especially since it came from the slopes in sight from our room. The occasion was serendipitous; it was serene and simple—and simply perfect.

But situations in Switzerland are like that. Vignettes to pull from the memory shelf at odd hours of the day or night, whenever and wherever a moment allows.

There are times when the bone-chilling cold of a freezing-drizzle on a winter day drove me from a cobbled street into the nearest *Stübli*, where—even when I knew none of the others—a cozy warm welcome wrapped around me. Even when I did not share the language, the universal "language" of smiles, looks and gestures sufficed to put hot coffee on the table while I watched what others were eating so I could make my choice by pointing to theirs.

At other times, with several friends, we walked and hiked, high in the mountains. Renegade patches of snow crunched under foot in some places; wildflowers proudly peeked from terrain that looked too bleak to bear such beautiful blooms in others. And, although niblets of chocolate never tasted better that when they were pulled from a pocket to be shared at a pause in our walk, they paled when confronted with the hearty luncheon served in an Alpine chalet, whose owners boldly built in what appeared to be a desolate mountain niche. The extraordinary achievement of creating such memorable meals in isolated specks buttoned onto steep mountain sides never ceases to amaze me. It's one of the many marvels of mountain life.

And there are mountain memories like the ones that come from the time, several years ago when my nephews and I tucked ourselves into one of my favorite Alpine places, an inn reached by walking through woods that are perfumed by the pines and other plants that thrive along the path. We stayed in a wonderful wood-walled bedroom, with fluffy duvets on each of our beds and red-checked curtains at windows that framed an astounding Alpine view. We were hiking mountain trails, enjoying exceptional meals and living in Switzerland the way it's possible for visitors to do when they break from the well-trod tourist routes and spend leisurely days in small villages.

But all generations can enjoy this country. On another memorable occasion, with my parents on my mother's birthday, we shared a bottle of special wine, greeted by the shy (but approving) smiles of those around us, as we all rode the train along the scenic route that stretches up and out from Montreux to pause at Zweisimmen, before sashaying strategically down to the lakeside town of Spiez. We were heading for Interlaken, where lakeboat journeys and train rides would take us back to Spiez to enjoy its castle and lakeside cafés, as well as to special sights in other lovely villages around the Thunersee.

Switzerland is made for memories. Any of us who have been to the country have a fortune of them.

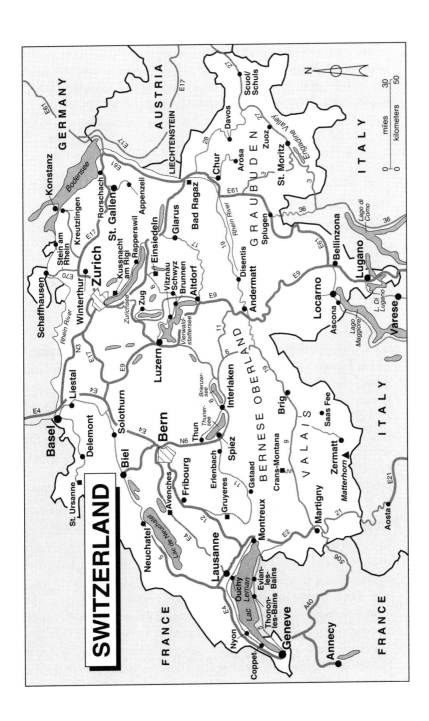

SWITZERLAND

COUNTRY IN CAPSULE

Confederatio Helvetica is Switzerland, the Confederation of the Helvetian tribes, whose descendants joined together to form an eternal pact on August 1, 1291. Today's Switzerland occupies 15,941 square miles, three-quarters of which is useful for agriculture or forestry. The country is about half the size of the state of Maine or twice the size of New Jersey, but what it may lack in border-to-border measure, it more than makes up for in vertical distance—and in scenery. Since 60% of the country is Alpine and the rest of the country is easily reached from and affected by the Alpine areas, this chapter includes observations about the entire country.

Graubünden (in German) claims southeastern Switzerland. The canton, or state, is also known as Grisons (French) and Grigioni (Italian). This largest canton includes well-known ski areas such as Davos, St. Moritz, Klosters, Arosa, Flims, Lenzerheide and Pontresina, as well as many little-known villages, especially those of the tradition-rich Engadine valley, where townspeople often wear their ancestral costumes for festival days. Taking its name from the Inn river, which runs through Innsbruck, Austria, to join the Danube and is known as the "En" in the region's unique Romansch language, the valley has two parts: Oberengadin (Upper Engadine) and Unterengadin (Lower Engadine). The far-eastern portion of Graubünden pokes into Italy, where Müstair, with its Catholic convent dating from the 9th century, has had year-round access to the rest of Switzerland only in this century. The neighboring town, Santa Maria, is where the Protestant Reformation was halted on its march south. The rugged National Park of Switzerland, near Zernez, is at the knuckle of this finger of land.

Ostschweiz, to German-speaking folks, is eastern Switzerland, also known as Suisse orientale to those speaking French and Svizzera orientale to those whose language is Italian. The region includes the cantons of Appenzell, St. Gallen, Schaffhausen, Thurgau and Glarus. The Rhein river—and the Bodensee (Lake Constance) that grows from it—made this area a major trading route in the Middle Ages. The rolling hills—both the areas around Schaffhausen and around Appenzell and St. Gallen to the east—are prized farming lands that become a patchwork of meadows, wildflowers and forests in spring, summer and fall, and are increasingly popular for cross-country skiing in winter. Swiss brown-gray cows graze happily in the meadows while cablecars stretch to impressive peaks such as Säntis and Hoher Kasten.

The canton of **Zürich** is much more than its capital, which is much more than the prosperous banking and commercial city that brings it worldwide fame. Hidden in the heart of Zürich is its Altstadt, the medieval city center that thrives today within a few steps of the chic and sophisticated Bahnhofstrasse. The canton of Zürich includes the vineyard-draped slopes of its Zürichsee, the lovely lake that sprouts sailboats as soon as the weather warms, as well as surrounding villages that thrive, quietly, in the orbit of the busy city.

Central Switzerland is the country's heartland, spreading from the shores of the Vierwaldstättersee, the lake of the four forest cantons that joined in the 13th and 14th centuries. Luzern is probably the best-known town, but there are several lovely villages, many of which are rural and quiet while others, especially the mountain areas, have become sports' resorts. In many villages, medieval buildings are testimony to a location on an early trading route through the mountains between northern Europe and Italy.

Northwestern Switzerland flares from its international city of Basel, a pivot point for three countries (Switzerland, France, and Germany). Supported by an affluent community and the world's major chemical companies, Basel is a city of museums and sophisticated cultural events. There is history along the Rhein, at the Roman ruins at Augst and the mineral springs that created the spa at Rheinfelden, as well as at Solothurn, which boasts St. Ursen Cathedral, the only Italian baroque building in Switzerland.

Bern and the **Bernese Oberland** are a microcosm of the best of Switzerland, with medieval buildings that date from 1191 and beautiful mountain scenery known from Interlaken ("between the lakes"), with the Thunersee to the west and the Brienzersee to the east. Here's where you'll find the Jungfrau, the Mönch, and the Eiger, as well as many other astounding peaks that lure hikers in summer and skiers in winter months. But the region also benefits from the Emmental, the valley of the Emmen river that is a lake-marked area of rolling hills and vast farmlands where cows produce the milk for the famed Emmenthaler cheese, known the world over as "Swiss cheese."

Fribourg, **Neuchâtel**, and the **Jura** region comprise a wedge that stretches west of mid-country to the northern border, where the Swiss Jura region mingles with the French. Fiercely independent and primarily French-speaking, Fribourg and Neuchâtel have been university towns since the Middle Ages. Many of their buildings, and those in neighboring villages, date from the 13th and 14th centuries, giving them a special atmosphere. A Celtic site at La Tène, on Lac de Neuchâtel, dates from the 5th century B.C.

Genève takes its cue from the United Nations and the dozens of multinational companies based here and its quality of life from its French-shared lake and the mountains of canton **Vaud** that have become playgrounds for the world's wealthy. Cosmopolitan and effectively French-Swiss, the region around Lac Léman, the lake of Genève, lives "the good life."

The **Valais**, where mountain tunnels and passes make links with France and Italy, takes its atmosphere from the Alps that rise impressively from the Rhône valley floor. Known to traders since the Bronze Age, the area is outdoor country with weathered wood chalets standing on stone foundations and cog-railways, modern lifts and cablecars stretching to awesome heights. This is the region of Zermatt, Saas Fee, Crans-Montana and dozens of other resorts.

Ticino is Italian Switzerland, where palm trees grow along the shores of lago di Lugano and lago Maggiore, and the lifestyle thrives on the sunny side of the Alps. Backed by high peaks, the Ticino looks south to Italy, for lifestyle, recipes and language, although its systems and currency are certainly Swiss. This is a region where mountainside dwellings are built from the gray-granite rocks, and flowers—and family-owned trattorias—provide bright spots for daily living.

HISTORIC HIGHLIGHTS

Relics from the Bronze Age indicate very early settlements. Prehistoric man is known to have lived in La Tène, at Chur, and near Solothurn, where early records tell of travels of Celtic tribes, later called Gauls, from the east, and of the Helvetti, who migrated through the flatlands between the Jura mountains and the Alps, around Genève's Lac Léman (Lake of Geneva).

Julius Caesar and his Romans swept through and around these lands as they sparred with the Gauls. Roman ruins can be seen in Genève, on its lakeshores at Bosceaz, and at Augst, a few minutes' drive or a short train ride from Basel. Avenches, south of Lac de Neuchâtel, was a Celtic town before it was a thriving Roman community known as Aventicum. The Alemanni, a Germanic tribe, made inroads near what is now the German border, and Burgundians, from what is now France, also claimed part of today's Switzerland.

When Charlemagne's empire dissolved in the 9th century, barons, lords and other large landholders began to grab the land for themselves and the fractionalization of Switzerland began. Local skirmishes between those with French or German allegiance continued near the borders for several hundred years.

The core of the country is near Schwyz, where representatives of the first three cantons (Uri, Schwyz and Unterwalden (which has grown to become Nidwalden and Obwalden) formed the perpetual alliance against the Habsburgs. Luzern, also threatened by Habsburg domination, joined the Confederation in 1332, making the four forest cantons that give the name to the Vierwaldstättersee, known better to English-speaking people as the lake of Lucerne.

Other cantons joined in subsequent years: Zürich in 1351, Glarus and Zug in 1352, Bern in 1353, Fribourg and Solothurn in 1481, Basel and Schaffhausen in 1501, and Appenzell in 1513, for a total of 13 cantons.

By the 16th century, the Swiss realized their location at the crossroads of Europe left them vulnerable to invasion by the world's hordes, who crisscrossed through Alpine passes. Neutrality was the route they chose. The unified cantons proclaimed that they would allow no further expansion, would wage no wars, and would, in fact, send their well-trained soldiers to fight on behalf of other causes, under their own banner and in their own uniforms. Swiss mercenaries have served in other nations since then, and military service is still compulsory for all males over the age of 18. The Swiss army can be quickly mobilized.

The original cantons comprised the boundaries of Switzerland until the early 1800s, when Napoleon restored the feudal system, adding the cantons of St. Gallen, Graubünden, Aargau, Thurgau, Ticino and Vaud, at the French border. This number held until Napoleon's fall from power and the Habsburg establishment of three new cantons—Valais, Neuchâtel and Genève in 1815. The most recent canton is the Jura, established in 1979 and composed of portions of the Jura mountain area that had been part of other cantons, especially of Bern.

The total of 26 cantons includes both parts of the two-part cantons of Unterwalden, Basel, and Appenzell.

POLITICAL PICTURE

Although the country has been a democracy since 1291, the present system took cues from the United States when, following a short civil war in 1848, the Swiss drew up a new federal constitution and Bern became the federal capital. Lausanne is the legislative capital and Zürich is the banking capital. Each canton operates as an independent republic with control over its educational system, public health, police, taxes and internal laws. Representatives to the States Council are roughly equivalent to U.S. Senators, while the National Council is similar to the U.S. House of Representatives. The Federal Council is appointed every year at the first meeting in December. It elects the president and vice president each year. Both men carry out their duties with little fanfare. The council's seven members are jointly responsible for the country's international role and overall government. Each canton has its capital, which is the home for the cantonal government, and its individual constitution, with independent legislative and executive bodies, much as is the case for the United States. Swiss citizenship is, in reality, citizenship in one of the communities.

LIFESTYLE

What is "Swiss"? Some think of the Swiss as "gray people," not easily defined, not overly enthusiastic or exciting or inventive. Not so. There is a Swiss reserve not unlike that of a New Englander in the U.S., but the Swiss don't talk about themselves much. Some say they don't have to: Quality speaks for itself. I've traveled countless miles in this country, confident in the knowledge that no matter where I stay, the place will be clean, the food good, the hospitality dependable, and—when I choose well—the traditions secure. Spontaneity may not be a Swiss trait, but dependability certainly is. Things work in this country and that's important for travelers. The Swiss go about their work—and their play—quietly, with an inner confidence that comes from living off the land. They have created their country and their wealth from their farms and, more recently, from the no-nonsense business acumen that seems to come naturally. As far as dress is concerned, conservative is the custom. Although you'll see a sprinkling of shocking colors on the mountainsides, on both skiers and hikers, the basic daily wear in cities is more likely nature's colors: beige, black, brown and gray.

AUTHOR'S OBSERVATION

The Swiss are the ones who taught me how to travel unencumbered. Watch them as they board trains and arrive in Alpine resorts. Seldom do they have more than one small suitcase, although they always seem appropriately dressed. Muted dark colors may seem boring, but they travel well and can go anywhere. Women can add some zip with a brightly colored scarf; men can concentrate on their neckties.

NATURAL SURROUNDINGS

Switzerland's landscape is, quite simply, spectacular, with 20 percent of the Alps within its borders. The valleys of the Rhône and the upper Rhein cut across the country, while the valleys of the Reuss and the Ticino seem to cut the mountains into northeastern, northwestern and southern ranges. The mountains are formed of granite and crystalline slate that appear as building materials as well as throughout the landscape, especially at the highest elevations, when they are no longer clothed with forests. Valleys, terraces, passes and pastures respond to the effects of ice-age glaciers, some still evident and a few popular for year-round skiing. Although most of the Alpine region seems like a national park, the official Swiss National Park stretches over acres of eastern Switzerland, with its headquarters in Zernez and walking paths threading much of the terrain.

For bird-watchers, the extremes in landscape, from lakes to high Alps and both northern and southern slopes, gives the country unique qualities. The Swiss National Park is one good area for birding, but there are many different species in the southern Ticino and along the shores of the Bodensee (Lake Constance), in the northeast. Further information about birding is available through the *Vogelwarte* in Sempach, on the Semperachersee, about 20 minutes northwest of Luzern.

PRACTICAL FACTS ABOUT SWITZERLAND

Count on orderly procedures everywhere. In spite of the fact that the southern Ticino canton benefits from a carefree Italian influence, its systems are securely Swiss.

INFORMATION SOURCES

Schweizerische Verkehrszentrale, the Central Tourist Office of Switzerland, is at *Bellariastrasse 38, Postfach, CH-8027 Zürich,* ☎ *41+1+288.11.11, FAX 41+1+288.12.05.* In North America, contact the **Swiss National Tourist Office**, *#2930, 150 N. Michigan Ave., Chicago, IL 60601,* ☎ *312+630-5840, FAX 312+630-5848; #1570, 222 N. Sepulveda Blvd., El Segundo, CA 90245,* ☎ *310+335-5980, FAX 310+335-5982; 608 Fifth Ave., New York, NY 10020,* ☎ *212+757-5944, FAX 212+262-6116; #610, 154 University Ave., Toronto, Ontario M5H 3Y9 Canada,* ☎ *416+971-9734, FAX 416+971.64.25.* In England, the office is the **Swiss Centre**, *New Coventry St., London W1V 8EE England,* ☎ *44+71+73.41.921, FAX 44+71+437.45.77.*

Information is also available from the regional tourism offices listed at the end of this chapter and from the local tourism offices, whose address and telephone number follow in parenthesis when places are mentioned under the "Places Worth Finding" heading, below.

Throughout the chapter, some words and all place names are spelled as they are in Switzerland. For translation of foreign words, refer to the back-of-the-book glossary.

CASH, CURRENCY AND CREDIT CARDS

The Swiss unit of currency is the Swiss Franc, which is made up of 100 centimes. The one-Franc coin, about the size of a U.S. quarter, is worth about U.S.$.65 at presstime, which means that U.S.$1.00 buys about SFr 1.50. There are convenient exchange booths at both Genève and Zürich airports and at major railway stations. The service charges at banks vary with the bank and may result in a sizeable chunk from a travelers cheque. Always ask about the per check charge when you exchange travelers cheques; it may be wise to cash high denominations and fewer cheques, when the charge seems substantial.

Most banks can arrange for purchase of travelers cheques in Swiss Franc denominations, which means your exchange rate has been established at the time of purchase and needn't be considered again. One dependable U.S.-based source for buying Swiss Franc travelers cheques is **Reusch International** *(1350 Eye Street, W., Washington, DC 20005;* ☎ *202+408-1200 or 800+424-2923; FAX 202+408+1211).*

Although credit cards are more widely used than a few years ago, they are not always accepted at country inns and other places when you travel outside the cities. Always ask in advance so that you can arrange to get Swiss cash while you are in, or traveling through, a city where exchange offices are obvious.

AUTHOR'S OBSERVATION

Switzerland has never been known as an inexpensive country, but you get what you pay for. When you live the Swiss way—lunch in a tea room, one-plate meal service, table wines and country inns—prices are reasonable and the experience is exceptional.

COMMUNICATIONS

Every Swiss is multilingual. The official national languages are four: German, French, Italian and Romansch, the language of a portion of southeastern Switzerland, especially the Engadine valley (with a version also spoken in a neighbor Italian valley), which is a form of Ladin, similar to what English-speaking people know as Latin. Add to this official roster the fact that all areas and some villages, have their own dialects of Schweizer Deutsch (Swiss-German), making a verbal medley. One result of the several languages is efficient sign-posting, which reduces the need to speak—in any language. (Even when the common language is fragmented, basic comforts are easily found.)

Although many people on the well-traveled tourist routes speak some English, some of the best places have not been inundated with English-speaking travelers. You'll often be surrounded by local dialect and will certainly find most food offerings presented only in the local language. For carefree travel it's a good idea to become familiar with the German, French and perhaps Italian words for the major transportation aids, food suggestions and lodging necessities, as well as for place names.

AUTHOR'S OBSERVATION

Gruezi is a word to know. It's pronounced something like "curtsey" with a "g," but ask a Swiss to say the word for you and adopt it as a part of your own vocabulary. It means "hello," "good day," "hi," or whatever is an appropriate greeting in the German-speaking part of Switzerland. (Its equivalent in the French-speaking area is bonjour.) The word is Swiss-German, idiomatic and spoken in towns and cities when you enter a store or restaurant as well as high in the mountains when you're passing someone on a hiking or walking trail.

PTT, which stands for *Post, Telefon, Telegraf,* can be found in every city, town, or village, usually near the railroad or bus station. It indicates much more than a place to mail letters, although it is that also. At the PTT office there's always a telephone from which you can dial directly any number in the world, after you have notified the clerk at the dispensing window. When the call is completed, simply go to the window and pay. If you're looking up the U.S. in the telephone book, it helps to know that it's listed as *Vereinigte Staaten von Amerika,* the German name, in most telephone books, and as *Etats Unis* for the French-speaking area.

Within Switzerland, you can easily telephone the U.S. from any phone, for the cost of a local call, through AT&T's *USADirect* system, or similar systems of MCI and Sprint. The AT&T code to reach the U.S. operator is 155.00.11. If you are an AT&T card holder, you can charge the call to your designated phone. If you use the services of another international carrier, check with them for details on their direct dial international service. For more information in the U.S., prior to your travels, contact your long distance carrier.

AUTHOR'S OBSERVATION

Telephone numbers in this chapter are given for direct dial from the U.S., with the addition of the country code. When in Switzerland, you'll need to begin dialing out-of-town numbers with a "0."

To telephone Switzerland from the United States, simply dial an international access code plus 41 for the country code, followed by the city or town code and the number, which usually has six digits but may have five or seven.

Facsimile is well known and widely used in Switzerland, especially by hotels and other businesses. Equipment can be found in many PTT offices to send faxes as easily as telephoning.

DOCUMENTS AND OTHER PAPERS

You'll need to show your passport at passport control when you enter the country, but it may be difficult/impossible to get it stamped. Swiss immigration officials have dispensed with the entry and departure stamps; they look and nod.

MEDICAL FACILITIES

Krankenhaus is the word for hospital in German, and Switzerland's medical facilties are acknowledged to be among the best in the world. There are special clinics and treatment centers throughout the country, as well as first-class spas at places such as Baden, within a few minutes' train ride or drive from Zürich, and elsewhere in the country.

TRAVEL FACTS

Getting to and around Switzerland is a pleasure in these days of often chaotic travel. The Swiss public transportation network is comfortable, convenient and effective, whether you choose to travel on trains, buses, lake or river boats, or all manner of cablecar, cog railway, or other mountain conveyance.

ARRIVAL

Both Genève and Zürich have international airports that are among the most "user-friendly" in the world. Not only have the Swiss taken security and airplane service into account, but they have supplied entire "towns" of shops, both outside the check-in area and (with slightly better, apparently "duty-free" prices for popular items) inside the secured area, after passengers pass through immigration. Both airports have efficient train stations on site, making it easy to travel anywhere in Switzerland, and throughout the Alpine area and the rest of Europe.

AUTHOR'S OBSERVATION

If your travel plans are unstructured when you arrive in Switzerland and you're planning to roam on public transportation, make the information desk at the Swiss Federal Railways your first stop. Their personnel are the best in Europe at providing accurate, helpful facts in a pleasant and efficient manner. You can also buy rail tickets through them, but purchase is not a requirement for getting information.

Swissair, the country's flag carrier, repeatedly earns top honors for service, on-time performance and food. Among the many special features for travelers are the "building blocks" program that allows you to tailor elements to your own travel plans and a Fly-luggage system that allows for luggage check-through from your overseas check-in point to your ultimate Swiss destination, using rail services for Swiss delivery. For details, ask your travel agent or check with Swissair.

AUTHOR'S OBSERVATION

Switzerland has the world's best national transportation system. I have traveled countless miles by all available methods of public transportation. The system is carefree—once you master the basic methods—and is clean, safe, comfortable and pleasant.

Balair is Swissair's sibling. The Swiss-based airline operates as a charter service, with scheduled flights and in-flight services that are comparable to Swissair's coach service. Well known to wise European travelers, Balair is not widely promoted in North America, but your travel agent can get details or you can contact their office *(608 Fifth Ave., New York, NY 10020; ☎ 212+581-3411).* **TRAVAC** *(☎ 800+872-8800)* is a reliable ticket consolidator that uses Balair and other carriers for good-value tickets for departures on specified days between North American cities and Zürich and/or Genève.

TOURING TIPS

The **Swiss Travel System** is the most efficient in Europe. Switzerland was the first European country to issue a national travel pass that could be used for unlimited travel on all trains, postal buses and most lakeboats for the number of days purchased. In recent years, the Swiss have splintered their former Swiss Holiday Pass into a *Swiss Pass*, which gives unlimited travel for 8 or 15 days or one month, as did the original pass; a less costly *Swiss Flexipass*, which is valid for travel on three nonconsecutive days in a 15-day period; a *Swiss Card*, which is a round-trip train ticket for travel between Zürich or Genève airports, or any Swiss border point, and an unlimited number of transportation tickets at half rate on all trains, postal buses and lakeboats for a period of one month. Other possibilities are a *Swiss Family Travel Plan*, where children under 16 can travel free when accompanied by at least one parent, and a *Fly-Rail Baggage* plan, wherein baggage can be checked from your U.S. departure point to your destination in Switzerland—a system I would trust only in Switzerland!

BIKES are available at most railroad stations at a modest daily rental fee. Most bikes are multispeed, modern and in excellent condition. You can rent for a day, to return the bike after you've had a leisurely ride around the lake, or for longer, taking your bike on and off trains and postal buses when the route gets too steep or you're pressed for time. SNTO can give you details about rentals.

BOATS offer an unexpected diversion, not only for a day's outing but also as a means of getting from "here" to "there" for lunch or dinner, perhaps returning by train. The lakeboat services on the Zürichsee make it possible to go, for example, from Zürich to Rapperswil or to Au for lunch and a walk, returning either by another boat or by train. In the western part of the country, on Lac Léman, you can go easily from Lausanne's lake-suburb of Ouchy to Evian in France several times daily and, during warm weather months, from Genève to Nyon, Coppet and other towns along the lakeside, as well as on all-day excursions as far as Lausanne and the far end of the lake, to Château Chillon, beyond Montreux.

On the Bodensee, you can ride between Switzerland, Austria and Germany. (Bring your passport.) Boats on the larger lakes have special excursions that include lunch, attractively served while you watch the passing scene. There are also boats plying the small lakes such as Lac de Morat and Lac de Neuchâtel and some that go along the rivers, as does the *Romadie* from Solothurn along the Aare to Biel/Bienne, where you can change to another boat for a ride to the far end of the Bielersee (also called, in French, the Lac de Bienne), to connect with another boat for a ride through a canal to the Lac de Neuchâtel. (That's an all day excursion, returning to Solothurn by train, perhaps from Yverdon.) With one of the Swiss transportation cards, you can hop on and off the lakeboats, as well as the trains, at whim, without bothering with reservations or on-the-spot ticket purchase.

BUS TRAVEL is excellent, pleasant and very comfortable, especially for travel through small villages in the high mountains, where the colorful yellow-and-white PTT buses are the main transportation link for the local folk. Not only do efficient buses snake up and around mountain passes, but they also tie charming villages to places that are easily reached by train. At Sion and Sierre, two towns on the Rhône Valley floor in the canton of Valais, several buses wait to take people into places such as Les Haudères, Evolène, Arolla, or up to Zinal. From Brig, a postal bus weaves up and out to Saas Fee, stopping at other villages on its route. Even from Zürich's Wiedikon depot, buses stretch to Landikon, while from the towns on the lake near Genève, city buses thread to Cartigny and Chancy as well as to Bossy and around the lake to Hermance, on the French border.

CARS make it easy to drive over any one of Switzerland's 22 Alpine passes, enjoying the dramatic scenery, secure in the knowledge that the weather postings (for times when the highest passes are not negotiable) are accurate. The only danger with driving is that the highways are so efficient and direct, you're apt to speed past lovely villages hidden from the main routes. Although clearly marked highways make almost straight routes between major cities, the secondary and lesser roads are the best, in my opinion, not only because they weave through farmers' fields, but also because they allow for slower transit, with time to pause at good walking places and lovely country inns.

A national patrol network puts "help" telephones at strategic points along the highways, and tunnel authorities monitor television cameras that quickly alert them to problems within tunnels, so help can be dispatched. Migros and other Swiss companies have roadside stopping places for food and facilities.

Rental cars are available, either chauffeured or drive-yourself, at many locations within Switzerland. Most firms prepay the highway tax, which you must pay if you plan to drive into the country from elsewhere in Europe. The cost is SFr30 at the border.

TRAINS are clean, efficient, comfortable, fast—and cradlelike, as they carry you from one place to the next. The SBB/CFF/FFS painted on the side of the railway cars signifies **Schweizerischen Bundesbahnen**, **Chemin de fer fédéraux suisses** and **Ferrovie federali svizzere**, in the three most popular languages of the country.

Although many trains offer both first and second-class compartments, the only real difference (in addition to the cost of the ticket) is the padding on and width of the seats. First class has slightly wider and plumper seats. During peak travel times, first class will be less crowded on the most popular international trains and your fellow seat mates will probably be Americans, Japanese and other visitors.

High-speed trains skim between Basel and Zürich on hourly departures for the 56-minute trip, or between Bern and Genève, via Fribourg, on hourly departures for the hour-and-42-minute ride. The journey between Genève and Lausanne, through vineyards along the lake, takes about 30 minutes; from Zürich to Lugano takes just under three hours—and that's almost the north-south expanse of the country.

AUTHOR'S OBSERVATION

A moveable food cart is pushed through most trains that cover any distance, giving you an opportunity to buy chocolates, coffee, tea and assorted other beverages as well as a sandwich and other snacks. Dining cars are only on long distance trains. One special car is the Käse Express, where you can enjoy fondue or raclette and other cheese offerings while you travel. An innovation in 1992 is a McDonalds car, with the typical U.S. style fastfood! If you want to be sure to have food, buy a sandwich at the station before you board.

Some regional trains offer exceptional sightseeing, which the Swiss officials have recognized by giving them special names and touring status. The *Brig-Visp-Zermatt* cog-railway that climbs its way between the Rhône Valley and Zermatt is a delightful reasonably short ride that is part of the better known all-day journey that links Zermatt and St. Moritz as the *Glacier Express*. The *Golden Pass* route is aboard the *Montreux-Oberland-Bernois*, known as MOB, line that wiggles up and over the mountains between Montreux on Lac Léman and Spiez on the Thunersee, pausing at Gstaad, Château d'Oex and other mountain resorts. The *William Tell Express* begins about mid-day, with a boat trip out of Luzern to connect with the train that goes up-out-and-around to Lugano or Locarno by late afternoon. And the *Bernina Express* travels on a corkscrew route in eastern Switzerland, from Pontresina through Bernina Hospiz to Poschaivo, terminating at Tirano, Italy, where you can wait a while for the train that retraces that route on a return journey or continue on for travels in the Italian Alps. Other train trips worth taking, among the many options, are the train that climbs the narrow route between Martigny and Le Châtelard, on the frontier with France, where the service links with the line that serves French Chamonix, about 30 minutes from Vallorbe, and the *Furka-Oberalp Railway* that is part of the Glacier Express route mentioned above, between Brig and Disentis, which is between the Rhône and the Rhein. Even the oldest railway cars are comfortable. Some have been beautifully maintained and are used on special routes for parties and other occasions. (Look for the vintage cars at the railway station in Chur, for example, where the *Rhaetian Railway*, an independent company, uses such cars for special private journeys to St. Moritz and other resorts.) For details on the *Orient Express*, refer to "Trains" under "Transportation" in the introductory chapter.

AUTHOR'S OBSERVATION

RailEurope (☎ *800-848-7245) is a commercial venture for the sale of railway tickets in North America. Although it is one source for purchase of the Swiss Travel Plans outside Switzerland, I have found the "busy-line" syndrome a nuisance. Call very early in the day for best results, or work through your travel agent, who can get full details through the computer system. Another source is* **DER Tours** *(☎ 800-782-2424). The best source, however, is a good travel agent, who can use the computer to give you all the details.*

DAILY LIVING

FOOD, WINE AND OTHER BEVERAGES

Mealtimes in Switzerland are festive occasions; they're not just for filling the stomach. Surroundings are special, whether you choose a venerable farmhouse or village inn or an elegant *haute cuisine* restaurant in a city. Each area of the country—and sometimes even each village or crossroads—has specialties and each master chef brings his or her special talent to the preparation and presentation. Freddie Girardet set a high standard, a few years ago, when his restaurant at Crissier, near French-speaking Lausanne, was "discovered," but the country has an amazing number of exceptional chefs.

One of my favorite restaurants is in Saas Fee, high in the Valais Alps. At their Waldhotel Fletschhorn, in a clearing that is a 20-minute walk through the woods, Irma and Hans-Jörg Deütsch-Grandjean combine their talents—hers from Gruyères, his from the Bodensee area—to serve exceptional meals and wines in memorable surroundings.

Dining in Switzerland can take its cue from what is known as French or Italian or German cuisine, but it is usually distinctly Swiss. You can spend as much on one good meal as you do for your room for overnight, but you can also eat well for the Swiss Franc equivalent of about $5 from the many stands that sell bratwurst and other snacks.

Among the traditional cooking styles is the hearty farm food of the German-speaking part of the country. The *Bernerplatte*, which takes its name from the federal capital, is a huge portion of fresh farm food, including home-cured pork, potatoes, sauerkraut and *hausgemacht* (homemade) sausage. *Züricher Geschnetzeltes* are chips of thinly sliced veal in an herbed light cream sauce; they are usually served with *Rösti*, Switzerland's unique potatoes that are grated and butter-browned into a crusty pancake. *Schublig* and *Bratwurst* are two popular sausages. In Graubünden, the regional plate is Bündnerteller, paper-thin slices of beef that have been dried in the mountain air. It is called *viande sechée* in French-speaking areas, or *assiette Valaisanne* in the French-speaking Valais, the region where special cheeses are used for *fondue* and *raclette*. Cheese fondue is grated cheese, melted with white wine, served piping hot so that those around the table can pierce cubes of bread on a long fork and dip into the mixture; raclette is broiled cheese scraped onto a plate to be served with small boiled potatoes and tart pickles.

When you're in mountain areas, it helps to know that *Alpenmagronen* is noodles flavored with cheese and onions in the style of the chef and that *Rösti* may appear as *Sennenrösti*, flavored with bits of ham and topped with cheese and an egg.

AUTHOR'S OBSERVATION

When you want the menu ask for the Karte or Speisekarte in the German-speaking area and carte in the French-speaking places. The word menu is the chef's choice of the meal for the day. If you say the word, you will have ordered it and, although it will certainly be good, it may not be what you had in mind.

The village of Meiringen (see "Places Worth Finding," below) is the source for crispy, airy, melt-in-your-mouth meringues, the egg-white and sugar confection that is popular plain or with ice cream and sauce.

The Swiss day usually begins with a hearty breakfast, which is included in the room charge at most hotels. Modern practice is to present a full buffet, with your choice of homemade breads and jams, wheat or oat cereals, piping hot coffee, tea, or chocolate and sometimes fresh fruit or juices. Eggs are available for those who want them, sometimes at an additional charge.

The one big meal may be lunch or dinner, depending on your choice. (Farmers traditionally ate the big meal midday; business folks often continue that practice, but there are many people these days who enjoy only a soup or a pastry and coffee for the mid-day meal.)

The Swiss custom of second servings at the major meal is yielding to the diet obsession of the '90s, but it is still part of the dining ceremony in the best restaurants. The main course is served to you two times. In the normal ritual, your table attendant presents an attractively prepared plate of food from a platter that is kept warm on a separate serving table. When you have finished, he or she will quietly appear with a second plate of the same food, in slightly smaller portions. You are expected to lift your utensils from the first (now empty) plate, holding them while the new (second) serving is put before you.

AUTHOR'S OBSERVATION

It's expected that you'll enjoy your second serving with the same enthusiasm you showed for the first. If you don't want the two-serving meal, look for Tellerservice. *It implies one-plate service and is usually available.*

Tagesteller or *Tagesplatte, assiette du jour,* or *piatto del giorno* is the daily "plate," or one-plate service that is the common practice in North American restaurants.

You'll notice a proliferation of pastry shops, called *Konditorei* or *patisserie,* in German or French respectively. And some small eateries are marked "Tea Room," in deference to the early 19th-century English tourists who caused them to come into being. Whatever these places are called, they are your source for mouth-watering pastries, open-faced sandwiches and other light-meal possibilities.

In Zürich, search out the *Zunfthaüser,* as the medieval guild halls are called. There are several along the banks of the Limmat river (the street is known as Limmatquai) and most post their mealtime offerings beside the entrance. Dining in the guildhalls is a unique experience and, even though most of your fellow dining companions will be Swiss, you are welcome.

LODGING

Acknowledged as the pacesetter for expert hotelkeeping, Switzerland's famous *École Hôtelière Lausanne,* the hotel-training school, is the source not only for the top hoteliers in Switzerland, but for the best innkeepers worldwide.

The country excels with traditional European-style luxury, which thrives in cities and most resorts. Switzerland also has a strong and honorable tradition of innkeeping, wherein entire families are involved with offering warm and welcoming hospitality, often through several generations.

APARTMENTS and **CHALETS** have grown in all the mountain resorts. The SNTO is one good source for general listings; the local tourist offices often have pictures of some of the apartment blocks. There are a few firms that specialize in apartment rentals. It's easy to find housekeeping supplies at the local grocery stores, especially the chain of Migros and Coop. One good source for rentals is **Interhome** *(124 Little Falls Rd., Fairfield, NJ 07004;* ☎ *201+882-6864; FAX 201+808-1742).* **Idyll Ltd.** *(341 West State St., Media, PA 19063;* ☎ *215+565-5242, FAX 215+565-5142)* a unique firm that specializes in rural holidays, based in farming villages in mountain areas of the Bernese Oberland, south of Luzern toward Thun. Accommodations are appealing, simple and focused on walking, hiking and enjoying country life.

CAMPING is strictly controlled, although there are many areas with designated campsites. The usual system in Europe is to rent a caravan, or RV, to drive from place to place, searching out the campgrounds from maps that can be purchased from bookshops in Switzerland and, occasionally, through travel bookshops elsewhere. If you're a serious camper and understand German, invest in *Der ADAC Camping Führer*, a comprehensive guidebook to campsites throughout Europe. The Swiss Tourist Office has copies of a series of "Camping" brochures that are published from time to time. Divided by regions, the brochures have tables with symbols indicating facilities at many campgrounds as well as line maps showing locations. Text is given in German, French, Italian and English.

FARMS offer another type of vacation. Known as *Urlaub am Bauernhof*, farm holidays are popular with many European visitors, but little known to Americans, partly due to potential language problems and also because farm holidays have not been effectively promoted in the North American market. Several regions print comprehensive booklets, however, with pictures and statistics about the various farms, all of which have been inspected prior to their listing. Most of the literature is printed only in German, which is your tip-off to the fact that knowledge of the language is worthwhile.

Sources for further information include the regional tourist offices and the SNTO.

HUTS and **MOUNTAIN LODGES** are dependably clean and comfortable. Swiss huts are maintained for serious climbers, not for weekend walkers. They have basic facilities, but nothing lavish. Mountain lodges, on the other hand, are quite comfortable, usually with excellent (and rib-sticking) food. Many are best reached by mountain transportation, such as cablecars, funiculars, cog-railways and other aerial methods, as well as by climbing.

Naturfreunde (Friends of Nature) also maintains huts in the Alps. For details on their huts and suggested walks and hikes, contact **Naturfreunde Schweiz** *(Birmensdorferstrasse 67, CH-8004 Zürich, Switzerland)*.

INNS and **SMALL HOTELS** are a specialty of the Alpine region and most are family owned and operated. Switzerland is freckled with them. Although many are independently operated and best found by arriving in a village and looking around, several are members of loosely affiliated groups. German-based **Romantik Hotels und Restaurants** *(Postfach 1144, D-63786 Karlstein/Main, Germany;* ☎ *49+61+88.50.20, FAX 49+61+88.60.07)* has several members in Switzerland. All *Romantik* properties are charming inns that occupy historic buildings. All are "under the management of the owner, have first-class cuisine, friendly service and a pleasant and comfortable atmosphere," as stated in their code of ethics. Several of the member properties are represented in the United States through **Romantik Tours and Europa Hotels** *(Box 1278, Woodinville, WA 98072;* ☎ *206+485-6985 or 800+826-0015, FAX 206+481-4079)*, a firm that plans itineraries in the Alpine area and elsewhere in Europe, using traditional properties. **Relais & Châteaux** *(#707, 11 East 44th, New York, NY 10017;* ☎ *212+856-0115 or 800+743-8033; FAX 212+856-0193)*, an association of attractive, well-run properties noted for good food and exceptional surroundings, also has several members in Switzerland. Although some are large properties, many members of the French-based **Relais du Silence** *(2 Passage du Guesclin, F-75015 Paris, France;* ☎ *33+1+4566.77.77; FAX 33+1+4065.90.09)* are pleasant inns. All are protective of a rural setting and high quality. Members of many of these associations are mentioned as appealing lodgings under "Places Worth Finding," below.

LUXURY HOTELS in Switzerland maintain the traditional European style, which is taught at *Ecole Hôtelière*, the Swiss Hotel School in Lausanne. There are several late 19th-century and early 20th-century hotels around the country that are beautifully maintained, with all modern comforts. Leading Hotels, the registered name for a group of privately owned properties that share elegance in classic style, is a Swiss company. The U.S. contact for some members of the group is **Leading Hotels of the World** *(737 Third Ave., New York, NY 10017;* ☎ *212+838-3110 or 800+223-6800, FAX 212+758+7367)*. There are almost two dozen members in this country: in Bad Ragaz, the Quellenhof; in Basel, the Drei König (Three Kings); in Bern, the Bellevue Palace and the Gauer Hôtel Schweizerhof; in Burgenstock, the Estate; in Genève, the Hôtel de la Paix, the Hôtel du Rhône, and the Hôtel le Richmond; in Grindelwald, the Hôtel Regina; in Gstaad, the Palace; in Interlaken, the Victoria-Jungfrau Grand Hôtel; in Kandersteg, the Royal Hôtel Bellevue; on the lake at Ouchy, below Lausanne, the Beau-Rivage Palace; in the hillside city, the Lausanne Palace; in Luzern, the Palace Luzern; in Lugano, the Splendide; in Montreux, Le Palace; in St. Moritz, Badrutt's Palace; at Vevey, the Hôtel des Trois Couronnes; in Zermatt, two Seiler family hotels, the Monte Rosa and the Mont Cervin; and in Zürich, the Baur au Lac and the hillside Dolder Grand. Most of the members of **Relais & Châteaux** (see above) are also in the luxury category, although they are usually smaller properties. Many properties that are members of **Relais du Silence** *(2 Passage du Guesclin, F-75015 Paris, France;* ☎ *33+1+4566.77.77; FAX 33+1+4065.90.09)* are large, luxurious hotels.

SPAS have offered the classiest vacation style since the time of the Romans and certainly through the era of emperors and kings. These days, they're open for anyone who can afford them and are very popular with Europeans who have a tradition of visiting spas. Programs are offered for weight loss, stress reduction and more serious ailments; each spa has its specialties. The best-known Swiss spas are at Bad Ragaz, Baden near Zürich, Lenk, Leukerbad and St. Moritz, which have linked for promotion purposes as the "Leading Spas of Switzerland." **Spa Trek Travel** *(475 Park Ave South, New York, NY 10016;* ☎ *212+779-3480 or 800+272-3480, FAX 212+779-3471)* and **Great Spas of World** *(#1404, 211 East 43rd St., New York, NY 10017;* ☎ *212+599-0382 or 800+826-8062, FAX 212+599-0380)* are two U. S.-based firms that can help with programs at Swiss spas.

PLACES WORTH FINDING

Bern, Basel, Genève, Zürich and other cities and towns with names you'll recognize, have highlights mentioned below, but these places are by no means the only ones where you can enjoy the Swiss lifestyle. Towns and villages on lakes and in the mountains hold untold riches in their chapels, churches and cathedrals, where impressive paintings, wood carvings, frescoes and stucco work praise the Lord; sports events bring fame to many of the mountain villages that are at their best—naturally—at other times; regular markets are ideal times to sample local recipes and to enjoy the work of local craftspeople; and almost every village has at least one inn that is the gathering place for the local folks and a welcoming restaurant or place to spend a few days when you are a visitor.

Many castles and fortresses were built in the 11th century when the traders and invaders created market villages and made fortified strongholds necessary as they crossed the Alps between Italy and northern Europe. Today the hilltop and lowland castles and mansions are often museums, occasionally hotels or restaurants and sometimes used as the venue for musical and other events.

In the following place names, the postal code (CH-0000) and the telephone number for the local tourist office (☎ 00+000.00.00) appears in parentheses. Telephone numbers have five, six, or seven digits. When dialing a number within Switzerland, begin by dialing 0, followed by the number; from outside the country, no 0 is required. CH stands for Confederatio Helvetica, the Latin name for Switzerland.

AUTHOR'S OBSERVATION

See "Touring Tips," above, for details about the Swiss travel passes that allow for carefree travel on trams and buses within many towns as well as for lakeboats and some regional trains. With pass in hand, you don't need to stand in line to buy tickets or worry about making change for token booths.

ANDERMATT

Andermatt *(CH-6490; ☎ 44+674.54, FAX 44+681.85)*, at the Gotthard pass, almost in the middle of the country, has always been a crossroads. Well before the Middle Ages, pack animals crossed the Alps through these mountains, linking northern Europe and the south. These days, trains corkscrew through the mountains, and highways burrow through once impregnable rock, from Göschenen, just north of Andermatt, to Italy. Andermatt's location, in a bowl of mountains at the northern "end" of the Italy-linking Gotthard pass, makes it a respected center for mountaineers as well as hikers and walkers. Surrounded by sensational ski runs and rock-climbing areas, the community has a small-town feeling, with many of its historic weathered-wood buildings still intact.

LODGING: Among the several small hotels (there are no large ones) is the **Drei Könige und Post** *(23 rooms; ☎ 44+672.03, FAX 44+676.66)*, which was the town's postal coach stop when horse-drawn carriages made the Alpine crossing. Conveniently located in the center of town, the hotel maintains traditional Alpine decor in its restaurant and in the bedrooms. The **Krone** *(50 rooms; ☎ 44+672.90; FAX 44+678.38)* is also historically appealing, with atmosphere maintained while modern conveniences have been added. The smaller, more modest **Hotel Schweizerhof** *(30 rooms; Gotthardstrasse; ☎ 44+671.89, FAX 44+687.89)* is a comfortable neighbor; and the very modest **Löwen** *(22 rooms; ☎ 44+672.23)* is a favorite of climbers and other outdoor types. (See "Sports," below, for information about activities.)

Also in this area, high in the mountains and favored by hikers and climbers, are the **St. Gotthard-Hospiz** *(34 beds; ☎ 94+88.12.35; FAX 94+88.18.11)* on the Gotthardpass, and the **Hotel Tiefenbach** *(25 beds; ☎ 94+6.73.22)* and the **Hotel Galenstock** *(26 beds; ☎ 94+6.77.60)*, both on the Furkapass. Only the Tiefenbach offers rooms with private bath.

ANZÈRE

Anzère *(CH-1972; ☎ 27+38.25.29, FAX 27+38.18.66)*, high in the Valais above Sion/Sierre, sits on a wide south-facing meadow. A few of the chalets are old; most are newly built as small cottages or large apartment-filled buildings. Most vacationers head here to enjoy walks and hikes in summer and skiing in winter, as well as swimming in a covered pool, the ice-skating rink, the tennis courts and—of course—the spectacular mountains. A well-maintained cross-country loop entertains winter sportsfolk; it's marked by signs that say both *Langlaufloipe* and *Piste de fond*, using the two languages (German and French) spoken in the area.

LODGING: The **Eden** *(100 rooms; ☎ 27+38.38.44, FAX 27+38.17.91)* is the main hotel in town, although its peak season rates (in February, and in July and early August) are very reasonable.

APPENZELL

Appenzell *(CH-9050; ☎ 71+87.41.11, FAX 71+87.52.66)*, in eastern Switzerland, is the name of both a town and a region. The town is nestled in the rolling hills above St. Gallen, which makes it easy to reach aboard the charming *Appenzellerbahn*, a regional train line that provides a pleasant day of sightseeing from its windows as well as transport for schoolchildren and others who live along its route. Noted for the folk-art painting on its buildings and inns, the village is a favorite for tours—and tourists. However, if you stay overnight, you'll be able to enjoy the typical (and traditional) farm village atmosphere. The name—derived from Abbatis cella, or Abbott's cell—refers to its settlement by monks from nearby St. Gallen. The **Heimatmuseum** on the second floor of the Rathaus has a collection of the naive paintings of farm scenes that are unique to this area as well as embroidery, lace and other crafts that are linked with the region and with farming.

The canton of Appenzell, established in 1513, has many charming villages that are home for farmers-turned-craftsmen as well as for artists who have been drawn to the rural region. It is also one of the two places in Switzerland where votes are cast in the traditional way by men who gather at the town square at election times to raise their swords in affirmation.

LODGING: The **Romantik Hotel Säntis** *(60 beds;* ☎ *71+87.87.22; FAX 71+87.48.42)* has been in the Heeb family for several generations. Photogenic, with its facade painted in regional style, the inn is decorated in country style. Fluffy duvets sit like clouds on the beds and rooms are perfumed with the pungent smell of the larch wood used for the interior walls. Also very pleasant, with plenty of atmosphere, the **Hotel Appenzell** *(20 rooms;* ☎ *71+87.42.11, FAX 71+87.42.84)* has an attractive restaurant and a convenient location in the middle of the village.

Near Appenzell, **Urnäsch** *(CH-9107;* ☎ *71+58.17.77)* has a small but very special **Museum fur Appenzeller Brauchtum** (Museum of Appenzell customs) where costumes, handicrafts and home furnishings are displayed in a typical wooden house.

LODGING: The small **Krone** *(20 rooms;* ☎ *71+58.15.15, FAX 71+58.23.81)* is photogenic, with a traditional wrought iron sign over its entry door. The country-style bedrooms may seem small, but they are cozy and comfortable.

AROSA

Arosa *(CH-7050;* ☎ *81+31.16.21, FAX 81+31.31.35)*, in eastern Switzerland's canton of Graubünden, stretches from its lake up a mountainside to offer viewful perches. Popular in both summer and winter as a resort favored by Europeans, the town is an ideal place for walks, hikes and general exploring of the region.

LODGING: Options range from the **Arosa Kulm** *(150 rooms;* ☎ *81+31.16.21; FAX 81+31.40.90)*, nestled in a wooded area on the hillside and the **Tschuggen Grand Hotel** *(125 rooms;* ☎ *81+31.02.21, FAX 81+31.41.75)*, also in the style that was the tradition for mountain resorts in the early 1900s, to small *garni* hotels such as the **Kaiser** *(54 beds;* ☎ *81+31.34.54, FAX 81+31.42.44)* and the **Obersee** *(40 beds;* ☎ *81+31.12.16; FAX 81+31.45.66).*

ASCONA

Ascona *(CH-6612;* ☎ *93+35.55.44, FAX 93+36.10.08),* in the Ticino, on Italian-shared Lago Maggiore, is a lovely town with medieval history, not far from Locarno, to which it is linked by lakeboat and local bus. Seriously flooded when unusual rains caused rivers to rush into the lake, in late September 1993, Ascona recovered quickly, and benefits from the thorough cleaning and the essential refurbishing (and rebuilding, in some cases) of places nearest the lakeside. Although the August-September music festival is the highlight of the cultural calendar, the town's worth visiting at all times of year. In warm weather months, lakefront cafés and shops welcome visitors, who sit amid the vestiges of what was a medieval fishing village. Ascona may seem crowded in summer, but it is peaceful and quiet at other times. Boats stretch from the dock to neighboring villages and to the gardens of Isole di Brissago.

Lodging choices include the **Romantik Hotel Tamaro** *(78 beds;* ☎ *93+35 02 82; FAX 93+35.29.28),* owned by Annetta and Paolo Witzig, where you'll find atmosphere, with good food and other comforts; the **Castello del Sol** *(125 beds;* ☎ *93+35.02.02; FAX 93+36.11.18),* with a country-club feeling that includes tennis among its offerings, a short walk inland from the lakes, and **Castello Seeschloss** *(65 beds;* ☎ *93+35.01.61; FAX 93+35.18.04),* on the lakefront promenade, which is ideal for scenery and convenience but can be noisy if you have a viewful room in the front of the castlelike building.

Inland, on the outskirts of Ascona, *Losone* claims the **Albergo Losone** *(50 rooms;* ☎ *93+35.01.31),* which has become a total vacation "experience." The original family inn has expanded through the years to accommodate families and sports-oriented vacationers. The Glaus-Somaini family has packaged many Ticinese customs and ceremonies to offer them for their guests. Rooms are comfortable; there's a pleasant pool on the premises; and management helps with tips about places worth visiting in the surrounding countryside.

AVENCHES

Avenches *(CH-1580;* ☎ *37+75.11.59, FAX 37+75.33.93),* in the canton of Vaud, a short drive south of Lac de Neuchâtel, was the Celtic capital of the Helvetians. Ruins of the amphitheater dating to the years when it was the thriving Roman city of Aventicum still stand. (The Roman town was destroyed by the Alemanni in the third century.) A museum holds a collection of Roman antiquities found on the site.

LODGING: Options include the modern **Lacotel** *(78 beds; ☎ 37+75.34.44; FAX 37+75.11.88)*, but also consider hotels far-more-charming Murten/Morat (see below), with a German/French name that indicates its location at one of Switzerland's language borders.

BAD RAGAZ

Bad Ragaz *(CH-7310; ☎ 81+302.10.61, FAX 81+302.62.90)*, in the Kanton St. Gallen, in eastern Switzerland, has been a respected spa since 1840, when thermal springs at the Tamina gorge were harnessed for therapeutic purposes. These days the town is a thriving resort, with daily concerts in summer months and an open-air thermal pool that is open year-round. In addition to the many activities centered around the Kursaal (where there's a band for dancing some evenings and a Swiss-style casino that may be disappointingly conservative to travelers expecting U.S.-style Las Vegas glitz), there's a cable car to take you 5000 feet above sea level to Pardiel-Pizol, an area noted for walking or skiing, depending on the season.

LODGINGS: are legion in this place, which has been a popular spa for centuries. The **Quellenhof** *(200 beds; ☎ 81+303.20.20, FAX 81+303+30.22)* is the social leader, offering an established European 19th century spa-resort's facilities, but there are a dozen members of the Swiss Hotel Association as well as several other pleasant places to stay that are comfortable and clean, but that are not Hotel Association members.

BASEL

Basel *(CH-4000; ☎ 61+261.50.50; FAX 61+261.59.44)* takes on aspects of a charming, sophisticated small town, for those of us enchanted by its exceptional museums, its cultural life and its surrounding countryside. It is, in fact, a very cosmopolitan large city that has played an important role in European history since the first Celtic settlement in the years before Christ. The **Münster** (cathedral), at Munsterhügel, is the heart of the matter, not only because of its embellished towers and the expressions on the faces of the delightful statues that live on its rosy red walls, but also because the view over the Rhein from its grounds is thought-provoking for the history it has known and the pastoral presence it still claims.

This is where a Raurician tribe settled and "Colonia Raurica" was founded by the Romans. (See below, for facts about the Roman ruins at nearby Augst.) And it's where the community named Basilia by Roman Emperor Valentinian I was established before the year 400, when he built a fortress on the site. German Emperor Heinrich II consecrated the first cathedral in 1019, recognizing the importance of the location, on a bluff overlooking the Rhein's curve.

By 1226, a bridge had been built over the Rhein and settlements began at Kleinbasel (Little Basel), on the other side. The prosperous town was shattered by an earthquake in 1356. Not long after it had been rebuilt, an illustrious former resident, Pope Pius II (Aeneas Silvius), gave it university status. The University that opened in 1460 became a lure for Erasmus and other great thinkers. Weaving ribbons and silk fabric popular with Europe's aristocracy brought wealth and fame to the city almost 200 years later, when the town fathers granted asylum to Protestant refugees, the Hugenots, fleeing from persecution that followed the revocation of the Edict of Nantes in 1685. By this time, the city was well known, not only for the much talked about theories expounded by its intellectuals, but also for the fine handcrafts and other skills of its craftsmen residents. Silk weaving and other intricate handwork created a new industry: the creation of dyes to make the beautiful colors then in vogue. And the expertise with dyes gave rise to the prosperous chemical companies that still enrich this city's coffers. (Ciba-Geigy was founded, as the J.R. Geigy company, in 1785; F. Hoffmann-La Roche is also based in Basel.) Basel joined the Swiss Confederation in 1501, and became two independent half cantons, Basel-Stadt and Baselland, in 1833.

Touring the city is easy aboard quick, efficient and carefree trams and buses, especially when you purchase the multiride ticket that allows you to get on and off at will or have some version of the prepaid Swiss Pass that permits limitless travel in most Swiss cities and towns. The **Altstadt** (old city) is best by foot, since it's clustered around the cathedral and is where you'll find several special museums along the narrow roads, within easy walking distance of each other.

Visiting the **Münster** in the early morning has distinct advantages, not only because the sun's first light casts an unusual tone on the rose-red stone, but also because it's easy to imagine this place when it was a center for European intellectuals in the Middle Ages. The 20th century does not intrude until 9 a.m. or later. Among the most Swiss of the city's many museums is the **Historisches Museum** (☎ *61+271.05.05)*, which is divided into several parts. My favorite, as much for the opportunity to be inside a once private home as for the treasures, is the **Haus zum Kirschgarten** (*Elisabethenstrasse 27-29;* ☎ *61+271.13.33)*, with a fascinating collection of porcelain painted by Swiss and other artists from the 16th century onwards as well as furniture and some paintings. Also worth noting is the **Barfüsserkirche** *(Barfüsserplatz;* ☎ *61+271.05.05)*, with a collection of crafts, art and artifacts from the Middle Ages and the Renaissance. Other parts of the Historisches Museum are the **Kutschen-und Schlittensammlung** *(Villa Merian in Bruglingen, St. Jakob, Basel;* ☎ *61+271.05.05)* and the **Musikinstrumenten-Sammlung** *(Leonhardsstrasse 8;* ☎ *061+271.05.05)*, with musical instruments.

The **Kunstmuseum** *(St. Alban-Graben 16;* ☎ *61+271.08.28)* is world famous, not only for the perspicacity of its director (who has melded finds from around the world into fascinating exhibits of interrelated arts) but also for its collection of Picassos, some given by the artist in gratitude for the funds raised by Basel's citizens when they realized they might lose many pieces of his work. The collection occupies several halls within the museum, as do masterworks of artists from the Middle Ages, the Renaissance and more recent times.

Three other museums that I find fascinating for their special focuses are the **Papiermuhle** *(St. Alban-Tal 35-37;* ☎ *61+272.96.52)*, a museum of writing and paper that is housed in an old papermill; the **Schweizerisches Schiffartsmuseum** *(Rheinhafen Kleinhuningen;* ☎ *61+66.33.49)*, at the harbor, with a collection of models, paintings, and other memorabilia from the shipping history of Switzerland and the **Spielzeug- und Dorfmuseum Riehen** *(in the Wettsteinhuas, Baselstrasse 34, Riehen;* ☎ *61+67.28.29)*, with a toy collection that includes generations of teddy bears.

The **Botanischer Garten der Universitäat Basel** *(Schonbeinstrasse 6, near the Spalentor;* ☎ *61+267.35.19)* is a lovely place for leisurely strolls past acres of plants, many of which have been brought from foreign countries. Although many European species are shown, the collection of Alpine flowers and plants is especially noteworthy. May is peak time for the garden, which is worth visiting anytime.

Spend at least one day in the countryside, an outing easily accomplished by tram, train, or rental car. The **Botanischer Garten** in Bruglingen *(St. Jakob;* ☎ *61+311.87.80)* is easily reached by tram #14, in about 20 minutes from the center of the city. Inquire about hours for visiting the Villa Merian. Two other goals that are slightly out of center city are **Schloss Binningen** *(*☎ *61+47.20.55)*, a restaurant in a moat-surrounded castle from the 13th century, and **Weiherschloss Bottmingen**, a suburban restaurant that can be reached by bus from Basel's Hauptbahnhof in less than 10 minutes.

Two small spots in Basel for informal dining are the **Cafe zum Isaak**, near the entrance of the Cathedral, with an inside room as well as a patio where tables sprout as soon as the weather warms, and the **Elisabethenstübli** (☎ 61+272.11.05), on *Elisabethstrasse 34*, not far from the Haus zum Kirschgarten, for light meals or hearty fare.

LODGING: For convenience as well as for comfort, Basel's legendary hotel is **Drei Könige am Rhein** (*75 rooms; Blumenrain 8;* ☎ *61+261.52.52; FAX 61+261.21.53*), with rooms overlooking the Rhein. The conveniently located **Euler Mainz Privacy** (*62 rooms; Centralbahnplatz 14,* ☎ *61+272.45.00; FAX 61+271.50.00*), on Centralbahnplatz, is a short walk from the railroad station. Another choice, close to the station, is the **Hotel St. Gotthard** (*Central-bahnstrasse 13;* ☎ *61+271.52.50; FAX 61+271.52.14*), which the family Albert Geyer-Arel has turned into a pleasant small hotel in spite of their capitulation to outright commercial ventures with a McDonalds fastfood outlet next to the street entrance. Although some bedrooms are tiny, they are modern, neat and quiet—when you select a room at the back of the house. Places near the railroad station are ideal for daytrips by train.

From Basel, *Augst* is less than 20 minutes by train to the nearest station (at Kaiseraugst). The **Romermuseum** (☎ *61+811.11.87*), on the site of a former Roman camp, is about 15 minutes' walk from the railroad station (and the Rhein river). Although the small museum is interesting, the ruins can be explored by simply strolling around them. The amphitheater is used for performances in warm-weather months. Ask the tourist office for a schedule if you're interested in attending one of the events.

In *Dornach*, 9 minutes by train from Basel, the **Goetheanum** (☎ *61+701.40.41 for tickets and information*) is a huge center honoring Goethe and devoted to the performing arts.

In *Liestal*, reached by frequent trains from Basel in less than 20 minutes, the **Kantonsmuseum Baselland**, in the Altes Zeughaus (*Zeughausplatz 28;* ☎ *61+925.59.86*), is as interesting for the tokens from times in the canton's history as for the historic building that hosts the museum. Convenient to Basel, the town of Liestal offers a pleasant change from the life of the city.

LODGING: The pleasant **Hotel Engel** (*35 rooms;* ☎ *61+921.25.11, FAX 61+921.25.16*), now popular with businessfolks, was a mail coach stop in earlier times. It's a short walk from the station and offers traditional appearance in spite of its many modern facilities and services.

BERN

Bern *(CH-3001; ☎ 31+311.66.11; FAX 31+312.12.33)*, the country's federal capital, is a living monument to the Middle Ages, with its arcaded streets, frequent outdoor markets, cafés and cozy inns for pleasant pausing places and easily accessible countryside for walks and memorable inns.

Founded in 1191 by Berchtold V von Zähringen, the town was rebuilt, mostly with sandstone, following a fire that devoured most of the wooden buildings in 1405. Many buildings date from the 15th century; the strategically placed town (on the peninsula of a hairpin curve in the river Aare) was a thriving market community from the 14th through the 16th centuries. Bern's university was established in 1834, several years after Napoleon's troops invaded the town (in 1798) and after the dissolution of the Ancien Regime. Bern joined the Swiss Confederation in 1353 and became the federal capital in 1848, but its quaint aspect, with the Tuesday- and Saturday-morning markets, make it seem more like a stage set than the active 20th-century city that it is.

Although the medieval part of the town is comfortably enjoyed by foot, public transportation spokes from the Bahnhof, an active transit point that can seem confusing to first-time visitors. Most of the pedestrian action at the Bahnhof is underground, where you'll need to pause for a couple of minutes to orient yourself and follow the signs, which are very clear once you find them. Taking a tram is the easiest way to cover longer distances in the city.

The **Altstadt** is a pleasant walk from the Bahnhof, heading out onto Bubenbergplatz and turning left, to stroll down Spitalgasse which becomes Marktgasse, then Kramgasse and Gerechtigkeitgasse, before you cross the Aare, over the Nydeggbrücke, to visit the **Bärengraben** (bears' pit), a traditional sight of the city. The arcaded medieval buildings that border your multi-named route house some of the city's hundreds of shops and restaurants; the streets are punctuated with the famed (and much photographed) clocktowers and fountains.

The medieval buildings, and the commerce among them, are so photogenic that strolling, with an occasional pause at a cozy *Stúbli*, can be a full-time occupation, but there are several sights worth seeing. The first, if you have time for only one, is the **Münster** and the tree-studded Munsterplatz, with its view over the river. (The best view rewards those who climb to the top of the cathedral tower.)

Other touchstones for the city include the **Kunstmuseum** *(Hodler-strasse 12;* ☎ *31+22.09.44),* with an outstanding collection of Swiss art, which was its sole focus from the time of its founding in 1879 until the 1930s when other European artists were added. The Kunstmuseum has more than 2000 works by Paul Klee. The **Historisches Museum** *(Helvetiaplatz 5;* ☎ *31+43.18.11)* has an enchanting collection of items from earliest Bernese history, plus 15th-century tapestries.

Among my favorite places for more esoteric subjects are the **Gutenbergmuseum** *(Zeughausgasse 2;* ☎ *31+22.31.61),* with a fascinating collection of old printing presses and examples of leather bookbinding; the **PTT-Museum** *(Helvetiastrasse 16;* ☎ *31+62.77.77),* with exhibits showing the history of the Swiss telecommunications system; and the **Alpines Museum** *(Helvetiaplatz 4;* ☎ *31+43.04.34),* on an upper floor of the same building, with exhibits and pictures of Alpine life through the centuries and some relief maps that make it easier to comprehend the interrelationships between mountain peaks and interlocking valleys.

In the nearby countryside, two castles worth visiting when they're open (May-October) are **Schloss Jegenstorf**, a 20-minute train ride on the SZB line, which has furnishings dating from the 17th to 19th centuries and beautiful grounds, and **Schloss Oberhofen** on the Thunersee, which can be reached by a dual-linked journey of train plus boat or local bus in about 30 minutes. Highlights here are the wall treatments, room furnishings and grounds of the beautifully maintained lakeside castle. The best way to arrive is by boat, with a ride before or after, around the **Thunersee**. There's boat service between Thun and Interlaken, with shorter cruises as well.

LODGING: Although there are several pleasant places to stay around the Thunersee, Bern can also be a good touring base, especially when you choose a hotel near the Bahnhof, so daily excursions by train are easy to negotiate. Choices are led by the **Schweizerhof** *(170 beds; Bahnhofplatz 11;* ☎ *31+311.45.01, FAX 31+312.21.79),* in my opinion, not only because the elegant family-owned hotel places fine antique furniture in rooms and public places and gorgeous flower arrangements are part of the decor, but also because it's convenient for train, tram and bus travel. Also top of the line is the **Bellevue Palace** *(223 beds; Kochergasse 3-5;* ☎ *31+320.45.45, FAX 31+311.47.43),* not far from the Bundeshaus, with a pleasant terrace on the far side of its lobby that has a sensational view, when the weather is clear, of distant mountains over the nearby rooftops of Bern.

Other comfortable places include the more modestly priced **Hotel Bären** *(46 roms; Schauplatzgasse 4; ☎ 31+311.33.67; FAX 31+311.69.83)* and **Hotel Bristol** *(72 rooms; Schauplatzgasse 10; ☎ 31+311.01.01; FAX 31+311.94.79)*, neighbors in the center of town and partners with membership in the Best Western reservations system. The stark modern decor of the bedrooms provides comforts but belies the history wrapped around the location. Both are within a few steps of the Bundeshaus, just off Bubenbergplatz (which the Bahnhof faces), and not far from the cathedral and other historic sights.

Not far away, in the village of **Worb**, the **Romantik Hotel Zum Löwen** *(Enggisteinstrasse 3, CH-3076 Worb; ☎ 31+839.23.03, FAX 31+839.48.77)* puts you in the mood of the region. Hans-Peter and Ursula Bernard are the 11th generation of the family to be affiliated with the one-time tavern, in a 600-year-old, Bernese-style building, with its distinctive, sturdy, overhanging shingled roof. The bedrooms have modern comforts.

BODENSEE

Bodensee (Lake Constance), shared by Germany and Switzerland, with a tiny Austrian portion at the east (refer to "Bregenz" in the Austrian chapter), is a lovely playground, especially in warm-weather months, when the lakeboats tie towns together and the lakefront inns serve at tables in the sunshine, with a view of the lake (see map of Bodensee in "Germany"). Although it's tempting to stay aboard the lakeboat, for the entire tour, it's also pleasant to pause at one or two villages on the route, to settle into one of the inns or to walk out into the hills.

Gottlieben *(CH-8274; ☎ 72+69.12.82)* has lured me on many occasions, not only because of its lakeside location, but mostly because of its **Romantik Hotel Krone** *(23 rooms; ☎ 72+69.23.23; FAX 72+69.24.56)*, a charming hotel where meals can be occasions and bedrooms offer all the comforts. Lunch, snacks and dinner are served at tables on a patch by the lake, when the weather warms; otherwise meals are served in the street level dining room, with breakfast offered for guests in an upstairs room. I prefer the original lakeview bedrooms; recently refurbished bedrooms at the back of the building have all modern comforts (including TV) with too much pattern, in my opinion. The tiny village's other hotel is the **Drachenburg & Waaghaus** *(54 rooms; ☎ 72+9.62.03)*, once the favorite, but now over-"restored." It's well known to business folks and has become a bit too commercial for my taste.

At **Rorschach** *(CH-9400; ☎ 71+41.70.34, FAX 71+41.70.36)*, on the hillside, above the lake, the **Parkhotel Waldau** *(40 rooms; ☎ 71+43.01.80; FAX 71+42.10.02)* has a swimming pool, tennis courts and fitness center in addition to a memorable dining room with slightly pretentious French offerings.

(See also "Schaffhausen" and "Stein am Rhein," below.)

CHUR

Chur *(CH-7000; ☎ 81+22.18.18, FAX 81+22.90.76)*, the capital of the canton of Graubünden, dates to the Bronze Age. Although a modern city has risen around the 2000-year-old historic heart, there are several medieval buildings clustered in the old town and they are worth visiting. Among them are the **Catholic Bishop's palace**, where the bishop for eastern Switzerland and Liechtenstein resides, the **Katedrale**, with an impressive 12th-century altar, the **Rathaus**, and the 15th-century **St. Martin Kirche**. Also in this area are some restaurants in historic buildings, my favorite of which is in the building to the left just after you pass through the arch into the Altstadt. Food is basic country style; the atmosphere will take you back in time.

Don't be put off by the first impression, when you arrive by road or train, of an industrial area that thrives in the wide Rhein (Rhine) valley. The **Altstadt** hides in the center, a short walk from the Bahnhof, with the station's main entrance at your back. The town is a pivot point for trains into the Engadine valley resorts (St. Moritz and Pontresina, for example) as well as for buses to Arosa, Flims and other mountain resorts in its orbit. Chur is also a possible starting point for a day on the *Glacier Express* excursion train, which reaches Zermatt late in the afternoon.

LODGING: Choices are led, in my opinion, by the **Romantik Hotel Stern** *(Reichgasse 11; ☎ 81+22.35.55, FAX 81+22.19.15)*, where Sandra and Walter Brunner-Decurtins continue the traditions put in place and maintained by the imagination and perseverance of Emil Pfister, who put 20th-century life into many of the Engadine region's most endearing customs. Not only are rooms furnished in traditional style, but the restaurant staff wear comfortable versions of the regional costume and the kitchen prepares historic recipes that are served in traditional ways.

COPPET

Coppet *(CH-1296)*, noteworthy for the **Château** of Mme. de Staël, is within minutes by train of Genève and a lovely boat ride from that city if you visit when the lakeboat schedule is in full swing (in warmest-weather months). Noted in documents from the time of Peter of Savoy (1268), the château is impressive in its own right, even without the fascinating tales about Mme. de Staël, born Germaine Necker, daughter of a minister to the court of French king Louis XVI. It is fully furnished and full of legends about the salons Mme. de Stäel held here when she had been exiled by Napoleon for her liberal ideas and outspoken manner. Chateaubriand referred to his visit here in 1805, and other noteworthy guests gathered with Mme. de Stael to discuss Jean-Jacques Rousseau and other literati of the time.

LODGING: If Coppet appeals enough for you to stay for a night or two, which it certainly will on the summer evenings when concerts are performed at the château, you'll be richly rewarded by the **Hôtel du Lac** *(23 rooms;* ☎ *22+776.15.21; FAX 22+776.53.46)*, with an exceptionally fine (and expensive) restaurant on the lakeside. Its unpretentious (less expensive) neighbor, **Hotel d'Orange** *(22 beds;* ☎ *22+776.10.37)* is also pleasant. Be sure to ask for a room with a lakeside view at both places; rooms on the front have a steady buzz of traffic.

(For nearby places, see "Genève" and "Lac Léman," below.)

CRANS-MONTANA

Crans-Montana *(CH-3963 Crans;* ☎ *27+41.21.32, FAX 27+ 41.17.94; CH-3962 Montana,* ☎ *27+41.30.41, FAX 27+41.74.60)* is two former Valais villages that have grown into each other, high on an Alpine hillside above the Rhône river valley. Thanks to rapid expansion, modern buildings mask what might have been historic about this heavily promoted area. The resort is mentioned only because its vast size, which includes dozens of places to stay, eat, dance and do sports, makes it popular with some families and other people who want everything in one place.

LODGING: Choices number in the dozens, with plenty of apartments clustered in over-sized buildings that have a pseudo-chalet style and are better for the views from some rooms than for their own appearnace. One small hotel in Montana, with a welcome Alpine focus, is **Les Quatres Canetons** *(50 beds;* ☎ *27+41.42.14)*, where the owners keep in touch with traditional activities in this busy area.

DAVOS

Davos *(CH-7270;* ☎ *81+45.21.21, FAX 81+45.21.00)*, at 5062 feet in eastern Switzerland, is the highest town in Europe. It's also the town made famous in Franz Kafka's signature novel, *Magic Mountain*, for its role as a health resort, used in the early 1900s for tuberculosis patients. These days, although still highly regarded for its healthy climate, the town sprawls along its shop-and-hotel bordered main street, with sensational places to walk, hike and ski within easy distance. Although Davos is a tourist and convention/conference town, daily life is centered on winter skiing and summer walking, hiking and mountaineering, with resting times (when many places are closed) in early spring and mid to late fall. While making the most of the fact that winter sports started in the canton of Graubünden in 1864, Davos has become a total sports center, with horseback riding, tennis tournaments, squash courts and many miles of hiking trails, 50 of which are open during winter months. Davos built its first T-bar skilift in 1904; the area now has 55 lifts. The longest of its 200 miles of ski runs is the one from the Weissfluh to Küblis, an area laced with beautiful walking and hiking paths when weather warms.

In the Alpine sense, Davos is a big and busy resort, in a narrow valley amid Alpine peaks, with most shops, cafés and restaurants bordering its Promenade, the main street and its side streets. Bus service operates frequently between the Bahnhof at Davos Dorf and the center of resort activities, at Davos Platz, for those who prefer to ride, although the distance can easily be covered by foot. Some buses continue on to the lake. Although not noted for its museums, since Davos delights in its sports, there are a few small museums worth visiting. The **Heimatmuseum Davos** (*Museumstrasse 1, Davos Dorf;* ☎ *81+46.26.66*), has a delightful collection of farmhouse interiors and items from the rural, farming life of the region. The **Bergbaumuseum Graubünden** (*Schmeizboden;* ☎ *81+43.63.66*), in one of the region's trademark stucco-style farmhouses, depicts the mining history of the region. The **Kirchner Museum** (*Promenade 43, Davos Platz;* ☎ *81+43.64.84*), opened in 1992, displays the works of Ernst Ludwig Kirchner, who lived here for 20 years and is buried in the forest cemetery in the direction of Frankenkirche (next to a gravel pit). The museum, across the road from the Steigenberger Belvédère hotel, has a small-but-noteworthy fine arts collection. Each of this trio of museums is open on specific days, from mid-June to the end of October, and at other times by appointment.

LODGINGS are legion, with the **Steigenberger Belvédère** (*125 rooms;* ☎ *81+44.12.81, FAX 81+43.11.71*) among the best for service, grand hotel style and comfortably furnished modern rooms, but a few of my favorites are the **Meierhof** (*75 rooms;* ☎ *81+47.12.85, FAX 81+46.39.82*), where a new wing was added to the traditional-style building in 1984, but the mountain-chalet atmosphere has been preserved and maintained. Balconies on the rooms face south, to take advantage of the sunshine. **Berghotel Schatzalp** *(100 rooms; CH-7270;* ☎ *81+44.13.31, FAX 81+43.13.44)*, built in utilitarian style, but blissfully quiet, with a pleasant atmosphere. Perched in the mountains, above the busyness of Davos, the Berghotel is easily reached by a 5-minute ride on the Schatzalp funicular. The Strela cablecars are nearby and the hotel is ideally situated for mountain walks, as well as for skiers. **Hotel Ochsen** *(Davos Platz;* ☎ *81+43.52.22; FAX 81+43.76.71)* isn't much to look at from the outside, but it's not far from the Platz railroad station and convenient to the shops and other in-town activities, with a cozy Alpine atmosphere within its walls. The restaurant is on the street level, with three levels of rooms above. The **Davoserhof** *(25 rooms;* ☎ *81+43.68.17, FAX 81+43.16.14)* across from the PTT at the Platz end of town, is known by wise visitors for its good food at reasonable prices amid Alpine surroundings. Even the newest rooms have been decorated in traditional style. Some bedrooms overlook the Jakobsbahn. The small-and-simply furnished **Zur Alten Post** *(20 rooms;* ☎ *81+43.54.03, FAX 81+43.62.39)* is the nearest neighbor, and the **Morosani Posthotel** *(94 rooms;* ☎ *81+44.11.61, FAX 81+43.16.47)*, near the main Post office (which has a winter sports-museum on its second floor), is popular with ski groups in winter months. Although there are stores on the street level, the restaurant and bedrooms are in traditional style. The **Golfhotel Waldhaus** *(62 rooms;* ☎ *81+47.11.31, FAX 81+46.39.39)*, on the lower lip of Davos, has charm, with a farm-country style helped along by half-curtains in the breakfast room, country-style furniture and a menu that features produce grown in and around Davos. On the upper side of the Promenade, the **Sonnenberg Hotel** *(37 rooms;* ☎ *81+46.10.22, FAX 81+46.57.97)*, at the Dorf end of town, is a pleasantly comfortable hotel, with modest prices, but with a swimming pool and warm-and-welcoming hospitality offered by owner Frau Gertrud Weber, who oversees a kitchen that served good regional food. The basically-furnished rooms open off a stark-looking hallway. The **Concordia** *(25 rooms;* ☎ *81+46.32.22, FAX 81+46.50.48)* is a pleasant 3-star hotel, on the view side of the valley, along the main street; the small **Trauffer**, a few shops away, on the same main street, has not completely lost its original chalet style.

RESTAURANTS are often in hotels, but **Fah**, near the main post office at the Platz end of town, is the signature *confiserie*, where "everyone" gathers for morning coffee, tea-time, and for light meals. **Bünderstübli**, a restaurant owned by Rudi and Rosita Fontanesi, is one place to enjoy excellent regional food served in a typically Alpine setting. At the top of the Weissfluh, the restaurant serves a spectacular view with standard fare.

DELÉMONT

Delémont *(CH-2800;* ☎ *66+53.13.58, FAX 66+22.87.81)*, in the Jura, north of the Alps and easily reached out of Basel, has all the atmosphere of neighboring France with the currency and comforts of Switzerland—and a history that dates from first mention in the 8th century. The railroad station is not the town's highlight. If you arrive by train, walk up the main road (with the station at your back) and curve to the left to find the historic *vieille ville* (old city), where you'll find the **Château**, built between 1717 and 1721 to serve as the summer residence of the prince-bishops (until the French Revolution); **L'Hotel de Ville**, built in Renaissance style a few years later; **L'eglise de Saint-Marcel**, with a small museum in its sacristy; and **Le Musée jurassien**, near the Château, with a collection that tells the history of the surrounding countryside and the town. Several historic fountains dot squares in the old part of the town.

LODGING: One of my favorite perches is the small **La Bonne Auberge** *(14 beds;* ☎ *66+22.17.58)*, better known for its restaurant than for the few simple bedrooms.

DISENTIS

Disentis *(CH-7180;* ☎ *81+947.58.22, FAX 81+947.49.37)*, in Graubünden and easily reached by heading out of the valley from Chur, claims the oldest monastery in Switzerland. Although it is now part of a widely respected school, the **Cathedral** holds remarkable paintings and elaborate gold and stucco embellishments that rival those that are easier to see in St. Gallen.

EINSIEDELN

Einsiedeln *(CH-8840;* ☎ *55+53.44.88, 55+53.25.10)*, easily reached by train from Zürich and not far from Schwyz, in central Switzerland, has a Benedictine **monastery** that was founded at the time of Charlemagne. The abbey church of the vast monastery holds the Black Madonna of Einsiedeln. The Festival of the Miraculous Dedication, with impressive candlelight procession, is held each year on September 14.

LODGING: Among the several hotels, the **Drei Könige** *(57 rooms;* ☎ *55+53.24.41, FAX 55+53.66.52)* is the town's best, with the **Bären Zunfthaus** *(42 rooms;* ☎ *55+53.28.76, FAX 55+53.65.06)* also convenient, on Hauptstrasse, and comfortable.

ENGADINE VALLEY

The Engadine Valley, in Graubünden, is unique, not only for its ski facilities but, more significantly, for the Romansch language that is traditionally spoken by its residents and for exceptional innkeeping and hospitality in a calm, natural style. The region claims the well-known resorts such as St. Moritz, Pontresina and others, as well as many little-known but lovely villages that still thrive with farming although they also appeal to visitors who want to settle into the rural lifestyle, to enjoy cross-country skiing, or long walks and hikes.

In the Unterengadin, as the lower Engadine is called in German, the architecture of farmhouses is unique, with straight lines, drab stucco color, and delightful geometric designs, etched into the wet stucco/cement, around wood-framed windows and doorways. The area also has a few castles, with **Schloss Tarasp** *(CH-7553 Tarasp; open May to mid-October, ☎ 84+993.68)* one of the most enchanting.

Bad Tarasp-Vulpera *(CH-7552 Vulpera; ☎ 84+909.44, FAX 84+909.45)* appears to be a confusing mixture of new and old communities that have grown together in recent years in response to the spa facilities, the winter sports activities and the fact that the communities are at the "end of the line" for the Rhaetian Railway's route to this part of the Italian border. To make things more confusing, the three original villages of Tarasp, Scuol and Vulpera are sliced by old roads and new highways. Although the river, with its curative springs, is deep in a narrow valley, buildings have grown from the valley floor up the mountainsides to the level of the train station and commercial hub, at a point where the valley widens. Rising from the top of a pinnacle of rocks, the **castle** is a lonely statement of an earlier, less cluttered time. Its Romanesque chapel dates from 1040, with additions in the 16th century. Although many of the frescoes are Romanesque, some of the apostles in the nave are from the 17th century. Established in the 11th century, the castle was claimed by the Counts of the Tirol in 1239. In 1803, Napoleon brought Tarasp into the Helvetian republic. After years of neglect, the castle was acquired by a Dr. Lingner in 1900, and extensively rebuilt, restored and revitalized, with a concert organ built within the castle and the grounds planted with hundreds of trees. Although Dr. Lingner died in 1916, before the restoration was completed, the property is now owned by princess Margaret of Hesse and is open on request as a museum of 16th to 18th century living with sturdy wooden furnishings and a banquet hall that has an elaborately carved ceiling.

LODGING: At *Bad Scuol-Tarasp*, the **Romantik Hotel Guardaval** (☎ *81+864.13.21, FAX 81+864.97.67*), owned by Peider Andri and Monika Regi, is a gem, although it may seem difficult to find with the convoluted road system. Be sure to ask, because meals served in the restaurant are rightfully praised and public rooms (and bedrooms) offer style and comforts.

La Punt, another farming village on the train and highway route between St. Moritz and Tarasp-Scuol-Vulpera, is nondescript, except for Waltraud and Eduard Hitzberger's **Romantik Restaurant Chesa Pirani**, nestled at 5577 feet at the foot of the Albula Pass in the Upper Engadine valley. The inn is a lovely luncheon goal amid walks in gorgeous countryside. The 1750 building is typical of the stark lines and whimsical trompe l'oeil-etched window decoration.

Among the other towns in the valley, discussed alphabetically in this section, are St. Moritz, Pontresina, and Zuoz.

FRIBOURG

Fribourg *(CH-1700; ☎ 37+81.31.75, FAX 37+22.35.27)* zigzags from hilltop to riverside, lining roadsides with a collection of more than 200 historic buildings. Although many date from the Middle Ages, there are also prized examples of baroque and classic French-style buildings. At the linguistic border, French is the language spoken by most; the spelling of the town's name translates as "free town," which is Freiburg in German. Always known for scholarly pursuits, the town is home to a number of language schools, as well as to the **University**, an impressive **Musée d'art et d'histoire** and many photogenic buildings that nestle against each other on the winding way from the hilltop to the riverside.

Founded in 1157 by Berchtold of Zähringen (Bertold in French), the city resisted the Reformation and remains staunchly Catholic. The country's only bilingual Catholic university was founded here in the late 1800s; the town continues to be a major learning center.

LODGING: Among the places to stay, the **Hotel Duc Bertold** *(60 beds; rue des Bouchers 112; ☎ 37+81.11.21, FAX 37+23.15.87)* is in a 19th-century patrician home that has been classified as a historic monument and the **Hotel de la Rose** *(42 rooms; pl. Notre Dame 179; ☎ 37+81.12.70, FAX 37+22.35.66)* claims portions of a 17th-century home, but most of the structure is of recent date with comfortable facilities and a good restaurant.

See "Gruyères" below, for one of many easy day trips from Fribourg.

GENÈVE

Genève *(CH-1201;* ☎ *22+738.52.00, FAX 22+731.90.56)*, tucked into the French border in the west, is more an international city than a Swiss one, insofar as traditional customs are concerned But there's no doubt about the city's excellent restaurants, hospitality, transportation and shops, or about its easy access to spectacular sites for walks, hikes, serious climbing, or simply leisure time in elegant surroundings with all comforts. Mont Blanc and its neighboring mountains provide the backdrop for Lac Léman (see below), also known as the lake of Genève, embroidered with several charming villages, many with cozy inns that may also be exceptional restaurants. Vineyards blanket the slopes that rise from Lac Léman, with vines that turn gold as the weather cools, and the grapes are harvested and pressed, in fall. Comfortable lakeboats lace the shoreside villages, with frequent summer service and some journeys on most weekends and holidays throughout the year, weather permitting.

Although the area around Genève's railroad station is the seediest part of town, when you walk through the underground passage or dart across the traffic-clogged streets, you can stroll down rue de Mont Blanc to the lake in less than 10 minutes—and step into the sophisticated life of the city. Across the lake, rising to the tower of its churches, is the *vieille ville*, with cobbled roads, pedestrian areas and a liberal sprinkling of cafés and small, wood-walled restaurants where the atmosphere is as good as the food.

The **Place de Bourg**, on the site where Julius Caesar gathered with his troops, is the heart of the *vieille ville*. Any one of its cafés is an ideal place to contemplate your next move, or the last, or the people around you—or nothing at all.

RESTAURANTS: A few of my favorites are in this area, namely **Au Pied au Couchon**, near Place de Bourg, and **Café-Restaurant l'Hôtel de Ville**, diagonally across from the Hôtel de Ville, as the town hall is called in French-speaking Genève, at the top of Grand' Rue. In warm-weather months, spring and fall weekends, plan to dine on one of the lakeboats, as it glides along its route, lacing villages together. Another memorable place, best known to the Genevoise, is **au Milan**, on rue Chaponnière, near the Post Office, just off rue de Mont Blanc.

LODGING: This city has a flock of luxury lodgings that offer skilled service in pace-setting Swiss style (at top cost). Four worth noting are the classic **Beau Rivage** *(172 beds;* ☎ *22+731.02.21; FAX 22+738.98.47)*, where the best rooms have balconies and a lake view,

Des Bergues *(185 beds;* ☎ *22+731.50.50; FAX 22+732.19.89)*, with a classic lobby of several small rooms, **De la Paix** *(152 beds;* ☎ *22+732.61.50; FAX 22+738.87.94)*, with a coveted location and a devoted following, and **Le Richmond** *(183 beds;* ☎ *22+731.14.00; FAX 22+731.67.09)*, which was totally refurbished recently, to emerge in modern, masculine, wood-and-marble style. The first-mentioned three of these four hotels are facing or near the city-splitting river and lakeboat dock; Le Richmond is bordering the river and farthest from the lake. Among my smaller favorites are the classy and comfortable **Hôtel de la Cigogne** *(50 rooms; 17 pl. Longmalle;* ☎ *22+21.42.42, FAX 22+21.40.65)*, a *Relais & Châteaux* member at the foot of the cobbled streets that lead up to the historic *vieille ville* and **Les Armures** *(52 beds; 1 Puits St. Pierre;* ☎ *22+310.91.72; FAX 22+310.98.46)*, on the hilltop in the old town. One modest nest that's been my home on several visits is **Le Chandèlier** *(22 rooms;* ☎ *22+21.56.88)*, which I first visited several years ago and still enjoy. Its narrow doorway is amid antique shops and bookstores on Grand' Rue, in the old town, neighbor to several cozy restaurants. When I have arrived in the city at a late hour, sometimes too tired to travel far, I have also folded into one of the rooms at the **Hotel Bernina** *(100 beds;* ☎ *22+731.49.50)*, on Place Cornavin across from the Hauptbahnhof. It's used by what appears to be lower echelon international folks from Europe and the Middle East, in town for business of some sort. Bedrooms vary in size, shape and upkeep, but mine have been spanking clean, reasonably comfortable and modestly priced. **Hotel d'Allèves** *(41 rooms; rue Kleberg 13,* ☎ *22+738.32.66, FAX 22+738.32.66)*, not far from the Hotel des Berges, and an easy walk from the railroad station and the lake, has been my home on recent visits. With small rooms, and a very convenient location, the hotel seems cozy and comfortable amid the city's activities.

For a country atmosphere with all the city's conveniences, visit **Auberge de Pinchat** *(32 Chemin de Pinchat, CH 1227 Carouge; 8 rooms;* ☎ *22+342.30.77; FAX 22+300.22.19)*. Best known locally for its restaurant, the inn is a lovely place to stay. The tram reaches nearby; a car is the most convenient way to get here.

In addition to the villages mentioned below (see "Lac Léman"), there are several pleasant excursions from Genève. The journey to **Hermance** passes Genève's classy hillside "suburb" of **Cologny**, where the elegant **Lion d'Or** is a restaurant worth noting both for food and for the terrace view.

GRINDELWALD

Grindelwald *(CH-3818;* ☎ *36+53.12.12, FAX 36+53.30.88)*, at 3393 ft (1034 m) in the Berner Oberland, is almost in the middle of the country, and easily reached by car and by train, out of Interlaken. The 35-minute train ride up and out from Interlaken is slow enough and pretty enough to set the mood for a mountain holiday. Although the one-time village has obviously cast its lot with tourism, and there are approximately 50 hotels and 500 apartments that range from luxurious to very modest, the mountain transport can lift you away from any clutter within a few minutes. The main road through town bends and weaves and is fringed with shops that sell clothes and trinkets as well as some that rent skiing and hiking equipment. The greatest asset of Grindelwald, in my opinion, is the fact that it nests in a mountain valley, with the **Jungfraujoch** (at 11,333 ft, or 3454 m) one of many enchanting, scenic excursions, via the cog-railway through Kleine Scheidegg. The 40-minute train ride from Grindelwald up to **Kleine Scheidegg** is spectacular in its own right, with the mountaintop station providing a sensational view of the north face of the Eiger mountain as well as of the Mönch and the Jungfrau, and the **Alpine garden** near the topmost station a delight for those who make the time to walk through it.

Other clear-day excursions easily accomplished from Grindelwald include taking the 6-person gondola up to First (pronounced "*Fearst*," a starting point for any of several enchanting walks. (It's possible, spectacular and relatively easy, to walk down from First to Grindelwald, but those of us who have done it are quick to warn of day-after shin-splints when you're not in shape.) **Männlichen** (7317 ft; 2230 m), with a view of far off mountain peaks that includes, like Kleine Scheidegg, the north face of the Eiger, the Mönch, and the Jungfrau is also a worthy goal, as is the **Schilthorn** (9748 ft; 2971 m), known as "Piz Gloria" in the James Bond movie "On Her Majesty's Secret Service." Piz Gloria is now the name of the revolving restaurant, which claims to offer a view of almost 200 Alpine peaks. The journey to the Schilthorn from Stechelberg to Mürren is on what's touted as the "longest cable-car of the Alps." For the fearless folks who ski down from the top in winter, the start is like skiing down the face of a needle. Also worth some time is the journey to **Bussalp** (5906 ft; 1792 m), a delightful postal bus ride for summer walks as well as for winter cross-country skiing and tobogganing. Obviously none of these excursions is much if weather prevents enjoying the view, unless—like me—you delight in heading up and out just for the fun of it, on the chance that the weather will lift (which it often does).

The tourist office provides details about well-planned walks and hikes, ranging from very easy to much more strenuous routes, with maps for those who want to strike out independently and guides available if arrangements are made a couple of days in advance. Concerts and folklore events are highlights of the busy summer and winter seasons; don't count on much evening activity during spring and fall, when many hotels and restaurants close for refurbishing and staff vacations.

LODGING: In addition to the hotels and apartments, there are several mountain hotels and five camp sites. The tourist office provides details and will make reservations (☎ *36+53.15.60, FAX 36+ 53.30.88).* The **Grand Hotel Regina** *(100 rooms; ☎ 36+54.54.55, FAX 36+53.47.17)* is the grande dame of the village, in addition to being a member of the prestigious *Leading Hotels of the World* group, with all the pomp that that implies. Convenient to everything, the classic property is at the upper end of the town's main road, across from the train station and within walking distance of the gondola station to ride up to First. Built as the 18th century became the 19th, in the style of that time, the hotel was purchased and completely refurbished in 1955. *La Pendule d'Or*, the deluxe restaurant, and the informal *Jägerstube*, serving Swiss specialties, are deservedly popular; guest facilities include two pools, tennis courts, sauna and massage services. Some of the hotel's multinight packages are very good value; the chalet-style **Regina Haus**, linked to the hotel, has 9 apartments. The **Hotel Kreuz & Post** *(82 beds; ☎ 36+54.54.92, FAX 36+53.43.19)* is also in the 5-star league, with rooms on the front of the 6-story building providing a lovely view (and street noises, when traffic is steady). Both hotels are in the grand tradition with crisp bed linens, attentive service and good food served in the formal dining rooms. At the other extreme, for in-town lodgings with Alpine atmosphere, the chalet-style **Bellevue** *(9 rooms; ☎ 36+53.12.34)* and the newer **Gasthof Steinbock** *(22 rooms, ☎ 36+53-10.10, FAX 36+53.34.94)*, also with chalet style, offer garni service (no meals), with cozy, small rooms in traditional decor and prices that are a fraction of the 5-star places. **Alpenblick** *(12 rooms; ☎ 36+53.11.05)*, better known for its restaurant and mountain-meadow location than for its cozy, comfortable bedrooms, is popular with walkers, hikers and others who enjoy being out of the mainstream and in the mountains.

GRUYÈRES

Gruyères *(CH-1663; ☎ 29+6.10.30)*, a medieval town not far from Fribourg (see above), gives its name to cheese and has a **Cheese-making Museum** at the base of its hill-climbing main street. But it's the renaissance houses that line the one street of the village and the **Schloss** (castle) to which the street leads, that linger in the memory. Decorated in styles familiar in the 15th to 17th centuries, the houses are now shops, restaurants and inns. The castle, a delightful example of Switzerland's castle culture, was built for the vassal lords of the kingdom of Burgundy in the Middle Ages and was home for the counts of Gruyères. Although tours can clog the town's street when weather is warm and sunny, there are a couple of charming inns where staying overnight can put you back in time, to enjoy the village when it settles back to quiet, after the tours have left. The small **Hostellerie St. Georges** *(34 beds; ☎ 29+6.22.46; FAX 29+6.33.13)* and the slightly larger **Hostellerie des Chevaliers** *(70 beds; ☎ 29+6.19.33, FAX 29+6.25.52)* are both in medieval buildings adapted for use by modern travelers.

GSTAAD

Gstaad *(CH-3780; ☎ 30+471.71, FAX 30+456.20)*, high in the western part of the Bernese Oberland, is a revered mountain resort, although it is still in farming country where a strict building code perpetuates traditional wood-chalet architecture. Respected as a ski resort, with 70 skilifts and mountain railways and almost 160 miles (250 km) of downhill trails in and around this and neighboring villages, the town appeals to famous names who want anonymity. Although the heart of the village is still at and around the Bahnhof, with its flower-filled window boxes, chalets and other homes have grown on the hillsides, both for view and exclusivity. One popular annual event is the **Musiksommer**, an exceptional program of concerts and other performances from the end of July through mid-September.

In addition to its acknowledged importance as a winter resort, the entire **Saanenland** region *(CH-3778 Schönried; ☎ 30+488.88, FAX 30+464.70)* is ideal for summer sport, including walks, hikes, climbing and even skiing on the glacier at Les Diablerets. This is also an area for ballooning, as well as for trout fishing in the Arnensee and the Saane river, outside of Gsteid/Feutersoey. Neighboring villages with rural appeal include **Saanen** *(CH-3792; ☎ 30+425.97; FAX 30+461.82)*, noteworthy for its frequent country markets and the tiny **Mauritiuskirche** that has well-preserved 15th century paintings;

Schönried (CH-3778; ☎ 30+488.88; FAX 30+464.70), popular with families because of its location in a wide valley with beautiful mountain views; *Saanenmöser* (CH-3777; ☎ 30+422.22, FAX 30+493.51), above Zweisimmen (where passengers change trains on the MOB train ride between Montreux and Spiez) with its golf course; **Gstei-d/Feutersoey** (CH-3785; ☎ 30+512.31), at the foot of Col du Pillon, with an Alpine railway to the glacier at Les Diablerets; and **Lauenen** (CH-3782; ☎ 30+533.30), with its neighboring **Geltental nature reserve**, the gorgeous **Geltenschuss** (waterfall), and the **Lauenensee** (lake).

LODGING: Gstaad's choices range from the ultra-chic, quietly-tony places known to (and for) celebrities to dozens of attractive small places, where bedrooms are clean and tidy and cost a fraction of the price that the famed places charge. The **Palace** *(107 rooms;* ☎ *30+831.31; FAX 30+433.44)* and the newer **Grand Hotel Park** *(83 rooms;* ☎ *30+833.77; FAX 30+444.14)* are the biggest hotels, both with full resort facilities, including swimming pool, sauna, squash and tennis courts. The **Hotel Christiania** *(25 rooms;* ☎ *30+451.21; FAX 30+471.09)*, near the tennis courts, is chalet style, with a terrace restaurant for summer months and a pleasant Alpine atmosphere throughout the year. Most rooms have a balcony; all have views; some cluster as apartments. The smaller, family-owned **Hotel Olden** *(15 rooms;* ☎ *30+434.44; FAX 30+461.64)* has more country charm than the bigger hotels. It also has a popular (very good) restaurant. Another small spot, with modest prices and Alpine chalet atmosphere, is the **Posthotel Rössli** *(20 rooms;* ☎ *30+434.12; FAX 30+461.90)*.

In Saanen, most hotels are small. A personal favorite is the small **Hotel Boo** *(17 rooms;* ☎ *30+414.41; FAX 30+440.27)*, with some apartments. It's popular, as are many places in this area, with vacationing British.

INTERLAKEN

Interlaken *(CH-3800;* ☎ *36+22.21.21; FAX 36+22.52.21)* is on every tourist itinerary, but don't let that scare you away. This town is a wonderful hub for stretching up to the mountains, to the Jungfrau, which you can see on a clear day from Interlaken, or by taking a lakeboat for a leisurely ride on either of two lovely lakes. The town name means "between the lakes," so it should be no surprise that you can walk to board a boat for the Thunersee/Lac de Thoune, capped with a castle, or the Brienzersee/Lac de Brienz, which takes its name from a town noted for a wood-carving tradition. The town is a tourist place, especially in summer months, but it claims its own personality in spring and fall. There are souvenir and other shops lining the main streets. One major reason for coming to town is the annual **Tellespiel**, an outdoor performance of the legend of William Tell, complete with cows, horses and costumed participants. Although the event is spoken in German, the story is perfectly clear to all. Inquire at the tourist office about dates and reservations.

LODGING: The pace is set by the huge **Victoria Jungfrau** *(400 beds;* ☎ *36+27.11.11; FAX 36+27.37.37).* Built in late 19th century style with a more modern wing, the hotel was known to Mark Twain and has been home for thousands of other American tourists. Restored to its turn-of-the-century appearance, the hotel offers all modern conveniences for bus tours and other groups. **Hôtel Du Lac** *(70 beds;* ☎ *36+22.29.22, FAX 36+22.29.15),* near the boat dock for rides on the Brienzersee, also caters to groups in summer season, but has a pleasant atmosphere. A personal favorite, shared by three generations of my family, is the **Gasthof Hirschen** *(20 rooms;* ☎ *36+22.15.45, FAX 36+23.37.45),* in **Matten**, a one-time village that's now glued to Interlaken. On the far side of a park, a reasonable walk from the shopping streets, the inn has a pleasant and cozy country-style restaurant on its street level. Athough the hotel's exterior is traditional farmhouse style and its restaurants maintain the old flavor, the bedrooms were modernized a few years ago and are clean and neat, but some seem spartan.

LAC LÉMAN

Lac Léman, known to most English-speaking folks as the lake of Geneva, is shared by the French and the Swiss. The lakeside is studded with castles that punctuate towns established in the Middle Ages. Important trading centers throughout the ages, most towns are now favored by visitors and residents for their shops, their sightseeing and their inns, many of which benefit from the wine produced in nearby vineyards. Several of the lakeside towns have large, well-equipped marinas; some have sailboats for rent.

From Genève, at the western end of the crescent moon-shaped lake, highlights include **Coppet** (see above), **Nyon**, **Rolle**, **Morges** and **Ouchy**, the lakeside "suburb" of hillside **Lausanne**. (See "Lausanne," below.) Many of the area's vintners open their cellars for visitors and several villages have exceptional museums hidden in their castles or villas. Walking paths follow the lakeside in most areas and thread through the vineyards on the sun-washed slopes. At the eastern end of the lake, beyond **Vevey** and **Montreux**, the imposing site of the

Château de Chillon moved Lord Byron to write his famous *Prisoner of Chillon*. Towns along the lake's French side—**Evian-les- Bains**, **Thonon-les-Bains** and others—are mentioned in the chapter on France.

LAGO MAGGIORE

Lago Maggiore, poking into Switzerland's southern canton of Ticino and shared with Italy, is embroidered with many charming villages that can be ideal pausing places during lakeside or hillside walks and hikes. Boats, which operate frequently in warm-weather months and on weekends and holidays throughout the year, are the best way to travel from village to village. The service, operated by an Italian company, is at an extra charge, even for those holding one of the otherwise-inclusive Swiss travel passes. One attraction of this area, for those in search of natural places, is the relaxed lifestyle at many valley villages and *grotti*, where homecooked meals and drinks can be enjoyed, often on vine-covered terraces pinned to the lakeside. Many are pleasant places to spend a few nights in comfortably rustic surroundings. A few can be reached only by boat. Not far from the lake, both the **Valle Maggia** and the **Val Verzasca** (see below) are flecked with rustic villages, usually with several traditional stone-slab houses, where flowers pour from windowboxes, and a small church. Although Locarno (see below) is a major Swiss town and its neighbor, Ascona (see above) is popular for its cafes, boutiques and summer music festival, there are many delightful villages on the lake and in the surrounding mountains. (For information about Italian villages, refer to the chapter on Italy.)

LAUSANNE

Lausanne *(CH-1000;* ☎ *21+617.73.21; FAX 21+616.86.47)*, a university town rising from the shores of Lac Léman, has a medieval *vieille ville* at its heart and counts among its attractions an exceptional art gallery, **La Fondation l'Hermitage** *(2, route du Signal,* ☎ *21+20.50.01)* that was once a private home. It's in a residential area, easily reached by bus 16 to the stop marked "La Croisée du Signal." The medieval center has grown around the **Place de la Cathedrale**, where you'll find several cozy (and excellent) restaurants, as well as much of historic interest. The **Musée des Arts Decoratifs** is a treasure chest of applied arts. Exhibits feature glassware, ceramics and folk art.

To fully appreciate the city, visit the **Musée Historique de Lausanne** *(Ancien Evêche, 4 Place de la Cathédrale)*, where there's a scale model of the Lausanne, in addition to paintings and other items identified with important periods throughout its history.

The new **Musée Olympique** *(1 quai d'Ouchy)* sits amid gardens, to the left as you leave the funicular that stretches between the hilltops of Lausanne and lakeside Ouchy. Opened with ceremonies on June 23, 1992, the museum holds the official collection for the Olympic committee, with memorabilia from all the Olympic games and documents from Olympic history. Designed by Mexican architect Pedro Ramirez Vazquez and Lausanne architect Jean-Pierre Cahen, the museum is built in tiers, from underground to high level windows that can give an awe-inspiring view of the Savoy Alps when the weather allows. Although the ultra-modern building raised some eyebrows when it was planted amid the venerable mansions that punctuate most of the lakeside landscape, the museum has become a focal point, not only for the events held here on the premises but also for the grounds and the exhibitions, including those that are animated with audio-visual aids. (Such a prestigious museum was envisioned by Pierre de Fredi, Baron de Coubertin, the father of the International Olympic Committee, which was founded in 1894, two years before the first Olympic games took place.)

While the city has grown to cover several hilltops and provide a full range of shops, cultural activities and hotels, *Ouchy*—the medieval fishing village that has become a thriving Lac Léman marina—still has small-town qualities (in addition to its lovely lakeside location). Ouchy is an ideal pivot point for lake and other touring, with the hillside train station linked to the sea by the *Métro*, a funicular that rachets up and down the hillside the lake, the station and the *vieille ville* on a steady, dependable schedule. (The public bus follows a similar route.)

LODGING: Both city and lakeside hotels have their special virtues. I prefer the lakeside, which gives easy access for spontaneous boat trips. In the city, the **Lausanne Palace** *(160 rooms; ☎ 21+331.31.31, FAX 21+323.25.71)* is the most luxurious, offering splendidly-Swiss service, in the best *École Hôtelière* tradition. Also maintaining the style known for the most elegant turn-of-the-century hotels, the lakeside **Beau Rivage** *(189 rooms; ☎ 21+617.17.17, FAX 21+617.78.78)* is a cherished property. Its dining room is elegant; its public rooms grand; and the nicely appointed bedrooms facing the lake overlook the gardens. An extensive refurbishing, modernization program over the past few years added TV and other 1990's touches to traditional decor. **La Résidence** *(52 rooms; ☎ 21+617.77.11; FAX 21+617.06.67)*, also elegant, with the feeling of a private manor house, is a neighbor at the lake. More than once I have nestled into the far less lavish rooms at the **Angleterre** (☎ 21+617.21.11; FAX 21+616.80.75), enjoying the fact that Byron stayed here—and that the restaurant serves good food within view of the lake, on a roadside promenade that allows for leisurely people-watching. Another choice, even less expensive, with very modest bedrooms, is the **Hôtel du Port** *(Place du Port,* ☎ 21+617.49.30), which is better known for its streetfront café restaurant than as a place to overnight.

From Lausanne-Ouchy, boats leave several times daily for France, for **Evian** across the lake (and discussed in the chapter on France). The wine-making village of **Cully**, is an easy excursion by lakeboat or by train, or perhaps going one way, lingering for a meal and returning with the alternate transport.

LODGING AND RESTAURANTS: Two of my favorite inns are neighbors in Cully. The **Major Davel** *(17 rooms;* ☎ 21+799.11.37, FAX 21+799.37.82) is at the lakeside, a few steps from the boat dock. The **Hôtel du Raisin** *(6 rooms;* ☎ 21+799.21.31, FAX 21+799.25.01), in the center of the tiny village and a few steps farther from the dock, is tonier, well-known to businessfolks and more expensive. Both places serve excellent meals; the formal dining room at du Raisin is more formal, with more elaborate cuisine.

(For other places on and near the lake, refer to Genève and Lac Léman.)

LOCARNO

Locarno *(CH-6600;* ☎ 93+31.03.33, FAX 93+31.90.70), the largest Swiss settlement on the Lago Maggiore (see above), is a popular town for tourism and retirement, as well as for banks. Nearby Ascona (see above), a onetime fishing village that is now a spruced up artists' colony, is also popular for summer excursions and cultural events.

LODGING in Locarno can be in a castle, a manor house, a large, early-19th century hotel, or in one of many small spots. My votes go to the **Schlosshotel** *(34 rooms;* ☎ 93+31.23.61, FAX 93+31.73.23) and the smaller **Minusio** *(26 rooms;* ☎ 93+33.19.13, FAX 93+33.77.04), where rooms have personality and the surroundings are appealing. Each is a short walk inland from the lake. For tonier, more traditionally elegant surroundings, the long-time leader is **Treff Hotel La Palma au Lac** *(74 rooms;* ☎ 93+33.01.71, FAX 93+33.39.74), used by bus tour groups that can affect the atmosphere. Its lakefront location is ideal, however, and convenient for the boat dock and shops as well as the railroad station.

LUGANO

Lugano *(CH-6900;* ☎ *91+21.46.64, FAX 91+22.76.53)*, resting beside lovely Lago Lugano in the southern Ticino, has long been a favorite place for retirees and others lured here by the springlike climate offered on the southern "sunny side of the Alps." The **Piazza Riforma** bristles with café tables whenever the weather is warm enough and is the prized lingering spot whether you choose to dine, drink or just rest. On market days, the square is covered with fruit, vegetable and other produce stalls from early morning through midday. The lakefront promenade is studded with benches, trimmed with gardens that include palm trees among their plantings and laced by boats, notably the popular lakeboats that thread nearby villages to the town. The railway station, on the hillside, is linked to the lake by funicular. An ideal touring base, Lugano is also connected to smaller communities by postal bus and by funiculars to high mountain villages. (Lugano is a comfortable, pleasant base for touring Italy's peripatetic city of Milano, a two-hour train ride away. See Italy's chapter for details about Milano.)

LODGING: Gaining a name for itself as a money hub by providing Swiss banking services to neighboring Italians and others, the town has its share of posh hotels. But the small spots offer the most typical hospitality. Among them, my home on several occasions has been the Müller family's pension-style **City Hotel** *(Crocicchio Cortogna 7;* ☎ *91+23.62.44)*, occupying the upper floors of a palacio a few steps from the central Piazza Reforma, not far from the railway station's funicular. Nearby, the **Romantik Hotel Ticino** *(Piazza Cioccaro 1; 23 rooms;* ☎ *91+22.77.72; FAX 91+23.62.78)*, in a 400-year-old house, maintains Ticinese traditions, with regional recipes offered in its restaurant, but staff seemed a bit standoffish when I recently visited.

Morcote is one of the lakeside highlights. The village is easily reached by postal bus and by lakeboat. Now clipped to the lakeside by a new highway, the faded pastel buildings, the arcaded lakeside street and the several café-restaurants and small hotels keep the village atmosphere intact.

LODGINGS: Among my favorites, for places to stay, are the **Carina-Carlton** *(25 rooms;* ☎ *91+69.11.31; FAX 91+69.19.29)*, recently purchased by new owners but with its comforts and small-hotel hospitality maintained, and its neighbor, the **Hotel Post** *(5 rooms;* ☎ *91+69.11.27; FAX 91+69.17.74)*. Both hotels have terrace restaurants hanging over the lake in additon to main house restaurants on the inland side of the lake-rimming road.

Castagnola is another gem of the village on the shore. Best known among art aficionados for Baron Hans Heinrich Thyssen-Bornemisza's **Villa Favorita**, which had held his private collection of exceptional art, the museum has reopened and, although the nucleus of the famous collection is no longer here, there are special exhibitions as well as an impressive collection of other art held by the family. (More than 750 of the most famous masterpieces are displayed in a new museum in Madrid, under terms worked out at the behest of the Spanish-born wife of the Baron.) Although a 20-room wing had been added to the 17th-century Villa Favorita from 1919-39 to hold the collection, it was not large enough to hold the works and emotional ties to Spain resulted first in the loan to Spain's Prado Museum, for ten years and now to the present display in the recently completed building in Madrid.

LODGING: Although the **Carlton Villa Moritz** *(52 rooms;* ☎ *91+51.38.12; FAX 91+51.38.14)* is favored by some, I've enjoyed the simple **Fischer's Seehotel** *(20 rooms;* ☎ *91+51.55.71; FAX 91+53.15.77)*.

Bosco Luganese *(CH-6935)*, about four miles from the lake, is noteworthy for its country atmosphere, and for the **Hotel Villa Margherita** *(31 rooms, 6 apartments;* ☎ *91+50.61.49, FAX 91+50.61.49)*, a country estate with many comforts. As a member of the *Relais & Châteaux*, the pool-punctuated villa is noted for its meals and services as well as for its pleasant rooms and rural setting.

The **Taler von Lugano** region, in the mountains above Lugano, claims several small villages that are ideal places for walks and hikes. Among them are **Vedeggio**, **Capriasca** and **Valcolla**, around **Taverne** *(CH-6807 Taverne;* ☎ *91+93.24.66)*, where tiled roofs cap stucco-walled houses clustered in small villages. Rivers and paths slice the mountainsides and meadows. Bus service links these villages with Lugano, making it possible to head out for a day of walking and a country lunch, to return to the bigger town by nightfall.

LUZERN

Luzern *(CH-6003;* ☎ *41+61.71.71; FAX 41+51.73.34)*, known as **Lucerne** to English-speaking travelers, was established centuries ago as a market town that appealed to travelers. Although mention is made of an 8th-century monastery in the area, the town began to grow when the pass to the south was opened in the 13th century and traders from northern Europe and southern Italy passed through. They left their imprint in building styles, monuments and legends. Today's "traders" also leave their imprint, especially in summer months, when the flood of tourists fills the streets (and shops) with English, Japanese, and other non-Swiss languages. Shops border most streets in the old town on both sides of the river that divides the town as it grows alongside the lake. Countless photographs have been taken through the years of all angles of the **Kapellbrücke**, one of the wood covered bridges that stretches across the river at the end of the lake. Destroyed by a mysterious fire in early spring 1993, the bridge has been rebuilt in the old style. Not as tragic as it first seemed, since sections of the bridge had been rebuilt throughout its recent history so little that burned was from the Middle Ages, the fire was thought to have started in a small boat placed under the bridge. Planned for reconstruction in the old style (although not completed at presstime), the bridge will once again claim its photogenic position, not far from the **Hauptbahnhof** (railway station) and the departure point for the lakeboats.

Restaurants and cafés line the waterfront and some of the cobblestone areas of the **Altstadt**. Most are tourist-oriented, with menus that cater to transient patrons. One joy of this town, in spite of its sometimes-overwhelming tourism, is its location, on the lake and within easy trainride, public bus journey, or drive from dozens of wonderfully scenic, rural areas. (See "Vierwaldstättersee" below.) It's possible to spend the day on a lakeboat, riding to the far end, to return by train, if your time is limited. It's also possible to take the lakeboat to one of the villages and to walk/hike along wall marked paths, or to take a mountain railway to higher points for viewful strolls, perhaps to an inn for lunch.

LODGING: Among the dozens of comfortable lodgings in Luzern, the lakeside **Grand Hotel National** (*78 rooms; Haldenstrasse 4;* ☎ *41+50.11.11, FAX 41+51.55.39*) is a member of the *Preferred Hotel* group, and its neighbor, the **Palace** (*152 rooms; Haldenstrasse 10;* ☎ *41+50.22.22, FAX 41+51.69.76*), belongs to the *Leading Hotels of the World*. Both properties continue the traditional Swiss "grand hotel" style, with top-of-the-line comforts. The National has an indoor pool. The **Wilden Mann** (*43 rooms; Bahnhofstrasse 30;* ☎ *41+23.16.66, FAX 41+23.16.29*) has been a long-time favorite, not only because it is convenient to the railroad station, lake, Altstadt, and everything else, but because it maintains a traditional atmosphere in its charming bedrooms and holds history in the wood-walled public rooms, including the street-level restaurants.

Among the smaller, cozy (and less expensive) properties, consider **zum Wiessen Kreuz** (*34 rooms; Furrengasse 19;* ☎ *41+51.40.40, FAX 41+51.40.60*), where I've stayed on several occasions, or the **Schiff**

(20 rooms; Brandgässli 9; ☎ *41+51.38.51, FAX 41+52.82.52)*, both just in from the river that runs from the lake, in the heart of the Altstadt. Although bedrooms are small, facilities are modern and adequate.

Above the busyness of town, **Château Gütsch** *(42 rooms;* ☎ *41+22.02.72, FAX 41+22.02.52)* clings to a viewful hillside and is linked to commerce by its own funicular. The hotel continues to provide a very specal atmosphere, with many luxurious elements.

MÜRREN

Mürren *(CH-3825;* ☎ *36+56.16.16, FAX 36+55.37.69)*, in the Bernese Oberland, can seem like paradise, especially on a clear day when the snow-capped mountain peaks are etched against the sky. Wisely off-limits to cars, the mountain resort is reached by a funicular tram that slices the mountainside from Lauterbrunnen (linked by train to Interlaken). Although the tram will take you all the way to Mürren, I've enjoyed getting off at an earlier stop to walk along well-maintained paths to the town. The view across the valley to the mountain peaks, as they reveal themselves along the path, is memorable. Primarily a sports resort, the town is alive both summer and winter, for hiking, walking, ballooning, skiing, mountainclimbing and more traditional sports such as tennis

LODGING: Choices are many. The **Eiger** *(48 rooms;* ☎ *36+55.13.31, FAX 36+55.39.31)* and the **Palace Mürren** *(57 rooms;* ☎ *36+55.24.24, FAX 36+55.24.17)* are top-rated, but I have settled happily into the smaller **Bellevue-Crystal** *(23 rooms;* ☎ *36+55.14.01, FAX 36+55.14.90)*, a garni hotel with a cozy atmosphere.

MURTEN/MORAT

Murten/Morat *(CH-3280;* ☎ *37+71.51.12; FAX 37+71.49.83)*, with its German/French names a hint of its split personality, is a gem. Not far from Fribourg, the town is about half-an-hour's drive from Bern, although it takes longer by train due to connections. Plan to be in town on a market day, when the produce stalls and other items are displayed much as they might have been in the 12th century when this town was founded by the Dukes of Zähringhen. Since most of the buildings have been restored to the style of the Middle Ages and some to the 18th century, it's easy to recall the past. Murten, to use its German name, seems most unusual when you stay overnight and wander the arcaded streets within the walled town. Beautifully placed, on a hilltop overlooking the small Lac de Morat, the town claims a **Schloss**, which holds the limited **Museum**

Historisches, with some items from the Roman times and others from other stages in the town's history.

LODGING within the walled town can be at a handful of choice spots. Two of my favorites are the **Hotel Murtenhof** *(23 rooms; ☎ 37+71.56.56, FAX 37+71.50.59)* which is in the walls at the castle, and the larger, slightly more elegant double-named **Krone/Couronne** *(52 roms; ☎ 37+71.52.52, FAX 37+71.36.10)*, which is in the middle of town and well-known for its prized location. On the shore of the Lac du Morat, at **Murten-Meyriez** (with the hyphen designating a "suburb" of Murten/Morat), the country house atmosphere of **Vieux Manoir au Lac** *(30 rooms; ☎ 37+71.12.83; FAX 37+71.31.88)* and its exceptional restaurant, which takes on added appeal in warm weather months when you can dine by the lake, gives the property special appeal. Below the arcaded winding streets of the medieval village of Murten/Morat, the inn is a good base for relaxing by the lake as well as for stepping back into time at the top of the hill.

NEUCHÂTEL

Neuchâtel *(CH-2000; ☎ 38+25.42.42; FAX 38+24.28.52)*, which dates from 1170, has the Jura mountains behind it and lovely Lac de Neuchâtel as its apron. The town's venerable history includes Charlemagne, the Kings of Burgundy and the wealthy medieval House of Fenis, during which time Ulrich II built the château (some portions date from the 12th century), the collegiate church and many medieval buildings. Just before becoming part of the Swiss confederation, the town was ruled by the Kings of Prussia. Each ruler has left his mark and all have contributed to a heritage of the "good life," with excellent wines—the cause for an annual fall festival—and cultural events that include museums, concerts and schools of higher learning. The town may seem overwhelming, at first glance, with its cluster of homes as well as buildings devoted to watch-making, wine and its university.

LODGING: The **Beaulac** *(50 rooms; ☎ 38+25.88.22; FAX 38+25.60.35)*, perched at the lake on Quai Leopold-Robert, has a favored location for those who enjoy the lake, but it's not much for atmosphere. Nearby in **Hauterive** *(CH-2068)*, **Les Vieux Toits** *(8 rooms; ☎ 38+33.42.42)* has more atmosphere, with a 16th-century heritage, but it's a trolley-bus ride from town.

La Neuveville *(CH-2520; ☎ 38+51.49.49)*, about 20 minutes' train ride from Nauchâtel, is pinned to the nearby **Bielersee**, which is also known as the **Lac du Bienne** in this two-language area. The once-charming medieval village, now threatened by elevated highways and lake-rimming railroad tracks, huddles within its ancient walls. Mentioned here because it was a favorite retreat for Jean Jacques Rousseau and it has a memorable inn, La Neuveville can be charming when you look to the lake for inspiration. Rousseau spent time in the area in the 1760s, when the area was peaceful and remote. For two months in 1765, he stayed on **St. Petersinsel**, an islet in the Lac du Bienne that is linked to Jolimont, near **Erlach**, by the **Heidenweg** (Pagan's Way), a narrow strip of land. The small isle, where Cluniac monks built a monastery in 1127, is also linked to La Neuveville. Guests to the monastery-turned-inn come to dine, to spend a few quiet days, or to walk the grounds, passing vineyards and, perhaps, spotting some of the birds that nest in the woods and the surrounding marshes.

LODGING is possible at the **Restaurant-Hôtel St. Petersinsel** *(10 rooms; CH-3235 Erlach;* ☎ *32+88.11.14)*, where the bedroom named for Jean Jacques Rousseau has a traditonal tile stove and rustic-style furnishings. The hotel's restaurant is a popular weekend goal for people who live in the area. The **Hôtel J. J. Rosseau** *(23 rooms;* ☎ *38+51.36.51, FAX 38+51.56.23)*, a lakeside inn I have enjoyed on several visits, also has comfortable bedrooms and appealing public rooms. Best known to nearby businessfolks and for weekend outings, the inn has a lake view dining room; the boat dock is a short stroll toward the village. A lakeside table for meals can be a special experience; the best bedrooms have a view of the lake.

SAAS-FEE

Saas-Fee *(CH-3906;* ☎ *28+57.14.57, FAX 28+57.18.60)*, high in the Valais mountains, branches off from the route that puts it at the tip of one end of an inverted Y. (Zermatt is at the tip of the other end.) Linked by yellow postal bus with Brig, on the Rhône valley floor, Saas-Fee keeps all cars at a neck of land paved for the purpose. Only electric carts are allowed in the village. Once devoted to farming, the village now concentrates on tourism, with tennis courts and swimming pools to supplement the astounding mountains that are the lure for most visitors. Shops, cozy restaurants and most of the chalet-style hotels gather in a knot a short walk below the modern postal bus station. Ski lifts and cablecars stretch from one end of town to the highest slopes, allowing for summer skiing and viewful hikes and walks, as well as challenging mountain climbing. Popular for family vacations, Saas-Fee offers concerts and folk festivals, as well as guide services for mountain activities.

LODGING can be in the heart of tourism-and-the-town, or on the outskirts at places that can seem quieter and cozier at the height of summer or winter seasons. Nothing is very far from anything else; an easy stroll puts everything in reach. **Waldhotel Fletschhorn** *(10 rooms;* ☎ *28+57.21.31; FAX 28+57.21.87)*, a unique-and-charming inn, tucked in a clearing about 20 minutes' walk through the woods from the village center, is a place where magical memories are made. Hans-Jörg and Irma Dütsch-Grandjean are perfect hosts, whether you choose to walk to their inn for a meal or to sit on their sun terrace for afternoon tea or settle into one of the cozy rooms for several days. With warm hospitality, gourmet meals and rare wine, this place is at the top of my list for Swiss hideaways.

GRAND ST.-BERNARD PASS

Grand St.-Bernard Pass gives its name to the legendary dogs. The pass leads through the high mountains between Switzerland's Martigny, in the Valais region, at a bend in the Rhône river, and Italy's Aosta, on the southern side of the Alps. Trained by monks of the Middle Ages to aid them with rescues during the difficult mountain crossings, the dogs are still bred at L'Hospice St. Bernard. Established by St. Bernard of Menthon in 1094, the hospice is now administered by Augustinian monks. The kennels can be visited, but advance reservations are suggested. Write to **L'Hospice St. Bernard** *(CH-1946 Bourg-St.-Pierre;* ☎ *26+87.12.36)*. Note that you will miss the location if you drive *through* the tunnel; you must take the up-and-over route through the pass to see the dogs. (The **Swiss Club of St. Bernard Dog Owners** can assist with further information. Contact its President, Roland Hans, who lives near Olten, just south of Basel *(7 Im Gnoed, CH-4614 Haegendorf, Switzerland,* ☎ *62+46.32.10)*.

LODGING: At L'Hospice, the monks operate a dormitory that is used by hikers and walkers during warm-weather months and by folks arriving on cross-country skis when snow covers the ground. Costs at the dormitory are about Sfr15 per night. The nearby village of **Orsières** has more traditional surroundings. A trio of mountain hotels include **Le Catogne** *(26 rooms;* ☎ *26+83.12.30)*, the smaller **de l'Union** *(14 rooms;* ☎ *26+83.11.38)* and the **Terminus** *(16 rooms;* ☎ *26+83.20.40)*.

ST. GALLEN

St. Gallen *(CH-9001;* ☎ *71+22.62.62, FAX 71+23.43.04)*, in eastern Switzerland, was well known throughout the 9th and 10th centuries, when the Abbey of St. Gall was noted for scholarship and art.

The community developed from the monastic cell of an Irish hermit, Gallus, who lived here in 612; a Benedictine monastery was built in the 8th century, and its monks are responsible for the impressive work on manuscripts, which they illuminated as they translated them from Latin to German. In keeping with the times and the town's artistic focus, the town's baroque architecture continues to set the style today. Although modern trappings surround the old town, which is in the bottom of a cup of hills, the **Klosterkirche** (cathedral built in 1755-68) is at its heart. Deceptively plain walls surround the exuberantly baroque interior. Nearby, the **Stiftsbibliothek** (Abbey Library) holds a valuable collection of more than 130,000 books and illuminated manuscripts, including the oldest documents in the German language. Visitors are required to put on slippers the size of elephant feet to move quietly over the highly polished wood floors, inlaid with elaborate designs. Long revered as a market town, now noted for modern shops, St. Gallen also has a captivating lace museum, with intricate work attractively displayed and an extensive library of patterns that is valued by students and other craftspeople. The town is surrounded by miles of farmland that yield some of the country's most popular cheeses.

LODGING in St. Gallen is limited to a few, fairly standard hotels. **Im Portner** *(Bankgasse 12; 22 rooms;* ☎ *71+22.97.44)*, with modernized rooms conveniently located in the center of the Altstadt is one choice, but I prefer the **Sonne Rotmonten** *(Guisanstrasse 94; 23 rooms;* ☎ *71+25.68.25, FAX 71+25.01.74)*, a bus ride up the hill in a suburban area. The comfortable neighborhood inn has clean and tidy rooms that may seem small, but the atmosphere is more typical of the area.

Among the several easy trips up into the hills above St. Gallen are a visit to ***Trogen*** *(CH-9403;* ☎ *71+94.13.16)*, aboard its own special train that weaves through town before climbing up to the hillside village, a half hour's ride with pastoral views. The **Hotel Krone** *(17 beds;* ☎ *71+94.13.16)* is an ideal place to spend a night, or arrange for luncheon in the second-floor dining room. (Lunch is better than dinner because you can enjoy the view. If you're staying overnight, the homecooked regional specialties are reason enough to linger.)

Other farm villages easily reached from St. Gallen include Appenzell (see above), ***Gais***, ***Herisau*** and ***Lichtensteig***, all settled amid vast green meadows where contented cows mark the landscape and scenery gives inspiration for the naïf paintings and other art that is a trademark of this part of eastern Switzerland. The Säntis mountain and others reached by cablecars are popular places for walks and hikes in warm-weather months and for skiing in winter.

ST. MORITZ

St. Moritz *(CH-7500,* ☎ *82+3.31.47),* in Graubünden, is the birthplace of Swiss winter sports, after a challenge to British visitors more than 100 years ago. With classy shops in its midtown area, the town is devoted to sports—both summer and winter. Although the lifts are clogged at town level, most skiers head to the high slopes for their day on the slopes, avoiding the bottleneck at the base. Nearby **Pontresina**, slightly less pretentious, and other villages in the Engadine valley continue to revel in the traditions that townsfolk enjoy with time-honored devotion.

AUTHOR'S OBSERVATION

One memorable day's outing, from either St. Moritz or Pontresina, is the Bernina Express train trip to Tirano, Italy, corkscrewing down the valley through Poschiavo. (It's possible to lunch in Tirano, near the terminal, before boarding a return train back to your homebase if you want to make the trip in one full day.)

RESTAURANTS: For dining in St. Moritz, tony **Chesa Veglia** *(2 via Veglia;* ☎ *82+335.96)* breaks the bank; its upstairs pizzeria has more reasonable (but still high) prices and a pleasing, less pretentious atmosphere. One of my favorite places is the **Landgasthof Meierei** *(52 via Dimle,* ☎ *82+320. 60),* a pleasant half hour walk around the lake. Another is **Konditorei Hanselmann** *(8 via Maistra;* ☎ *82+338.64),* in the heart of town, where the social set gathers at tea time—and discreetly for other meals.

LODGING: The top of the list is classy **Badrutt's Palace** *(220 rooms;* ☎ *82+211.01, FAX 82+377.39),* with its Chesa Veglia restaurant and traditional, elegant atmosphere. As a member of the prestigious *Leading Hotels of the World* group, the management and services are the best you can get, even when the traditional European service has to yield to North American and other convention groups, as sometimes happens at this property. Also elegant, on the west side of town, **Suvretta House** *(217 rooms;* ☎ *82+211.21, FAX 82+385.24)* has an indoor swimming pool, sauna, tennis courts and a full ski facility. Worth noting in this sports-focused town are the two all-inclusive, action-packed **Club Méditeranée**'s, namely **Roi Soleil** *(*☎ *82+323.23, FAX 82+391.61)* and **Victoria** *(*☎ *82+340.32, FAX 82+380.84),* both better known to European vacationers than to Americans. With inclusive pricing, the friendly, relaxed atmosphere of the Clubs lend themselves to participation in various lessons, walks, hikes and evening activities. One pleasant, less-pretentious spot within convenient walking distance of the top social centers is the **Albana** *(65 rooms;* ☎ *82+331.21, FAX 82+315.43).*

In **Pontresina**, I've spent pleasant days at the **Steinbock** *(30 rooms;* ☎ *82+663.71, FAX 82+679.22),* at the top of the hill road that slants down past shops and other hotels.

ST. URSANNE

St. Ursanne *(CH-2882;* ☎ *66+55.37.16),* on the Doubs, near Basel, takes its name from an Irish monk, Ursicinus, who made his way here in the 6th century. He was followed, in the 7th century, by a pilgrim named Wadrille who discovered his tomb and established a monastery on the site. The town is a gem, with its medieval appearance preserved thanks to status as a national monument. The centerpiece of the church, which has grown from its remarkable 12th-century core, with tombstones in its cloister from the 7th and 8th centuries. The soft ocher of the building stones sets the tone for the town. Note the tympanum on the south portal and the charming statues of the Virgin and Child and St. Ursanne, in two niches on that side. Also worth some time are the three town gates, namely the **Porrentruy gate**, also known as St. Paul's gate, which was rebuilt in 1664; the **Bridge Gate**, a.k.a. St. John's gate, built in 1728, with a 17th-century upper level; and the **Lorette Gate**, a.k.a. St. Peter's gate, which was built in 1552 and modified in 1665. The **Hôtel de Ville** has been restored to its 15th-century style, and there are several historic buildings lining the narrow lanes of the town, near the church. On the north side of town, up in the hills, the **Hermitage** of St. Ursanne dates from the 18th and 19th centuries and is a good walkers' goal, both for view and for exercise.

SCHAFFHAUSEN

Schaffhausen *(CH-8200;* ☎ *53+25.51.41; FAX 53+25.51.43),* on the Bodensee (Lake Constance), near the Rhein falls, in the northeast, received a city charter in 1045 and maintains its many medieval buildings, with painted facades and oriel windows, as a living museum of early Alpine architecture. The town became important as a transit point, where riverboats off-loaded their cargo for transportation around the treacherous waterfalls. The **Münsterkirche** (church) dates from the 11th century, and the **Kloster Allerheiligen** holds a valuable collection of 17th-century silver and gold craftmanship as well as paintings. An old wall of the St. Johanneskapelle, dating from 1064, has been incorporated into one of the exhibit rooms.

LODGING AND DINING: For an exceptional experience, make a reservation at **Rheinhotel Fischerzunft** *(Rheinquai 8;* ☎ *53+25.32.81; FAX 53+24.32.85),* a member of the prestigious *Relais et Châteaux.* Bordering the promenade along the Rhein river's edge, the hotel's claim to fame is Andre Jaeger's restaurant, which draws cognescenti from far away. The dozen bedrooms are elegantly furnished and ideally situated for walks, riverboat rides and other ways of enjoying the surrounding countryside, which includes the Rhein river, the Bodensee, and its many lakeside villages. (See "Bodensee" above and "Stein am Rhein," below.)

SOLOTHURN

Solothurn *(CH-4500;* ☎ *65+22.19.24, FAX 65+23.16.32),* just north of Bern, was a Roman settlement as well as a residence for 16th- and 17th-century ambassadors to France. Although it is north of the Alpine area, its history is tied to the region. The town has an impressive **Kathedrale St. Ursen**, designed in baroque style by 18th-century Ticinese artists, from the once Italian part of Switzerland. The **Marktplatz**, with its 16th-century fountains, has a clock that dates to the 14th century. In a residential area on the fringe of town, **Museum Blumstein** holds treasures from earlier times, including stained-glass windows with town maps.

During warm-weather months, the "Romadie" travels along the Aare river, from Solothurn to Biel/Bienne, a dual-language town at the German-speaking/French-speaking "border." (If you'd like to spend a day on the water, check boat schedules to change at Biel/Bienne to the lakeboat that travels across the Bielersee, to pass through a canal that links it to Las Neuchâtel. If you schedule it right, and don't mind returning after dark, it's possible to return from Yverdon to Solothurn by train on a day that's "free" with a version of the Swiss travel card. (See "Touring Tips," above.)

LODGING: One of my favorite inns is Solothurn's **Hotel Krone** *(60 beds; Hauptgasse;* ☎ *65+22.44.12, FAX 65+22.37.24),* at the steps of the cathedral, with an excellent restaurant, comfortable rooms and a location that's convenient for the town's market, shops and river excursions. Other places to consider include the **Roter Turn** *(40 beds; Hauptgasse;* ☎ *65+22.96.21, FAX 65+22.98.65),* with a modern interior and river-viewing dining room that belies the medieval entrance near the market square.

SPIEZ

Spiez *(CH-3700;* ☎ *33+54.21.38; FAX 33+54.21.92),* on the Thunersee, not far from either Interlaken or Thun, slants from its hilltop Bahnhof to the Schifflande at its lakeside. It's a charming town that is a personal favorite, shared with three generations of my family. The castle, popular for weddings, has a small museum, but check in advance if entrance seems important. The outside is so picturesque that the interior seems a bit of a letdown, except for the views from its windows. The castle is open in warm-weather months, but can be enjoyed from the outside year-round.

LODGING: The lake, the region and the town are the reasons for settling here. It's an ideal pivot point, especially if you're content, as I have been more than once, at the small **Bellevue Hotel** *(20 rooms;* ☎ *33+54.84.64, FAX 33+54.84.48)*, a family-run place that is popular with the village, on the main road between Bahnhof and the boat dock. Slightly tonier, and a farther walk from the two depots, is the **Strandhotel Belvédère Hotel** *(30 rooms;* ☎ *33+54.33.33, FAX 33+54.66.33)*, a member of the *Relais du Silence*, with an excellent dining room (with view of the lake), high ceilings and a turn-of-the-century aspect with modern facilities.

SPLÜGEN

Splügen *(CH-7435;* ☎ *81+62.13.32, FAX 81+62.18.26)*, high in the mountains at 4789 ft (1460 m), is a wonderfully quiet place for walks, hikes, and winter cross-country skiing.

LODGING: A place I have stayed happily is the **Posthotel Bodenhaus** *(47 beds;* ☎ *81+62.11.21, FAX 81+62.18.80)*, a short walk from the PTT bus stop and well located for walks, with a picnic planned with help from the local bakery. The hotel is shoebox-style, with efficiently-furnished rooms intended for sporting types who prefer to be out in the mountains. Don't count on luxury, but do count on cozy surroundings and good food.

STEIN AM RHEIN

Stein am Rhein *(CH-8260;* ☎ *54+41.28.35, FAX 54+41.51.46)*, near Schaffhausen in northeastern Switzerland, is near the point where the Rhein flows into the Untersee, eventually to widen to the Bodensee (Lake Constance). The town lures visitors, who parade up and down its few streets looking at the painted facades of the 15th- and 16th-century buildings. The **Rathaus** dates from 1539, and the elaborate painting on its walls is a favorite feature for photographs. A top-floor museum features 16th- and 17th-century stained glass and armor. A favorite walking goal is **Burg Hohenklingen**, a hill-capping castle, with a restaurant and a wonderful view over the roofs of the riverside town.

LODGING: Although there's only one 4-star hotel, there are several appealing small spots with modestly appointed rooms and easy access to the boat dock. The **Closterhof** *(85 rooms; ☎ 54+42.42.42, FAX 54+41.13.37)* is popular with tour groups, as well as with those who want the most modern surroundings. It is at one end of town. The smaller **Adler** *(25 rooms; ☎ 54+42.61.61, FAX 54+41.44.40)* has more personality, in my opinion. Although it is small and some bedrooms are tiny, it's location on Rathausplatz puts it in the center of things.

THUN

Thun *(CH-3600; ☎ 33+22.23.40; FAX 33+22.83.23)*, nestled at one end of the Thunersee, caps its hilltop with a **Schloss**, reached by a covered staircase and holding the **Historisches Museum** that has tapestries in its knights hall and furniture and pottery on display. Concerts are sometimes held in the castle. The river that splits the town is spanned by bridges that contribute to the town's pleasant atmosphere. Convenient on train routes and linked by lakeboat to Interlaken, Thun is a touring base.

LODGING: Choices are more utilitarian than charming, now that the town has become a minor touring center. The best hotel, in my opinion, is the **Krone** *(60 beds; ☎ 33+22.82.82; FAX 33+22.45.87)*, in the center of town. Although modernized to almost antiseptic standards, the location on Rathausplatz puts shops and the town-crowning castle within pleasant walking distance.

VALLE MAGGIA

The Valle Maggia *(CH-6600 Maggia)*, in the Ticino, stretches northwest as far as Robiei. It is one of that southern canton's unique valleys, long neglected but now appealing to city folk from elsewhere in search of peacefully rural surroundings. Postal buses link Locarno (see above) to the valley villages. Favored for its waterfalls, rivers, lakes, verdant glens and lush pastures as well as for the rugged climbing required to reach the glaciers at **Cavergno**, **Basodino** and **Cavagnoli**, the area has the highest peaks in the Ticino. A cablecar reaches **Robiei** in 15 minutes from San Carlo, at the "end" of a finger valley.

LODGING: Alloggio Robiei *(20 rooms; ☎ 93+99.12.26)* has a good restaurant and clean, neat rooms for those who want to be high in the mountains.

Along the valley, **Cevio**, **Broglio**, **Prato** and **Campo** have many of the Ticino's typical stone-walled, slate-roofed houses. In the chapel at **Maggia** there are 15th-century paintings; at Cevio, the **Cappella**

della Rovana has charming stuccowork; and all through the valley, small chapels yield surprising paintings and other treasures.

VAL VERZASCA

Val Verzasca, a rural Ticino valley, is another charming southern area with clusters of piled-stone houses and dramatic scenery that lures those in search of a quiet, rural life. In spite of recent growth for holiday homes, there are many places where time seems to stand still. The yellow postal coaches are the main transport for residents.

VIERWALDSTÄTTERSEE

The Vierwaldstättersee, known to English-speaking travelers as the Lake of Lucerne, is actually the "lake of the four forest cantons," so named for the three original communities—Uri, Schwyz and Unter-walden—that joined to form the kernel of present-day Switzerland on August 1, 1291, and were later joined by Luzern. With its well-known tourist town of Luzern, the lake is a prized touring area, especially aboard one of the lakeboats to watch the passing scenery. There are several pretty towns pinned to the lake.

Brunnen (CH-6440; ☎ 43+31.17.77, FAX 43+31.17.78) is the nearest lakeside dock for the village of Schwyz, to which it's linked by public bus service. Although busy during warm-weather months, the peak of the tourist season, the lakeside town is pleasant in spring and fall when the weather is still warm enough to enjoy the lake. Several cozy restaurants and tea rooms stand at the roadside, near the lake, along with shops selling tourist items. The **Hotel Schmid am See** (45 beds; ☎ 43+31.18.82) is actually three roadside buildings, one of which holds the *Stübli* and others with additional rooms. The simple hotel is family-owned and operated; speaking German is helpful.

Another, **Kussnacht am Rigi** (CH-6403; ☎ 41+81.33.30; FAX 41+81.34.30) is sometimes troubled by the fact that it is on a well-traveled lakeside road that can be traffic-clogged in mid-summer. The village has a few pleasant inns that can seem far removed from the tourism of Luzern, however. **DuLac/Seehof** (17 rooms; ☎ 41+81.10.12, FAX 41+81.34.30) is ideally located, right at lakeside, within a few steps of the boat dock. Not only do some bedrooms have a lovely view of the lake, but the restaurant that moves inside for the cooler winter months has a lakeside terrace that is ideal for lingering when the weather is warm. The long-established **Hotel Hirschen** (65 beds; ☎ 41+81.10.27; FAX 41+81.68.80), a few steps inland, at the main "square" (where the local bus stops) is historic and photogenic, but seems to have turned to pizza and other moderate-priced tourist customs. It's worth looking before booking.

Among the other places on the Vierwaldstättersee, covered elsewhere in this section, are Luzern and Vitznau.

VITZNAU

Vitznau *(CH-6354; ☎ 41+83.13.55; FAX 41+83.17.83)* is not only an appealing small village with a popular lakeboat dock, but it is also the pivot point for the trainride to the top of the Rigi mountain, where many go for walks, hikes—or to pause at the restaurant at one of the stops en route to the top, or perhaps at the top itself. Vitznau can be a pleasant, relaxing base for excursions into Luzern by boat, or by bus, or bus-and-train, as well as for journey's up the Rigi and by lakeboat to other villages, perhaps for a walk around some of the **Swiss Path**, which was inaugurated on the 700th anniversary of the country's founding and has segments sponsored by each of the Swiss cantons (states).

LODGING: The **Park Hotel Vitznau** *(98 rooms; ☎ 41+83.01.00, FAX 41+83.13.97)* on the lake shore, is one of the best places to stay. It has a heated swimming pool, a lovely garden area, sensational views from most of its rooms and elegant dining in its more formal restaurant. The facilities are elegant, and maintained with style. I have enjoyed staying at the **Terrasse am See** *(30 rooms; ☎ 41+83.10.33, FAX 41+83.21.55)*, where rooms are modestly furnished, but the location—at the Rigibahn station and the lakeboat dock— makes excursions easy. Other pleasant in-town places include the family-style **Hotel Kreuz** *(45 beds; ☎ 41+83.13.05)* and, at modest cost, the **Hotel Rigi** *(48 beds; ☎ 41+83.13.61)* and the **Hotel Waldheim** *(15 beds; ☎ 41+83.11.74)*. The small **Berghotel Wissifluh** *(38 beds; ☎ 41+83.13.27)* is chalet style, with a sun terrace that is pleasant when the weather is. It's reached by cablecar, for those who prefer not to walk up or down.

WINTERTHUR

Winterthur *(CH-8410; ☎ 52+212.00.88; FAX 52+212.00.72)*, an easy excursion north of Zürich by train (20 minutes' on an express) or car, claims one of the country's exceptional collections of European masters, in the once private home of Oskar Reinhart. Known as the **Sammlung Oskar Reinhart am Römerholz**, the museum is about 20 minutes' leisurely walk up the hillside from the railroad station. (Taxis are also available.) Dr. Reinhart's collection was given to the city in 1951. The art is displayed almost the way he enjoyed it, in the several rooms of his hillside home. Because the artists' use of light intrigued the doctor, he collected work that emphasized light by Toulouse-Lautrec, Tintoretto, Utrillo, Renoir, Rubens, Pissaro, Picasso, and many other well-known names. Two of the salons have skylights to take advantage of the way the natural light enhances the paintings. The collection proves a lure for schoolchildren, matrons from nearby towns, walkers and hikers, some of whom have jogged around the nearby Vitaparcours, a trail with exercise stations that is a gift of the Vita insurance company. There's a small café/restaurant and, weather permitting, a relaxing and pleasant outdoor terrace where you can sit in the sun to read the museum guide and reflect on the paintings.

In the center of town, at the **Rathaus**, another town resident has donated his private collection of clocks for public viewing. Known as the **Uhrensammlung Konrad Kellenberger**, the museum holds an amazing collection of timepieces, many of them with historic connections. Also worth noting is the **Museum im Lindengut**, on *Römerstrasse 8*, noted for its collection of typical tiled stoves of earlier times as well as some maps and pictures of Winterthur from the 17th to the 19th centuries. Nearby Steinberggasse is the site for the Tuesday and Friday **market**, when farmers from nearby villages sell their produce—in a town better known to the Swiss (and some others) as the home for the industrial giant, Sulzer and other firms.

Although masked by modern development, the city's medieval core was a Habsburg stronghold under Rudolf, when it was part of the Austro-Hungarian empire. Barely surviving as an independent town (between 1415 and 1442), Winterthur was linked to Zürich for much of its past. Now, as the sixth largest town in Switzerland, it includes the villages of Toss, Veltheim, Oberwinterthur, Seen and Wulflingen.

LODGING: One noteworthy inn is the **Krone** *(Marktgasse 49;* ☎ *52+213.25.21, FAX 52+213.48.08),* with a cozy restaurant and small but comfortable rooms.

ZERMATT

Zermatt *(CH-3920;* ☎ *28+66.11.81; FAX 28+66.11.85),* high in the mountains of the Valais, is much more than the sight of the Matterhorn, although that is admittedly what draws many people to this spot. Although the place is unabashedly tourist-conscious in midwinter, when skiers flock to the town and in midsummer, when holiday-seekers make their pilgrimage, life can be more relaxing in spring, when the first wildflowers peep through the snow, and even in the fall, when some hotels are closed and others are in the midst of their annual refurbishing.

AUTHOR'S OBSERVATION

No transit cars are allowed in the village. They must be parked at the vast expanses made available at the railway station in Täsch, lower in the valley. In spite of that fact, a proliferation of electric carts and assorted other vehicles make strolling on the main road a constant leaping game from the road to the very narrow sidewalk.

On the train ride (or drive) up to Täsch, where all cars must be parked-and-left for the train link to Zermatt, there's a relatively new and certainly awesome sight of a rock slide. In fact, during two horrifying interludes in spring of '91, a mountain-slide poured into the valley at the village of Randa, blocking the river (and thereby flooding the village) and covering both road and railway. Within days, a secondary road was built and a bus link was put in place, to link the trains below with the trains to Zermatt above. Although gigantic rock-moving equipment looked like ants on a rockpile when the incredible task was underway, a new railway and permanent road was quickly built, the river was rerouted through an underground tunnel and life returned to normal. The mountains are constantly monitored by Swiss technicians and the always-respectful residents gained new understanding of the fragility of their surroundings. These days, you'll notice huge piles of rock to the right as you ride up to Zermatt; fortunately only a few small barns were buried in the avalanches.

LODGING: Zermatt has a long list of places to stay. At the top of anyone's list, for chic spots, is the **Mont Cervin** *(228 beds;* ☎ *28+66.11.22; FAX 28+67.28.78)*, but I also enjoy the smaller **Monte Rosa** *(89 beds;* ☎ *28+66.11.31; FAX 28 67.11.60)*, which has a spectacular view of the Matterhorn out some of its bedroom windows. Tops for countrystyle atmosphere, with good food in its restaurants and very comfortable rooms, is the **Walliserhof** *(60 beds;* ☎ *28+67.11.74; FAX 28+67.55.31)*, where I have stayed during several visits. Also worth noting is the **Romantik Hotel Julen** *(37 beds;* ☎ *28+67.14.81; FAX 28+67.14.81)*, built in the 1930s and rebuilt in 1981. Although bedrooms are modern and comfortable, the chalet style building near the town-splitting river bed, is in the midst of shops, hotels and restaurants and not far from the cablecar sheds.

ZUG

Zug *(CH-6300;* ☎ *42+21.00.78, FAX 42+23.18.23)*, about 30 minutes south of Zürich, is best known to assorted businessmen and entrepreneurs. Though modern multi-story buildings cluster near its

Bahnhof, the town has a charming medieval **Altstadt**, with narrow streets and many buildings that have been meticulously restored to their 16th-century appearance. To find them, walk from the railroad station down Alpenstrasse to the Zugersee (lake), to bear left and follow its shores, keeping the **Zytturm** (clocktower) in view.

LODGING: The **Hotel zum Ochsen** *(72 beds; 11 Kolinplatz;* ☎ *42+21.32.32, FAX 42+21.30.32)* was a favorite of Goethe, as well as other noteworthy travelers. At *Fischmarkt*, the **Hecht** *(*☎ *42+21.01.93)* overlooks the lake and provides an ideal place to enjoy a leisurely meal.

Pleasant excursions, in addition to the lakeboats that head out to Walchwil, Arth and other ports from spring through fall are the 3255-foot **Zugerberg** rises nearby and a reasonable hour-plus climb from lakeside. (It can also be reached by bus from the Bahnhof to Shoenegg, where a cablecar stretches to the mountaintop.)

LODGING: The small **Hotel Zugerberg** *(*☎ *42+21.05.06)* serves meals along with a lovely view over the Zugersee and tidbits of Luzern's Vierwaldstättersee.

ZUOZ

Zuoz *(CH-7524;* ☎ *82+715.10; FAX 82+733.34)*, in the Upper Engadine valley, is a cluster of 16th-century stone houses that puts you into times gone by, if you stay in the Crusch Alva, near the church and at the village center. Although the old town is surrounded by modern holiday apartments, they fade from view when you are in the heart of the village. Walking tours through the village unlock the secrets of village history. Check with the tourist office for dates and times. Although the village takes on a festive flurry when it becomes the finish line for the amazing Engadine Marathon, a ski event that is mentioned under "Sports," below, and is active during summer months, life is low-key and relaxed during the shoulder seasons.

LODGING can be at the **Posthotel Enbgiadine** *(40 rooms;* ☎ *82+710.21, FAX 82+733.03)*, which is the most elegant hotel in town, or at the delightful **Crusch Alva** *(12 rooms;* ☎ *82+713.19, FAX 82+724.59)*, where the public restaurants on the street level put you into the town's mainstream and the more formal dining room upstairs serves excellent meals with full (and correct) Swiss service. The bedrooms are comfortable with modern facilities and views into the past from the windows.

ZÜRICH

Zürich *(CH-8000; ☎ 1+211.40.00; FAX 1+212.01.41)*, with its lovely Zürichsee, is better known for banking, business and buying than for its **Altstadt** and the villages that rim its lake. Zürich is a liveable city, with classy stores, excellent restaurants, good music, opera, art galleries and museums—plus a lovely lake, an historic Altstadt and a convenient location. From Zürich you can be almost anywhere else in Switzerland within a few hours aboard good fast trains and anywhere else in Europe by train or plane.

AUTHOR'S OBSERVATION

This city has long been one of my European touchstones, especially for its Altstadt and the Zürichsee. But the past few years have seen dramatic changes in what had been an orderly and beautiful place. Although the seedy drug park has been closed (it was an unfortunate experiment by the liberal city fathers, located behind the important Landesmuseum near the railroad station), its troubled inhabitants now wander and sprawl elsewhere in the city. And the Hauptbahnhof, which has been under extensive reconstruction for several years, has been "modernized," with an underground system of tracks and other additions, so that it may be more efficient, but it seems to me that it has lost its soul. These two points having been made, I return to Zürich each time I am in its orbit because I like the city in spite of its encounters with the world's ills.

Public transportation is easy to use, with trams, buses, trains and lakeboats threading the city and its suburbs. Multiride tickets can be purchased at vending machines and/or booths at strategic places. One source is the **Hauptbahnhof**, which also has a vast underground shopping area and is the headquarters for the Zürich Tourist Office, the best source for answers to all your questions.

Schifflände, the lakeboat dock, is at Bürkliplatz, at the lake-end of Bahnhofstrasse, the city's famous (and most expensive) shopping street. It's a source of great pleasure, whether you choose to sit on one of the benches to watch the swans, the people and the boat activity, or whether you want to read the posted schedules and board a *schiff* (boat) for an enchanting ride around the Zürichsee.

Although there are many areas of Zürich that are interesting, my favorite is the **Altstadt**, a maze of narrow streets on both sides of the Limmat river, where some medieval houses have become shops and restaurants and others are still used as dwellings, the best of which have very modern interiors.

Two important museums to set the stage for Alpine touring are the **Schweizerisches Landesmuseum**, the Swiss National Museum, to the right as you face the Hauptbahnhof, and the **Wohnmuseum**, on Basteiplatz, just off a midpoint on the Bahnhofstrasse. The Landes-museum is vast, as you'd expect of the national museum, but among its several rooms are some that have been taken board-by-board from ancient houses around the country to be rebuilt within the museum. These places provide an excellent "schoolroom" for traditional lifestyles and crafts. There are also many interesting paintings, not only of early Zürich and other Swiss cities, but also of the countryside, some of which look like places you can see today. Favorite among the treasures are the tiled stoves, like those still in use in some of the country's inns. When the fire was stoked inside the stove, the tiles warmed the room as well as providing a decorative element. Stoves were often built in a common corner, so that several rooms could benefit from the "central heating."

The **Wohnmuseum** (house museum) is, in fact, two patrician houses that were moved from nearby Bärengasse to make way for a modern bank. Both have been restored and are filled with memorabilia from Zürich households of the 18th and 19th centuries. Rooms have been redecorated, but the original woodwork and doorways have been left intact. Note the linens in the baby's room and the antiques that punctuate most rooms. Porcelain and tableware are displayed in cabinets. Interesting prints and diagrams on the walls show what the city looked like at the time the houses were built.

Among other sights to see are **Grossmünster**, literally the "big church," whose two towers are landmarks for the city. Known as "the most important Romanesque religious structure in Switzerland," Grossmunster was started in the early 1100s. It is the church of Ulrich Zwingli, a religious reformer who studied with Erasmus and was somewhat softer in his espousal of Protestantism than Martin Luther, whom he met in 1529. Charlemagne, whose statue is in an alcove on one of the towers, established a church on this site, noted as the place where legendary Felix and Ursula, brother and sister, collapsed after being martyred on the place where the Wasserkirche now stands.

Follow any of the narrow lanes that stretch from Grossmünster to find the antique shops and many boutiques and shops along both sides of the Limmat river, or the guildhalls, known as **Zunfthaüser** (see below), where you can enjoy a meal in historic surroundings.

Across the Limmat is the **Fraumünster** ("Lady church"), a 13th-century building with frescoes in its cloister that describe the legend of the two daughters of Ludwig the German, who were led to this site by a stag with candles burning in its antlers. Hildegard and Bertha, as they were called, became the first abbesses of the church. But it is the windows by Marc Chagall that draw the most attention. Designed in 1968, the windows were executed by a studio in Rheims and installed in Fraumünster, after the 83-year-old Chagall had painted the figures and shadows in grisaille technique. His theme for the windows is the sources of love, as shown in the five windows, dedicated to the Prophets, Jacob, Christ, Zion, and Law.

The square of the Fraumünster is one of my favorites, not only for the window-boxed buildings around its fringes, but for the wonderful small shops that line the narrow lanes that stretch out from the site, for the **Zunfthaus zum Meisen-Keramische Sammlung**, the exceptional museum of porcelain that occupies the first level of the guildhall facing the church, and nearby **Sprüngli**, a Bahnhofstrasse confectionary shop with an upstairs "tearoom" that is one of my Zürich haunts. Established in 1836, the store was in the family through five generations and has recently been brought into the Lindt/Sprüngli enterprise. Tearoom procedure dictates that you hang your coat on one of the coatracks and take a seat at a table, passing the case full of delicious pastries on your way. There's a *karte* for choices or you can get up, after a waitress has taken your order for drinks and other choices made from the karte, to choose a selection from the display of small sandwiches and pastries. Pay at the counter for your choices and take them back to your table. Although upstairs is for leisurely sipping and supping, the street level of Sprüngli, except for the small café to the left of the main shop, is for buying to take home.

RESTAURANTS: Mealtimes in Zürich can be memorable. Although most of the best restaurants seem to be tucked into hard-to-find side streets with sometimes intimidating doorways, quietly enter and settle into your table for a special experience. You can dine, for example, at several of the medieval guildhalls, most of which can be found in the Altstadt, on or near Limmatquai, the road that borders the Limmat river, near where the Zürichsee begins its route to the River Aare. Check the **Zunfthaus Schmieden** *(Marktgasse 20)*, or the **Zunfthaus Königstuhl** *(Stussihofstaat)* or the **Zunfthaus Rüden** *(Limmatquai 42)*, as well as others, following the steps up to the first-floor dining room from the menu posted by the arcaded street-level door.

Among other restaurants worth noting are the **Goethestube**, an ancient café upstairs in the Weinstube zur Gorssen Reblaube, in a building where the German philosopher-poet-intellectual Goethe came to see his friend Lavater, who had an office here in the 18th century.

LODGING: Although the list of hotels in Zürich is a long one, my list of favorites is a special few. For grand living in the best Swiss style, it's hard to beat the **Baur au Lac** *(210 beds;* ☎ *1+221.16.50; FAX 1+212.81.39)*, perched near the lake with a fleet of Mercedes and other luxury cars at its entrance. Up in the hills, overlooking the lake but linked to town by its own funicular, is the **Dolder Grand** *(300 beds; 1+251.62.31; FAX 1+251.88.29)*, with a golf course and an atmosphere that seems far removed from city life. My own home, on more occasions than I can count, has been the **Hotel Florhof** *(56 beds; 4 Florhofgasse;* ☎ *1+261.44.70; FAX 1+261.46.11)*, next to the music conservatory, on the fringe of the Altstadt, with small and tidy rooms, a dining room where delicious meals are served and an "insider" atmosphere.

Zürichsee, the lake of Zürich, is a lovely playground in all kinds of weather. If there's a lakeboat leaving, get on it—just to ride around watching the activity. Among the many worthy halting places are **Au**, for a walk up the winding path to the **Halbinsel Au** *(20 beds;* ☎ *1+781.10.10; FAX 1+781.10.90)*, a pleasant inn that is best known locally for its restaurant; **Erlenbach**, across the lake, where you can dine or overnight at the **Erlenbacherhof** *(34 beds;* ☎ *1+910.55.22; FAX 1+910.33.25)*; and **Obermeilen**, where the small **Hirschen** *(35 beds;* ☎ *1+923.65.51)* is a pleasant inn. Crown jewel of the lakeside towns is at the far end from Zürich, however, where you can get off at **Rapperswil** *(CH-8640;* ☎ *55+27.70.00)*, to wander around, climb to the **castle** and perhaps stay overnight at the **Schwanen** *(38 beds;* ☎ *55+21.91.81; FAX 55+27.77.77)*, where the best rooms overlook the lake.

SPORTS

Ever since the middle of the 19th century when the British began to visit this country for their holidays, the Swiss mountains and lakes have been the focal point for outdoor activities. The most rugged Alps are in the south and southeast, although the northern foothills corrugate most of the country. In the eastern sector, the National Park is carefully maintained as a preserve for flora and fauna. In the northwest, north of the Alps, the Jura mountains undulate over the border with France.

Swiss lakes surprise many who expect only towering mountains. In fact, the high Alpine lakes around St. Moritz are favorites for boaters and the large and international Lac Léman (lake of Geneva) is dotted with boat-building yards and dozens of marinas.

Vita Parcours is a name to know if you practice aerobics or like to jog and exercise. It's a regimen of exercises and walking or jogging, following instructions posted along the route of the outdoor courses originally sponsored by the Vita Insurance Company in the 1960s. *Vita Parcours* are everywhere, even in green-belt areas of cities. Your on-the-spot source for facts is the local tourist office.

BALLOONING

"High Alpine Ballooning Weeks" are held in Mürren in late June/early July each year. Flims has an "International Ballooning Week" in September, and it's also possible to enjoy balloon rides in the valley below Laax. Château d'Oex, high in the Alpine area of canton Vaud, has a "Winter Alpine Balloon Festival" that draws as many as 50 balloons from more than 15 countries. For ballooning tours from North America, contact the **Bombard Society** *(6727 Curran St., McLean, VA 22101,* ☎ *800+862-8537 or 703+448-9407, FAX 703+883-0985).*

BICYCLING

In addition to privately owned shops, the Swiss Travel System has a "**Rail Fitness**" program where new-model bicycles are rented from almost 300 railway stations throughout the country. The Swiss Railway prints a booklet called *Rent A Bike* which is available free of charge at railway station information offices. The French edition, with a subtitle "Découvrez la Suisse en train et à vélo," gives details about several itineraries where you can use the railway system bikes for a combination of train and bike excursions. The bicycle rental charge for a half-day is Sfr 8, full day is Sfr 14, and 7 days is Sfr 56. It's wise to reserve a week in advance at peak seasons and European vacation times. Bicycles can be shipped between stations on the train and on some postal buses. Be sure to allow enough time for bike check-in, which takes a bit longer than simply boarding the train. Mountain-biking is becoming popular in some of the Alpine resorts, notably the Obergoms valley and in the Engadine, where **Mountain-Bike-Tours** are offered *(***Vereinigte Verkehrsvereine Obergoms***, CH-3985 Münster;* ☎ *28+ 73.22.54; FAX 28+73.24.97).* Another Swiss-based firm, **Eurotrek** *(Malzstrasse 17, Case Postale, CH-8036 Zürich;* ☎ *48+02.14.35)* plans cycling tours with the Swiss Railways, as well as many other adventure holidays. Itineraries are arranged around the Bodensee (Lake Constance) as well as in the Ticino, using lakeboats for some distances.

CANOEING/KAYAKING

The sport is popular on several rivers. Three of the most noteworthy are the Doubs in the northwest's Jura region, the Rhein (Rhine) around Laax and Flims, and the Inn near St.Moritz, in eastern Switzerland. One firm with international qualifications is Euroraft, which operates as **Swissraft**, through Cheziére & Co. in Flims-Laax *(CH-7032 Laax-Murschetg;* ☎ *86+ 3.41.41)*, Gstaad-Saanenland *(CH-3792 Saanen;* ☎ *30+4.50.80)*, along the Inn river *(CH-7550 Scuol;* ☎ *84+9.99.44)*, and along almost 9 miles (14 km) of the young Rhône in the Obergoms valley *(CH-3985 Münster;*

☎ *28+73.22.54).* Swiss-based **Eurotrek** *(Malzstrasse 17, Case Postale, CH-8036 Zürich;* ☎ *48+02.14.35)*, mentioned above for cycling tours, also plans canoe and rafting holidays, including train travel to the appropriate rivers and lakes. The upper Engadine is one area; portions of the Rhein is another.

FISHING

Regulations vary from place to place and according to type of fish, but licenses are required and can usually be obtained through the local police department, with the assistance of the tourist office. Contact the local tourist offices well in advance of your planned arrival if you are planning to bring equipment and other essentials with you. It's possible to buy fishing gear (there's at least one excellent store in Zürich, near the lake, not far from Bahnhofstrasse), but there's not much for rent. Places range from large Lac Léman and Lago Maggiore to places for trout fishing near Davos and little-known lakes like the Bergsee near Bivio, not far from St. Moritz. Both are in the eastern canton of Graubünden. The Rhône, which flows through the Valais in the south, is good for fishing in some segments, as are other rivers such as the Aare, Reuss, Linth, Simme, Thur, Doubs, Töss and Inn, which is known as the Enn in the Engadine.

GOLF

Crans/Montana, high in the Valais Alps, has hosted the **Ebel European Master Swiss Open** at its challenging course in September. There are 32 golf courses throughout Switzerland, including one at Riederalp that claims to be the highest golf course in the world and is interrupted by a farmer's pasture. (With true Swiss independence, he refused to capitulate to the overtures of developers.) Among other places where some hotels offer golf packages are Genève, Luzern, Montreux and Lugano. Guest privileges are possible on the challenging 18-hole course in Davos, for members of golf clubs elsewhere, and the Dolder Grand Hotel, on a Zürich hillside, has its own golf course.

HANG GLIDING OR SOARING

The sport is growing rapidly, as enthusiasts recognize the fascination of suitable air currents around the Alps. Noteworthy areas include from Rochers de Naye to Montreux, in the mountains above Lac Léman; from Corviglia to St. Moritz in eastern Graubünden and the area of Kleine Scheidegg, which is easily reached by cog-railway from Interlaken. Verbier, in the Val de Bagnes, also offers hang-gliding, as does Davos in the canton of Graubünden. *(Details from the* **Delta- und Gleitschirm-Flugschule Davos***, c/o Hans Guler, CH-7270;* ☎ *81+43.60.43.)*

HIKING

Since hiking and walking are part of the lifestyle for most Swiss and a rapidly increasing number of visitors, the Swiss National Tourist Office has complete and detailed information. The country claims 30,000 miles of marked paths. Known as *Wandern, Tourisme Pedestre,* or *Tourismo Pedestre,* in the three main languages of the country, the activity is helped along by a detailed system of *Wanderwege* (walking paths) that are clearly posted, with both the hours and the minutes it takes to walk to the noted place. The times are given, in true Swiss accuracy, for a moderate but steady walk that any reasonably fit person can easily accomplish. Some North American firms, usually sparked by one enthusiastic hiker, plan and guide hikes and walks with a small group of compatible people. Participants usually spend each night in a comfortable, cozy Alpine inn, with daily walks/hikes that are planned to meet the needs and wishes of the group. Although most hiking holidays are planned during warm-weather months, the few that are planned for early spring and fall can be the most interesting. For details, contact **Fred Jacobson's Alpine Trails Ltd.** *(c/o Chappaqua Travel, Inc., South Greeley Ave., Chappaqua, NY 10514;* ☎ *914+238-5151 or 800+666-5161, FAX 914+238-5533).* Its owner was one of the first Americans to organize hikes. Also contact **Ryder-Walker Alpine Trails** *(Box 947, 5 Lake Fork Junction, Telluride, CO 81435;* ☎ *303+728-6481),* started by people who learned the ropes from Fred, and **Wanderweg Holidays** *(519 Kings Croft, Cherry Hill, NJ 08034;* ☎ *609+321-1040 or 800+270-2577, FAX 609+321-1040),* which is planned and manned by Phil Scheidt, a thorough researcher. **Travent International** *(Box 711, Bristol, VT 05443;* ☎ *802+453-5710 or 800+325-3009, FAX 802+453-4806)* is another firm with organized itineraries in Switzerland. Although the Valais has long been a popular hiking area, there are also holidays planned for the Bernese Oberland, Graubünden, and the Ticino.

Most town and village tourist offices provide information about and sometimes guides for walks and hikes in specific areas. Some also organize more ambitious walking tours, sometimes using postbus links or cablecars to reach starting points. Experienced hikers should ask about the Upper Valais and about hiking along the "Haute Route" from Chamonix (in France) via Zermatt to Saas Fee, spending overnights in mountain refuges. In addition to a system for "real" hiking, bordering on (and sometimes becoming) mountaineering, almost every town has at least a few posted walks. Grindelwald, in the Berner Oberland, boasts 180 miles (300 km) of mountain paths, maintained for hiking and/or walking. As with many mountain centers, postal buses and mountain transport (cablecars, gondolas, chair lifts, and funiculars) conquer long distances, putting you at the start of a noted walk.

For information about hiking trails, and the "Programm der Schweizer Wanderwege," contact the **Schweizer Wanderwege** *(Swiss Walking Ways, Im Hirshalm 49, CH-4125 Riehen).* (For more information see "Walking" below.)

HORSEBACK RIDING

The Swiss National Tourist Office has listings of riding schools, the best of which are in the rolling hills of the Jura, in the northwestern part of the country and in some of the Alpine valleys. The annual horse auction and show, held in August in the Jura village of Saignelegier, lures enthusiasts from all over the world. In Maienfeld, not far from Chur and best known for its mention in the "Heidi" legend, there is a riding school with resident programs in dressage and other techniques for adults and children.

HUNTING

Although all Swiss men have full shooting equipment stowed at home as part of their responsibility as members of the Swiss armed forces, hunting is not easy for visitors to arrange. If you have personal friends who hunt, let them do all the planning. Otherwise, head for other countries for this sport.

MOUNTAINEERING/CLIMBING

Even before Edward Whymper conquered the Matterhorn in 1865, man has been challenging the Alps, but since that year the numbers of climbers have increased each season. It's wise to firm up details well in advance and to be in very good shape if you want to climb the Matterhorn, starting from Zermatt. The tourist office assists with details and with finding appropriate guides.

Expert guides and comprehensive mountaineering schools can be found in many Alpine towns and villages in the Valais and in the Bernese Oberland, especially at Zermatt, Saas Fee, Andermatt and Kandersteg. The **Schweizerischer Alpen Club** *(Swiss Alpine Club, Box 1, CH-3920 Zermatt)* and **Club Alpin Suisse** *(rue Beau-Sejour 24, CH-1003 Lausanne)* are your best sources for information about membership, use of huts and details about routes.

Among the best sources for information for experienced climbers is the **Alpine Sportschule Gotthard** *(Postfach 108, CH-6490 Andermatt;* ☎ *44+ 6.77.88)*, which has special summer and winter programs, with ski touring offered from January through May. Special *Bergsteigerschule Uri* "Mountain Reality" programs, where you'll ski on unbroken snow (and be outfitted with an Autophon avalanche radio) are offered by **Alex Clapasson** *(CH-6490 Andermatt;* ☎ *44+6.71.44)*. Up-to-date information on winter ski conditions is provided on a 24-hour basis by the Swiss National Tourist Office *(*☎ *212+757-6336)*.

Out of Grindelwald, in the Berner Oberland, the **Mountaineering Centre** *(*☎ *36+53.52.00, FAX 36+53.12.22)* plans guided walks in winter and summer, as well as glacier descents and high-altitude ice-climbs in winter.

PARAGLIDING

You can spot the colorful parachutes from the ground as you drive, ride, or walk in many mountain areas. Grindelwald, in the Berner Oberland, is one of many places with a **Paragliding School** *(*☎ *36+55.15.47 or 77+ 56.53.34)*, where you can learn the sport or enjoy it as a professional.

RIVER RAFTING

As is the case with "Canoeing" above, some rivers are especially challenging for rafting. Among the most noteworthy are the Rhein through Flims and Laax, the Rhône in the Obergoms valley around Munster, the

Inn at Scuol and the Saane from Gstaad. One source for details about expeditions is **Schlauchbootzentrum** *(Cheziëre & Co., CH-7031 Laax)*.
Another Swiss-based firm, **Eurotrek** *(Malzstrasse 17, Case Postale, CH-8036
Zürich;* ☎ *48+02.14.35)* arranges river-rafting holidays, using trains to get
to starting points for the Inn river as well as the "Grand Canyon de Suisse," on the Rhein between Ilanz and Reichenau, in the canton of
Graubünden, in eastern Switzerland.

ROWING

The sport, as it's practiced with crew-and-sheel, is mainly for spectators,
with regattas at Fribourg and on the Rotsee, the small lake "behind" Luzern. It's possible to rent row boats, however, on most of the larger lakes,
especially at the lakeside in Zürich and in Genève, Lausanne-Ouchy and
some other lake-bordering towns for Lac Léman, and at St. Moritz.

SAILING

International races are held on Lac Léman. One source for information
is at the tourist office in Ouchy, the lakeside town that is linked with hillside Lausanne. Yacht Club members should check about reciprocal privileges with Ouchy's Yacht Club. On the Thunnersee, between Thun and
Interlaken, there's a sailing school at Hilterfingen, and Spiez is one of the
many towns with marinas on that lake. In eastern Switzerland, Silvaplaner-
see (lake Silvaplanna) is respected for its brisk winds—and its regattas. **Eurotrek**
(Malzstrasse 17, Case Postale, CH-8036 Zürich; ☎ *48+02.14.35)*, mentioned
elsewhere for their adventure holidays planned with rail transportation
links, arranges sailing holidays on Lago Maggiore in the Ticino.

SKIING

There's summer skiing on the highest mountain glaciers. Of particular
interest are Mittelallalin above Saas Fee, the Klein Matterhorn above Zermatt, and the Plaine Morte above Crans/Montana in the Valais. Other
places include the glacier above Les Diablerets, easily reached from Gstaad
and other resorts in its area where Vaud canton mingles with the Bernese
Oberland, Mont Fort above Verbier, and Vorab above Flims and Laax, as
well as Diavolezza above Pontresina, and Mt. Corvatsch above St. Moritz.
All these are in eastern Switzerland. A challenge for experienced skiers is
spring ski touring along the "Haute Route," following a pattern first cut
by three skiers from Chamonix, France, in 1903. The week-long excursion
stretches between either Saas Fee or Zermatt and Chamonix. **Mountain
Travel-Sobek** *(6420 Fairmont Ave., El Cerrito, CA 94530;* ☎ *510+527-8100
or 800+227-2384, FAX 510+525-7710)* plans a spring "Skiing the Haute
Route" tour. For winter skiing, ask about special ski week tickets that may
be available in areas of interest. They usually include lift tickets for several
neighboring runs, in addition to transportation passes between areas.

Der Engadiner, an annual event that lures thousands of participants from
around the world, is an annual ski marathon-race that takes place on a
mid-March Sunday, from Maloja, southwest of Sils, through St. Moritz
and Pontresina, to the northeast side of Zuoz, almost to S-chanf, a distance

of about 25 miles (42 km), which is the official marathon length. Started in 1969, with 945 registered skiers, the March 1993 race included approximately 12,000 participants, plus thousands of on-lookers.

Clusters of nearby mountain resorts gather together to offer a regional skipass. For example, in the Berner Oberland, Grindelwald has a *Swisski Package* that includes 7 nights at a hotel or apartment, with a 6-day skipass for the Jungfrau region at a special price, from early January through mid-April. details are available through the tourist office or the **Swiss Ski School Grindelwald** *(☎ 36+53.20.21, FAX 36+53.20.26)*.

SWIMMING

The Swiss enjoy swimming in their lakes. The Zürichsee has places for swimming when the summer weather warms, as do Lac Lëman and most of the other big lakes. One of the loveliest lakes is the Brienzersee, which touches Interlaken, but the lakes at and around St. Moritz, in eastern Switzerland, are also wonderful in summer and early fall. You can count on finding pools at many Swiss spas and also at many resorts without curative springs. Many newer hotels have pools, no matter where they are located.

TENNIS

Most resort centers have several tennis courts in excellent shape. Sass Fee and St. Moritz have complete tennis programs, as do many of the other ski resorts. Gstaad's annual "Swiss Open" tournament is held in early July, but the village has a tennis focus throughout the summer.

WALKING/TREKKING

"Panoramic Walks" are so much a part of Swiss life that the PTT, the Swiss Postbus system, devoted a series of booklets to several areas. All the booklets, written by region, are sold in the PTT offices for 3SFr. The buses thread up and out of the mountain valleys to several good (and high) starting points, where you can stroll, walk, or hike to another place to pick up a bus for return to your hometown if your walk doesn't take you there. The Swiss system of *Wanderwege* cobwebs the country. The signs are yellow and marked with the hours and minutes it takes to walk at a reasonable pace to the noted destination. The network of *Wanderwege* is outlined on maps that are usually posted at the railway station and always at the tourist office (where you can pick up handy maps to carry on your route). For walks focused on wildflowers, contact the tourist offices in the Alpine areas and purchase a small *Alpenblumen* (Alpine flowers) guidebook on the spot. Many regions have promotional material with suggested walks. Walks in the Berner Oberland, a region that includes Interlaken, the Brienzersee and the Thunersee, are defined in **Berner Wanderwege** *(Postfach, Nordring 10a, CH-3013 Bern 25; ☎ 31+42.37.66)*.

Since 1991, the year of celebration of the 500th anniversary of the founding of Switzerland (on August 1, 1291), the classic walk for this country, known as the **Via Svizra/Voie Suisse/Via Svizzera/Weg der Schweiz** in the four Swiss languages, is a well-posted scenic route that skirts most of the Vierwaldstättersee, as the Lake of the Four Forest Cantons is known in its locally-spoken German. Although a walk around the entire route can take many hours, segments can be walked by most reasonably fit people who can pause at appropriate inns and other places along the route. The delight of this route is that everyone can participate. There are some paved areas, suitable for wheel chair travel, as well as many areas that are much more strenuous, climbing through forested areas. Day-long segments of the route will include portions of paved paths as well as walking through meadows and some up and down, depending on your starting and finishing points. You can buy a helpful guidebook that explains the walks; maps are readily available in the area. Most of the tourist offices at lakeside villages have information.

Among the North American firms planning guided walks and hikes are **Mountain Travel-Sobek** *(6420 Fairmont Ave., El Cerrito, CA 94530;* ☎ *510+527-8100 or 800+227-2384, FAX 510+525-7710),* which has some strenuous excursions, plus **Ryder-Walker Alpine Trails** *(Box 947, 5 Lake Fork Junction, Telluride, CO 81435;* ☎ *303+728-6481),* **Fred Jacobson Alpine Adventures** *(c/o Chappaqua Travel, Inc., South Greeley Ave., Chappaqua, NY 10514;* ☎ *914+238-5151 or 800+666-5161, FAX 914+238-5533),* **Travent International** *(Box 711, Bristol, VT 05443;* ☎ *802+453-5710 or 800+325-3009, FAX 802+453-4806),* which has had a walk between the Matterhorn and the Jungfrau (from Zermatt to Interlaken) in recent summer programs, and **Wanderweg Holidays** *(519 Kings Croft, Cherry Hill, NJ 08034;* ☎ *609+321-1040 or 800+270-2577, FAX 609+321-1040),* which offers several varied and well-planned itineraries.

WATERSKIING

The love of winter skiing has expanded to include waterskiing. Although dozens of places have good facilities, among the best are the Paradiso area of Lugano for Lago di Lugano in the southern Ticino region, out of Montreux on Lac Léman, the lake shared with France; and from Günten on the Thunersee, a lovely lake that links Thun and Interlaken. The *Wasserskiclub* in Herrliberg, on the Zürichsee and a few minutes away from the city by local train or by car and slightly longer aboard a lakeboat, is one source for information and lessons.

WINDSURFING/BOARDSAILING

The sport has taken over in most of the Alpine countries where accomplished skiers are looking for a fast sport for warmer months, and Switzerland is no exception. You can count on seeing boardsailors on most of the Swiss lakes, especially the Thunersee and, of course, the Zürichsee and Lac Léman, as well as on the Vierwaldstättersee (Lake Lucerne), where there's a center at Vitznau. The unofficial course for many boardsailors seems to closely follow that of the scheduled ferries that tie lakeside towns together, which means that many lakeboat passengers can capture colorful photographs, especially on sunny days. The Champferer See, above St. Moritz, and the Obersee in Arosa, both in the mountains, are two of many small lakes where the sport is popular. To rent boards, check far enough in advance through your hotel as well as with the local tourist office. It's not always easy and sometimes not even possible, to find boards for rent—and you'll want a wet suit for the sport on many of the lakes, especially when they are made lively by brisk to very cold winds over snowy mountain fields.

TREASURES AND TRIFLES

Quality is unquestioned in Switzerland, whether you are buying clothes, clocks, candy, or anything else. Watches, clocks and other precision products are the first things that come to mind for many, and stores in all cities and most towns, and many villages, have timepieces for sale. Prices are stable, no matter where you shop. If there is a price difference, it is probably because the inner workings are different. The famous watch-making names—*Baume & Mercier, Rolex, Piaget, Bucherer,* and *Omega,* plus *Heuer* for sport watches—are all here, as is the ubiquitous *Swatch,* Switzerland's answer to cheap Japanese watches. It's wise to have some idea of what you're looking for, but be prepared for a wider selection of styles at shops in Switzerland. Only a small percentage of available items are exported, and some items that are made exclusively for the U.S. market are not available in Switzerland.

You will see Swiss army knives in more styles and sizes than you ever thought possible. Prices are standard throughout the country and the knives (and many other items) are sold at shops everywhere, including those at both major airports (Zürich and Genève).

Heimatwerk is a name to look for. It translates as "homework," but implies quality handicrafts. Among the typical items are pottery, woven place mats and other items, children's clothes with embroidery and smocking, handkerchiefs, men's clothes such as neckties and jackets worn in farm country, wood blocks and furniture, paintings in the naif style popular in the Appenzell region, and enamel, silver, and other handcrafted jewelry. There are *Heimatwerk* stores in most cities and some towns, but they are not part of a chain. Each store does its own buying, and although some merchandise overlaps, each store carries merchandise made by craftspeople in the immediate vicinity. In Zürich, find the **Schweizerische Heimatwerk** on Rudolf Brun-Brucke, bordering the Limmat River, or at Bahnhofstrasse, near the head of the Zürichsee; in Bern, the **Heimatwerk** is nestled under the arcades on Spitalgasse, the main fountain-punctuated street in town; in Luzern, the **Innerschweizer Heimatwerk** is on Franziskannerplatz 14, not far from the Hauptbahnhof (main railroad station) and the Wilden Mann Hotel. Be on the lookout for other handicraft shops wherever you wander; the merchandise is unique and of highest quality.

Department stores yield treasures. In Zürich and most of German-speaking Switzerland, **Jelmoli** (pronounced "yell-mole-ee") and Globus are two stores to find. (Both are just off Bahnhofstrasse in Zürich.) In Genève, look for **Innovation**, near the old city. That chain is known as **Inovazione** in the Italian-speaking canton of Ticino. Also look at **Migros** (pronounced "mee-grow") and **Coop** (say "cope"), two food-store chains that carry much more than groceries, although many of the specialty foods are fun to bring home as gifts. Department stores are arranged much as those in North America, making it easy to shop by looking at merchandise, checking price tags and speaking few words. In most cases, there will be someone who speaks English, but don't count on everyone to do so.

Opportunities for airport shopping are endless. Not only are there excellent food stores, where many gourmet items make welcome gifts, but there are clothing stores and toy stores as well as electronic centers that have a wide assortment of items in all price ranges.

AUTHOR'S OBSERVATION

When you are buying an expensive item, it's worthwhile asking about the tax refund plan for items for use outside the country. Some stores are prepared to fill out the necessary forms for partial refund of the Warenumsatzteuer, known as WUST. It is the store "turn-over" tax. When you leave the country, you must present the form to the Swiss customs officer and show him the item. He then verifies the form and files it. A check in Swiss francs will be mailed to you at a later date. The system is only practical at airports; it's difficult to find customs officials at the railroad station and time-consuming at border crossings when you travel by car.

ADDITIONAL INFORMATION SOURCES

The following addresses for central tourism offices are listed, according to the cantons they serve. To send a letter, use the following form:

Verkehrsburo (of the pertinent city)
Street address
CH-0000 town name
SWITZERLAND

CANTON OF GRAUBÜNDEN
Verkehrsverein Graubünden, *Alexanderstrasse 24, Postfach 256, CH-7001 Chur;* ☎ *81+22.13.60.*

APPENZELL, GLARUS, ST. GALLEN, SCHAFFHAUSEN, THURGAU, AND LIECHTENSTEIN
Verkehrsverband Ostschweiz and Fürstentum Liechtenstein, *Bahnhofplatz 1a, CH-9001 St. Gallen;* ☎ *71+23.43.04; FAX 71+23.43.04.*

ZÜRICH CITY AND ENVIRONS
Verkehrsverein Zürich, *Bahnhofplatz 15, CH-8023 Zürich;* ☎ *1+211.40.00; FAX 1+212.01.41.*

URI, SCHWYZ, OBWALDEN, NIDWALDEN, LUZERN, ZUG
Verkehrsverband Zentralschweiz, *Alpenstrasse 1, CH-6002 Luzern;* ☎ *41+51.18.91; FAX 41+51.72.60.*

AARGAU, BASELLAND, SOLOTHURN
Argauische Tourismum Kommission, *c/o Verkehrsburo Baden, Bahnhofstrasse 50, CH-5400 Baden;* ☎ *56+22.53.18; FAX 56+22.53.90.*

CITY OF BASEL AND ENVIRONS
Offizielles Verkehrsburo Basel, *Blumenrais 2, Schifflande, CH-4001 Basel;* ☎ *61+261.50.50; FAX 61+261.59.44.*

BERNESE OBERLAND
Verkehrsverband Berner Oberland, *Jungfraustrasse 38, CH-3800 Interlaken;* ☎ *36+22.26.21; FAX 36+22.57.16.*

FRIBOURG AREA
Union fribourgeoise du tourisme, *Case postal 921, CH-1701 Fribourg;* ☎ *37+24.56.44; FAX 37+24.31.19.*

NEUCHÂTEL AREA
Fédération Neuchâteloise du tourisme, *9 rue du Treson (Place des Halles), CH-2001 Neuchâtel;* ☎ *38+25.17.89; FAX 38+24.49.40.*

JURA AREA
Fédération du tourisme de la Republique et Canton de Jura, *12 Place de la Gare, CH-2800 Délémont;* ☎ *66+22.99.77; FAX 66+22.68.03.*

BERNESE JURA REGION
Office du Tourisme du Jura Bernois, *26 ave. de la Poste, CH-2740 Moutier;* ☎ *32+93.64.66; FAX 32+93.61.56.*

LAKE GENEVA REGION/CANTON OF VAUD
Office du tourisme du canton de Vaud, *60 av. d'Ouchy, CH-1000 Lausanne-Ouchy;* ☎ *21+617.72.02; FAX 21+617.72.40.*

CANTON OF VALAIS/WALLIS
Union valaisanne du tourisme, *15 rue de Lausanne, CH-1951 Sion 1;* ☎ *27+22.31.61; FAX 27+23.15.72.*

CANTON OF TICINO
Ente Ticinese per il turismo, *Villa Turrita, Caselle postale 1441, CH-6501 Bellinzona;* ☎ *92+25.70.56; FAX 92+25.36.14.*

BERNESE MIDDLELAND
Verkehrsverband Berner Mittelland, c/o **Verkehrsburo Bern**, *P.O.B., CH-3001 Bern;* ☎ *31+22.12.12; FAX 31+21.08.20.*

GENEVA AREA
Office du tourisme de Genève, *Gare Cornavin, CH-1201 Genève;* ☎ *22+738.52.00; FAX 22+21.89.65.*

GLOSSARY

English	German	French	Italian	Slovene
PLACE NAMES:				
Austria, or East Flank	Österreich	Autriche		Austrija
Archduke	Erzherzog	Archiduc		Vojvoda
Bavarian	Bayerisches	Bavarois		Bavarska
Carinthia (Austrian state)	Kärnten	Corinthe		Koroška
Danube (river)	Donau	Danube		Donava
Geneva	Genf	Genève	Ginevra	Ženeva
king	König	roi	rey	kralj
Lake Constance	Bodensee	lac de Constance		Jezero Konstanca
Lower Austria (Austrian state)	Niederösterreich	basse Autriche		
Lucerne	Luzern	Lucerne	Lucerna	Lucern
Milan	Milano	Milan	Milano	Milano
Mont Blanc (mountain)	Monte Bianco	Mont Blanc	Monte Bianco	Mont Blanc
Munich	München	Munich		Minhen
Piedmont (region)		Piedmont	Piemonte	Piemont
Rhine river	Rhein	Le Rhin		Ren
states or provinces	Länder (Austrian)	etat/la province	stati/provincie	Pokrajina
	Canton (Switzerland)			

English	German	French	Italian	Slovene
Slovenia				Slovenija
Styria (Austrian state)	Steiermark			Štajerska
Turin	Torino	Turin	Torino	Torino
Upper Austria (Austrian state)	Oberösterreich	Haut Autriche		
Valais (Swiss canton)	Wallis	Valais	Valese	Valais
Venice	Venedig	Venise	Venezia	Benetke
Vienna (Austria's capital)	Wien (pronounced "veen")	Vienne	Wien	Dunaj
GENERAL WORDS/TERMS				
entrance	Eingang	entrée	entrata	Vhod
exit	Ausgang	sortie	uscita	Izhod
excuse me	entschuldigen Sie	pardonez-moi	permesso	Oprostite
foundation (as in charity)	Stiftung	charité	fondazione	
good day (hello)	guten Tag	bonjour	buon giorno	dobro jutro
good evening	gut Nacht	bon soir	buona sera	dober večer
good-bye	auf Wiederschen	au revoir	arrivederci	nasvidenje
'bye (informal)	wiedersehen	salut	ciao	adijo
good morning	guten Morgen	bonjour	buon giorno	dobro jutro
high (as in Alps)	Ober	haute	alto	visok
left	links	gauche	sinistra	levo
low	unter	bas	basso	pod

English	German	French	Italian	Slovene
many thanks	danke viel mal	merci beaucoup	molte grazie	Huala Lepa
no	nicht	non	no	ne
please	bitte	s'il vous plait	per piacere	prosim
please (don't mention it)	keine Ursache	il n'y a pas de quoi	prego	
old (as in ancient/historic)	alt	vieille	vecchio	star zgodovinski
right	recht	droit	destra	desno
thank you	danke schöen	merci	grazie	hvala
yes	ja	oui	si	da
LODGING AND RESTAURANTS				
bed-and-breakfast places	Zimmer frei	chambre d'hôtes	stanze libere	prenocisce zajtrk
bill (cost for meal)	Die Rechnung	l'addition	il conto	račun
breakfast	Fruhstück	petit dejeuner	prima colazione	zajtrk
dinner (evening meal)	Abendessen	diner	cena	vecerja
guest house, or inn	Gasthof (pl. -höfe)	auberge	albergo	gostilna/prenocišča
hotel	das Hotel	l'hôtel	l'hotel	hotel
house	Haus	maison	casa	hiša
household inn, often farm	Wirtschaft	gîtes	albergo	gostilna/prenocišča
inn	Gasthof	auberge	locanda or osteria	prenocisce or gostilna
luncheon	Mittagessen	dejeuner	il pranzo	kosilo
menu in restaurants	Spieskarte	carte	il menù	Jedilni list

English	German	French	Italian	Slovene
restaurant	Restaurant	restaurant	ristorante	restavracija
room (bedroom)	Zimmer	chambre	una camera	soba
service (tip)	Inbegriffen	service	servizio	napitnina
TRAVEL TERMS				
airport	Flughafen	aeroport	aeroporto	letališče
arrival	Ankunft	arrivée	arrivo	prihod
boat	Schiff	bateau	barca	čoln
booking office (for reservations)	Verkaufsstellen	réservation	l'uffico di prenotazione	rezervacije
bus	Autobus	autobus	autobus	avtobus
departure	Abfahrt	départ	partenze	odhod
excursion	Ausflug	excursion	excursioni	izlet
hand luggage	Handgepäck	baggage a main	borsa a mano	ročna prtljaga
holiday	Ferien	vacances	vacanza	počitnice
hospital	das Krankenhaus	l'hôpital	l'ospedale	Bolnišnica
inn or guest house	Gasthof (pl. -höfe)	auberge	locanda	motel ali privatne sobe
journey, as in trip	Reisen	voyage	excursioni	potovanje
luggage	Gepäck	bagage	bagaglio	prtljaga
luggage cart	Handgepäck-roller	caddie	charlots bagages	prtljažni list
meals en route (train service)	Speisen beim Reisen	repas en route	carrozza ristorante	
money exchange	Geldwechsel	change	cambio	menjalnica

English	German	French	Italian	Slovene
rail (for trains, pl. rails)	Bahn (pl. Bahnen)	train	ferrovie/treno	postaja
rent-a-bike	Mietvelo	location de vélo	affitto bicicletta	najem kolesa
seat	Platz	siège	sedia	sedež
seat reservations	Platzreservierung	reservation de siège	prenotazione	rezervacija sedeža
station	Bahnhof	station	stazione	postaja
street or way	Strasse	rue	strada/viale	cesta
spa (also bath, as in tub)	Bad	station thermale	terme	zdravilišče
sundries shop	Tabak	tabac	tabac	
telephone	Telefon	téléphone	telefono	telefon
tickets	Fahrschein	billette	biglietto	vozovnica
timetable	Fahrplan	horaire	orario	vozni red
tourist office	Verkehrsbüro	office de tourisme	l'ufficio di turismo	turistični biro
track (for train)	Gleis	quai	binario	tir
train (pl. trains)	Zug (pl. Zuge)	train	ferrovie	vlak (vlaki)
train station (railhouse)	Bahnhof	gare	stazione	železniška postaja
train station - main	Hauptbahnhof	gare central	stazione centrale	glavna postaja
travel or journey	Reisen	voyage	viaggiatori	popotovanje
SIGHTS				
castle	Schloss or die Burg	le château	castello	grad
cathedral	Dom	le cathédrale	duomo	katedrala

English	German	French	Italian	Slovene
church	die Kirche	l'église	la chiesa	cerkev
forest	Wald	fôret	foresta	gozd
fortress (or castle)	die Festung	la forteresse	castello/fortezza	trdnjava
glacier	Gletsche	glace	ghiacciaio	ledenik
hall (large room)	Saal	salon	salone	salon
homeland or local museum	Heimatmuseum	musée local	museo	muzej
high meadow	Alp	patûrages	alpi	
hill, or height	Höhe	collines	collina	hrib
historic city	Altstadt	vieille ville	città antica	stari del mesta
island	Insel	île	Isola	otok
little, small	Klein	petit	piccolo	majhen
lake	See	lac	lago	jezero
large, great	Gross	grand	grande	velik
mansion	Wohnhaus	palais	il palazzo	dvorec
map or, in restaurants, menu	Karte	carte	mappa	menu
mineral "bath" or spa	Bad	spa	minerale terme	zdravilišče
meadow (usually Alpine)	Alm	prairie		
mountain	Berg	mont	montagne	gora
museum	Museum	musée	il museo	muzej
museum of the state/province	Landesmuseum	musée	museo principale	muzej

English	German	French	Italian	Slovene
museum/picture gallery	Pinakothek	la galerie	la galleria or pinacoteca	galerija
tourist office	Verekehrsburo	l'office du tourisme	l'ufficio di turismo	turistični biro
old	Alt	vieille	antica	star
pass (mountain)	Joch (also Sattel)	col	passo	prehod
path	Steig	chemin	sentiero	steza pot
pointed peak	Horn	sommet	la vetta	najvišja točka
ridge	Grat	crête	passaggio	sleme
river	Ache/Fluss	rivière	fiume	reva
riverside	Ufer	quai	quai	obala
side valley	Grund	vallée	sponda	pobočje
stream or brook	Bach	courant	fiumiciattolo	tok
square (as in Town square)	Platz	place	piazza	trg
town	Dorf	ville	città	mesto
town hall	Rathaus	hôtel de ville	il municipio	mesta hiša
valley	Tal	vallée	val	dolina
view	Blick	vue	vista	pogled
wall paintings (exterior)	Lüftlmalerei	peinture extérieure		freske
way or path	Weg	chemin	sentiero	steza pot

English	German	French	Italian	Slovene
SPORTS				
bicycle	Fahrrad	velo	bicicletta	kolo
boat(s)	Schiff	batteau(x)	barca	čoln
fishing	Fischen	pêche	pesca	ribolov
hang-gliding	Deltafliegen	vol libre	paracaoutismo alpino	jadranje letalom
hunting	Jagen	la chasse	caccia	lov
horseback riding	Reiten	équestre	equitazione	jahanje
off-trail (as in skiing)	Tiefschnee skifahren	hors-piste	fuori-pista	steza
parachuting	Fallschirmsprigen	parachutisme	paracaoutismo	padalstvo
rent-a-bike	Fahrrad Vermietung	location de vélo	affittare bicicletta	najem kolesa
sailing	Segeln	voile	vela	jadranje
ski trail	Piste	piste	pista da sci	steza
waterskiing	Wasserskifahren	ski nautique	sci d'acqua	vodno smučanje
walking/hiking path	Wanderweg	excursions sentier	passeggiare	planinarjenje

INDEX

Introducing the 1994 Fielding Travel Guides— fresh, fascinating and fun!

An incisive new attitude and an exciting new look! All-new design and format. In-depth reviews. Fielding delivers travel information the way frequent travelers demand it—written with sparkle, style and humor. Candid insights, sage advice, insider tips. No fluff, no filler, only fresh information that makes the journey more fun, more fascinating, more Fielding. Start planning your next great adventure today!

Australia 1994	**$16.95**
Belgium 1994	**$16.95**
Bermuda/Bahamas 1994	**$16.95**
Brazil 1994	**$16.95**
Britain 1994	**$16.95**
Budget Europe 1994	**$16.95**
Caribbean 1994	**$16.95**
Europe 1994	**$16.95**
Far East 1994/95	**$16.95**
France 1994	**$16.95**
The Great Sights of Europe 1994	**$16.95**
Hawaii 1994	**$16.95**
Holland 1994	**$16.95**
Italy 1994	**$16.95**
Mexico 1994	**$16.95**
New Zealand 1994	**$16.95**
Scandinavia 1994	**$16.95**
Spain & Portugal 1994	**$16.95**
Switzerland & the Alpine Region 1994	**$16.95**
Worldwide Cruises 1994	**$16.95**
Shopping Europe	**$12.95**

To place an order: call toll-free
1-800-FW-2-GUIDE
add $2.00 shipping & handling, allow 2-6 weeks.

ALPINE NEWSLETTER

In spite of the fact that the region is centuries old and many of the buildings—and even hotels and restaurants—are wonderfully constant in their quality and their family heritage, there's always news. From the time this manuscript went to press, there've been some changes, frequently with promotional airfares and sometimes with new inns and special activities in villages, towns and cities of the Alpine area. Often, in my travels, I discover places that may have been around for ages, but are new to me—and perhaps to you. I share them in the "Alpine Newsletter."

If you'd like to keep in touch with "news" from this remarkable region, fill in the form below and send this page with a stamped self-addressed envelope, to:

> Alpine Newsletter
> c/o **GeoMedia**; #316
> 1771 Post Road East
> Westport, CT 06880

We'll send you a free copy of the "Alpine Bulletin" and let you know how to get the insider information.

Name:

Street:

City, State and Zip Code:

We're interested in making this book as useful as possible for your travels. For that reason, we'd appreciate having some information about you, as well as your suggestions.

Special interest for travel: (festivals, inns, nature, hiking, other?)

Preferred style of lodging:
Luxury _____ ; Inn _____ ; Budget_____

Month of intended Alpine visit:

Country (or countries) of interest:

Intended length of stay:

Anticipated budget, minus airfare, for the vacation:

Number of people in your party (including yourself)

Approximate age of travelers:
under 25 _____ ; from 26-39 ____; from 40-55 ____ ; over 60____

Suggestions and/or comments:

Favorite People, Places & Experiences

ADDRESS:	NOTES:

Name

Address

Telephone

Name

Address

Telephone

Name

Address

Telephone

Name

Address

Telephone

Name

Address

Telephone

Name

Address

Telephone

Name

Address

Telephone

Favorite People, Places & Experiences

ADDRESS:	NOTES:

Name

Address

Telephone

Name

Address

Telephone

Name

Address

Telephone

Name

Address

Telephone

Name

Address

Telephone

Name

Address

Telephone

Name

Address

Telephone